Contents

CONTINUUM & THE PUBLISHERS ASSOCIATION

DIRECTORY OF PUBLISHING

2011

UNITED KINGDOM AND THE REPUBLIC OF IRELAND

continuum

Continuum
The Tower Building
11 York Road
London SE1 7NX

80 Maiden Lane
Suite 704
New York, NY 10038

© Continuum 2010

Thirty-sixth Edition 2010

British Library Cataloguing-in-Publication Data
A catalogue entry for this book is available from the British Library.

ISBN: 9781441184429

Research and editing by First Edition Translations, Cambridge
Text processing and typesetting by John Ainslie Consultancy
Printed and bound in Great Britain by MPG Books Group

1 Introduction

FOREWORD

The 36th edition of the *Directory of Publishing*, published by Continuum in association with The Publishers Association, provides an indispensable guide to book publishing in the United Kingdom and Republic of Ireland and contains details of nearly 900 publishers. In addition to the detailed entries on publishers, the *Directory* offers in depth coverage of the wider UK book trade, and lists over 500 organizations associated with the industry, including packagers, distributors, library suppliers, authors' agents and translation services. An appendix analyses publishers by field of speciality. Indexes include ISBN prefix numbers; names of key personnel and publishers' imprints; and a listing of UK publishers by postcode.

The directory is updated annually. Previous entrants are sent last year's entry and new entrants a questionnaire. We are grateful to all those who have provided information for this edition. We have done all we can to ensure accuracy and completeness, but cannot accept responsibility for errors or omissions that escaped us. New entrants either approached the publisher or were discovered by monitoring various sources – the trade press, publishers' catalogues, exhibitions, book fairs, and the files of the Publishers Association itself.

As in the previous edition we have not excluded all organizations which have failed to reply to our mailings. Instead we have re-run their 2010 entries (in abbreviated form) and marked them with an asterisk. However, such organizations will be deleted from the next edition if they fail to update their entries for the second year running.

Underlined entries are members of the Publishers Association.

We welcome all comments and suggestions from readers for improvements. We are also happy to receive details of possible new entries, but please note these must meet our criteria for inclusion. Publishers must either be a Publishers Association or Foilsiú Éireann member or be of a certain size, publishing at least 5 new titles a year or employing at least 4 people.

All organizations are entered free of charge.

Continuum

HOW TO OBTAIN BRITISH BOOKS

This introduction is particularly intended for booksellers ordering from a British publisher for the first time.

HOW TO ORDER
1   If you have not previously ordered from a publisher, you should write for details on:
   trade discounts;
   credit facilities;
   catalogue mailing.
Please enclose in your letter information including:
   name and address of your bank;
   names and addresses of one or two publishers, preferably British, with whom you already do business. In certain circumstances you may be directed to a local stockist, agent or representative.

2   When the publisher agrees to supply you, your order should include:
   your full name and address;
   order date and order number;
   dispatch instructions: where you want the books to be sent and where you want the invoice sent;
   carriage instructions:
      surface post
      special carrier (e.g. shipper)
      air freight
   invoicing instructions:
      if you want a separate invoice by airmail
      minimum number of copies you require
   full details of the book:
      number of copies you need
      title
      author/editor
      cased/limp/paperback
      international standard book number (ISBN)

3   Orders Clearing, Mardev Ltd, Quadrant House, The Quadrant, Sutton, Surrey SM2 5AS (tel: +44 (0)20 8652 3899, fax: +44 (0)20 8652 4597, email: enquiries@mardev.com, web site: http://www.mardevlists.com) have an Orders Clearing system: by sending all your orders for different publishers to the one address, you can save yourself money. Similarly, Orders Clearing operates a service for the payment of publishers' accounts, the Overseas Booksellers' Clearing House (OBCH). Booksellers may send one cheque for various accounts and OBCH will then distribute the payments to the different publishers.

4   An Orders Clearing Service is also offered by the Booksellers Order Distribution Ltd (BOD). Their address is 49 Victoria Road, Aldershot, Hampshire GU11 1SJ (tel: +44 (0)1252 20697, fax: +44 (0)1252 20697).

5   Nielsen BookNet provides a range of e-commerce services that allow electronic trading between booksellers, distributors, publishers, libraries and other suppliers, regardless of their size and location. Services include BookNet for booksellers and publishers/distributors, TeleOrdering and EDI messaging. Contact Nielsen BookData, 3rd Floor, Midas House, 62 Goldsworth Road, Woking, GU21 6LQ (tel: +44 (0)870 777 8710, fax: +44 (0)870 777 8711, email: sales@nielsenbookdata.co.uk, website: http://www.bookdata.co.uk).

FOR REFERENCE
1   **Nielsen BookData:**
Provides monthly and quarterly content-rich book information for English-language titles published internationally. Available on CD-ROM and online by subscription from Nielsen BookData, 3rd Floor, Midas House, 62 Goldsworth Road, Woking, GU21 6LQ (tel: +44 (0)870 777 8710, fax: +44 (0)870 777 8711, email: sales@nielsenbookdata.co.uk, website: http://www.bookdata.co.uk).

2   **The Bookseller:**
The British book trade journal, published weekly by Bookseller Publications, containing correspondence, articles, trade news, together with a list of books published each week (web site: http://www.theBookseller.com). See also section 6.12 for details of other periodicals and reference books of the trade.

3   **British National Bibliography:**
A subject list of new British books arranged by Dewey classification. Published weekly with interim cumulations and an annual cumulation by the British Library, National Bibliographic Service, Boston Spa, Wetherby, West Yorkshire LS23 7BQ (tel: +44 (0)1937 546585, fax: +44 (0)1937 546586, email: nbs-info@bl.uk, web site: http://www.bl.uk).

4   Individual publishers will normally provide catalogues of their own publications on request.

HOW TO PAY
You can pay by:
   cheque, bank draft or letter of credit
   bill of exchange drawn by the publisher on your giro or postal account
   international money order/postal order

IMPORTANT
Please make sure that:
   the publisher receives the *full amount* of the invoice value, free of all bank charges and transfer fees;
   you pay *promptly*;
   if you have any problems, raise them *promptly*;
   if you have any difficulty in paying, consult your local bank manager, or the British Embassy, Consulate or High Commission.

WHEN YOU HAVE DIFFICULTY IN OBTAINING BRITISH BOOKS

1   If you have a problem of a *general* nature, please write to the Publishers Association, 29b Montague Street, London WC1B 5BH (email: mail@publishers.org.uk, tel: +44 (0)20 7691 9191, fax: +44 (0)20 7691 9199). The Association cannot intervene in problems which may arise between individual booksellers and publishers.

2   British Council

Your nearest office may be able to help you with enquiries about UK publishing. Details of its network of offices are available from: British Council Information Centre, tel: +44 (0)161 957 7755, fax: +44 (0) 161 957 7762, email: general.enquiries@britishcouncil.org, minicom: +44 (0)161 957 7188, web site: http://www.britishcouncil.org.

PUBLISHERS' ABBREVIATED ANSWERS

Most publishers use one of the answers below when books are not available, and give an explanation of their answer codes at the bottom of the invoice.

NK	Not known, not ours, or so far in the future or so long out of print that it is unknown to the trade department
OO/TF	On order, to follow shortly
B8 *or* **BDG8**	Binding, will be available in August
B/ND	Binding (no date)
RP/June *or* **RP/6**	Reprint available in June
RP/2M	Reprint available in 2 months
NYP	Not yet published
NEP	New edition in preparation
RPUC	Reprint under consideration
OP	Out of print
OO/USA	On order, to be supplied by USA
TOP	Temporarily out of print

OS	Out of stock
RP/ND	Reprinting, no date

TECHNICAL TERMS

Firm

Books are normally supplied 'firm'. This means you will accept the books, pay for them, and will not be able to return them.

See-safe or On approval

Some publishers are prepared to supply books on the basis that they are paid for at normal credit terms, but if the books remain unsold they may be returned with the publisher's authorization for crediting against future orders. You will be expected to return the books at your own expense. You should always obtain in writing details from publishers of any such agreements they are prepared to offer to their customers.

Standing Orders

Some publishers operate a scheme which allows a bookseller automatically to receive books in given subjects as they are published. These are normally supplied 'on approval'. You should write to individual publishers for details of their schemes.

Continuation Orders

Continuation Orders can be placed for books published in series and multi-volume works. This means that each new volume that appears will be sent to you automatically.

Pro-forma Invoice

Some publishers may prefer to supply initial orders by means of a pro-forma invoice which has to be paid before the books are sent.

THE PUBLISHERS ASSOCIATION

29b Montague Street, London WC1B 5BW
Telephone: +44 (0)20 7691 9191 **Fax:** +44 (0)20 7691 9199
Email: mail@publishers.org.uk
Web site: http://www.publishers.org.uk

Chief Executive: Richard Mollet
Director of Educational, Academic & Professional Publishing:
  Graham Taylor
Director of International Services: Emma House

Making the case for UK publishers

– **The Publishers Association** is the leading organisation working on the behalf of book, journal and electronic publishers based in the UK. We bring publishers together to discuss the critical issues facing the industry and to define the practical policies, which will drive our lobbying and campaigns in the UK and Internationally. The aim of The Publishers Association is to ensure a secure future for the UK publishing industry.

– **Acting for the Industry:** The PA's mission is to strengthen the trading environment for UK publishers by ensuring that the needs and concerns of the industry are heard at all levels of Government in the UK, in Europe and internationally. We are actively involved in issues such as: copyright legislation, the adaptation of legislation to digital technology, copyright licensing arrangements for education, business, and public bodies, legislation on VAT, e-commerce and other issues affecting publishers, funding for learning and information resources in schools, colleges and universities, the promotion of books and reading, export promotion of books and journals, anti-piracy campaigns (terrestrial and internet), efficiency in supply and marketing, the protection of freedom to publish.

– **Front Line Information:** PA posts front line information to our website and communicates with members through our regular e-mail bulletins. The Members Only section of the PA website contains detailed information prepared exclusively for members including: the latest market statistics, copyright law updates, comments on current government policy, PA briefs and reports on market concerns, anti-piracy action updates, digital rights information, updates on EU legislation.

Home and Export Markets

Market development is at the heart of the PA's activities, which include:

– **International trade fairs**, operating with UK Trade & Investment a subsidy scheme for companies wishing to exhibit. Additionally, our TurnKey Exhibition Services offer publishers a complete exhibition service for major fairs.

– **Market intelligence**, including free online access to the Global Publishing Information website (http://www.publishers.org.uk/gpi.nsf), and exclusive access to the Aid Digest.
– **Trade delegations and seminars** organised with UK Trade & Investment support, to gain knowledge of and exposure in growth markets such as China, Africa, Asia and Eastern Europe.
– **Home trade initiatives**, such as World Book Day, which result in a significant increase in sales, particularly of children's books, during the period of promotion.

Join the PA now – add your voice, have your say

As a PA member you can add your voice and have your say on the vital issues affecting our industry today. Membership is open to any company registered in the UK engaged in book, journal or electronic publishing as a bona fide and continuing operation. Subscription rates are based on turnover, with special introductory rates for new members and discounted rates for journal publishers.

The International Division

The International Division actively supports the international sales activities of PA members. We act against piracy, and on copyright and trade barrier issues, organise trade missions and UK representation at international trade fairs.

Trade Publishers Council

The Trade Publishers Council determines PA policy on consumer market matters, and acts on specific issues with the objectives of expanding the market and increasing efficiency. Other trade groups include our Children's Book Group and Religious Books Group.

Academic and Professional Publishing

The Academic and Professional Division provides a forum for higher education, monograph, journal and reference publishers. We represent publishers' concerns to key stakeholders, conduct market research and run a number of events.

The Educational Publishers Council (EPC)

The Educational Publishers Council provides a voice for school and college publishers. We campaign for better funding for learning resources and represent the industry in the development of the electronic market, as well as running seminars and compiling market statistics.

Digital Publishing Forum

Provides support for on-line and off-line electronic publishers, and organises a programme of seminars and meetings.

2 Publishers

2001 ▬▬▬▬

AA PUBLISHING
[trading as AA Media Ltd]
Fanum House, Basingstoke, Hants
RG21 4EA
Telephone: 01256 491578
Fax: 01256 322575
Email: AAPublish@TheAA.com
Web Site: www.theAA.com

Distribution (UK):
Littlehampton Book Services Ltd,
Faraday Close, Durrington, Worthing,
West Sussex BN13 3RB

Personnel:
R. C. A. Miles (Chief Executive)
D. Watchus (Publisher)
T. A. Lee (Sales & Marketing Director)
R. Firth (Production Director)
L. Hopkins (Finance Director)
S. Gold (Human Resources Director)

Atlases & Maps; Guide Books; Natural
History; Photography; Transport; Travel &
Topography

Imprints, Series & ISBNs:
Automobile Association: 978 0 7495, 978 0
    86145
Travel Series: Citypacks: 978 0 7495
Travel Series: Essentials: 978 0 7495
Travel Series: Key Guides: 978 0 7495
Travel Series: Spiral Guides: 978 0 7495

Distributor for:
AAA Road Maps of USA, Canada, Mexico;
    Thomas Cook; Scottish Tourist Board

2002 ▬▬▬▬

ACAIR LTD
Unit 7, 7 James Street, Stornoway,
Isle of Lewis HS1 2QN
Telephone: 01851 703020
Fax: 01851 703294
Email: info@acairbooks.com
Web Site: www.acairbooks.com

Distribution:
BookSource, 50 Cambuslang Road,
Glasgow G32 8NB
Telephone: 0845 370 0067
Fax: 0845 370 0068

Personnel:
Norma Macleod (Editor)
Margaret Anne Macleod (Designer)
Margaret Martin (Administrator)
Donalda Riddell (Stock)

Children's Books; Educational & Textbooks;
Fiction; History & Antiquarian; Poetry

New Titles: 5 (2009) , 6 (2010)

No of Employees: 5
Annual Turnover: £95,000

Imprints, Series & ISBNs:
978 0 86152

Book Trade Association Membership:
Publishing Scotland; Booksellers
Association

2003 ▬▬▬▬

ACCENT PRESS LTD
The Old School, Upper High Street,
Bedlinog CF46 6RY
Telephone: 01443 710930
Fax: 01443 710940
Email: info@accentpress.co.uk
Web Site: www.accentpress.co.uk

Distribution:
Macmillan Distribution (MDL), Brunel Road,
Houndmills, Basingstoke, Hants RG21 6XS
Telephone: 01256 802692
Email: trade@macmillan.co.uk

Personnel:
Hazel Cushion (Managing Director)
Robert Cushion (Finance Director)
Karen Smart (Administration)
Alison Stokes (Production)

Biography & Autobiography; Children's
Books; Cookery, Wines & Spirits; Crafts &
Hobbies; Crime; Educational & Textbooks;
Fiction; Guide Books; Humour; Industry,
Business & Management; Medical (incl. Self
Help & Alternative Medicine); Poetry

Associated Companies:
Curriculum Concepts UK; Green Fuse;
    Wedding Bible Co; Xcite Books

Overseas Representation:
All Arab countries: Peter Ward
Australia & New Zealand: Exisle Publishing
Central & Eastern Europe: Tony Moggach
Indian Sub Continent: Maya Publishers
Singapore, Malaysia, Thailand & Indonesia:
    PMS Publishers Marketing Services,
    Singapore
Spain, Portugal & Gibraltar: Iberian Book
    Services

Book Trade Association Membership:
Booksellers Association; Independent
Publishers Guild

2004 ▬▬▬▬

ACUMEN PUBLISHING LTD
4 Saddler Street, Durham DH1 3NP
Telephone: 0191 383 1889
Fax: 0191 386 2542
Email:
    steven.gerrard@acumenpublishing.co.uk

Web Site: www.acumenpublishing.co.uk

**Warehouse, Trade Enquiries, Orders &
Distribution:**
Marston Book Services, 160 Milton Park,
Abingdon, Oxon OX14 4YN
Telephone: 01235 465521
Fax: 01235 465555
Email: trade.orders@marston.co.uk
Web Site: www.marston.co.uk

Personnel:
Steven Gerrard (Publisher)
Kate Williams (Prepress Manager)
Tristan Palmer (Senior Editor)

Academic & Scholarly; Biography &
Autobiography; Educational & Textbooks;
History & Antiquarian; Philosophy; Politics &
World Affairs; Reference Books, Directories
& Dictionaries; Religion & Theology;
Sociology & Anthropology

New Titles: 25 (2009) , 30 (2010)

Imprints, Series & ISBNs:
978 1 84465, 978 1 902683

Overseas Representation:
Australia & New Zealand: Palgrave
    Macmillan, South Yarra, Vic, Australia
Austria, Germany & Switzerland: Bernd
    Feldmann, Oranienburg, Germany
Belgium, Luxembourg & Netherlands:
    Kemper Conseil Publishing, De Star,
    Netherlands
Botswana, Lesotho, Namibia, South Africa,
    Swaziland & Zimbabwe: The African
    Moon Press, Kelvin, South Africa
Brunei, Cambodia, Indonesia, Laos,
    Philippines, Singapore, Thailand &
    Vietnam: APD Singapore Pte Ltd,
    Singapore
China, Hong Kong, Korea & Taiwan: Asia
    Publishers Services Ltd, Hong Kong
France, Italy, Portugal & Spain: Flavio
    Marcello Publishers' Agents &
    Consultants, Padua, Italy
Greece, Cyprus & Malta: Charles Gibbes
    Associates, Louslitges, France
India: Maya Publishers Pvt Ltd, New Delhi,
    India
Middle East: Avicenna Ltd, Oxford, UK
Scandinavia: Colin Flint Ltd, Harlow, UK
USA & Canada: McGill-Queen's University
    Press, Montreal, PQ, Canada

Book Trade Association Membership:
Independent Publishers Guild

2005 ▬▬▬▬

ADAM MATTHEW DIGITAL LTD
Pelham House, London Road,
Marlborough, Wiltshire SN8 2AA
Telephone: 01672 511921

Fax: 01672 511663
Email: david@amdigital.co.uk
Web Site: www.amdigital.co.uk

Personnel:
William Pidduck (Chairman)
David Tyler (Managing Director)
Khal Rudin (Sales & Marketing Director)

Academic & Scholarly; Electronic
(Educational); Electronic (Professional &
Academic); Gender Studies; History &
Antiquarian; Literature & Criticism; Military
& War

Parent Company:
Hanfrageo Holdings Ltd

Associated Companies:
Adam Matthew Publications Ltd

Overseas Representation:
Italy: Licosa SPA, Florence, Italy
Japan: Maruzen Co Ltd, Tokyo, Japan
Korea: GDI, Seoul, Republic of Korea
Taiwan: Transmission Books & Microforms
    Co Ltd, Taipei, Taiwan

2006 ▬▬▬▬

**ADAM MATTHEW PUBLICATIONS
LTD**
Pelham House, London Road,
Marlborough, Wiltshire SN8 2AA
Telephone: 01672 511921
Fax: 01672 511663
Email: david@ampltd.co.uk
Web Site: www.ampltd.co.uk

Personnel:
William Pidduck (Chairman)
David Tyler (Managing Director)
Khal Rudin (Sales & Marketing Director)

Academic & Scholarly; Economics; Gender
Studies; History & Antiquarian; Literature &
Criticism; Reference Books, Directories &
Dictionaries

Imprints, Series & ISBNs:
978 1 85711

Parent Company:
Hanfrageo Holdings Ltd

Associated Companies:
Adam Matthew Digital Ltd

Overseas Representation:
Japan: Maruzen Co Ltd, Tokyo, Japan
Taiwan: Transmission Books & Microforms
    Co Ltd, Taipei, Taiwan

2007

ADAMSON PUBLISHING LTD
8 The Moorings, Norwich NR3 3AX
Telephone: 01603 623336
Fax: 01603 624767
Email: stephen@adamsonbooks.com
Web Site: www.adamsonbooks.com

Personnel:
Stephen Adamson (Chairman)

Educational & Textbooks; Electronic
(Educational); Reference Books, Directories
& Dictionaries

New Titles: 4 (2009) , 4 (2010)
Annual Turnover: £110,000

Imprints, Series & ISBNs:
978 0 948543

2008

ADLARD COLES NAUTICAL
36 Soho Square, London W1D 3QY
Telephone: 020 7758 0200
Fax: 020 7758 0333
Web Site: www.adlardcoles.com

Personnel:
Janet Murphy (Editorial Director)
David Wightman (Sales Director)
Jill Coleman (Managing Director)

Nautical

Imprints, Series & ISBNs:
978 0 7136, 978 0 85177

Parent Company:
A. & C. Black (Publishers) Ltd

Associated Companies:
Thomas Reed Publications; Reeds Almanac

Overseas Representation:
See: A. & C. Black (Publishers) Ltd, London,
UK

2009

ADVANCE MATERIALS
41 East Hatley, Sandy, Bedfordshire
SG19 3JA
Telephone: 01767 652140
Fax: 01767 652937
Email: office@advancematerials.co.uk
Web Site: www.advancematerials.co.uk

Orders:
NBN International, Estover Road, Plymouth,
Devon PL6 7PY
Telephone: 01752 202300
Fax: 01752 202330
Email: orders@nbninternational.com
Web Site: www.nbninternational.com

Personnel:
Mrs Jennifer Ollerenshaw (Director)
Dr Timothy Ollerenshaw (IT Manager)
Mrs Helen Edwards (Administrator)

Educational & Textbooks; Languages &
Linguistics

New Titles: 11 (2009) , 5 (2010)
No of Employees: 4

Imprints, Series & ISBNs:
978 0 9532440, 978 0 9547695, 978 0
9559265, 978 0 9565431

Overseas Representation:
Australia & New Zealand: Foreign Language
Bookshop Pty Ltd, Melbourne, Vic,
Australia
North America: IB Source, Chicago, IL, USA

Book Trade Association Membership:
Independent Publishers Guild

2010

AEON BOOKS
118 Finchley Road, London W5 4YX
Telephone: 020 7431 1075
Fax: 020 7435 9076
Email: shop@karnacbooks.com
Web Site: www.karnacbooks.com

Warehouse, Distribution:
NBN International, Estover Road, Plymouth
PL6 7PY
Telephone: 01752 202301
Fax: 01752 202333
Email: orders@nbninternational.com
Web Site: nbninternational.com

Personnel:
Oliver Rathbone (Managing Director)

Magic & the Occult

New Titles: 15 (2009) , 15 (2010)
No of Employees: 8

Imprints, Series & ISBNs:
978 1 904658

Overseas Representation:
USA: Stylus Publishing Inc, Sterling, VA, USA

Book Trade Association Membership:
Booksellers Association

2011

AGE UK BOOKS
1268 London Road, Norbury, London
SW16 4ER
Telephone: 020 8765 7200
Fax: 020 8765 7211
Email: acil.orders@ageuk.org.uk
Web Site: www.ageuk.org.uk

Trade Distributor:
Orca Book Services, Stanley House,
3 Fleets Lane, Poole, Dorset BH15 3AJ
Telephone: 01202 665432
Fax: 01202 666219
Email: orders@orcabookservices.co.uk
Web Site: www.orcabookservices.co.uk

Personnel:
Emma Jessop (National Resources Manager)
Donna Colbourne (Information
Communication Manager)

Academic & Scholarly; Accountancy &
Taxation; Computer Science; Educational &
Textbooks; Guide Books; Health & Beauty;
Medical (incl. Self Help & Alternative
Medicine); Photography; Reference Books,
Directories & Dictionaries

Imprints, Series & ISBNs:
978 0 86242
Can do computing
We've Made It Easy
Your Rights (series)

Associated Companies:
Age Concern; Help the Aged

Book Trade Association Membership:
Independent Publishers Guild

2012

AIR-BRITAIN (HISTORIANS) LTD
41 Penshurst Road, Leigh, Tonbridge, Kent
TN11 8HL
Telephone: 01732 835637
Fax: 01732 835637
Email: mike@absales.demon.co.uk
Web Site: www.air-britain.com

Personnel:
Michael Graham Rice (Sales Director)
Howard Nash (Director)
Dr Chris Chatfield (Director)
Don Schofield (Treasurer)
Geoff Negus (Chairman)

Aviation; Military & War

New Titles: 12 (2009) , 12 (2010)
No of Employees: 4
Annual Turnover: £207,000

Imprints, Series & ISBNs:
978 0 85130

Overseas Representation:
Australia & New Zealand: Aviation
Worldwide, Oamaru, New Zealand

2013

**AL-FURQAN ISLAMIC HERITAGE
FOUNDATION**
22A Old Court Place, London W8 4PL
Telephone: 020 3130 1530
Fax: 020 7937 2540
Email: info@al-furqan.com
Web Site: www.al-furqan.com

Personnel:
Susan John-Richards (Office Manager)

Academic & Scholarly; History &
Antiquarian; Mathematics & Statistics;
Religion & Theology

Imprints, Series & ISBNs:
Al-Furqan Publications: 978 1 873992

Book Trade Association Membership:
Publishers Association; Booksellers
Association

2014

ALBAN BOOKS LTD
14 Belford Road, Edinburgh EH4 3BL
Telephone: 0131 226 2217
Fax: 0131 225 5999
Email: sales@albanbooks.com
Web Site: www.albanbooks.com

**Warehouse, Invoicing, Customer
Services:**
c/o Marston Book Services
Telephone: 01235 465500
Fax: 01235 465555

Personnel:
Jane Grounsell (Managing Director)
Nigel Parkinson (Sales Manager)
Elaine Reid (Marketing Executive)
Margaret Reid (Accounts & Special Orders)
Katie Gordon (Sales & Marketing Assistant)
Alison Wilson (Sales & Marketing Assistant)

Academic & Scholarly; Children's Books;
Educational & Textbooks; Fiction;
Philosophy; Reference Books, Directories &
Dictionaries; Religion & Theology

Distributor for:
USA: Abingdon Press; Augsburg Fortress
Publishers; Ave Maria Press; Baylor
University Press; Wm B. Eerdmans
Publishing Co; Hendrickson Publishers;
Orbis Books; Templeton Foundation
Press; Westminster John Knox Press

2015

ALBYN PRESS
2 Caversham Street, Chelsea, London
SW3 4AH
Telephone: 020 7351 4995
Fax: 020 7351 4995
Email:
leonard.holdsworth@btopenworld.com

Personnel:
James Hughes (Editorial Director)
Leonard Holdsworth (Production)
Margaret Fletcher (Sales)

Fiction; Fine Art & Art History; Geography &
Geology; Guide Books; History &
Antiquarian; Illustrated & Fine Editions;
Literature & Criticism; Poetry; Reference

Books, Directories & Dictionaries; Transport

Imprints, Series & ISBNs:
978 0 284

Parent Company:
Christchurch Publishers Ltd

Associated Companies:
Charles Skilton Publishing Group; Tallis
Press

Book Trade Association Membership:
Independent Publishers Guild

2016

IAN ALLAN PUBLISHING LTD
Riverdene Business Park, Molesey Road,
Hersham, Surrey KT12 4RG
Telephone: 01932 266600
Fax: 01932 266601
Email: info@ianallanpublishing.co.uk
Web Site: www.ianallanpublishing.com

Distribution:
Littlehampton Book Services,
Faraday Close, Durrington, Worthing,
West Sussex BN13 3RB
Telephone: 01903 828800 (trade orders)
Fax: 01903 828802
Email: orders@lbsltd.co.uk

Mail Order:
Midland Counties Publications,
4 Watling Drive, Hinckley, Leics LE10 3EY
Telephone: 01455 254450
Fax: 01455 233737
Email: orders@midlandcounties.com
Web Site:
www.midlandcountiessuperstore.com

Representation (England & Wales):
Amalgamated Book Services,
The Old Mill House, Mill Lane, Uckfield,
East Sussex TN22 5AA
Telephone: 01825 746050
Fax: 01825 764925

Representation (Scotland):
Alan Scollan, Earnockmuir Cottage,
Meikle Earnock Road, Hamilton ML3 8RL
Telephone: 01698 459371

Personnel:
David Allan (Chairman)
Iain Aitken (Managing Director)
Jonathan King (Sales & Marketing Director)
Nick Grant (Publisher)
Nigel Passmore (Sales Manager)
Sue Frost (Marketing Manager)
Alan Butcher (Production Manager)

Atlases & Maps; Aviation; Biography &
Autobiography; History & Antiquarian;
Military & War; Nautical; Reference Books,
Directories & Dictionaries; Sports & Games;
Transport

Imprints, Series & ISBNs:
Aerofax: 978 1 85780
Ian Allan: 978 0 7110
Classic Publications: 978 1 903223
Lewis: 978 0 85318
Lewis Masonic (only available from Midland
Counties Publications): 978 0 85318
Midland Publishing: 978 1 85780
OPC: 978 0 86093

Parent Company:
Ian Allan Group Ltd

Distributor for:
KRB (formerly Kestrel Railway Books);
Millstream; Noodle Books; Pendragon;
Polygon Press; Red Kite; Runpast; John
Sullivan

Overseas Representation:
Australia, New Zealand, New Guinea &
Papua: DLS Australia (Pty) Ltd, Braeside,
Vic, Australia

Austria, Belgium, France, Germany, Netherlands & Switzerland: European Marketing Services, London, UK
Canada: Vanwell Publishing Ltd, St Catharines, Ont, Canada
Central & Eastern Europe: Tony Moggach, InterMedia Americana (IMA) Ltd, London, UK
Middle & Far East: Julian Ashton, Ashton International Marketing Services, Sevenoaks, Kent, UK
Republic of Ireland & Northern Ireland: Sales Office, Ian Allan Publishing Ltd, Hersham, UK
Scandinavia: Gill Angell & Stewart Siddall, Angell Eurosales, Berwick-on-Tweed, UK
Spain, Portugal, Gibraltar, Italy, Malta, Greece, Slovenia, Croatia, Bosnia & Montenegro: Bookport Associates, Corsico (MI), Italy
USA (Aviation titles only): Specialty Press, North Branch, MN, USA
USA (Masonic titles only): Atlas Books (a division of BookMasters Inc), Ashland, OH, USA
USA (Military titles only): Casemate Publishers & Book Distributors LLC, Havertown, PA, USA

Book Trade Association Membership:
Booksellers Association; Independent Publishers Guild

2017

PHILIP ALLAN PUBLISHERS LTD
Market Place, Deddington, Oxon OX15 0SE
Telephone: 01869 338652
Fax: 01869 338803
Email: sales@philipallan.co.uk
Web Site: www.philipallan.co.uk

Personnel:
Paul Cherry *(Editorial Director)*
Ceri Jenkins *(Marketing Manager)*

Educational & Textbooks

New Titles: 180 (2009) , 200 (2010)
No of Employees: 26
Annual Turnover: £>4M

Imprints, Series & ISBNs:
Philip Allan Updates: 978 0 86003, 978 1 84489

Parent Company:
Hodder Education

Book Trade Association Membership:
Educational Publishers Council

2018

J. A. ALLEN
[an imprint of Robert Hale Ltd]
45–47 Clerkenwell Green, London EC1R 0HT
Telephone: 020 7251 2661
Fax: 020 7490 4958
Email: allen@halebooks.com
Web Site: www.allenbooks.co.uk

Warehouse & Shipping:
Combined Book Services Ltd, Units I/K, Paddock Wood Distribution Centre, Paddock Wood, Tonbridge, Kent TN12 6UU
Telephone: 01892 837171
Fax: 01892 837272
Email: orders@combook.co.uk

Personnel:
Lesley Gowers *(Publisher)*

Animal Care & Breeding; Sports & Games; Veterinary Science

New Titles: 12 (2010)

Imprints, Series & ISBNs:
978 0 85131

Parent Company:
Robert Hale Ltd

Overseas Representation:
See: Robert Hale Ltd, London, UK

2019

ALLISON & BUSBY
13 Charlotte Mews, London W1T 4EJ
Telephone: 020 7580 1080
Fax: 020 7580 1180
Email: susie@allisonandbusby.com
Web Site: www.allisonandbusby.com

Warehouse/Distribution:
Turnaround Publisher Services Ltd, Unit 3, Olympia Trading Estate, Coburg Road, London N22 6TZ
Telephone: 020 8829 3000
Fax: 020 8881 5088
Email: orders@turnaround-uk.com

Personnel:
Susie Dunlop *(Publishing Director & UK Sales)*
Chiara Priorelli *(Publicity & Online Marketing Manager)*
Lara Crisp *(Managing Editor)*
Lesley Crooks *(Sales & Digital Manager)*
Louise Watson *(Editor)*
Christina Griffiths *(Art Editor)*

Biography & Autobiography; Crime; Fiction; Humour; Literature & Criticism; Science Fiction

New Titles: 90 (2009) , 90 (2010)
No of Employees: 6

Imprints, Series & ISBNs:
978 0 7490, 978 0 85031

Parent Company:
Spain: Editorial Prensa Iberica SA

Overseas Representation:
Africa, Middle East & Gulf: InterMedia Americana (IMA) Ltd, London, UK
Australia: DLS Australia
Canada: Georgetown Publications Inc, Toronto, Ont, Canada
France, Belgium & Netherlands: Michael Geoghegan, London, UK
Germany: Gabriele Kern Publishers Services, Frankfurt-am-Main, Germany
India: Maya Publishers Pvt Ltd, New Delhi, India
Italy: Ted Dougherty, London, UK
Scandinavia: Angell Eurosales, Berwick-on-Tweed, UK
South & South East Europe, Eastern Europe & Egypt: IMA
Spain, Portugal & Malta: Peter Prout Iberian Book Services, Madrid, Spain
USA: International Publishers Marketing Inc, Sterling, VA, USA

Book Trade Association Membership:
Independent Publishers Guild

2020

ALMA BOOKS LTD
London House,
243–253 Lower Mortlake Road, Richmond, Surrey TW9 2LL
Telephone: 020 8948 9550
Fax: 020 8948 5599
Email: info@almabooks.com
Web Site: www.almabooks.com

Personnel:
Alessandro Gallenzi *(Managing Director)*
Elisabetta Minervini *(Sales & Marketing Director)*

Biography & Autobiography; Crime; Fiction; Humour; Poetry

New Titles: 14 (2009) , 14 (2010)
No of Employees: 4

Annual Turnover: £400,000

Imprints, Series & ISBNs:
978 1 84688

Associated Companies:
UK: Herla Publishing

Overseas Representation:
Australia: Macmillan, Australia
South Africa: SG Distributors, South Africa
USA & Canada: Trafalgar Square Publishing / IPG, Chicago, IL, USA

Book Trade Association Membership:
Independent Publishers Guild

2021

ALPHA SCIENCE INTERNATIONAL LTD
7200 The Quorum,
Oxford Business Park North, Garsington Road, Oxford OX4 2JZ
Telephone: 01865 481433
Fax: 01865 481482
Email: info@alphasci.com
Web Site: www.alphasci.com

Trade Orders:
Marston Book Services,
Trade Order Department, PO Box 269, Abingdon, Oxon OX14 4YN
Telephone: 01235 465500
Fax: 01235 465655
Email: direct.trade@marston.co.uk

Personnel:
Sascha Mehra *(Director)*

Academic & Scholarly; Biology & Zoology; Chemistry; Computer Science; Educational & Textbooks; Electronic (Educational); Electronic (Professional & Academic); Engineering; Environment & Development Studies; Mathematics & Statistics; Medical (incl. Self Help & Alternative Medicine); Physics; Reference Books, Directories & Dictionaries; Scientific & Technical

Imprints, Series & ISBNs:
978 1 84265

Distributor for:
India: Narosa Publishing House Pvt Ltd

Book Trade Association Membership:
Publishers Association; Independent Publishers Guild

2022

AMBERWOOD PUBLISHING LTD
Unit 4, Stirling House, Sunderland Quay, Culpeper Close, Medway City Estate, Rochester, Kent ME2 4HN
Telephone: 01634 290115
Fax: 01634 290761
Email: books@amberwoodpublishing.com
Web Site:
www.amberwoodpublishing.com

Warehouse:
Mulberry Court, Stour Road, Bournemouth, Dorset
Telephone: 01202 488333
Fax: 01202 476872
Email: pauline@bio-health.co.uk

Personnel:
June Crisp *(Managing Director)*
Henry Crisp *(Company Secretary)*
Victor Perfitt *(Chairman)*
Pauline Parrot *(Administration & Accounts, Dispatch)*

Health & Beauty; Medical (incl. Self Help & Alternative Medicine)

Imprints, Series & ISBNs:
978 0 9517723, 978 1 899308

2023

AMERICAN PSYCHIATRIC PUBLISHING INC
5 Victoria House, 138 Watling Street East, Towcester NN12 6BT
Telephone: 01327 357770
Fax: 01327 359572
Email: appi@oppuk.co.uk
Web Site: www.appi.org

Warehouse & Distribution:
NBN International, Estover Road, Plymouth PL6 7PY
Telephone: 01752 202301
Fax: 01752 202331
Email: orders@nbninternational.com
Web Site: www.nbninternational.com

Personnel:
Gary Hall *(Manager)*

Academic & Scholarly; Educational & Textbooks; Medical (incl. Self Help & Alternative Medicine); Psychology & Psychiatry; Reference Books, Directories & Dictionaries

New Titles: 25 (2009) , 40 (2010)

Imprints, Series & ISBNs:
978 0 89042, 978 1 58562

Parent Company:
USA: American Psychiatric Publishing Inc

2024

AMNESTY INTERNATIONAL INTERNATIONAL SECRETARIAT
1 Easton Street, London WC1X 0DW
Telephone: 020 7413 5500
Fax: 020 7956 1157
Email: amnestyis@amnesty.org & orderpubs@amnesty.org
Web Site: www.amnesty.org & shop.amnesty.org

Personnel:
Irene Khan *(Secretary General)*
Sarah Wilbourne *(Director, Publications Program)*

Academic & Scholarly; Law; Politics & World Affairs

Imprints, Series & ISBNs:
978 0 86210

Overseas Representation:
see website: www.amnesty.org, UK

2025

A.M.S. EDUCATIONAL LTD
38 Parkside Road, Leeds LS6 4NB
Telephone: 0113 275 9900
Fax: 0113 275 7799
Email: admin@amseducational.co.uk
Web Site: www.amseducational.com

Orders (for Senter & Propagator):
38 Parkside Road, Leeds LS6 4NB
Telephone: 0113 275 9900
Fax: 0113 275 7799
Email: www.amseducational.co.uk
Web Site: www.senter.co.uk

Personnel:
Stan Sharp *(Managing Director)*
Margaret Sharp *(Finance Director)*
Victoria Keys *(Publishing Manager)*

Aviation; Biography & Autobiography; Children's Books; Educational & Textbooks; History & Antiquarian; Military & War; Poetry

New Titles: 12 (2009) , 27 (2010)
No of Employees: 4

Imprints, Series & ISBNs:
A.M.S. Educational: 978 1 86029
Educational Fun Factory: 978 1 86029
Falconwood Series: 978 1 900899
Leopard Learning: 978 1 899929
New Education Press (N.E.P.): 978 0 946947
Propagator Press: 978 1 86029
Senter Series: 978 1 902751

Distributor for:
Prim-Ed Publishing
New Zealand: Sunshinebooks UK
UK: Claire Publications; Desktop
 Publications

Book Trade Association Membership:
Independent Publishers Guild

2026

ANDERSEN PRESS LTD
20 Vauxhall Bridge Road, London
SW1V 2SA
Telephone: 020 7840 8701
Fax: 020 7233 6263
Email:
 andersenpublicity@randomhouse.co.uk
Web Site: www.andersenpress.co.uk

Warehouse, Orders & Payments:
TBS Ltd, Colchester Road, Frating Green,
Colchester, Essex CO7 7DW
Telephone: 01206 255678
Fax: 01206 255930

Address for Returns Requests:
Sales Department,
Random House Children's Books,
61-63 Uxbridge Road, London W5 5SA
Telephone: 020 8231 6800
Fax: 020 8231 6767
Web Site: www.andersenpress.co.uk

Personnel:
Klaus Flugge *(Managing & Publisher)*
P. W. Durrance *(Director)*
Rona Selby *(Editorial Director)*
Mark Hendle *(Company Secretary)*
Sarah Pakenham *(Rights & Permission)*
Eloise King *(Marketing & Publicity)*

Children's Books

Imprints, Series & ISBNs:
Andersen Artists (greetings cards): 978 0
 86264, 978 0 905478, 978 1 84270, 978
 1 84939
Andersen Press: 978 0 86264, 978 0
 905478, 978 1 84270, 978 1 84939
Andersen Young Readers' Library: 978 0
 86264, 978 0 905478, 978 1 84270, 978
 1 84939
Children's Picture Books: 978 0 86264, 978
 0 905478, 978 1 84270, 978 1 84939

Associated Companies:
Random House

Overseas Representation:
Other overseas markets See: Random
 House Group Ltd, London, UK
USA: Lerner Publishing Group, USA

2027

**PETER ANDREW PUBLISHING CO
LTD**
4 Charlecot Road, Droitwich, Worcs
WR9 7RP
Telephone: 01905 778543
Email: sales@peterandrew.com
Web Site: www.peterandrew.com

Personnel:
Philip Checkley *(Director)*
Joan Checkley *(Sales Director)*

*Academic & Scholarly; Accountancy &
Taxation; Economics; Engineering; Health &
Beauty; Industry, Business & Management;
Law; Sports & Games; Theatre, Drama &
Dance*

Imprints, Series & ISBNs:
978 0 946796

Book Trade Association Membership:
Book Data

2028

**CHRIS ANDREWS PUBLICATIONS
LTD**
15 Curtis Yard, North Hinksey Lane, Oxford
OX2 0LX
Telephone: 01865 723404
Fax: 01865 725294
Email: chris.andrews1@btclick.com
Web Site: www.cap-ox.co.uk

Personnel:
Chris Andrews *(Director)*
Virginia Andrews *(Director)*
Annabel Matthews *(Personal Assistant)*

Travel & Topography

New Titles: 5 (2009) , 6 (2010)
No of Employees: 3

Imprints, Series & ISBNs:
978 0 9509643, 978 0 9540331, 978 1
 905385, 978 1 906725

Book Trade Association Membership:
Independent Publishers Guild

2029

ANGLO-SAXON BOOKS
Hereward, 11 Black Bank Road,
Little Downham, Cambs CB6 2UA
Telephone: 07576 4552901
Email: tony@asbooks.co.uk
Web Site: www.asbooks.co.uk

Personnel:
Tony Linsell *(Contact)*

*Academic & Scholarly; Educational &
Textbooks; History & Antiquarian;
Languages & Linguistics; Military & War;
Poetry; Reference Books, Directories &
Dictionaries*

New Titles: 4 (2009) , 4 (2010)

Imprints, Series & ISBNs:
Anglo-Saxon Books: 978 1 898281
Athelney: 978 1 903313

Overseas Representation:
USA & Canada: The David Brown Book Co,
 Oakville, CT, USA

2030

ANN ARBOR PUBLISHERS LTD
PO Box 1, Belford, Northumberland
NE70 7JX
Telephone: 01668 214460
Fax: 01668 214484
Email: enquiries@annarbor.co.uk
Web Site: www.annarbor.co.uk

Personnel:
Peter D. Laverack *(Managing Director)*

*Academic & Scholarly; Educational &
Textbooks; Psychology & Psychiatry*

No of Employees: 4
Annual Turnover: £500,000

Imprints, Series & ISBNs:
978 0 87879, 978 0 931421, 978 1 900506

Distributor for:
Academic Therapy Publications; Ann Arbor
 Publishers; High Noon Books; PAR; Pro-
 Ed; SlossEn; Western Psychological
 Services

Book Trade Association Membership:
BEEA

2031

ANOVA BOOKS
The Old Magistrates Court,
10 Southcombe Street, London W14 0RA
Telephone: 0207 605 1400
Fax: 0207 605 1401
Email: customerservices@anovabooks.com
Web Site: www.anovabooks.com

Warehouse, Trade orders & enquiries:
HarperCollins, Westerhill Road,
Bishopbriggs, Glasgow G64 2QT
Telephone: 0141 306 3100
Email: uk.orders@harpercollins.co.uk

Personnel:
Mr Jonathan White *(Sales & Marketing
 Director)*
Ms Komal Patel *(Senior Publicity &
 Marketing Manager)*
Miss Joanna Hutchinson *(Digital Marketing
 Executive)*
Ms Sinead Hurley *(Head of Foreign Rights)*

*Animal Care & Breeding; Architecture &
Design; Children's Books; Cinema, Video,
TV & Radio; Cookery, Wines & Spirits;
Crafts & Hobbies; Do-It-Yourself; Fashion &
Costume; Fine Art & Art History;
Gardening; History & Antiquarian;
Humour; Military & War; Music;
Photography; Sports & Games*

New Titles: 160 (2009) , 160 (2010)
No of Employees: 60

Imprints, Series & ISBNs:
Batsford
Collins & Brown: 978 1 84340
Conway: 978 1 84486
National Trust
Pavilion: 978 1 86205
Portico
Robson: 978 1 86105
Salamander (packager)

Overseas Representation:
Australia: HarperCollins Publishers, Pymble,
 NSW, Australia
*Belgium, France, Netherlands &
 Luxembourg:* Ted Dougherty, London,
 UK
Carribbean, Mexico & Central America:
 Humphrys Roberts Associates, London,
 UK
Central & Eastern Europe: CLB Marketing
 Services, Budapest, Hungary
Far East: Ashton International Marketing,
 Kent, UK
Germany, Switzerland & Austria: Gabriele
 Kern Publishers Services, Frankfurt,
 Germany
Italy, Greece, Spain, Portugal & Cyprus:
 Padovani Books, Italy
New Zealand: HarperCollins Publishers (NZ),
 Glenfield, Auckland, New Zealand
Scandinavia: McNeish Publishing Services,
 East Sussex, UK
Singapore & Malaysia: Pansing Distribution,
 Times Centre, Singapore
South Africa (Batsford, Conway, Robson):
 Trinity Books, Randburg, South Africa
*South Africa (Collins & Brown, National
 Trust, Pavilion, Portico, Simplicity Books):*
 Wild Dog Press, Johannesburg, South
 Africa
*USA & Canada (Batsford, Collins & Brown,
 Conway):* Sterling Distribution, New
 York, NY, USA
*USA & Canada (National Trust, Pavilion,
 Portico, Robson, Simplicity Books):*
 Trafalgar Square, IPG, Chicago, IL, USA

Book Trade Association Membership:
Independent Publishers Guild

2032

ANSHAN LTD
6 Newlands Road, Tunbridge Wells, Kent
TN4 9AT

Telephone: 01892 557767
Fax: 01892 530358
Email: info@anshan.co.uk
Web Site: www.anshan.co.uk

Warehouse:
CBS, Unit Y,
Paddock Wood Distribution Centre,
Paddock Wood, Tonbridge, Kent TN12 6UU
Telephone: 01892 837171
Fax: 01892 837272
Email: orders@combook.co.uk
Web Site: www.combook.co.uk

Representation (UK):
Quantum Publishing Solutions Ltd,
2 Cheviot Road, Paisley PA2 8AN

Personnel:
Shân White *(Managing Director)*
Andrew White *(Sales Director)*

*Academic & Scholarly; Biography &
Autobiography; Chemistry; Computer
Science; Educational & Textbooks;
Engineering; Environment & Development
Studies; Mathematics & Statistics; Medical
(incl. Self Help & Alternative Medicine);
Physics; Psychology & Psychiatry; Reference
Books, Directories & Dictionaries; Scientific
& Technical*

New Titles: 28 (2009) , 40 (2010)
No of Employees: 0

Imprints, Series & ISBNs:
978 1 848290, 978 1 904798, 978 1
 905740

Overseas Representation:
Australia & New Zealand: All Things
 Medical
Central Europe & Ireland: Durnell
 Marketing Ltd, Tunbridge Wells, UK
China: China Publishers Services Ltd, Hong
 Kong
Greece & Eastern Europe: Philip Tyers
Japan (Medical titles): Nankodo Co Ltd,
 Tokyo, Japan
Japan (Science titles): United Publishers
 Services Ltd, Tokyo, Japan
Scandinavia: Colin Flint Ltd, Harlow, UK
Taiwan: Unifacmanu Trading Co Ltd, Taipei,
 Taiwan
USA: Princeton Selling Group Inc, Wayne,
 PA, USA

2033

ANTHEM PRESS
[an imprint of Wimbledon Publishing Co]
75–76 Blackfriars Road, London SE1 8HA
Telephone: 020 7401 4200
Fax: 020 7401 4225
Email: info@wpcpress.com
Web Site: www.anthempress.com

Personnel:
Tej Sood *(Managing Director)*

*Academic & Scholarly; Atlases & Maps;
Chemistry; Economics; Educational &
Textbooks; Electronic (Educational);
Electronic (Professional & Academic);
Engineering; Environment & Development
Studies; Gender Studies; Geography &
Geology; Industry, Business &
Management; Law; Literature & Criticism;
Mathematics & Statistics; Medical (incl. Self
Help & Alternative Medicine); Physics;
Poetry; Politics & World Affairs; Reference
Books, Directories & Dictionaries; Scientific
& Technical*

New Titles: 70 (2009) , 120 (2010)

Imprints, Series & ISBNs:
Anthem Press: 978 1 84331, 978 1 898855
Anthem Press India: 978 81 905835, 978 81
 907570
Wimbledon Publishing Co: 978 1 84331
WPC Classics: 978 1 898855

Parent Company:
UK: Wimbledon Publishing Co

Book Trade Association Membership:
Independent Publishers Guild

2034 ▬▬▬▬▬

ANTIQUE COLLECTORS' CLUB LTD
Sandy Lane, Old Martlesham, Woodbridge,
Suffolk IP12 4SD
Telephone: 01394 389950
Fax: 01394 389999
Email: sales@antique-acc.com
Web Site: www.antique-acc.com

Personnel:
Diana Steel *(Managing Director)*
Sarah Smye *(Marketing Director)*
Vanessa Shorten *(Financial Director)*
James Smith *(Sales Director)*
Marco Jellinek *(Business Development Director)*
John Brancati *(General Manager, USA)*

Antiques & Collecting; Architecture & Design; Children's Books; Cookery, Wines & Spirits; Fashion & Costume; Fine Art & Art History; Gardening; Humour; Natural History; Photography; Reference Books, Directories & Dictionaries

New Titles: 30 (2009) , 33 (2010)
No of Employees: 32
Annual Turnover: £3.5M

Imprints, Series & ISBNs:
978 0 902028, 978 0 907462, 978 1 85149, 978 1 870673

Distributor for:
Acanthus Press; ACR Edition; Adelson Galleries; Umberto Allemandi; Arnoldsche Verlagsanstalt; Arsenale Editrice; Artmedia Press; The Azur Corporation Ltd; Chris Beetles; Beta Plus; George Braziller; Centro Di; Images; Lannoo; Naanders; New Cavendish; PI Global; River Books; Scala; Stichting Kunstboe

Overseas Representation:
All other territories: Antique Collectors' Club, Woodbridge, Suffolk, UK
Australia: Peribo Pty Ltd, Mount Kuring-Gai, NSW, Australia
Central Europe (excluding Russia): Csaba & Jackie Lengyel de Bagota, Budapest, Hungary
Far East (including Hong Kong, Taiwan, Philippines & China): Asia Publishers Services Ltd, Hong Kong
France: Interart SARL, Paris, UK
Germany, Austria & Switzerland: Michael Klein, Vilsbiburg, Germany
India: The Variety Book Depot, New Delhi, India
Iran: Jahan Adib Publishing, Tehran, Iran
Italy, Spain, Portugal & Greece: Penny Padovani, London, UK
Japan & South Korea: Ralph & Sheila Summers, Woodford Green, Essex, UK
Malaysia: APD Kuala Lumpur Pte Ltd, Selangor, Malaysia
Near & Middle East & Turkey: Avicenna Partnership, Dumfries, UK
Netherlands: Libridis Group / Nilsson & Lamm BV, Weesp, Netherlands
New Zealand: Book Reps NZ Ltd, Auckland, New Zealand
Republic of Ireland & Northern Ireland: Robert Towers, Monkstown, Co Dublin, Republic of Ireland
Scandinavia & Iceland: Elisabeth Harder-Kreimann, Hamburg, Germany
South & Central America, Caribbean & Mexico: InterMedia Americana (IMA) Ltd, London, UK
South Africa: Peter Hyde Associates (Pty) Ltd, Cape Town, South Africa
South East Asia (including Singapore,

Thailand, Vietnam, Cambodia, Indonesia & Brunei): APD Singapore Pte Ltd, Singapore
USA: Antique Collectors Club, New York, NY, USA
West, Central & East Africa (excluding Sudan): InterMedia Africa Ltd (IMA), London, UK

Book Trade Association Membership:
Independent Publishers Guild

2035 ▬▬▬▬▬

ANVIL PRESS POETRY LTD
Neptune House, 70 Royal Hill, London
SE10 8RF
Telephone: 020 8469 3033
Fax: 020 8469 3363
Email: anvil@anvilpresspoetry.com
Web Site: www.anvilpresspoetry.com

Distributors:
Littlehampton Book Services,
Columbia Building, Faraday Close,
Durrington, Worthing, West Sussex
BN13 3RB
Telephone: 01903 828800
Fax: 01903 828801 & 828802
Email: orders@lbsltd.co.uk
Web Site: www.lbsltd.co.uk

Personnel:
Peter Jay *(Managing Director: Editorial, Administration & Production)*
Kit Yee Wong *(Administrative Manager)*

Poetry

Imprints, Series & ISBNs:
Anvil Editions: 978 0 85646, 978 0 900977
Poetica: 978 0 85646, 978 0 900977

Overseas Representation:
Australia: Eleanor Brasch Enterprises, Artarmon, NSW, Australia
Eastern Europe, Greece & Israel: Tony Moggach, InterMedia Americana (IMA) Ltd, London, UK
France, Benelux, Germany, Austria & Switzerland: Ted Dougherty, London, UK
Republic of Ireland: Robert Towers, Monkstown, Co Dublin, Republic of Ireland
Spain: Peter Prout Iberian Book Services, Madrid, Spain
USA: Consortium Book Sales & Distribution Inc, Minneapolis, MN, USA

Book Trade Association Membership:
Independent Publishers Guild

2036 ▬▬▬▬▬

APEX PUBLISHING LTD
PO Box 7086, Clacton-on-Sea, Essex
CO15 5WN
Telephone: 01255 428500
Email: mail@apexpublishing.co.uk
Web Site: www.apexpublishing.co.uk

Personnel:
Jackie Bright *(Marketing Manager)*
Chris Cowlin *(Managing Editor)*

Academic & Scholarly; Biography & Autobiography; Children's Books; Crafts & Hobbies; Crime; Fiction; Fine Art & Art History; Guide Books; Health & Beauty; Humour; Medical (incl. Self Help & Alternative Medicine); Military & War; Philosophy; Poetry; Politics & World Affairs; Reference Books, Directories & Dictionaries; Religion & Theology; Science Fiction; Sports & Games

Imprints, Series & ISBNs:
978 1 904444, 978 1 906358

Book Trade Association Membership:
Independent Publishers Guild

2037 ▬▬▬▬▬

APPLETREE PRESS LTD
The Old Potato Station,
14 Howard Street South, Belfast BT7 1AP
Telephone: 028 9024 3074
Fax: 028 9024 6756
Email: reception@appletree.ie
Web Site: www.appletree.ie

Distribution:
BookSource, 50 Cambuslang Road,
Cambuslang, Glasgow G32 8NB
Telephone: 0141 642 9182
Fax: 0141 641 9181

Personnel:
John Murphy *(Managing Director)*
Jean Brown *(Editor)*
Paul McAvoy *(Production Manager)*
Mark Elliott *(Sales Manager)*

Cookery, Wines & Spirits; Guide Books; History & Antiquarian; Humour; Reference Books, Directories & Dictionaries; Sports & Games; Travel & Topography

New Titles: 12 (2009) , 6 (2010)
No of Employees: 9

Imprints, Series & ISBNs:
978 0 86281, 978 0 904651

Overseas Representation:
Australia & New Zealand: Peribo Pty Ltd, Mount Kuring-Gai, NSW, Australia
France, Belgium, Scandinavia, Germany, Austria, Switzerland & Spain: Appletree Press, Belfast, UK
Greece, Cyprus, Israel, Russia, Eastern Europe & the Baltic States: IMA, Greece
Italy: Penguin Italia srl, Milan, Italy
Netherlands: Novelty Books, Weesp, Netherlands
Republic of Ireland: Compass Independent Book Sales Ltd, Naas, Co Kildare, Republic of Ireland
USA & Canada: Independent Publishers Group (IPG), Chicago, IL, USA

Book Trade Association Membership:
Publishing Ireland (Foilsiú Éireann)

2038 ▬▬▬▬▬

ARC PUBLICATIONS LTD
Nanholme Mill, Shaw Wood Road,
Todmorden, Lancs OL14 6DA
Telephone: 01706 812338
Fax: 01706 818948
Email: arc.publications@btconnect.com
Web Site: www.arcpublications.co.uk

Personnel:
Tony Ward *(Publishing Director)*
Angela Jarman *(Development Director)*

Music; Poetry

Imprints, Series & ISBNs:
978 0 902771, 978 0 946407, 978 1 900072, 978 1 904614, 978 1 906570

Overseas Representation:
Australia & New Zealand: Eleanor Brasch Enterprises, Artarmon, NSW, Australia

Book Trade Association Membership:
Independent Publishers Guild

2039 ▬▬▬▬▬

ARCADIA BOOKS LTD
15–16 Nassau Street, London W1W 7AB
Telephone: 020 7436 9898
Email: info@arcadiabooks.co.uk
Web Site: www.arcadiabooks.co.uk

Distribution:
Turnaround, Unit 3, Olympia Trading Estate,
Coburg Road, London N22 6TZ

Telephone: 020 8829 3000
Fax: 020 8881 5088
Email: orders@turnaround-uk.com
Web Site: www.turnaround-uk.com

Personnel:
Gary Pulsifer *(Publisher)*
Daniela de Groote *(Associate Publisher)*
Angeline Rothermundt *(Editor)*

Biography & Autobiography; Crime; Fiction; Gay & Lesbian Studies; Gender Studies; Photography; Politics & World Affairs; Travel & Topography

Imprints, Series & ISBNs:
978 1 900850, 978 1 905147
BlackAmber
Bliss Books
EuroCrime
The Maia Press

Overseas Representation:
Australia: Tower Books Pty Ltd, Brookvale, NSW, Australia
Israel (selected titles only): Steimatzky Ltd, Bnei Brak, Israel
New Zealand: Addenda Ltd, Grey Lynn, New Zealand
North America: Independent Publishers Group (IPG), Chicago, IL, USA
South Africa: Quartet Sales & Marketing, Johannesburg, South Africa

Book Trade Association Membership:
Independent Publishers Guild; Hite Research Foundation; English PEN – Writers in Prison & Books to Prisoners Committee; BTBS (The Book Trade Charity)

2040 ▬▬▬▬▬

ARCHAEOPRESS LTD
Gordon House, 276 Banbury Road, Oxford
OX2 7ED
Telephone: 01865 311914
Fax: 01865 311914
Email: bar@archaeopress.com
Web Site: www.archaeopress.com

Personnel:
Dr David Davison *(Director)*

Archaeology

New Titles: 170 (2009) , 150 (2010)
No of Employees: 4

Imprints, Series & ISBNs:
Archaeopress: 978 1 905739
British Archaeological Reports: 978 1 4073

Overseas Representation:
Worldwide: Hadrian Books Ltd, Oxford, UK

2041 ▬▬▬▬▬

ARCHETYPE PUBLICATIONS LTD
6 Fitzroy Square, London W1T 5HJ
Telephone: 020 7380 0800
Fax: 020 7380 0500
Email: info@archetype.co.uk
Web Site: www.archetype.co.uk

Personnel:
James Black *(Managing Director)*

Academic & Scholarly; Archaeology; Fine Art & Art History; Scientific & Technical

New Titles: 11 (2009) , 12 (2010)
No of Employees: 3
Annual Turnover: £250,000

Imprints, Series & ISBNs:
978 1 873132, 978 1 904982

Overseas Representation:
USA (All titles): Antique Collectors Club Ltd, Easthampton, MA, USA; JG Publishing Services, Los Angeles, CA, USA

2042

ARCHITECTURAL ASSOCIATION PUBLICATIONS
36 Bedford Square, London WC1B 3ES
Telephone: 020 7887 4021
Fax: 020 7414 0782
Email: publications@aaschool.ac.uk
Web Site: www.aaschool.ac.uk

Personnel:
Marilyn Sparrow (Sales & Marketing Manager)
Kirsten Morphet (Publications Co-ordinator)
Pamela Johnston (Editor)
Thomas Weaver (Editor)

Architecture & Design

New Titles: 10 (2009), 10 (2010)
No of Employees: 4
Annual Turnover: £150,000

Imprints, Series & ISBNs:
978 1 870890, 978 1 902902

Parent Company:
Architectural Association Inc

Overseas Representation:
Australia: Robyn Ralton, Collingwood, Vic, Australia
France: Muriel Fischer, Paris, France
Germany & Austria: Kurt Salchli, Berlin, Germany
Netherlands & Belgium: Berend Bosch, Noordwijk, Netherlands
Southern Europe: Bookport Associates, Milan, Italy

Book Trade Association Membership:
Publishers Association

2043

ARENA BOOKS (PUBLISHERS)
6 Southgate Green, Bury St Edmunds, Suffolk IP33 2BL
Telephone: 01284 754123
Fax: 01284 754123
Email: arenabooks@tiscali.co.uk
Web Site: www.arenabooks.co.uk

Personnel:
James Farrell (Managing Director)
Robert Corfe (Director)
Russell Corfe (Editor)
June Hardy (Sales Manager)

Academic & Scholarly; Economics; Fiction; History & Antiquarian; Industry, Business & Management; Literature & Criticism; Military & War; Philosophy; Politics & World Affairs; Religion & Theology; Science Fiction; Sociology & Anthropology; Travel & Topography

New Titles: 12 (2009), 10 (2010)
No of Employees: 4

Imprints, Series & ISBNs:
978 0 9538460, 978 0 9543161, 978 0 9556055, 978 1 906791

Overseas Representation:
Egypt: Abdul Radder Al-Bakkar, Cairo, Egypt
Poland: Graal Sp, Warsaw, Poland
USA: Ingram Publisher Services, La Vergne, TN, USA

Book Trade Association Membership:
Independent Publishers Guild

2044

ARRIS PUBLISHING LTD
12 Main Street, Adlestrop, Moreton in Marsh, Glos GL56 0YN
Telephone: 01608 659328
Email: gcs@arrisbooks.com
Web Site: www.arrisbooks.com

Distribution (for Arris titles):
Orca Book Distribution, Unit A3, Fleets Corner, Poole, Dorset BH17 0HL
Telephone: 01202 665432
Fax: 01202 666219

Distribution (for Chastleton titles – Travel):
Portfolio Books (for Chastleton imprint), 2nd Floor, Westminster House, Richmond, Surrey TW9 2ND
Telephone: 020 8334 1730
Email: info@portfoliobooks.com

Personnel:
Geoffrey Smith (Joint Managing Director)
Victoria Huxley (Editorial Director)

Guide Books; History & Antiquarian; Natural History; Politics & World Affairs; Travel & Topography

Imprints, Series & ISBNs:
978 1 84437
Chastleton Travel: 978 1 905214

Overseas Representation:
Germany, Eastern Europe, Switzerland, Austria, Italy & Greece: Portfolio Books, Brentford, UK

2045

ASHGATE PUBLISHING LTD
Wey Court East, Union Road, Farnham, Surrey GU9 7PT
Telephone: 01252 736600
Fax: 01252 736736
Email: info@ashgatepublishing.com
Web Site: www.ashgate.com

Warehouse & Mailing Shop, Orders:
Ashgate Publishing Direct Sales, Bookpoint Ltd, 39 Milton Park, Abingdon, Oxon OX14 4TD
Telephone: 01235 400400
Fax: 01235 400454

Personnel:
Nigel Farrow (Chairman)
Rachel Lynch (Managing Director)
John Smedley (Publisher: History (Variorum))
Jonathan Norman (Publisher: Business (Gower))
Lucy Myers (Managing Director – Lund Humphries)
Adrian Shanks (Social Sciences & Digital Director)
Darren Wise (Finance/Accounting Director)
Anne Nolan (Ashgate Marketing Director)
Richard Dowling (Sales Director)
Jo Burges (Editorial & Production Director)

Academic & Scholarly; Architecture & Design; Aviation; Bibliography & Library Science; Economics; Educational & Textbooks; Electronic (Professional & Academic); Environment & Development Studies; Fine Art & Art History; Gender Studies; Geography & Geology; History & Antiquarian; Illustrated & Fine Editions; Industry, Business & Management; Law; Literature & Criticism; Military & War; Music; Philosophy; Politics & World Affairs; Reference Books, Directories & Dictionaries; Religion & Theology; Sociology & Anthropology; Theatre, Drama & Dance; Transport

New Titles: 746 (2009), 762 (2010)
No of Employees: 119

Imprints, Series & ISBNs:
Arena: 978 1 85742
Ashgate Publishing: 978 0 7546, 978 1 84014
Avebury: 978 0 291, 978 1 85628, 978 1 85972
Dartmouth: 978 1 85521
Gower Publishing: 978 0 566, 978 1 85904
Gregg International: 978 0 576
Gregg Revivals: 978 0 7512

Lund Humphries: 978 0 85331
Scolar Press: 978 0 85967, 978 1 85928
Variorum: 978 0 86078
Wildwood House: 978 0 7045

Parent Company:
Ashgate Publishing Group

Associated Companies:
Gower Publishing Co Ltd; Lund Humphries; Scolar Fine Art Ltd
USA: Ashgate Publishing Co

Overseas Representation:
Australia, South East Asia, Malaysia, Philippines, China, Hong Kong, Taiwan, Myanmar (Burma) & South Korea: Ashgate Publishing Asia-Pacific, Newport, NSW, Australia
India: Maya Publishers Pvt Ltd, New Delhi, India
Japan: United Publishers Services Ltd, Tokyo, Japan
USA: Ashgate Publishing Co, Burlington, VT, USA

Book Trade Association Membership:
Independent Publishers Guild

2046

ASHGROVE PUBLISHING
27 John Street, London WC1N 2BX
Telephone: 020 7242 4820
Email: ashgrovepublishing@googlemail.com
Web Site: www.ashgrovepublishing.com

Warehouse & Distribution:
Orca Book Services, Unit 3A, Fleets Corner Industrial Estate, Fleetsbridge, Poole, Dorset BH17 0HL
Telephone: 01202 785714
Fax: 01202 672076
Email: tradeorders@orcabookservices.co.uk
Web Site: www.orcabookservices.co.uk

Personnel:
Brad Thompson (Managing Director)

Audio Books; Biography & Autobiography; Cookery, Wines & Spirits; Fiction; Health & Beauty; Medical (incl. Self Help & Alternative Medicine); Military & War; Psychology & Psychiatry; Religion & Theology

New Titles: 10 (2010)
No of Employees: 2
Annual Turnover: £35,000

Imprints, Series & ISBNs:
978 0 906798, 978 1 85398

Parent Company:
Hollydata Publishers Ltd

Associated Companies:
Childrens Corner Ltd

2047

ASHMOLEAN MUSEUM PUBLICATIONS
Ashmolean Museum, Beaumont Street, Oxford OX1 2PH
Telephone: 01865 278010
Fax: 01865 278106
Email: publications@ashmus.ox.ac.uk
Web Site: www.ashmolean.org

Warehouse, Trade Enquiries & Orders:
Antique Collectors Club, Sandy Lane, Old Martlesham, Woodbridge, Suffolk IP12 4SD
Telephone: 01394 389950
Fax: 01394 389999
Email: sales@antique-acc.com
Web Site: www.accdistribution.com

Personnel:
D. McCarthy (Commercial Manager)
E. Jolliffe (Deputy, Editorial, Production, Web Editor Publishing Manager)
K. Wodehouse (Picture Library Manager)

Academic & Scholarly; Archaeology; Fine Art & Art History; History & Antiquarian

New Titles: 8 (2010)
No of Employees: 2

Imprints, Series & ISBNs:
978 0 900090, 978 0 907849, 978 1 85444

Parent Company:
Ashmolean Museum, University of Oxford

Overseas Representation:
Australia: Inbooks, c/o James Bennett Pty Ltd, Belrose, NSW, Australia
Europe: Antique Collectors Club, Suffolk, UK
USA: Antique Collectors Club Ltd, Easthampton, MA, USA

Book Trade Association Membership:
Booksellers Association; Independent Publishers Guild; Museums & Galleries Publishing Group

2048

ASSOCIATION FOR LEARNING TECHNOLOGY
Gipsy Lane, Headington, Oxford OX3 0BP
Telephone: 01865 484125
Fax: 01865 484165
Email: admin@alt.ac.uk
Web Site: www.alt.ac.uk

Personnel:
Seb Schmoller (Chief Executive)

Academic & Scholarly

Imprints, Series & ISBNs:
Beyond Control (Research Proceeding): 978 0 9545870

2049

ASSOCIATION FOR SCOTTISH LITERARY STUDIES
c/o Dept of Scottish Literature, University of Glasgow, 7 University Gardens, Glasgow G12 8QH
Telephone: 0141 330 5309
Fax: 0141 330 5309
Email: office@asls.org.uk
Web Site: www.asls.org.uk

Trade Enquiries:
BookSource, 50 Cambuslang Road, Glasgow G32 8NB
Telephone: 0845 370 0063
Fax: 0845 370 0064
Email: orders@booksource.net
Web Site: www.booksource.net

Personnel:
Mr Duncan Jones (General Manager)

Academic & Scholarly; Educational & Textbooks; Languages & Linguistics; Literature & Criticism; Poetry; Theatre, Drama & Dance

New Titles: 4 (2009), 6 (2010)
No of Employees: 2
Annual Turnover: £129,203

Imprints, Series & ISBNs:
978 0 948877, 978 1 906841
ASLS Annual Volumes (series)
New Writing Scotland (series)
Occasional Papers (series)
Scotnotes (series)

Book Trade Association Membership:
Publishing Scotland

2050

ATLANTIC BOOKS
Ormond House, 26–27 Boswell Street,
London WC1N 3JZ
Telephone: 020 7269 1610
Fax: 020 7430 0916
Email: enquiries@groveatlantic.co.uk
Web Site: www.atlantic-books.co.uk

Distribution:
TBS Ltd, Colchester Road, Frating Green,
Colchester, Essex CO7 7DW
Telephone: 01206 255678
Fax: 01206 255930
Email: sales@tbs-ltd.co.uk
Web Site: www.thebookservice.co.uk

Personnel:
Guy Newton (Company Financial Officer)
Toby Mundy (Chief Executive Officer &
 Publisher)
Daniel Scott (Commercial Director)
Nicolas Cheetham (Publishing Director,
 Corvus)
Sarah Castleton (Editorial Director)
Alan Craig (Production)
Valerie Duff (Rights)
Karen Duffy (Publicity)
Ravi Mirchandani (Editor-in-Chief)

Biography & Autobiography; Crime;
Economics; Fiction; History & Antiquarian;
Humour; Industry, Business &
Management; Law; Literature & Criticism;
Mathematics & Statistics; Military & War;
Music; Natural History; Philosophy; Poetry;
Politics & World Affairs; Psychology &
Psychiatry; Reference Books, Directories &
Dictionaries; Religion & Theology; Science
Fiction; Sports & Games; Transport

New Titles: 90 (2009) , 200 (2010)
No of Employees: 20

Imprints, Series & ISBNs:
978 1 84354

Associated Companies:
USA: Grove/Atlantic Inc

Overseas Representation:
Australia: Penguin, Scoresby, Vic, Australia
Caribbean: David Willians, InterMedia
 Americana (IMA) Ltd, London, UK
Europe: Faber & Faber, London, UK
Far East: Julian Ashton, Ashton
 International Marketing Services,
 Sevenoaks, Kent, UK
New Zealand: Penguin Books (New
 Zealand) Ltd, Auckland, New Zealand
Republic of Ireland: Repforce Ireland,
 Irishtown, Dublin, Republic of Ireland
South Africa: Penguin Group SA, Rosebank,
 South Africa

Book Trade Association Membership:
Independent Publishers Guild

2051

**ATLANTIC EUROPE PUBLISHING CO
LTD**
Greys Court Farm, Greys Court,
Henley on Thames, Oxon RG9 4PG
Telephone: 01491 628188
Fax: 01491 628189
Email: info@atlanticeurope.com
Web Site: www.AtlanticEurope.com &
 www.CurriculumVisions.com

Personnel:
Dr B. J. Knapp (Director)

Chemistry; Children's Books; Educational &
Textbooks; Electronic (Educational);
Environment & Development Studies;
Geography & Geology; History &
Antiquarian; Mathematics & Statistics;
Physics; Reference Books, Directories &
Dictionaries; Religion & Theology; Scientific
& Technical

Imprints, Series & ISBNs:
978 1 86214, 978 1 869860

2052

ATTIC PRESS
[an imprint of Cork University Press]
c/o Cork University Press,
Youngline Industrial Estate, Pailaduff Road,
Togher, Cork, Republic of Ireland
Telephone: +353 (021) 490 2980
Fax: +353 (021) 431 5329
Web Site: www.corkuniversitypress.com

**Representation (Republic of Ireland &
Northern Ireland):**
Mullet Fitzpatrick, 58 New Vale Cottages,
Shankhill, Dublin, Republic of Ireland

Orders & Distribution:
Gill & Macmillan, Hume Avenue,
Park West, Dublin 12, Republic of Ireland

Personnel:
Mike Collins (Publications Director)

Biography & Autobiography; Cookery,
Wines & Spirits; Gender Studies; Music;
Politics & World Affairs

Imprints, Series & ISBNs:
978 0 946211, 978 0 9535353, 978 1
 85594

Parent Company:
Republic of Ireland: Cork University Press

Overseas Representation:
Netherlands & Germany: Brigitte Axster,
 Frankfurt, Germany
UK: Quantum Publishing Solutions Ltd,
 Paisley, UK
UK (excluding Northern Ireland): Marston
 Book Services Ltd, Abingdon, UK
USA: Dufour Editions Inc, Chester Springs,
 PA, USA

Book Trade Association Membership:
Publishing Ireland (Foilsiú Éireann)

2053

**AUDIO-FORUM – THE LANGUAGE
SOURCE**
World Microfilms, PO Box 35488,
St John's Wood, London NW8 6WD
Telephone: 020 7586 4499
Email: microworld@ndirect.co.uk
Web Site: www.microworld.uk.com

Personnel:
S. C. Albert (Director)

Academic & Scholarly; Languages &
Linguistics

Imprints, Series & ISBNs:
with Sussex Publications: 978 1 86013

Associated Companies:
Sussex Publications Ltd; World Microfilms
 Publications Ltd

2054

AURELIAN INFORMATION LTD
4(A) Alexandra Mansions, West End Lane,
London NW6 1LU
Telephone: 020 7794 8609
Fax: 020 7794 8609
Email: aurelian@dircon.co.uk
Web Site: www.dircon.co.uk/aurelian/

Distribution:
Wyvern DM Ltd, Harrier House,
Sedgeway Business Park, Witchford, Ely,
Cambs CB6 2HY
Telephone: Database enquiries: 01353
667733
Fax: 01353 669030 (Database enquiries)
Web Site: www.dircon.co.uk/aurelian/

Personnel:
Paul Petzold (Director)
Julia Kaufmann OBE (Company Secretary)

Industry, Business & Management;
Reference Books, Directories & Dictionaries

Imprints, Series & ISBNs:
Aurelian: 978 1 899247
National Charities Database: 978 1 899247

2055

AUREUS PUBLISHING LTD
Castle Court, Castle-upon-Alun,
St Bride's Major, Vale of Glamorgan
CF32 0TN
Telephone: 01656 880033
Fax: 01656 880033
Email: info@aureus.co.uk
Web Site: www.aureus.co.uk

Personnel:
Meuryn Hughes (Director)

Biography & Autobiography; Fine Art & Art
History; Music; Sports & Games

New Titles: 2 (2009) , 2 (2010)

Imprints, Series & ISBNs:
978 1 899750

2056

**AURORA METRO PUBLICATIONS
LTD**
67 Grove Avenue, Twickenham, London
TW1 4HX
Telephone: 020 3261 0000
Fax: 020 8898 0735
Email: info@aurorametro.com
Web Site: www.aurorametro.com

Distribution:
Central Books, 99 Wallis Road, Hackney,
London E9 5LN
Telephone: 020 8986 4854
Fax: 020 8533 5821
Email: info@centralbooks.com &
orders@centralbooks.com
Web Site: www.centralbooks.com

Personnel:
Cheryl Robson (Publisher)
Steve Robson (Sales & Marketing)
Rebecca Gillieron (Editor)
Stacey Crawshaw (Administrator)

Academic & Scholarly; Children's Books;
Cinema, Video, TV & Radio; Cookery, Wines
& Spirits; Educational & Textbooks; Fiction;
Gay & Lesbian Studies; Gender Studies;
Humour; Reference Books, Directories &
Dictionaries; Theatre, Drama & Dance;
Travel & Topography

Imprints, Series & ISBNs:
Aurora Metro Press: 978 0 9515877, 978 0
 9536757, 978 0 9542330, 978 0
 9546912, 978 0 9551566, 978 1 906582

Overseas Representation:
Canada: Playwrights Press Canada, Toronto,
 Ont, Canada
South Africa: Quartet Sales & Marketing,
 Johannesburg, South Africa
USA: TCG/Consortium, St Paul, MN, USA

Book Trade Association Membership:
Independent Publishers Guild

2057

AURUM PRESS
7 Greenland Street, London NW1 0ND
Telephone: 020 7284 7160
Fax: 020 7485 4902
Email:
 firstname.secondname@aurumpress.co.
 uk
Web Site: www.aurumpress.co.uk

Distribution & Warehouse:
Littlehampton Book Services,
Columbia Building, Faraday Close,
Durrington, Worthing, West Sussex
BN13 3RB
Telephone: 01903 828800
Fax: 01903 828801

Personnel:
W. J. McCreadie (Managing Director)
Graham Eames (Sales Director)
Graham Coster (Editorial Director)

Architecture & Design; Biography &
Autobiography; Cinema, Video, TV &
Radio; Cookery, Wines & Spirits; Crafts &
Hobbies; Fashion & Costume; Gardening;
Health & Beauty; Humour; Military & War;
Music; Natural History; Photography;
Sports & Games; Transport; Travel &
Topography

New Titles: 46 (2009) , 48 (2010)
No of Employees: 12
Annual Turnover: £4.5M

Imprints, Series & ISBNs:
978 1 84513, 978 1 85410, 978 1 902538,
 978 1 903221, 978 1 906417

Parent Company:
Quarto Group Plc

Overseas Representation:
Africa (excluding South Africa) & Eastern
 Europe: InterMedia Americana (IMA) Ltd,
 London, UK
Australia: Bookwise International, Adelaide,
 SA, Australia
Canada: Manda Group, Toronto, Ont,
 Canada
Europe: Bill Bailey Publishers
 Representatives, Newton Abbot, UK
Far East: Ashton International Marketing
 Services, Sevenoaks, Kent, UK
Latin America & Caribbean: Humphrys
 Roberts Associates, London, UK
New Zealand: Hachette Livre New Zealand,
 Auckland, New Zealand
Scandinavia: McNeish Publishing
 International, East Sussex, UK
South Africa: Trinity Books CC, Randburg,
 South Africa
USA: IPG Trafalgar Square, Chicago, IL, USA

Book Trade Association Membership:
Independent Publishers Guild

2058

**AUSTIN & MACAULEY PUBLISHERS
LTD**
CGC-33–01, 25 Canada Square,
Canary Wharf, London E14 5LB
Telephone: 020 7038 8212
Fax: 020 7038 8100
Email: editors@austinmacauley.com
Web Site: www.austinmacauley.com

Personnel:
Annette Longman (Chief Editor)
Serena Brotherton (Executive Editor)
Ross Malik (Marketing Executive)

Academic & Scholarly; Accountancy &
Taxation; Agriculture; Animal Care &
Breeding; Antiques & Collecting; Audio
Books; Bibliography & Library Science;
Biography & Autobiography; Biology &
Zoology; Children's Books; Cinema, Video,
TV & Radio; Computer Science; Cookery,
Wines & Spirits; Crime; Crime; Do-It-
Yourself; Economics; Educational &
Textbooks; English as a Foreign Language;
Environment & Development Studies;
Fashion & Costume; Fiction; Fine Art & Art
History; Gardening; Gay & Lesbian Studies;
Health & Beauty; Humour; Industry,
Business & Management; Literature &
Criticism; Magic & the Occult; Mathematics
& Statistics; Medical (incl. Self Help &

Alternative Medicine); Military & War; Natural History; Nautical; Philosophy; Poetry; Politics & World Affairs; Psychology & Psychiatry; Reference Books, Directories & Dictionaries; Religion & Theology; Science Fiction; Scientific & Technical; Sociology & Anthropology; Sports & Games; Theatre, Drama & Dance; Travel & Topography; Vocational Training & Careers

New Titles: 50 (2009) , 100 (2010)

2059

AUTHENTIC MEDIA
500 Avebury Boulevard, Milton Keynes
MK9 2BE
Email: info@authenticmedia.co.uk
Web Site: www.authenticmedia.co.uk

Orders:
STL Distribution, IBS-STL UK, PO Box 300,
Kingstown Broadway, Carlisle, Cumbria
CA3 0HA
Telephone: 01228 512512
Fax: 01228 514949
Web Site: www.stldistribution.co.uk

Personnel:
Mark Finnie *(Publisher)*
Malcolm Down *(Fiction & Children Publisher)*
Sarah Gallagher *(Marketing Co-ordinator, Authentic (General) – Administration)*
Mike Parsons *(Paternoster (Academic) Editorial)*
Liz Williams *(Authentic (General) – Editorial)*
Peter Little *(Production Controller)*
Richard Durham *(Data Administrator)*

Academic & Scholarly; Biography & Autobiography; Children's Books; Religion & Theology

No of Employees: 6

Imprints, Series & ISBNs:
Authentic Bibles: 978 0 85009
Authentic Lifestyle: 978 1 85078, 978 1 86024
Authentic US Lifestyle
Paternoster: 978 1 84227, 978 1 85364

Overseas Representation:
India: OM Book Services, Delhi, India
USA: STL Inc, Waynesboro, GA, USA

2060

AUTHORHOUSE UK LTD
500 Avebury Boulevard, Milton Keynes,
Bucks MK9 2BE
Telephone: 01908 309250
Fax: 01908 309259
Web Site: www.authorhouse.co.uk

Personnel:
Tim Davies *(Managing Director)*
Daniel Cooke *(Business Development Director)*

Biography & Autobiography; Children's Books; Cookery, Wines & Spirits; Crime; Fiction; Humour; Poetry; Religion & Theology; Science Fiction

Imprints, Series & ISBNs:
978 1 4208, 978 1 4259, 978 1 4343

Parent Company:
USA: Author Solutions Inc

Associated Companies:
USA: Authorhouse (USA); iUniverse; Trafford; Wordclay; Xlibris

2061

AVA PUBLISHING (UK) LTD
56A Chapel Road, Worthing, West Sussex
BN11 1BE
Telephone: 01903 204455

Fax: 01903 237346
Email: enquiries@avabooks.com
Web Site: www.avabooks.com

Personnel:
Brian Morris *(Publisher)*
Terry Hancock *(Finance Manager)*
Caroline Walmsley *(Editor in Chief)*

Architecture & Design; Cinema, Video, TV & Radio; Educational & Textbooks; Electronic (Educational); Fashion & Costume; Industry, Business & Management; Photography; Reference Books, Directories & Dictionaries

New Titles: 23 (2009) , 20 (2010)

Imprints, Series & ISBNs:
978 2 88479, 978 2 940373, 978 2 940411, 978 2 940439

Parent Company:
Switzerland: AVA Publishing SA

Overseas Representation:
USA & Canada: Ingram Publisher Services, La Vergne, TN, USA
World (excluding North America): Thames & Hudson Ltd, London, UK

2062

AWARD PUBLICATIONS LTD
The Old Riding School, Welbeck Estate,
Worksop, Notts S80 3LR
Telephone: 01909 478170
Fax: 01909 484632
Email: info@awardpublications.co.uk
Web Site: www.awardpublications.co.uk

Personnel:
Anna Wilkinson *(Managing Director)*
Richard Carman *(International Sales Director)*
David Meggs *(UK Sales Director)*
Ian Day *(Southern UK Sales Representative)*

Children's Books

New Titles: 50 (2009) , 50 (2010)
No of Employees: 16
Annual Turnover: £NA

Imprints, Series & ISBNs:
978 0 86163, 978 1 84135

2063

B & D PUBLISHING
PO Box 4658, Stratford upon Avon,
Warwickshire CV37 1EP
Telephone: 01789 417824
Fax: 01789 417826
Email: postmaster@banddpublishing.co.uk
Web Site: www.banddpublishing.co.uk

Academic & Scholarly; Educational & Textbooks

Book Trade Association Membership:
Publishers Association

2064

B SMALL PUBLISHING LTD
The Book Shed, 36 Leyborne Park, Kew,
Richmond, Surrey TW9 3HA
Telephone: 020 8948 2884
Fax: 020 8948 6458
Email: (via website)
Web Site: www.bsmall.co.uk

Sales Representation, UK Trade Enquiries & Orders:
Bounce! Sales & Marketing Ltd,
14 Greville Street, London EC1N 8SB
Telephone: 020 7138 3650
Fax: 020 7138 3658
Email: sales@bouncemarketing.co.uk
Web Site: www.bouncemarketing.co.uk

Personnel:
Catherine Bruzzone *(Publisher & Managing Director)*

Children's Books; Languages & Linguistics

Imprints, Series & ISBNs:
978 1 874735, 978 1 902915, 978 1 905710

Overseas Representation:
Australia (languages only): Intext Book Co Pty Ltd, Hawthorn, Vic, Australia
South Africa: Phambili Agencies CC, Johannesburg, South Africa

Book Trade Association Membership:
Independent Publishers Guild

2065

BERNARD BABANI (PUBLISHING) LTD
The Grampians, Shepherds Bush Road,
London W6 7NF
Telephone: 020 7603 2581/7296
Fax: 020 7603 8203
Email: enquiries@babanibooks.com
Web Site: www.babanibooks.com

Personnel:
Michael H. Babani *(Sales, Production, Managing Director)*

Computer Science; Crafts & Hobbies; Educational & Textbooks; Electronic (Educational); Electronic (Entertainment); Electronic (Professional & Academic); Engineering; Mathematics & Statistics; Scientific & Technical

New Titles: 25 (2009) , 30 (2010)

Imprints, Series & ISBNs:
Babani Press: 978 0 85934, 978 0 900162

Associated Companies:
Bernards (Publishers) Ltd

Book Trade Association Membership:
Independent Publishers Guild

2066

BACK-IN-PRINT BOOKS LTD
PO Box 47057, London SW18 1YW
Telephone: 020 8637 0975
Email: rolf@backinprint.co.uk
Web Site: www.backinprint.co.uk

Orders:
Gardners Books, 1 Whittle Drive,
Eastbourne BN23 6QH

Orders:
Bertrams, Norwich

Personnel:
Rolf Stricker *(Director)*
Gillian Cutress *(Director)*

Biography & Autobiography; Crime; Educational & Textbooks; Fiction; Guide Books; Literature & Criticism; Military & War

Imprints, Series & ISBNs:
978 1 903552

Associated Companies:
Italy: Editoriale Shopping Italia srl

2067

BADGER PUBLISHING LTD
Suite G08, Business & Technology Centre,
Bessemer Drive, Stevenage SG1 2DX
Telephone: 01438 791037
Fax: 01438 791036
Email: enquiries@badger-publishing.co.uk
Web Site: www.badger-publishing.co.uk

Personnel:
David Jamieson *(Director & Publisher)*
Jean Constantine *(Sales & Marketing Manager)*
Danny Pearson *(Editor)*

Children's Books; Educational & Textbooks

Imprints, Series & ISBNs:
978 1 84424, 978 1 84691, 978 1 85880

Parent Company:
UK: Haven Books Ltd

Book Trade Association Membership:
Publishers Association; Educational Publishers Council

2068

DUNCAN BAIRD PUBLISHERS
Castle House, 6th Floor,
75–76 Wells Road, London W1T 3QH
Telephone: 020 7323 2229
Fax: 020 7580 5692
Email: enquiries@dbp.co.uk
Web Site: www.dbp.co.uk

Personnel:
Duncan Baird *(Managing Director)*
Bob Saxton *(Editorial Director)*
Roger Walton *(Art Director)*
Ryan Tring *(Finance Director)*
Severine Jeauneau *(Foreign Rights Director)*

Architecture & Design; Cookery, Wines & Spirits; Fine Art & Art History; Health & Beauty; Magic & the Occult; Medical (incl. Self Help & Alternative Medicine); Natural History; Philosophy; Reference Books, Directories & Dictionaries; Religion & Theology

Imprints, Series & ISBNs:
978 1 84483

Associated Companies:
Watkins Publishing

Overseas Representation:
Australia: Simon & Schuster (Australia) Pty Ltd, Pymble, NSW, Australia
Canada: Raincoast Book Distribution Ltd, Vancouver, BC, Canada
New Zealand: HarperCollins (NZ) Ltd, Glenfield, Auckland, New Zealand

2069

THE BANNER OF TRUTH TRUST
3 Murrayfield Road, Edinburgh EH12 6EL
Telephone: 0131 337 7310
Fax: 0131 346 7484
Email: info@banneroftruth.co.uk
Web Site: www.banneroftruth.co.uk

Warehouse:
17 Bankhead Drive,
Sighthill Industrial Estate, Edinburgh
EH11 4DW
Telephone: 0131 442 2945
Fax: 0131 442 2945

Personnel:
John Rawlinson *(General Manager)*
Jonathan Watson *(Editor)*

Religion & Theology

New Titles: 26 (2009) , 28 (2010)
No of Employees: 10
Annual Turnover: £1M

Imprints, Series & ISBNs:
978 0 85151, 978 1 84871

Associated Companies:
USA: The Banner of Truth

Overseas Representation:
New Zealand: Sovereign Grace Books, Auckland, New Zealand

Nigeria: Amazing Grace Ltd, Kano, Nigeria
Philippines: Evangelical Outreach Inc,
Quezon City, Philippines
South Africa: Barnabas Book Room, Durban
North, South Africa; Farel Distributors
(Pty) Ltd, North Riding, South Africa
USA: The Banner of Truth, Carlisle, PA, USA

2070

THE BANTON PRESS
Rosebank, Cordon, Isle of Arran KA27 8NQ
Telephone: 01770 600416
Fax: 01770 600416
Email: bantonpress@ndo.co.uk
Web Site: www.bantonpress.co.uk

Personnel:
Mark Brown *(Managing Director)*

*Fiction; History & Antiquarian; Magic & the
Occult; Philosophy; Religion & Theology*

New Titles: 1 (2009) , 2 (2010)
No of Employees: 1

Imprints, Series & ISBNs:
978 1 85652

2071

BARDDAS
Pen-Rhiw, 71 Pentrepoeth Road, Morriston,
Swansea SA6 6AE
Telephone: 01792 792829
Fax: 01792 792829
Email: alan.llwyd@googlemail.com

Assistant Officer:
Bod Aeron, Heol Pen-Sarn, Y Bala,
Gwynedd LL23 7SR
Telephone: 01678 521051
Fax: 01678 521051
Email: elwyn@barddas.fsnet.co.uk
Web Site: www.barddas.com

Personnel:
Alan Llwyd *(Administrative Officer)*
Elwyn Edwards *(Assistant Officer)*

Poetry

Imprints, Series & ISBNs:
978 1 900437

2072

BAREFOOT BOOKS
124 Walcot Street, Bath BA1 5BG
Telephone: 01225 322400
Fax: 01225 322499
Email: info@barefootbooks.com
Web Site: www.barefootbooks.com

Trade Sales (Orders):
Littlehampton Book Services Ltd,
Faraday Close, Durrington, Worthing,
West Sussex BN13 3RB
Telephone: 01903 828800
Fax: 01903 828801

Personnel:
Tessa Strickland *(Editor-in-Chief)*
Nancy Traversy *(Managing Director)*
Sarah Spencer *(Rights Manager)*
Kay Celtel *(UK Business Development
Manager)*
Jen McDerra *(Public Relations)*

*Audio Books; Children's Books; Educational
& Textbooks*

New Titles: 24 (2009) , 26 (2010)
No of Employees: 35

Imprints, Series & ISBNs:
978 1 84148, 978 1 84686, 978 1 898000,
978 1 901223, 978 1 902283, 978 1
905236

Overseas Representation:
Australia: Willow Connection Pty Ltd,
Brookvale, NSW, Australia
East Africa: A–Z Africa Book Services,
Rotterdam, Netherlands
*Europe (Trade), Indian Sub-Continent &
Middle East:* Gabriele Kern Publishers
Services, Frankfurt-am-Main, Germany;
Jenny Padovani, Barcelona, Spain; Penny
Padovani, Montanare di Cortona, Italy
Latin America & Caribbean: David Williams,
InterMedia Americana (IMA) Ltd,
London, UK
New Zealand: Addenda Ltd, Grey Lynn,
New Zealand
Republic of Ireland & Northern Ireland:
Conor Hackett, Dublin, Republic of
Ireland
South Africa: Phambili Agencies CC,
Germiston, South Africa; Salmonberry
Press, South Africa
*South East Asia, Far East, North Asia, Hong
Kong, Singapore, Brunei & Malaysia
(Libraries), Singapore, Brunei & Malaysia
(Trade & Special Sales):* Chris Ashdown,
Publishers Marketing Services Pte Ltd,
Singapore
South East, Far East & North Asia:
Publishers International Marketing,
London, UK
USA: Barefoot Books Inc, Cambridge, MA,
USA

2073

BARNY BOOKS
Hough on the Hill, Grantham NG32 2BB
Telephone: 01400 250246
Fax: 01400 251737
Email: barnybooks@hotmail.co.uk
Web Site: www.barnybooks.biz

Invoices:
76 Cotgrave Lane, Tollerton, Nottingham
NG12 4FY
Telephone: 0115 937 5147
Email: barnybooks@hotmail.co.uk
Web Site: www.barnybooks.biz

Personnel:
Molly Burkett *(Editor)*
Jayne Thompson *(Business Manager)*

*Biography & Autobiography; Children's
Books; Fiction; History & Antiquarian;
Humour; Industry, Business &
Management; Medical (incl. Self Help &
Alternative Medicine); Military & War;
Transport*

New Titles: 8 (2009) , 12 (2010)
No of Employees: 2
Annual Turnover: £12,000

Imprints, Series & ISBNs:
978 0 948204, 978 1 906542
Events, People to be Remembered (Joseph
Banks – Sir John Hawrins)
Once upon a Wartime (Series): 978 1
903172

2074

BATSFORD
[an imprint of Anova Books Group]
10 Southcombe Street, London W14 0RA
Telephone: 020 7605 1400
Fax: 020 7605 1401
Email: reception@anovabooks.com
Web Site: www.anovabooks.com

Distribution, Warehouse & Enquiries:
HarperCollins Distribution, Campsie View,
Westerhill Road, Bishopbriggs, Glasgow
G64 2QT
Telephone: 0141 306 3100
Fax: 0141 306 3767

Personnel:
Tina Persaud *(Publisher)*
Komal Patel *(Marketing Manager)*
Sinead Hurley *(Head of International Rights)*

*Archaeology; Architecture & Design; Crafts
& Hobbies; Fashion & Costume;
Gardening; History & Antiquarian*

Imprints, Series & ISBNs:
978 0 7134

Parent Company:
Anova Books Co Ltd

Overseas Representation:
Australia: Capricorn Link (Australia) Pty Ltd,
Windsor, NSW, Australia
Canada: Sterling Publishing Co Inc, New
York, NY, USA
Eastern Europe: Tony Moggach, InterMedia
Americana (IMA) Ltd, London, UK
Far East: Ashton International Marketing
Services, Sevenoaks, Kent, UK
France, Netherlands & Luxembourg: Ted
Dougherty, London, UK
Germany, Switzerland & Austria: Gabriele
Kern Publishers Services, Frankfurt-am-
Main, Germany
Mexico & Central America: Christopher
Humphrys, Humphrys Roberts
Associates, London, UK
New Zealand: HarperCollins (NZ) Ltd,
Glenfield, Auckland, New Zealand
Scandinavia & Italy: McNeish Publishing
International, East Sussex, UK
Singapore: Pansing Distribution Sdn Bhd,
Singapore
South Africa: Trinity Books CC, Randburg,
South Africa
South America: Terry Roberts, Cotia SP,
Brazil
Spain, Portugal, Malta & Greece: Penny
Padovani, London, UK

Book Trade Association Membership:
Independent Publishers Guild

2075

BBC AUDIOBOOKS LTD
St James House, The Square,
Lower Bristol Road, Bath BA2 3BH
Telephone: 01225 878000
Fax: 01225 310771
Email: jan.paterson.01@bbc.com
Web Site: www.bbcaudiobooks.com

Personnel:
Mike Bowen *(Managing Director)*
Jan Paterson *(Publishing & Marketing
Director)*
Sam Newman *(Sales Director)*
Tracy Leeming *(Operations Director)*
Bradley Whittock *(Finance Director)*

Audio Books

Imprints, Series & ISBNs:
Cover to Cover Cassettes (Audio Cassettes
& CDs): 978 1 85549
Radio Collection (Audio Cassettes, CDs &
MP3 CDs): 978 0 563
Word for Word (Audio Cassettes & CDs)

Parent Company:
BBC Worldwide

Overseas Representation:
USA: BBC Audiobooks America, USA

2076

BBH PUBLISHING LTD
[trading as The Francis Frith Collection]
Frith's Barn, Teffont, Salisbury, Wilts
SP3 5QP
Telephone: 01722 716376
Fax: 01722 716881
Email: sales@francisfrith.co.uk
Web Site: www.francisfrith.co.uk

Personnel:
John Buck *(Managing Director)*
Jason Buck *(Development Director)*
John Brewer *(Financial Controller)*
Julia Skinner *(Managing Editor)*

Isobel Buck *(IP Rights Manager)*
Sandra Sanger *(Office Sales Manager)*

*History & Antiquarian; Photography; Travel
& Topography*

New Titles: 30 (2009) , 30 (2010)
No of Employees: 14
Annual Turnover: £750,000

Imprints, Series & ISBNs:
978 1 84589, 978 1 85937

2077

BEAM EDUCATION
Delta Place, 27 Bath Road, Cheltenham
GL53 7TH
Telephone: 01242 278100
Fax: 01242 278650
Email: info@beam.co.uk
Web Site: www.beam.co.uk

Personnel:
Adrian Maddison *(Manager)*
Liz Free *(Professional Development Lead)*
Holly Haynes *(Professional Development
Admin.)*
Ellie Hanwell *(BEAM Administrator)*

*Educational & Textbooks; Mathematics &
Statistics*

Imprints, Series & ISBNs:
978 1 906224
Peter Clarke: 978 1 906224

Parent Company:
UK: Nelson Thornes Ltd

2078

RUTH BEAN PUBLISHERS
Victoria Farmhouse, Carlton, Bedford
MK43 7LP
Telephone: 01234 720356
Fax: 01234 720590
Email: ruthbean@onetel.com

Personnel:
Ruth Bean *(Publisher)*
Nigel Bean *(Sales Manager)*

*Academic & Scholarly; Antiques &
Collecting; Crafts & Hobbies; Fashion &
Costume; Theatre, Drama & Dance*

Imprints, Series & ISBNs:
978 0 903585

Book Trade Association Membership:
Independent Publishers Guild

2079

BEAUTIFUL BOOKS LTD
36–38 Glasshouse Street, London W1B 5DL
Telephone: 020 7734 4448
Fax: 020 3070 0764
Email: simon@beautiful-books.co.uk
Web Site: www.beautiful-books.co.uk

Sales & Distribution:
Turnaround Publisher Services, Unit 3,
Olympia Trading Estate, Coburg Road,
London N22 6TZ
Telephone: 020 8829 3000
Fax: 020 8881 5088
Email: claire@turnaround-uk.com
Web Site: www.turnaround-uk.com

Personnel:
Simon Petherick *(Publisher)*
Tamsin Griffiths *(Production Manager)*
Ryan Davies *(Publicity Manager)*
Sara Di Girolamo *(Rights Officer)*

*Audio Books; Biography & Autobiography;
Fiction; Humour; Literature & Criticism;
Music; Psychology & Psychiatry; Travel &
Topography*

New Titles: 24 (2009) , 30 (2010)
No of Employees: 4
Annual Turnover: £500,000

Imprints, Series & ISBNs:
Beautiful Books: 978 1 905636, 978 1 907616
Bloody Books: 978 1 905636, 978 1 907616
Burning House: 978 1 905636, 978 1 907616

Overseas Representation:
Australia & New Zealand: Peribo Pty Ltd, Mount Kuring-Gai, NSW, Australia
Europe (including Ireland): Turnaround Publisher Services Ltd, London, UK

2080

BEDFORD FREEMAN WORTH (BFW)
at Palgrave Macmillan, Houndmills, Basingstoke, Hants RG21 6XS
Telephone: 01256 302983

Trade Orders & Warehouse:
Macmillan Direct, Customer Services, Brunel Road, Houndmills, Basingstoke, Hants RG21 6XS
Telephone: 01256 302699
Fax: 01256 364733
Email: mdl@macmillan.co.uk
Web Site: www.macmillan-mdl.co.uk

Personnel:
Margaret Hewinson *(Publishing Director (College))*

Academic & Scholarly; Biology & Zoology; Chemistry; Geography & Geology; Mathematics & Statistics; Physics; Psychology & Psychiatry

Imprints, Series & ISBNs:
978 0 7167

Parent Company:
USA: W. H. Freeman & Co

Distributor for:
Palgrave Macmillan; University Science Books; Worth Publishers
USA: Sinauer Associates

Overseas Representation:
Australia & New Zealand: Macmillan Education Australia, South Yarra, Vic, Australia
USA: W. H. Freeman & Co, New York, USA

Book Trade Association Membership:
International Group of Scientific, Medical & Technical Publishers

2081

THE BELMONT PRESS
29 Tenby Avenue, Harrow HA3 8RU
Telephone: 020 8907 4700
Fax: 020 8907 7354
Web Site: www.waterways.co.uk & www.belmont1948.co.uk

Personnel:
John Lawes *(Managing Director)*
Mark Lawes *(Technical Director)*

Atlases & Maps; Children's Books; History & Antiquarian; Nautical; Transport; Travel & Topography

New Titles: 6 (2009) , 6 (2010)
No of Employees: 3

Imprints, Series & ISBNs:
Belmont series of books: 978 0 905366
Navigator series of maps: 978 0 905366
Working Waterways series: 978 0 905366

Parent Company:
Belmont (1948) Ltd

Associated Companies:
Belmont Books; Chris Deucher; John Reeve; Waterway Books; Waterways Book Service

Distributor for:
Enigma Publishing; Remus Publishing; W.H. Walker & Bros; Robert Wilson Designs; Working Waterways Series

2082

BENE FACTUM PUBLISHING LTD
PO Box 58122, London SW8 5WZ
Telephone: 020 7720 6767
Email: inquiries@bene-factum.co.uk
Web Site: www.bene-factum.co.uk

Representation:
Compass DSA, 13 Progress Business Park, Whittle Parkway, Slough SL1 6DQ
Telephone: 01628 559500
Fax: 01628 663876
Email: sales@compass-dsa.co.uk

Distribution:
Marston Book Services, PO Box 269, Abingdon, Oxon OX14 4YN
Telephone: 01235 465500
Fax: 01235 465555
Email: direct.orders@marston.co.uk

Personnel:
Anthony Weldon *(Managing Director)*

Aviation; Biography & Autobiography; Children's Books; Cookery, Wines & Spirits; Fine Art & Art History; Gardening; History & Antiquarian; Humour; Illustrated & Fine Editions; Industry, Business & Management; Law; Medical (incl. Self Help & Alternative Medicine); Military & War; Poetry; Reference Books, Directories & Dictionaries; Travel & Topography; Vocational Training & Careers

New Titles: 5 (2009) , 10 (2010)

Imprints, Series & ISBNs:
978 0 9522754, 978 1 903071

Book Trade Association Membership:
Independent Publishers Guild

2083

BERG PUBLISHERS
1st Floor, Angel Court, 81 St Clements Street, Oxford OX4 1AW
Telephone: 01865 245104
Fax: 01865 791165
Email: kearle@bergpublishers.com
Web Site: www.bergpublishers.com

Distribution & Returns:
Macmillan Distribution Ltd (MDL), Brunel Road, Houndmills, Basingstoke, Hants RG21 6XS
Telephone: 01256 302692
Fax: 01256 812521/812558 (Home), 01256 842084 (Export)
Email: trade@macmillan.co.uk
Web Site: www.macmillandistribution.co.uk

Also at:
A. & C. Black, 36 Soho Square, London W1D 3QY
Telephone: 020 7758 0200
Fax: 020 7758 0222
Email: salesoffice@acblack.com
Web Site: www.acblack.com

Personnel:
Kathryn Earle *(Managing Director)*
Geraldine Billingham *(Editorial Director)*
Jennifer Howell *(Head of Marketing)*
Ken Bruce *(Head of Production)*

Academic & Scholarly; Architecture & Design; Cinema, Video, TV & Radio; Educational & Textbooks; Electronic

(Professional & Academic); Fashion & Costume; Fine Art & Art History; Photography; Sociology & Anthropology

New Titles: 41 (2009) , 34 (2010)
No of Employees: 18

Imprints, Series & ISBNs:
978 0 485, 978 0 85496, 978 1 84520, 978 1 84788, 978 1 85973

Parent Company:
A. & C. Black

Distributor for:
USA: Fairchild Books

Overseas Representation:
Australia & New Zealand: Allen & Unwin, Sydney, Australia
China & Hong Kong: [no rep]
Europe: Andrew Durnell Marketing Ltd, Tunbridge Wells, UK
India: Maya Publishers Pvt Ltd, New Delhi, India
Japan: United Publishers Services Ltd, Tokyo, Japan
Korea: Information & Culture Korea (ICK), Seoul, Republic of Korea
Middle East & Africa: International Publishing Services (IPS) Middle East Ltd, Dubai, UAE
Pakistan: World Press, Lahore, Pakistan
Philippines: AdBox Distributors, Quezon City, Philippines
South Africa: Book Promotions, Cape Town, South Africa
Taiwan: Unifacmanu Trading Co Ltd, Taipei, Taiwan
USA: Palgrave Macmillan, New York, NY, USA

Book Trade Association Membership:
Publishers Association; Independent Publishers Guild

2084

BERGHAHN BOOKS
3 Newtec Place, Magdalen Road, Oxford OX4 1RE
Telephone: 01865 250011
Fax: 01865 250056
Email: publisher@berghahnbooks.com
Web Site: www.berghahnbooks.com

Warehouse & Orders:
Marston Book Services, PO Box 269, Abingdon, Oxon OX14 4YN
Telephone: 01235 465500
Fax: 01235 465555
Email: enquiries@marston.co.uk

Also at:
150 Broadway, Suite 812, New York, NY 10038, USA
Telephone: +1 (212) 233 6004
Fax: +1 (212) 233 6007
Web Site: berghahnbooks.com

Personnel:
Marion Berghahn *(Managing Director)*
Mark Stanton *(Managing Editor)*
Kayleigh Chalcroft *(Publicity/Marketing Associate)*
Lore Cortis *(Rights Manager)*
Rupert Jones-Parry *(International Sales Director)*
Vivian Berghahn *(Editorial Director)*
Melissa Spinelli *(Production Manager)*
Ann Przyzycki *(Editorial Associate)*
Martha Hoffman *(Journal Manager)*
Katherine Elgart *(Publicity/Marketing Assistant)*
Gabriel Stuart *(Journal Marketing Assistant)*

Academic & Scholarly; Biography & Autobiography; Cinema, Video, TV & Radio; Economics; Electronic (Professional & Academic); Environment & Development Studies; Gender Studies; History &

Antiquarian; Languages & Linguistics; Literature & Criticism; Military & War; Politics & World Affairs; Religion & Theology; Sociology & Anthropology; Theatre, Drama & Dance; Travel & Topography

New Titles: 85 (2009) , 100 (2010)
No of Employees: 11
Annual Turnover: £1.4M

Imprints, Series & ISBNs:
978 1 57181, 978 1 84545

Distributor for:
India: Social Science Press
Israel: Yad Vashem
UK: Durkheim Press

Overseas Representation:
Australia & New Zealand: Woodslane Pty Ltd, Warriewood, NSW, Australia
Benelux: Jos de Jong, Belgium
Canada: Renouf Books, Ottawa, Ont, Canada
China & Hong Kong: Inspirees Bowen, Beijing, P. R. of China
Eastern Europe: László Horváth Publishers Representative, Budapest, Hungary
Europe: Berghahn Books, Oxford, UK
Germany (stockholding): Missing Link International Booksellers, Bremen, Germany
Greece & Cyprus: Charles Gibbes Associates, London, UK
India: Sara Books Pvt Ltd, New Delhi, India
Italy & France: Flavio Marcello Publishers' Agents & Consultants, Padua, Italy
Japan (stockholding): United Publishers Services Ltd, Tokyo; Kinokuniya Ltd, Tokyo, Japan
Latin/Central America: Cranbury International LLC, Montpelier, VT, USA
Middle East & Turkey: Avicenna Partnership, Oxford, UK
Scandinavia: David Towle International, Stockholm, Sweden
South Africa: The African Moon Press, South Africa
Spain & Portugal: Iberian Book Services, Madrid, Spain
Taiwan: Unifacmanu Trading Co Ltd, Taipei, Taiwan

2085

BIBLE READING FELLOWSHIP
15 The Chambers, Vineyard, Abingdon, Oxon OX14 3FE
Telephone: 01865 319700
Fax: 01865 319701
Email: enquiries@brf.org.uk
Web Site: www.brf.org.uk

Distribution:
STL Distribution, Kingstown, Broadway, Carlisle CA3 0HA
Telephone: 01228 512512
Fax: 01228 514949
Email: info@stl.org
Web Site: www.stldistribution.co.uk

Personnel:
R. Fisher *(Chief Executive Officer)*
Karen Laister *(General Manager)*
Sue Doggett *(Commissioning Editor)*
Naomi Starkey *(Commissioning Editor)*

Children's Books; Educational & Textbooks; Religion & Theology

New Titles: 54 (2009) , 64 (2010)
No of Employees: 24

Imprints, Series & ISBNs:
978 0 7459, 978 0 85746, 978 1 84101
Barnabas
Day by Day with God
Guidelines
New Daylight
People's Bible Commentary Series
Quiet Spaces

The Upper Room

Overseas Representation:
Australia: Willow Connection Pty Ltd,
Brookvale, NSW, Australia
New Zealand: Scripture Union Wholesale,
Wellington, New Zealand
USA: The Bible Reading Fellowship, Winter
Park, FL, USA

2086 ━━━━━━━

JOSEPH BIDDULPH PUBLISHER
32 Strŷd Ebeneser, Pontypridd CF37 5PB
Telephone: 01443 662559

Personnel:
Joseph Biddulph *(Sole Proprietor)*

*Academic & Scholarly; Architecture &
Design; Languages & Linguistics*

New Titles: 1 (2009) , 1 (2010)

Imprints, Series & ISBNs:
Joseph Biddulph Publisher: 978 1 897999
Languages Information Centre: 978 0
948565

2087 ━━━━━━━

**BIOHEALTHCARE PUBLISHING
(OXFORD) LTD**
TBAC Business Centre, Avenue 4,
Station Lane, Witney, Oxon OX28 4BN
Telephone: 01993 848726
Fax: 01865 884448
Email: info@biohealthcarepublishing.com
Web Site:
www.biohealthcarepublishing.com

Personnel:
Dr Glyn Jones *(Managing Director)*
Melinda Taylor *(Finance Director)*

*Academic & Scholarly; Industry, Business &
Management; Scientific & Technical*

New Titles: 15 (2009) , 25 (2010)
No of Employees: 10

Imprints, Series & ISBNs:
978 1 907568

2088 ━━━━━━━

BIRLINN LTD
West Newington House,
10 Newington Road, Edinburgh EH9 1QS
Telephone: 0131 668 4371
Fax: 0131 668 4466
Email: info@birlinn.co.uk
Web Site: www.birlinn.co.uk

Distribution:
BookSource, 50 Cambuslang Road,
Glasgow G32 8NB
Telephone: 0845 370 0067
Fax: 0845 370 0068
Email: info@booksource.net
Web Site: www.booksource.net

Personnel:
Hugh Andrew *(Managing Director)*
Rona Stewart *(Finance)*
Liz Short *(Production)*
Neville Moir *(Publisher)*
Andrew Simmons *(Editorial)*
Helen Stanton *(Sales)*
Maria White *(Rights)*
Jan Rutherford *(Publicity)*
Bob Smith *(Sales Key Accounts Manager)*

*Fiction; Guide Books; History &
Antiquarian; Humour; Illustrated & Fine
Editions; Military & War*

New Titles: 170 (2009) , 200 (2010)
No of Employees: 14

Imprints, Series & ISBNs:
Birlinn: 978 1 84158, 978 1 874744

Birlinn General (Military & Adventure titles):
978 1 84341
John Donald: 978 0 85976
John Donald (Print on demand titles): 978 1
904607
Mercat: 978 1 84183
Polygon: 978 0 7486, 978 0 9544075, 978
1 84697, 978 1 904598

Associated Companies:
John Donald Publishers Ltd; Polygon

Distributor for:
Clar; Maclean Press

Overseas Representation:
Australia: UNIREPS University and Reference
Publishers' Services, Sydney, NSW,
Australia
*Austria, Belgium, France, Germany, Greece,
Italy, Luxembourg, Netherlands &
Switzerland:* Ted Dougherty, London, UK
Canada: Vanwell Publishing Ltd, St
Catharines, Ont, Canada
*Denmark, Finland, Iceland, Norway,
Portugal, Spain, Sweden & Eastern
Europe:* Bill Bailey Publishers
Representatives, Newton Abbot, UK
USA (academic): Interlink Publishing Group
Inc, Northampton, MA, USA
USA (for military & adventure titles only):
Casemate Publishers & Book Distributors
LLC, Havertown, PA, USA

Book Trade Association Membership:
Independent Publishers Guild

2089 ━━━━━━━

BITTER LEMON PRESS
37 Arundel Gardens, London W11 2LW
Telephone: 020 7727 7927
Fax: 020 7460 2164
Email: books@bitterlemonpress.com
Web Site: www.bitterlemonpress.com

Crime; Fiction

Book Trade Association Membership:
Independent Publishers Guild

2090 ━━━━━━━

BLACK ACE BOOKS
PO Box 7547, Perth PH2 1AU
Telephone: 01821 642822
Fax: 01821 642101
Web Site: www.blackacebooks.com

Personnel:
Hunter Steele *(Publisher & Rights)*
Boo Wood *(Publicity & Sales)*

*Academic & Scholarly; Biography &
Autobiography; Fiction; History &
Antiquarian; Philosophy*

Imprints, Series & ISBNs:
978 1 872988

Overseas Representation:
Italy: Piergiorgio Nicolazzini Literary Agency,
Milan, Italy
Japan: The English Agency (Japan) Ltd,
Tokyo, Japan

2091 ━━━━━━━

BLACK DOG PUBLISHING LTD
10A Acton Street, London WC1X 9NG
Telephone: 020 7713 5097
Fax: 020 7713 8682
Web Site: www.blackdogonline.com

Warehouse & Distribution:
Marston Book Services, PO Box 269,
Abingdon, Oxon OX14 4YN
Telephone: 01235 465500
Fax: 01235 465555
Email: direct.orders@marston.co.uk

Architecture & Design; Cinema, Video, TV &

Radio; Crafts & Hobbies; Environment &
Development Studies; Fashion & Costume;
Fine Art & Art History; Gardening;
Illustrated & Fine Editions; Music;
Photography; Travel & Topography

New Titles: 30 (2009) , 40 (2010)
No of Employees: 14

Imprints, Series & ISBNs:
978 1 904772, 978 1 906155, 978 1
907317
Architecture & Urbanism (Serial books): 978
1 901033
Artworld
-De, -Dis, -Ex: 978 1 901033
Labels Unlimited
Revisions: 978 1 901033
Serial Books Design: 978 1 901033

Overseas Representation:
Australia & New Zealand: Peribo Pty Ltd,
Mount Kuring-Gai, NSW, Australia
Canada & USA: Perseus Group, Jackson,
TN, USA
Europe, Asia & New Zealand: Marston Book
Services Ltd, Abingdon, UK
France: Critiques Livres Distribution,
Bagnolet, France
Germany: Bugrim, Berlin, Germany

2092 ━━━━━━━

BLACK SPRING PRESS LTD
Curtain House, 134–146 Curtain Road,
London EC2A 3AR
Telephone: 020 7613 3066
Fax: 020 7613 0028
Email: general@blackspringpress.co.uk
Web Site: www.blackspringpress.co.uk

Distribution:
Turnaround Publisher Services Ltd, Unit 3,
Olympia Trading Estate, Coburg Road,
London N22 6TZ
Telephone: 020 8829 3000
Fax: 020 8881 5088
Email: orders@turnaround-uk.com
Web Site: www.turnaround-psl.com

Personnel:
Robert Hastings *(Publisher)*

*Biography & Autobiography; Cinema,
Video, TV & Radio; Fiction; Music*

Imprints, Series & ISBNs:
978 0 948238

Overseas Representation:
Europe, Middle East & Far East: Turnaround
Publisher Services Ltd, London, UK

2093 ━━━━━━━

A. & C. BLACK (PUBLISHERS) LTD
36 Soho Square, London W1D 3QY
Telephone: 020 7758 0200
Fax: 020 7758 0222
Email: rbortoli@acblack.com
Web Site: www.acblack.com

Distribution:
Macmillan Distribution (MDL), Brunel Road,
Houndmills, Basingstoke, Hants RG21 6XT
Telephone: 01256 302699
Fax: 01256 812521
Email: direct@acblack.com

Personnel:
Nigel Newton *(Chairman)*
Jill Coleman *(Managing Director)*
Jonathan Glasspool *(Deputy Managing
Director)*
Janet Murphy *(Adlard Coles Nautical
Director)*
Oscar Heini *(Production Director)*
David Wightman *(Rights, Sales & Marketing
Director)*
Colin Adams *(Group Finance Director)*
Chris Facey *(Finance Director)*

Jayne Parsons *(Children's Books Director)*
Rosanna Bortoli *(Head of Publicity &
Marketing)*

*Architecture & Design; Children's Books;
Crafts & Hobbies; Educational & Textbooks;
English as a Foreign Language; Fashion &
Costume; Fine Art & Art History; Health &
Beauty; Humour; Music; Natural History;
Nautical; Reference Books, Directories &
Dictionaries; Sports & Games; Theatre,
Drama & Dance*

Imprints, Series & ISBNs:
Adlard Coles Nautical
The Arden Shakespeare
Andrew Brodie Publications
Featherstone Education
Know the Game
Methuen Drama
New Mermaids
Thomas Reeds
Whitaker's Almanacks
Who's Who
Wisden Cricketer's Almanack

Parent Company:
Bloomsbury Plc

Distributor for:
Little Tiger Press; V & A Publications;
Wisden

Overseas Representation:
Australia & New Zealand: Allen & Unwin Pty
Ltd, Crows Nest, NSW, Australia
Canada (excluding V&A titles): Penguin
Group Canada, Toronto, Ont, Canada
Central & Eastern Europe: Grazyna
Soszynska, Penguin Poland, Poznan-
Baranowo, Poland
France (excluding V&A titles): Jean-Luc
Morel, Penguin France, Paris, France
Germany: Edith Strommen, Penguin Books
Deutschland GmbH, Frankfurt am Main,
Germany
Germany & Austria: Klaus Melz, Penguin
Books Deutschland GmbH, Mannheim,
Germany
India (excluding V&A titles): Penguin Books
India, New Delhi, India
Italy: Umberto Vigoni, Penguin Italia srl,
Milan, Italy
Laos, Cambodia, Vietnam & Thailand: Keith
Hardy, International Sales Dept, Penguin
UK, London, UK
Malaysia (excluding V&A titles): Penguin
Books Malaysia, c/o Pearson Malaysia
Sdn Bhd, Selangor Darul Ehsan, Malaysia
*Middle East, Hong Kong, Thailand &
Indonesia:* Sarah Davison-Aitkins,
International Sales Dept, Penguin UK,
London, UK
Netherlands, Belgium & Luxembourg: Feico
Deutekom, Penguin Books BV,
Amsterdam, Netherlands
Portugal: Adelino Abrantos, Penguin Books
SA, Madrid, Spain
Republic of Ireland: Brian Blennerhassett,
Butler Sims Ltd, Dublin, Republic of
Ireland
Scandinavia & Latin America: Tamsin
Pagella, International Sales Dept,
Penguin UK, London, UK
Singapore (excluding V&A titles): Penguin
Books Singapore, c/o Pearson Education
South Asia Pte Ltd, Singapore
South America, Latin America & Caribbean:
David Williams, InterMedia Americana
(IMA) Ltd, London, UK
South East Europe & Africa: Amy Elkington,
International Sales Dept, Penguin UK,
London, UK
*South Korea, Taiwan, Japan, China &
Philippines:* Yvonne Francis, International
Sales Dept, Penguin UK, London, UK
Southern Africa: Book Promotions (Pty) Ltd/
Horizon Books (Pty) Ltd, Cape Town,
South Africa
Spain: Javier Rivera, Penguin Books SA,
Madrid, Spain

Switzerland & Malta: Kathy John, International Sales Dept, Penguin UK, London, UK
USA (excluding V&A titles): Consortium Book Sales & Distribution, Minneapolis, MN, USA

Book Trade Association Membership:
Educational Publishers Council; Music Publishers Association

2094

BLACKHALL PUBLISHING
Lonsdale House, Avoca Avenue, Blackrock, Co Dublin, Republic of Ireland
Telephone: +353 (01) 278 5090
Fax: +353 (01) 278 4800
Email: blackhall@eircom.net
Web Site: www.blackhallpublishing.com

Personnel:
Gerard O'Connor *(Managing Director)*
Elizabeth Brennan *(Commissioning Editor)*
Conor O'Mahony *(Financial Controller)*
Eileen O'Brien *(Editor)*
Zoe Faulder *(Marketing)*
Benil Shah *(Typesetting Manager)*

Academic & Scholarly; Accountancy & Taxation; Economics; Electronic (Professional & Academic); Industry, Business & Management; Law; Medical (incl. Self Help & Alternative Medicine); Psychology & Psychiatry; Sociology & Anthropology

New Titles: 17 (2009) , 19 (2010)
No of Employees: 5

Imprints, Series & ISBNs:
978 1 84218, 978 1 901657

Overseas Representation:
UK: Gill & Macmillan, Dublin, Republic of Ireland

Book Trade Association Membership:
Publishing Ireland (Foilsiú Éireann)

2095

BLACKSTAFF PRESS
4C Heron Wharf, Sydenham Business Park, Belfast BT3 9LE
Telephone: 028 9045 5006
Fax: 028 9046 6237
Email: info@blackstaffpress.com
Web Site: www.blackstaffpress.com

Distribution (UK & Northern Ireland):
Gill & Macmillan, Hume Avenue, Park West, Dublin 12, Republic of Ireland
Telephone: +353 (01) 500 9500
Fax: +353 (01) 500 9599
Email: sales@gillmacmillan.ie
Web Site: www.gillmacmillan.ie

Personnel:
Patricia Horton *(Managing Editor)*
Helen Wright *(Editor)*
Michelle Griffin *(Production Editor)*
Sarah Bowers *(Publicist)*

Academic & Scholarly; Agriculture; Archaeology; Biography & Autobiography; Cinema, Video, TV & Radio; Cookery, Wines & Spirits; Crime; Fiction; Geography & Geology; Guide Books; Health & Beauty; History & Antiquarian; Humour; Illustrated & Fine Editions; Literature & Criticism; Mathematics & Statistics; Medical (incl. Self Help & Alternative Medicine); Military & War; Music; Natural History; Photography; Poetry; Politics & World Affairs; Reference Books, Directories & Dictionaries; Religion & Theology; Sports & Games; Theatre, Drama & Dance; Travel & Topography

New Titles: 8 (2010)
No of Employees: 5

Imprints, Series & ISBNs:
978 0 85640

Parent Company:
CDS

Overseas Representation:
All other areas: Blackstaff Press, Belfast, UK
USA: Dufour Editions Inc, Chester Springs, PA, USA

Book Trade Association Membership:
Publishing Ireland (Foilsiú Éireann); Booksellers Association; Independent Publishers Guild

2096

BLACKTHORN PRESS
Blackthorn House, Middleton Road, Pickering, North Yorks YO18 8AL
Telephone: 01751 474043
Email: blackthornpress@yahoo.com
Web Site: www.blackthornpress.com

Personnel:
Alan Avery *(Proprietor)*

Fine Art & Art History; History & Antiquarian; Literature & Criticism

New Titles: 6 (2009) , 6 (2010)
No of Employees: 2
Annual Turnover: £68,000

Imprints, Series & ISBNs:
978 0 9540535

2097

JOHN BLAKE PUBLISHING LTD
[incorporating Smith Gryphon Publishers Ltd & Metro Publishing Ltd]
3 Bramber Court, 2 Bramber Road, London W14 9PB
Telephone: 020 7381 0666
Fax: 020 7381 6868
Email: rosie@blake.co.uk
Web Site: www.johnblakepublishing.co.uk

Distribution:
Littlehampton Book Services, Faraday Close, Durrington, Worthing, West Sussex BN13 3RB
Telephone: 01903 828800
Fax: 01903 828802
Email: orders@lbsltd.co.uk
Web Site: www.lbsltd.co.uk

Personnel:
John Blake *(Managing Director)*
Rosie Virgo *(Deputy Managing Director)*
Ray Mudie *(Sales Director)*
Michelle Signore *(Editor-in-Chief)*
Joanna Kennedy *(Accounts Executive)*
Clare Tillyer *(Head of Marketing)*
Stuart Finglass *(Sales & Logistics Manager)*
John Wordsworth *(Editor)*
Moira Ashcroft *(Production)*
Liz Mallett *(Head of Publicity)*

Audio Books; Biography & Autobiography; Cookery, Wines & Spirits; Crime; Humour; Music; Sports & Games

New Titles: 100 (2009) , 120 (2010)
No of Employees: 14

Imprints, Series & ISBNs:
978 1 84358, 978 1 84454, 978 1 85782

Associated Companies:
Metro Books; Smith Gryphon Publishers Ltd

Overseas Representation:
Australia & New Zealand: Alpa Books, St Agnes, Australia
Germany: Michael Mellor, Munich, Germany
South Africa: Peter Hyde Associates (Pty) Ltd, Cape Town, South Africa
USA: Trafalgar Publishing, Chicago, IL, USA

Book Trade Association Membership:
Booksellers Association; Independent Publishers Guild

2098

BLOODAXE BOOKS LTD
Highgreen, Tarset, Northumberland NE48 1RP
Telephone: 01434 240500 (editorial) 01678 521550 (sales)
Fax: 01434 240505 (editorial) 01678 521544 (sales)
Email: editor@bloodaxebooks.com (editorial), sales@bloodaxebooks.com
Web Site: www.bloodaxebooks.com

Warehouse, Trade Enquiries & Orders:
Littlehampton Book Services, Faraday Close, Durrington, Worthing, West Sussex BN13 3RB
Telephone: 01903 828800
Fax: 01903 828802
Email: orders@lbsltd.co.uk

Personnel:
Simon Thirsk *(Chairman)*
Neil Astley *(Managing Director)*
Alison Davis *(Company Secretary)*
Bethan Jones *(Finance Manager)*
Christine Macgregor *(Publicity Manager)*
Suzanne Fairless-Aitken *(Permissions & Foreign Rights)*
Jean Smith *(Finance & Sales Assistant)*
Rebecca Hodkinson *(Prizes & Administration)*
Annette Charpentier *(Marketing)*

Literature & Criticism; Poetry

New Titles: 32 (2009)
No of Employees: 6

Imprints, Series & ISBNs:
Bloodaxe Books: 978 0 906427, 978 1 85224
Pandon Press: 978 1 85557

Associated Companies:
Pandon Press Ltd

Overseas Representation:
Australia: John Reed Book Distribution, Tea Gardens, NSW, Australia
Caribbean: Hugh Dunphy, Kingston, Jamaica
Europe: Michael Geoghegan, London, UK
India: Surit Mitra, New Delhi, India
Italy, Spain & Portugal: Penny Padovani, London, UK
North America: Dufour Editions Inc, Chester Springs, PA, USA
Republic of Ireland: Repforce Ireland, Irishtown, Dublin, Republic of Ireland
South & Central America, Africa (excluding South Africa), Eastern Europe, Middle East, Turkey, Israel, Greece & Cyprus: InterMedia Americana (IMA) Ltd, London, UK

2099

BLOOMSBURY PUBLISHING PLC
36 Soho Square, London W1D 3QY
Telephone: 020 7494 2111
Fax: 020 7434 0151
Web Site: www.bloomsbury.com

Distributor:
Macmillan Distribution (MDL), Houndmills, Basingstoke, Hants RG21 6XS
Telephone: 01256 329242
Fax: 01256 364733

Personnel:
Nigel Newton *(Chief Executive Director)*
Richard Charkin *(Executive Director)*
Alexandra Pringle *(Editor-in-Chief)*
Kathleen Furran *(Marketing Director)*
Colin Adams *(Finance Director)*
Ruth Logan *(Rights Director)*
Colin Midson *(Publicity Director)*

Penny Edwards *(Production Director)*
David Ward *(Sales Director)*
Sarah Odedina *(Children's Director)*

Audio Books; Biography & Autobiography; Children's Books; Cinema, Video, TV & Radio; Cookery, Wines & Spirits; Fiction; Health & Beauty; History & Antiquarian; Humour; Literature & Criticism; Military & War; Music; Politics & World Affairs; Reference Books, Directories & Dictionaries; Theatre, Drama & Dance

Imprints, Series & ISBNs:
978 0 7475

Parent Company:
USA: Bloomsbury

Associated Companies:
A & C Black
Germany: Berlin Verlag

Overseas Representation:
Africa & Middle East: Penguin International Sales, London, UK
Australia & New Zealand: Allen & Unwin Pty Ltd, Sydney, NSW, Australia
Canada: Penguin Group Canada, Toronto, Ont, Canada
Central & Eastern Europe: Grazyna Soszynska, Penguin Poland, Poznan-Baranowo, Poland
France, Morocco, Tunisia & Algeria: Jean-Luc Morel, Penguin Group, Roissy, France
Germany & Austria: Uli Hoernemann, Berlin Verlag, Berlin, Germany
Hong Kong, Macau, China, Philippines, Thailand, Indonesia, Vietnam, Cambodia, Taiwan & Korea: Yvonne Francis, Penguin International Sales, London, UK
India: Penguin Books India, New Delhi, India
Italy: Penguin Italia srl, Milan, Italy
Japan: Lisa Finch, Bloomsbury International Sales, Bloomsbury Publishing, London, UK
Netherlands, Belgium & Luxembourg: Penguin Books BV, Amsterdam, Netherlands
Pakistan: Julian Russ, Tula Publishing Ltd, Oxford, UK
Republic of Ireland & Northern Ireland: Louise Dobbin, Repforce Ireland, Irishtown, Dublin, Republic of Ireland
Scandinavia: Sarah Davison-Aitkens, Penguin International Sales, London, UK
Singapore & Malaysia: Penguin Books Malaysia, c/o Pearson Malaysia Sdn Bhd, Selangor Darul Ehsan, Malaysia; Penguin Books Singapore, c/o Pearson Education South Asia Pte Ltd, Singapore
South Africa: Jonathan Ball Publishers (Pty) Ltd, Johannesburg, South Africa
South East Europe, Cyprus, Greece, Gibraltar, Turkey, Israel, Caribbean & Latin America: Tamsin Pagella, Penguin International Sales, London, UK
Spain & Portugal: Geraldine Kilpatrick, Penguin Books SA, Madrid, Spain
Sri Lanka: Shan Rajaguru, Colombo, Sri Lanka
Switzerland & Malta: Kathy John, Penguin International Sales, London, UK

Book Trade Association Membership:
Publishers Association; Independent Publishers Guild

2100

BLUE OCEAN PUBLISHING
St John's Innovation Centre, Cowley Road, Cambridge CB4 0WS
Telephone: 01763 208887
Email: blueoceanpublishing@btconnect.com
Web Site: www.blueoceanpublishing.biz

Academic & Scholarly; Children's Books; Cookery, Wines & Spirits; Crafts & Hobbies; Educational & Textbooks; Industry, Business & Management; Poetry; Religion &

Theology; Theatre, Drama & Dance

New Titles: 6 (2009) , 5 (2010)
No of Employees: 1
Annual Turnover: £>100,000

Imprints, Series & ISBNs:
978 0 9556430, 978 1 907527

2101

BLUE SKY PRESS
57 Longfield Avenue, Fareham, Hants
PO14 1BU
Telephone: 07816 411341
Fax: 01329 221969
Email: press@mrbluesky.net
Web Site: www.mrbluesky.net,
www.thealicefactor.com &
www.blueskypress.co.uk

Personnel:
Victoria Stone *(Executive Assistant)*
Cfyn Markwick-Day *(Managing Editor)*

Fiction; Music; Poetry

Parent Company:
Mr Blue Sky Ltd

2102

BLUEBERRY PRESS LTD
17 Cheltenham Avenue, Catshill,
Bromsgrove, Worcs B61 0RU
Telephone: 07795 360294
Web Site: www.blueberrypress.co.uk

Book Trade Association Membership:
Publishers Association

2103

BML
St Andrew's House,
18–20 St Andrew Street, London
EC4A 3AG
Telephone: 020 7832 1782
Email: jo@bookmarketing.co.uk
Web Site: www.bookmarketing.co.uk

Personnel:
Jo Henry *(Managing Director)*
Steve Bohme *(Research Director)*

*Academic & Scholarly; Electronic
(Professional & Academic); Reference
Books, Directories & Dictionaries*

New Titles: 2 (2009) , 2 (2010)

Parent Company:
UK: Bowker

Book Trade Association Membership:
Publishers Association; Booksellers
Association; Independent Publishers Guild

2104

BODLEIAN LIBRARY PUBLISHING
Osney One, Osney Mead, Oxford OX2 0EW
Telephone: 01865 283850
Fax: 01865 277260
Email: publishing@bodleian.ox.ac.uk
Web Site: www.bodleianbookshop.co.uk

Trade Enquiries & Orders:
Turpin Distribution Ltd, Pegasus Drive,
Stratton Business Park, Biggleswade, Beds
SG18 8TQ
Telephone: 01767 604968
Fax: 01767 601640
Email: custserv@turpin-distribution.com
Web Site: www.turpin-distribution.com

Representation (UK Book Trade):
Yale University Press

Personnel:
Samuel Fanous *(Publisher)*
Deborah Susman *(Managing Editor)*

*Academic & Scholarly; Antiques &
Collecting; Architecture & Design;
Biography & Autobiography; Children's
Books; Fine Art & Art History; History &
Antiquarian; Humour; Literature &
Criticism; Military & War; Natural History;
Politics & World Affairs; Reference Books,
Directories & Dictionaries; Sports & Games*

New Titles: 8 (2009) , 11 (2010)

Imprints, Series & ISBNs:
978 1 85124
Original Rules
Postcards from...
Treasures of the Bodleian Library

Parent Company:
University of Oxford

Overseas Representation:
USA & Canada: Chicago University Press,
Chicago, IL, USA

Book Trade Association Membership:
Independent Publishers Guild; Association
of Cultural Enterprises

2105

BOOK CASTLE PUBLISHING LTD
2a Sycamore Business Park, Copt Hewick,
North Yorkshire HG4 5DF
Telephone: 01582 344321
Fax: 01582 344318
Email: info@bookcastlepublishing.co.uk
Web Site: www.book-castle.co.uk

Personnel:
Paul Bowes *(Publisher, Manager)*
Sally Siddons *(External Sales & Marketing
Production Manager)*

*Biography & Autobiography; History &
Antiquarian; Travel & Topography*

New Titles: 3 (2009) , 3 (2010)
No of Employees: 4

Imprints, Series & ISBNs:
978 0 9509773, 978 1 871199, 978 1
903747, 978 1 906632

Book Trade Association Membership:
Booksellers Association

2106

BORTHWICK PUBLICATIONS
Borthwick Institute, University of York,
Heslington, York YO10 5DD
Telephone: 01904 321160
Web Site: www.york.ac.uk/borthwick

Personnel:
Sara Slinn *(Publications Manager)*

*Academic & Scholarly; Archaeology;
Educational & Textbooks; History &
Antiquarian; Law; Religion & Theology*

New Titles: 5 (2009) , 5 (2010)

Imprints, Series & ISBNs:
Borthwick List & Indexes: 978 0 903857
Borthwick Papers: 978 0 903857
Borthwick Publications: 978 1 09
Borthwick Studies in History: 978 0 903857
Borthwick Texts & Calendars: 978 0 903857
Borthwick Wallets: 978 0 903857
Monastic Research Bulletin: 978 0 903857

Parent Company:
University of York

2107

BOSSINEY BOOKS LTD
Hillside, Langore, Launceston, Cornwall
PL15 8LD
Telephone: 01566 774176
Email: bossineybooks@btinternet.com

Web Site: www.bossineybooks.com

Distribution:
Tor Mark Press, PO Box 4, Redruth,
Cornwall TR16 5YX
Telephone: 01209 822101
Fax: 01209 822035
Email: office@tormark.co.uk
Web Site: www.tormark.co.uk

Personnel:
Jane White *(Director)*
Paul White *(Director)*

*Cookery, Wines & Spirits; Guide Books;
History & Antiquarian; Magic & the Occult*

Imprints, Series & ISBNs:
978 1 899383, 978 1 906474
Tamar Books

Book Trade Association Membership:
Independent Publishers Guild

2108

BOWKER (UK) LTD
St Andrew's House,
18–20 St Andrew Street, London
EC4A 3AG
Telephone: 020 7832 1770
Fax: 020 7832 1710
Email: sales@bowker.co.uk
Web Site: www.bowker.com

Personnel:
Doug McMillan *(Managing Director)*
Pam Roud *(Sales Director)*
Jo Grange *(Marketing Manager)*

*Academic & Scholarly; Bibliography &
Library Science; Electronic (Educational);
Electronic (Professional & Academic);
Reference Books, Directories & Dictionaries*

Imprints, Series & ISBNs:
978 0 8352

Associated Companies:
USA: R. R. Bowker LLC; Cambridge
Information Group

Overseas Representation:
see: www.bowker.co.uk, UK

Book Trade Association Membership:
Booksellers Association; Data Publishers
Association

2109

MARION BOYARS PUBLISHERS LTD
24 Lacy Road, London SW15 1NL
Telephone: 020 8788 9522
Fax: 020 8789 8122
Email: catheryn@marionboyars.com
Web Site: www.marionboyars.co.uk

Distribution:
Central Books, 99 Wallis Road, London
E9 5LN
Telephone: 020 8986 4854
Fax: 020 8533 5821
Email: orders@centralbooks.com

Personnel:
Catheryn Kilgarriff *(Managing Director)*
Rebecca Gillieron *(Editorial Manager)*
Katharine Bright-Holmes *(Editorial
Manager)*
Kit Maude *(Sales Co-ordinator Manager)*

*Biography & Autobiography; Children's
Books; Cinema, Video, TV & Radio; Fiction;
Literature & Criticism; Music; Philosophy;
Theatre, Drama & Dance*

Imprints, Series & ISBNs:
978 0 7145

Associated Companies:
USA: Marion Boyars Publishers Inc

Overseas Representation:
Australia & New Zealand: Tower Books Pty
Ltd, Frenchs Forest, NSW, Australia
France, Germany & Switzerland: Michael
Geoghegan, London, UK
Italy, Spain, Portugal & Greece: Penny
Padovani, London, UK
South Africa: Stephan Phillips (Pty) Ltd,
Cape Town, South Africa
USA: Consortium Book Sales & Distribution
Inc, MN, USA

Book Trade Association Membership:
Independent Publishers Guild

2110

BOYDELL & BREWER LTD
PO Box 9, Woodbridge, Suffolk IP12 3DF
Telephone: 01394 610600
Fax: 01394 610316
Email: trading@boydell.co.uk
Web Site: www.boydell.co.uk

Personnel:
P. Clifford *(Managing Director)*
M. J. Richards *(Sales Director)*
C. L. Palmer *(Editorial Director)*
W. Ellis *(Accounts Director)*
J. M. Jordan *(Customer Orders Manager)*
M. L. Webb *(Production Manager)*

*Academic & Scholarly; Archaeology;
Architecture & Design; History &
Antiquarian; Literature & Criticism; Military
& War; Music; Philosophy; Reference
Books, Directories & Dictionaries; Travel &
Topography*

Imprints, Series & ISBNs:
Boydell Press: 978 0 85115
D. S. Brewer: 978 0 85991
Camden House: 978 1 57113
Companion Guides: 978 1 900639
James Currey: 978 1 84701
Tamesis: 978 1 85566

Associated Companies:
USA: Boydell & Brewer Inc; University of
Rochester Press

Distributor for:
Bedfordshire Historical Record Society;
Henry Bradshaw Society; Burke's
Peerage; Canterbury & York Society;
Church of England Record Society; Early
English Text Society; Ecclesiastical History
Society; Lincoln Records Society;
Plumbago Books; Royal Society of
Literature; Suffolk Records Society;
Surtees Society; Victoria County History;
Yorkshire Archaeological Society
USA: Toccata Press; University of Rochester
Press

Overseas Representation:
Australia: DA Information Services Pty Ltd,
Mitcham, Vic, Australia
Belgium, Luxembourg & Netherlands:
Kemper Conseil Publishing,
Leidschendam, Netherlands
Eastern Europe: Marek Lewinson, Warsaw,
Poland
France: Mare Nostrum, Paris, France
Germany, Austria & Switzerland: Bernd
Feldmann, Oranienburg, Germany
Greece & Cyprus: Charles Gibbes
Associates, Louslitges, France
India & Sri Lanka: Viva Group, New Delhi,
India
Italy: David Pickering, Mare Nostrum
Publishing Consultants, Rome, Italy
Middle East & North Africa: Publishers
International Marketing, Storrington, UK
Pakistan: T.M.L. Publishers' Consultants &
Representatives, Lahore, Pakistan
Philippines: Edwin Makabenta, Quezon
City, Philippines
Republic of Ireland: Mullett Fitzpatrick,
Shankill, Co Dublin, Republic of Ireland

Scandinavia: Colin Flint Ltd, Publishers
Scandinavian Consultancy, Cambridge,
UK
South East Asia & Korea: Publishers
International Marketing, London, UK
Spain & Portugal: Iberian Book Services,
Madrid, Spain

2111

BRADT TRAVEL GUIDES LTD
23 High Street, Chalfont St Peter, Bucks
SL9 9QE
Telephone: 01753 893444
Fax: 01753 892333
Email: info@bradtguides.com
Web Site: www.bradtguides.com

British Orders (Distributor):
NBN International, 10 Estover Road,
Plymouth PL6 7PY
Telephone: 01752 202301
Fax: 01752 202331
Email: orders@nbninternational.com

Personnel:
Donald Greig *(Executive Director)*
Peter Jay *(Finance Director)*
Adrian Phillips *(Publishing Director)*

Guide Books; Travel & Topography

New Titles: 31 (2009) , 35 (2010)
No of Employees: 15
Annual Turnover: £1M

Imprints, Series & ISBNs:
Backpacking Guide Series: 978 1 84162,
978 1 898323
Eccentric Series: 978 1 84162, 978 1
898323
Guide to Series: 978 1 84162, 978 1
898323
Mini Guide Series: 978 1 84162
Rail Guide Series: 978 1 84162, 978 1
898323
Wildlife Series: 978 1 84162, 978 1 898323

Overseas Representation:
*Africa (excluding South Africa, Namibia, &
Zimbabwe):* A–Z Africa Book Services,
Rotterdam, Netherlands
Australia: Woodslane Pty Ltd, Warriewood,
NSW, Australia
Austria: Freytag & Berndt, Vienna, Austria
Belgium: Craenen bvba, Herent (Winksele),
Belgium
Eastern Europe: CLB Marketing Services,
Budapest, Hungary
France: Cartothèque EGG, Notre Dame
D'Oé, France
Germany & Luxembourg: Durnell
Marketing Ltd, Tunbridge Wells, UK
Israel: Steinhard Katzir, Netanya, Israel
Netherlands: Nilsson & Lamm BV, Weesp,
Netherlands
Portugal: Iberian Book Services, Madrid,
Spain
Scandinavian Europe: Angell Eurosales,
Berwick-on-Tweed, UK
Singapore: Pansing Distribution Pte Ltd,
Singapore
South & Central America: David Williams,
InterMedia Americana (IMA) Ltd,
London, UK
South Africa: Jacana Media, Johannesburg,
South Africa
Spain: Altair, Barcelona, Spain
Switzerland: Distribution OLF SA, Fribourg,
Switzerland
USA & Canada: Globe Pequot Press,
Guilford, CT, USA

Book Trade Association Membership:
Independent Publishers Guild

2112

BRANDBOOKS LTD
PO Box 650, Aylesbury, Bucks HP22 4YY
Telephone: 01926 682210

Email: sales@brandbooks.co.uk
Web Site: www.brandbooks.co.uk

*Academic & Scholarly; Educational &
Textbooks*

Book Trade Association Membership:
Publishers Association

2113

**BRANDON/MOUNT EAGLE
PUBLICATIONS**
PO Box 32, Dingle, Co Kerry,
Republic of Ireland
Telephone: +353 (066) 915 1463
Fax: +353 (066) 915 1234
Web Site: www.brandonbooks.com

Warehouse, Trade Orders:
Gill & Macmillan, Hume Avenue,
Park West, Dublin 12, Republic of Ireland
Telephone: +353 (01) 500 9500
Fax: +353 (01) 500 9599
Email: sales@gillmacmillan.ie

Personnel:
Steve MacDonogh *(Publisher & Managing
Director)*

*Biography & Autobiography; Fiction;
Literature & Criticism; Politics & World
Affairs; Travel & Topography*

Imprints, Series & ISBNs:
Brandon: 978 0 86322
Mount Eagle: 978 1 902011

Associated Companies:
Republic of Ireland: Brandon Book
Publishers Ltd

Overseas Representation:
UK (excluding Northern Ireland):
Turnaround Publisher Services Ltd,
London, UK
USA: Dufour Editions Inc, Chester Springs,
PA, USA

Book Trade Association Membership:
Publishing Ireland (Foilsiú Éireann)

2114

NICHOLAS BREALEY PUBLISHING
3–5 Spafield Street, London EC1R 4QB
Telephone: 020 7239 0360
Fax: 020 7239 0370
Email: rights@nicholasbrealey.com
Web Site: www.nicholasbrealey.com

Orders & Warehouse:
TBS Ltd, Colchester Road, Frating Green,
Colchester, Essex CO7 7DW
Telephone: 01206 256000
Fax: 01206 819587

Personnel:
Nicholas Brealey *(Managing Director)*
Andrew Menniss *(Sales Manager)*
Sally Lansdell *(Publishing Manager)*

*Biography & Autobiography; Economics;
Industry, Business & Management;
Psychology & Psychiatry; Travel &
Topography; Vocational Training & Careers*

New Titles: 25 (2009) , 30 (2010)
No of Employees: 4

Imprints, Series & ISBNs:
Nicholas Brealey: 978 1 85788
Nicholas Brealey International
Davies-Black: 978 0 89106
Industrial Society (acquired titles): 978 0
85290
Intercultural Press

Parent Company:
UK: NB Ltd

Associated Companies:
USA: NB Publishing Inc

Overseas Representation:
Asia (excluding Singapore & Malaysia):
Sales East, Bangkok, Thailand
Australia: Allen & Unwin Pty Ltd, Sydney,
NSW, Australia
*Europe (excluding Scandinavia) &
Switzerland:* Michael Geoghegan,
London, UK
India: Research Press, New Delhi, India
Republic of Ireland: Gill Simpson, Dublin,
Republic of Ireland
Scandinavia: Angell Eurosales, Berwick-on-
Tweed, UK
Singapore & Malaysia: Horizon Books Pte
Ltd, Singapore
South Africa: Wild Dog Press, Highlands
North, South Africa
USA: National Book Network, Lanham, MD,
USA; Nicholas Brealey Publishing North
America, Boston, MA, USA

Book Trade Association Membership:
Independent Publishers Guild

2115

BREWIN BOOKS LTD
Doric House, 56 Alcester Road, Studley,
Warwickshire B80 7LG
Telephone: 01527 854228
Fax: 01527 852746
Email: admin@brewinbooks.com
Web Site: www.brewinbooks.com

Warehouse:
Supaprint Works, Unit 19,
Enfield Industrial Estate, Redditch, Worcs
B97 6BZ
Telephone: 01527 62212
Fax: 01527 60451
Email: admin@supaprint.com
Web Site: www.supaprint.com

Personnel:
Alan Brewin *(Managing Director)*
Alistair Brewin *(Art, Book Design &
Production Director)*
Julie Brewin *(Company Secretary)*

*Biography & Autobiography; Fiction;
History & Antiquarian; Military & War;
Transport*

New Titles: 25 (2009) , 30 (2010)
No of Employees: 5

Imprints, Series & ISBNs:
Alton Douglas Books: 978 1 85858
Brewin Books: 978 0 947731, 978 0
9505570, 978 1 85858
History-into-Print: 978 1 85858

Distributor for:
City of Birmingham Libraries; Hunt End
Books

2116

BRIDGE BOOKS
61 Park Avenue, Wrexham LL12 7AW
Telephone: 01978 358661 & 0845 166
2851
Email: enquiries@bridgebooks.co.uk

Personnel:
W. Alister Williams *(Partner)*
Susan A. Williams *(Partner)*

*Aviation; History & Antiquarian; Military &
War; Travel & Topography*

Imprints, Series & ISBNs:
978 0 9508285, 978 1 84494, 978 1
872424

Associated Companies:
Maelor Interactive Publishing

2117

BRILLIANT PUBLICATIONS
Unit 10, Sparrow Hall Farm, Edlesborough,
Dunstable LU6 2ES
Telephone: 01525 222292
Fax: 01525 222720
Email: info@brilliantpublications.co.uk
Web Site: www.brilliantpublications.co.uk

Sales & Distribution:
BEBC Distribution, Albion Close, Parkstone,
Poole, Dorset BH12 3LL
Telephone: 01202 712910
Fax: 0845 130 9300
Email: brilliant@bebc.co.uk

Personnel:
Priscilla Hannaford *(Publisher)*
Richard Dorrance *(Finance Director)*
Alison Marshall *(Marketing)*

*Educational & Textbooks; Languages &
Linguistics*

New Titles: 28 (2009) , 25 (2010)
No of Employees: 5

Imprints, Series & ISBNs:
978 0 85747, 978 1 897675, 978 1
903853, 978 1 905780

Book Trade Association Membership:
Educational Publishers Council;
Independent Publishers Guild

2118

**BRITISH ASSOCIATION FOR
ADOPTION & FOSTERING**
[BAAF]
Saffron House, 6–10 Kirby Street, London
EC1N 8TS
Telephone: 020 7421 2602
Fax: 020 7421 2601
Email: shaila.shah@baaf.org.uk
Web Site: www.baaf.org.uk

Trade Enquiries:
Turnaround Distribution, Unit 3,
Olympia Trading Estate, Coburg Road,
London N22 6TZ
Telephone: 020 8829 3000
Fax: 020 8881 5088
Email: orders@turnaround-uk.com

Personnel:
David Holmes *(Chief Executive)*
Shaila Shah *(Director of Publications)*

*Academic & Scholarly; Children's Books;
Psychology & Psychiatry; Reference Books,
Directories & Dictionaries; Sociology &
Anthropology*

New Titles: 30 (2009) , 30 (2010)
No of Employees: 100

Imprints, Series & ISBNs:
978 0 903534, 978 1 873868, 978 1
903699, 978 1 905664, 978 1 907585

Overseas Representation:
Australia (selected titles): Innovative
Resources, Bendigo, Vic, Australia

Book Trade Association Membership:
The Publishers Forum for the Voluntary
Sector

2119

BRITISH GEOLOGICAL SURVEY
Keyworth, Nottingham NG12 5GG
Telephone: 0115 936 3241 (sales) & 0115
936 3147 (returns)
Fax: 0115 936 3488
Email: sales@bgs.ac.uk & ikp@bgs.ac.uk
(returns)
Web Site: www.bgs.ac.uk &
www.geologyshop.com (online shop)

Distribution & Representation:
Cordee Ltd, 11 Jacknell Road,
Dodswell Bridge Industrial Estate, Hinckley,
Leics LE10 3BS
Telephone: 01455 611185
Fax: 01455 635687
Email: info@cordee.co.uk
Web Site: www.cordee.co.uk

Personnel:
Prof John Ludden (Director)
Jim Rayner (Head of Graphics
    Communication)
Chris Luton (Copyright & IPR)
Ms Elaine Mason (Head of Sales)
Ivan Page (Sales Manager (returns))

Atlases & Maps; Geography & Geology;
Guide Books; Scientific & Technical

New Titles: 50 (2009) , 55 (2010)
No of Employees: 700

Imprints, Series & ISBNs:
British Geological Survey (Books & Reports):
    978 0 85272
British Geological Survey (Maps): 978 0
    7518

Parent Company:
Natural Environment Research Council

Distributor for:
Durham County Council; Journal of Mines
    & Minerals

2120 ▬▬▬▬

BRITISH LIBRARY
96 Euston Road, London NW1 2DB
Telephone: 020 7412 7535
Fax: 020 7412 7768
Email: blpublications@bl.uk
Web Site: www.bl.uk

Orders:
The British Library, Turpin Distribution Ltd,
Stratton Business Park, Pegasus Drive,
Biggleswade, Beds SG18 8QB
Telephone: 01767 604955
Fax: 01767 601640
Email: custserv@turpin-distribution.com
Web Site: www.turpin-distribution.com

Personnel:
David Way (Head of Publishing)
Catherine Britton (Editorial & Rights)
Martin Oestreicher (Sales)
Lara Speicher (Editorial)

Academic & Scholarly; Bibliography &
Library Science; Biography &
Autobiography; Fine Art & Art History;
History & Antiquarian; Illustrated & Fine
Editions

New Titles: 30 (2009) , 35 (2010)

Imprints, Series & ISBNs:
Bibliography of British Newspapers: 978 0
    7123
The British Library: 978 0 7123
British Library Guides: 978 0 7123
British Library Occasional Papers: 978 0
    7123
The British Library Studies in Medieval
    Culture: 978 0 7123
The British Library Studies in the History of
    the Book: 978 0 7123
Corpus of British Medieval Library
    Catalogues: 978 0 7123
The Panizzi Lectures: 978 0 7123

Parent Company:
The British Library

Overseas Representation:
Australia: InBooks, Belrose, NSW, Australia
USA & Canada: University of Chicago Press,
    Chicago, IL, USA

Book Trade Association Membership:
Publishers Association; Booksellers
Association; Independent Publishers Guild

2121 ▬▬▬▬

BRITISH MUSEUM PRESS
38 Russell Square, London WC1B 3QQ
Telephone: 020 7323 1234
Fax: 020 7436 7315
Email: rbradley@britishmuseum.co.uk
Web Site: www.britishmuseum.org

Trade Distributor:
Littlehampton Book Services,
Faraday Close, Durrington, Worthing,
West Sussex BN13 3RB
Telephone: 01903 828501
Fax: 01903 828801/2
Email: enquiries@lbsltd.co.uk

Personnel:
Brian Oldman (Managing Director)
Helen Watts (Finance & Administration
    Director)
Rosemary Bradley (Publishing Director)
Teresa Francis (Editorial)
Susan Walby (Production)
Sheila McKenna (Head of Sales, Marketing
    & Rights)
Victoria Benjamin (Marketing/Publicity)

Academic & Scholarly; Antiques &
Collecting; Archaeology; Children's Books;
Fine Art & Art History; Natural History;
Reference Books, Directories &
Dictionaries; Sociology & Anthropology

Imprints, Series & ISBNs:
978 0 7141

Parent Company:
The British Museum Co Ltd

Overseas Representation:
USA (Trade orders): British Museum Press,
    London, UK
Worldwide (excluding USA): Thames &
    Hudson (Distributors) Ltd, Farnborough,
    Hants, UK

Book Trade Association Membership:
Publishers Association

2122 ▬▬▬▬

BROOKLANDS BOOKS LTD
PO Box 146, Cobham, Surrey KT11 1LG
Telephone: 01932 865051
Fax: 01932 868803
Email: sales@brooklands-books.com
Web Site: www.brooklands-books.com

Personnel:
I. Dowdeswell (Director)
J. Powell (Director)
B. Cleveland (Sales Manager)

Aviation; Military & War; Transport

New Titles: 50 (2010)
No of Employees: 6

Imprints, Series & ISBNs:
978 1 85520

Parent Company:
USA: Robert Bentley Publishers; Cartech;
    SA Design

Distributor for:
USA: Robert Bentley Inc; SA Design

Overseas Representation:
Southern Europe: Bookport Associates,
    Corsico (MI), Italy

2123 ▬▬▬▬

BROWN DOG BOOKS
6 The Old Dairy, Melcombe Road, Bath
BA2 3LR

Telephone: 01225 478444
Fax: 01225 478440
Email: sales@manning-partnership.co.uk
Web Site: www.manning-
    partnership.co.uk

Personnel:
Garry Manning (Managing Director)
Roger Hibbert (Sales & Marketing Director)
Heather Morris (Editorial Director)
Karen Twissell (Office Manager)
James Wheeler (Sales Manager)

Children's Books; Cookery, Wines & Spirits;
Humour; Sports & Games

Imprints, Series & ISBNs:
Brown Dog Books: 978 1 903056
Nightingale: 978 1 903222

Parent Company:
Manning Partnership Ltd

Distributor for:
Australia: Brimax; Five Mile Press
UK: Carroll & Brown; Interpet Publishing;
    Nightingale Press; Tony Potter; Search
    Press
USA: Globe Pequot Press; Mathew Price;
    Source Books

2124 ▬▬▬▬

BROWN, SON & FERGUSON, LTD
4–10 Darnley Street, Glasgow G41 2SD
Telephone: 0141 429 1234/5922
Fax: 0141 420 1694
Email: info@skipper.co.uk
Web Site: www.skipper.co.uk

Personnel:
T. Nigel Brown (Chairman & Production
    Director)
R. P. B. Brown (Sales Manager)

Nautical; Theatre, Drama & Dance

New Titles: 4 (2009) , 2 (2010)
No of Employees: 12

Imprints, Series & ISBNs:
978 0 85174, 978 1 84927

Associated Companies:
James Munro & Co

Book Trade Association Membership:
Publishing Scotland

2125 ▬▬▬▬

BROWN & WHITTAKER PUBLISHING
Stronsaule, Tobermory, Isle of Mull
PA75 6PR
Telephone: 01688 302381
Email: olivebrown@msn.com
Web Site: www.brown-whittaker.co.uk

Personnel:
Olive Brown (Partner)
Jean Whittaker (Partner)

Archaeology; Biography & Autobiography;
Biology & Zoology; Cookery, Wines &
Spirits; Guide Books; History &
Antiquarian; Natural History; Poetry

New Titles: 2 (2009) , 2 (2010)
Annual Turnover: £15,000

Imprints, Series & ISBNs:
978 0 9528428, 978 0 9532775, 978 1
    904353

Book Trade Association Membership:
Publishing Scotland

2126 ▬▬▬▬

BRYNTIRION PRESS
Bryntirion, Bridgend, Mid Glamorgan
CF31 4DX

Telephone: 01656 655886
Fax: 01656 665919

Representation:
Evangelical Press, Faverdale North,
Darlington DL3 0PH
Telephone: 01325 380232
Fax: 01325 466153
Email: sales@evangelical-press.org

Personnel:
Huw Kinsey (Press Officer)

Religion & Theology

New Titles: 5 (2009) , 4 (2010)
No of Employees: 1

Imprints, Series & ISBNs:
Evangelical Library of Wales: 978 0 900898,
    978 0 9502686, 978 1 85049
Evangelical Movement of Wales: 978 0
    900898, 978 1 85049
Evangelical Press of Wales: 978 0 900898,
    978 1 85049

Parent Company:
Evangelical Movement of Wales

Distributor for:
Association of Christian Teachers of Wales;
    Evangelical Library (London); Yr Undeb
    Cristnogol

Book Trade Association Membership:
Booksellers Association; Undeb
Cyhoeddwyr a Llyfrwerthwyr Cymru (The
Union of Welsh Publishers and Booksellers)

2127 ▬▬▬▬

BURNS & OATES
see: Continuum International Publishing
Group

2128 ▬▬▬▬

BUSINESS EDUCATION PUBLISHERS
evolve Business Centre, Cygnet Way,
Rainton Bridge Business Park,
Houghton-le-Spring, Tyne & Wear
DH4 5QY
Telephone: 0191 305 5165
Fax: 0191 305 5504
Email: info@bepl.com
Web Site: www.bepl.com

Warehouse:
Unit 18, Hartlepool Workshops,
Usworth Road Industrial Estate,
Usworth Road, Hartlepool, Cleveland
TS25 1PD
Telephone: 01429 234153
Fax: 01429 234153

Personnel:
Paul Callaghan (Managing Director)
Andrea Murphy (Publications Manager)
Joe McQuilling (Warehouse Manager)

Academic & Scholarly; Biography &
Autobiography; Computer Science;
Educational & Textbooks; History &
Antiquarian; Industry, Business &
Management; Law; Military & War

Imprints, Series & ISBNs:
978 0 907679, 978 1 901888

Book Trade Association Membership:
Booksellers Association; Book Data

2129 ▬▬▬▬

BUTTERFINGERS BOOKS
The Rose House, 19 Tor View Avenue,
Glastonbury, Somerset BA6 8AE
Telephone: 01458 832035
Email: laurie@butterfingersbooks.co.uk
Web Site: www.butterfingers.co.uk

Personnel:
L. H. R. Collard (*Rights Director*)

Educational & Textbooks; Sports & Games

New Titles: 1 (2009) , 1 (2010)
No of Employees: 1

Imprints, Series & ISBNs:
978 0 9513240, 978 1 898591

Distributor for:
Germany: Die Jonglerie
UK: Circustuff
USA: Brian Dubé Inc; Finesse Press;
Renegade Juggling

Overseas Representation:
North America: Brian Dube Inc, New York,
NY, USA

2130

CABI
Nosworthy Way, Wallingford, Oxon
OX10 8DE
Telephone: 01491 832111
Fax: 01491 833508 & 829292 (order
fulfilment)
Email: publishing@cabi.org
Web Site: www.cabi.org/

Personnel:
Ms Caroline McNamara (*Executive &
Commercial Director*)
Ms Andrea Powell (*Executive & Publishing
Director*)
Shaun Hobbs (*Database Publishing Director*)
Elizabeth Dodsworth (*Knowledge for
Development Director*)
Nigel Farrar (*Books Publisher*)

*Academic & Scholarly; Agriculture; Animal
Care & Breeding; Biology & Zoology;
Environment & Development Studies;
Medical (incl. Self Help & Alternative
Medicine); Scientific & Technical; Veterinary
Science*

New Titles: 74 (2009) , 70 (2010)
No of Employees: 100

Imprints, Series & ISBNs:
978 0 85198, 978 0 85199, 978 1 84593

Parent Company:
CAB International

Distributor for:
International Food Information Service;
Royal Society of Edinburgh

Overseas Representation:
Africa: CABI Africa, Nairobi, Kenya
All other areas: Commercial Department,
Wallingford, UK
Asia: CABI South East & East Asia, Serdang,
Malaysia
*Australia, New Zealand & Papua New
Guinea:* DA Information Services Pty Ltd,
Mitcham, Vic, Australia
Canada: CABI North America, Cambridge,
MA, USA
Caribbean: CABI Caribbean & Latin
America, Curepe, Trinidad
*Denmark, Finland, Iceland, Norway &
Sweden:* Colin Flint Ltd, Harlow, UK
Germany, Austria & Switzerland: Missing
Link International Booksellers, Bremen,
Germany
India: Book Marketing Services, Chennai,
India
Middle East (excluding Iran): James & Lorin
Watt Ltd, Publishing Consultants,
Oxford, UK
South Africa: Academic Marketing Services
(Pty) Ltd, Craighall, South Africa
*USA, Central America, Caribbean, Mexico,
Puerto Rico & Guam:* Oxford University
Press, Cary, NC, USA

Book Trade Association Membership:
Booksellers Association

2131

CALYPSO PUBLICATIONS
2 Gatcombe Road, London N19 4PT
Telephone: 020 7281 4948
Fax: 020 7281 4948
Email: Gerald@calypso.org.uk &
enquiries@calypso.org.uk
Web Site: www.calypso.org.uk/ourbooks &
www.calypso.org.uk/bookshop

Personnel:
G. H. Jennings (*Proprietor*)

*Academic & Scholarly; Animal Care &
Breeding; Biology & Zoology; Crafts &
Hobbies; Educational & Textbooks; Natural
History; Reference Books, Directories &
Dictionaries; Scientific & Technical; Travel &
Topography; Veterinary Science*

New Titles: 4 (2009) , 4 (2010)
No of Employees: 2

Imprints, Series & ISBNs:
978 0 906301, 978 1 902788

Parent Company:
The Calypso Organization

Overseas Representation:
Australia: Andrew Isles Bookshop,
Melbourne, Vic, Australia
Cyprus: Soloneion Book Centre, Nicosia,
Cyprus
USA: The Aquatic Bookshop, Placerville,
CA, USA

2132

**CAMBRIDGE ARCHIVE EDITIONS
LTD**
7 Ashley House, The Broadway,
Farnham Common, Slough SL2 3PQ
Telephone: 01753 646633
Fax: 01753 646746
Email: info@archiveeditions.co.uk
Web Site: www.archiveeditions.co.uk

Personnel:
Jeanette Wood (*Head of Customer
Relations & Finance*)
Ann Greenwood (*Production Manager*)
Jessica Lagan (*Publisher*)

*Academic & Scholarly; History &
Antiquarian; Politics & World Affairs*

New Titles: 3 (2009) , 2 (2010)
No of Employees: 5

Imprints, Series & ISBNs:
978 1 84097, 978 1 85207

Parent Company:
UK: Cambridge University Press

2133

CAMBRIDGE UNIVERSITY PRESS
The Edinburgh Building, Shaftesbury Road,
Cambridge CB2 8RU
Telephone: 01223 312393
Fax: 01223 315052
Email: information@cambridge.org
Web Site: www.cambridge.org

Orders:
Telephone: 01223 325577
Fax: 01223 325151
Email: intcustserve@cambridge.org
Web Site: www.cambridge.org

Personnel:
Stephen R. R. Bourne (*Chief Executive of the
Press*)
Christopher Boughton (*Managing Director,
Asia-Pacific Press Board*)

Andrew Brown (*Managing Director,
Academic Press Board*)
Hanri Pieterse (*Managing Director,
Cambridge Learning Press Board*)
Andrew Gilfillan (*Managing Director,
Europe, Middle East & Africa Press Board*)
Steven Miller (*Chief Financial Officer Press
Board*)
Richard Ziemacki (*President, Americas Press
Board*)
Ron Bennett (*Legal Services Director*)
Peter Davison (*Corporate Affairs Director*)
Richard Fisher (*Academic & Professional
Director*)
David Harrison (*ELT Group Director, EMEA*)
Ron Ragsdale (*ELT Editorial Director*)
Maralyn Johnson (*Chief Technology Officer*)
Simon Ross (*Journals Director*)
Rohan Seery (*Academic Sales & Marketing
Director*)
Simon Read (*Education Director*)
Howard Buckley (*Chief Financial Officer,
EMEA*)
Cheryl Park (*Human Resources Director*)
Andy Williams (*Production Director,
Academic & Professional*)
Geoff Staff (*Global Publishing Operations
Director, Cambridge Learning*)
Sandra Ward (*Executive Director of
Operations*)
Mark Maddocks (*Chief Information Officer*)

*Academic & Scholarly; Accountancy &
Taxation; Agriculture; Archaeology;
Architecture & Design; Bibliography &
Library Science; Biography &
Autobiography; Biology & Zoology;
Chemistry; Children's Books; Computer
Science; Economics; Educational &
Textbooks; Electronic (Educational);
Electronic (Professional & Academic);
Engineering; English as a Foreign
Language; Environment & Development
Studies; Fine Art & Art History; Gender
Studies; Geography & Geology; History &
Antiquarian; Industry, Business &
Management; Languages & Linguistics;
Law; Literature & Criticism; Mathematics &
Statistics; Medical (incl. Self Help &
Alternative Medicine); Music; Natural
History; Philosophy; Physics; Politics &
World Affairs; Psychology & Psychiatry;
Reference Books, Directories &
Dictionaries; Religion & Theology; Scientific
& Technical; Sociology & Anthropology;
Theatre, Drama & Dance*

New Titles: 4200 (2009) , 36300 (2010)
No of Employees: 1960
Annual Turnover: £205.1M

Imprints, Series & ISBNs:
978 0 521

Associated Companies:
Greece: Cambridge University Press
(Greece) EPE
Hong Kong: Cambridge Knowledge (China)
Ltd; United Publishers Services Ltd
India: Cambridge University Press India (Pvt)
Ltd
Japan: Cambridge University Press Japan
KK; Kabushiki Kaisha Phoenic
Mexico: ELT Trading SA de CV
South Africa: Cambridge University Press
South Africa (Pty) Ltd
UK: Cambridge Global Grid for Learning;
Cambridge Hitachisoft Educational
Solutions PLC; Cambridge Printing
Services Ltd; Cambridge University Press
(Holdings) Ltd; Greenwich Medical
Media Ltd; Oncoweb Ltd

Overseas Representation:
Contact: Chris Boughton, Managing
Director, Asia-Pacific, Cambridge
University Press, Cambridge, UK; Richard
Ziemacki, President, The Americas,
Cambridge University Press, Cambridge,
UK

Book Trade Association Membership:
Publishers Association; Booksellers
Association; Educational Publishers
Council; International Group of Scientific,
Medical & Technical Publishers;
Independent Publishers Guild; Association
of Learned & Professional Society
Publishers; BML; IBD

2134

CAMERON BOOKS
PO Box 1, Moffat, Dumfriesshire DG10 9SU
Telephone: 01683 220808
Fax: 01683 220012
Email: jh@cameronbooks.co.uk
Web Site: www.cameronbooks.co.uk

Personnel:
Jill Hollis (*Director*)

*Antiques & Collecting; Architecture &
Design; Fine Art & Art History; Natural
History*

New Titles: 1 (2009) , 1 (2010)
No of Employees: 2

Imprints, Series & ISBNs:
Cameron & Hollis: 978 0 906506

2135

CAMRA BOOKS
230 Hatfield Road, St Albans, Herts
AL1 4LW
Telephone: 01727 867201
Fax: 01727 867670
Email: camra@camra.org.uk
Web Site: www.camra.org.uk

UK Distribution:
Macmillan Distribution (MDL), Houndmills,
Basingstoke, Hampshire RG21 6XS
RG21 6XS
Telephone: 01256 329242
Fax: 01256 328339

Personnel:
Louise Ashworth (*Head of Marketing*)
Simon Hall (*Managing Editor*)
Kim Carvey (*Marketing Manager*)

*Biography & Autobiography; Cookery,
Wines & Spirits; Guide Books; Reference
Books, Directories & Dictionaries; Travel &
Topography*

New Titles: 7 (2009) , 6 (2010)
No of Employees: 25

Imprints, Series & ISBNs:
Good Beer Guides: 978 1 85249
Pub Walks: 978 1 85249

Parent Company:
Campaign for Real Ale Ltd

Overseas Representation:
USA: Trafalgar (Pan Macmillan), Chicago, IL,
USA

Book Trade Association Membership:
Independent Publishers Guild

2136

CANONGATE BOOKS
14 High Street, Edinburgh EH1 1TE
Telephone: 0131 557 5111
Fax: 0131 557 5211
Email: info@canongate.co.uk
Web Site: www.meetatthegate.com

Warehouse & Orders:
The Book Service Ltd, Distribution Centre,
Colchester Road, Frating Green, Colchester,
Essex CO7 7DW
Telephone: 01206 256000
Fax: 01206 255715
Email: helpdesk@tbs-ltd.co.uk
Web Site: www.thebookservice.co.uk

Personnel:
Jamie Byng *(Publisher)*
Kathleen Anderson *(Finance Director)*
Caroline Gorham *(Production Director)*
Polly Collingridge *(Rights Director)*
Jenny Todd *(Sales & Marketing Director)*
Anya Serota *(Publishing Director (Fiction))*
Nick Davies *(Editorial Director (Non-Fiction))*
Norah Perkins *(Managing Editor)*

Audio Books; Biography & Autobiography; Crime; Fiction; Fine Art & Art History; Guide Books; History & Antiquarian; Humour; Illustrated & Fine Editions; Literature & Criticism; Music; Philosophy; Poetry; Politics & World Affairs

Imprints, Series & ISBNs:
Canongate: 978 0 86241, 978 1 84195
Canongate Classics: 978 0 86241, 978 1 84195
Myths: 978 0 86241, 978 1 84195

Associated Companies:
Australia: Text Publishing
USA: Canongate US

Overseas Representation:
Australia: Penguin Books Australia Ltd, Camberwell, Vic, Australia
Canada: Penguin Group Canada, Toronto, Ont, Canada
Eastern Europe: Csaba & Jackie Lengyel de Bagota, Budapest, Hungary
Far East: Julian Ashton, Ashton International Marketing Services, Sevenoaks, Kent, UK
India: Rave Media, Nandan Jha, India
Latin America & Caribbean: InterMedia Americana (IMA) Ltd, London, UK
Netherlands, Africa & Pakistan: Export Sales Department, Canongate Books, Edinburgh, UK
New Zealand: Penguin Books (New Zealand) Ltd, Auckland, New Zealand
Northern Europe: Bridget Lane, Faber & Faber, London, UK
South Africa: Penguin Books South Africa, Gardenview, South Africa
Southern Europe: Melissa Elders, Faber & Faber, London, UK
USA: Publishers Group West, Berkeley, CA, USA

Book Trade Association Membership:
Publishing Scotland; Independent Publishers Guild

2137 ━━━━━━━

CAPALL BANN PUBLISHING
Auton Farm, Milverton, Somerset TA4 1NE
Telephone: 01823 401528
Fax: 01823 401529
Email: enquiries@capallbann.co.uk
Web Site: www.capallbann.co.uk

Personnel:
Jon Day *(Sales & Rights Publisher)*
Julia Day *(Administration & Editorial Publisher)*

Animal Care & Breeding; Archaeology; Cookery, Wines & Spirits; Crafts & Hobbies; Educational & Textbooks; Environment & Development Studies; Gardening; Gender Studies; Guide Books; Health & Beauty; History & Antiquarian; Magic & the Occult; Medical (incl. Self Help & Alternative Medicine); Music; Natural History; Philosophy; Psychology & Psychiatry; Religion & Theology; Theatre, Drama & Dance

New Titles: 30 (2009) , 46 (2010)

Imprints, Series & ISBNs:
978 1 86163, 978 1 898307

Overseas Representation:
Australia (New Age): Brumby Books Holdings Pty Ltd, Kilsyth South, Vic, Australia
South Africa: Bacchus Books, Cresta, South Africa
USA: Holmes Publishing Group, Edmunds, WA, USA; New Leaf Distributing Co, Lithia Springs, GA, USA

2138 ━━━━━━━

CAPITAL TRANSPORT PUBLISHING
PO Box 250, Harrow, Middlesex HA3 5ZH
Email: info@capitaltransport.com
Web Site: www.capitaltransport.com

Trade Orders:
The Trade Counter,
Mendlesham Industrial Estate,
Norwich Road, Mendlesham, Norfolk
IP14 5NA
Telephone: 01449 766629
Fax: 01449 767122
Email: orders@tradecounter.co.uk

Personnel:
James Whiting *(Publisher)*

Transport

Imprints, Series & ISBNs:
Capital History: 978 1 85414
Capital Transport: 978 1 85414

Book Trade Association Membership:
Independent Publishers Guild

2139 ━━━━━━━

CAPSTONE GLOBAL LIBRARY LTD
Halley Court, Jordan Hill, Oxford OX2 8EJ
Telephone: 01865 311366
Fax: 01865 314272
Email: information@cambridge.org
Web Site: www.heinemannlibrary.co.uk

Academic & Scholarly; Educational & Textbooks

Book Trade Association Membership:
Publishers Association

2140 ━━━━━━━

CAPUCHIN CLASSICS
128 Kensington Church Street, London W8 4BH
Telephone: 020 7221 7166
Fax: 020 7792 9288
Email: info@capuchin-classics.co.uk
Web Site: www.capuchin-classics.co.uk

Representation (UK):
DJ Segrue Ltd, London

Personnel:
Max Scott *(Director)*
Emma Howard *(Editor-at-Large)*
Christopher Ind *(Editor)*
David Birkett *(Sales & Marketing)*

Fiction

New Titles: 16 (2009) , 20 (2010)
No of Employees: 10

Parent Company:
Stacey Arts Ltd

Overseas Representation:
Asia: PIM, London, UK
Australia: Peribo, NSW, Australia
Europe: Durnell Marketing, Tunbridge Wells, UK
South Africa: Stephan Philips, Cape Town, South Africa
South America & Caribbean: Intermedia Americana, London, UK
USA: IPG, Chicago, IL, USA

Book Trade Association Membership:
Independent Publishers Guild

2141 ━━━━━━━

CAREERS EUROPE
72–74 Godwin Street, Bradford BD1 3PT
Telephone: 01274 829600
Fax: 01274 829610
Email: info@careerseurope.co.uk
Web Site: www.careerseurope.co.uk

Personnel:
Michael Carey *(Manager)*
Leila Shkodra *(Sales & Business Development Manager)*

Educational & Textbooks

Imprints, Series & ISBNs:
Gap Year Resource Pack: 978 1 899483
Languages & Careers Pack: 978 1 899483
Science & Careers Pack: 978 1 899483

Associated Companies:
UK: Aspire-i Ltd

2142 ━━━━━━━

CAREL PRESS
4 Hewson Street, Carlisle, Cumbria CA2 5AU
Telephone: 01228 538928
Fax: 01228 591816
Email: info@carelpress.com
Web Site: www.carelpress.com & www.shortershakespeare.com

Personnel:
Chas White *(Publisher)*

Atlases & Maps; Educational & Textbooks; Electronic (Educational); Languages & Linguistics; Literature & Criticism; Mathematics & Statistics; Reference Books, Directories & Dictionaries; Sports & Games; Theatre, Drama & Dance

Imprints, Series & ISBNs:
978 1 872365, 978 1 905600

Distributor for:
Arc Theatre Co; ODT Inc (Maps); One Page Book Co

Book Trade Association Membership:
Independent Publishers Guild

2143 ━━━━━━━

CARLTON PUBLISHING GROUP
20 Mortimer Street, London W1T 3JW
Telephone: 020 7612 0400
Fax: 020 7612 0408
Email: sales@carltonbooks.co.uk
Web Site: www.carltonbooks.co.uk

Distribution:
HarperCollins Publishers, PO Box Glasgow G4 0NB
Telephone: 0141 306 3100
Fax: 0141 306 3767
Email: uk.orders@harpercollins.co.uk

Personnel:
J. Goodman *(Chairman/Publisher)*
B. Rasmussen *(Managing Director)*
P. Murray Hill *(Publishing Director)*
R. Porter *(Design Director)*
A. Whitton *(Financial Director)*
J. Greenhough *(Sales Director)*

Antiques & Collecting; Architecture & Design; Biography & Autobiography; Children's Books; Cinema, Video, TV & Radio; Cookery, Wines & Spirits; Crafts & Hobbies; Crime; Electronic (Entertainment); Fashion & Costume; Fine Art & Art History; Health & Beauty; History & Antiquarian; Humour; Illustrated & Fine Editions; Military & War; Music; Natural History; Photography; Sports & Games; Transport

New Titles: 100 (2009) , 100 (2010)

Imprints, Series & ISBNs:
978 1 85868
Carlton Books: 978 1 84222
Andre Deutsch: 978 0 233
Goodman Books: 978 1 84796
Prion: 978 1 85375

Parent Company:
Jonathan Goodman Publishing

Overseas Representation:
All Other Markets: Gunnar Lie & Associates Ltd, London, UK
Australia & New Zealand: c/o Jonathan Goodman, Carlton Publishing Group, London, UK
North America & Foreign Language: c/o Belinda Rasmussen, Carlton Publishing Group, London, UK

2144 ━━━━━━━

CARNEGIE PUBLISHING LTD
Carnegie House, Chatsworth Road, Lancaster LA1 4SL
Telephone: 01524 840111
Fax: 01524 840222
Email: anna@carnegiepublishing.com
Web Site: www.carnegiepublishing.com

Personnel:
Alistair Hodge *(Managing Director)*
Anna Goddard *(Marketing Director)*

Academic & Scholarly; Agriculture; Archaeology; Cookery, Wines & Spirits; History & Antiquarian; Industry, Business & Management; Military & War; Natural History

New Titles: 16 (2009) , 18 (2010)
No of Employees: 7
Annual Turnover: £500,000

Imprints, Series & ISBNs:
Carnegie Publishing Ltd: 978 1 85936
Crucible Books: 978 1 905472
Palatine Books: 978 1 874181
Scotforth Books: 978 1 904244

Book Trade Association Membership:
Independent Publishers Guild

2145 ━━━━━━━

JON CARPENTER PUBLISHING
Alder House, Market Street, Charlbury OX7 3PH
Telephone: 01608 819117
Fax: 01608 811969
Email: jon@joncarpenter.co.uk

Trade Orders:
Central Books, 99 Wallis Road, London E9 5LN
Telephone: 020 8986 4854
Fax: 020 8533 5821
Email: orders@centralbooks.com

Personnel:
Jon Carpenter *(Publisher)*

Academic & Scholarly; Cookery, Wines & Spirits; Economics; Environment & Development Studies; History & Antiquarian; Medical (incl. Self Help & Alternative Medicine); Philosophy; Politics & World Affairs; Sociology & Anthropology

New Titles: 8 (2009) , 8 (2010)
No of Employees: 1

Imprints, Series & ISBNs:
Jon Carpenter: 978 0 9549727, 978 1 897766, 978 1 906067
Wychwood Press: 978 1 902279

Distributor for:
Australia: Envirobook Pty

Overseas Representation:
Australia: Envirobook, Annandale, NSW, Australia
South Africa: New Horizon Distributors, Claremont, South Africa
USA: Independent Publishers Group (IPG), Chicago, IL, USA

Book Trade Association Membership:
Booksellers Association

2146

CARROLL & BROWN LTD
20 Lonsdale Road, London NW6 6RD
Telephone: 020 7372 0900
Fax: 020 7372 0460
Email: mail@carrollandbrown.co.uk
Web Site: www.carrollandbrown.co.uk

Personnel:
Amy Carroll (*Managing Director*)
Chrissie Lloyd (*Art Director*)
Simonne Waud (*Sales, Rights Director*)
Derek Thornhill (*UK Sales Director*)

Animal Care & Breeding; Cookery, Wines & Spirits; Health & Beauty; Medical (incl. Self Help & Alternative Medicine)

New Titles: 10 (2009) , 15 (2010)
No of Employees: 11

Imprints, Series & ISBNs:
978 1 903258, 978 1 904760

Associated Companies:
Carroll & Brown Publishers Ltd

Overseas Representation:
Worldwide: Derek Thornhill, Carroll & Brown Ltd, London, UK

Book Trade Association Membership:
Independent Publishers Guild; Book Packagers Association

2147

CATCHER LTD
Honeysuckle Cottage,
4 Weaverhead Close, Thaxted, Essex
CM6 2PP
Telephone: 01371 831087
Email: juliaheron@btinternet.com
Web Site: www.catcher.me

Personnel:
Julia Heron (*Managing Director*)

Biography & Autobiography; Children's Books; Educational & Textbooks; Electronic (Educational); Fiction; Poetry; Science Fiction

Imprints, Series & ISBNs:
Memorycatcher Books: 978 0 9554992
Storycatcher Books / children's fiction: 978 0 9544619

Overseas Representation:
Canada: Martine Jacquot, Canada
China: David Zou / CNN, P. R. of China
USA: Pinnock & Co, USA

2148

THE CATHOLIC TRUTH SOCIETY
40–46 Harleyford Road, London SE11 5AY
Telephone: 020 7640 0042
Fax: 020 7640 0046
Email: info@cts-online.org.uk
Web Site: www.cts-online.org.uk

Retail Bookshop & Mail Order:
25 Ashley Place, London SW1P 1LT
Telephone: 020 7834 1363
Fax: 020 7821 7398
Email: bookshop@cts-online.org.uk
Web Site: www.cts-online.org.uk

Personnel:
Rt Rev Paul Hendricks (*Chairman*)
Fergal Martin (*General Secretary, Publisher, Rights & Permissions, Accounts, Editorial*)
John Dilger (*Hon Treasurer & Director*)
Stephen Campbell (*Production*)
Richard Brown (*Sales*)
Carlo Boi (*Systems*)

Biography & Autobiography; Children's Books; Educational & Textbooks; Guide Books; History & Antiquarian; Religion & Theology

New Titles: 60 (2009) , 70 (2010)
No of Employees: 25
Annual Turnover: £1.2M

Imprints, Series & ISBNs:
The Incorporated Catholic Truth Society: 978 1 86082
CTS Publications: 978 1 86082

Distributor for:
Vatican City: Osservatore Romano

Overseas Representation:
Australia & New Zealand: St Pauls Publications, Strathfield, NSW, Australia
North America: Ignatius Press, CA, USA

Book Trade Association Membership:
Booksellers Association

2149

JOHN CATT EDUCATIONAL LTD
12 Deben Mill Business Centre, Melton, Woodbridge, Suffolk IP12 1BL
Telephone: 01394 389850
Fax: 01394 386893
Email: enquiries@johncatt.co.uk
Web Site: www.johncatt.com

Personnel:
Jonathan Evans (*Managing Director*)
Christine Evans (*Information Director*)
Derek Bingham (*Publishing Director*)

Academic & Scholarly; Educational & Textbooks

Imprints, Series & ISBNs:
978 1 901577, 978 1 904724

Book Trade Association Membership:
Periodical Publishers' Association

2150

CAXTON PUBLISHING GROUP LTD
20 Bloomsbury Street, London WC1B 3JH
Telephone: 020 7636 7171
Fax: 020 7636 1922
Email: office@caxtonpublishing.com
Web Site: www.caxtonpublishing.com

Personnel:
Finbarr McCabe (*Managing Director*)
James Birney (*Sales Director*)

Antiques & Collecting; Architecture & Design; Atlases & Maps; Aviation; Children's Books; Cookery, Wines & Spirits; Crafts & Hobbies; Crime; Do-It-Yourself; Fiction; Fine Art & Art History; Gardening; Magic & the Occult; Medical (incl. Self Help & Alternative Medicine); Military & War; Natural History; Reference Books, Directories & Dictionaries; Transport

Annual Turnover: £2.5M

Imprints, Series & ISBNs:
Brockhampton Press: 978 1 84186
Caxton Editions: 978 1 84067
Chaucer Press: 978 1 904449
Knight Paperbacks: 978 1 84067
Mercury Books: 978 1 904668
TimeLife: 978 1 84447

2151

CBD RESEARCH LTD
Chancery House, 15 Wickham Road, Beckenham, Kent BR3 5JS
Telephone: 020 8650 7745
Fax: 020 8650 0768
Email: cbd@cbdresearch.com
Web Site: www.cbdresearch.com

Crime; Reference Books, Directories & Dictionaries

Imprints, Series & ISBNs:
978 0 9554514
CBD Research: 978 0 900246
Chancery House Press: 978 0 900246

Book Trade Association Membership:
Independent Publishers Guild; Data Publishers Association

2152

CENGAGE LEARNING EMEA LTD
Cheriton House, North Way, Andover, Hants SP10 5BE
Telephone: 01264 332424
Fax: 01264 342745
Web Site: www.cengage.co.uk

Personnel:
Jill Jones (*Chief Executive Officer & President*)
Chad Bonney (*Chief Financial Officer*)
Andrew Robinson (*Sales Director*)
Diane Thomas (*Sales Director*)
Rossella Proscia (*Marketing Director*)
Linden Harris (*Publishing Director*)
Pedja Paulicic (*Digital Solutions Director*)

Academic & Scholarly; Accountancy & Taxation; Educational & Textbooks; English as a Foreign Language; Industry, Business & Management; Vocational Training & Careers

Distributor for:
Brooks/Cole; Cengage Learning; Delmar Learning; Gale; Heinle; South Western; Wadsworth

Book Trade Association Membership:
Publishers Association

2153

CENTRE FOR ALTERNATIVE TECHNOLOGY PUBLICATIONS
Machynlleth, Powys SY20 9AZ
Telephone: 01654 705980
Fax: 01654 702782
Email: allan.shepherd@cat.org.uk
Web Site: www.cat.org.uk/catpubs

Distribution:
Central Books, 99 Wallis Road, London E9 5LN
Telephone: 0845 458 9911
Fax: 0845 458 9912
Email: contactus@centralbooks.com
Web Site: www.centralbooks.com

Personnel:
Graham Preston (*Production Manager*)
Allan Shepherd (*Publisher*)
Annika Lundqvist (*Publishing Assistant*)

Architecture & Design; Do-It-Yourself; Educational & Textbooks; Environment & Development Studies; Gardening; Travel & Topography

New Titles: 1 (2009) , 3 (2010)
No of Employees: 3
Annual Turnover: £100,000

Imprints, Series & ISBNs:
New Futures: 978 1 898049, 978 1 902175

Overseas Representation:
USA & Canada: New Society Publishers, Gabriola Island, BC, Canada

Book Trade Association Membership:
Independent Publishers Guild

2154

CENTRE FOR ECONOMIC POLICY RESEARCH
53–56 Great Sutton Strreet, London EC1V 0DG
Telephone: 020 7183 8801
Fax: 020 7183 8820
Email: cepr@cepr.org
Web Site: www.cepr.org

Personnel:
Stephen Yeo (*Chief Executive Officer*)
Anil Shamdasani (*Publications Manager*)

Academic & Scholarly; Economics; Industry, Business & Management; Politics & World Affairs

New Titles: 10 (2009) , 10 (2010)
No of Employees: 16

Imprints, Series & ISBNs:
978 0 9557009, 978 1 898128, 978 1 907142

Overseas Representation:
USA & Canada: The Brookings Institution, Washington, DC, USA

2155

CENTRE FOR POLICY ON AGEING
25–31 Ironmonger Row, London EC1V 3QP
Telephone: 020 7553 6500
Fax: 020 7553 6501
Email: cpa@cpa.org.uk
Web Site: www.cpa.org.uk/

Warehouse, Trade Enquiries & Orders:
Central Books, 99 Wallis Road, London E9 5LN
Telephone: 0845 458 9911
Fax: 0845 458 9912
Email: orders@centralbooks.com
Web Site: www.centralbooks.co.uk

Personnel:
Gillian Crosby (*Director*)
Angela Clark (*Manager*)

Academic & Scholarly; Electronic (Professional & Academic); Sociology & Anthropology

Imprints, Series & ISBNs:
978 0 904139, 978 1 901097

Book Trade Association Membership:
Independent Publishers Guild

2156

CHALKSOFT LTD
PO Box 49, Spalding, Lincs PE11 1NZ
Telephone: 01775 769518
Fax: 01775 762618
Email: chalksoft@clara.co.uk
Web Site: www.chalksoft.clara.co.uk

Personnel:
David Baldwin (*Managing Director*)
Mrs Gillian Baldwin (*Sales & Rights, Office Manager*)

Academic & Scholarly; Animal Care & Breeding; Children's Books; Educational & Textbooks; Electronic (Educational); Gardening; Geography & Geology; Mathematics & Statistics; Music; Natural History; Scientific & Technical

Imprints, Series & ISBNs:
Chalksoft: 978 1 85116
Nene Valley Publishing: 978 1 85116
School Garden Co: 978 1 85116
SGC Books: 978 1 85116

Associated Companies:
Nene Valley Publishing; School Garden Co

Book Trade Association Membership:
Independent Publishers Guild

2157 ▬▬▬▬▬

CHAMBERS HARRAP PUBLISHERS LTD
7 Hopetoun Crescent, Edinburgh EH7 4AY
Telephone: 0131 556 5929
Fax: 0131 556 5313
Email: admin@chambersharrap.co.uk
Web Site: www.chambersharrap.com

Distributor:
Bookpoint, 130 Milton Park, Abingdon,
Oxon OX14 4SB
Telephone: 01235 400400
Fax: 01235 400401

Personnel:
Patrick White (Managing Director &
  Publisher)
Jane Camillin (Sales & Marketing Manager)
Ian Scott (Production Manager)
Vivian Marr (Editorial Manager)

Reference Books, Directories & Dictionaries

Imprints, Series & ISBNs:
Chambers: 978 0 550
Harrap: 978 0 245

Parent Company:
France: Hachette Livre

Overseas Representation:
Africa: Anita Zih, A–Z Africa Book Services,
  Rotterdam, Netherlands
All other international enquiries: Hema
  Shah, Export Sales Dept, Hodder,
  London, UK
Australia: Hachette Livre Australia, Sydney,
  NSW, Australia
Caribbean: Christopher Humphrys,
  Humphrys Roberts Associates, London,
  UK
China: Ian Taylor Associates Ltd, London, UK
Eastern Europe: Jacek Lewinson, Warsaw,
  Poland
Europe & Middle East (schools enquiries):
  Gill Dee, International Schools Sales
  Manager, Hodder, London, UK
France & French-speaking countries:
  Larousse, Paris, France
Germany, Austria & Switzerland: Giana
  Elyea, Hodder, London, UK
Greece, Malta & Cyprus: Zitsa Seraphimidi,
  J & L Watt, Paleo Faliro, Greece
Hong Kong, Taiwan & Japan: Andrew
  White, The White Partnership, Tunbridge
  Wells, UK
India: Sunil Sachdev, Allied Publishers Ltd,
  New Delhi, India
Italy, Spain & Portugal: Anna Kelsall,
  Hodder, London, UK
Korea: Information & Culture Korea (ICK),
  Seoul, Republic of Korea
Middle East: James & Lorin Watt Ltd,
  Publishing Consultants, Oxford, UK
New Zealand: Hachette Livre New Zealand,
  Auckland, New Zealand
Pakistan: Salahuddin Iqbal, Paramount
  Books (Pvt) Ltd, Karachi, Pakistan
Scandinavia & Benelux: Bea Dorning,
  Hodder, London, UK
Singapore, Malaysia & Brunei (schools only):
  APD Malaysia, Malaysia
Singapore, Malaysia & Brunei (trade): MPH
  Distributors, Singapore
South Africa: Pan Macmillan SA Pty Ltd,
  Hyde Park, South Africa
South America: Terry Roberts, Humphrys
  Roberts Associates, Cotia SP, Brazil
USA: Katrina Kruse, Houghton Mifflin,
  Boston, MA, USA

Book Trade Association Membership:
Publishing Scotland

2158 ▬▬▬▬▬

CHANNEL VIEW PUBLICATIONS LTD
St Nicholas House, 31–34 High Street,
Bristol BS1 2AW
Telephone: 0117 315 8562
Fax: 0117 315 8563
Email: info@channelviewpublications.com
Web Site:
  www.channelviewpublications.com

Distribution:
Marston Book Services, PO Box 269,
Unit 160, Milton Park, Abingdon
OX14 4YN
Telephone: 01235 465500
Fax: 01235 465555
Email: trade.order@marston.co.uk
Web Site: www.marston.co.uk

Personnel:
Tommi Grover (Managing Director)
Anna Roderick (Editorial Director)
Elinor Robertson (Marketing Manager)
Sarah Williams (Production Manager)

Academic & Scholarly; Educational &
Textbooks; Environment & Development
Studies; Languages & Linguistics;
Psychology & Psychiatry; Sociology &
Anthropology; Travel & Topography

New Titles: 48 (2009) , 45 (2010)
No of Employees: 4
Annual Turnover: £750,000

Imprints, Series & ISBNs:
Channel View Publications: 978 1 84541
Multilingual Matters: 978 0 905028, 978 1
  84769, 978 1 85359

Overseas Representation:
Australia: DA Information Services Pty Ltd,
  Mitcham, Vic, Australia
Canada: University of Toronto Press, North
  York, Ont, Canada
China: Sarah Zhao, Meme Media, P. R. of
  China
Hong Kong: Aromix Books, Hong Kong
Iran: Kowkab Publishers, Tehran, Iran
Japan: Koro Komori, Japan
Korea: Se-Yung Jun, Seoul, Republic of
  Korea
Malaysia: PMS Marketing Services,
  Selangor, Malaysia
Singapore: Publishers Marketing Services
  Pte Ltd, Singapore
USA: UTP, Tonawanda, NY, USA

Book Trade Association Membership:
Independent Publishers Guild; Association
of Learned & Professional Society
Publishers; UK Serials Group

2159 ▬▬▬▬▬

**CHARTERED INSTITUTE OF
PERSONNEL & DEVELOPMENT**
151 The Broadway, London SW19 1JQ
Telephone: 020 8612 6570
Fax: 020 8543 4371
Email: publishing@cipd.co.uk
Web Site: www.cipd.co.uk/bookstore

Distribution:
McGraw-Hill Education,
McGraw-Hill House,
Shoppenhangers Road, Maidenhead, Berks
SL6 2QL
Telephone: 01628 502700
Fax: 01628 770224
Web Site: www.cipd.co.uk/bookstore

Personnel:
Ruth Lake (Head of Publishing)
Margaret Marriott (Commissioning
  Manager)
Caroline Windle (Operations Manager)
Dawn Wood (Sales & Marketing Manager)
Georgie Smith (Operations Co-ordinator)
Sinead Burke (Senior Sales & Marketing
  Executive)

Roger Dickens (Sales & Marketing Executive)
Lynette Marx (Sales & Marketing
  Administrator)
Robert Williams (Senior Operations
  Executive)
Andrea Blue (Senior Commissioning Editor)
Ruth Anderson (Senior Commissioning
  Editor)
Kirsty Smy (Assistant Commissioning Editor)
Lindsay Anderson (Online Content Editor)
Abi Sugden (Development Editor)
Rob Jones (Commissioning Administrator)

Academic & Scholarly; Educational &
Textbooks; Industry, Business &
Management

New Titles: 12 (2009) , 22 (2010)
No of Employees: 17
Annual Turnover: £2.5M

Imprints, Series & ISBNs:
978 0 85292, 978 1 84398

2160 ▬▬▬▬▬

**THE CHARTERED INSTITUTE OF
PUBLIC FINANCE & ACCOUNTANCY**
3 Robert Street, London WC2N 6RL
Telephone: 020 7543 5600
Fax: 020 7543 5607
Email: sara.hackwood@cipfa.org.uk
Web Site: www.cipfa.org.uk/shop

Personnel:
Ms Sara Hackwood (Publications Manager)

Accountancy & Taxation; Economics

New Titles: 30 (2009) , 30 (2010)

Imprints, Series & ISBNs:
978 0 85299, 978 1 84508

2161 ▬▬▬▬▬

CHATHAM PUBLISHING
3 Barham Avenue, Elstree, Herts WD6 3PW
Telephone: 020 8455 5559
Email: michael@frontline-books.com
Web Site: www.chathampublishing.com

Trade Enquiries & Orders:
Bookpoint Ltd, 39 Milton Park, Abingdon,
Oxon OX14 4TD
Telephone: 01235 400400

Personnel:
Lionel Leventhal (Publisher)

Military & War; Nautical; Transport

Imprints, Series & ISBNs:
978 1 86176

Parent Company:
Lionel Leventhal Ltd

Overseas Representation:
Australia & New Zealand: Peribo Pty Ltd,
  Mount Kuring-Gai, NSW, Australia
Austria, Switzerland, Czech & Slovak
  Republics, Hungary, Poland, Croatia,
  Slovenia, Spain (including Gibraltar) &
  Portugal: Sandro Salucci, Florence, Italy
Belgium: De Krijger, Erps, Belgium
Canada: Vanwell Publishing Ltd, St
  Catharines, Ont, Canada
France & Netherlands: Casemate Books,
  Newbury, UK
Germany: Robbert J. Pleysier, Heerde,
  Netherlands
India: Knowledge World International,
  Delhi, India
Middle East & Far East: Publishers
  International Marketing, Burmarsh, UK
New Zealand: South Pacific Books (Imports)
  Ltd, Auckland, New Zealand
South Africa: Peter Renew, Titles SA,
  Johannesburg, South Africa
USA: MBI Publishing Co, St Paul, MN, USA

2162 ▬▬▬▬▬

CHEMCORD LTD
16 Inch Keith, St Leonards, East Kilbride,
Glasgow G74 2JZ
Telephone: 01355 235447
Fax: 01355 235447
Email: office@chemcord.co.uk
Web Site: www.chemcord.co.uk

Personnel:
Jim Melrose (Director)
Douglas Buchanan (Director)
Pat Buchanan (Sales Manager & Company
  Secretary)

Educational & Textbooks

2163 ▬▬▬▬▬

CHICKEN HOUSE PUBLISHING LTD
2 Palmer Street, Frome, Somerset
BA11 1DS
Telephone: 01373 454488
Fax: 01373 454499
Email: chickenhouse@doublecluck.com
Web Site: www.doublecluck.com

Warehouse, Trade Enquiries & Orders:
HarperCollins Publishers,
  Customer Services, 103 Westerhill Road,
Bishopbriggs, Glasgow G64 2QT
Telephone: 0844 576 8121
Fax: 0844 576 8131
Email: uk.orders@harpercollins.co.uk

Personnel:
Barry Cunningham (Managing Director)
Rachel Hickman (Deputy Managing
  Director)
Imogen Cooper (Fiction Editor)
Elinor Bagenal (Rights Manager)
Esther Waller (Publishing Manager)
Claire Skuse (Publishing Officer)

Children's Books

New Titles: 20 (2009) , 23 (2010)

Imprints, Series & ISBNs:
978 1 903434, 978 1 904442, 978 1
  905294

Parent Company:
USA: Scholastic

Overseas Representation:
Bermuda: Mary Winchell, Flatts, Bermuda
Central & Eastern Europe & Israel: Vincent
  Walsh, Yellow Brick Media, Scarborough,
  UK
Hong Kong & China: Jolie Li, Scholastic
  Asia, Causeway Bay, Hong Kong
Jamaica & other Caribbean Islands: Sharon
  Neita, The Book Merchant Ltd, Kingston,
  Jamaica
Japan: Keiko Niwano, Scholastic, Saitama,
  Japan
Korea: Helen Yang, Scholastic Asia, Seoul,
  Republic of Korea
Latin America: Janine Kelly, Scholastic,
  Buenos Aires, Argentina
Middle East & Northern Africa: Michelle
  Alwan & Bassem Badran, Bab Idriss,
  Beirut, Lebanon
Philippines: Henry Chua, Scholastic, Makati
  City, Philippines
Puerto Rico: Darlene Vazquez, Caribe
  Grolier/Scholastic Inc, Santurce, Puerto
  Rico
Singapore, Malaysia & Indonesia: Selina
  Lee, Scholastic, Kuala Lumpur, Malaysia
Southern & East Africa: Brian Mey,
  Scholastic, Cape Town, South Africa
Taiwan: Sonia Dung, Scholastic, Taipei,
  Taiwan
Thailand: Maneerat Kurdmanee, Scholastic
  Asia, Bangkok, Thailand
West Africa: Joyce Agyare, Scholastic,
  Tema, Ghana

2164

CHILD'S PLAY (INTERNATIONAL) LTD
Ashworth Road, Bridgemead, Swindon, Wilts SN5 7YD
Telephone: 01793 616286
Fax: 01793 512795
Email: allday@childs-play.com
Web Site: www.childs-play.com

Personnel:
Neil Burden *(Publisher, Chief Executive)*
Paul Gerrish *(Sales Director)*
Claire Matthews *(Production Manager)*
Beth Cox *(Education Manager)*
Adriana Twinn *(Chair)*

Children's Books

Imprints, Series & ISBNs:
Child's Play: 978 0 85953, 978 1 84643, 978 1 904550

Overseas Representation:
Australia: Child's Play Australia, Terrey Hills, NSW, Australia
Canada: Monarch Books of Canada Ltd, Downsview, Ont, Canada
New Zealand: Educational Equipment Wholesale Ltd, Auckland, New Zealand
South Africa: Phambili Agencies CC, Germiston, South Africa
United Arab Emirates: Child's Play Dubai, Dubai, UAE
USA: Child's Play Inc, Auburn, ME, USA

Book Trade Association Membership:
Educational Publishers Council; Independent Publishers Guild

2165

CHRISTIAN EDUCATION
1020 Bristol Road, Selly Oak, Birmingham B29 6LB
Telephone: 0121 472 4242
Fax: 0121 472 7575
Email: enquiries@christianeducation.org.uk
Web Site: www.christianeducation.org.uk

Personnel:
Peter Fishpool *(Chief Executive Officer)*
Azhar Lodhi *(Design & Production)*
Anstice Hughes *(Publications Team Leader)*
Gill Neuenhaus *(Finance Officer)*
Diane Horton *(Office, Sales & Administration Manager)*
Harvinder Rai *(Marketing Manager)*
Pete Johnson *(Sales Administrator)*

Academic & Scholarly; Children's Books; Educational & Textbooks; Religion & Theology

Imprints, Series & ISBNs:
Christian Education Publications: 978 1 904024, 978 1 905893
International Bible Reading Association: 978 1 904024
RE Today Services: 978 1 904024

Associated Companies:
Christian Education Publications; RE Today Services

Book Trade Association Membership:
Publishers Association; Educational Publishers Council; Christian Booksellers Convention

2166

CHRISTIAN FOCUS PUBLICATIONS
Geanies House, Fearn, Tain, Ross-shire IV20 1TW
Telephone: 01862 871011
Fax: 01862 871699
Email: info@christianfocus.com
Web Site: www.christianfocus.com

Distribution:
STL Distribution, PO Box 300, Kingstown Broadway, Carlisle, Cumbria CA3 0QS
Telephone: 0800 282728
Email: info@stl.org
Web Site: www.stldistribution.co.uk

Personnel:
William MacKenzie *(Managing Director)*
Anthony Gosling *(Sales & Marketing Manager)*
Willie Mackenzie *(Publishing Director (Adult Editorial))*
Jonathan Dunbar *(Production Manager)*
Catherine Mackenzie *(Children's Editor)*
Daniel van Straaten *(Design Manager)*
Philip Magee *(Marketing Manager)*

Biography & Autobiography; Children's Books; Educational & Textbooks; History & Antiquarian; Religion & Theology; Sports & Games

New Titles: 80 (2009) , 80 (2010)
No of Employees: 15

Imprints, Series & ISBNs:
978 0 906731, 978 1 84550, 978 1 85792, 978 1 871676
Christian Focus
Christian Focus 4 Kids
Christian Heritage
Mentor

Parent Company:
UK: Balintore Holdings

Overseas Representation:
Australia: CLC Australia, Kippa-Ring, Qld, Australia; Koorong, Blackburn South, Vic, Australia; Reformers Bookshop, Stanmore, Australia; Word, Nunawading, Vic, Australia
Far East: Chris Ashdown, Publishers' International Marketing, Ferndown, Dorset, UK
New Zealand: Soul Distributors, Auckland, New Zealand
South Africa: Struik Christian Books, Cape Town, South Africa
USA & Canada: Revelation Team, Greenville, USA; STL Distribution, Elizabethton, TN, USA

Book Trade Association Membership:
Evangelical Christian Publishers Association (USA); Christian Booksellers Association (USA)

2167

CHURCH HOUSE PUBLISHING
The Archbishops' Council, Church House, Great Smith Street, London SW1P 3AZ
Telephone: 020 7898 1451
Fax: 020 7898 1449
Email: publishing@c-of-e.org.uk
Web Site: www.chpublishing.co.uk

Sales, Customer Service & Warehouse:
Norwich Books & Music, St Mary's Works, St Mary's Plain, Norwich NR3 3BH
Telephone: 01603 612914
Fax: 01603 624483
Email: orders@norwichbooksandmusic.co.uk
Web Site: www.chpublishing.co.uk

See also:
SCM-Canterbury Press

Personnel:
Thomas Allain-Chapman *(Publishing Manager)*

Reference Books, Directories & Dictionaries; Religion & Theology

New Titles: 15 (2009) , 20 (2010)

Imprints, Series & ISBNs:
978 0 7151
In association with Saint Andrew Press: 978 0 9562821

Parent Company:
UK: The Archbishops' Council

Associated Companies:
UK: Hymns Ancient & Modern Ltd

Overseas Representation:
Australia & New Zealand: Rainbow Book Agencies, Preston, Vic, Australia
Canada: Bayard/Novalis Distribution, Toronto, Ont, Canada
USA: Westminster John Knox Press, Louisville, KY, USA

Book Trade Association Membership:
Independent Publishers Guild; Christian Suppliers' Group

2168

CHURCH OF IRELAND PUBLISHING
Church of Ireland House, Church Avenue, Rathmines, Dublin 6, Republic of Ireland
Telephone: +353 (01) 492 3979
Fax: +353 (01) 492 4770
Email: susan.hood@rcbdub.org
Web Site: www.cip.ireland.anglican.org

Personnel:
Susan Hood *(Publications Officer)*

Academic & Scholarly; History & Antiquarian; Religion & Theology

New Titles: 5 (2009) , 4 (2010)
No of Employees: 1

Imprints, Series & ISBNs:
978 1 904884

Book Trade Association Membership:
Publishing Ireland (Foilsiú Éireann)

2169

CICERONE PRESS LTD
2 Police Square, Milnthorpe, Cumbria LA7 7PY
Telephone: 015395 62069
Fax: 015395 63417
Email: info@cicerone.co.uk
Web Site: www.cicerone.co.uk

Personnel:
Jonathan Williams *(Managing Director)*
Lesley Williams *(Sales & Marketing Director)*

Guide Books; Sports & Games; Travel & Topography

New Titles: 30 (2009) , 30 (2010)
No of Employees: 9
Annual Turnover: £1.2M

Imprints, Series & ISBNs:
978 0 902363, 978 1 84965, 978 1 85284

Overseas Representation:
Europe: Bill Bailey Publishers Representatives, Newton Abbot, UK
France: Editeur, Vaison la Romaine, France
Netherlands: Nilsson & Lamm BV, Houten, Netherlands
Spain: Map Iberia FeB SL, Avila, Spain
USA: Midpoint Trade Books Inc, New York, USA

Book Trade Association Membership:
Independent Publishers Guild

2170

CILT, THE NATIONAL CENTRE FOR LANGUAGES
111 Westminster Bridge Road, London SE1 7HR
Telephone: 0845 612 5885

Fax: 0845 612 5995
Email: books@cilt.org.uk
Web Site: www.cilt.org.uk

Distribution & Orders:
Central Books Ltd, 99 Wallis Road, London E9 5LN
Telephone: 0845 458 9911
Fax: 0845 458 9912
Email: mo@centralbooks.com
Web Site: www.centralbooks.com

Personnel:
Teresa Tinsley *(Director, Communications)*
Tamzin Caffrey *(Head of Marketing, Press & Publishing)*
Rick Sutton *(Publishing Manager)*
Julie Manandhar *(Marketing Co-ordinator)*

Academic & Scholarly; Educational & Textbooks; Languages & Linguistics; Vocational Training & Careers

New Titles: 6 (2009) , 6 (2010)
No of Employees: 66

Imprints, Series & ISBNs:
Advanced Pathfinder
Classic Pathfinder
Curriculum Guides
Info Tech
New Pathfinder
Pathfinder
Reflections on Practice
Resource File
Young Pathfinder

Book Trade Association Membership:
Educational Publishers Council

2171

CLAIRE PUBLICATIONS
Unit 8, Tey Brook Centre, Great Tey, Colchester, Essex CO6 1JE
Telephone: 01206 211020
Fax: 01206 212755
Email: mail@clairepublications.com
Web Site: www.clairepublications.com

Personnel:
Noel Graham *(Production Managing Director)*
Luba Medcalf *(Finance)*
Dorcas Smith *(Rights)*

Educational & Textbooks; Electronic (Educational); Languages & Linguistics; Mathematics & Statistics

Book Trade Association Membership:
British Educational Supplies Association

2172

CLAIRVIEW BOOKS LTD
Hillside House, The Square, Forest Row, East Sussex RH18 5ES
Telephone: 0870 486 3526
Email: office@clairviewbooks.com
Web Site: www.clairviewbooks.com

Personnel:
Sevak Gulbekian *(Chief Editor)*

Agriculture; Cookery, Wines & Spirits; Environment & Development Studies; Health & Beauty; Medical (incl. Self Help & Alternative Medicine); Military & War; Politics & World Affairs; Religion & Theology

New Titles: 5 (2009) , 5 (2010)
No of Employees: 1
Annual Turnover: £70,000

Imprints, Series & ISBNs:
978 1 905570

Overseas Representation:
Australia: Footprint Books, Melbourne, Vic, Australia

Canada: Tri-Fold Books, Ont, Canada
New Zealand: Ceres Books, Auckland, New Zealand
South Africa: Stephan Phillips Ltd, Cape Town, South Africa
USA: Steinerbooks, New York, NY, USA

Book Trade Association Membership:
Independent Publishers Guild

2173

T. & T. CLARK
see: Continuum International Publishing Group

2174

JAMES CLARKE & CO
PO Box 60, Cambridge CB1 2NT
Telephone: 01223 350865
Fax: 01223 366951
Email: publishing@jamesclarke.co.uk & orders@jamesclarke.co.uk
Web Site: www.james.clarke.co.uk

Personnel:
Adrian Brink *(Managing Director)*
Rowan Binney *(Customer Service)*
Penny Bull *(Accounts Department)*
Ilaria Tassistro *(Sales & Publicity)*
Michelle Priestley *(Sales & Publicity)*
Aidan van de Weyer *(Editorial)*
Ian Bignall *(Editorial)*
Elaine Proudlove *(Editorial)*

Academic & Scholarly; Bibliography & Library Science; Biography & Autobiography; History & Antiquarian; Literature & Criticism; Philosophy; Reference Books, Directories & Dictionaries; Religion & Theology

New Titles: 31 (2009) , 40 (2010)
No of Employees: 8

Imprints, Series & ISBNs:
978 0 227

Associated Companies:
The Lutterworth Press

Overseas Representation:
Asia: Access Asia Media Services, Shanghai, P. R. of China
Philippines: Edwin Makabenta, Quezon City, Philippines
USA: The David Brown Book Co (DBBC), Oakville, CT, USA

Book Trade Association Membership:
Educational Publishers Council; Independent Publishers Guild

2175

CLASS PUBLISHING
The Exchange, Express Park, Bristol Road, Bridgwater, Somerset TA6 4RR
Telephone: 01278 427800
Fax: 01278 421077
Email: post@class.co.uk
Web Site: www.class.co.uk

Trade Enquiries & Orders & Distribution:
Macmillan Distribution (MDL), Brunel Road, Houndmills, Basingstoke, Hants RG21 6XS
Telephone: 01256 329242
Fax: 01256 331413
Email: mdl@macmillan.co.uk
Web Site: www.macmillan-mdl.co.uk

Personnel:
Richard Warner *(Managing Director)*
Rebecca Hirst *(Healthcare Marketing Manager)*
Sylvia Hotchin *(Legal Customer Services Manager)*
Lorna Downing *(European Manager, Jones & Bartlett International)*

Health & Beauty; Law; Medical (incl. Self Help & Alternative Medicine)

Imprints, Series & ISBNs:
978 1 85959, 978 1 872362

Associated Companies:
Class Health; Class Legal; Jones & Bartlett International; Jones & Bartlett Learning

Book Trade Association Membership:
Independent Publishers Guild

2176

CLASSICAL COMICS LTD
PO Box 7280, Litchborough, Towcester, Northants NN12 9AR
Telephone: 0845 812 3000
Fax: 0845 812 3005
Email: info@classicalcomics.com
Web Site: www.classicalcomics.com

Personnel:
Clive Bryant *(Chairman)*
Jo Wheeler *(Creative Director)*

Children's Books; Educational & Textbooks; English as a Foreign Language; Fiction; Literature & Criticism; Theatre, Drama & Dance

New Titles: 22 (2009) , 12 (2010)
No of Employees: 3
Annual Turnover: £240,000

Imprints, Series & ISBNs:
978 1 906332, 978 1 907127

Parent Company:
UK: Providence Press

Overseas Representation:
Australia, New Zealand & Fiji: Book & Volume, Birregurra, Vic, Australia
USA & Canada: Publishers Group West, Berkeley, CA, USA

Book Trade Association Membership:
Independent Publishers Guild

2177

CLEAR ANSWER MEDICAL PUBLISHING LTD
128A Queens Court, Queensway, London W2 4QS
Telephone: 020 7229 0893
Email: info@camp-books.com

Personnel:
Dr Frank Seibert-Alves *(Managing Director)*
Mrs Catarina A. Seibert-Alves *(Company Secretary)*

Academic & Scholarly; Biology & Zoology; Educational & Textbooks; Medical (incl. Self Help & Alternative Medicine)

New Titles: 2 (2009) , 2 (2010)

Imprints, Series & ISBNs:
978 1 903573

Book Trade Association Membership:
Independent Publishers Guild

2178

CLÓ IAR-CHONNACHTA
Indreabhán, Conamara, Co Galway, Republic of Ireland
Telephone: +353 (091) 593307
Fax: +353 (091) 593362
Email: cic@iol.ie
Web Site: www.cic.ie

Representation:
AIS, 31 Fenian Street, Dublin 2, Republic of Ireland

Telephone: +353 (01) 661 6522
Fax: +353 (01) 661 2378

Personnel:
Micheal Ó Conghaile *(Managing Director, Rights)*
Bridget Bhreathnach *(Sales & Marketing)*
Deirdre Ní Thuathail *(General Manager)*

Audio Books; Biography & Autobiography; Children's Books; Educational & Textbooks; Fiction; Gay & Lesbian Studies; History & Antiquarian; Languages & Linguistics; Literature & Criticism; Music; Photography; Poetry; Theatre, Drama & Dance; Travel & Topography

New Titles: 12 (2009) , 12 (2010)
No of Employees: 5

Imprints, Series & ISBNs:
978 1 874700, 978 1 900693, 978 1 902420, 978 1 905560

Overseas Representation:
USA: Dufour Editions Inc, Chester Springs, PA, USA

Book Trade Association Membership:
Publishing Ireland (Foilsiú Éireann)

2179

COACHWISE LTD
Chelsea Close, off Amberley Road, Armley, Leeds LS12 4HP
Telephone: 0113 231 1310
Fax: 0113 203 8826
Email: enquiries@coachwise.ltd.uk
Web Site: www.coachwise.ltd.uk

Personnel:
Tony Byrne *(Managing Director)*
Kath Leonard *(Commercial Director)*
Melanie Mallinson *(Marketing & Mail Order Director)*
Martin Betts *(Head of Publications & Design)*
Terry Hartley *(Print Manager)*

Academic & Scholarly; Children's Books; Educational & Textbooks; Electronic (Educational); Sports & Games

Imprints, Series & ISBNs:
978 1 905540, 978 1 902523

Parent Company:
UK: The National Coaching Foundation

Distributor for:
UK: The Association for Physical Education; The National Coaching Foundation

Overseas Representation:
USA: Soccer Learning Systems, Pleasanton, CA, USA

2180

COASTAL PUBLISHING
The Studio, Puddletown Road, Wareham, Dorset BH20 6AE
Telephone: 01929 554195
Fax: 01929 554502
Email: orders@coastalpublishing.co.uk
Web Site: www.coastalpublishing.co.uk

Academic & Scholarly

Book Trade Association Membership:
Publishers Association

2181

COIS LIFE
62 Páirc na Rós, Ascaill na Cille, Dún Laoghaire, Co Dublin, Republic of Ireland
Telephone: +353 (01) 280 7951
Fax: +353 (01) 280 7951
Email: eolas@coislife.ie
Web Site: www.coislife.ie

Trade - Wholesaler:
Áis, 31 Fenian Street, Dublin 2, Republic of Ireland
Telephone: +353 (01) 661 6522

Personnel:
C. Nic Pháidín *(Company Secretary)*
S. Ó Cearnaigh *(Chairman)*

Academic & Scholarly; Audio Books; Children's Books; Educational & Textbooks; Fiction; Languages & Linguistics; Literature & Criticism; Poetry; Theatre, Drama & Dance

Imprints, Series & ISBNs:
978 1 901176, 978 1 907494

Book Trade Association Membership:
Publishing Ireland (Foilsiú Éireann)

2182

COLLINS & BROWN
Anova Books, 10 Southcombe Street, London W14 0RA
Telephone: 020 7605 1400
Fax: 020 7605 1401
Email: customerservices@anovabooks.com
Web Site: www.anovabooks.com

Warehouse & Trade Orders:
HarperCollins, Glasgow
Telephone: 0141 306 3100
Fax: 0141 306 1401

Personnel:
Katie Cowan *(Associate Publisher)*
Jonathan White *(Head of Sales & Marketing)*

Animal Care & Breeding; Cookery, Wines & Spirits; Crafts & Hobbies; Do-It-Yourself; Fashion & Costume; Fiction; Health & Beauty; Magic & the Occult; Medical (incl. Self Help & Alternative Medicine); Music; Photography; Reference Books, Directories & Dictionaries; Sports & Games; Theatre, Drama & Dance

Imprints, Series & ISBNs:
978 1 84340

Parent Company:
Anova Books

Overseas Representation:
Australia: HarperCollins Publishers, Pymble, NSW, Australia
Belgium, France, Netherlands & Luxembourg: Anova Books, London, UK
Caribbean, Mexico & Central America: Christopher Humphrys, Humphrys Roberts Associates, London, UK
Eastern Europe: Csaba Lengyel de Bagota, CLB Marketing Services, Budapest, Hungary
Far East: Julian Ashton, Ashton International Marketing Services, Sevenoaks, Kent, UK
Germany, Switzerland & Austria: Gabriele Kern Publishers Services, Frankfurt-am-Main, Germany
India: Mr Seshadri, Overleaf, New Delhi, India
Italy, Spain, Portugal & Greece: Padovani Books Ltd, London, UK
New Zealand: HarperCollins (NZ) Ltd, Glenfield, Auckland, New Zealand
Pakistan: Tahir M. Lodhi, Lahore, Pakistan
Russia & Baltic States: Tony Moggach, InterMedia Americana (IMA) Ltd, London, UK
Scandinavia: Katie McNeish, McNeish Publishing International, East Sussex, UK
Singapore & Malaysia: Pansing Distribution Sdn Bhd, Singapore
South Africa: Trinity Books CC, Randburg, South Africa
South America: Terry Roberts, Humphrys Roberts Associates, Cotia SP, Brazil

USA & Canada: Sterling Publishing Co Inc, New York, NY, USA

Book Trade Association Membership:
Independent Publishers Guild

2183 ▬▬▬

COLLINS GEO
[a division of HarperCollins Publishers]
Westerhill Road, Bishopbriggs, Glasgow
G64 2QT
Telephone: 0141 306 3576
Fax: 020 8237 4209
Email:
elizabeth.mclachlan@harpercollins.co.uk
Web Site: www.collinsbartholomew.com

Personnel:
Sheena Barclay *(Managing Director)*
James Graves *(Production Director)*
Judith Norse *(Marketing Manager)*
David Alford *(Commercial Director)*

Atlases & Maps; Educational & Textbooks; Electronic (Educational); Environment & Development Studies; Geography & Geology; Guide Books; Travel & Topography

Imprints, Series & ISBNs:
Bartholomew: 978 0 7028
Collins Cartographic: 978 0 00
Collins Longman: 978 0 00
Nicholson: 978 0 7028
Times Books: 978 0 7230

Parent Company:
HarperCollins

Overseas Representation:
Australia: HarperCollins Publishers, Pymble, NSW, Australia
Canada: HarperCollins Publishers, Toronto & Scarborough, Ont, Canada
Denmark: Scanvik Books ApS, Copenhagen, Denmark
France: Editions Geographiques Generales, Paris, France
Germany & Austria: Internationales Landkartenhaus Geocenter, Stuttgart, Germany
India: Maya Publishers Pvt Ltd, New Delhi, India; Rupa, New Delhi, India
Italy: InterOrbis Media Distribution srl Ed, Corsico (Milan), Italy
Japan: Maruzen Co Ltd, Tokyo, Japan
Netherlands: Nilsson & Lamm BV, Weesp, Netherlands
New Zealand: HarperCollins (NZ) Ltd, Glenfield, Auckland, New Zealand
Singapore & Malaysia: MPH Distributors, Singapore
South Africa: Jonathan Ball, HarperCollins Publishers, Johannesburg & Jeppestown, South Africa
Sweden: Lantmateriet Kartbutiken, Stockholm & Vällingby, Sweden
Thailand: Asia Book Co Ltd, Bangkok, Thailand
USA: Hammond Inc, Maplewood, NJ, USA

Book Trade Association Membership:
Publishers Association; Publishing Scotland

2184 ▬▬▬

COLOUR HEROES LTD
Unit 6, LongbridgeHouse Farm,
Stillington Road, Easingwold, York
YO61 3UZ
Telephone: 01347 824459
Fax: 01347 822543
Email: info@colourheroes.com
Web Site: www.colourheroes.com

Personnel:
Lorraine Ives *(Sales & Marketing Director)*
Les Ives *(Creative Director)*
Nichola Theakstone *(Business Development Manager)*

Archaeology; Educational & Textbooks; Fiction; Guide Books; History & Antiquarian; Military & War; Natural History

New Titles: 6 (2009) , 6 (2010)
No of Employees: 5
Annual Turnover: £200,000

2185 ▬▬▬

COLOURPOINT BOOKS
Colourpoint House, Jubilee Business Park,
21 Jubilee Road, Newtownards, Co Down
BT23 4YH
Telephone: 028 9182 6339
Fax: 028 9182 1900
Email: info@colourpoint.co.uk
Web Site: www.colourpoint.co.uk

Representation:
Bookworld, Unit 10, Hodfar Road,
Sandy Lane Industrial Estate,
Stourport on Severn, Worcs DY13 9QB
Telephone: 01299 823330

Distribution:
MIMO Distribution (as principal address)
Telephone: 028 9182 0505
Email: sales@mimodistribution.co.uk

Personnel:
Norman Johnston *(Partner)*
Sheila Johnston *(Partner)*
Wesley Johnston *(Editorial Partner)*
Malcolm Johnston *(Finance Partner)*
Denise Martin *(Company Administrator)*

Biography & Autobiography; Educational & Textbooks; Fiction; History & Antiquarian; Transport

Imprints, Series & ISBNs:
978 1 898392, 978 1 904242, 978 1 906578

Distributor for:
MIMO Distribution

Book Trade Association Membership:
Irish Educational PA

2186 ▬▬▬

COLUMBA
55A Spruce Avenue,
Stillorgan Industrial Park, Blackrock,
Co Dublin, Republic of Ireland
Telephone: +353 (01) 294 2556
Fax: +353 (01) 294 2564
Email: info@columba.ie
Web Site: www.columba.ie

Personnel:
Séan O Boyle *(Managing Director & Publisher)*
Cecilia West *(Sales Director)*
Michael Brennan *(Sales Manager)*

History & Antiquarian; Religion & Theology

New Titles: 40 (2009) , 40 (2010)
No of Employees: 7

Imprints, Series & ISBNs:
The Columba Press: 978 0 948183, 978 1 85607
Currach Press: 978 1 85607

Overseas Representation:
Australia: Rainbow Books, Melbourne, Vic, Australia
Canada: Bayard Distribution, Toronto, Ont, Canada
New Zealand: Pleroma, Central Hawkes Bay, New Zealand
USA: Dufour Editions Inc, Chester Springs, PA, USA

Book Trade Association Membership:
Publishing Ireland (Foilsiú Éireann);
Booksellers Association

2187 ▬▬▬

COMMONWEALTH SECRETARIAT
Marlborough House, Pall Mall, London
SW1Y 5HX
Telephone: 020 7747 6342
Fax: 020 7839 9081
Email: g.bentham@commonwealth.int
Web Site: www.thecommonwealth.org

Orders:
BEBC Distribution, Albion Close, Parkstone,
Poole, Dorset BH12 3LL
Telephone: 01202 724292
Email: commonwealth@bebc.co.uk
Web Site: www.bebcdistribution.co.uk

Personnel:
Guy Bentham *(Publications Manager)*
Nicola Perou *(Publications Assistant)*

Academic & Scholarly; Agriculture; Economics; Electronic (Educational); Environment & Development Studies; Gender Studies; Industry, Business & Management; Law; Politics & World Affairs; Reference Books, Directories & Dictionaries; Scientific & Technical

New Titles: 30 (2009) , 30 (2010)
No of Employees: 300

Imprints, Series & ISBNs:
978 0 85092, 978 1 84859, 978 1 84929

Overseas Representation:
Canada: Renouf Publishing Co Ltd, Ottawa, Ont, Canada
Ghana: F. Reimmer Book Services, Accra, Ghana
Hong Kong: Transglobal Publishers Services Ltd, Hong Kong
Iberia: Iberian Book Services, Madrid, Spain
India: Parrot Reads Publishers, New Delhi, India
Malaysia: Globe Enterprise, Selangor, Malaysia; MDC Publishers, Kuala Lumpur, Malaysia
Middle East, Mediterranean & North Africa: Avicenna Partnership, Oxford, UK
Nigeria: Mosuro The Booksellers Ltd, Ibadan, Nigeria
Pakistan: Book Bird Publishers Representatives, Lahore, Pakistan
Singapore: Horizon Books Pte Ltd, Singapore; Select Books Pte Ltd, Singapore
South Africa: Hargraves Library Service, Claremont & Cape Town, South Africa
USA: Stylus Publishing Inc, Sterling, VA, USA

Book Trade Association Membership:
Publishers Association; Independent Publishers Guild

2188 ▬▬▬

COMPENDIUM PUBLISHING LTD
43 Frith Street, London W1D 4SA
Telephone: 02072874570
Fax: 08451303173
Email: info@compendiumpublishing.com
Web Site:
www.compendiumpublishing.com

Personnel:
Alan Greene *(Managing Director)*
Simon Forty *(Editor)*
Bill Lucas *(Sales Director)*

Architecture & Design; History & Antiquarian; Military & War; Music; Philosophy; Photography; Travel & Topography

New Titles: 30 (2009) , 25 (2010)
No of Employees: 10
Annual Turnover: £14M

Imprints, Series & ISBNs:
Compendium Publishing

Overseas Representation:
Australia: Herron, Queensland, Australia
Central & South America, Caribbean: David Williams, London, UK
Europe excluding Germany: Book Port Associates, Corsico, Italy
Germany, Austria & Switzerland: Publishers Services, Frankfurt, Germany
Hong Kong & China: United Century Book Services, Chaiwan, Hong Kong
India, Bangladesh & Sri Lanka: Research Press, New Delhi, India
Middle East, North Africa & Israel: Peter Ward Book Exports, London, UK
Philippines, Korea & Taiwan: Marketing Services for Publishers, Pasig City, Philippines
Singapore, Malaysia, Indonesia & Brunei: Marketing Services for Publishers Pte Ltd, Singapore
South Africa: Wild Dog Press, Lyndhurst, South Africa

2189 ▬▬▬

CONRAN OCTOPUS
Endeavour House,
189 Shaftesbury Avenue, London
WC2H 8JY
Telephone: 020 7632 5400
Web Site: www.octopusbooks.co.uk

Distribution:
Littlehampton Book Services Ltd,
Faraday Close, Durrington, Worthing,
West Sussex BN13 3TG
Telephone: 01903 828500
Fax: 01903 828802

Personnel:
Lorraine Dickey *(Publisher)*
Jonathan Christie *(Art Director)*

Architecture & Design; Cookery, Wines & Spirits; Crafts & Hobbies; Gardening

Parent Company:
Hachette UK

Overseas Representation:
See: Octopus Publishing Group, London, UK

2190 ▬▬▬

CONSTABLE & ROBINSON LTD
3 The Lanchesters,
162 Fulham Palace Road, London W6 9ER
Telephone: 020 8741 3663
Fax: 020 8748 7562
Email: general@constablerobinson.com &
sales@constablerobinson.com
Web Site: www.constablerobinson.com

Warehouse & Distribution:
TBS Ltd, Colchester Road, Frating Green,
Colchester, Essex CO7 7DW
Telephone: 01206 256000
Fax: 01206 819587

Personnel:
Nick Robinson *(Publisher)*
Pete Duncan *(Managing Director)*
Nova Jayne Robinson *(Online-publishing Director)*
Adrian Andrews *(Finance Director)*
Martin Palmer *(Group Sales Director)*
Leo Hollis *(History Editor)*
Eryl Humphrey Jones *(Rights Director)*
Sam Evans *(Publicity Director)*
Haydn Jones *(Sales Director)*
Rob Nichols *(Marketing Director)*
Krystyna Green *(Senior Commissioning Editor: Robinson – Crime – Fiction & Non-Fiction)*
Duncan Proudfoot *(Non-Fiction Editor)*
James Gurbutt *(Publisher, Corsair imprint)*
Andreas Campomar *(Editorial Director, Non-Fiction)*
Fritha Saunders *(Editor, Psychology)*
Hugh Barker *(Special Sales Manager)*

Biography & Autobiography; Fiction; Gardening; Humour; Illustrated & Fine Editions; Medical (incl. Self Help & Alternative Medicine); Military & War; Psychology & Psychiatry; Science Fiction

New Titles: 150 (2009) , 170 (2010)
No of Employees: 34

Imprints, Series & ISBNs:
Constable: 978 1 84901, 978 1 84119, 978
   1 84529, 978 1 85487
Corsair: 978 1 84901
Magpie Books: 978 1 84901, 978 1 84119,
   978 1 85487
Right Way: 978 0 7160
Robinson: 978 1 84901, 978 1 84119, 978
   1 84529, 978 1 85487

Overseas Representation:
*Australia (Constable & Robinson – Library
   Supplies):* DLS Australia (Pty) Ltd,
   Braeside, Vic, Australia
Australia (Constable & Robinson – Retail):
   Scribo Group Pty Ltd, Frenchs Forest,
   NSW, Australia
*Central & Eastern Europe, Russia, CIS,
   Middle East, North & Central America:*
   Tony Moggach, IMA, London, UK
France: Anselm Robinson, London, UK
India: Maya Publishers Pvt Ltd, New Delhi,
   India
Italy & Greece: Ted Dougherty, London, UK
Japan & China: Timberham, Ferndown, UK
Japan, China & South East Asia: Publishers
   International Marketing, London, UK
Middle East: Ray Potts, Polfages, France
New Zealand: Southern Publishers Group,
   Auckland, New Zealand
Republic of Ireland: Vivienne Lavery,
   Blackrock, Co Dublin, Republic of Ireland
Scandinavia & Iceland: McNeish Publishing
   International, East Sussex, UK
South Africa: Penguin Books South Africa,
   Parklands, South Africa
Spain & Portugal: Iberian Book Services,
   Madrid, Spain
West Indies & West Africa: Kelvin van
   Hasselt Publishing Services, Briningham,
   Norfolk, UK
Western Europe: Michael Geoghegan,
   London, UK

Book Trade Association Membership:
Publishers Association; Independent
Publishers Guild

2191 ▬▬▬▬▬

**THE CONTINUUM INTERNATIONAL
PUBLISHING GROUP LTD**
The Tower Building, 11 York Road, London
SE1 7NX
Telephone: 020 7922 0880
Fax: 020 7922 0881
Email: info@continuumbooks.com
Web Site: www.continuumbooks.com

Distribution:
Orca Book Services, Stanley House,
3 Fleets Lane, Poole, Dorset BH15 3AJ
Telephone: 01202 665432
Fax: 01202 666219
Web Site: www.orcabookservices.co.uk

Personnel:
Oliver Gadsby *(Chief Executive)*
Bob Marsh *(Finance Director)*
Robin Baird-Smith *(Publishing Director)*
Ken Rhodes *(Sales & Marketing Director)*
Anna Fleming *(Publisher)*
Sarah Campbell *(Publisher)*
Elizabeth White *(Special Sales & Rights
   Manager)*
Louise Cameron *(Production Director)*

*Academic & Scholarly; Bibliography &
Library Science; Biography &
Autobiography; Cinema, Video, TV &
Radio; Economics; Educational &*

*Textbooks; Electronic (Educational);
Electronic (Professional & Academic);
History & Antiquarian; Languages &
Linguistics; Literature & Criticism; Music;
Philosophy; Politics & World Affairs;
Reference Books, Directories &
Dictionaries; Religion & Theology; Theatre,
Drama & Dance*

New Titles: 600 (2009) , 600 (2010)
No of Employees: 65
Annual Turnover: £10M

Imprints, Series & ISBNs:
Athlone: 978 0 485
A. & C. Black (New Testament
   Commentaries): 978 0 7136
Burns & Oates: 978 0 86012
Cassell Academic: 978 0 304
Cassell Reference: 978 0 304
Geoffrey Chapman: 978 0 225
Claridge Press: 978 0 582
T. & T. Clark International: 978 0 567
Continuum: 978 0 8264, 978 1 4411
Continuum Collection: 978 1 84714
Hambledon Continuum: 978 1 84725
Leicester University Press: 978 0 7185
Mansell: 978 0 7201
Mowbray: 978 0 264
Network Continuum Education: 978 1
   85539
Pinter
Sheed & Ward: 978 0 7220
Sheffield Academic Press: 978 1 84127, 978
   1 85075
Thoemmes Continuum: 978 1 84371, 978
   1 85506
Trinity Press International: 978 1 56338

Associated Companies:
USA: The Continuum International
   Publishing Group Inc

Overseas Representation:
Australia: Palgrave Macmillan, Melbourne,
   Vic, Australia
Australia (Religion titles only): Rainbow
   Books, Melbourne, Vic, Australia
Austria, Greece & Cyprus: Tyers Book Sales,
   UK
Eastern Europe: Jacek Lewinson, Warsaw,
   Poland
India & Sri Lanka: Palgrave Macmillan, New
   Delhi, India
Japan: United Publishers Services Ltd,
   Tokyo, Japan
Korea: Information & Culture Korea (ICK),
   Seoul, Republic of Korea
Mexico, Central & South America:
   Cranbury International LLC, Montpelier,
   VT, USA
Middle East, North Africa & Malta:
   International Publishing Services (IPS)
   Middle East Ltd, Dubai, UAE
*Netherlands, Belgium, Germany, France,
   Switzerland, Italy, Israel & Caribbean:*
   The Continuum International Publishing
   Group Ltd, London, UK
Nigeria: Bounty Press Ltd, Ibadan, Nigeria
Pakistan: T.M.L. Publishers' Consultants &
   Representatives, Lahore, Pakistan
Scandinavia: Colin Flint Ltd, Publishers
   Scandinavian Consultancy, Cambridge,
   UK
Southeast & East Asia: Taylor & Francis Asia
   Pacific, Singapore
Southern Africa: Book Promotions (Pty) Ltd/
   Horizon Books (Pty) Ltd, Cape Town,
   South Africa
Spain, Portugal & Gibraltar: Iberian Book
   Services, Madrid, Spain

Book Trade Association Membership:
Independent Publishers Guild

2192 ▬▬▬▬▬

CONWAY
10 Southcombe Street, London W14 0RA
Telephone: 020 7605 1400
Fax: 020 7605 1401

Email: jlee@anovabooks.com
Web Site: www.anovabooks.com

Distribution:
HarperCollins, Campsie View,
Westerhill Road, Bishopbriggs, Glasgow
G64 2QT
Telephone: 0141 306 3100
Fax: 0141 306 3767

Personnel:
John Lee *(Associate Publisher)*
Komal Patel *(Publicity & Marketing
   Manager)*

*Aviation; Engineering; History &
Antiquarian; Military & War; Nautical;
Politics & World Affairs; Transport*

Imprints, Series & ISBNs:
978 1 84486
Brassey's (UK): 978 1 85753
Conway Maritime Press: 978 0 85177
Putnam Aeronautical Books: 978 0 85177

Overseas Representation:
Australia: Capricorn Link (Australia) Pty Ltd,
   Windsor, NSW, Australia
Canada: Vanwell Publishing Ltd, St
   Catharines, Ont, Canada
Caribbean: Humphrys Roberts Associates,
   London, UK
Eastern Europe: CLB Marketing Services,
   Budapest, Hungary
Far East: Ashton International Marketing
   Services, Sevenoaks, Kent, UK
France, Netherlands & Luxembourg: Anova
   Books, London, UK
Germany, Austria & Switzerland: Gabriele
   Kern Publishers Services, Frankfurt-am-
   Main, Germany
New Zealand: HarperCollins (NZ) Ltd,
   Glenfield, Auckland, New Zealand
Russia & Baltic States: Tony Moggach,
   InterMedia Americana (IMA) Ltd,
   London, UK
Scandinavia: McNeish Publishing
   International, East Sussex, UK
Singapore & Malaysia: Pansing Distribution
   Sdn Bhd, Singapore
South Africa: Trinity Books CC, Randburg,
   South Africa
South America: Terry Roberts, Cotia SP,
   Brazil
Spain, Portugal, Malta, Greece & Italy:
   Padovani Books Ltd, London, UK
USA: Casemate Publishers & Book
   Distributors LLC, Havertown, PA, USA

2193 ▬▬▬▬▬

DAVID C COOK (UK)
Lottbridge Drove, Eastbourne, East Sussex
BN23 6NT
Telephone: 01323 437700
Fax: 01323 411970
Email: books@kingsway.co.uk
Web Site: www.kingsway.co.uk

Personnel:
John Paculabo *(Chief Executive Officer)*
Richard Herkes *(UK Publishing Director)*
Bill Owen *(Finance & Administration
   Manager)*
Miriam Doherty *(Trade Books Manager)*

*Biography & Autobiography; Religion &
Theology*

Imprints, Series & ISBNs:
Great Ideas
Honor
Kingsway: 978 0 85476, 978 0 85491, 978
   0 86065, 978 0 86239, 978 0 902088,
   978 1 84291
Life Journey
Nexgen
Riveroak
Survivor
Victor

Distributor for:
Barbour; Charisma House; Harrison House;
Lifeway, Broodman & Holmon; New Leaf
Press; Regal

Overseas Representation:
Australia: Kennedy International, NSW,
   Australia
Canada: David C. Cook Distribution
   Canada, Paris, Ont, Canada
South Africa: Struik Christian Books Pty Ltd,
   Maitland, Cape Town, South Africa

2194 ▬▬▬▬▬

**COORDINATION GROUP
PUBLICATIONS LTD (CGP LTD)**
Kirkby-in-Furness, Cumbria LA17 7WZ
Telephone: 01229 715700
Fax: 01229 716958
Email: customerservices@cgpbooks.co.uk
Web Site: www.cgpbooks.co.uk

Personnel:
Graham Servante *(Managing Director)*
Jane Barnes *(Publishing Director)*

Educational & Textbooks

Imprints, Series & ISBNs:
978 1 84146, 978 1 84762

Associated Companies:
USA: CGP Study; Coordination Group
   Publications Inc (trading as CGP
   Education)

2195 ▬▬▬▬▬

COPPER BEECH PUBLISHING LTD
PO Box 159, East Grinstead, Sussex
RH19 4FS
Telephone: 01342 314734
Fax: 01342 312196
Email: sales@copperbeechpublishing.co.uk
Web Site:
   www.copperbeechpublishing.co.uk

Personnel:
Jan Barnes *(Rights)*
Julie Hird *(Editorial)*
Elizabeth Moreira *(Finance)*

*Cookery, Wines & Spirits; Fashion &
Costume; Gardening; History &
Antiquarian; Sports & Games; Transport*

Imprints, Series & ISBNs:
978 0 9516295, 978 1 898617
English Eccentricities
The Etiquette Collection

Book Trade Association Membership:
Independent Publishers Guild

2196 ▬▬▬▬▬

CORK UNIVERSITY PRESS
Youngline Industrial Estate, Pailaduff Road,
Togher, Cork, Republic of Ireland
Telephone: +353 (021) 490 2980
Fax: +353 (021) 431 5329
Email: corkuniversitypress@ucc.ie
Web Site: www.corkuniversitypress.com

**Orders & Distribution (Republic of
Ireland, Northern Ireland & Europe):**
Gill & Macmillan Distribution,
Hume Avenue, Park West, Dublin 12,
Republic of Ireland
Telephone: +353 (01) 500 9500
Fax: +353 (01) 500 9596

**Representation (Republic of Ireland &
Northern Ireland):**
Robert Towers, 2 The Crescent,
Monkstown, Co Dublin, Republic of Ireland
Telephone: +353 (01) 280 6532
Fax: +353 (01) 280 6020

Personnel:
Mike Collins (*Publications Director*)
Maria O'Donovan (*Production Editor*)

Academic & Scholarly; Archaeology;
Architecture & Design; Atlases & Maps;
Environment & Development Studies; Fine
Art & Art History; Gay & Lesbian Studies;
Gender Studies; History & Antiquarian;
Literature & Criticism; Music; Philosophy;
Photography

Imprints, Series & ISBNs:
Atrium
Attic Press
Field Day Essays: 978 0 902561, 978 1
85918
Irish Narratives: 978 0 902561, 978 1
85918
Undercurrents: 978 0 902561, 978 1 85918

Overseas Representation:
Germany, Austria & Switzerland (Rights only): Brigitte Axster, Frankfurt, Germany
Japan: United Publishers Services Ltd,
Tokyo, Japan
North America: Stylus Publishing LLC,
Herndon, VA, USA
UK & Europe: Quantum Publishing
Solutions Ltd, Paisley, UK
*UK (excluding Northern Ireland)
(Distribution):* Marston Book Services Ltd,
Abingdon, UK

Book Trade Association Membership:
Publishing Ireland (Foilsiú Éireann)

2197

CORNWALL EDITIONS LTD
8 Langurtho Road, Fowey, Cornwall
PL23 1EQ
Telephone: 01726 832483
Fax: 01726 832483
Email: info@cornwalleditions.co.uk
Web Site: www.cornwalleditions.co.uk

Personnel:
Ian Grant (*Publisher*)
Judy Martin (*Customer Services Manager*)

Archaeology; Children's Books; Fiction;
History & Antiquarian; Natural History

Imprints, Series & ISBNs:
Cornwall Editions: 978 1 904880
Ian Grant Publishers: 978 1 904880

Book Trade Association Membership:
Independent Publishers Guild

2198

COUNCIL FOR BRITISH ARCHAEOLOGY
St Mary's House, 66 Bootham, York
YO30 7BZ
Telephone: 01904 671417
Fax: 01904 671384
Email: books@britarch.ac.uk
Web Site: www.britarch.ac.uk

Distribution:
Central Books Ltd, 99 Wallis Road, London
E9 5LN
Telephone: 0845 458 9910
Fax: 0845 458 9912
Email: mo@centralbooks.com
Web Site: www.centralbooks.com

Personnel:
Michael Heyworth (*Director*)
Peter Olver (*Finance Director*)
Gill Chitty (*Head of Conservation*)
Donald Henson (*Head of Education*)
Lynne Walker (*Listed Buildings Officer*)
Dan Hull (*Head of Information & Communications*)
Marcus Smith (*Information Officer*)
Sophie Cringle (*Marketing & Events Officer*)
Nicky Milsted (*Young Archaeologists' Club Magazine Editor*)

Mike Pitts (*British Archaeology Magazine Editor*)
Catrina Appleby (*Publications Officer*)
Suzie Thomas (*Community Archaeology Support Officer*)

Archaeology

New Titles: 6 (2009) , 8 (2010)
No of Employees: 25

Imprints, Series & ISBNs:
Archaeology of York
British and Irish Archaeological Bibliography
British Archaeology
CBA Research Reports: 978 1 902771
Practical Handbooks in Archaeology: 978 1
902771

Book Trade Association Membership:
Association of Learned & Professional
Society Publishers

2199

COUNTRYSIDE BOOKS
2 Highfield Avenue, Newbury, Berks
RG14 5DS
Telephone: 01635 43816
Fax: 01635 551004
Email: info@countrysidebooks.co.uk
Web Site: www.countrysidebooks.co.uk

Personnel:
Nicholas Battle (*Publisher*)
Suzanne Battle (*Partner*)
Jackie Arrowsmith (*Sales Manager*)
Paula Leigh (*Managing Editor*)

Architecture & Design; Aviation; Guide
Books; History & Antiquarian; Humour;
Military & War; Reference Books,
Directories & Dictionaries; Sociology &
Anthropology; Transport; Travel &
Topography

Imprints, Series & ISBNs:
978 0 86368, 978 0 905392, 978 1 84674,
978 1 85306, 978 1 85455

Parent Company:
Countryside Book UK

Distributor for:
Boomerang Family Ltd; Cube Publications
Ltd; The Dovecote Press; Historical
Publications Ltd; Kent County Council;
Meridian Books; Power Publications

Overseas Representation:
USA & Canada: The David Brown Book Co,
Oakville, CT, USA

Book Trade Association Membership:
Independent Publishers Guild

2200

COUNTYVISE LTD
14 Appin Road, Birkenhead CH41 9HH
Telephone: 0151 647 3333
Fax: 0151 647 8286
Email: info@birkenheadpress.co.uk
Web Site: www.countyvise.co.uk

Personnel:
John Emmerson (*Managing Director*)
Jean Emmerson (*Director*)

Academic & Scholarly; Biography &
Autobiography; Children's Books; Crime;
Fiction; History & Antiquarian; Humour;
Natural History; Nautical; Poetry; Religion &
Theology; Sports & Games; Transport

New Titles: 34 (2009) , 30 (2010)
No of Employees: 3
Annual Turnover: £61,386

Imprints, Series & ISBNs:
978 0 907768, 978 1 901231, 978 1
906823

Appin Press: 978 1 906205
Liver Press: 978 1 871201
Merseyside Port Folios: 978 0 9516129
Picton Press (Liverpool): 978 1 873245

2201

CRÉCY PUBLISHING LTD
Unit 1A, Ringway Trading Estate,
Shadowmoss Road, Manchester M22 5LH
Telephone: 0161 499 0024
Fax: 0161 499 0298
Email: books@crecy.co.uk
Web Site: www.crecy.co.uk

Personnel:
Jeremy M. Pratt (*Managing Director*)
Gill Richardson (*Customer Services Manager*)
Chris Tordoff (*Marketing Manager*)

Aviation; History & Antiquarian; Military &
War; Nautical; Transport

New Titles: 5 (2009) , 10 (2010)
No of Employees: 3

Imprints, Series & ISBNs:
Airdata Publications: 978 0 85979
Airplan Flight Equipment Ltd: 978 1 874783
Crécy: 978 0 947554
Flight Recorder Publications
Goodall Publications: 978 0 907579
Hikoki Publications: 978 1 902109

Distributor for:
Air Research Publications; Airplan Flight
Equipment Ltd; Airtime Publishing;
Aviation Publications Inc; Camber
Publications Ltd; Independent Books;
Pacific Century; Specialty Press

Overseas Representation:
Australia: J. B. Wholesalers, Bibra Lake, WA,
Australia
Canada: Vanwell Publishing Ltd, St
Catharines, Ont, Canada
Eastern Europe: Tony Moggach, UK
Europe: Bookport Associates, Corsico (MI),
Italy
New Zealand: South Pacific Books (Imports)
Ltd, Auckland, New Zealand
USA: Specialty Press, North Branch, MN,
USA
Western Europe: Anselm Robinson, UK

2202

CRESSRELLES PUBLISHING CO LTD
10 Station Road Industrial Estate, Colwall,
Malvern WR13 6RN
Telephone: 01684 540154
Fax: 01684 540154
Email: simon@cressrelles.co.uk
Web Site: www.cressrelles.co.uk

Personnel:
Simon Smith (*Sales Director*)
Leslie Smith (*Director*)

Theatre, Drama & Dance

New Titles: 15 (2009) , 20 (2010)
No of Employees: 2

Imprints, Series & ISBNs:
978 0 903653, 978 0 906660
Actinic Press
Cressrelles: 978 0 85956
J. Garnet Miller: 978 0 85343
Kenyon-Deane: 978 0 7155
New Playwrights' Network: 978 0 86319

Distributor for:
USA: Anchorage Press Inc

Overseas Representation:
Australia: Origin Theatrical, Sydney, NSW,
Australia
New Zealand: Play Bureau of New Zealand
Ltd, New Plymouth, New Zealand

Republic of Ireland: Drama League of
Ireland, Dublin, Republic of Ireland
South Africa: Dalro (Pty) Ltd, Braamfontein,
South Africa
USA: Bakers Plays, Quincy, MA, USA

2203

CRIMSON PUBLISHING
2nd Floor, Westminster House, Kew Road,
Richmond, Surrey TW9 2ND
Telephone: 020 8334 1600
Fax: 020 8334 1601
Email: info@crimsonpublishing.co.uk
Web Site: www.crimsonpublishing.co.uk

Bookshop Orders:
Portfolio Books, 2nd Floor,
Westminster House, Kew Road, Richmond,
Surrey TW9 2ND
Telephone: 020 8334 1730
Fax: 020 8334 1609
Email: info@portfoliobooks.com
Web Site: www.portfoliobooks.com

Personnel:
David Lester (*Managing Director*)
Allison Harper (*Financial Director*)
Jo Jacomb (*Production Manager – Trotman*)
Sally Rawlings (*Production Manager – Crimson*)
Lucy Smith (*Marketing Director*)
Alison Yates (*Senior Commissioning Editor*)
Hugh Brune (*Sales Director*)

Biography & Autobiography; Crafts &
Hobbies; Educational & Textbooks;
Electronic (Educational); Guide Books;
Health & Beauty; Industry, Business &
Management; Reference Books, Directories
& Dictionaries; Travel & Topography;
Vocational Training & Careers

New Titles: 122 (2009) , 99 (2010)
No of Employees: 20

Imprints, Series & ISBNs:
Crimson / Vacation Work / Pathfinder
Guides / Crimson Short Walks: 978 1
85458
Pocket Bibles
Trotman: 978 1 84455
Trotman Education: 978 1 906041
White Ladder

Overseas Representation:
Australia: Woodslane Pty Ltd, Warriewood,
NSW, Australia
Benelux: Nilsson & Lamm BV, Weesp,
Netherlands
South Africa: Trinity Books CC, Randburg,
South Africa
USA: Letter Soup Rights Agency, Woodbury,
MN, USA

2204

CROSSBOW EDUCATION LTD
41 Sawpit Lane, Brocton, Staffs ST17 0TE
Telephone: 01785 660902
Fax: 01785 661431
Email: sales@crossboweducation.co.uk
Web Site: www.crossboweducation.co.uk

Also at:
Crossbow Education Ltd,
Tollgate Business Centre, Tollgate Drive,
Stafford ST16 3HS
Telephone: 0845 269 7272
Email: orders@crossboweducation.co.uk
Web Site: crossboweducation.com

Personnel:
Robert Hext (*Co-Director: UK & USA*)
Anne Hext (*Co-Director: UK & USA*)
Pelle Johansson (*UK General Manager*)
Ruth Johansson (*UK Finance & Wages*)
Mark Poyser (*UK General Sales*)
Robin York (*US Manager*)

Academic & Scholarly; Educational &
Textbooks

New Titles: 1 (2009)
No of Employees: 7
Annual Turnover: £500,000

Imprints, Series & ISBNs:
978 1 900891

Overseas Representation:
USA: Crossbow Education Corp, Cornelius, NC, USA

Book Trade Association Membership:
Educational Publishers Council

2205

CROWN HOUSE PUBLISHING LTD
Crown Buildings, Bancyfelin, Carmarthenshire SA33 5ND
Telephone: 01267 211345
Fax: 01267 211882
Email: books@crownhouse.co.uk
Web Site: www.crownhouse.co.uk

Personnel:
David Bowman *(Managing Director)*
Caroline Lenton *(Sales & Marketing Director)*

Academic & Scholarly; Medical (incl. Self Help & Alternative Medicine); Psychology & Psychiatry

New Titles: 25 (2009) , 25 (2010)
No of Employees: 12
Annual Turnover: £1.25M

Distributor for:
UK: The Developing Co; The Quest Institute
USA: Free Spirit; Kagan Professional Development; Kendall Hunt Publishing; Meta Publications; Science & Behaviour Books; Westwood Publishing

Overseas Representation:
Australasia: Footprint Books Pty Ltd, NSW, Australia
Central & Eastern Europe: IMA Publishers' Sales Representation, London, UK
China: China Publishers Marketing, Shanghai, P. R. of China
Hong Kong & Macau: Transglobal Publishers Services Ltd, Hong Kong
India: Research Press, New Delhi, India
Malaysia: Publishers Marketing Services Pte Ltd, Malaysia
Nordic Territories: McNeish Publishing Services, Hastings, UK
Philippines, Korea & Taiwan: I. J. Sagun Enterprises Inc, Philippines
Singapore: Publishers Marketing Services Pte Ltd, Singapore
South Africa: Juta & Co, Claremont, South Africa
Spain, Portugal & Gibraltar: Iberian Book Services, Spain

Book Trade Association Membership:
Booksellers Association; Independent Publishers Guild

2206

THE CROWOOD PRESS LTD
The Stable Block, Crowood Lane, Ramsbury, Marlborough, Wiltshire SN8 2HR
Telephone: 01672 520320
Fax: 01672 520280
Email: enquiries@crowood.com
Web Site: www.crowood.com

Distribution:
Grantham Book Services, Trent Road, Grantham, Lincs NG31 7XQ
Telephone: 01476 541000
Fax: 01476 541060
Email: orders@gbs.tbs-ltd.co.uk
Web Site: www.crowood.com

Personnel:
John Dennis *(Chairman)*

Ken Hathaway *(Managing Director)*
Julie Sankey *(Sales & Marketing)*

Agriculture; Animal Care & Breeding; Antiques & Collecting; Aviation; Crafts & Hobbies; Do-It-Yourself; Gardening; Military & War; Natural History; Nautical; Sports & Games; Theatre, Drama & Dance; Transport

Imprints, Series & ISBNs:
978 0 946284, 978 1 84797, 978 1 85223, 978 1 86126

Overseas Representation:
Australia: Peribo Pty Ltd, Mount Kuring-Gai, NSW, Australia
Canada: Vanwell Publishing Ltd, St Catharines, Ont, Canada
Scandinavia: Angell Eurosales, Berwick-on-Tweed, UK
Singapore, Malaysia & Brunei: Publishers Marketing Services Pte Ltd, Singapore
South Africa: Peter Hyde Associates (Pty) Ltd, Cape Town, South Africa
Southern Europe: Bookport Associates, Corsico (MI), Italy
USA: Trafalgar Square Publishing, North Pomfret, VT, USA
Western Europe: Anselm Robinson, London, UK

2207

G. L. CROWTHER
224 South Meadow Lane, Preston PR1 8JP
Telephone: 01772 257126

Personnel:
G. L. Crowther *(Sole Proprietor/Executive)*

Atlases & Maps; Geography & Geology; Transport

New Titles: 4 (2009) , 17 (2010)
Annual Turnover: £3000

Imprints, Series & ISBNs:
National Series of Waterway Tramway and Railway Atlases: 978 1 85615

2208

CRW PUBLISHING LTD
6 Turville Barns, Eastleach, Cirencester, Glos GL7 3QB
Telephone: 01367 850448
Fax: 0870 751 7073
Email: clive.reynard@btinternet.com
Web Site: www.collectors-library.com

Trade Orders:
Macmillan Distribution (MDL), Brunel Road, Basingstoke, Hants RG21 6XS
Telephone: 01256 302692 & 0845 070 5656 (automated line – orders & availability)
Fax: 01256 812558
Email: orders@macmillan.co.uk

Personnel:
Ken Webb *(Production Director)*
Marus Clapham *(Editorial Director)*
Clive Reynard *(Sales Director)*
Cameron Brown *(Chairman, Director)*

Children's Books; Fiction; Humour

New Titles: 15 (2009) , 15 (2010)
No of Employees: 6
Annual Turnover: £1M

Imprints, Series & ISBNs:
Collector's Library: 978 1 904633, 978 1 904919, 978 1 905716, 978 1 907360
Collector's Library Editions/Cases/Omnibus Editions: 978 1 904633, 978 1 904919, 978 1 905716

Overseas Representation:
Australia: The Scribo Group, NSW, Australia
Far East: Pan Macmillan Asia, Hong Kong
Germany, Eastern Europe, Russia, Benelux,

Austria & Switzerland: Pan Macmillan, London, UK
Greece: Bookport Associates
New Zealand: David Bateman Ltd, Auckland, New Zealand
Scandinavia: Anglo-Nordic Books Ltd
Spain, Portugal & Italy: Penguin Books SA, Madrid, Spain

2209

CSA WORD
[the trading name for CSA Telltapes Ltd]
6a Archway Mews, London SW15 2PE
Telephone: 020 8871 0220
Fax: 020 8877 0712
Email: info@csaword.co.uk
Web Site: www.csaword.co.uk

Distribution:
Orca Book Services, Unit A3, Fleets Corner, Poole, Dorset BH17 0HL
Telephone: 01202 665432
Fax: 01202 666219
Email: orders@orca-book-services.co.uk

Personnel:
Clive Stanhope *(Managing Director)*
Victoria Williams *(Sales Manager)*
Vanessa Brown *(Production Manager)*

Audio Books

Imprints, Series & ISBNs:
978 1 873859, 978 1 901768, 978 1 904605, 978 1 906147, 978 1 934997

Overseas Representation:
USA & Canada: Publishers Group West, Berkeley, CA, USA

2210

CUALANN PRESS
6 Corpach Drive, Dunfermline, Fife KY12 7XG
Telephone: 01383 733724
Fax: 01383 733724
Email: info@cualann.com & cualann@btinternet.com
Web Site: www.cualann.com

Personnel:
Brid Hetherington *(Director)*

Biography & Autobiography; History & Antiquarian; Military & War; Sports & Games; Travel & Topography

Annual Turnover: £6000

Imprints, Series & ISBNs:
978 0 9535036, 978 0 9544416, 978 0 9554273

2211

CURRACH PRESS
55A Spruce Avenue, Stillorgan Industrial Park, Blackrock, Co Dublin, Republic of Ireland
Telephone: +353 (01) 294 2556
Fax: +353 (01) 294 2564
Email: jo@currach.ie
Web Site: www.currach.ie

Trade Enquiries & Orders:
CMD Book Source
Telephone: +353 (01) 294 2560
Fax: +353 (01) 294 2564
Email: cmd@columba.ie

Personnel:
Jo O'Donoghue *(Publisher)*
Gráinne Ross *(Publicity Officer)*
Michael Brennan *(Sales Manager)*

Biography & Autobiography; Cinema, Video, TV & Radio; Cookery, Wines & Spirits; Guide Books; History &

Antiquarian; Humour; Music; Photography; Psychology & Psychiatry; Sports & Games; Transport; Travel & Topography

Imprints, Series & ISBNs:
978 1 85607

Parent Company:
Republic of Ireland: The Columba Bookservice Ltd

Overseas Representation:
Australia: Rainbow Books, Fairfield, Vic, Australia
Europe: Andrew Durnell Marketing Ltd, Tunbridge Wells, UK
New Zealand: Pleroma Christian Supplies, Otane, Central Hawkes Bay, New Zealand
USA & Canada: Dufour Editions Inc, Chester Springs, PA, USA

Book Trade Association Membership:
Publishing Ireland (Foilsiú Éireann)

2212

CYHOEDDIADAU'R GAIR
Ael y Bryn, Chwilog, Pwllheli, Gwynedd LL53 6SH
Telephone: 01766 819120
Fax: 01766 819120
Email: aled@ysgolsul.com
Web Site: www.ysgolsul.com

Personnel:
Aled Davies *(Director)*

Children's Books; Religion & Theology

Imprints, Series & ISBNs:
978 1 85994

Parent Company:
Welsh Sunday School Council

Overseas Representation:
Worldwide: Welsh Books Council, Aberystwyth, UK

Book Trade Association Membership:
Independent Publishers Guild

2213

DANCE BOOKS LTD
The Old Bakery, 4 Lenten Street, Alton, Hants GU34 1HG
Telephone: 01420 86138
Fax: 01420 86142
Email: dwl@dancebooks.co.uk
Web Site: www.dancebooks.co.uk

Warehouse, Trade Enquiries & Orders:
Vine House Distribution, Waldenbury, North Common, Chailey, East Sussex BN8 4DR
Telephone: 01825 723398
Fax: 01825 724188
Email: sales@vinehouseuk.co.uk
Web Site: www.vinehouseuk.co.uk

Personnel:
John O'Brien *(Chairman)*
David Leonard *(Managing, Editorial & Production Director)*
Richard Holland *(Sales Director)*

Academic & Scholarly; Music; Theatre, Drama & Dance

Imprints, Series & ISBNs:
978 0 903102, 978 1 85273

Distributor for:
USA: Dance Horizons; Princeton Book Co

Overseas Representation:
Australia: Footprint Books Pty Ltd, Warriewood, NSW, Australia
USA: Princeton Book Co, Hightstown, NJ, USA

Book Trade Association Membership:
Booksellers Association

2214 ━━━━━

DARTON, LONGMAN & TODD LTD
1 Spencer Court,
140–142 Wandsworth High Street, London
SW18 4JJ
Telephone: 020 8875 0155
Fax: 020 8875 0133
Email: audep@darton-longman-todd.co.uk
Web Site: www.dltbooks.com

Distribution:
Norwich Books and Music,
St Mary's Works, St Mary's Plain, Norwich
NR3 3BH
Telephone: 01603 612914

Personnel:
Margot Crowther (Accounts Director)
Brendan Walsh (Editorial Director)
Helen Porter (Managing Editor Director)
Ken Ruskin (Production Director)
Aude Pasquier (Sales & Marketing Director)

Academic & Scholarly; Biography &
Autobiography; Educational & Textbooks;
Philosophy; Psychology & Psychiatry;
Religion & Theology

Imprints, Series & ISBNs:
978 0 232

Overseas Representation:
Africa, Caribbean Commonwealth, Far East
& South Africa: Kelvin van Hasselt
Publishing Services, Briningham, Norfolk,
UK
Australia: Rainbow Books, Fairfield, Vic,
Australia
Canada: Novalis Inc, Toronto, Ont, Canada
Malta: Preca Library, Societas Doctrinae
Christianae, M.U.S.E.U.M., Bajda, Malta
New Zealand: Pleroma Christian Supplies,
Otane, Central Hawkes Bay, New Zealand

2215 ━━━━━

THE DAVENANT PRESS
PO Box 323, Burford OX18 4XN
Telephone: 01865 292148
Fax: 01993 824129
Email: judith@history.u-net.com
Web Site: www.davenantpress.co.uk

Personnel:
Judith Ann Loades (Proprietor)

Academic & Scholarly; Animal Care &
Breeding; Archaeology; Biography &
Autobiography; Educational & Textbooks;
History & Antiquarian; Literature &
Criticism; Politics & World Affairs; Religion
& Theology

New Titles: 12 (2009) , 26 (2010)
No of Employees: 1

Imprints, Series & ISBNs:
Davenant Press (General Academic Titles):
978 1 85944
Notes on English Literature: 978 1 85944
Notes on History: 978 1 85944
Notes on Politics: 978 1 85944

Book Trade Association Membership:
Booksellers Association

2216 ━━━━━

DAY ONE PUBLICATIONS
Ryelands Road, Leominster HR6 8NZ
Telephone: 01568 613740
Fax: 01568 611473
Email: info@dayone.co.uk
Web Site: www.dayone.co.uk

Personnel:
John Roberts (Director)

Mark Roberts (Managing Director)
Jim Holmes (Marketing & Sales Manager)

Audio Books; Biography & Autobiography;
Children's Books; Guide Books; Religion &
Theology; Travel & Topography

New Titles: 43 (2009) , 45 (2010)
No of Employees: 5

Imprints, Series & ISBNs:
978 0 902548, 978 1 84625, 978 1 903087

Parent Company:
Day One Christian Ministries

Overseas Representation:
Canada: Sola Scriptura Ministries, Guelph,
Ont, Canada
USA: Day One Christian Ministries (Inc),
Greenville, SC, USA

Book Trade Association Membership:
Booksellers Association; Christian
Booksellers Convention (UK); CBA (USA)

2217 ━━━━━

DEDALUS LTD
Langford Lodge, St Judith's Lane, Sawtry,
Cambs PE28 5XE
Telephone: 01487 832382
Email: info@dedalusbooks.com
Web Site: www.dedalusbooks.com

Distribution, Warehouse & Invoicing:
Central Books Ltd, 99 Wallis Road, London
E9 5LN
Telephone: 0845 458 9911
Fax: 0845 458 9912
Email: orders@centralbooks.com

UK Sales:
Turnaround Publisher Services Ltd, Unit 3,
Olympia Trading Estate, Coburg Road,
London N22 6TZ
Telephone: 020 8829 3000
Fax: 020 8881 5088

Personnel:
Robert Irwin (Editorial Director)
Juri Gabriel (Chairman & Rights Director)
Eric Lane (Managing Director)
Mike Mitchell (Translations Director)

Biography & Autobiography; Cookery,
Wines & Spirits; Fiction; Gardening;
Literature & Criticism; Travel & Topography

New Titles: 12 (2009) , 12 (2010)
No of Employees: 2
Annual Turnover: £150,000

Imprints, Series & ISBNs:
Dedalus Concept Books: 978 1 903517,
978 1 907650
Dedalus Euro Shorts
Dedalus European Classics: 978 0 946626,
978 1 873982
Empire of the Senses: 978 0 946626, 978 1
873982
Europe 1992–2012: 978 0 946626, 978 1
873982
Modern English Fiction: 978 0 946626, 978
1 873982

Overseas Representation:
Australia & New Zealand: Peribo Pty Ltd,
Mount Kuring-Gai, NSW, Australia
Canada: Disticor Book Division, Toronto,
Ont, Canada
France, Belgium, Germany, Switzerland,
Austria, Netherlands & Eastern Europe:
Michael Geoghegan, London, UK
Scandinavia: Angel Eurosales, Berwick-on-
Tweed, UK
Spain, Portugal, Greece & Italy: Penny
Padovani, London, UK
USA: SCB Distributors, Gardena, CA, USA

Book Trade Association Membership:
Independent Publishers Guild

2218 ━━━━━

DELANCEY PRESS LTD
23 Berkeley Square, London W1J 6HE
Telephone: 020 7665 6605
Email: delanceypress@aol.com
Web Site: www.delanceypress.co.uk &
www.peoplesbookprize.com

Personnel:
Tatiana Wilson (Managing Director:
Marketing)
Jackie Naish (Finance)
Rupert Jones-Parry (Rights Manager)
Alexandra Shelly (Editor)
Rashmi Shastri (PA to Managing Director)

Children's Books; Fiction; Humour;
Psychology & Psychiatry

Imprints, Series & ISBNs:
978 0 9539119, 978 1 907205

Book Trade Association Membership:
Publishers Association; Booksellers
Association; Independent Publishers Guild

2219 ━━━━━

DELTA ALPHA PUBLISHING LTD
19H John Spencer Square, London N1 2LZ
Telephone: 020 7359 1822
Fax: 020 7359 1822
Email: dap@deltaalpha.com
Web Site: www.deltaalpha.com

Personnel:
Damien Abbott (Director)
Deborah Lloyd (Marketing Manager)
John Knox (Marketing Manager)

Economics; Law; Photography; Reference
Books, Directories & Dictionaries

No of Employees: 2

Imprints, Series & ISBNs:
978 0 9668946

Associated Companies:
USA: Delta Alpha Publishing

Overseas Representation:
Australia: Delta Alpha, Scarborough, Qld,
Australia
USA: Port City Fulfilment, Kimball, MI, USA

Book Trade Association Membership:
Independent Publishers Guild; Publisher
Marketing Association, USA; Australian PA

2220 ━━━━━

DELTA ELT PUBLISHING LTD
Hoe Lane, Peaslake, Surrey GU5 9SW
Telephone: 01306 731770
Web Site: www.deltapublishing.co.uk

Educational & Textbooks; English as a
Foreign Language; Languages & Linguistics

New Titles: 10 (2009) , 10 (2010)
No of Employees: 2

Imprints, Series & ISBNs:
978 1 900783, 978 1 905085

2221 ━━━━━

RICHARD DENNIS PUBLICATIONS
The Old Chapel, Shepton Beauchamp,
Ilminster, Somerset TA19 0LE
Telephone: 01460 240044
Fax: 01460 242009
Email:
books@richarddennispublications.com
Web Site:
www.richarddennispublications.com

Personnel:
Richard Dennis (Production)
Sharon Pearce (Administration)
Tracie Welch (Account)
Magnus Dennis (Photographer)
Buchan Dennis (Marketing)

Academic & Scholarly; Antiques &
Collecting; Architecture & Design;
Biography & Autobiography; Fine Art & Art
History; History & Antiquarian; Illustrated &
Fine Editions

New Titles: 1 (2009) , 1 (2010)
No of Employees: 5

Imprints, Series & ISBNs:
978 0 903685, 978 0 9553741

Overseas Representation:
USA: Antique Collectors Club Ltd,
Easthampton, MA, USA

2222 ━━━━━

DENOR PRESS LTD
PO Box 12913, London N12 8ZR
Telephone: 07768 855995
Fax: 020 8446 4504
Email: denor@dial.pipex.com
Web Site: www.denorpress.com

Personnel:
Lucille Leader (Production & Editorial
Director)
Dr Geoffrey Leader (Director)
Philip Woolfson (Consultant/Accountant)

Academic & Scholarly; Biography &
Autobiography; Educational & Textbooks;
Fiction; Medical (incl. Self Help & Alternative
Medicine); Music

New Titles: 3 (2009) , 3 (2010)
No of Employees: 1

Imprints, Series & ISBNs:
978 0 9526056

Distributor for:
UK: Leading Note Productions

Overseas Representation:
USA: Lightning Source Inc (US), Lavergne,
TN, USA

2223 ━━━━━

J M DENT
[imprint of The Orion Publishing Group Ltd]
Orion House, 5 Upper St Martins Lane,
London WC2H 9EA
Telephone: 020 7240 3444
Fax: 020 7240 4822

Trade Counter & Warehouse:
Littlehampton Book Services Ltd,
Faraday Close, Durrington, Worthing,
West Sussex BN13 3RB
Telephone: 01903 828500
Fax: 01903 828625

Academic & Scholarly; Biography &
Autobiography; Children's Books;
Economics; Fiction; Gardening; History &
Antiquarian; Law; Literature & Criticism;
Music; Reference Books, Directories &
Dictionaries; Scientific & Technical

Imprints, Series & ISBNs:
J M Dent: 978 0 460
Everyman Paperbacks: 978 0 460

Parent Company:
The Orion Publishing Group Ltd

Overseas Representation:
see: The Orion Publishing Group Ltd,
London, UK

2224

THE DERBY BOOKS PUBLISHING CO LTD
3 The Parker Centre, Mansfield Road, Derby DE21 4SZ
Telephone: 01332 384235
Fax: 01332 292755
Email: sales@dbpublishing.co.uk
Web Site: www.derbybooks.co.uk

Personnel:
Stephen Caron (*Chairman & Managing Director*)
Jane Caron (*Finance Director*)
Alex Morton (*Publishing Manager, Editorial*)
Jo Rush (*Sales & Marketing*)
Carole Vernon (*Administration*)

Biography & Autobiography; Sports & Games; Transport

New Titles: 60 (2010)
No of Employees: 13

Imprints, Series & ISBNs:
978 0 907969, 978 1 85983, 978 1 873626

2225

DIONYSIA PRESS LTD
7 Duddingston House Courtyard, 127 Milton Road West, Edinburgh EH15 1JG

Personnel:
Eve Smith (*Director*)
Denise Smith (*Director: Marketing, Editorial, Secretary*)

Literature & Criticism

New Titles: 5 (2009) , 6 (2010)
No of Employees: 6

Imprints, Series & ISBNs:
978 1 903171

Distributor for:
Greece: Dionysia Press

Overseas Representation:
Greece: Dionysia Zervanou, Athens, Greece

Book Trade Association Membership:
Publishing Scotland

2226

DISCOVERY WALKING GUIDES LTD
10 Tennyson Close, Dallington, Northampton NN5 7HJ
Web Site: www.walking.demon.co.uk

Also at:
DWG Ltd, c/o Mailshot Services, 21 Upper Priory Street, Northampton NN1 2PT

Personnel:
David Brawn (*Company Secretary*)
Ros Brawn (*Director*)

Atlases & Maps; Guide Books; Travel & Topography

New Titles: 16 (2009) , 6 (2010)

Imprints, Series & ISBNs:
Drive! Touring Maps: 978 1 904946
Tour & Trail Maps: 978 1 904946
Walk! Guide Books: 978 1 904946

Overseas Representation:
Spain: Map Iberia FeB SL, Avila, Spain

2227

DITTO INTERNATIONAL LTD
7 Regents Hall, St Mary's Avenue, Stony Stratford, Bucks MK11 1EB
Telephone: 01908 563766

Email: info@dittointernational.co.uk

Academic & Scholarly; Educational & Textbooks

Book Trade Association Membership:
Publishers Association

2228

ERIC DOBBY PUBLISHING LTD
Random Acres, Slip Mill Lane, Hawkhurst, Kent TN18 5AD
Telephone: 01580 753387
Fax: 01580 753387
Email: eric@ericdobbypublishing.com

Distribution:
Publishers Group UK, 8 The Arena, Mollison Avenue, Enfield, Middx EN3 7NL
Telephone: 020 8804 0400
Fax: 020 8804 0044
Web Site: www.pguk.co.uk

Personnel:
Eric Dobby (*Managing Director, Sales & Rights*)
Tracey Dobby (*Director Administration*)

Architecture & Design; Crime; Fashion & Costume; Military & War; Reference Books, Directories & Dictionaries

New Titles: 10 (2009) , 6 (2010)
No of Employees: 2
Annual Turnover: £75,000

Imprints, Series & ISBNs:
978 1 85882

Associated Companies:
Medway Publishing Ltd

Overseas Representation:
Australia: Woodslane, Mona Vale, NSW, Australia
Benelux: Jos de Jong, Just in Time Promotions, Heenstal, Netherlands
Eastern Europe: Dr László Horváth Publishers Representative, Budapest, Hungary
Italy, Greece & Cyprus: Charles Gibbes Associates, London, UK
Middle East & Malta: Avicenna Partnership, Oxford, UK
Scandinavia: David Towle International
South Africa: Palgrave Macmillan, Johannesburg, South Africa
South East Asia: Asia Publishers Services Ltd, Hong Kong
South West Asia: APD Singapore Pte Ltd, Singapore
Spain, Portugal & Gibraltar: Iberian Book Services, Madrid, Spain

2229

DONHEAD PUBLISHING LTD
Lower Coombe, Donhead St Mary, Shaftesbury, Dorset SP7 9LY
Telephone: 01747 828422
Fax: 01747 828522
Web Site: www.donhead.com

Personnel:
Jill Pearce (*Managing Director & Publisher*)
Chris Hall (*Finance Director*)

Architecture & Design; Scientific & Technical

New Titles: 6 (2009) , 5 (2010)
No of Employees: 4

Imprints, Series & ISBNs:
978 1 873394

Overseas Representation:
Germany, Switzerland, Austria: Fraunhofer IRB, Stuttgart, Germany
USA: Port City Fulfilment, Kimball, MI, USA

Book Trade Association Membership:
Independent Publishers Guild

2230

THE DOVECOTE PRESS
Stanbridge, Wimborne Minster, Dorset BH21 4JD
Telephone: 01258 840549
Fax: 01258 840958
Email: online@dovecotepress.com
Web Site: www.dovecotepress.com

Personnel:
David Burnett (*Managing Director*)
Elizabeth Dean (*Secretary*)

Archaeology; Biography & Autobiography; Geography & Geology; Guide Books; History & Antiquarian; Military & War; Natural History; Transport; Travel & Topography

New Titles: 11 (2009) , 12 (2010)
No of Employees: 2
Annual Turnover: £170,000

Imprints, Series & ISBNs:
978 0 946159, 978 1 874336, 978 1 904349

2231

ASHLEY DRAKE PUBLISHING LTD
PO Box 733, Cardiff CF14 7ZY
Telephone: (029) 2021 8187
Email: post@ashleydrake.com
Web Site: www.ashleydrake.com

Distribution:
NBN International, Estover Road, Plymouth PL6 7PY
Web Site: www.nbninternational.com

Personnel:
Ashley Drake (*Managing Director*)
Siwan Wyn (*Company Secretary*)

Academic & Scholarly; Biography & Autobiography; Children's Books; Cookery, Wines & Spirits; Educational & Textbooks; History & Antiquarian; Industry, Business & Management; Languages & Linguistics; Literature & Criticism; Military & War; Politics & World Affairs; Psychology & Psychiatry; Sports & Games; Theatre, Drama & Dance

New Titles: 3 (2009) , 8 (2010)

Imprints, Series & ISBNs:
Y Ddraig Fach: 978 1 899877
Gwasg Addysgol Cymru: 978 1 899869
Hisarlik Press: 978 1 874312
Morgan Publishing: 978 1 903532
Scandinavian Academic Press: 978 1 904609
St David's Press (formerly Ashley Drake Publishing): 978 1 902719
Welsh Academic Press: 978 1 86057

Overseas Representation:
North America: ISBS, Portland OR, USA

2232

DRAMATIC LINES
PO Box 201, Twickenham TW2 5RQ
Telephone: 020 8296 9502
Fax: 020 8296 9503
Email: mail@dramaticlinespublishers.co.uk
Web Site: www.dramaticlines.co.uk

Personnel:
John Nicholas (*Managing Editor*)
Heather Stephens (*Sales, Marketing & Production*)
Irene Palko (*Development*)

Children's Books; Educational & Textbooks; History & Antiquarian; Theatre, Drama & Dance

New Titles: 1 (2009) , 1 (2010)

2233

DREF WEN CYF/LTD
28 Church Road, Whitchurch, Cardiff CF14 2EA
Telephone: 029 2061 7860
Fax: 029 2061 0507
Email: gwilym@drefwen.com
Web Site: www.drefwen.com

Personnel:
Roger Boore (*Director*)
Anne Boore (*Director*)
Gwilym Boore (*Director*)
Alun Boore (*Director*)
Rhys Boore (*Director*)

Audio Books; Children's Books; Educational & Textbooks; Fiction

New Titles: 42 (2009) , 40 (2010)

Imprints, Series & ISBNs:
978 0 85596, 978 0 946962

Book Trade Association Membership:
Cwlwm Cyhoeddwyr Cymru (Union of Welsh Publishers)

2234

GERALD DUCKWORTH & CO LTD
90–93 Cowcross Street, London EC1M 6BF
Telephone: (020) 7490 7300
Fax: (020) 7490 0080
Email: info@duckworth-publishers.co.uk
Web Site: www.ducknet.co.uk

Distribution:
Grantham Book Services, Trent Road, Grantham, Lincs NG31 7XQ

Personnel:
Peter Mayer (*Owner & Managing Director*)
Ray Davies (*Production Director*)
Deborah Blake (*Academic Editorial Director*)
Nina Woods (*Sales & Marketing Executive*)
Suzannah Rich (*Publicity Manager*)

Academic & Scholarly; Archaeology; Architecture & Design; Biography & Autobiography; Crime; Fashion & Costume; Fiction; Fine Art & Art History; History & Antiquarian; Humour; Literature & Criticism; Military & War; Philosophy; Politics & World Affairs; Reference Books, Directories & Dictionaries; Religion & Theology; Science Fiction; Theatre, Drama & Dance; Travel & Topography

No of Employees: 6

Imprints, Series & ISBNs:
Bristol Classical Press: 978 1 85399
Duckworth: 978 0 7156

Overseas Representation:
Australia & New Zealand (Academic): Palgrave Macmillan, South Yarra, VIC, Australia
Australia (General): The Scribo Group, Frenchs Forest, NSW, Australia
Europe: Bill Bailey Publishers Representatives, Newton Abbot, UK
Middle East & Indian Subcontinent: Publishers International Marketing, France
New Zealand (General): Addenda Publishing, Auckland, New Zealand
South Africa: Book Promotions Pty Ltd, Diep River, South Africa
South East Asia & North East Asia: Publishers International Marketing, Dorset, UK
USA & Canada (Academic): Publishers International Marketing, Dulles, VA, USA

Book Trade Association Membership:
Independent Publishers Guild

2235

DUNEDIN ACADEMIC PRESS
Hudson House, 8 Albany Street, Edinburgh
EH1 3QB
Telephone: 0131 473 2397
Fax: 01250 870920
Email: mail@dunedinacademicpress.co.uk
Web Site:
www.dunedinacademicpress.co.uk

Representation (UK):
Compass Academic Ltd,
The Barley Mow Centre,
10 Barley Mow Passage, Chiswick, London
W4 4PH
Telephone: 020 8994 6477
Fax: 020 8400 6132
Email: AS@compass-academic.co.uk

**Distribution (excluding North America
& Australasia):**
Dunedin Academic Press, c/
o Turpin Distribution, Pegasus Drive,
Stratton Business Park, Biggleswade, Beds
SG18 8TQ
Telephone: 01767 604951
Fax: 01767 601640
Email: books@turpin-distribution.com

Personnel:
Anthony Kinahan *(Director)*
Norman Steven *(Director)*

*Academic & Scholarly; Geography &
Geology; Languages & Linguistics;
Sociology & Anthropology*

New Titles: 13 (2009) , 15 (2010)
No of Employees: 0

Imprints, Series & ISBNs:
978 1 903765, 978 1 906716

Overseas Representation:
Arab World & Iran: Dar Kreidieh, Beirut,
Lebanon
Australasia: Inbooks, c/o James Bennett Pty
Ltd, Belrose, NSW, Australia
Benelux: Netwerk Academic Book Agency,
Rotterdam, Netherlands
Hong Kong & Macau: Transglobal
Publishers Services Ltd, Hong Kong
India: Overseas Press India Pvt Ltd, New
Delhi, India
Korea South, Taiwan & Philippines: Edwin
Makabenta, Quezon City, Philippines
North America: International Specialized
Book Services Inc, Portland, OR, USA
*Republic of Ireland (including Northern
Ireland):* Brookside Publishing Services,
Dublin, Republic of Ireland
Scandinavia: Jan Norbye, Ølstykke,
Denmark
Spain & Portugal: Chris Humphrys, Gaucin,
Spain

Book Trade Association Membership:
Publishing Scotland

2236

EAGLE PUBLISHING LTD
3–4 The Drove, West Wilts Trading Estate,
Westbury, Wilts BA13 4JE
Telephone: 01225 899141
Fax: 01225 768811
Email: eaglepublishing@btconnect.com

Distributors:
IVP Books, Norton Street, Nottingham
NG7 3HR
Telephone: 0115 978 1054
Fax: 0115 942 2694
Web Site: www.ivpbooks.com

Personnel:
David Wavre *(Managing Director)*

Religion & Theology

Imprints, Series & ISBNs:
978 0 86347

Overseas Representation:
Australia & South Africa: IVP Books,
Nottingham, UK
New Zealand: Scripture Union Wholesale,
Wellington, New Zealand
Republic of Ireland: Columba Book Service,
Blackrock, Co Dublin, Republic of Ireland

2237

EARTHSCAN
Dunstan House, 14A St Cross Street,
London EC1N 8XA
Telephone: 020 7841 1930
Fax: 020 7242 1474
Email: earthinfo@earthscan.co.uk
Web Site: www.earthscan.co.uk

Distribution:
Macmillan Distribution (MDL), Brunel Road,
Houndmills, Basingstoke, Hants RG21 6XS
Telephone: 01256 329242
Fax: 01256 842084
Email: orders@macmillan.co.uk

Personnel:
Edward Milford *(Executive Chairman)*
Jonathan Sinclair Wilson *(Managing
Director)*
Gina Mance *(Head of Production)*
Veruschka Selbach *(Head of Sales &
Marketing)*

*Academic & Scholarly; Agriculture;
Architecture & Design; Atlases & Maps;
Biology & Zoology; Economics; Educational
& Textbooks; Electronic (Professional &
Academic); Engineering; Environment &
Development Studies; Geography &
Geology; Industry, Business &
Management; Law; Natural History; Politics
& World Affairs; Reference Books,
Directories & Dictionaries; Scientific &
Technical; Sociology & Anthropology;
Transport*

New Titles: 138 (2009) , 180 (2010)
No of Employees: 30

Imprints, Series & ISBNs:
Earthscan: 978 1 84407, 978 1 85383
James & James: 978 0 907383, 978 1
873936, 978 1 902916

Overseas Representation:
Africa (excluding North & South Africa):
Tony Moggach, InterMedia Africa Ltd
(IMA), London, UK
*Australia, New Zealand & Papua New
Guinea:* New South Books, Moorebank,
NSW, Australia
Canada: UBC Press, Georgetown, Ont,
Canada
China & Hong Kong: China Publishers
Services Ltd, Hong Kong
India: Vinod Vasishtha, Viva Books, New
Delhi, India
Japan: Tim Burland, Tokyo, Japan; United
Publishers Services Ltd, Tokyo, Japan
Korea: Se-Yung Jun, Information & Culture
Korea (ICK), Seoul, Republic of Korea
Latin America & Caribbean: Ethan Atkin,
Cranbury International LLC, Montpelier,
VT, USA
Malaysia & Brunei: UBSD, Selangor,
Malaysia
Middle East & North Africa: Zoe Kaviani,
International Publishing Services (IPS)
Middle East Ltd, Dubai, UAE
Pakistan, Afghanistan & Tajikistan: Book
Bird Publishers Representatives, Lahore,
Pakistan
Philippines: Megatexts Phil Inc, Cebu City,
Philippines
South Africa: Jacana Media, Johannesburg,
South Africa
Taiwan: Unifacmanu Trading Co Ltd, Taipei,
Taiwan

USA: Stylus Publishing LLC, Herndon, VA,
USA

Book Trade Association Membership:
Independent Publishers Guild

2238

ECO-LOGIC BOOKS
Mulberry House, 19 Maple Grove, Bath
BA2 3AF
Telephone: 01225 484472
Fax: 0871 522 7054
Web Site: www.eco-logicbooks.com

Personnel:
Peter Andrews *(Senior Executive)*

*Agriculture; Architecture & Design; Crafts &
Hobbies; Crafts & Hobbies; Environment &
Development Studies; Gardening*

New Titles: 3 (2009) , 3 (2010)

Imprints, Series & ISBNs:
978 1 899233

Distributor for:
Australia: Holmgren Design Services
UK: Common Ground; Verey & von Kanitz
Rural Classics
USA: Alan C. Hood & Co Inc; Mole
Publishing Co; Oasis Design; Post
Carbon Publishing; Trucking Turtle
Publishing

2239

**ECO PUBLISHING INTERNATIONAL
LTD**
PO Box 56891, London N13 9AJ
Email:
mail@ecopublishinginternational.com
Web Site:
www.ecopublishinginternational.com

Personnel:
Malcolm Watson *(Chairman)*

*Educational & Textbooks; Environment &
Development Studies*

New Titles: 48 (2009) , 50 (2010)
No of Employees: 3
Annual Turnover: £50,000

Imprints, Series & ISBNs:
978 1 947049

Book Trade Association Membership:
Publishers Association

2240

EDINBURGH UNIVERSITY PRESS
22 George Square, Edinburgh EH8 9LF
Telephone: 0131 650 4218
Fax: 0131 650 3286
Email: marketing@eup.ed.ac.uk
Web Site: www.euppublishing.com

Trade Enquiries:
Marston Book Services, PO Box 269,
Abingdon, Oxon OX14 4YN
Telephone: 01235 465500
Fax: 01235 465655
Web Site: www.marston.co.uk

Personnel:
Timothy Wright *(Chief Executive)*
Jackie Jones *(Deputy Chief Executive & Head
of Book Publishing)*
Ian Davidson *(Head of Production)*
Jan Thomson *(Head of Finance &
Subscription Management)*
Catriona Murray *(Head of Sales &
Marketing)*
Sarah Edwards *(Head of Journals)*
Wendy Gardner *(Marketing Manager)*
Anna Glazier *(Marketing Manager)*
Avril Buckler *(Sales & Digital Administrator)*

Naomi Farmer *(Marketing Executive)*
Bekah Mackenzie *(Project Manager)*

*Academic & Scholarly; Archaeology;
Cinema, Video, TV & Radio; Educational &
Textbooks; Electronic (Professional &
Academic); Gender Studies; History &
Antiquarian; Languages & Linguistics; Law;
Literature & Criticism; Philosophy; Politics &
World Affairs; Reference Books, Directories
& Dictionaries; Religion & Theology;
Sociology & Anthropology*

New Titles: 110 (2009) , 129 (2010)
No of Employees: 23
Annual Turnover: £2.3M

Imprints, Series & ISBNs:
Edinburgh University Press: 978 0 7486, 978
0 85224
Keele University Press: 978 1 85331
Polygon @ Edinburgh: 978 1 902930

Parent Company:
University of Edinburgh

Overseas Representation:
Australia & New Zealand: NewSouth Books,
Sydney, NSW, Australia
Benelux: Kemper Conseil Publishing,
Voorburg, Netherlands
Caribbean & Latin America: InterMedia
Americana, London, UK
China: Ian Taylor Associates Ltd, London, UK
Cyprus (Turkish), Malta & Middle East:
James & Lorin Watt Ltd, Publishing
Consultants, Oxford, UK
East & South East Asia: Taylor & Francis Asia
Pacific, Singapore
Eastern Europe: Marek Lewinson, Warsaw,
Poland
Germany, Austria & Switzerland: SHS
Publishers' Consultants and
Representatives, Oranienberg, Germany
Greece: Charles Gibbes Associates,
Louslitges, France
India: Maya Publishers Pvt Ltd, New Delhi,
India
Iran: Vijeh Nashr Co, Tehran, Iran
Italy & France: Mare Nostrum Publishing
Consultants, Rome, Italy
Japan: United Publishers Services Ltd,
Tokyo, Japan
Korea: Se-Yung Jun, Seoul, Republic of
Korea
Pakistan: World Press, Lahore, Pakistan
Scandinavia: Colin Flint Ltd, Harlow, UK
South Africa: Academic Marketing Services
(Pty) Ltd, Craighall, South Africa
Spain & Portugal: Mare Nostrum Publishing
Consultants, Madrid, Spain
Sub-Saharan Africa: InterMedia Africa Ltd,
London, UK
*USA & Canada (most titles, enquiries &
orders):* Columbia University Press, New
York, USA

Book Trade Association Membership:
Publishers Association; Publishing
Scotland; Independent Publishers Guild;
Association of Learned and Professional
Society Publishers

2241

**EDUCATIONAL PLANNING BOOKS
LTD**
PO Box 63, Hathersage, Hope Valley,
Derbyshire S32 1DJ
Telephone: 01433 651010
Fax: 01433 650000
Email: sales@epb-ltd.co.uk

Warehouse:
Bamford Works, Bamford, Hope Valley,
Derbyshire S33 0EB
Telephone: 01433 651010
Fax: 01433 650000
Email: sales@epb-ltd.co.uk
Web Site: www.edplanbooks.com

Personnel:
G. N. S. Garner (Managing Director)

Educational & Textbooks

No of Employees: 8
Annual Turnover: £1.6M

Book Trade Association Membership:
Publishers Association

2242

EGMONT UK LTD
239 Kensington High Street, London
W8 6SA
Telephone: 020 7761 3500
Fax: 020 7761 3510
Email: info@euk.egmont.com
Web Site: www.egmont.co.uk

Egmont Press & Sales Departments:
3rd Floor, Beaumont House,
Kensington Village, Avonmore Road,
London W14 8TS
Telephone: 020 7605 6600
Fax: 020 7605 6601

Personnel:
Rob McMenemy (Senior Vice-President,
  Egmont English Language & Central
  Europe)
Jimmy Weir (Chief Financial Officer)
Gillian Laskier (Group Sales Director)
Cally Poplak (Managing Director, Egmont
  Press)
David Riley (Managing Director, Egmont
  Publishing Group)
Debbie Cook (Director of Magazines)

Children's Books

No of Employees: 220
Annual Turnover: £49.7M

Imprints, Series & ISBNs:
Dean: 978 0 603
Egmont: 978 1 4052
Mammoth: 978 0 7497
Methuen: 978 0 416

Parent Company:
Denmark: Egmont Fonden

Book Trade Association Membership:
Publishers Association; Booksellers
Association

2243

EGON PUBLISHERS LTD
618 Leeds Road, Outwood, Wakefield
WF1 2LT
Telephone: 01924 871697
Fax: 01924 871697
Email: information@egon.co.uk
Web Site: www.egon.co.uk

Personnel:
Colin Redman (Managing Director)
Mrs Rachel Redman (Company Secretary)

Educational & Textbooks

New Titles: 6 (2009) , 3 (2010)
No of Employees: 2
Annual Turnover: £50,000

Imprints, Series & ISBNs:
978 0 905858, 978 1 899998, 978 1
  904160, 978 1 907656

Associated Companies:
UK: SEN Marketing

Distributor for:
UK: Brand Books

Overseas Representation:
Australia: Silvereye Publications, Avalon,
  NSW, Australia

New Zealand: Acquila Enterprises,
  Auckland, New Zealand
Singapore: September 21, Braddell Tech,
  Singapore

2244

ELAND PUBLISHING LTD
3rd Floor, 61 Exmouth Market, London
EC1R 4QL
Telephone: 020 7833 0762
Fax: 020 7833 4434
Email: info@travelbooks.co.uk
Web Site: www.travelbooks.co.uk

Trade Distribution:
Grantham Book Services, Trent Road,
Grantham, Lincs NG31 7XG
Telephone: 01476 541080
Fax: 01476 541061
Email: orders@gbs.tbs-ltd.co.uk

Trade Representation (UK):
Publishers Group UK, 8 The Arena,
Mollison Avenue, Enfield, Middx EN3 7NL
Telephone: 020 8804 0400
Fax: 020 8804 0044
Email: info@pguk.co.uk
Web Site: www.pguk.co.uk

Personnel:
Rose Baring (Production Director)
Barnaby Rogerson (Co-Publisher)
Stephanie Allen (Publicity Director)

Travel & Topography

New Titles: 10 (2009) , 9 (2010)
No of Employees: 6
Annual Turnover: £300,000

Imprints, Series & ISBNs:
978 0 907871

Associated Companies:
UK: Baring & Rogerson; Sickle Moon Books

Overseas Representation:
Australia & New Zealand: New South
  Books, NSW, Australia
Eastern Europe, Russia & Sub-Saharan
  Africa: Tony Moggach, London, UK
France, Benelux, Germany, Austria &
  Switzerland: Ted Dougherty, London, UK
Italy, Spain, Portugal, Greece & Gibraltar:
  Jenny & Penny Padovani, London, UK
Mexico, Central & Southern America: David
  Williams, InterMedia Americana (IMA)
  Ltd, London, UK
Middle East, North Africa, Turkey & Iran:
  Peter Ward Book Exports, London, UK
Thailand, Burma, Laos & Vietnam: Orchid
  Press, Bangkok, Thailand
USA & Canada: Dufour Editions Inc, Chester
  Springs, PA, USA

Book Trade Association Membership:
Independent Publishers Guild

2245

ELECTRIC WORD PLC
33–41 Dallington Street, London EC1V 0BB
Telephone: 020 7954 3420
Fax: 0845 450 6140
Web Site: www.electricwordplc.com

Academic & Scholarly

Book Trade Association Membership:
Publishers Association

2246

EDWARD ELGAR PUBLISHING LTD
The Lypiatts, 15 Lansdown Road,
Cheltenham, Glos GL50 2JA
Telephone: 01242 226934
Fax: 01242 262111
Email: info@e-elgar.co.uk
Web Site: www.e-elgar.co.uk

Distribution:
Marston Book Services Ltd, PO Box 269,
Abingdon, Oxon OX14 4YN
Telephone: 01235 465500
Fax: 01235 465555
Email: client@marston.co.uk
Web Site: www.marston.co.uk

Personnel:
Edward Elgar (Chairman)
Tim Williams (Managing Director)
Sandy Elgar (Personnel Director & Secretary)
Alex Pettifer (Editorial Director)
Julie Leppard (Head of Editorial &
  Production Service)
Francine O'Sullivan (Senior Commissioning
  Editor)
Ruth Kirk (Rights & Permissions)
Hilary Quinn (Marketing, Publicity & Sales)

Academic & Scholarly; Agriculture;
Economics; Educational & Textbooks;
Electronic (Professional & Academic);
Environment & Development Studies;
Industry, Business & Management; Law;
Reference Books, Directories &
Dictionaries; Transport

New Titles: 274 (2009) , 302 (2010)

Imprints, Series & ISBNs:
978 1 84064, 978 1 84376, 978 1 84542,
  978 1 84720, 978 1 84844, 978 1
  85278, 978 1 85898

Associated Companies:
USA: Edward Elgar Publishing Inc

Overseas Representation:
Japan: United Publishers Services Ltd,
  Tokyo, Japan
North & South America: Edward Elgar
  Publishing Inc, Northampton, MA, USA
Singapore, Malaysia, Thailand, Indonesia,
  Philippines, Brunei, Vietnam, Myanmar,
  Laos & Cambodia: Taylor & Francis Asia
  Pacific, Singapore

2247

ELLIOTT & THOMPSON
27 John Street, London WC1N 2BX
Telephone: 020 7831 5013
Fax: 020 7831 5011
Email: mark@eandtbooks.com
Web Site: www.eandtbooks.com

Personnel:
Lorne Forsyth (Chairman)
Mark Searle (Publisher)
Ellen Marshall (Executive)

Cookery, Wines & Spirits; History &
Antiquarian; Industry, Business &
Management; Military & War; Music;
Natural History; Sports & Games

New Titles: 10 (2009) , 20 (2010)
No of Employees: 3
Annual Turnover: £500,000

Imprints, Series & ISBNs:
978 1 904027, 978 1 907642

Book Trade Association Membership:
Independent Publishers Guild

2248

ELM PUBLICATIONS
Seaton House, Kings Ripton, Huntingdon
PE28 2NJ
Telephone: 01487 773359
Fax: 01487 773359
Email: elm@elm-training.co.uk
Web Site: www.elm-training.co.uk

Personnel:
Sheila Ritchie (Home & Export Sales
  Managing Director)
Duncan Ritchie (IT Director/Secretary)
Jacqueline Wieczovek (Sales Manager)

Educational & Textbooks; Electronic
(Educational); Industry, Business &
Management; Transport; Travel &
Topography

Imprints, Series & ISBNs:
978 0 946139, 978 0 9505828, 978 1
  85450

Parent Company:
Elm Consulting Ltd

Book Trade Association Membership:
Booksellers Association

2249

ELSEVIER LTD
The Boulevard, Langford Lane, Kidlington,
Oxford OX5 1GB
Telephone: 01865 843000
Fax: 01865 853010
Email: initial.surname@elsevier.com
Web Site: www.elsevier.com

Also at:
32 Jamestown Road, London NW1 7BY
Telephone: 020 7424 4200
Fax: 020 7424 4431

Also at:
20–22 East Street, Edinburgh EH7 4BQ
Telephone: 0131 524 1700
Fax: 0131 524 1800

Academic & Scholarly; Chemistry;
Educational & Textbooks; Medical (incl. Self
Help & Alternative Medicine); Scientific &
Technical

Imprints, Series & ISBNs:
Academic Press: 978 0 12
Churchill-Livingstone: 978 0 443
Elsevier Advanced Technology: 978 0 08
Elsevier Applied Science: 978 0 08
Elsevier Trends Journals: 978 0 08
Harcourt Health Sciences
Harcourt Ltd
Harcourt Publishers Ltd
Mosby: 978 0 7243
Pergamon: 978 0 08
W. B. Saunders: 978 0 7020
Scutari Press

Parent Company:
Netherlands: Elsevier BV

Associated Companies:
USA: Elsevier Inc

Overseas Representation:
Australia: Elsevier Australia, Marrickville,
  NSW, Australia
Brazil: Editora Campus Ltda, Rio de Janeiro,
  Brazil
India: Elsevier India, New Delhi, India
Japan: Elsevier Japan, Tokyo, Japan
Korea: Elsevier, Seoul, Republic of Korea
Pakistan: Rae & Sons Publishers
  Representatives, Lahore, Pakistan

Book Trade Association Membership:
Publishers Association; International Group
of Scientific, Medical & Technical
Publishers; STM

2250

EMERALD GROUP PUBLISHING LTD
Howard House, Wagon Lane, Bingley,
West Yorkshire BD16 1WA
Telephone: 01274 777700
Web Site: www.emeraldinsight.com

Personnel:
Martin Fojt (Chairman)
John Peters (Chief Executive Officer)
Niki Haunch (Head of Editorial)
Moyna Keenan (Head of Corporate
  Communications)

Academic & Scholarly; Accountancy &

Taxation; Archaeology; Computer Science; Economics; Educational & Textbooks; Electronic (Educational); Electronic (Professional & Academic); Engineering; Environment & Development Studies; Industry, Business & Management; Languages & Linguistics; Philosophy; Psychology & Psychiatry; Sociology & Anthropology; Transport; Vocational Training & Careers

No of Employees: +200

2251

ENCYCLOPAEDIA BRITANNICA (UK) LTD
2nd Floor, Unity Wharf, 13 Mill Street, London SE1 2BH
Telephone: 020 7500 7800
Fax: 020 7500 7578
Email: enquiries@britannica.co.uk
Web Site: www.britannica.co.uk

Distributors:
Encyclopaedia Britannica (UK) Ltd, Unit Y, Paddock Wood Distribution Centre, Paddock Wood, Tonbridge, Kent TN12 6UU
Telephone: 01892 839814
Fax: 01892 837272
Email: britannica@combook.co.uk

Personnel:
Ian Grant (Managing Director)
Jane Helps (Operations Vice-President)
Patrick McGuire (Sales & Distribution Manager)
Diane Franklyn (Consumer Sales Director)
Chrysandra Halstead (Marketing Executive Manager)

Atlases & Maps; Children's Books; Electronic (Educational); Reference Books, Directories & Dictionaries

New Titles: 25 (2010)
No of Employees: 25
Annual Turnover: £5M

Imprints, Series & ISBNs:
978 0 85229, 978 1 59339, 978 1 84326, 978 2 85229

Parent Company:
USA: Encyclopaedia Britannica Inc

Distributor for:
France: Encyclopaedia Universalis

Overseas Representation:
Germany, Austria, Switzerland & Netherlands: Ted Dougherty, London, UK
Italy: Mare Nostrum Publishing Consultants, Rome, Italy
Scandinavia: Colin Flint Ltd, Harlow, UK
South-East Europe, North Africa & Middle East (excluding GCC): Avicenna Partnership, Oxford, UK
Spain & Portgual: Iberian Book Services, Madrid, Spain
Sub-Saharan Africa (excluding South Africa), Eastern Europe (excluding Russia): InterMedia Americana (IMA) Ltd, London, UK

Book Trade Association Membership:
Independent Publishers Guild

2252

ENERGY INSTITUTE
61 New Cavendish Street, London W1G 7AR
Telephone: 020 7467 7100
Fax: 020 7255 1472
Web Site: www.energypublishing.org

Personnel:
Erica Sciolti (Publishing Manager)

Academic & Scholarly; Aviation; Chemistry; Electronic (Professional & Academic); Engineering; Environment & Development Studies; Industry, Business & Management; Reference Books, Directories & Dictionaries; Scientific & Technical

New Titles: 18 (2009), 25 (2010)
No of Employees: 50

Imprints, Series & ISBNs:
978 0 85293

Book Trade Association Membership:
Association of Learned & Professional Society Publishers

2253

ENGLISH HERITAGE
Kemble Drive, Swindon SN2 2GZ
Telephone: 01793 414619
Fax: 01793 414769
Email: robin.taylor@english-heritage.org.uk
Web Site: www.english-heritage.org.uk

Distribution:
Central Books, 99 Wallis Road, London E9 5LN
Telephone: 0845 458 9910
Fax: 020 8533 5821
Email: eh@centralbooks.com

Personnel:
Robin Taylor (Managing Editor)
John Hudson (Head of Publishing)
Clare Blick (Sales & Publicity Manager)

Academic & Scholarly; Archaeology; Architecture & Design; Children's Books; Educational & Textbooks; Guide Books; History & Antiquarian; Military & War; Scientific & Technical; Travel & Topography

New Titles: 17 (2009), 16 (2010)
No of Employees: 11

Imprints, Series & ISBNs:
978 1 84802, 978 1 85074, 978 1 873592, 978 1 905624

Overseas Representation:
Australia: James Bennett Pty Ltd, Belrose, NSW, Australia
Benelux: Roy de Boo, Hooge Mierde, Netherlands
Scandinavia: Jan Norbye, Olstykke, Denmark
Spain and Portugal: Peter Prout, Iberian Book Services, Madrid, Spain
USA: The David Brown Book Co, Oakville, CT, USA

Book Trade Association Membership:
Association of Learned & Professional Society Publishers

2254

ENITHARMON PRESS
26B Caversham Road, London NW5 2DU
Telephone: 020 7482 5967
Fax: 020 7284 1787
Email: books@enitharmon.co.uk
Web Site: www.enitharmon.co.uk

Warehouse:
Central Books, 99 Wallis Road, London E9 5LN
Telephone: 020 8986 4854
Fax: 020 8533 5821

Personnel:
Stephen Stuart-Smith (Director)
Jacqueline Gabbitas (Marketing Manager)
Isabel Britten (Editorial Manager)

Fiction; Illustrated & Fine Editions; Literature & Criticism; Poetry

Imprints, Series & ISBNs:
978 1 870612, 978 1 900564, 978 1 904634

Associated Companies:
Enitharmon Editions Ltd

Overseas Representation:
USA & Canada: Dufour Editions Inc, Chester Springs, PA, USA

Book Trade Association Membership:
Independent Publishers Guild

2255

EQUINOX PUBLISHING LTD
1 Chelsea Manor Studios, Flood Street, London SW3 5SR
Telephone: 020 7823 3748
Fax: 020 7823 3748
Email: jjoyce@equinoxpub.com
Web Site: www.equinoxpub.com

Distribution:
Marston Book Services Ltd, PO Box 269, Abingdon, Oxon OX14 4YN
Telephone: 01235 465521
Fax: 01235 465555
Email: trade.orders@marston.co.uk

Personnel:
Janet Joyce (Publisher)
Valerie Hall (Editorial & Rights)
Yvonne Nazareth (Journals)

Academic & Scholarly; Archaeology; Biography & Autobiography; Cookery, Wines & Spirits; Educational & Textbooks; Electronic (Professional & Academic); Gender Studies; History & Antiquarian; Languages & Linguistics; Music; Philosophy; Reference Books, Directories & Dictionaries; Religion & Theology; Sociology & Anthropology

New Titles: 50 (2009), 50 (2010)
No of Employees: 3

Imprints, Series & ISBNs:
Equinox: 978 1 84553, 978 1 904768
Southover Press: 978 1 87096

Distributor for:
J R Collis Publications; Contact Pastoral Trust

Overseas Representation:
Australia & New Zealand: Eleanor Brasch Enterprises, Artarmon, NSW, Australia
China, Hong Kong & Taiwan: Ian Taylor & Associates, Beijing, P. R. of China
Europe: Andrew Durnell Marketing Ltd, Tunbridge Wells, UK
India: Maya Publishers Pvt Ltd, New Delhi, India
Japan: United Publishers Services Ltd, Tokyo, Japan
Middle East: Avicenna Partnership Ltd, Oxford, UK
North America: The David Brown Book Co, Oakville, CT, USA
Singapore, Malaysia & Brunei: Publishers Marketing Services Pte Ltd, Singapore
South Africa, Botswana, Lesotho, Namibia, Swaziland & Zimbabwe: Chris Reinders, The African Moon Press, Kelvin, South Africa

Book Trade Association Membership:
Independent Publishers Guild; Association of Learned & Professional Society Publishers (UK Serials Interest Group)

2256

THE ERSKINE PRESS
The White House, Sandfield Lane, Eccles, Norwich, Norfolk NR16 2PB
Telephone: 01953 887277
Fax: 01953 888361

Email: erskpres@aol.com
Web Site: www.erskine-press.com

Personnel:
Crispin de Boos (Director)
Lesley de Boos (Commissioning Editor)

Academic & Scholarly; Biography & Autobiography; History & Antiquarian; Illustrated & Fine Editions; Medical (incl. Self Help & Alternative Medicine); Military & War; Natural History; Travel & Topography

New Titles: 3 (2009), 5 (2010)
Annual Turnover: £50,000

Imprints, Series & ISBNs:
Archival Facsimiles: 978 0 948285, 978 1 85297
Erskine Press: 978 0 948285, 978 1 85297

Parent Company:
jack afrika Publishing Ltd

2257

ETHICS INTERNATIONAL PRESS LTD
[publishes for Centre for Business & Public Sector Ethics]
St Andrews Castle,
St Andrews Street South, Bury St Edmunds, Suffolk IP33 3PH
Telephone: 01954 710086
Fax: 01954 710103
Email: info@ethicspress.com
Web Site: www.ethicspress.com

Personnel:
Dr Rosamund Thomas (Director)
Robert Willis (Marketing Manager)
Christopher Thomas (General Manager)

Academic & Scholarly; Educational & Textbooks; Electronic (Educational); Electronic (Professional & Academic); Environment & Development Studies; Industry, Business & Management; Law; Politics & World Affairs; Vocational Training & Careers

New Titles: 1 (2010)

Imprints, Series & ISBNs:
978 1 871891
Teaching Ethics (Book series)

Associated Companies:
Ethics International MultiMedia Ltd

Book Trade Association Membership:
Publishers Association

2258

EUROMONITOR INTERNATIONAL
60–61 Britton Street, London EC1M 5UX
Telephone: 020 7251 8024
Fax: 020 7608 3149
Email: info@euromonitor.com
Web Site: www.euromonitor.com

Personnel:
Trevor Fenwick (Managing Director)
Robert Senior (Chairman)
David Gudgin (Director)

Economics; Industry, Business & Management; Reference Books, Directories & Dictionaries

Imprints, Series & ISBNs:
978 0 86338, 978 1 84264

Associated Companies:
Dubai: Euromonitor International
Lithuania: Euromonitor International
P. R. of China: Euromonitor International (Shanghai) Co Ltd
Singapore: Euromonitor International (Asia) Pte Ltd
USA: Euromonitor International Inc

31

Book Trade Association Membership:
Data Publishers Association; European Association of Directory Publishers

2259

EVANS PUBLISHING GROUP
2A Portman Mansions, Chiltern Street, London W1U 6NR
Telephone: 020 7487 0920
Fax: 020 7487 0921
Email: sales@evansbrothers.co.uk
Web Site: www.evansbooks.co.uk

Trade Office:
Zero to Ten, Suite 1.3, Coomb House, 7 St John's Road, Isleworth, Middx TW7 6NH
Telephone: 020 8758 9777
Fax: 020 8758 9888
Web Site: www.evansbooks.co.uk

Personnel:
Stephen Pawley (Managing Director)
Brian Jones (International Director)
Andrew Macmillan (UK Sales Director)
Ms Alex Evans (Marketing Director)
Ms Su Swallow (UK Publisher)
Danny Daly (Accountant)
Ms Jenny Mulvanny (Production Manager)
Ms Britta Martins-Simon (Foreign Rights Manager)
Jason McGovern (Export Sales Manager)

Children's Books; Educational & Textbooks; Electronic (Educational)

Imprints, Series & ISBNs:
Cherrytree: 978 1 84234
Evans: 978 0 237
Zero to Ten: 978 1 84089

Associated Companies:
Kenya: Evans Brothers (Kenya) Ltd
Nigeria: Evans Brothers (Nigeria Publishers) Ltd
Sierra Leone: Evans Brothers (Sierra Leone) Ltd

Book Trade Association Membership:
Publishers Association; Educational Publishers Council

2260

EVERYMAN'S LIBRARY
Northburgh House, 10 Northburgh Street, London EC1V 0AT
Telephone: 020 7566 6350
Fax: 020 7490 3708
Email: books@everyman.uk.com

Trade Orders & Enquiries:
Grantham Book Services, Trent Road, Grantham, Lincs NG31 7XQ
Telephone: 01476 541000
Fax: 01476 541061
Web Site: www.granthambookservices.co.uk

Personnel:
David Campbell (Managing Director)
Clémence Jacquinet (Editorial (Travel Guides))
Jane Holloway (Editorial (Classics))

Academic & Scholarly; Children's Books; Fiction; Guide Books; Illustrated & Fine Editions; Literature & Criticism; Philosophy; Poetry; Science Fiction; Travel & Topography

Imprints, Series & ISBNs:
Everyman Children's Classics
Everyman Classics
Everyman Guides
Everyman Pocket Classics
Everyman Pocket Poets
Everyman Wodehouse

Parent Company:
USA: Alfred A. Knopf

Overseas Representation:
Worldwide (excluding North America): Random House International (Everyman's Library), UK

2261

EX LIBRIS PRESS
16A New St John's Road, St Helier, Jersey JE2 3LD
Telephone: 01534 780488
Fax: 01534 780488
Email: roger.jones@ex-librisbooks.co.uk
Web Site: www.ex-librisbooks.co.uk

Stockists:
Gardners Books, 1 Whittle Drive, Willingdon Drove, Eastbourne, East Sussex BN23 6QH
Telephone: 01323 521777
Fax: 01323 521666

Personnel:
Roger Jones (Proprietor)

Archaeology; Biography & Autobiography; Cookery, Wines & Spirits; Gardening; Geography & Geology; Guide Books; History & Antiquarian; Natural History; Nautical; Poetry; Transport; Travel & Topography

New Titles: 10 (2009) , 10 (2010)

Imprints, Series & ISBNs:
978 1 906641
ELSP (Ex Libris Self Publishing)
Seaflower Books: 978 0 948578, 978 0 9506563, 978 1 903341

2262

EXECUTIVE GRAPEVINE INTERNATIONAL LTD
Rosanne House, Parkway, Welwyn Garden City AL8 6HG
Telephone: 01707 351451
Fax: 01707 390143
Email: enquiries@executive-grapevine.co.uk
Web Site: www.askgrapevine.com

Personnel:
Helen Barrett (Chief Executive Officer)
Anna Weston (Managing Director)
Sabrina Ponte (Director, Sales & Marketing)
Sally Griffin (Director of Finance)

Industry, Business & Management; Reference Books, Directories & Dictionaries

New Titles: 2 (2009) , 2 (2010)

Imprints, Series & ISBNs:
978 1 903530, 978 1 903550

Book Trade Association Membership:
Data Publishers Association

2263

EXLEY PUBLICATIONS LTD
16 Chalk Hill, Watford, Herts WD19 4BG
Telephone: 01923 474480
Fax: 01923 818733
Web Site: www.helenexleygiftbooks.com

Warehouse:
Trade Counter, The Airfield, Norwich Road, Mendlesham, Suffolk IP14 5NA
Telephone: 01449 766629
Fax: 01449 767122

Personnel:
Helen M. Exley (Managing Director & Editorial)
Richard A. Exley (Finance & Production Director)
Lincoln Exley (Associate/Export Sales Director)

Charlotte Smith (Head of UK Sales Manager)
Keith Allen-Jones (Foreign Rights Director)

Humour

New Titles: 10 (2009) , 10 (2010)

Imprints, Series & ISBNs:
978 1 84634, 978 1 85015, 978 1 86187

Associated Companies:
France: Exley SA
USA: Exley Giftbooks

Overseas Representation:
Australia: Card & Paper House, Australia; New Holland Publishers Pty Ltd, French's Forest, NSW, Australia
Canada: Pierre Belvedere, Montreal, Canada
Hong Kong: Pacific Century Distribution Ltd, Hong Kong
India: Maya Publishers Pvt Ltd, New Delhi, India
Israel: Astra Agency, Jerusalem, Israel
Korea: Union Enterprise Co Ltd, Seoul, Republic of Korea
Lebanon: Librarie Samir Editeur, Beirut, Lebanon
Malta: Audio Visual Centre Ltd, Sliema, Malta
New Zealand: David Bateman Ltd, Auckland, New Zealand
Pakistan: Mackwin & Co, Karachi, Pakistan
Philippines: Balatbat & Sons International, Filinvest, Philippines
Republic of Ireland: Island Publications Ltd, Dublin, Republic of Ireland
Singapore: Cards n Such Pte Ltd, Singapore
Southern Africa: Struik Book Distributors, Johannesburg, South Africa
Spain: Editorial Edaf SA, Madrid, Spain
Vietnam: Fahasa Companie, Ho Chi Minh City, Vietnam

Book Trade Association Membership:
Independent Publishers Guild

2264

EXPRESS NEWSPAPERS
The Northern and Shell Building, 10 Lower Thames Street, London EC3R 6AE
Telephone: 0871 520 7887
Fax: 0871 434 7966
Email: leila.palmer@express.co.uk
Web Site: www.express.co.uk

Personnel:
Leila Palmer (Head of Enterprise)

Atlases & Maps; Biography & Autobiography; Crime; Do-It-Yourself; Gardening; Guide Books; Health & Beauty; Humour; Illustrated & Fine Editions; Poetry; Reference Books, Directories & Dictionaries; Sports & Games; Transport; Travel & Topography

Imprints, Series & ISBNs:
978 0 85079

Parent Company:
Northern and Shell Media

Overseas Representation:
Canada: Canadian Manda Group, Toronto, Ont, Canada
India: Wilco International, India

2265

F+W MEDIA INTERNATIONAL (FORMERLY DAVID & CHARLES)
[A subsidiary of F+W Media, Inc.]
Brunel House, Newton Abbot, Devon TQ12 4PU
Telephone: 01626 323200
Fax: 01626 323317
Web Site: www.davidandcharles.co.uk

Trade Orders and Enquiries to::
Customer Services, Trade Department, GBS, Trent Road, Grantham, Lincolnshire NG31 7QX
Telephone: 01476 541080
Fax: 01176 541061
Email: orders@gbs.tbs-ltd.co.uk

Personnel:
James Woollam (Managing Director)
Richard Dodman (Sales & New Business Director and Trade Community Leader)
Ali Myer (Craft Community Leader)

Crafts & Hobbies; Do-It-Yourself; Fine Art & Art History; History & Antiquarian; Humour; Military & War; Natural History; Photography

Imprints, Series & ISBNs:
David & Charles: 978 0 7153
Pevensey Press: 978 0 907115

Parent Company:
USA: F+W Media, Inc.

Distributor for:
UK: Reader's Digest Books
USA: Adams Media; Dover Publications; F+W Media (North Light Books, Writer's Digest Books, Betterway Books); Krause Publications

Overseas Representation:
Asia, Middle East: Michelle Morrow Curreri, Beverly, MA, USA
Australia: Capricorn Link (Australia) Pty Ltd, Windsor, NSW, Australia
Belgium, France & Netherlands: Ted Dougherty, London, UK
Cyprus, Gibraltar, Spain and Portugal: Jenny Padovani Frias, Barcelona, Spain
Denmark, Finland, Norway, Sweden & Netherlands (Foreign Rights Agent): Candida Buckley, Leeds, Kent, UK
Denmark, Sweden, Norway & Finland: Angell Eurosales, Berwick-on-Tweed, UK
Germany, Austria & Switzerland: Gabriele Kern Publishers Services, Frankfurt-am-Main, Germany
India, Bangladesh, Nepal & Sri Lanka: Maya Publishers Pvt Ltd, New Delhi, India
Italy & Greece: Penny Padovani, London, UK
Latin America & Caribbean: David Williams, London, UK
Mauritius, Kenya, Gambia, Botswana & Zimbabwe: Export Sales Manager, David & Charles Ltd, Newton Abbot, UK
New Zealand: David Bateman Ltd, Auckland, New Zealand
Poland, Croatia, Hungary, Czech Republic, Romania, Slovak Republic, Yugoslavia, Bulgaria, Slovenia & Bosnia: Bill Bailey Publishers Representatives, Newton Abbot, UK
South Africa: Trinity Books CC, Randburg, South Africa
USA & Canada: F & W Media Ltd, Cincinnati, USA

Book Trade Association Membership:
Independent Publishers Guild

2266

FABER & FABER LTD
Bloomsbury House, 74–77 Great Russell Street, London WC1B 3DA
Telephone: 020 7927 3800
Fax: 020 7927 3801
Email: mailbox@faber.co.uk
Web Site: www.faber.co.uk

Accounts:
16 Burnt Mill, Elizabeth Way, Harlow, Essex CM20 2HX
Fax: 01279 417366
Web Site: www.faber.co.uk

Distribution & Orders:
TBS Ltd, Colchester Road, Frating Green,
Colchester, Essex CO7 7DW
Telephone: 01206 256004
Fax: 01206 255912

Personnel:
Stephen Page *(Chief Executive)*
Walter Donohue *(Publisher & Film Director)*
Valerie Eliot *(Director)*
Julian Loose *(Editorial, Fiction & Non-Fiction Director)*
Lee Brackstone *(Director)*
David Tebbutt *(Finance Director)*
Nigel Marsh *(Publishing Services Director)*
Jason Cooper *(Rights Director)*
Will Atkinson *(Sales & Marketing Director)*
Rachel Alexander *(Publicity Director)*
Belinda Matthews *(Music Director)*
Paul Keegan *(Editorial: Poetry)*
Julia Haydon-Wells *(Editorial: Children's)*
Dinah Wood *(Editorial: Plays)*

Biography & Autobiography; Children's Books; Cinema, Video, TV & Radio; Cookery, Wines & Spirits; Fiction; Literature & Criticism; Music; Poetry; Politics & World Affairs; Theatre, Drama & Dance

New Titles: 270 (2009)
No of Employees: 90

Imprints, Series & ISBNs:
978 0 571

Associated Companies:
USA: Faber & Faber Inc

Distributor for:
De la Mare Publishing Ltd; Sanctuary
Publishing; Screenpress Publishing
USA: Faber & Faber Inc

Overseas Representation:
Argentina, Bermuda, Bolivia, Brazil, Central America, Chile, Columbia, Ecuador, French West Indies, Jamaica, Mexico, Paraguay, Peru, Uruguay & Venezuela: InterMedia Americana (IMA) Ltd, London, UK
Asia (including Japan, Korea, Taiwan & Hong Kong): Julian Ashton, Sevenoaks, Kent, UK
Australia: Allen & Unwin Pty Ltd, Crows Nest, NSW, Australia
Canada: Penguin Group Canada, Toronto, Ont, Canada
Central Europe, Netherlands, Belgium, Luxembourg, Switzerland & Scandinavia: Bunmi Oke, Faber & Faber, London, UK
Eastern Europe (excluding Russia & Baltic States): Csaba Lengyel de Bagota, Budapest, Hungary
France, Germany & Austria: Patrick Keogh, Faber & Faber, London, UK
India: Penguin Books India, New Delhi, India
Italy: Penguin Italia srl, Milan, Italy
Middle East (including Israel & Iran), North Africa, Malta & Turkey: Peter Ward Book Exports, London, UK
New Zealand: Allen & Unwin Pty Ltd, Auckland, New Zealand
Pakistan: Faber & Faber, London, UK
Republic of Ireland: Gill Hess Ltd, Skerries, Co Dublin, Republic of Ireland
Singapore & Malaysia: Penguin Singapore, Singapore
Southern Africa: Book Promotions Pty Ltd, Cape Town, South Africa
Spain & Portugal: Penguin Spain, Madrid, Spain
Thailand, Cambodia, Laos, Vietnam & Myanmar: Keith Hardy, Hardy Bigfoss International Co Ltd, Bangkok, Thailand
USA: Faber & Faber Inc, A Division of Farrer, Strauss & Giroux, New York, USA

Book Trade Association Membership:
Publishers Association

2267

FABIAN SOCIETY
11 Dartmouth Street, London SW1H 9BN
Telephone: 020 7227 4900
Fax: 020 7976 7153
Email: info@fabian-society.org.uk
Web Site: www.fabians.org.uk

Personnel:
Sunder Katwala *(General Secretary)*
Phil Mutero *(Sales)*
Tom Hampson *(Editorial Director)*

Academic & Scholarly; Economics; Environment & Development Studies; Philosophy; Politics & World Affairs

New Titles: 7 (2009) , 7 (2010)
No of Employees: 12
Annual Turnover: £835,000

Imprints, Series & ISBNs:
Fabian Pamphlet: 978 0 7163

Associated Companies:
NCLC Publishers Ltd

Distributor for:
NCLC Publishers Ltd

Book Trade Association Membership:
Booksellers Association

2268

FACET PUBLISHING
7 Ridgmount Street, London WC1E 7AE
Telephone: 020 7255 0590
Fax: 020 7255 0591
Email: info@facetpublishing.co.uk
Web Site: www.facetpublishing.co.uk

Warehouse:
Bookpoint Ltd, 130 Milton Park, Abingdon,
Oxon OX14 4SB
Telephone: 01235 827702
Fax: 01235 827703
Email: facet@bookpoint.co.uk

Personnel:
John Woolley *(Managing Director (CILIP Enterprises))*
Helen Carley *(Publisher)*
Sarah Busby *(Commissioning Editor)*
James Williams *(Marketing Manager)*
Kathryn Beecroft *(Production Manager)*
Rohini Ramachandran *(Sales Manager)*
Lin Franklin *(Desk Editor)*
June York *(Typesetter)*

Academic & Scholarly; Bibliography & Library Science; Educational & Textbooks; Electronic (Professional & Academic); Reference Books, Directories & Dictionaries

No of Employees: 7

Imprints, Series & ISBNs:
978 1 85604

Parent Company:
CILIP (Chartered Institute of Library and
Information Professionals)

Overseas Representation:
Australia & New Zealand: Inbooks, c/o James Bennett Pty Ltd, Belrose, NSW, Australia
Canada & USA: Neal-Schuman Publishers Inc, New York, NY, USA
Eastern Europe: Marek Lewinson, Warsaw, Poland
India: Book Marketing Services, Chennai, India
Japan: United Publishers Services Ltd, Tokyo, Japan
Middle East: International Publishing Services (IPS) Middle East Ltd, Dubai, UAE
South East Asia: Taylor & Francis Asia Pacific, Singapore

Spain & Portugal: Iberian Book Services,
Madrid, Spain

Book Trade Association Membership:
Publishers Association; Independent
Publishers Guild

2269

FAMILY PUBLICATIONS
Denis Riches House, 66 Sandford Lane,
Kennington, Oxford OX1 5RP
Telephone: 0845 0500 879
Fax: 01865 321325
Email: sales@familypublications.co.uk
Web Site: www.familypublications.co.uk

Personnel:
Colin Mason *(Managing Director)*

Biography & Autobiography; History & Antiquarian; Religion & Theology

New Titles: 12 (2009) , 12 (2010)
No of Employees: 5
Annual Turnover: £300,000

Imprints, Series & ISBNs:
978 1 871217, 978 1 907380

Overseas Representation:
Australia: Freedom Publishing, North
Melbourne, Vic, Australia

2270

A. & A. FARMAR
78 Ranelagh Village, Dublin 6,
Republic of Ireland
Telephone: +353 (01) 496 3625
Fax: +353 (01) 497 0107
Email: afarmar@iol.ie
Web Site: www.farmarbooks.com

Trade Orders (Republic of Ireland):
Gill and Macmillan, HUme Avenue,
Park West, Dublin 12, Republic of Ireland
Telephone: +353 (01) 500 9599
Fax: +353 (01) 500 9599

Personnel:
Anna Farmar *(Editorial)*
Tony Farmar *(Production)*

Academic & Scholarly; History & Antiquarian

New Titles: 10 (2009) , 12 (2010)
No of Employees: 2

Imprints, Series & ISBNs:
978 1 899047, 978 1 906353

Overseas Representation:
UK (Trade Orders): Central Books Ltd,
London, UK

Book Trade Association Membership:
Publishing Ireland (Foilsiú Éireann)

2271

FASTPRINT
9 Culley Court, Bakewell Road,
Orton Southgate, Peterborough PE2 6XD
Telephone: 01733 237867
Fax: 01733 234309
Email: info@upfrontpublishing.com
Web Site: www.upfrontpublishing.com

Personnel:
Andy Cork *(Managing Director)*
Simon Potter *(Publishing Manager)*
Pauline Tebbott *(Publishing Assistant)*

Biography & Autobiography; Fiction; Poetry; Religion & Theology

New Titles: 100 (2009) , 120 (2010)

Imprints, Series & ISBNs:
Fastprint: 978 1 84426

Upfront: 978 1 84426

Parent Company:
Print on Demand – Worldwide

Book Trade Association Membership:
Independent Publishers Guild

2272

FEATHER BOOKS
PO Box 438, Shrewsbury SY3 0WN
Telephone: 01743 872177
Fax: 01743 872177
Email: john@jjwfeather.uk.com
Web Site: www.waddysweb.freeuk.com

Personnel:
Revd John Waddington-Feather *(Sales & Marketing Director)*
Sheila Waddington-Feather *(Production Manager)*
Paul Evans *(Sub-Editor, Production Manager)*
Tony Reavill *(Recording & Drama Producer)*
David Grundy *(Music Director & Editor)*
Anna Waddington-Feather *(Public Relations & Sub-Editor)*
Janet Evans *(Sub-Editor)*

Academic & Scholarly; Audio Books; Biography & Autobiography; Children's Books; Crime; Fiction; Humour; Literature & Criticism; Music; Poetry; Religion & Theology; Theatre, Drama & Dance

New Titles: 20 (2009) , 10 (2010)

Imprints, Series & ISBNs:
Christianity & Literature Series: 978 1 84175
Feather Books Biography Series: 978 1 84175
Feather Books Drama Series: 978 0 947718, 978 1 84175
Feather Books Music Series: 978 1 84175
Feather Books Poetry Series: 978 1 84175

Associated Companies:
Moorside Words & Music

2273

FHG GUIDES LTD
Abbey Mill Business Centre, Seedhill,
Paisley PA1 1TJ
Telephone: 0141 887 0428
Fax: 0141 889 7204
Email: admin@fhguides.co.uk
Web Site: www.holidayguides.com

Book Trade Representative:
Martin Kaye, Kuperard Publishers,
59 Hutton Grove, London N12 8DS
Telephone: 020 8446 2440
Fax: 020 8446 2441
Email: martin@kuperard.co.uk

Personnel:
G. Pratt *(Publishing Director)*

Guide Books; Sports & Games; Travel & Topography

Imprints, Series & ISBNs:
978 1 85055

Parent Company:
Kuperard Publishers

Book Trade Association Membership:
Periodical Publishers Association

2274

FIELL PUBLISHING LTD
51 Sulgrave Road, London W6 7QH
Telephone: 020 7603 4247
Fax: 020 7602 4268
Web Site: www.fiell.com

Architecture & Design; Fashion & Costume; Photography; Travel & Topography

Book Trade Association Membership:
Publishers Association

2275

FILAMENT PUBLISHING LTD
16 Croydon Road, Waddon, Croydon,
Surrey CR0 4PA
Telephone: 020 8688 2598
Fax: 020 7183 7186
Email: info@filamentpublishing.com
Web Site: www.filamentpublishing.com

Representation (UK):
Gardners Books, 1 Whittle Drive,
Eastbourne, East Sussex BN23 6QH

Personnel:
Christopher Day *(Director)*
Bernard Marchant *(Finance)*
Zara Thatcher *(Editor)*
Andrew White *(Production)*

Audio Books; Biography & Autobiography;
Educational & Textbooks; Electronic
(Professional & Academic); Industry,
Business & Management; Medical (incl. Self
Help & Alternative Medicine); Philosophy;
Religion & Theology; Sports & Games;
Theatre, Drama & Dance; Vocational
Training & Careers

No of Employees: 5
Annual Turnover: £160,000

Imprints, Series & ISBNs:
978 1 905493

Book Trade Association Membership:
Publishers Association; Independent
Publishers Guild

2276

FINDHORN PRESS LTD
Delft Cottage, Dyke, Forres, Moray
IV36 2TF
Telephone: 01309 690582
Fax: 0131 777 2711
Email: info@findhornpress.com
Web Site: www.findhornpress/

Personnel:
Thierry Bogliolo *(Publisher)*
Carol Shaw *(Marketing & Publicity*
Manager)
Sabine Weeke *(Rights, Editorial Manager)*

Animal Care & Breeding; Cookery, Wines &
Spirits; Gardening; Gay & Lesbian Studies;
Guide Books; Health & Beauty; Medical
(incl. Self Help & Alternative Medicine);
Religion & Theology

New Titles: 30 (2009) , 45 (2010)
No of Employees: 5
Annual Turnover: £607,573

Imprints, Series & ISBNs:
978 0 905249, 978 1 84409, 978 1 899171

Overseas Representation:
Australia: Brumby Books Holdings Pty Ltd,
Kilsyth South, Vic, Australia
New Zealand: Ceres Books, Ellerslie, New
Zealand
North America: Independent Publishers
Group (IPG), Chicago, IL, USA
Republic of Ireland & Europe: Deep Books
Ltd, London, UK
Singapore: Pen International Ltd,
Singapore, Singapore
South Africa: Faradawn CC, Saxonwold,
South Africa
USA: New Leaf Distributing Co, Lithia
Springs, GA, USA

Book Trade Association Membership:
Independent Publishers Guild

2277

FIRST & BEST IN EDUCATION
Earlstrees Court, Earlstrees Road, Corby,
Northants NN17 4HH
Telephone: 01536 399011 (Orders &
Accounts), 399004 (Editorial)
Fax: 01536 399012
Email: sales@firstandbest.co.uk
Web Site: www.shop.firstandbest.co.uk

Personnel:
Jane Edmonds *(Finance Manager)*
Tony Attwood *(Managing Director)*
Anne Cockburn *(Senior Editor)*

Educational & Textbooks; Electronic
(Educational)

Imprints, Series & ISBNs:
978 1 86083

Book Trade Association Membership:
Educational Publishers Council

2278

FIVE LEAVES PUBLICATIONS
PO Box 8786, Nottingham NG1 9AW
Telephone: 0115 969 3597
Email: info@fiveleaves.co.uk
Web Site: www.fiveleaves.co.uk

Personnel:
Ross Bradshaw *(Publisher)*

Academic & Scholarly; Children's Books;
Crime; Fiction; History & Antiquarian;
Poetry; Theatre, Drama & Dance

New Titles: 20 (2009) , 12 (2010)
No of Employees: 1

Imprints, Series & ISBNs:
Bromley House Editions: 978 1 905512
Crime Express: 978 1 905512
Five Leaves Publications: 978 0 907123, 978
1 905512
New London Editions: 978 1 905512
Richard Hollis: 978 1 905512

2279

FLAMBARD PRESS
Holy Jesus, City Road, Newcastle upon Tyne
NE1 2AJ
Telephone: 0191 233 3865
Email: editor@flambardpress.co.uk
Web Site: www.flambardpress.co.uk

Personnel:
Peter Lewis *(Company Secretary)*
Margaret Lewis *(Editor)*
Will Mackie *(Managing Editor)*

Biography & Autobiography; Crime;
Fiction; Fine Art & Art History;
Photography; Poetry

New Titles: 9 (2009) , 9 (2010)

Imprints, Series & ISBNs:
978 1 873226, 978 1 906601

Book Trade Association Membership:
Independent Publishers Guild

2280

FLORAMEDIA UK LTD
Global House, Global Park, Moorside,
Eastgates, Colchester CO1 2TW
Telephone: 01206 771040
Email: info@floramedia.co.uk
Web Site: www.floramedia.co.uk

Personnel:
N. Mathias *(Managing Director)*

Gardening

Imprints, Series & ISBNs:
978 0 903001

Parent Company:
Netherlands: Floramedia Group BV

Overseas Representation:
Australia: Macbird Floraprint Pty Ltd,
Scoresby, Vic, Australia
Austria: Floramedia GmbH, Vienna, Austria
Belgium: Floramedia NV, Antwerp, Belgium
Canada: John Markham Associates, Sidney,
BC, Canada
France: Floramedia, Lille, France
Germany: Verlagsgesellschaft Grun ist
Leben mbH, Pinneberg, Germany
Liechtenstein: Floramedia Group AG,
Vaduz, Liechtenstein
Netherlands: Floramedia Group BV,
Zaandam, Netherlands
New Zealand: Floramedia New Zealand,
Wellington, New Zealand
Republic of Ireland: Carleys Bridge Potteries
Ltd, Enniscorthy, Republic of Ireland
South Africa: Floramedia Southern Africa,
Florida, South Africa
Spain: Floramedia España, Valencia, Spain
Switzerland: Floramedia AG, Rapperswil-
Jona, Switzerland

2281

FLORIS BOOKS
15 Harrison Gardens, Edinburgh EH11 1SH
Telephone: 0131 337 2372
Fax: 0131 347 9919
Email: floris@florisbooks.co.uk
Web Site: www.florisbooks.co.uk

Warehouse & Orders:
BookSource, 50 Cambuslang Road,
Glasgow G32 8NB
Telephone: 0845 370 0067
Fax: 0845 370 0068
Email: orders@booksource.net

Personnel:
Christian Maclean *(Chief Executive)*
Katy Lockwood-Holmes *(Marketing)*
Sally Martin *(Editorial)*

Academic & Scholarly; Children's Books;
Crafts & Hobbies; Gardening; Health &
Beauty; Medical (incl. Self Help &
Alternative Medicine); Philosophy; Religion
& Theology

Imprints, Series & ISBNs:
978 0 86315, 978 0 903540, 978 0 906155

Distributor for:
Lindisfarne Press
USA: Biodynamic Farming & Gardening
Association

Overseas Representation:
Australia: Footprint Books Pty Ltd,
Warriewood, NSW, Australia
New Zealand: Ceres Books, Ellerslie, New
Zealand
USA (34 Children's & Parents' titles):
Gryphon House Inc, Beltsville, MD, USA
USA (all titles): Steiner Books Inc, Herndon,
VA, USA

Book Trade Association Membership:
Publishing Scotland

2282

FOLENS LTD
Waterslade House, Thame Road,
Haddenham, Bucks HP17 8NT
Telephone: 0870 609 1235 (order hotline),
1237 (customer services)
Fax: 0870 609 1236 (order hotline)
Email: folens@folens.com
Web Site: www.folens.com

Personnel:
David Moffatt *(Chairman)*

Adrian Cockell *(Managing Director)*
Peter Burton *(Publishing Director)*
Jacqui Dilley *(Marketing Director)*
John Cadell *(Group Managing Director)*

Atlases & Maps; Educational & Textbooks;
Electronic (Educational); English as a
Foreign Language; Reference Books,
Directories & Dictionaries

Imprints, Series & ISBNs:
Belair Publications: 978 1 84163, 978 1
84191, 978 1 84303, 978 1 85008, 978
1 85276, 978 1 86202

Overseas Representation:
Australia: Educational Supplies Pty Ltd,
Australia
Bahrain: The Bookcase, Manama, Bahrain
Canada: Bacon & Hughes Ltd, Ottawa, Ont,
Canada
Egypt: International Language Bookshop,
Egypt
Hong Kong: Transglobal Publishers Services
Ltd, Hong Kong
Jamaica: The Book Merchant Ltd, Kingston,
Jamaica
Jordan: Al-Kashkool Bookshop, Amman,
Jordan; Philadelphia Book Gallery, Jordan
Kuwait: Saeed & Samir Bookstore Co Ltd,
Kuwait
Malaysia: Extrazeal, Malaysia; University
Book Store (M) Sdn Bhd, Malaysia
Malta: Agius & Agius Ltd, Valletta, Malta
New Zealand: South Pacific Books (Imports)
Ltd, Auckland, New Zealand
Oman: Al Manahil Educational Consultancy,
Oman
Saudi Arabia: Elmia Bookstores, Al Khobar,
Saudi Arabia
Singapore: September 21 Enterprise Pte
Ltd, Singapore
South Africa: Everybody's Books, Durban,
South Africa
Spain: TEK Books (Bookworld Espana),
Spain
United Arab Emirates: All Prints Distributors
& Publishers, UAE; Jashanmal National,
UAE; Magrudy Enterprises, Dubai, UAE
USA: Social Studies School Service (USA),
USA

Book Trade Association Membership:
Publishers Association; Educational
Publishers Council

2283

FOOD TRADE PRESS LTD
Station House, Hortons Way, Westerham,
Kent TN16 1BZ
Telephone: 01959 563944
Fax: 01959 561285
Web Site: www.foodtradepress.com

Personnel:
Adrian Binsted *(Publishing Director)*

Agriculture; Chemistry; Reference Books,
Directories & Dictionaries

Imprints, Series & ISBNs:
978 0 900379, 978 0 903962

Associated Companies:
Attwood & Binsted Ltd

Distributor for:
Campden & Chorleywood Research
Association; Leatherhead Food Research
Association
Denmark: Mercantila Publishing AS
Italy: Chiriotti Editori Srl
Spain: Montagud Editores SA
Switzerland: Binsted Frères SA
USA: American Association of Cereal
Chemists; American Institute of Baking;
Chemical Publishing Co Inc; CTI
Publications Inc; Food & Nutrition Press
Inc; Food Processors Institute; Edward E.
Judge & Sons

2284

FOOTPRINT TRAVEL GUIDES
6 Riverside Court, Lower Bristol Road, Bath
BA2 3DZ
Telephone: 01225 469141
Fax: 01225 469461
Email: contactus@footprintbooks.com
Web Site: www.footprinttravelguides.com

UK Trade Sales Agent:
GeoCenter International Ltd,
Meridian House, Churchill Way West,
Basingstoke, Hants RG21 6YR
Telephone: 01256 817987
Fax: 01256 817988
Email: sales@geocenter.co.uk
Web Site: www.geocenter.co.uk

Personnel:
Andy Riddle (Managing Director)
Patrick Dawson (Commercial Director)
Alan Murphy (Publisher)
Liz Harper (Marketing Manager)

Guide Books; Sports & Games; Travel &
Topography

New Titles: 38 (2009) , 38 (2010)
No of Employees: 10

Imprints, Series & ISBNs:
978 0 900751
Footprint Handbooks: 978 1 900949, 978 1
903471, 978 1 904777, 978 1 906098

Parent Company:
USA: Morris Communications LLC

Associated Companies:
UK: Compass Maps Ltd
USA: Globe Pequot Press

Distributor for:
UK: Wexas International
USA: Globe Pequot Press; Insiders' Guides

Overseas Representation:
Australia & New Zealand: Woodslane Pty
Ltd, Warriewood, NSW, Australia
Belgium: Craenen bvba, Herent (Winksele),
Belgium
Canada: Manda Group, Toronto, Ont,
Canada
Europe: Bill Bailey Publishers
Representatives, Newton Abbot, UK
Israel: SKP, Tel Aviv, Israel
Latin America: InterMedia Americana (IMA)
Ltd, London, UK
Middle East: Peter Ward Book Exports
Netherlands: Nilsson & Lamm BV, Weesp,
Netherlands
Singapore & Malaysia: Pansing Distribution
Pte Ltd, Singapore
South Africa: Faradawn CC, Saxonwold,
South Africa
South East Asia: DDP, Paris, France
USA: Globe Pequot Press, Guilford, CT, USA

2285

FORENSIC SCIENCE SOCIETY
Clarke House, 18A Mount Parade,
Harrogate HG1 1BX
Telephone: 01423 506068
Fax: 01423 566391
Email: journal@forensic-science-
society.org.uk
Web Site: www.forensic-science-
society.org.uk

Personnel:
Dr Niamh Nic Daéid (Hon. Editor)

Scientific & Technical

2286

FORWARD PRESS
Remus House, Coltsfoot Drive, Woodston,
Peterborough PE2 9JX
Telephone: 01733 890099

Fax: 01733 313524
Email: info@forwardpress.co.uk
Web Site: www.forwardpress.co.uk

Personnel:
Morgan Walton (Marketing Manager)

Poetry

New Titles: 500 (2009) , 500 (2010)

Imprints, Series & ISBNs:
afterschoolclub.net
Bookprinting UK
Leavers Books
Need2Know
New Fiction
Poetry Rivals
Pond View
Proprint
School Artists
School Products
Spotlight Poets
Writers' Bookshop
Young Writers

Parent Company:
Forward Press

Book Trade Association Membership:
Booksellers Association

2287

THE FOSTERING NETWORK
87 Blackfriars Road, London SE1 8HA
Telephone: 020 7620 6400
Fax: 020 7620 6401

Personnel:
Robert Tapsfield (Director)
Lucy Peake (Head of External Affair)
Ruth Richards (Publishing)

Children's Books; Educational & Textbooks;
Psychology & Psychiatry; Sociology &
Anthropology; Vocational Training &
Careers

Imprints, Series & ISBNs:
978 0 946015

2288

W. FOULSHAM & CO LTD
The Oriel, Thames Valley Court,
183–187 Bath Road, Slough, Berks
SL1 4AA
Telephone: 01753 526769
Fax: 01753 535003
Email: reception@foulsham.com
Web Site: www.foulsham.com

Distribution:
Macmillan Distribution (MDL), Houndmills,
Basingstoke RG21 2XS
Telephone: 01256 329242
Fax: 01256 812558
Email: mdl@macmillan.co.uk
Web Site: www.mdl.macmillan.co.uk

Personnel:
Barry Belasco (Managing Director)
Graham Kitchen (Financial Director)
Roy Mantel (Production Director)
Wendy Hobson (Editorial Director)

Accountancy & Taxation; Antiques &
Collecting; Children's Books; Cookery,
Wines & Spirits; Crafts & Hobbies; Crime;
Educational & Textbooks; Gardening; Guide
Books; Health & Beauty; Humour; Industry,
Business & Management; Magic & the
Occult; Medical (incl. Self Help & Alternative
Medicine); Military & War; Poetry;
Reference Books, Directories &
Dictionaries; Religion & Theology; Travel &
Topography

Imprints, Series & ISBNs:
Arcturus: 978 0 572

Foulsham: 978 0 572
Quantum: 978 0 572

Overseas Representation:
Australia: Capricorn Link (Australia) Pty Ltd,
Windsor, NSW, Australia
Belgium, Germany, Luxembourg,
Netherlands, Switzerland & Austria:
Robbert J. Pleysier, Heerde, Netherlands
Cambodia, Laos, Myanmar, Thailand,
Philippines & Vietnam: Ashton
International Marketing Services,
Sevenoaks, Kent, UK
Canada: Codasat, Vancouver, BC, Canada
Caribbean: Macmillan Caribbean Ltd,
Oxford, UK
Central & Eastern Europe: Dr László Horváth
Publishers Representative, Budapest,
Hungary
Central & South America: InterMedia
Americana (IMA) Ltd, London, UK
Far East, Singapore & Malaysia: Ashton
International Marketing Services,
Sevenoaks, Kent, UK
France, Gibraltar, Greece, Italy, Spain &
Portugal: Sandro Salucci, Florence, Italy
India: Maya Publishers Pvt Ltd, New Delhi,
India
Middle East: Richard Carman Associates,
Northwich, UK
New Zealand: Southern Publishers Group,
Auckland, New Zealand
South Africa: Alternative Books CC,
Ferndale, South Africa
Sub Saharan Africa: InterMedia Africa Ltd
(IMA), London, UK
USA: Associated Publishers Group,
Nashville, TN, USA

2289

FOUR COURTS PRESS
7 Malpas Street, Dublin 8,
Republic of Ireland
Telephone: +353 (01) 453 4668
Fax: +353 (01) 453 4672
Email: info@fourcourtspress.ie
Web Site: www.fourcourtspress.ie

Distribution:
Gill & Macmillan, Hume Avenue,
Park West, Dublin 12, Republic of Ireland
Telephone: +353 (01) 500 9555
Fax: +353 (01) 500 9599
Email: info@fourcourtspress.ie
Web Site: www.fourcourtspress.ie

Personnel:
Martin Healy (Managing Director)
Anthony Tierney (Marketing)
Martin Fanning (Editorial)

Academic & Scholarly; Archaeology; Fine
Art & Art History; History & Antiquarian;
Law; Literature & Criticism; Military & War;
Music; Philosophy; Religion & Theology

Imprints, Series & ISBNs:
978 0 906127, 978 1 84682, 978 1 85182
Four Courts Press
Open Air

Overseas Representation:
USA: International Specialized Book
Services Inc, Portland, OR, USA

2290

SAMUEL FRENCH LTD
52 Fitzroy Street, London W1T 5JR
Telephone: 020 7387 9373
Fax: 020 7387 2161
Email: theatre@samuelfrench-
london.co.uk
Web Site: www.samuelfrench-
london.co.uk

Personnel:
Leon F. Embry (Chairman)
Vivien Goodwin (Managing Director)
Amanda Smith (Director)
Paul Taylor (Director)

Theatre, Drama & Dance

Imprints, Series & ISBNs:
978 0 573

Parent Company:
Samuel French Inc

Distributor for:
USA: Samuel French Inc

Overseas Representation:
Australia: The Dominie Group, Brookvale,
NSW, Australia
East Africa: Phoenix Players Ltd, Nairobi,
Kenya
Malta: Dingli Co International, Valletta,
Malta
New Zealand: Play Bureau of New Zealand
Ltd, New Plymouth, New Zealand
Republic of Ireland: Drama League of
Ireland, Dublin, Republic of Ireland
South Africa, Namibia, Swaziland,
Botswana & Lesotho: Dalro (Pty) Ltd,
Braamfontein, South Africa
Zimbabwe: National Theatre Organization,
Harare, Zimbabwe

Book Trade Association Membership:
Publishers Association; Booksellers
Association

2291

FRIENDS OF THE EARTH
26–28 Underwood Street, London N1 7JQ
Telephone: 020 7490 1555
Fax: 020 7490 0881
Web Site: www.foe.co.uk

Personnel:
Adam Bradbury (Publications Manager)

Academic & Scholarly; Educational &
Textbooks; Environment & Development
Studies; Gardening; Reference Books,
Directories & Dictionaries; Transport

Imprints, Series & ISBNs:
978 1 85750

2292

GADFLY ENTERTAINMENT LTD
15–19 Cavendish Square, London
W1G 0DD
Email: info@gadfly-ent.com
Web Site: www.gadfly-ent.com

2293

GALACTIC CENTRAL PUBLICATIONS
25a Copgrove Road, Leeds, West Yorkshire
LS8 2SP
Telephone: 0113 248 8124
Email: philsp@philsp.com
Web Site: www.philsp.com

Personnel:
Phil Stephensen-Payne (Publisher)

Bibliography & Library Science

No of Employees: 0

Imprints, Series & ISBNs:
978 1 871133

Overseas Representation:
USA: Chris Drumm, Polk City, IA, USA

2294

THE GALLERY PRESS
Loughcrew, Oldcastle, Co Meath,
Republic of Ireland
Telephone: +353 (049) 854 1779
Fax: +353 (049) 854 1779
Email: gallery@indigo.ie
Web Site: www.gallerypress.com

Personnel:
Peter Fallon (*Editorial, Production Director*)
Jean Barry (*Administration*)
Suella Wynne (*Administration*)
Anne Duggan (*Sales & Accounts*)

Fiction; Poetry; Theatre, Drama & Dance

New Titles: 11 (2009) , 11 (2010)
No of Employees: 4

Imprints, Series & ISBNs:
978 0 902996, 978 0 904011, 978 1 85235

2295

GALORE PARK PUBLISHING LTD
19–21 Sayers Lane, Tenterden, Kent
TN30 6BW
Telephone: 01580 764242
Fax: 01580 764142
Email: info@galorepark.co.uk
Web Site: www.galorepark.co.uk

Personnel:
Nicholas Oulton (*Managing Director*)
Aidan Gill (*Publishing Director*)
Natalie Friend (*Marketing Manager / Public
Relations*)
Helen Standen (*Financial Controller*)

Children's Books; Educational & Textbooks

New Titles: 70 (2009) , 65 (2010)
No of Employees: 15
Annual Turnover: £1.3M

Imprints, Series & ISBNs:
Galore Park Publishing: 978 1 902984
Gresham Books
Iseb Publications: 978 1 902984

Parent Company:
Galore Park (Holdings) Ltd

Associated Companies:
Gresham Books Ltd

Book Trade Association Membership:
Publishers Association; Booksellers
Association; Educational Publishers
Council; Independent Publishers Guild

2296

GARNET PUBLISHING LTD
8 Southern Court, South Street, Reading
RG1 4QS
Telephone: 0118 959 7847
Fax: 0118 959 7356 (Trade Enquiries &
Orders)
Email: dan@garnetpublishing.co.uk
Web Site: www.garnetpublishing.co.uk

Personnel:
Dan Nunn (*Permissions, Rights & Editorial
Manager*)
Nick Holroyd (*Office, Production & Finance
Manager*)
Val Eve (*Sales Manager*)

*Academic & Scholarly; Architecture &
Design; Cookery, Wines & Spirits;
Economics; Electronic (Professional &
Academic); Fiction; Gender Studies; Guide
Books; History & Antiquarian; Literature &
Criticism; Photography; Politics & World
Affairs; Religion & Theology; Sociology &
Anthropology; Travel & Topography*

Imprints, Series & ISBNs:
Garnet Publishing: 978 1 85964, 978 1
873938, 978 1 902932
Ithaca Press: 978 1 85964, 978 1 873938,
978 1 902932
South Street Press: 978 1 85964, 978 1
873938, 978 1 902932

Associated Companies:
Garnet Education; Ithaca Press; South
Street Press

Overseas Representation:
Australia: InBooks, Frenchs Forest, NSW,
Australia
Europe: Andrew Durnell Marketing Ltd,
Tunbridge Wells, UK
USA (Academic): International Specialized
Book Services Inc, Portland, OR, USA
USA (Trade): IPM, Dulles, VA, USA

Book Trade Association Membership:
Independent Publishers Guild

2297

GATEHOUSE MEDIA LTD
PO Box 965, Warrington, Cheshire
WA4 9DE
Telephone: 01925 267778
Fax: 01925 267778
Email: info@gatehousebooks.com
Web Site: www.gatehousebooks.com

Personnel:
Catherine White (*Managing Director*)
Mark White (*Director*)

*Audio Books; Educational & Textbooks;
English as a Foreign Language*

Imprints, Series & ISBNs:
Gatehouse Books: 978 1 84231

Overseas Representation:
Canada: Grass Roots Press, Edmonton, Alb,
Canada
USA: Peppercorn Books Press, Snow Camp,
NC, USA

Book Trade Association Membership:
Publishers Association

2298

GEDDES & GROSSET
144 Port Dundas Road, Glasgow G4 0HZ
Telephone: 0141 567 2830
Fax: 0141 567 2831
Email: info@geddesandgrosset.co.uk &
liz@waverley-books.co.uk
Web Site: www.geddesandgrosset.co.uk

Warehouse:
Peter Haddock Ltd, Industrial Estate,
Pinfold Lane, Bridlington YO16 5BT
Telephone: 01262 678121
Fax: 01262 400043

Personnel:
Ron Grosset (*Publisher*)
Liz Small (*Sales & Marketing*)

*Atlases & Maps; Children's Books; Cookery,
Wines & Spirits; History & Antiquarian;
Magic & the Occult; Medical (incl. Self Help
& Alternative Medicine); Reference Books,
Directories & Dictionaries*

New Titles: 30 (2009) , 30 (2010)
No of Employees: 7
Annual Turnover: £2M

Imprints, Series & ISBNs:
978 1 85534, 978 1 902407

Parent Company:
D. C. Thomson & Co Ltd

Associated Companies:
Waverley Books Ltd

Overseas Representation:
Africa & Caribbean: Kelvin van Hasselt
Publishing Services, Briningham, Norfolk,
UK
Central & South America: InterMedia
Americana Ltd (IMA), Gibraltar
Southern Africa: Book Promotions Pty Ltd,
Cape Town, South Africa

Book Trade Association Membership:
Publishing Scotland

2299

GEOCENTER INTERNATIONAL LTD
Meridian House, Churchill Way West,
Basingstoke, Hants RG21 6YR
Telephone: 01256 817987
Fax: 01256 817988
Email: sales@geocenter.co.uk
Web Site: www.geocenter.co.uk

Distribution:
Grantham Book Services, Trent Road,
Grantham, Lincs NG31 7XQ
Telephone: 01476 541080
Fax: 01476 541061

Public Relations:
Julia Spence, 29 St Mary's Street,
Wallingford, Oxon OX10 0ET
Telephone: 01491 824524
Fax: 01491 824694
Email: juliaspence.pr@googlemail.com

Personnel:
Ian MacDonald (*Sales & Marketing Director*)
Andy Casey (*Sales Manager*)
Petra Hourd (*Marketing Manager – Insight
Guides*)
Donna Burridge (*Marketing Manger –
Cartography*)
Sam Bufton (*Marketing Manager – Berlitz
Language*)
Diane McEntee (*Marketing Manager –
Berlitz Travel*)
Hayley Whitlock (*Marketing Manager –
Ullmann*)

*Academic & Scholarly; Architecture &
Design; Atlases & Maps; Cookery, Wines &
Spirits; Fine Art & Art History; Gardening;
Guide Books; Languages & Linguistics;
Photography; Reference Books, Directories
& Dictionaries; Transport; Travel &
Topography*

New Titles: 238 (2009) , 159 (2010)
No of Employees: 14
Annual Turnover: £6M

Imprints, Series & ISBNs:
AMC Maps & Atlases: 978 0 8416
Berlitz: 978 981 246, 978 981 268
Berlitz Earworms
BSM
Dino's Illustrated Maps: 978 0 9549056
Everyman: 978 1 84159
GeoCenter Maps / Baedeker: 978 3 575,
978 3 8279, 978 3 8297
Hg2: 978 0 9547878, 978 1 905428
Horizon Press: 978 1 84306
Insight Guides: 978 981 234, 978 981 258
Langenscheidt Dictionaries: 978 0 88729,
978 1 58573, 978 3 468
Nelles Maps: 978 3 86574, 978 3 88618
Periplus Maps: 978 0 7946, 978 962 593
Ullmann: 978 3 8290, 978 3 8331

Parent Company:
Germany: Langenscheidt KG

Distributor for:
AMC Maps & Atlases; Apa Guides (Insight
Guides); Berlitz; Berlitz Earworms; BSM;
Dino's Illustrated Maps; Everyman; Filmer
Ltd (Hg2); Footprint; Globe Pequot
Press; Horizon Press; Langenscheidt
Dictionaries; Luxe; Monaco Books; Nelles
Verlag (Guides & Maps); Not for Tourists;
Periplus Editions (Periplus Maps); RV
Verlag (GeoCenter Maps & Baedeker
Guides); Ullmann

Overseas Representation:
Europe: Bill Bailey Publishers
Representatives, Newton Abbot, UK
South America: InterMedia Americana Ltd
(IMA), Gibraltar

Book Trade Association Membership:
Book Data Subscriber

2300

THE GEOGRAPHICAL ASSOCIATION
160 Solly Street, Sheffield S1 4BF
Telephone: 0114 296 0088
Fax: 0114 296 7176
Email: info@geography.org.uk
Web Site: www.geography.org.uk

Personnel:
David Lambert (*Chief Executive*)
John Lyon (*Programme Director*)
Richard Gill (*Business Manager*)
Ruth Totterdell (*Publications Manager*)
Dorcas Turner (*Assistant Editor*)
Anna Grandfield (*Production Editor*)
Nicola Donkin (*Editorial Assistant*)

*Atlases & Maps; Educational & Textbooks;
Electronic (Educational); Geography &
Geology; Guide Books; Travel & Topography*

Imprints, Series & ISBNs:
978 0 900395, 978 0 948512, 978 1
84377, 978 1 899085, 978 1 903448

Book Trade Association Membership:
Educational Publishers Council

2301

GEOGRAPHY PUBLICATIONS
24 Kennington Road, Templeogue,
Dublin 6W, Republic of Ireland
Telephone: +353 (01) 456 6085
Fax: +353 (01) 456 6085
Email: books@geographypublications.com
Web Site:
www.geographypublications.com

Personnel:
William Nolan (*Contact*)

*Academic & Scholarly; Archaeology; Atlases
& Maps; Biography & Autobiography;
Educational & Textbooks; Geography &
Geology; History & Antiquarian; Languages
& Linguistics; Reference Books, Directories
& Dictionaries*

New Titles: 2 (2009) , 3 (2010)

Imprints, Series & ISBNs:
History & Society Series: 978 0 906602

2302

**GEOLOGICAL SOCIETY PUBLISHING
HOUSE**
Unit 7, Brassmill Enterprise Centre,
Brassmill Lane, Bath BA1 3JN
Telephone: 01225 445046
Fax: 01225 442836
Email: sales@geolsoc.org.uk
Web Site: www.geolsoc.org.uk/bookshop

Personnel:
Neal Marriott (*Director of Publishing*)
Alison Tucker (*Marketing Assistant*)
Angharad Hills (*Commissioning Editor*)
Sarah Gibbs (*Senior Production Editor*)
Dawn Angel (*Sales & Customer Services
Supervisor*)

*Academic & Scholarly; Engineering;
Environment & Development Studies;
Geography & Geology; Scientific &
Technical*

Imprints, Series & ISBNs:
Geological Society: 978 0 903317, 978 1
86239, 978 1 897799

Distributor for:
USA: American Association of Petroleum
Geologists; Geological Society of
America; SEPM

Overseas Representation:
India: EWP, New Delhi, India
South East Asian Territories: The White
Partnership

Spain & Portugal: Iberian Book Services, Madrid, Spain
USA: AAPG, Tulsa, USA; Princeton Selling Group Inc, Wayne, PA, USA

Book Trade Association Membership:
Association of Learned & Professional Society Publishers

2303

STANLEY GIBBONS
399 Strand, London WC2R 0LX
Telephone: 020 7836 8444
Fax: 020 7836 8444
Email: enquiries@stanleygibbons.co.uk
Web Site: www.stanleygibbons.com

Publishing, Mail Order:
7 Parkside, Christchurch Road, Ringwood, Hants BH24 3SH
Telephone: 01425 472363
Fax: 01425 470247
Email: ahalligan@stanleygibbons.co.uk
Web Site: www.stanleygibbons.com

Personnel:
Michael Hall *(Chief Executive)*
Mark Henley *(Finance Director)*
Ann-Marie Halligan *(Publishing Director)*
Donal Duff *(Chief Operating Officer)*
Richard Purkis *(Company Secretary)*
Keith Heddle *(Sales & Marketing Director)*

Crafts & Hobbies; Reference Books, Directories & Dictionaries

New Titles: 28 (2009) , 30 (2010)
No of Employees: 110
Annual Turnover: £23M

Imprints, Series & ISBNs:
978 0 85259

Parent Company:
UK: Stanley

Associated Companies:
UK: Fraser's

Overseas Representation:
Australia: Renniks Publications Pty Ltd, Banksmeadow, NSW, Australia
Belgium: N. V. deZittere (DZT)/Davo, Tielt (Brabant), Belgium
Canada: Unitrade Associates, Toronto, Ont, Canada
Denmark: Samlerforum/Davo, Karup, Denmark
Finland: Davo C/o Kapylan, Helsinki, Finland
France: ARPHI/Davo, Viroflay, France
Germany: Schaubek Verlag Leipzig, Markranstaedt, Germany
Italy: Ernesto Marini SRL, Genoa, Italy
Japan: Japan Philatelic, Tokyo, Japan
Netherlands: Uitgeverij Davo BV, Deventer, Netherlands
New Zealand: House of Stamps, Paraparaumu, New Zealand; Philatelic Distributors, New Plymouth, New Zealand
Norway: Skanfil A/S, Haugesund, Norway
Saudi Arabia: Arabian Stamp Centre, Riyadh, Saudi Arabia
Singapore: C S Philatelic Agency, Singapore
Sweden: Chr Winther Sorensen AB, Knaered, Sweden
USA: Filatco, Appleton, WI, USA

2304

GIBSON SQUARE
Please See Website
Telephone: 020 7096 1100
Fax: 020 7993 2214
Email: info@gibsonsquare.com
Web Site: www.gibsonsquare.com

Warehouse:
Littlehampton Book Services, Faraday Close, Durrington, Worthing, West Sussex BN13 3RB

Telephone: 01903 828500
Fax: 01903 828802
Email: orders@lbsltd.co.uk
Web Site: www.lbsltd.co.uk

Personnel:
Camille Pandian

Biography & Autobiography; Cinema, Video, TV & Radio; Crime; Economics; Fine Art & Art History; Gay & Lesbian Studies; Health & Beauty; History & Antiquarian; Humour; Medical (incl. Self Help & Alternative Medicine); Philosophy; Politics & World Affairs; Psychology & Psychiatry; Sociology & Anthropology; Theatre, Drama & Dance; Travel & Topography

Imprints, Series & ISBNs:
978 1 903933, 978 1 906142

Overseas Representation:
Australia: Tower Books Pty Ltd, Frenchs Forest, NSW, Australia
Canada & USA: NBN, Blue Ridge Summit, PA, USA
New Zealand: Addenda Ltd, Grey Lynn, New Zealand

Book Trade Association Membership:
Independent Publishers Guild

2305

GILL & MACMILLAN LTD
Hume Avenue, Park West, Dublin 12, Republic of Ireland
Telephone: +353 (01) 500 9500
Fax: +353 (01) 500 9599
Email: ftobin@gillmacmillan.ie
Web Site: www.gillmacmillan.ie

Personnel:
M. H. Gill *(Chairman)*
M. D. O'Dwyer *(Managing Director)*
A. Murray *(Educational Publishing Director)*
P. A. Thew *(Marketing & Sales Director)*
B. D. Curtin *(Company Secretary/Financial Director)*
M. O'Keeffe *(Production Director)*
F. M. Tobin *(General Publishing Director)*
J. Manning *(Distribution Director)*

Academic & Scholarly; Biography & Autobiography; Cookery, Wines & Spirits; Economics; Educational & Textbooks; Guide Books; History & Antiquarian; Humour; Politics & World Affairs; Psychology & Psychiatry; Reference Books, Directories & Dictionaries

New Titles: 120 (2009) , 100 (2010)
No of Employees: 65
Annual Turnover: €9M

Imprints, Series & ISBNs:
Newleaf: 978 0 7171
RíRá: 978 0 7171

Overseas Representation:
Australia: Brumby Books Holdings Pty Ltd, Kilsyth South, Vic, Australia
India, Pakistan & Sri Lanka: Pan Macmillan, New Delhi, India
Middle East, South East & North Asia: Pan Macmillan Asia, Hong Kong
New Zealand: New Holland Publishers (NZ) Ltd, Auckland, New Zealand
South Africa: Pan Macmillan SA Pty Ltd, Johannesburg, South Africa
UK: Bounce! Sales & Marketing Ltd, London, UK

Book Trade Association Membership:
Publishing Ireland (Foilsiú Éireann)

2306

GLASGOW MUSEUMS PUBLISHING
Glasgow Museums Resource Centre, 200 Woodhead Road, Glasgow G53 7NN
Telephone: 0141 276 9452

Fax: 0141 276 9305
Email: susan.pacitti@csglasgow.org
Web Site: www.glasgowmuseums.com

Personnel:
Susan Pacitti *(Managing Editor)*

Archaeology; Fashion & Costume; Fine Art & Art History; History & Antiquarian; Transport

Imprints, Series & ISBNs:
978 0 902752

Parent Company:
Culture & Sport Glasgow

Book Trade Association Membership:
Publishing Scotland

2307

GLMP LTD
GLMP House, PO Box 225, Abergele, Conwy County LL18 9AY
Telephone: 01745 832863
Fax: 01745 826606
Web Site: www.studymates.co.uk

Warehouse, Trade Enquiries & Orders:
NBN International, 10 Estover Road, Plymouth PL6 9PY
Telephone: 01752 202301
Fax: 01752 202331
Email: orders@nbninternational.com

Representation (UK):
Compass Academic Ltd,
West Newington House,
10 Newington Road, Edinburgh EH9 1QS
Telephone: 0131 668 3777

Personnel:
Dr Graham Lawler *(Managing Director)*
Dr Judith Lawler *(Finance Director)*

Academic & Scholarly; Audio Books; Biology & Zoology; Chemistry; Educational & Textbooks; Electronic (Educational); English as a Foreign Language; History & Antiquarian; Industry, Business & Management; Languages & Linguistics; Law; Literature & Criticism; Mathematics & Statistics; Medical (incl. Self Help & Alternative Medicine); Military & War; Physics; Poetry; Politics & World Affairs; Religion & Theology; Scientific & Technical; Sociology & Anthropology; Theatre, Drama & Dance

New Titles: 20 (2009)

Imprints, Series & ISBNs:
Aber Education: 978 1 84285
Mr Educator: 978 1 84285
Studymates Professional: 978 1 84285

Overseas Representation:
Australia & New Zealand: Footprint Books Pty Ltd, Sydney, NSW, Australia
Caribbean: David Williams Intermedia Ltd, UK

Book Trade Association Membership:
Independent Publishers Guild

2308

GLOWWORM BOOKS & GIFTS LTD
Unit 4, Bishopsgate Business Park, Broxburn EH52 5LH
Telephone: 01506 857570
Fax: 01506 858100
Web Site: www.glowwormbooks.co.uk

Personnel:
Katrena Allan *(Managing Director)*
Gordon Allan *(Production Director)*

Children's Books

New Titles: 1 (2010)

No of Employees: 5

Imprints, Series & ISBNs:
978 0 9557559, 978 1 871512

Book Trade Association Membership:
BSA

2309

ALAN GODFREY MAPS
Prospect Business Park, Leadgate, Consett DH8 7PW
Telephone: 01207 583388
Fax: 01207 583399
Email: godfreyedition@btinternet.com
Web Site: www.alangodfreymaps.co.uk

Personnel:
Alan Godfrey *(Contact)*

Atlases & Maps; History & Antiquarian

New Titles: 125 (2009) , 125 (2010)
No of Employees: 4

Imprints, Series & ISBNs:
978 0 85054, 978 0 907554, 978 1 84151, 978 1 84784

Overseas Representation:
Australia: Mapworks, North Essendon, Vic, Australia
Germany: GeoCenter Touristik Medienservice GmbH, Stuttgart, Germany

Book Trade Association Membership:
British Cartographic Society

2310

GODSFIELD PRESS LTD
Endeavour House,
189 Shaftesbury Avenue, London WC2H 8JY
Telephone: 020 7632 5400
Email: publisher@godsfieldpress.com
Web Site: www.octopusbooks.co.uk/godsfield-press

Personnel:
Jo Hemmings *(Publisher)*
Steven Edney *(UK Sales & Marketing)*
Clare Churly *(Managing Editor)*
John Saunders-Griffiths *(Head of Foreign Rights)*

Magic & the Occult; Medical (incl. Self Help & Alternative Medicine); Religion & Theology

Imprints, Series & ISBNs:
978 1 84181, 978 1 899434

Parent Company:
Octopus Publishing Group

Associated Companies:
Bounty; Cassell Illustrated; Conran; Gaia; Hamlyn; Millers; Mitchell Beazley; Philip's; Spruce

2311

THE GOLDSMITH PRESS LTD
Newbridge, Co Kildare, Republic of Ireland
Telephone: +353 (045) 433613
Fax: +353 (045) 434648

Personnel:
Vivienne Abbott *(Director)*
Breda Ennis *(Secretary)*

Academic & Scholarly; Biography & Autobiography; Cookery, Wines & Spirits; English as a Foreign Language; Fine Art & Art History; Literature & Criticism; Poetry

Imprints, Series & ISBNs:
978 1 870491

Book Trade Association Membership:
Publishing Ireland (Foilsiú Éireann)

2312 ▬▬▬

VICTOR GOLLANCZ LTD
Orion House, 5 Upper St Martins Lane,
London WC2H 9EA
Telephone: 020 7240 3444
Fax: 020 7240 5822
Web Site: www.orionbooks.co.uk

Warehouse, Trade Enquiries & Orders:
see The Orion Publishing Group Ltd

Personnel:
Lisa Milton (Managing Director)
Dallas Manderson (Group Sales Director)
Mark Streatfeild (Export Sales Director)
Mark Prior (Finance Director)
Dominic Smith (UK Sales Director)
Simon Spanton (Deputy Publishing Director)
Jo Fletcher (Associate Publisher)
Gillian Redfearn (Senior Commissioning
Editor)

Fiction; Science Fiction

Imprints, Series & ISBNs:
Victor Gollancz Ltd: 978 0 575
VGSF: 978 0 575

Parent Company:
The Orion Publishing Group Ltd

Overseas Representation:
see: The Orion Publishing Group Ltd,
London, UK

2313 ▬▬▬

GOMER
Llandysul, Ceredigion SA44 4JL
Telephone: 01559 363090
Fax: 01559 363758
Email: meinir@gomer.co.uk
Web Site: www.gomer.co.uk

Personnel:
J. H. Lewis (Executive Director)
Jonathan Lewis (Managing Director)
Roderic Lewis (Director)
Carol Bignell (Accounts)
Meinir James (Head of Marketing)

Biography & Autobiography; Children's
Books; History & Antiquarian; Languages &
Linguistics; Literature & Criticism;
Photography; Poetry; Reference Books,
Directories & Dictionaries; Sports & Games;
Transport

New Titles: 120 (2009) , 115 (2010)
No of Employees: 12

Imprints, Series & ISBNs:
978 1 84851
Pont (English language publications for
children): 978 0 85088, 978 0 86383,
978 1 84323, 978 1 85902

Parent Company:
J. D. Lewis & Sons Ltd

Associated Companies:
Lewis Printers

Book Trade Association Membership:
Booksellers Association; Independent
Publishers Guild; Cwlwm Cyhoeddwyr
Cymru (Welsh Publishers)

2314 ▬▬▬

GOTHIC IMAGE PUBLICATIONS
PO Box 2568, Glastonbury, Somerset
BA6 8XR
Telephone: 01458 831281
Fax: 01458 833385
Email: publications@gothicimage.co.uk
Web Site: www.gothicimage.co.uk

Trade Orders:
Deep Books Ltd, Unit 3,
Goose Green Trading Estate,
47 East Dulwich Road, London SE22 9BN
Telephone: 020 8693 0234
Fax: 020 8693 1400
Email: sales@deep-books.co.uk

Personnel:
Frances Howard-Gordon (Editorial &
Commissioning Director)
Jamie George (Export Sales Director)
Diana Macleash (Financial Controller)

Biography & Autobiography; Fine Art & Art
History; Guide Books; Magic & the Occult;
Philosophy; Politics & World Affairs;
Psychology & Psychiatry; Religion &
Theology; Travel & Topography

Imprints, Series & ISBNs:
Traveller's Guide Series: 978 0 906362

Associated Companies:
UK: Gothic Image Ltd (Retail Shop); Gothic
Image Tours (Tour Operator)

Overseas Representation:
Europe: Deep Books Ltd, London, UK
USA: SCB Distributors, Gardena, CA, USA

Book Trade Association Membership:
Booksellers Association

2315 ▬▬▬

GOWER PUBLISHING CO LTD
Wey Court East, Union Road, Farnham,
Surrey GU9 7PT
Telephone: 01252 331551
Fax: 01252 736736
Email: info@gowerpublishing.com
Web Site: www.gowerpublishing.com

**Customer Service Department/World
Distribution:**
Bookpoint Ltd, 39 Milton Park, Abingdon,
Oxon OX14 4TD
Telephone: 01235 400400
Fax: 01235 400454
Email: gower@bookpoint.co.uk
Web Site: www.gowerpub.com

Personnel:
N. A. E. Farrow (Chairman)
Rachel Lynch (Managing Director)
Darren Wise (Finance Director)
Richard Dowling (Sales Director)
Josephine Burgess (Director - Publishing
Systems)
Jonathan Norman (Publishing Director -
Training Resources & Business Books)
Susan White (Marketing Manager)
K. Towndrow (Foreign Rights)

Accountancy & Taxation; Architecture &
Design; Educational & Textbooks;
Engineering; Industry, Business &
Management; Vocational Training & Careers

Imprints, Series & ISBNs:
Ashgate: 978 0 7546
Gower: 978 0 566
Lund Humphries: 978 0 85331

Parent Company:
Ashgate Publishing Co Ltd

Associated Companies:
USA: Ashgate Publishing Co

Overseas Representation:
Africa (excluding South Africa & North
Africa): InterMedia Africa Ltd (IMA),
London, UK
Central & Eastern Europe: Dr László Horváth
Publishers Representative, Budapest,
Hungary
India: Maya Publishers Pvt Ltd, New Delhi,
India
Iran: Kowkab Publishers, Tehran, Iran

Japan: United Publishers Services Ltd,
Tokyo, Japan
Korea: Information & Culture Korea (ICK),
Seoul, Republic of Korea
Middle East: Publishers International
Marketing, Burmarsh, UK
North & South America: Ashgate Publishing
Co, Burlington, VT, USA
Pakistan: Book Bird Publishers
Representatives, Lahore, Pakistan
South East Asia, Myanmar (Burma), China,
Hong Kong, South Korea, Australia &
New Zealand: Ashgate Publishing Asia-
Pacific, Newport, NSW, Australia

Book Trade Association Membership:
Independent Publishers Guild

2316 ▬▬▬

GRACEWING PUBLISHING
Gracewing House, 2 Southern Avenue,
Leominster, Herefordshire HR6 0QF
Telephone: 01568 616835
Fax: 01568 613289
Email: gracewingx@aol.com
Web Site: www.gracewing.co.uk

Personnel:
Tom Longford (Managing Director)
Jo Ashworth (Publishing Manager)
Adrian Hodnett (Customer Service
Manager)
Mary Clewer (Accounts Manager)
Monica Manwaring (Publicity Manager)

Academic & Scholarly; Architecture &
Design; Biography & Autobiography; Guide
Books; History & Antiquarian; Philosophy;
Religion & Theology

Imprints, Series & ISBNs:
978 0 85244

Distributor for:
Ignatius Press; Mercer University Press;
Newman House; OSV; Smyth & Helwys;
St Bedes; Templegate

Overseas Representation:
Australia: Freedom Publishing, North
Melbourne, Vic, Australia
USA: Liturgy Training Publications, Chicago,
IL, USA

2317 ▬▬▬

GRAFFEG
2 Radnor Court, 256 Cowbridge Road East,
Cardiff CF5 1GZ
Telephone: 029 2037 7312
Fax: 029 2039 8101
Email: info@graffeg.com
Web Site: www.graffeg.com

Representation (Wales only):
Welsh Books Council, Castell Brychan,
Aberystwyth, Ceredigion SY23 2JB

Personnel:
Peter Gill (Managing Director)
Vanessa Bufton (Marketing Manager)
Sarah Evans (Sales & Marketing Executive)

Architecture & Design; Cookery, Wines &
Spirits; Gardening; Geography & Geology;
Guide Books; Natural History;
Photography; Travel & Topography

New Titles: 3 (2009) , 4 (2010)
No of Employees: 2

Imprints, Series & ISBNs:
978 0 9544334, 978 1 905582

Overseas Representation:
USA & Canada: Antique Collectors' Club,
Woodbridge, Suffolk, UK

Book Trade Association Membership:
Independent Publishers Guild

2318 ▬▬▬

**W. F. GRAHAM (NORTHAMPTON)
LTD**
2 Pondwood Close, Moulton Park,
Northampton NN3 6RT
Telephone: 01604 645537
Fax: 01604 648414
Email: books@wfgraham.co.uk
Web Site: www.wfgraham.co.uk

Personnel:
Tim Graham (Managing Director)
Ian Wilson (General Manager)

Children's Books

New Titles: 5 (2010)
No of Employees: 6

Imprints, Series & ISBNs:
978 1 85128

Overseas Representation:
West Indies: Humphrys Roberts Associates,
London, UK

2319 ▬▬▬

GRANADA LEARNING
The Chiswick Centre,
414 Chiswick High Road, London W4 5TF
Telephone: 020 8996 3333
Fax: 020 8742 8546
Email: info@granadalearning.co.uk
Web Site: www.gl-assessment.co.uk

Educational & Textbooks

Book Trade Association Membership:
Publishers Association

2320 ▬▬▬

GRANTA BOOKS
12 Addison Avenue, London W11 4QR
Telephone: 020 7605 1360
Fax: 020 7605 1361
Email: rights@granta.com
Web Site: www.granta.com

Trade Orders:
TBS Ltd, Distribution Centre,
Colchester Road, Frating Green, Colchester,
Essex CO7 7DW
Telephone: 01206 255678
Fax: 01206 255930
Email: mdl@macmillan.co.uk

Representation (UK):
Faber & Faber Ltd, Bloomsbury House,
74–77 Great Russell Street, London
WC1B 3DA
Telephone: 020 7927 3800
Fax: 020 7927 3801
Email: sales@faber.co.uk

Personnel:
Brigid Macleod (Sales)
Pru Rowlandson (Publicity)
Sarah Wasley (Production)
Angela Rose (Rights)
Sara Holloway (Editorial)

Biography & Autobiography; Fiction;
Politics & World Affairs; Travel &
Topography

Imprints, Series & ISBNs:
Granta Books: 978 1 86207
Granta Magazine

Parent Company:
Granta Publications

Associated Companies:
Granta Magazine

Overseas Representation:
Australia & New Zealand: Allen & Unwin Pty
Ltd, Sydney, NSW, Australia

Canada: House of Anansi, Toronto, Ont, Canada
Europe: International Sales Director, Miles Poynton, Faber & Faber, London, UK
Indian Subcontinent: Penguin Books India, New Delhi, India
Northern Europe: Bridget Lane, Faber & Faber, London, UK
Republic of Ireland: Repforce Ireland, Irishtown, Dublin, Republic of Ireland
South Africa: Penguin Books South Africa (Pty) Ltd, Johannesburg, South Africa
Southern Europe: Melissa Elders, Faber & Faber, London, UK
USA, Middle East, Eastern Europe, Africa (excluding South Africa), Latin America & Caribbean: sales@granta.com, UK

2321

GRANTA EDITIONS
25–27 High Street, Chesterton, Cambridge CB4 1ND
Telephone: 01223 352790
Fax: 01223 460718
Email: granta@bpccam.co.uk
Web Site: www.grantaeditions.co.uk

Personnel:
Colin Walsh *(Managing Director)*
Susan Buck *(Accounts Manager)*
Jo Littlechild *(Marketing Manager)*
Jo'e Coleby *(Editorial Project Manager)*

Academic & Scholarly; Accountancy & Taxation; Agriculture; Antiques & Collecting; Archaeology; Architecture & Design; Atlases & Maps; Aviation; Biography & Autobiography; Cookery, Wines & Spirits; Do-It-Yourself; Economics; Educational & Textbooks; Engineering; Environment & Development Studies; Fashion & Costume; Fine Art & Art History; Guide Books; Health & Beauty; History & Antiquarian; Illustrated & Fine Editions; Industry, Business & Management; Law; Medical (incl. Self Help & Alternative Medicine); Music; Natural History; Nautical; Photography; Physics; Psychology & Psychiatry; Reference Books, Directories & Dictionaries; Scientific & Technical; Sociology & Anthropology; Sports & Games; Theatre, Drama & Dance; Transport; Travel & Topography; Veterinary Science

New Titles: 3 (2009) , 10 (2010)
No of Employees: 4

Imprints, Series & ISBNs:
978 0 906782, 978 1 85757

Parent Company:
Book Production Consultants Ltd

Associated Companies:
Book Connections Ltd

2322

GREEN BOOKS
Foxhole, Dartington, Totnes, Devon TQ9 6EB
Telephone: 01803 863843 & 863260
Fax: 01803 863843
Email: sales@greenbooks.co.uk
Web Site: www.greenbooks.co.uk

UK Trade Distribution:
Central Books, 99 Wallis Road, London E9 5LN
Telephone: 0845 458 9911
Fax: 0845 458 9912
Email: info@centralbooks.com
Web Site: www.centralbooks.com

Personnel:
John Elford *(Publisher)*
Bee West *(Sales Manager)*
Amanda Cuthbert *(Commissioning Editor)*
Stacey Despard *(Marketing & Publicity Manager)*

Architecture & Design; Biography & Autobiography; Cookery, Wines & Spirits; Do-It-Yourself; Economics; Environment & Development Studies; Fine Art & Art History; Gardening; Guide Books; Health & Beauty; Literature & Criticism; Natural History; Philosophy; Poetry; Politics & World Affairs; Reference Books, Directories & Dictionaries; Travel & Topography

Imprints, Series & ISBNs:
Green Books: 978 1 903998, 978 1 907448
Green Books & Resurgence Books: 978 1 870098
Green Earth Books: 978 1 900322
Themis Books: 978 0 9527302

Distributor for:
USA: Chelsea Green Publishing Co

Overseas Representation:
Australia: Brumby Books Holdings Pty Ltd, Kilsyth South, Vic, Australia
New Zealand: Ceres Books, Ellerslie, New Zealand
USA: Chelsea Green Publishing Co, White River Junction, VT, USA

Book Trade Association Membership:
Independent Publishers Guild

2323

W. GREEN THE SCOTTISH LAW PUBLISHER
[a Thomson Reuters Company]
21 Alva Street, Edinburgh EH2 4PS
Telephone: 0131 225 4879
Fax: 0131 225 2104
Email: Alan.Bett@thomson.com
Web Site: www.wgreen.thomson.com

Personnel:
Mrs Gilly Grant *(Director)*
Alan Bett *(Marketing Manager)*
Mrs Jill Hyslop *(Publisher)*

Law

New Titles: 32 (2009) , 30 (2010)
No of Employees: 25

Imprints, Series & ISBNs:
978 0 414

Parent Company:
International Thomson Corporation

Overseas Representation:
Australia: The Law Book Co Ltd, North Ryde, Australia
Bangladesh: Karim International, Dhaka, Bangladesh
Botswana: Kerrison Book Services, Gabarone, Botswana
Canada: Carswell Publishing Ltd, Scarborough, Ont, Canada
Ghana: J. A. Amoah, Accra, Ghana
India: N. M. Tripathi Pte Ltd, Bombay, India
Israel: Steimatzky Ltd, Bnei Brak, Israel
Japan: Macmillan Shuppan KK, Tokyo, Japan
Kenya, Tanzania, Uganda & Mauritius: Kelvin van Hasselt Publishing Services, Briningham, Norfolk, UK
Malawi, Zambia & Zimbabwe: Barbie Keene, Harare, Zimbabwe
Malaysia, Singapore & Brunei: Malayan Law Journal Pte Ltd, Singapore
Pakistan: Pakistan Law House, Karachi, Pakistan

Book Trade Association Membership:
Publishing Scotland

2324

GREENHILL BOOKS / LIONEL LEVENTHAL LTD
5A Accommodation Road, London NW11 8ED
Telephone: 020 8455 5559

Email: michael@frontline-books.com
Web Site: www.greenhillbooks.com

Warehouse:
Bookpoint Ltd, 39 Milton Park, Abingdon, Oxon OX14 4TD
Telephone: 01235 400400
Fax: 01235 832068

Personnel:
Michael Leventhal *(Director)*

Aviation; History & Antiquarian; Military & War

Overseas Representation:
Australia & New Zealand: Peribo Pty Ltd, Mount Kuring-Gai, NSW, Australia
Austria, Switzerland, Czech & Slovak Republics, Hungary, Poland, Croatia, Slovenia, Spain (including Gibraltar) & Portugal: Sandro Salucci, Florence, Italy
Belgium: De Krijger, Erps, Belgium
Canada: Vanwell Publishing Ltd, St Catharines, Ont, Canada
France & Netherlands: Casemate Books, Newbury, UK
Germany: Robbert J. Pleysier, Heerde, Netherlands
India: Knowledge World International, Delhi, India
Middle East & Far East: Publishers International Marketing, Burmarsh, UK
New Zealand: South Pacific Books (Imports) Ltd, Auckland, New Zealand
South Africa: Peter Renew, Titles SA, Johannesburg, South Africa
USA: MBI Publishing Co, St Paul, MN, USA

2325

GREENLEAF PUBLISHING
Aizlewood's Mill, Nursery Street, Sheffield S3 8GG
Telephone: 0114 282 3475
Fax: 0114 282 3476
Email: sales@greenleaf-publishing.com
Web Site: www.greenleaf-publishing.com

Personnel:
Jayney Bown *(Office Manager)*
Dean Bargh *(Editorial Director)*
John Stuart *(Managing Director)*

Academic & Scholarly; Educational & Textbooks; Environment & Development Studies; Industry, Business & Management; Scientific & Technical

New Titles: 15 (2009) , 15 (2010)

Imprints, Series & ISBNs:
978 1 874719, 978 1 906093

Overseas Representation:
Australia: DA Information Services Pty Ltd, Mitcham, Vic, Australia
India: Viva Books, New Delhi, India
Taiwan: Unifacmanu Trading Co Ltd, Taipei, Taiwan
USA & Canada: Renouf Publishing Co Ltd, Ottawa, Ont, Canada

2326

GRESHAM BOOKS LTD
19–21 Sayers Lane, Tenterden, Kent TN30 6BW
Telephone: 01580 767596
Fax: 01580 764142
Email: info@gresham-books.co.uk
Web Site: www.gresham-books.co.uk

Personnel:
Nicholas Oulton *(Managing Director)*

History & Antiquarian; Music; Religion & Theology

Imprints, Series & ISBNs:
978 0 905418, 978 0 946095, 978 0 9502121

Parent Company:
UK: Galore Park Publishing Ltd

Book Trade Association Membership:
Publishers Association; Booksellers Association; Educational Publishers Council; Independent Publishers Guild

2327

GRUB STREET
4 Rainham Close, London SW11 6SS
Telephone: 020 7924 3966 & 7738 1008
Fax: 020 7738 1009
Email: post@grubstreet.co.uk
Web Site: www.grubstreet.co.uk

Distribution:
Littlehampton Book Services Ltd, Faraday Close, Durrington, Worthing, West Sussex BN13 3RB
Telephone: 01903 828500
Fax: 01903 828802
Email: ...@lbsltd.co.uk
Web Site: www.lbsltd.co.uk

Personnel:
John Davies *(Director)*
Anne Dolamore *(Sales & Marketing)*

Aviation; Cookery, Wines & Spirits; Military & War

New Titles: 32 (2009) , 36 (2010)
No of Employees: 5
Annual Turnover: £900,000

Imprints, Series & ISBNs:
978 0 948817, 978 1 898697, 978 1 902304, 978 1 904010, 978 1 904943, 978 1 906502

Overseas Representation:
Asia & Middle East: Grub Street, London, UK
Australia: Capricorn Link (Australia) Pty Ltd, Windsor, NSW, Australia
Canada: Vanwell Publishing Ltd, St Catharines, Ont, Canada
New Zealand: Nationwide Book Distributors, New Zealand
North & West Europe: EMS (Anselm Robinson), London, UK
Republic of Ireland: Vivienne Lavery, Blackrock, Co Dublin, Republic of Ireland
Scandinavia: Angell Eurosales, Berwick-on-Tweed, UK
South Africa: Penguin Books South Africa (Pty) Ltd, Johannesburg, South Africa
Southern Europe: Jenny & Penny Padovani, London, UK
USA: Casemate Publishers & Book Distributors LLC, Havertown, PA, USA

Book Trade Association Membership:
Independent Publishers Guild; BA (Associate Member)

2328

GUILDHALL PRESS
Unit 15, Rath Mor Centre, Bligh's Lane, Derry BT48 0LZ
Telephone: 028 7136 4413
Fax: 028 7137 2949
Email: info@ghpress.com
Web Site: www.ghpress.com

Personnel:
Paul Hippsley *(Project & Managing Editor, Marketing Manager)*

Academic & Scholarly; Biography & Autobiography; Children's Books; Crime; Educational & Textbooks; Fiction; Gay & Lesbian Studies; Guide Books; History & Antiquarian; Humour; Literature & Criticism; Music; Photography; Poetry; Politics & World Affairs; Theatre, Drama & Dance

Imprints, Series & ISBNs:
978 0 946451

Overseas Representation:
Australia: Irish Book Centre, Melbourne, Australia
USA: Irish Books & Media Inc, Minneapolis, MN, USA

Book Trade Association Membership:
Publishing Ireland (Foilsiú Éireann)

2329

GULLANE CHILDREN'S BOOKS
See: Meadowside Children's Books

2330

GWASG CARREG GWALCH
12 Iard yr Orsaf, Llanrwst, Conwy LL26 0EH
Telephone: 01492 642031
Fax: 01492 641502
Email: llyfrau@carreg-gwalch.com
Web Site: www.carreg-gwalch.com

Personnel:
Myrddin ap Dafydd (Manager)
Gordon Jones (Editor)

Imprints, Series & ISBNs:
978 0 86381, 978 1 84524, 978 1 84527

Overseas Representation:
Worldwide: Welsh Book Centre, Aberystwyth, UK

Book Trade Association Membership:
Welsh PA

2331

GWASG GWENFFRWD
PO Box 21, Corwen LL21 9WZ
Telephone: 0845 330 6754

Personnel:
Dr H. G. A. Hughes (Director of Research)

Academic & Scholarly; Bibliography & Library Science; Biography & Autobiography; Children's Books; Educational & Textbooks; Electronic (Professional & Academic); English as a Foreign Language; History & Antiquarian; Languages & Linguistics; Literature & Criticism; Poetry; Politics & World Affairs; Reference Books, Directories & Dictionaries; Religion & Theology; Sociology & Anthropology; Travel & Topography

New Titles: 6 (2009) , 6 (2010)
No of Employees: 4

Imprints, Series & ISBNs:
978 0 9501861, 978 1 85651

2332

GWASG GWYNEDD
Hafryn, Llwyn Hudol, Pwllheli, Gwynedd LL53 5YE
Telephone: 01758 612483

Personnel:
Alwyn Elis (Managing Director)
Nan Elis (Editor)

Biography & Autobiography; Children's Books

Imprints, Series & ISBNs:
978 0 86074

2333

HACHETTE CHILDREN'S BOOKS
338 Euston Road, London NW1 3BH
Telephone: 020 7873 6000
Fax: 020 7873 6024
Email: gm@hachettechildrens.co.uk

Distribution Centre:
Bookpoint Ltd, 130 Milton Park, Abingdon, Oxon OX14 4SB
Telephone: 01235 400400
Fax: 01235 400445

Personnel:
Marlene Johnson (Managing Director)
Les Phipps (Group Sales Director)
Andrew Sharp (Group Rights Director)
Charmian Allwright (Group Production Director)
Anne McNeil (Publishing (Picture Books & Fiction) Director)
Susan Barry (Marketing Director)
Rachel Cooke (Franklin Watts Director)
Anne Marimuthu (Finance Director)
Paul Litherland (Trade Sales Director)
Penny Morris (Orchard Books Director)

Audio Books; Children's Books; Educational & Textbooks; Fiction; Fine Art & Art History; Poetry; Reference Books, Directories & Dictionaries

New Titles: 1500 (2009) , 1100 (2010)
No of Employees: 110

Imprints, Series & ISBNs:
Aladdin/Watts
Animal Ark Series
Felicity Wishes range
Franklin Watts
Hodder Children's Books: 978 0 340
Hodder Home Learning Series
Hodder Wayland
Kipper range: 978 0 340
Orchard Books
Rainbow Magic

Parent Company:
Hachette UK

Distributor for:
Aladdin

Overseas Representation:
Africa, West Indies, South & Central America: Tony Moggach, InterMedia Americana (IMA) Ltd, London, UK
Australia: Hachette Livre Australia, Sydney, NSW, Australia
Australia & New Zealand: Watts ANZ, Sydney, NSW, Australia
Brazil (paperbacks): Agencia Siciliano de Livros, São Paulo, Brazil
Canada (trade & paperbacks): McArthur & Co Publishers Ltd, Toronto, Ont, Canada
Eastern Europe: David Williams, InterMedia Americana (IMA) Ltd, London, UK
Germany, Switzerland & Austria: Gabriele Kern Publishers Services, Frankfurt-am-Main, Germany
Hong Kong: Publishers' Associates Ltd, Hong Kong
India: Ajay Parmar, New Delhi, India
Israel: Steimatzky Ltd, Bnei Brak, Israel
Italy, Spain, Portugal & Gibraltar: Penny Padovani, London, UK
Japan & Korea: Yasy Murayama, Ageo, Japan
Netherlands (trade): Nilsson & Lamm BV, Weesp, Netherlands
New Zealand: Hachette Livre New Zealand, Auckland, New Zealand
Norway, Sweden, Finland, Denmark, Iceland, Netherlands & France: Angell Eurosales, Berwick-on-Tweed, UK
Pakistan (paperbacks): Liberty Books (Pvt) Ltd, Karachi, Pakistan
Republic of Ireland & Northern Ireland: Repforce Ireland Ltd, Monkstown, Republic of Ireland
Singapore & Malaysia: APD Singapore Pte Ltd, Singapore
South Africa: Jonathan Ball Publishers (Pty) Ltd, Jeppestown, South Africa; Pan Macmillan SA Pty Ltd, Hyde Park, South Africa
South Africa & Southern Africa (Wayland): Pan Macmillan SA Pty Ltd, Hyde Park, South Africa

Southern Africa (trade): Jonathan Ball Publishers (Pty) Ltd, Johannesburg, South Africa

Book Trade Association Membership:
Publishers Association; Educational Publishers Council

2334

HACHETTE SCOTLAND
2A Christie Street, Paisley PA1 1NB
Telephone: 0141 552 8082
Email:
bob.mcdevitt@hachettescotland.co.uk
Web Site: www.hachettescotland.co.uk

Personnel:
Bob McDevitt (Publisher)
Gillian McKay (Regional Sales Manager)

Biography & Autobiography; Cookery, Wines & Spirits; Crime; Fiction; History & Antiquarian; Humour; Military & War; Music; Sports & Games

Imprints, Series & ISBNs:
978 0 7553

Parent Company:
UK: Hachette UK

Overseas Representation:
British Commonwealth of Nations (including Canada): Darragh Deering, Headline Export Sales, London, UK

Book Trade Association Membership:
Publishers Association; Publishing Scotland

2335

PETER HADDOCK PUBLISHING
Pinfold Lane, Bridlington, East Yorkshire YO16 6BT
Telephone: 01262 678121
Fax: 01262 400043
Email: sales@phpublishing.co.uk
Web Site: www.phpublishing.co.uk

Personnel:
Rodney Noon (Managing Director)
Peter Thornton (Shipping Manager)
Jason Hickey (Customer Services Manager)
Carolyn Meah (Commercial Director)

Children's Books; Reference Books, Directories & Dictionaries

New Titles: 40 (2009) , 50 (2010)

Imprints, Series & ISBNs:
978 0 7105
Big Time

Parent Company:
D. C. Thomson & Co Ltd

Book Trade Association Membership:
Booksellers Association

2336

HALBAN PUBLISHERS
22 Golden Square, Piccadilly, London W1F 9JW
Telephone: 020 7437 9300
Fax: 020 7437 9512
Email: books@halbanpublishers.com
Web Site: www.halbanpublishers.com

Distribution:
Littlehampton Book Services, Faraday Close, Durrington, Worthing, West Sussex BN13 3RB
Telephone: 01903 828842
Fax: 01903 828621
Email: rose.mellish@lbsltd.co.uk

Personnel:
Peter Halban (Director)
Martine Halban (Director)

Biography & Autobiography; Fiction; History & Antiquarian; Literature & Criticism; Philosophy; Politics & World Affairs; Religion & Theology

New Titles: 4 (2009) , 4 (2010)

Imprints, Series & ISBNs:
978 1 870015, 978 1 905559

Overseas Representation:
Australia: Allen & Unwin Pty Ltd, Crows Nest, NSW, Australia
Canada: McArthur & Co Publishers Ltd, Toronto, Ont, Canada
Caribbean: Humphrys Roberts Associates, London, UK
East & West Africa: Richard Carman Associates, Northwich, UK
Europe (excluding Scandinavia & Netherlands): c/o Florence Chatelain, The Orion Publishing Group Ltd, London, UK
India, Sri Lanka & Bangladesh: Maya Publishers Pvt Ltd, New Delhi, India
Japan, South East Asia, Far East & Pakistan: Ralph & Sheila Summers, Woodford Green, Essex, UK
Middle East & North Africa: Peter Ward Book Exports, London, UK
Netherlands: Consul Books, Blaricum, Netherlands
New Zealand: Hodder Moa Beckett Publishers (NZ) Ltd, Auckland, New Zealand
Republic of Ireland: Gill Hess Ltd, Skerries, Co Dublin, Republic of Ireland
Russia, Baltic States & former USSR: Tony Moggach, IMA, London, UK
Scandinavia: Pernille Larsen (Books for Europe), Roskilde, Denmark
South Africa: Jonathan Ball Publishers (Pty) Ltd, Johannesburg, South Africa
South America: Humphrys Roberts Associates, Cotia SP, Brazil
USA & other territories: Export Department, The Orion Publishing Group Ltd, London, UK
Yugoslavia, Bosnia, Romania, Poland, Bulgaria, Hungary, Czech Republic, Slovakia, Slovenia & Croatia: Csaba & Jackie Lengyel de Bagota, Budapest, Hungary

Book Trade Association Membership:
Independent Publishers Guild

2337

HALDANE MASON LTD
PO Box 34196, London NW10 3YB
Telephone: 020 8459 2131
Fax: 020 8728 1216
Email: info@haldanemason.com
Web Site: www.haldanemason.com

Warehouse, Trade Enquiries & Orders:
Vine House Distribution Ltd, The Old Mill House, Mill Lane, Uckfield, East Sussex TN22 5AA
Telephone: 01825 767396
Fax: 01825 765649
Email: sales@vinehouseuk.co.uk

Personnel:
Ron Samuel (Director)
Ms Sydney Francis (Director)

Children's Books; Cookery, Wines & Spirits; Crafts & Hobbies; Educational & Textbooks; Health & Beauty; Medical (incl. Self Help & Alternative Medicine); Natural History; Sports & Games

Imprints, Series & ISBNs:
978 1 902463, 978 1 905339
Haldane Mason
Red Kite Books

Book Trade Association Membership:
Independent Publishers Guild

2338

ROBERT HALE LTD
Clerkenwell House,
45–47 Clerkenwell Green, London
EC1R 0HT
Telephone: 020 7251 2661
Fax: 020 7490 4958
Email: enquire@halebooks.com
Web Site: www.halebooks.com

Warehouse & Returns:
Combined Book Services, Units I/K,
Paddock Wood Distribution Centre,
Paddock Wood, Tonbridge, Kent TN12 6UU
Telephone: 01892 837171
Fax: 01892 837272
Email: orders@combook.co.uk

Personnel:
John Hale (*Managing Director*)
Robert Kynaston (*Finance Director*)
Nick Chaytor (*Rights Manager*)
Gill Jackson (*General Manager*)
Robert Hale (*Production Manager*)

Animal Care & Breeding; Antiques & Collecting; Biography & Autobiography; Cinema, Video, TV & Radio; Crafts & Hobbies; Crime; Fiction; Humour; Magic & the Occult; Military & War; Music; Natural History; Photography; Politics & World Affairs; Reference Books, Directories & Dictionaries; Travel & Topography

Imprints, Series & ISBNs:
J. A. Allen: 978 0 85131
NAG Press: 978 0 7090, 978 0 7091, 978 0 7198

Distributor for:
Phoenix

Overseas Representation:
Australia: DLS Australia (Pty) Ltd, Braeside, Vic, Australia
France, Germany, Netherlands, Austria & Switzerland: Ted Dougherty, London, UK
Italy, Spain, Portugal, Greece & Gibraltar: Penny Padovani, London, UK
New Zealand: South Pacific Books (Imports) Ltd, Auckland, New Zealand
South Africa: Trinity Books CC, Randburg, South Africa
USA: Trafalgar Square Publishing, North Pomfret, VT, USA

Book Trade Association Membership:
Independent Publishers Guild

2339

HALSGROVE
Halsgrove House, Ryelands Estate,
Bagley Road, Wellington, Somerset
TA21 9PZ
Telephone: 01823 653777
Fax: 01823 665294
Email: sales@halsgrove.com
Web Site: www.halsgrove.com

Personnel:
Julian Davidson (*Managing Director*)
Steven Pugsley (*Chairman*)
Simon Butler (*Publisher*)

Archaeology; Aviation; Biography & Autobiography; Fine Art & Art History; Guide Books; History & Antiquarian; Illustrated & Fine Editions; Military & War; Natural History; Travel & Topography

New Titles: 200 (2009) , 150 (2010)

Imprints, Series & ISBNs:
Halsgrove: 978 1 84114
Halstar: 978 0 906690
Rylands: 978 0 906551

Parent Company:
UK: D. A. A. Halsgrove Ltd

Associated Companies:
UK: Halstar Ltd

Distributor for:
UK: Halsgrove; Halstar; Ryelands

2340

HAMBLEDON CONTINUUM LTD
see: Continuum International Publishing Group

2341

HAMMERSMITH PRESS LTD
14 Greville Street, London EC1N 8SB
Telephone: 020 7736 9132
Fax: 020 7348 7521
Email: gmb@hammersmithpress.co.uk
Web Site: www.hammersmithpress.co.uk

Distribution:
Combined Book Services, Unit Y,
Paddock Wood Distribution Centre,
Paddock Wood, Tonbridge, Kent TN12 6UU
Telephone: 01892 837171
Fax: 01892 837272
Email: orders@combook.co.uk
Web Site: www.combook.co.uk

Personnel:
Georgina Bentliff (*Director*)

Biography & Autobiography; Health & Beauty; Medical (incl. Self Help & Alternative Medicine)

Imprints, Series & ISBNs:
978 1 905140

Book Trade Association Membership:
Independent Publishers Guild

2342

HANBURY PLAYS
Keeper's Lodge, Broughton Green,
Droitwich, Worcs WR9 7EE
Telephone: 01527 821564
Email: hanburyplays@tiscali.co.uk
Web Site: www.hanburyplays.co.uk

Personnel:
Brian J. Burton (*Proprietor*)

Theatre, Drama & Dance

New Titles: 4 (2009) , 2 (2010)
Annual Turnover: £13,000

Imprints, Series & ISBNs:
978 0 85197, 978 0 907926, 978 1 85205

Distributor for:
USA: Contemporary Drama Service; Pioneer Drama Service

Overseas Representation:
Australia: The Dominie Group, Brookvale, NSW, Australia
Malta: Dingli Co International, Valletta, Malta
New Zealand: Play Bureau of New Zealand Ltd, New Plymouth, New Zealand

2343

HARDEN'S LTD
14 Buckingham Street, London WC2N 6DF
Telephone: 020 7839 4763
Fax: 020 7839 7561
Email: rh@hardens.com
Web Site: www.hardens.com

Personnel:
Richard Harden (*Director*)
Peter Harden (*Director*)

Guide Books; Reference Books, Directories & Dictionaries

Imprints, Series & ISBNs:
978 1 873721

2344

HARLEQUIN MILLS & BOON LTD
Eton House, 18–24 Paradise Road,
Richmond, Surrey TW9 1SR
Telephone: 020 8288 2800
Fax: 020 8288 2899
Web Site: www.millsandboon.co.uk

Personnel:
Mandy Ferguson (*Managing Director*)
Stuart Barber (*Finance & IS Director, Company Secretary*)
Karin Stoecker (*Editorial Director*)
Jackie McGee (*Human Resources Director*)
Clare Somerville (*Retail Sales & Marketing Director*)
Angela Meredith (*Retail Operations & Production Director*)
Tim Cooper (*Direct Marketing Director*)
Ian Roberts (*Sales Director*)

Fiction

Book Trade Association Membership:
Publishers Association

2345

JOHN HARPER PUBLISHING
27 Palace Gates Road, London N22 7BW
Telephone: 020 8881 4774
Email: orders@johnharperpublishing.co.uk
Web Site:
www.johnharperpublishing.co.uk

Book Orders:
Turpin Distribution Services Ltd,
Stratton Business Park, Pegasus Drive,
Biggleswade SG18 8QB
Telephone: 01767 604951
Email: custserv@turpin-distribution.com

Academic & Scholarly; Educational & Textbooks; Politics & World Affairs

New Titles: 3 (2009) , 5 (2010)
No of Employees: 1

Imprints, Series & ISBNs:
978 0 9543811, 978 0 9551144, 978 0 9556202, 978 0 9564508

Book Trade Association Membership:
Independent Publishers Guild

2346

HARPERCOLLINS PUBLISHERS LTD
77–85 Fulham Palace Road, London
W6 8JB
Telephone: 020 8741 7070
Fax: 020 8307 4440
Email: enquiries@harpercollins.co.uk
Web Site: www.harpercollins.co.uk

Registered Office (Warehouse, Trade Orders & Distribution, Finance):
Westerhill Road, Bishopbriggs, Glasgow
G64 2QR
Telephone: 0141 772 3200
Fax: 0141 772 3200 x3119

Personnel:
Victoria Barnsley (*Chief Executive Officer*)
Keith Mullock (*Chief Operating Officer*)
Charlie Redmayne (*Executive Vice-President & Chief Digital Officer*)
Robert Scriven (*Managing Director, Languages*)
Mario Santos (*Managing Director, Children's*)
Belinda Budge (*Managing Director & Publisher, Harper Fiction & Harper Non-Fiction*)
John Bond (*Managing Director, Press Books*)
David Roche (*Managing Director, Group Sales & Trade Marketing*)

Nigel Ward (*Managing Director, Education*)
Katie Fulford (*Managing Director, Special Projects*)
James Graves (*Global Sourcing Director*)
Lucy Vanderbilt (*Rights Director*)
Sylvia May (*Group International Sales Director*)
Helen Ellis (*Publicity Director, Harper Press*)
Julian Thomas (*Information Technology Director*)
Sean Plunkett (*Group Supply Chain Director*)
Ed Kielbasiewicz (*Finance Director*)
Siobhan Kenny (*Communications Director*)
Julia Wisdom (*Harper Fiction, Crime Publishing Director*)
Susan Watt (*Harper Fiction Publishing Director*)
Jonathan Taylor (*Harper Sport Publishing Director*)
Jane Johnson (*Harper Fiction, Voyager Publishing Director*)
Nick Pearson (*Fourth Estate Publishing Director*)
David Brawn (*Tolkien & Estates Publishing Director*)
Ann-Janine Murtagh (*Publisher, Children's Books*)
Clare Smith (*Harper Press Fiction Publishing Director*)
Arabella Pike (*Harper Press Non-Fiction Publishing Director*)
Lynne Drew (*Harper Fiction Publishing Director*)

Academic & Scholarly; Animal Care & Breeding; Antiques & Collecting; Architecture & Design; Atlases & Maps; Audio Books; Biography & Autobiography; Biology & Zoology; Chemistry; Children's Books; Cinema, Video, TV & Radio; Cookery, Wines & Spirits; Crafts & Hobbies; Crime; Do-It-Yourself; Economics; Educational & Textbooks; Electronic (Educational); Electronic (Entertainment); Electronic (Professional & Academic); English as a Foreign Language; Environment & Development Studies; Fiction; Fine Art & Art History; Gardening; Gender Studies; Geography & Geology; Guide Books; Health & Beauty; History & Antiquarian; Humour; Illustrated & Fine Editions; Industry, Business & Management; Languages & Linguistics; Literature & Criticism; Magic & the Occult; Medical (incl. Self Help & Alternative Medicine); Military & War; Music; Natural History; Photography; Physics; Poetry; Politics & World Affairs; Psychology & Psychiatry; Reference Books, Directories & Dictionaries; Religion & Theology; Science Fiction; Scientific & Technical; Sports & Games; Travel & Topography

Imprints, Series & ISBNs:
Collins
Collins Classics
Collins Crime
Collins Dictionaries COBUILD
Collins New Naturalist Library
Collins Teacher
Collins/Times Maps & Atlases
CollinsEducation
CollinsGems
Fourth Estate
Harper Perennial
Harper Sport
Harper Thorsons/Harper Element
HarperCollins
HarperCollins Audio
HarperCollins Children's Books
HarperCollins Entertainment
HarperCollins Non-Fiction
Janes
Times Books
Tolkien
Voyager

Parent Company:
News Corporation

Overseas Representation:
Australia: HarperCollins Publishers, Pymble, NSW, Australia
Canada: HarperCollins Publishers, Toronto & Scarborough, Ont, Canada
India: HarperCollins Publishers India Pvt Ltd, New Delhi, India
New Zealand: HarperCollins (NZ) Ltd, Glenfield, Auckland, New Zealand
USA: HarperCollins Publishers, New York, USA
Worldwide (except countries listed): HarperCollins Publishers Ltd, Glasgow & London, UK

Book Trade Association Membership:
Publishers Association

2347

HARRIMAN HOUSE
3A Penns Road, Petersfield, Hants GU32 2EW
Telephone: 01730 233870
Fax: 01730 233880
Email: info@harriman-house.com
Web Site: www.harriman-house.com

Personnel:
Myles Hunt *(Managing Director)*
Suzanne Anderson *(Rights)*
Louise Hinchen *(Publicity & Marketing)*
Nick Read *(Head of Production)*
Craig Pearce *(Editor)*
Chris Parker *(Sales & New Media)*

Accountancy & Taxation; Economics; Industry, Business & Management

New Titles: 40 (2009) , 60 (2010)

Imprints, Series & ISBNs:
978 0 85719, 978 1 897597, 978 1 905641, 978 1 906659

Overseas Representation:
Central & Eastern Europe: Tony Moggach, Publishers Sales Representation, London, UK
Spain, Portugal & Gibraltar: Peter Prout, Iberian Book Services, Madrid, Spain
West Africa: Joseph Makope, InterMedia Americana (IMA) Ltd, London, UK
Western Europe (including Austria, Belgium, France, Germany, Greece, Italy, Luxembourg, Malta, Netherlands & Switzerland): Ted Dougherty, London, UK

2348

HART PUBLISHING
16C Worcester Place, Oxford OX1 2JW
Telephone: 01865 517530
Fax: 01865 510710
Email: mail@hartpub.co.uk
Web Site: www.hartpub.co.uk

Personnel:
Richard Hart *(Joint Owner & Managing Director)*
Jane Parker *(Joint Owner, Sales & Marketing Director)*

Academic & Scholarly; Law

New Titles: 93 (2009) , 120 (2010)

Imprints, Series & ISBNs:
978 1 84113, 978 1 84946, 978 1 901362

Distributor for:
Belgium: Intersentia

Overseas Representation:
Benelux: Intersentia, Antwerp, Belgium
Canada: Codasat, c/o University Toronto Press Distribution, Downsview, Ont, Canada
Central & Eastern Europe: Jacek Lewinson, Poland
Greece, Turkey, Arab Middle East & North Africa: Avicenna Partnership Ltd, UK

Italy & France: Mare Nostrum Publishing Consultants, Rome, Italy
Scandinavia: Colin Flint Ltd, Harlow, UK
South East Asia: STM Publisher Services Pte Ltd, Singapore
Spain & Portugal: Peter Prout Iberian Book Services, Madrid, Spain
USA: International Specialized Book Services Inc, Portland, OR, USA

Book Trade Association Membership:
Independent Publishers Guild

2349

HARVARD UNIVERSITY PRESS
Fitzroy House, Chenies Street, London WC1E 7EY
Telephone: 020 7306 0603
Fax: 020 7306 0604
Email: info@HUP-MITpress.co.uk
Web Site: www.hup.harvard.edu

Orders & Warehouse:
c/o John Wiley & Sons,
Southern Cross Trading Estate,
1 Oldlands Way, Bognor Regis, West Sussex PO22 9SA
Telephone: 01243 779777
Fax: 01243 829121
Email: cs-books@wiley.co.uk

Personnel:
Ann Sexsmith *(Managing Director)*
Rebekah White *(Publicity & Promotion Manager)*

Academic & Scholarly; Biography & Autobiography; Biology & Zoology; Cinema, Video, TV & Radio; Economics; Fine Art & Art History; Gender Studies; Health & Beauty; History & Antiquarian; Law; Literature & Criticism; Military & War; Music; Natural History; Philosophy; Politics & World Affairs; Psychology & Psychiatry; Reference Books, Directories & Dictionaries; Religion & Theology; Sociology & Anthropology

New Titles: 150 (2009) , 150 (2010)

Imprints, Series & ISBNs:
Belknap: 978 0 674
Harvard University Press: 978 0 674
Loeb Classical Library: 978 0 674

Parent Company:
USA: Harvard University Press

Overseas Representation:
China: Everest International Publishing Services, Beijing, P. R. of China
Germany, Austria, Switzerland & Italy: Uwe Lüdemann, Berlin, Germany
Hong Kong: Jane Lam, Aromix Books, Hong Kong
India: Mediamatics, Calcutta, India
Israel: Rodney Franklin Agency, Tel Aviv, Israel
Japan: Rockbook, Tokyo, Japan
Malaysia: Simon Tay, Apex Knowledge, Selangor, Malaysia
Middle East (excluding Greece & Israel): Avicenna Partnership, Oxford, UK
North America, Mexico & Central America: Harvard University Press, Cambridge, MA, USA
Poland, Hungary, Croatia, Slovenia, Slovakia, Czech Republic, Russia, Lithuania, Latvia, Estonia, Romania, Serbia, Albania & Bosnia Herzegovina: Ewa Ledóchowicz, Konstancin-Jeziorna, Poland
Scandinavia, Netherlands, Luxembourg, Belgium & France: Fred Hermans, Bovenkarspel, Netherlands
South Africa: Cory Voigt Associates, Johannesburg, South Africa
South East Asia: Joseph Goh, IGP Services, Singapore
South Korea: Se-Yung Jun & Min-Hwa Yoo, Seoul, Republic of Korea

Spain & Portugal: Chris Humphrys, Gaucin, Spain
Taiwan: B. K. Norton, Taipei, Taiwan

Book Trade Association Membership:
Independent Publishers Guild

2350

HARVEY MAP SERVICES LTD
12–22 Main Street, Doune, Perthshire FK16 6BJ
Telephone: 01786 841202
Fax: 01786 841098
Email: sh@harveymaps.co.uk
Web Site: www.harveymaps.co.uk

Personnel:
Susan Harvey *(Managing Director)*
Jacci Cameron *(Office Manager)*

Atlases & Maps; Sports & Games

New Titles: 7 (2009) , 7 (2010)
No of Employees: 7
Annual Turnover: £650,000

Imprints, Series & ISBNs:
978 1 85137

Distributor for:
Canada: Chrismar Inc
Denmark: Compukort
South Africa: Jacana Media

Book Trade Association Membership:
International Map Trade Association

2351

HAWKER PUBLICATIONS
Culvert House, Culvert Road, London SW11 5DH
Telephone: 020 7720 2108
Fax: 020 7498 3023
Email: kate@hawkerpublications.com
Web Site: www.careinfo.org

Distribution:
NBN Plymbridge Ltd, Estover Road, Plymouth, Devon PL6 7PZ
Telephone: 01752 202300

Personnel:
Dr R. Hawkins *(Managing Director)*
P. Petker *(Sales Director)*

Health & Beauty; Medical (incl. Self Help & Alternative Medicine); Vocational Training & Careers

Imprints, Series & ISBNs:
Better Care Guides: 978 1 874790
Hawker Publications: 978 1 874790

Overseas Representation:
Australia: Basing House Books, Hammondville, NSW, Australia

2352

HAWTHORN PRESS
Hawthorn House, 1 Lansdown Lane, Stroud, Glos GL5 1BJ
Telephone: 01453 757040
Fax: 01453 751138
Email: info@hawthornpress.com
Web Site: www.hawthornpress.com

Distribution & Sales:
BookSource, 50 Cambuslang Road, Glasgow G32 8NB
Telephone: 0845 370 0063
Fax: 0845 370 0064
Email: orders@booksource.net

Personnel:
Martin Large *(Director)*
Judy Large *(Director)*
Farimah Englefield *(Finance Manager)*
Claire Percival *(Administrator)*

Academic & Scholarly; Children's Books; Crafts & Hobbies; Educational & Textbooks; Gardening; Gender Studies; Industry, Business & Management; Medical (incl. Self Help & Alternative Medicine); Music; Politics & World Affairs; Psychology & Psychiatry; Religion & Theology; Sociology & Anthropology

Imprints, Series & ISBNs:
978 1 903458, 978 1 907359
Conflict & Peace Building: 978 1 869890
Early Years Education: 978 1 869890
Family Activities & Crafts: 978 1 869890
Parenting & Child Health: 978 1 869890
Psychology & Self Help: 978 1 869890
Rudolf Steiner Education: 978 1 869890

Overseas Representation:
Australia: Footprint Books Pty Ltd, Warriewood, NSW, Australia
Canada: Tri-fold Books, Guelph, Ont, Canada
New Zealand: Ceres Books, Ellerslie, New Zealand
South Africa: Peter Hyde Associates (Pty) Ltd, Cape Town, South Africa; Rudolf Steiner Publications, Bryanston, South Africa
USA (all titles): Steiner Books Inc, Herndon, VA, USA

Book Trade Association Membership:
Independent Publishers Guild

2353

HAYNES PUBLISHING
Sparkford, Nr Yeovil, Somerset BA22 7JJ
Telephone: 01963 440635
Fax: 01963 440825
Email: sales@haynes.co.uk
Web Site: www.haynes.co.uk

Customer Services (Trade):
Telephone: 01963 442080
Fax: 01963 440001

Personnel:
J. Haynes *(Chairman)*
James Bunkum *(Finance Director & Group Company Secretary)*
Jeremy Yates-Round *(Managing & Sales Director)*
Nigel Clements *(Production Director)*
Matthew Minter *(Motor Trade, Editorial Director)*
Mark Hughes *(Book Division, Editorial Director)*
Graham Cook *(Overseas Sales & Rights Director)*
Eric Oakley *(Chief Executive)*

Animal Care & Breeding; Architecture & Design; Atlases & Maps; Aviation; Biography & Autobiography; Children's Books; Computer Science; Crafts & Hobbies; Crime; Do-It-Yourself; Electronic (Professional & Academic); Gardening; Guide Books; Health & Beauty; History & Antiquarian; Medical (incl. Self Help & Alternative Medicine); Military & War; Music; Nautical; Photography; Reference Books, Directories & Dictionaries; Scientific & Technical; Sports & Games; Transport; Travel & Topography

New Titles: 111 (2009) , 109 (2010)
No of Employees: 77
Annual Turnover: £35.3M

Imprints, Series & ISBNs:
G. T. Foulis: 978 0 85429, 978 0 85733
Haynes: 978 1 84425, 978 1 85010, 978 1 85960
J. H. Haynes & Co Ltd: 978 0 85696, 978 0 900550
Oxford Illustrated Press: 978 0 902280, 978 0 946609, 978 1 85509
Patrick Stephens Ltd: 978 0 85059, 978 1 85260

Parent Company:
UK: Haynes Publishing Group Plc

Distributor for:
USA: David Bull Publishing

Overseas Representation:
Australia: Haynes Manuals Inc, Padstow, NSW, Australia
New Zealand: Pace Publications, Wanganui, New Zealand
Sweden: Haynes Publishing Nordiska AB, Uppsala, Sweden
USA: Haynes Manuals Inc, Newbury Park, CA, USA
USA (non-Manual titles only): MBI Publishing Co, St Paul, MN, USA

Book Trade Association Membership:
Booksellers Association

2354 ▬▬▬▬

HAYWARD PUBLISHING
Southbank Centre, Belvedere Road, London SE1 8XX
Telephone: 020 7921 0826
Fax: 020 7921 0700
Email:
deborah.power@southbankcentre.co.uk
Web Site: www.southbankcentre.co.uk

Personnel:
Deborah C. Power *(Sales Manager)*
Amy Botfield *(Publications Co-ordinator)*
Mary Richards *(Art Publisher)*

Architecture & Design; Fine Art & Art History; Photography

New Titles: 8 (2009) , 6 (2010)

Imprints, Series & ISBNs:
978 1 85332

Book Trade Association Membership:
Booksellers Association

2355 ▬▬▬▬

HEART OF ALBION PRESS
2 Cross Hill Close, Wymeswold, Loughborough LE12 6UJ
Telephone: 01509 880725
Email: albion@indigogroup.co.uk
Web Site: www.hoap.co.uk

Personnel:
R. N. Trubshaw *(Owner)*

Archaeology; Electronic (Educational); Guide Books; History & Antiquarian; Magic & the Occult; Philosophy; Psychology & Psychiatry; Religion & Theology; Sociology & Anthropology

Imprints, Series & ISBNs:
Alternative Albion: 978 1 872883, 978 1 905646
Explore Books: 978 1 872883, 978 1 905646
Heart of Albion: 978 1 872883, 978 1 905646

2356 ▬▬▬▬

ROGER HEAVENS
125 Keddington Road, Louth, Lincolnshire LN11 0BL
Telephone: 01507 606102
Fax: 01507 606102
Web Site: www.booksoncricket.net

Personnel:
Roger Heavens *(Proprietor)*
Sally Heavens *(Editor)*
Roger Packham *(Editor)*

Academic & Scholarly; Sports & Games

New Titles: 3 (2009) , 5 (2010)
No of Employees: 1

Annual Turnover: £20,000

Imprints, Series & ISBNs:
Roger Heavens: 978 1 900592
RH Business Books: 978 1 900592

Overseas Representation:
Australia: Roger Page, Yallambe, Vic, Australia

2357 ▬▬▬▬

HELION & CO LTD
26 Willow Road, Solihull, West Midlands B91 1UE
Telephone: 0121 705 3393
Fax: 0121 711 4075
Email: info@helion.co.uk
Web Site: www.helion.co.uk

Personnel:
Duncan Rogers *(Managing Director)*
Wilfrid Rogers *(General Manager)*

Academic & Scholarly; History & Antiquarian; Military & War

New Titles: 23 (2009) , 35 (2010)

Imprints, Series & ISBNs:
978 1 874622, 978 1 906033, 978 1 907677

Distributor for:
Aegis Consulting/Aberjona Press; Eagle Editions; Reid Air Publishing; Vanwell Publishing

Overseas Representation:
Australia & New Zealand: Crusader Trading Pty Ltd, Weston, ACT, Australia
Austria, France, Switzerland, Benelux, Germany, Eastern Europe, Greece, Italy, Portugal, Spain, Gibraltar, Slovenia & Croatia: Casemate Publishing UK, Newbury, UK
Canada: Vanwell Publishing Ltd, St Catharines, Ont, Canada
USA: Casemate Publishers & Book Distributors LLC, Havertown, PA, USA

2358 ▬▬▬▬

HELTER SKELTER PUBLISHING LTD
PO Box 50497, London W8 9FA
Telephone: 0794 1206045
Email: sales@helterskelterpublishing.com
Web Site:
www.helterskelterpublishing.com

Personnel:
Graeme Milton *(Director)*
Michael O'Connell *(Company Secretary)*

Music

New Titles: 5 (2009) , 6 (2010)
No of Employees: 1
Annual Turnover: £75,000

Imprints, Series & ISBNs:
978 1 900924, 978 1 905139

2359 ▬▬▬▬

HEMMING INFORMATION SERVICES
32 Vauxhall Bridge Road, London SW1V 2SS
Telephone: 020 7973 6604
Fax: 020 7233 5053
Email: l.alderson@hgluk.com
Web Site: www.hgluk.com

Also at:
8 The Old Yarn Mills, Sherborne, Dorset DT9 3RQ
Telephone: 01935 816030
Fax: 01935 817200
Email: info@hisdorset.com

Also at:
Church House Business Centre, Church House, Church Road, Croydon CR0 1SB
Telephone: 020 8680 4200
Fax: 020 8680 8400

Personnel:
Graham Bond *(Managing Director)*
Linda Alderson *(Production Director)*
Mike Burton *(Editorial Director (Local Government titles))*
Emma Sabin *(Sales Director)*
Dean Wanless *(Senior Editor)*

Reference Books, Directories & Dictionaries

Imprints, Series & ISBNs:
978 0 7079

Parent Company:
Hemming Group Ltd

Book Trade Association Membership:
Data Publishers Association; European Directory Publishers Association

2360 ▬▬▬▬

IAN HENRY PUBLICATIONS LTD
20 Park Drive, Romford, Essex RM1 4LH
Telephone: 01708 749119
Fax: 01708 736213
Email: info@ian-henry.com
Web Site: www.ian-henry.com

Personnel:
Ian Wilkes *(Publisher & Managing Director)*

Cookery, Wines & Spirits; Educational & Textbooks; Fiction; History & Antiquarian; Humour; Medical (incl. Self Help & Alternative Medicine); Theatre, Drama & Dance; Transport

Imprints, Series & ISBNs:
978 0 86025

Distributor for:
UK: Havering Museum

2361 ▬▬▬▬

THE HERBERT PRESS
[an imprint of A. & C. Black]
36 Soho Square, London W1D 3QY
Telephone: 020 7758 0263
Email: sjames@acblack.com

Personnel:
Nigel Newton *(Chairman)*
Jill Coleman *(Managing Director)*
Susan James *(Publisher)*

Architecture & Design; Fashion & Costume; Fine Art & Art History; Illustrated & Fine Editions

Imprints, Series & ISBNs:
Design Handbooks: 978 0 7136, 978 0 906969, 978 1 871569
The Herbert History of Art & Architecture: 978 0 7136, 978 0 906969, 978 1 871569

Parent Company:
A. & C. Black Plc

Associated Companies:
Bloomsbury

Overseas Representation:
Australia: Allen & Unwin Pty Ltd, Sydney, NSW, Australia
Europe: Penguin Group, London, UK
USA: Bloomsbury Academic USA

2362 ▬▬▬▬

NICK HERN BOOKS
The Glasshouse, 49a Goldhawk Road, London W12 8QP

Telephone: 020 8749 4953
Fax: 020 8735 0250
Email: info@nickhernbooks.demon.co.uk
Web Site: www.nickhernbooks.co.uk

Distribution:
Grantham Book Services Ltd, Trent Road, Grantham, Lincs NG31 7XQ
Telephone: 01476 541000
Fax: 01476 541060
Email: orders@gbs.tbs-ltd.co.uk

Personnel:
Nick Hern *(Managing Director)*
Matt Applewhite *(Production Editor)*
Robin Booth *(Marketing & Publicity Manager)*
Ian Higham *(Sales Manager)*

Cinema, Video, TV & Radio; Theatre, Drama & Dance

New Titles: 55 (2009) , 65 (2010)
No of Employees: 8

Imprints, Series & ISBNs:
978 1 84842, 978 1 85459

Distributor for:
Canada: Playwrights Press Canada
USA: Drama Book Publishers; Theatre Communications Group

Overseas Representation:
Australia: Currency Press, Sydney, Australia
Canada: Playwrights Press Canada, Toronto, Ont, Canada
USA: Theatre Communications Group, New York, USA

Book Trade Association Membership:
Independent Publishers Guild

2363 ▬▬▬▬

HIGHLAND BOOKS
Two High Pines, Knoll Road, Godalming, Surrey GU7 2EP
Telephone: 01483 424560
Fax: 01483 424388
Email: info@highlandbks.com
Web Site: www.highlandbks.com

Distribution / Trade Orders:
STL Distribution, PO Box 300, Kingstown Broadway, Carlisle, Cumbria CA3 0QS
Telephone: 01228 611511
Fax: 01228 514949
Web Site: www.stldistribution.co.uk

Personnel:
Philip Ralli *(Director)*

Biography & Autobiography; Children's Books; Fiction; Religion & Theology

New Titles: 3 (2009) , 8 (2010)
No of Employees: 2
Annual Turnover: £40,000

Imprints, Series & ISBNs:
Highland: 978 0 946616, 978 1 897913
Usharp: 978 1 905496

Overseas Representation:
South Africa: Methodist Wholesale, Cape Town, South Africa

2364 ▬▬▬▬

HINTON HOUSE PUBLISHERS LTD
Newman House, 4 High Street, Buckingham MK18 1NT
Telephone: 01280 822557
Fax: 0560 313 5274
Email: info@hintonpublishers.com
Web Site: www.hintonpublishers.com

Personnel:
Sarah Miles *(Publisher)*

Educational & Textbooks; Languages & Linguistics; Medical (incl. Self Help & Alternative Medicine); Psychology & Psychiatry

New Titles: 7 (2009) , 8 (2010)

Imprints, Series & ISBNs:
978 1 906531

Distributor for:
Canada: Pembroke Publishers Ltd
USA: Stenhouse Publishers

Book Trade Association Membership:
Publishers Association

2365 ■

HIPPOPOTAMUS PRESS
22 Whitewell Road, Frome, Somerset
BA11 4EL
Telephone: 01373 466653
Fax: 01373 466653
Email: rjhippopress@aol.com

Personnel:
R. John *(Publisher)*
M. Pargitter *(Editor)*
Anna Martin *(Editorial Assistant)*

Literature & Criticism; Poetry

Imprints, Series & ISBNs:
978 0 904179

Distributor for:
Austria: University of Salzburg Press

2366 ■

HISTORICAL PUBLICATIONS LTD
32 Ellington Street, London N7 8PL
Telephone: 020 7607 1628
Fax: 020 7609 6451
Email:
richardson@historicalpublications.co.uk

Distribution:
Countryside Books, 2 Highfield Avenue,
Newbury, Berks RG14 5DS
Telephone: 01635 43816
Fax: 01635 551004
Email: info@countrysidebooks.co.uk
Web Site: www.countrysidebooks.co.uk

Personnel:
John Richardson *(Managing Director)*
Helen English *(Secretary)*

Academic & Scholarly; Architecture & Design; History & Antiquarian; Travel & Topography

New Titles: 6 (2009) , 5 (2010)
No of Employees: 3

Imprints, Series & ISBNs:
978 0 948667, 978 1 905286

2367 ■

HOBNOB PRESS
PO Box 1838, East Knoyle, Salisbury
SP3 6FA
Telephone: 01747 830015
Email: john@hobnobpress.co.uk
Web Site: www.hobnobpress.co.uk

Personnel:
John Chandler *(Sole Trader)*

Academic & Scholarly; Archaeology; Guide Books; History & Antiquarian; Literature & Criticism; Travel & Topography

New Titles: 8 (2009) , 10 (2010)
No of Employees: 110

Imprints, Series & ISBNs:
978 0 946418, 978 1 906978

Distributor for:
Ex Libris Press; Wiltshire Buildings Record; Wiltshire Record Society

2368 ■

HODDER EDUCATION
338 Euston Road, London NW1 3BH
Telephone: 020 7873 6000
Fax: 020 7873 6299 & 6325
Web Site: www.hoddereducation.co.uk

Distribution Centre:
Bookpoint Ltd, 130 Milton Park, Abingdon,
Oxon OX14 4SB
Telephone: 01235 400400
Fax: 01235 400445

Personnel:
Thomas Webster *(Chief Executive Director)*
Elisabeth Tribe *(Managing Director, Schools)*
C. P. Shaw *(Managing Director, Tertiary)*
Alyssum Ross *(Business Operations Director)*
David Swarbrick *(Managing Director, Consumer Learning)*
John Mitchell *(Scotland – Hodder Gibson Director)*
Robert Sulley *(Editorial Director, Science & International)*
Tim Mahar *(Sales & Marketing Director, Trade)*
Janice Tolan *(Schools & FE, Sales & Marketing Director)*
Jim Belben *(Schools Director (Humanities & Modern Languages))*
Steve Connolly *(Editorial Digital Publishing Director)*
Alex Jones *(Finance Director)*
Paul Cherry *(Philip Allan Director)*
Vivian Marr *(Editorial Director, Consumer Languages)*

Academic & Scholarly; Accountancy & Taxation; Animal Care & Breeding; Antiques & Collecting; Archaeology; Atlases & Maps; Audio Books; Aviation; Biology & Zoology; Chemistry; Cinema, Video, TV & Radio; Computer Science; Cookery, Wines & Spirits; Crafts & Hobbies; Do-It-Yourself; Economics; Educational & Textbooks; Electronic (Educational); Electronic (Professional & Academic); English as a Foreign Language; Environment & Development Studies; Gardening; Gender Studies; Geography & Geology; Health & Beauty; History & Antiquarian; Industry, Business & Management; Languages & Linguistics; Law; Literature & Criticism; Mathematics & Statistics; Medical (incl. Self Help & Alternative Medicine); Natural History; Philosophy; Physics; Politics & World Affairs; Psychology & Psychiatry; Reference Books, Directories & Dictionaries; Religion & Theology; Scientific & Technical; Sociology & Anthropology; Sports & Games; Vocational Training & Careers

New Titles: 721 (2009) , 1002 (2010)
No of Employees: 192

Imprints, Series & ISBNs:
Philip Allan: 978 0 86003, 978 1 84489
Arnold: 978 0 7131
Chambers: 978 0 550
Harrap: 978 0 245
Hodder & Stoughton: 978 0 340
Hodder & Stoughton Educational: 978 0 340
Hodder Arnold: 978 0 340
Hodder Gibson: 978 0 7169
Hodder Murray: 978 0 340
John Murray: 978 0 7195
Teach Yourself: 978 0 340

Parent Company:
Hodder Headline Plc/Hachette Livre

Associated Companies:
Headline Book Publishing Ltd; Hodder & Stoughton

Overseas Representation:
All other international queries: Rebecca Duprey, International Sales Manager, Hodder, London, UK
Antigua (School FE Medical Trade): The Best of Books, St John's, Antigua
Argentina (School): Kel Ediciones SA (Agents), Buenos Aires, Argentina
Australia (FE/Medical/Trade): Hachette Livre Australia, Sydney, NSW, Australia
Australia (Livewires): Cambridge University Press, Australia
Australia (School – excluding Livewires): Cengage (Australia), NSW, Australia
Bangladesh (School/FE/Medical/Trade): Ansania Mission Book Distribution House, Bangladesh
Barbados (School/FE/Medical/Trade): Julie White, Barbados
Benelux, Italy & Scandinavia (FE Medical Trade): Ben Doming, Hodder, London, UK
Cameroon (School/FE/Medical/Trade): Macmillan Publishers Cameroon Ltd, Limbe, Cameroon
Canada (FE/Medical/Trade, excluding Teach Yourself): Oxford University Press Canadian Branch, Don Mills, Ont, Canada
Canada (School – excluding Modern Languages): Bacon & Hughes Ltd, Ottawa, Ont, Canada
Canada (School – Modern Languages only): The Resource Centre, Waterloo, Canada
Canada (Teach Yourself): McGraw-Hill, Canada
Caribbean (Trade) & South America (School/FE/Medical/Trade): Humphrys Roberts Associates, London, UK
China (School/FE/Medical/Trade): Ian Taylor Associates Ltd, London, UK
Egypt (School): Macmillan Publishers Egypt Ltd, Cairo, Egypt
Ethiopia (School/FE/Medical/Trade): Etcon Ltd, Ethiopia
Europe (School): Gill Dee, International Schools Sales Manager, Hodder, London, UK
France, Spain & Portugal (FE/Medical/Trade): Anne Kelsall, Hodder, London, UK
Germany, Austria & Switzerland (School/FE/Medical/Trade): Giana Elyea, Hodder, London, UK
Ghana (School/FE/Medical/Trade): EPP Book Services Ltd, Accra, Ghana
Greece & Cyprus (FE/Medical/Trade): Zitsa Seraphimidi, J & L Watt, Paleo Faliro, Greece
Hong Kong (School/FE/Medical/Trade) & Taiwan (School): Asia Publishers Services Ltd, Hong Kong
Hong Kong (School): Pilot Publishers Services Ltd, Kowloon, Hong Kong
India (School/FE/Trade, excluding Teach Yourself): Viva Group, New Delhi, India
India (Medical): Jaypee Brothers Medical Publishers (Pte) Ltd, New Delhi, India
India (Teach Yourself): Hachette India, New Delhi, India
Iran (FE/Medical/Trade): Farhad Maftoon, Tehran, Iran
Israel (FE/Medical/Trade): Rodney Franklin Agency, Tel Aviv, Israel
Jamaica (School/FE/Medical/Trade): Kingston Bookshop, Kingston, Jamaica
Japan (School/FE/Trade): United Publishers Services Ltd, Tokyo, Japan
Japan (Medical): Nankodo Co Ltd, Tokyo, Japan
Korea (School/FE/Medical/Trade): Information & Culture Korea (ICK), Seoul, Republic of Korea
Malawi (School/FE/Medical/Trade): Bookland International, Malawi
Maldives (School/FE/Medical/Trade): Asrafee Bookshop, Maldives
Mauritius (School/FE/Medical/Trade): Editions le Printemps, Vacoas, Mauritius
Middle East (FE/Medical/Trade): James & Lorin Watt Ltd, Publishing Consultants, Oxford, UK
Middle East (School): Gill Dee, Hodder, London, UK

Namibia, Swaziland, Botswana, Lesotho & South Africa (School/FE/Medical): Macmillan South Africa Publishers (Pty) Ltd, Braamfontein, South Africa
Namibia, Swaziland, Botswana, Lesotho, South Africa & Zimbabwe (Trade): Pan Macmillan SA Pty Ltd, Hyde Park, South Africa
New Zealand (School/FE/Medical/Trade): Hachette Livre New Zealand, Auckland, New Zealand
Nigeria (School/FE/Medical/Trade): Bounty Press Ltd, Ibadan, Nigeria
Pakistan (School/FE/Medical/Trade): Andrew White, The White Partnership, Tunbridge Wells, UK
Republic of Ireland (School/FE/Medical/Trade): Vivienne Lavery, Blackrock, Co Dublin, Republic of Ireland
Scandinavia, Benelux & Eastern Europe (FE/Medical/Trade): Jacek Lewinson, Warsaw, Poland
Singapore, Indonesia, Brunei, Malaysia, Thailand & Philippines (School/FE/Medical): APD Malaysia, Malaysia; APD Singapore Pte Ltd, Singapore
Singapore, Indonesia, Brunei, Malaysia, Thailand & Philippines (Trade): Pansing Distribution Pte Ltd, Singapore
St Lucia (School FE Medical Trade): Nathaniel's Books, St Lucia
Tanzania (School/FE/Medical/Trade): Macmillan Aidan Ltd, Dar es Salaam, Tanzania
Trinidad & Tobago (School/FE/Medical/Trade): RIK Services Ltd, San Fernando, Trinidad
Turkey (Medical): Nobel Tip Kitabevlen, Turkey
Uganda (School/FE/Medical/Trade): Macmillan Uganda Ltd, Kampala, Uganda
USA (FE/Medical): Oxford University Press Inc USA, New York, NY, USA
USA (Teach Yourself): McGraw-Hill, Chicago, IL, USA
USA (Trade – excluding Teach Yourself): Trafalgar Square Publishing / IPG, Chicago, IL, USA
Zambia (School/FE/Medical/Trade): Macmillan Zambia, Lusaka, Zambia

Book Trade Association Membership:
Educational Publishers Council; International Group of Scientific, Medical & Technical Publishers

2369 ■

HODDER FAITH
338 Euston Road, London NW1 3BH
Telephone: 020 7873 6000
Fax: 020 7873 6059
Email: hodderfaith-sales@hodder.co.uk
Web Site: www.hodderfaith.com

Distribution Centre:
Bookpoint Ltd, 130 Milton Park, Abingdon,
Oxon OX14 4SB
Telephone: 01235 400400
Fax: 01235 400445

Personnel:
Wendy Grisham *(Publishing Director)*
Jean Whitnall *(Sales Director)*
Ian Metcalfe *(Publisher, Bibles & Digital Media)*

Biography & Autobiography; Children's Books; Fiction; History & Antiquarian; Humour; Religion & Theology

New Titles: 30 (2009) , 30 (2010)
No of Employees: 10

Imprints, Series & ISBNs:
Hodder & Stoughton: 978 0 340
New International Version: 978 0 340

Parent Company:
Hachette UK Ltd

Associated Companies:
Edward Arnold Ltd; Hachette Livre;
Headline Book Publishing Ltd

Overseas Representation:
Australia: Hachette Livre Australia, Sydney,
NSW, Australia
Canada (Christian trade): R. G. Mitchell
Family Books Inc, Kitchener, Ont, Canada
Canada (General trade): McArthur & Co
Publishers Ltd, Toronto, Ont, Canada
India: Hachette India, Mumbai, India
New Zealand: Hachette Livre New Zealand,
Auckland, New Zealand
Singapore: Pansing Distribution Sdn Bhd,
Singapore
Southern Africa: Jonathan Ball Publishers
(Pty) Ltd, Johannesburg, South Africa
USA: Trafalgar Square Publishing, North
Pomfret, VT, USA

Book Trade Association Membership:
Publishers Association; Booksellers
Association; ECPA

2370

HODDER GIBSON
[part of Hodder Education]
2A Christie Street, Paisley PA1 1NB
Telephone: 0141 848 1609
Fax: 0141 889 6315
Email: hoddergibson@hodder.co.uk
Web Site: www.hoddereducation.co.uk

Distribution:
Bookpoint, 130 Milton Park, Abingdon,
Oxon OX14 4SB
Telephone: 01235 400400
Fax: 01235 400454
Email: education@bookpoint.co.uk

Personnel:
John Mitchell *(Managing Director)*
Jim Donnelly *(Sales Manager)*
Katherine Bennett *(Commissioning Editor)*
Elizabeth Hayes *(Project Editor)*
Ian MacLean *(Sales Representative)*

*Academic & Scholarly; Educational &
Textbooks*

New Titles: 30 (2009) , 31 (2010)
No of Employees: 5

Imprints, Series & ISBNs:
formerly Robert Gibson & Sons: 978 0 7169
Hodder: 978 0 340

Parent Company:
Hachette UK

Book Trade Association Membership:
Publishing Scotland; Educational Publishers
Council

2371

HODDER & STOUGHTON GENERAL
338 Euston Road, London NW1 3BH
Telephone: 020 7873 6000
Fax: 020 7873 6195

Distribution Centre:
Bookpoint Ltd, 130 Milton Park, Abingdon,
Oxon OX14 4SB
Telephone: 01235 400400
Fax: 01235 400445

Personnel:
Jamie Hodder-Williams *(Managing Director)*
Lisa Highton *(Publisher)*
Lucy Hale *(Sales Director)*
Karen Geary *(Publicity Director)*
Auriol Bishop *(Creative Director)*
Helen Dance *(Chief Operating Officer)*
Carolyn Mays *(Fiction Director)*
Rowena Webb *(Non-Fiction Director)*
Rupert Lancaster *(Audio Director)*
Carole Welch *(Sceptre Director)*
Jason Bartholomew *(Subsidiary Rights)*

*Audio Books; Biography & Autobiography;
Cinema, Video, TV & Radio; Cookery, Wines
& Spirits; Crime; Fiction; History &
Antiquarian; Humour; Military & War;
Politics & World Affairs; Science Fiction;
Sports & Games*

New Titles: 400 (2009) , 400 (2010)
No of Employees: 110
Annual Turnover: £55M

Imprints, Series & ISBNs:
Hodder & Stoughton: 978 0 340
Mobius: 978 0 340
Sceptre: 978 0 340

Parent Company:
Hachette UK Ltd

Associated Companies:
Headline Book Publishing Ltd
France: Hachette Livre

Overseas Representation:
Australia: Hachette Australia, Sydney, NSW,
Australia
Canada (trade & paperbacks): Hachette
Canada, Toronto, Ont, Canada
New Zealand: Hachette New Zealand,
Auckland, New Zealand
Pakistan (paperbacks): Liberty Books (Pvt)
Ltd, Karachi, Pakistan
Singapore: Pansing Distribution Sdn Bhd,
Singapore
Southern Africa (trade): Jonathan Ball
Publishers (Pty) Ltd, Jeppestown, South
Africa

2372

ALISON HODGE PUBLISHERS
2 Clarence Place, Penzance, Cornwall
TR20 8XA
Telephone: 01736 368093
Email: info@alison-hodge.co.uk
Web Site: www.alison-hodge.co.uk

Distribution:
Tormark, Redruth, Cornwall TR16 5HY
Telephone: 01209 822101
Fax: 01209 822035
Email: sales@tormark.co.uk

Personnel:
Alison Hodge *(Publisher)*

*Biography & Autobiography; Cookery,
Wines & Spirits; Fine Art & Art History;
Gardening; Geography & Geology; Natural
History; Photography; Sports & Games;
Travel & Topography*

New Titles: 5 (2009) , 6 (2010)

Imprints, Series & ISBNs:
978 0 906720
The County Gardens Guides Inspirations
Series
Pocket Cornwall

Overseas Representation:
Europe: Bill Bailey Publishers
Representatives, Newton Abbot, UK

2373

HOLLAND PUBLISHING PLC
18 Bourne Court, Southend Road,
Woodford Green, Essex IG8 8HD
Telephone: 020 8551 7711
Fax: 020 8551 1266
Email: sales@holland-publishing.co.uk
Web Site: www.holland-publishing.co.uk

Personnel:
J. W. Holland *(Managing Director)*
Mrs S. M. Holland *(Company Secretary)*

*Children's Books; Educational & Textbooks;
Electronic (Educational); Electronic
(Entertainment)*

Imprints, Series & ISBNs:
978 1 85038
Christmas is Fun
Colouring is Fun
Creative Colouring
Doodle Design
Halloween is Fun
Learning is Fun
Little Star Creations
Phonics is Fun
Puzzle Zone

2374

HOLO BOOKS
Clarendon House, 52 Cornmarket, Oxford
OX1 3HJ
Telephone: 01865 513681
Fax: 01865 554199
Email: holobooks@yahoo.co.uk
Web Site: www.holobooks.co.uk

Orders:
Central Books, 99 Wallis Road, London
E9 5LN
Telephone: 020 8986 4854
Fax: 020 8533 5821
Email: orders@centralbooks.com
Web Site: www.centralbooks.co.uk

Personnel:
Susanna Hoe *(Partner)*
Derek Roebuck *(Partner)*
Leonie Harries *(Manager)*

*Academic & Scholarly; Archaeology;
Biography & Autobiography; Gender
Studies; Guide Books; History &
Antiquarian; Humour; Law; Travel &
Topography*

Imprints, Series & ISBNs:
The Arbitration Press
Of Islands and Women Series
The Women's History Press

Distributor for:
Hong Kong: Roundhouse Publications
(Asia)
USA: Bear Creek Books

Overseas Representation:
Hong Kong: Far East Media, Hong Kong
USA: Wm. W. Gaunt & Sons Inc, Holmes
Beach, FL, USA

2375

HONNO (WELSH WOMEN'S PRESS)
Unit 14, Creative Units,
Aberystwyth Arts Centre, Penglais Campus,
Aberystwyth, Ceredigion SY23 3GL
Telephone: 01970 623150
Fax: 01970 623150
Email: post@honno.co.uk
Web Site: www.honno.co.uk

Secretary (Honorary):
Ailsa Craig, Heol y Cawl, Dinas Powys,
Vale of Glamorgan CF6 4AH
Telephone: 029 2051 5014
Fax: 029 2051 5014
Email: (as above)
Web Site: (as above)

Personnel:
Helena Earnshaw *(Marketing Manager)*
Caroline Oakley *(Editor)*
Lesley Rice *(Production & Administration)*
Fran Lewis *(Finance)*

Biography & Autobiography; Crime; Fiction

New Titles: 10 (2009) , 11 (2010)
No of Employees: 4

Imprints, Series & ISBNs:
Honno Classic Fiction: 978 1 870206, 978 1
906784
Honno Modern Fiction: 978 1 870206, 978
1 906784

Honno Voices: 978 1 870206, 978 1
906784

Book Trade Association Membership:
Independent Publishers Guild; Union of
Welsh Booksellers & Publishers

2376

**HOPSCOTCH EDUCATIONAL
PUBLISHING**
St Jude's Church, Dulwich Road, Herne Hill,
London SE24 0PB
Telephone: 020 7738 5454
Fax: 020 7778 8317
Email: angela.s@markallengroup.com
Web Site: www.hopscotchbooks.com

Sales & Distribution:
Telephone: 01722 716935
Email: sales@hopscotchbooks.com

Personnel:
Angela Shaw *(Associate Publisher)*

Educational & Textbooks

Imprints, Series & ISBNs:
978 1 902239, 978 1 904307, 978 1
905390

Parent Company:
UK: Mark Allen Group

Book Trade Association Membership:
BESA

2377

THE HORIZON PRESS
The Oaks, Moor Farm Road West,
Ashbourne, Derbyshire DE6 1HD
Telephone: 01335 347349
Fax: 01335 347303

Trade Enquiries:
Grantham Book Services, Trent Road,
Grantham, Lincs NG31 7XQ
Telephone: 01476 541080

Trade Enquiries (alternative):
Tiptree Book Services

Personnel:
Lindsey Porter *(Managing Director)*
Chris Gilbert *(Sales & Marketing Manager)*
Stella Porter *(Office Manager)*

*Antiques & Collecting; Aviation; Guide
Books; History & Antiquarian; Nautical;
Transport; Travel & Topography*

New Titles: 20 (2009) , 20 (2010)
No of Employees: 4

Imprints, Series & ISBNs:
Landmark Collectors Library: 978 1 84306
Landmark Countryside Collection: 978 1
84306
Landmark Visitors Guides: 978 1 84306

2378

HOW TO BOOKS LTD
Spring Hill House, Spring Hill Road,
Begbroke, Oxford OX5 1RX
Telephone: 01865 375794
Fax: 01865 379162
Email: info@howtobooks.co.uk
Web Site: www.howtobooks.co.uk

Customer Services:
Grantham Book Services, Trent Road,
Grantham, Lincs NG31 7XG
Telephone: 01476 541080
Fax: 01476 541061
Email: orders@gbs.tbs-ltd.co.uk
Web Site: www.howtobooks.co.uk

Sales Representation (UK & Ireland):
Compass DSA Ltd,
13 Progress Business Centre,
Whittle Parkway, Slough SL1 6DQ
Telephone: 01628 559500
Fax: 01628 663876
Email: sales@compass-dsa.co.uk

Personnel:
Giles Lewis *(Managing Director)*
Nikki Read *(Editorial)*
Rosalind Loten *(Rights Manager & Sales)*
Bill Antrobus *(Production)*
Martin Wilkinson *(Finance)*

*Antiques & Collecting; Cookery, Wines &
Spirits; Educational & Textbooks;
Gardening; Guide Books; Industry, Business
& Management; Literature & Criticism;
Medical (incl. Self Help & Alternative
Medicine); Reference Books, Directories &
Dictionaries; Travel & Topography;
Vocational Training & Careers*

Imprints, Series & ISBNs:
How To Books: 978 1 84528, 978 1 85703,
978 1 905862
Spring Hill: 978 1 84528, 978 1 85703, 978
1 905862

Parent Company:
UK: How To Ltd

Overseas Representation:
Africa: Kelvin van Hasselt Publishing
Services, Briningham, Norfolk, UK
Australia & New Zealand: Footprint Books
Pty Ltd, Sydney, NSW, Australia
Austria, Germany & Benelux: Robbert J.
Pleysier, Heerde, Netherlands
*China, Hong Kong, Indonesia, Japan, Korea,
Philippines & Thailand:* Chris Ashdown,
Ferndown, UK
Eastern Europe & Greece: Tony Moggach,
InterMedia Americana (IMA) Ltd,
London, UK
France, Switzerland, Italy & Malta: Ted
Dougherty, Export Sales Agency, London,
UK
Latin America & West Indies: David
Williams, InterMedia Americana (IMA)
Ltd, London, UK
Malaysia & Singapore: Pansing Distribution
Pte Ltd, Singapore
Middle East & Turkey: Publishers
International Marketing, Polfages, France
South Africa: Phambili CC, Kensington,
South Africa
Spain & Portugal: Peter Prout Iberian Book
Services, Madrid, Spain
USA: Parkwest Publications Inc, Miami, FL,
USA

Book Trade Association Membership:
Independent Publishers Guild

2379 ▬▬▬▬▬▬

HUMAN KINETICS EUROPE LTD
107 Bradford Road, Stanningley, Leeds
LS28 6AT
Telephone: 0113 255 5665
Fax: 0113 255 5885
Email: hk@hkeurope.com
Web Site: www.humankinetics.com/

Personnel:
Sara Cooper *(Managing Director)*
Sian Partridge *(Sales Manager)*
Graham Wilson *(Finance Manager)*
Karen Ingram *(Customer Services Manager)*
Rory Aspell *(Marketing Manager)*
Peter Murphy *(Editorial Manager)*

*Academic & Scholarly; Educational &
Textbooks; Electronic (Educational);
Electronic (Professional & Academic);
Health & Beauty; Medical (incl. Self Help &
Alternative Medicine); Psychology &
Psychiatry; Scientific & Technical; Sports &
Games; Theatre, Drama & Dance*

New Titles: 150 (2009) , 150 (2010)
No of Employees: 16
Annual Turnover: £2.2M

Imprints, Series & ISBNs:
978 0 7360, 978 0 87322, 978 0 88011,
978 0 918438, 978 0 931250

Parent Company:
USA: Human Kinetics Inc

Associated Companies:
Australia: Human Kinetics
Canada: Human Kinetics
New Zealand: Human Kinetics

Overseas Representation:
Australia: Human Kinetics (Australia),
Torrens Park, SA, Australia
Brazil (academic): Tecmedd, São Paulo,
Brazil
Canada: Human Kinetics (Canada),
Windsor, Ont, Canada
China (including Hong Kong): AA Media
Services, Shanghai, P. R. of China
India: Disvan Enterprises, New Delhi, India
Iran: Kowkab Publishers, Tehran, Iran
Japan: Eureka Press, Kyoto, Japan
Korea: Daehan Media Co Ltd, Seoul,
Republic of Korea
New Zealand: Human Kinetics (New
Zealand), Auckland, New Zealand
Singapore & Malaysia: Icon Books
Singapore Pte Ltd, Singapore
South Africa (academic): Academic &
Professional Book Distributor,
Johannesburg, South Africa
South Africa (trade): Real Books CC,
Johannesburg, South Africa
Taiwan: Unifacmanu Trading Co Ltd, Taipei,
Taiwan
*Thailand, Indonesia, Bangladesh, Brunei &
Philippines:* Alkem Co (S) Pte Ltd,
Singapore
USA: Human Kinetics, Champaign, IL, USA

Book Trade Association Membership:
Independent Publishers Guild

2380 ▬▬▬▬▬▬

JOHN HUNT PUBLISHING LTD
c/o O Books, The Bothy, Deershot Lodge,
Park Lane, Ropley, Hants SO24 0BE
Fax: 01962 773769
Web Site: www.o-books.net

Personnel:
John Hunt *(Publisher)*
Kate Rowlandson *(Manager)*
Catherine Harris *(Sales Manager)*

*Children's Books; Fiction; Magic & the
Occult; Philosophy; Psychology &
Psychiatry; Religion & Theology*

New Titles: 110 (2009) , 200 (2010)
No of Employees: 3
Annual Turnover: £900,000

Imprints, Series & ISBNs:
Circle Books
John Hunt: 978 1 84298
O-Books: 978 1 903816
Zero Books

Overseas Representation:
Australia: Brumby Books Holdings Pty Ltd,
Kilsyth South, Vic, Australia
New Zealand: Peaceful Living Publications,
Auckland, New Zealand
Singapore: STP Distributors Pte Ltd,
Singapore
South Africa: Alternative Books CC,
Ferndale, South Africa
USA & Canada: NBN, Blue Ridge Summit,
PA, USA

Book Trade Association Membership:
Independent Publishers Guild

2381 ▬▬▬▬▬▬

C. HURST & CO (PUBLISHERS) LTD
41 Great Russell Street, London WC1B 3PL
Telephone: 020 7255 2201
Email: michael@hurstpub.co.uk
Web Site: www.hurstpub.co.uk

Distribution:
Marston Book Services, PO Box 269,
Abingdon, Oxon OX14 4YN
Telephone: 01235 465500
Fax: 01235 465555

Personnel:
Michael Dwyer *(Managing Director &
Publisher)*
Kathleen May *(Marketing Director)*
Daisy Leitch *(Managing Editor)*

*Academic & Scholarly; Gender Studies;
Military & War; Politics & World Affairs;
Religion & Theology; Sociology &
Anthropology*

Imprints, Series & ISBNs:
978 0 903983, 978 0 905838, 978 1 85065

Distributor for:
Signal Books

Overseas Representation:
Australia: UNIREPS University and Reference
Publishers' Services, Sydney, NSW,
Australia
Benelux, France & Suisse Romande:
Michael Geoghegan, London, UK
China & Hong Kong: Access Asia Media
Services, Beijing, P. R. of China
Eastern Europe: Ewa Ledóchowicz,
Konstancin-Jeziorna, Poland
Greece, Malta, Italy & Cyprus: Charles
Gibbes Associates, Louslitges, France
Japan: United Publishers Services Ltd,
Tokyo, Japan
Middle East: Avicenna Partnership, Oxford,
UK
Nordic countries: Colin Flint Ltd, Harlow, UK
Republic of Ireland: Geoff Bryan, Dublin,
Republic of Ireland
South East Asia: Horizon Books Pte Ltd,
Singapore
Southern Africa: Bacchus Books,
Johannesburg, South Africa
Spain & Portugal: Iberian Book Services,
Madrid, Spain

Book Trade Association Membership:
Independent Publishers Guild

2382 ▬▬▬▬▬▬

HYMNS ANCIENT & MODERN LTD
13–17 Long Lane, London EC1A 9PN
Telephone: 020 7776 7551
Fax: 020 7776 7556
Web Site: www.hymnsam.co.uk

Warehouse & Distribution:
Norwich Books & Music,
13a Hellesdon Park Road, Norwich, Norfolk
NR6 5DR
Telephone: 01603 785900
Fax: 01603 785915
Web Site:
www.norwichbooksandmusic.co.uk

Personnel:
Dominic Vaughan *(Group Chief Executive
Officer)*
Michael Addison *(Sales & Marketing
Director)*
Christine Smith *(Commissioning Director)*
Stephen Rogers *(Production Manager)*
Brenda Medhurst *(Financial Controller)*
Aude Pasquier *(UK Sales Manager)*
Rebecca Hills *(Rights Administrator)*
Natalie Watson *(SCM Press Commissioning
Editor)*

Academic & Scholarly; Biography &

*Autobiography; Educational & Textbooks;
Gay & Lesbian Studies; Gender Studies;
Music; Philosophy; Reference Books,
Directories & Dictionaries; Religion &
Theology; Travel & Topography*

New Titles: 120 (2009) , 120 (2010)
No of Employees: 15
Annual Turnover: £2.5M

Imprints, Series & ISBNs:
Canterbury Press, Norwich: 978 1 85311
Church House Publishing: 978 0 7151
Hymns Ancient & Modern: 978 0 907547
Religious and Moral Education Press: 978 0
900274, 978 1 85175
SCM Press: 978 0 334

Distributor for:
Acora; Cairns; Church House Publishing;
Church Publishing Inc; Churches
Together in Britain & Ireland; Concilium;
Darton, Longman & Todd; Epworth
Press; HarperCollins Religious; Joint
Liturgical Studies; RSCM; SLG Press

Overseas Representation:
Australia (Canterbury Press, Norwich):
Rainbow Books, Fairfield, Vic, Australia
*Canada (SCM Press & Canterbury Press,
Norwich):* Novalis Inc, Toronto, Ont,
Canada
*Continental Europe (Canterbury Press &
SCM Press):* Durnell Marketing Ltd,
Tunbridge Wells, UK
New Zealand (Canterbury Press, Norwich):
Church Book Stores, Auckland, New
Zealand
*Republic of Ireland (Canterbury Press & SCM
Press):* Columba Book Service, Blackrock,
Co Dublin, Republic of Ireland
South Africa (SCM Press): Pearson, South
Africa
*USA (SCM Press & Canterbury Press,
Norwich):* Westminster John Knox Press,
Louisville, KY, USA

Book Trade Association Membership:
Publishers Association; Independent
Publishers Guild

2383 ▬▬▬▬▬▬

HYPATIA PUBLICATIONS
[including Patten Press & Jamieson Library
imprints]
Trevelyan House, 16 Chapel Street,
Penzance, Cornwall TR18 4AW
Telephone: 01736 366597
Fax: 01736 333307
Email: info@hypatia-trust.org.uk
Web Site: www.hypatia-trust.org.uk

Warehouse:
Jamieson Library, Old Post Office, Newmill,
Penzance, Cornwall TR20 8XN
Telephone: 01736 360549
Email: booksales@hypatia-trust.org.uk
Web Site: www.hypatia-trust.org.uk

Personnel:
Dr Melissa Hardie *(Director)*
Dr Phil Budden *(Finance Director)*
Donna Anton *(IT Director)*
Peter Waverly *(P/A)*

*Academic & Scholarly; Bibliography &
Library Science; Biography &
Autobiography; Educational & Textbooks;
Fine Art & Art History; History &
Antiquarian; Reference Books, Directories &
Dictionaries*

New Titles: 1 (2009) , 4 (2010)
No of Employees: 3
Annual Turnover: £10,000

Imprints, Series & ISBNs:
978 1 872229

Parent Company:
UK: The Hypatia Trust

Associated Companies:
UK: Jamieson Library; Patten Press

Overseas Representation:
USA: Malcolm Summers, VT, USA

2384

ICHEME
165–189 Railway Terrace, Rugby
CV21 3HQ
Telephone: 01788 578214
Fax: 01788 560833
Email: claudia@icheme.org
Web Site: www.icheme.org

Personnel:
Claudia Flavell-While *(Publications Director)*
Jacqueline Cressey *(Marketing Manager)*

Engineering; Scientific & Technical

New Titles: 6 (2009) , 7 (2010)
No of Employees: 50
Annual Turnover: £500,000

Imprints, Series & ISBNs:
978 0 85295

Overseas Representation:
Australia & New Zealand: DA Information
Services Pty Ltd, Mitcham, Vic, Australia
USA & Canada: Princeton Selling Group Inc,
Wayne, PA, USA

2385

ICON BOOKS LTD
Omnibus Business Centre,
39–41 North Road, London N7 9DP
Telephone: 020 7700 9964
Fax: 020 7697 9501
Email: info@iconbooks.co.uk
Web Site: www.iconbooks.co.uk

Distribution:
TBS Distribution Centre, Colchester Road,
Frating Green, Colchester, Essex CO7 7DW
Telephone: 01206 255678 (UK trade) &
255644 (Export)
Fax: 01206 255930 (UK trade) & 255916
(Export)
Email: sales@tbs-ltd.co.uk & export@tbs-
ltd.co.uk

UK Rights (Icon & Wizard titles):
The Marsh Agency, 50 Albemarle Street,
London W1S 4BD
Telephone: 020 7493 4361
Fax: 020 7495 8961
Email: steph@patersonmarsh.co.uk

Sales Representation (UK):
Faber & Faber, Bloomsbury House,
74–77 Great Russell Street, London
WC1B 3DA
Telephone: 020 7465 0045
Fax: 020 7465 0034
Email: sales@faber.co.uk

Personnel:
Peter Pugh *(Chairman)*
Simon Flynn *(Managing Director)*
Duncan Heath *(Editorial Director)*
Andrew Furlow *(Sales & Marketing Director)*
Najma Finlay *(Publicity Director)*

*Academic & Scholarly; Aviation; Biography
& Autobiography; Chemistry; Children's
Books; Crime; Economics; Educational &
Textbooks; Fiction; Gender Studies;
Geography & Geology; Health & Beauty;
History & Antiquarian; Humour; Languages
& Linguistics; Literature & Criticism;
Mathematics & Statistics; Military & War;
Natural History; Philosophy; Physics;
Poetry; Politics & World Affairs; Psychology
& Psychiatry; Reference Books, Directories &
Dictionaries; Religion & Theology; Science
Fiction; Scientific & Technical; Sociology &
Anthropology; Sports & Games*

New Titles: 60 (2009) , 70 (2010)
No of Employees: 8
Annual Turnover: £2.5M

Imprints, Series & ISBNs:
978 1 84046, 978 1 84831

Associated Companies:
Wizard Books

Overseas Representation:
Australasia: Allen & Unwin Pty Ltd, Sydney,
NSW, Australia
Canada: Penguin Group Canada, Toronto,
Ont, Canada
Singapore & Malaysia: Penguin Books
Singapore, Jurong, Singapore
South Africa: Book Promotions Ltd,
Johannesburg, South Africa
USA (Rights - Icon & Wizard titles): Carol
Mann Agency, New York, NY, USA
USA (Totem Books): Consortium,
Minneapolis, MN, USA

Book Trade Association Membership:
Independent Publishers Guild

2386

**ICSA INFORMATION & TRAINING
LTD**
16 Park Crescent, London W1B 1AH
Telephone: 020 7612 7020
Fax: 020 7323 1132
Email: publishing@icsa.co.uk
Web Site: www.icsabookshop.co.uk

**Distribution, Orders, Customer Service
& Accounts:**
Marston Book Services Ltd, PO Box 269,
Abingdon, Oxon OX14 4YN
Telephone: 01235 465500
Fax: 01235 465555
Email: direct.order@marston.co.uk

Personnel:
Clare Grist Taylor *(Joint Managing Director)*
Susan Richards *(Joint Managing Director)*

Industry, Business & Management

New Titles: 15 (2009) , 15 (2010)
No of Employees: 12
Annual Turnover: £800,000

Imprints, Series & ISBNs:
978 0 902197, 978 1 85418, 978 1 86072

Book Trade Association Membership:
Independent Publishers Guild

2387

IHS BRE PRESS
Garston, Watford, Herts WD25 9XX
Telephone: 01923 664761
Fax: 01923 662477
Email: brepress@ihs.com
Web Site: www.brebookshop.com

Sales & Customer Service:
IHS BRE Press, Willoughby Road, Bracknell,
Berks RG12 8FB
Telephone: 01344 328038
Fax: 01344 328005
Email: brepress@ihs.com
Web Site: www.brebookshop.com

Personnel:
Nick Clarke *(Publisher)*

*Architecture & Design; Environment &
Development Studies; Scientific & Technical*

New Titles: 50 (2009) , 60 (2010)

Imprints, Series & ISBNs:
BRE Press: 978 1 86081
IHS BRE Press: 978 1 84806

Parent Company:
UK: IHS Global Ltd

2388

IHS JANE'S
163 Brighton Road, Coulsdon, Surrey
CR5 2YH
Telephone: 020 8700 3745
Fax: 020 8763 1006
Web Site: www.IHS.com

Personnel:
Michael Dell *(Director)*
Amanda Castle *(Public Relations)*
Sean Howe *(Publishing Director)*

*Aviation; Electronic (Professional &
Academic); Industry, Business &
Management; Military & War; Nautical;
Politics & World Affairs; Reference Books,
Directories & Dictionaries; Transport*

No of Employees: 200

Imprints, Series & ISBNs:
978 0 7106

Parent Company:
IHS

Overseas Representation:
Australia & New Zealand: IHS Jane's,
Rozelle, NSW, Australia
Egypt: IHS Jane's, Cairo, Egypt
India: IHS Jane's, New Delhi, India
*Indonesia, Korea, Malaysia, Singapore &
Taiwan:* IHS Jane's, Singapore
Japan: IHS Jane's, Japan
Kuwait & Saudi Arabia: IHS Jane's, Dubai,
UAE
North & South America: IHS Jane's,
Alexandria, VA, USA
Worldwide (excluding countries listed): IHS
Jane's, UK

Book Trade Association Membership:
Data Publishers Association

2389

THE ILEX PRESS LTD
210 High Street, Lewes, East Sussex
BN7 2NS
Telephone: 01273 487440
Fax: 01273 487441
Web Site: www.ilex-press.com

**Sales & Distribution, Trade Enquiries &
Orders:**
Trade Distribution & Accounts,
Thames & Hudson (Distributors),
44 Clockhouse Road, Farnborough, Hants
GU14 7QZ
Telephone: 01252 541602
Fax: 01252 541602
Email:
customerservices@thameshudson.co.uk

Personnel:
Alastair Campbell *(Publisher Director)*
Stephen Paul *(Managing Director)*
Peter Bridgewater *(Creative Director)*

*Crafts & Hobbies; Electronic
(Entertainment); Fine Art & Art History;
Industry, Business & Management;
Photography*

Imprints, Series & ISBNs:
978 1 904705

2390

IMMUNISATION INFORMATION
Department of Health, Skipton House,
80 London Road, London SE1 6LH
Telephone: 020 7972 3809
Fax: 020 7972 5240
Web Site: www.dh.gov.uk

*Academic & Scholarly; Educational &
Textbooks; Medical (incl. Self Help &
Alternative Medicine)*

Book Trade Association Membership:
Publishers Association

2391

IMPERIAL COLLEGE PRESS
57 Shelton Street, Covent Garden, London
WC2H 9HE
Telephone: 020 7836 3954
Fax: 020 7836 2020
Email: edit@icpress.co.uk
Web Site: www.icpress.co.uk

Trade Enquiries & Orders:
World Scientific Publishing,
57 Shelton Street, Covent Garden, London
WC2H 9HE
Telephone: 020 7836 0888
Fax: 020 7836 2020
Email: sales@wspc.co.uk
Web Site: www.wspc.co.uk

Personnel:
Prof K. K. Phua *(Chairman)*
Laurent Chaminade *(Publisher)*
Lance Sucharov *(Senior Commissioning
Editor)*
Lizzie Bennett *(Senior Editor)*

*Academic & Scholarly; Biology & Zoology;
Chemistry; Computer Science; Economics;
Electronic (Educational); Electronic
(Professional & Academic); Engineering;
Environment & Development Studies;
Industry, Business & Management;
Mathematics & Statistics; Medical (incl. Self
Help & Alternative Medicine); Physics;
Scientific & Technical*

Imprints, Series & ISBNs:
978 1 86094

Parent Company:
Singapore: World Scientific

Overseas Representation:
Hong Kong: World Scientific Publishing
(HK) Co Ltd, Hong Kong
India: World Scientific Publishing Co Pte Ltd,
Bangalore, India
Singapore: World Scientific Publishing Co
Pte Ltd, Singapore
Taiwan: World Scientific Publishing Co Pte
Ltd, Taipei, Taiwan
USA: World Scientific Publishing Co Inc,
River Edge, NJ, USA

2392

IMPRINT ACADEMIC
PO Box 200, Exeter, Devon EX5 5HY
Telephone: 01392 851550
Fax: 01392 851178
Email: sandra@imprint.co.uk
Web Site: www.imprint.co.uk

Personnel:
J. K. B. Sutherland *(Partner)*
K. A. Sutherland *(Partner)*
A. Freeman *(Managing Editor)*
S. Good *(Administrator)*
D. Hall *(Print Processor)*
A. Roppert *(Print Manager)*
J. Pomroy *(Binder)*

*Academic & Scholarly; Philosophy; Politics &
World Affairs; Psychology & Psychiatry;
Religion & Theology; Scientific & Technical;
Sociology & Anthropology*

New Titles: 120 (2009) , 100 (2010)
No of Employees: 5

Imprints, Series & ISBNs:
Idealist Studies: 978 0 907845, 978 1
84540
Imprint Art: 978 0 907845, 978 1 84540
Societas: 978 0 907845, 978 1 84540

Overseas Representation:
USA: Ingram Publisher Services Inc,

Chambersburg, PA, USA; Philosophy Documentation Center, Charlottesville, VA, USA

2393 ▬▬▬▬

IMRAY LAURIE NORIE & WILSON LTD
Wych House, The Broadway, St Ives, Huntingdon PE27 5BT
Telephone: 01480 462114
Fax: 01480 496109
Email: enquiries@ imray.com
Web Site: www.imray.com

Personnel:
William Wilson *(Managing Director)*
Mrs E. N. Wilson *(Director)*
Ian Rippington *(Sales Director)*
Mrs Emma Woodfield *(Accountant)*

Geography & Geology; Nautical; Sports & Games; Transport; Travel & Topography

New Titles: 10 (2009) , 10 (2010)
No of Employees: 23

Imprints, Series & ISBNs:
978 0 85288, 978 1 84623

Associated Companies:
Stanfords Charts

Distributor for:
Ordnance Survey; J. M. Pearson & Sons; RCC Pilotage Foundation; RYA Royal Yachting Association; United Kingdom Hydrographic Office
France: Editions du Briel; Editions Vagnon; Euromapping; Fluviacarte
Netherlands: ANWB; Hydrographic Office
Norway: Hydrographic Office
Republic of Ireland: Irish Cruising Club
UK: Clyde Cruising Club; Royal Yachting Association
USA: Cruising Guide Publications; Seaworthy Publications; University of Hawaii Press

Overseas Representation:
Australia: Boat Books (Australia) Pty Ltd, Melbourne, Vic, Australia; Boat Books (Australia) Pty Ltd, Sydney, NSW, Australia
Belgium: The Boathouse, Nieuwpoort, Belgium
France: Accastillage Diffusion, St-Martin de Crau, France; Groupe Calade Diffusion, Aix-en-Provence, France
Greece: AP Marine, Thessaloniki, Greece; Contract Yacht Services, Levkas, Greece; Lalizas, Piraeus PC, Greece; Tecrep Marine SA, Piraeus, Greece
Italy: Edizioni Il Frangente, Verona, Italy
Netherlands: Vrolijk Watersport BV, Scheveningen, Netherlands
New Zealand: Trans-Pacific Marine Ltd, Auckland, New Zealand
Republic of Ireland: Viking Marine, Dublin, Republic of Ireland
Spain: Flint Suministros SL, Barcelona, Spain
USA: Bluewater Books and Charts, Fort Lauderdale, FL, USA; Robert Hale; Seaworthy Publications Inc, Port Washington, WI, USA; Weems & Plath, Annapolis, MD, USA

Book Trade Association Membership:
International Map Trade Association

2394 ▬▬▬▬

IN EASY STEPS LTD
5C Southfield Road, Southam, Warks CV47 0FB
Telephone: 01926 817999
Fax: 01926 817005
Email: sevanti@ineasysteps.com
Web Site: www.ineasysteps.com

Distribution:
Bookpoint Ltd, 130 Milton Park, Abingdon, Oxon OX14 4SB
Telephone: 01235 400400
Fax: 01235 832068

Personnel:
Sevanti Kotecha *(Business Development Director)*
Harshad Kotecha *(Publishing Director)*

Accountancy & Taxation; Computer Science; Crafts & Hobbies; Educational & Textbooks; Electronic (Professional & Academic); Industry, Business & Management; Photography; Reference Books, Directories & Dictionaries; Scientific & Technical; Vocational Training & Careers

New Titles: 16 (2009) , 24 (2010)

Imprints, Series & ISBNs:
Complete Guides: 978 1 874029
In Easy Steps: 978 1 84078, 978 1 874029

Overseas Representation:
Australia & New Zealand: Woodslane Pty Ltd, Warriewood, NSW, Australia
South Africa: Intersoft Simon (Pty) Ltd, Johannesburg, South Africa
South East Asia: STP Distributors Pte Ltd, Singapore
USA: Publishers Group West, Berkeley, CA, USA

Book Trade Association Membership:
Independent Publishers Guild

2395 ▬▬▬▬

INCORPORATED COUNCIL OF LAW REPORTING FOR ENGLAND AND WALES
Megarry House, 119 Chancery Lane, London WC2A 1PP
Telephone: 020 7242 6471
Fax: 020 7831 5247
Email: postmaster@iclr.co.uk
Web Site: www.lawreports.co.uk

Binding Dept & Warehouse:
3 Star Yard, London WC2A 2JL
Telephone: 020 7242 8632
Fax: 020 7405 4898
Email: postmaster@iclr.co.uk
Web Site: www.lawreports.co.uk

Personnel:
Kevin Laws *(Secretary)*
Graham Chapman *(Office Manager)*
Stephen Mitchell *(Binding Manager)*
Clive Scowen *(Editor)*
Helen Yates *(Assistant to Permissions Secretary)*
Louise Carlin *(Marketing Administrator)*
Claire Honey *(Subscription Administrator)*

Law

Overseas Representation:
Australia: LBC Information Services, Rozelle, NSW, Australia
Canada: Carswell Publishing Ltd, Scarborough, Ont, Canada

2396 ▬▬▬▬

INDEPENDENT MUSIC PRESS
PO Box 69, Church Stretton, Shropshire SY6 6WZ
Telephone: 01694 720049
Email: martin@impbooks.com
Web Site: www.impbooks.com

Biography & Autobiography; Fashion & Costume; Music

New Titles: 6 (2009) , 7 (2010)

2397 ▬▬▬▬

INDEPENPRESS PUBLISHING LTD
25 Eastern Place, Brighton BN2 1GJ
Telephone: 0845 108 0530
Fax: 01273 261434
Email: info@penpress.co.uk
Web Site: www.penpress.co.uk, www.pulppress.co.uk & www.indepenpress.co.uk

Personnel:
Lynn Ashman *(Director)*
Grace Rafael *(Director)*
Kathryn Harrison *(Production Manager)*
Linda Lloyd *(Senior Editor)*
Danny Bowman *(Pulp Press Rights)*

Biography & Autobiography; Children's Books; Cookery, Wines & Spirits; Crafts & Hobbies; Crime; Do-It-Yourself; Educational & Textbooks; Fiction; Gay & Lesbian Studies; Health & Beauty; Humour; Industry, Business & Management; Literature & Criticism; Magic & the Occult; Medical (incl. Self Help & Alternative Medicine); Military & War; Music; Philosophy; Poetry; Politics & World Affairs; Reference Books, Directories & Dictionaries; Religion & Theology; Science Fiction; Sports & Games; Theatre, Drama & Dance; Travel & Topography

New Titles: 90 (2009) , 110 (2010)
No of Employees: 5

Imprints, Series & ISBNs:
978 1 900796, 978 1 904018, 978 1 904754, 978 1 905203, 978 1 906206, 978 1 906710, 978 1 907172, 978 1 907499
Indepenpress
Pen Press
Pink Press
Pulp Press

Book Trade Association Membership:
Booksellers Association; Independent Publishers Guild

2398 ▬▬▬▬

INSTANT-BOOKS UK LTD
10 Tennyson Close, Dallington, Northampton NN5 7HJ
Email: instant.books@ntlworld.com
Web Site: www.instant-books.org

Personnel:
David Brawn *(Company Secretary, Director)*
Ros Brawn *(Director)*
P. Tomlinson *(Director)*
J. Cawley *(Director)*
N. Robbins-Cherry *(Director)*
G. Robbins-Cherry *(Director)*

Atlases & Maps; Crafts & Hobbies; Environment & Development Studies; Guide Books; Travel & Topography

New Titles: 50 (2009) , 150 (2010)
No of Employees: 2

Imprints, Series & ISBNs:
Instant-Book Editions: 978 1 84834
Tour & Trail Maps: 978 1 84834
Walk! Guidebooks: 978 1 84834

2399 ▬▬▬▬

INSTITUTE FOR EMPLOYMENT STUDIES
Sovereign House, Church Street, Brighton BN1 1UJ
Telephone: 01273 763400
Fax: 01273 763401
Email: iesbooks@employment-studies.co.uk
Web Site: www.employment-studies.co.uk

Distributors:
Gardners Books Ltd, 1 Whittle Drive, Eastbourne BN23 6QH
Telephone: 01323 521555
Fax: 01323 521666
Email: sales@gardners.com
Web Site: www.gardners.com

Personnel:
Richard James *(Publications & Marketing Manager)*

Industry, Business & Management

New Titles: 20 (2009) , 20 (2010)
No of Employees: 67
Annual Turnover: £5M

Imprints, Series & ISBNs:
IES Report Series: 978 1 85184

2400 ▬▬▬▬

INSTITUTE OF ACOUSTICS
77A St Peter's Street, St Albans, Herts AL1 3BN
Telephone: 01727 848195
Fax: 01727 850553
Email: ioa@ioa.org.uk
Web Site: www.ioa.org.uk

Personnel:
Kevin Macan-Lind *(Chief Executive)*
Ian Bennett *(Editor)*
Dennis Baylis *(Advertising Manager)*

Academic & Scholarly; Scientific & Technical

No of Employees: 10
Annual Turnover: £1M

2401 ▬▬▬▬

INSTITUTE OF DEVELOPMENT STUDIES
University of Sussex, Brighton, Sussex BN1 9RE
Telephone: 01273 915637
Fax: 01273 621202
Email: bookshop@ids.ac.uk & g.edwards@ids.ac.uk (Subscription enquiries)
Web Site: www.ids.ac.uk/go/bookshop/

Personnel:
Nick Perkins *(Communications Manager)*
Alison Norwood *(Production Co-ordinator)*
Gary Edwards *(Marketing & Database Co-ordinator)*

Academic & Scholarly; Agriculture; Bibliography & Library Science; Economics; Educational & Textbooks; Environment & Development Studies; Gender Studies; Industry, Business & Management; Politics & World Affairs; Sociology & Anthropology

Imprints, Series & ISBNs:
Bridge Reports: 978 0 903715
Bulletin: 978 0 903715
Development Bibliographies: 978 0 903715
Discussion Papers: 978 0 903715
IDS Commisioned Studies: 978 0 903715
Institute of Development Studies: 978 0 903354, 978 1 85864
Research Reports: 978 0 903715
Working Papers: 978 0 903715

2402 ▬▬▬▬

INSTITUTE OF EDUCATION (PUBLICATIONS), UNIVERSITY OF LONDON
20 Bedford Way, London WC1H 0AL
Telephone: 020 7911 5383
Email: ioepublications@ioe.ac.uk
Web Site: www.ioe.ac.uk/publications

Trade Enquiries, Orders & Distribution:
Central Books Ltd, 99 Wallis Road, London E9 5LN
Telephone: 0845 458 9911

Fax: 0845 458 9912
Email: info@centralbooks.com
Web Site: www.centralbooks.com

Personnel:
Jim Collins *(Publisher)*
Dr Nicole Edmondson *(Assistant Publications Editor)*
Ms Sally Sigmund *(Marketing Manager)*

Academic & Scholarly; Educational & Textbooks; Sociology & Anthropology; Vocational Training & Careers

New Titles: 13 (2009) , 11 (2010)

Imprints, Series & ISBNs:
Bedford Way Papers (series): 978 0 85473
Inaugural Professorial Lectures (series): 978 0 85473
Issues in Practice (series): 978 0 85473
Viewpoints (series): 978 0 85473

Overseas Representation:
North America: Stylus Publishing Inc, Sterling, VA, USA

Book Trade Association Membership:
Independent Publishers Guild

2403

INSTITUTE OF EMPLOYMENT RIGHTS
50–54 Mount Pleasant, Liverpool L3 5SD
Telephone: 0151 702 6925
Fax: 0151 702 6935
Email: office@ier.org.uk
Web Site: www.ier.org.uk

Brighton Office:
Phelim MacCafferty,
Projects & Events Officer,
179 Preston Road, Brighton BN1 6AG
Telephone: 01273 330819
Email: phelim@ier.org.uk

Personnel:
Carolyn Jones *(Director)*
Treena Johnson *(Administration & Publications Officer)*
Phelim MacCafferty *(Projects & Events Officer)*

Academic & Scholarly; Economics; Law; Politics & World Affairs

New Titles: 7 (2009) , 9 (2010)
No of Employees: 3
Annual Turnover: £150,000

2404

INSTITUTE OF FOOD SCIENCE & TECHNOLOGY
5 Cambridge Court,
210 Shepherds Bush Road, London W6 7NJ
Telephone: 020 7603 6316
Fax: 020 7602 9936
Email: info@ifst.org
Web Site: www.ifst.org

Personnel:
Helen Wild *(Chief Executive)*
Angela Winchester *(Team Executive)*

Scientific & Technical

Imprints, Series & ISBNs:
978 0 905367

Book Trade Association Membership:
Association of Learned Society Publishers

2405

THE INSTITUTE OF MATHEMATICS AND ITS APPLICATIONS
Catherine Richards House,
16 Nelson Street, Southend-on-Sea, Essex SS1 1EF
Telephone: 01702 354020

Fax: 01702 354111
Email: post@ima.org.uk
Web Site: www.ima.org.uk

Personnel:
David Youdan *(Executive Director)*

Mathematics & Statistics

Imprints, Series & ISBNs:
978 0 905091

Book Trade Association Membership:
Association of Learned & Professional Society Publishers

2406

INSTITUTE OF PHYSICS & ENGINEERING IN MEDICINE
Fairmount House, 230 Tadcaster Road, York YO24 1ES
Telephone: 01904 610821
Fax: 01904 612279
Email: office@ipem.ac.uk
Web Site: www.ipem.ac.uk

Personnel:
R. W. Neilson *(General Secretary)*
M. Goodall *(Publications Co-ordinator)*

Engineering; Medical (incl. Self Help & Alternative Medicine); Physics; Scientific & Technical

Imprints, Series & ISBNs:
IPEM Report Series: 978 1 903613

Book Trade Association Membership:
Association of Learned & Professional Society Publishers

2407

INSTITUTION OF ENGINEERING AND TECHNOLOGY (IET)
Michael Faraday House, Six Hills Way, Stevenage, Herts SG1 2AY
Telephone: 01438 767328
Fax: 01438 765515
Email: books@theiet.org
Web Site: www.theiet.org

Trade Enquiries & Orders:
PO Box 96, Stevenage, Herts SG1 2SD
Telephone: 01438 767328
Fax: 01438 767375
Email: sales@theiet.org
Web Site: www.theiet.org

Warehouse:
7 Fulton Close, Argyle Way, Stevenage, Herts
Telephone: 01438 355029
Fax: 01438 355034

Personnel:
Steven Mair *(Managing Director)*
Amanda Weaver *(Publishing Director)*
Bianca Campbell *(Sales Manager)*

Academic & Scholarly; Computer Science; Educational & Textbooks; Electronic (Professional & Academic); Engineering; Industry, Business & Management; Scientific & Technical

New Titles: 20 (2009) , 16 (2010)

Imprints, Series & ISBNs:
978 0 85296, 978 0 86341, 978 0 901223, 978 0 906048, 978 1 84919

Associated Companies:
Peter Peregrinus Ltd
USA: INSPEC Inc

Overseas Representation:
Far East: Clarke Associates Ltd, Bristol, UK
USA & Canada: Princeton Selling Group Inc, Wayne, PA, USA

Book Trade Association Membership:
Booksellers Association; International Group of Scientific, Medical & Technical Publishers; Association of Learned & Professional Society Publishers

2408

INTELLECT LTD
The Mill, Parnall Road, Fishponds, Bristol BS16 3JG
Telephone: 0117 958 9910
Fax: 0117 958 9911
Email: info@intellectbooks.com
Web Site: www.intellectbooks.com/

Distribution:
Gardners Books, 1 Whittle Drive, Eastbourne BN23 6QH
Telephone: 01323 521777
Fax: 01323 521666
Email: custcare@gardners.com
Web Site: www.gardners.com

Personnel:
Masoud Yazdani *(Chairman & Editor-in-Chief)*
May Yao *(Associate Publisher)*

Academic & Scholarly; Architecture & Design; Cinema, Video, TV & Radio; Computer Science; Educational & Textbooks; Electronic (Educational); Electronic (Professional & Academic); Environment & Development Studies; Gender Studies; History & Antiquarian; Languages & Linguistics; Literature & Criticism; Philosophy; Scientific & Technical; Sociology & Anthropology; Theatre, Drama & Dance

Imprints, Series & ISBNs:
978 0 89391, 978 1 56750, 978 1 84150, 978 1 871516
Advances in Art & Urban Futures
Advances in Human Computer Interaction
Bahá'í Books (series)
Changing Media, Changing Europe (series)
Computer and the History of Art (series)
Decode Books (series)
ECREA (series)
Elm Bank Publications
European Studies Series
Intellect Play Series
Progress in Neural Networks
Readings in Art and Design Education (series)
Studies in Popular Culture (series)
Theatre & Consciousness (series)
Trends in Functional Programming
Venton

Overseas Representation:
Australasia: Inbooks, Sydney, NSW, Australia
North America: University of Chicago Press, Chicago, IL, USA
Singapore: Book Editions, Singapore

Book Trade Association Membership:
Independent Publishers Guild

2409

INTERNATIONAL MEDICAL PRESS
36 St Mary at Hill, London EC3R 8DU
Telephone: 020 7398 0700
Fax: 020 7398 0701
Email: info@intmedpress.com
Web Site: www.intmedpress.com

Academic & Scholarly; Electronic (Professional & Academic); Medical (incl. Self Help & Alternative Medicine)

Imprints, Series & ISBNs:
978 1 901769

Book Trade Association Membership:
Publishers Association

2410

INTERNATIONAL NETWORK FOR THE AVAILABILITY OF SCIENTIFIC PUBLICATIONS (INASP)
58 St Aldates, Oxford OX1 1ST
Telephone: 01865 249909
Fax: 01865 251060
Email: inasp@inasp.info
Web Site: www.inasp.info/

Personnel:
Tag McEntegart *(Executive Director)*
Julie Walker *(Head of Publishing Support Senior Programme)*
Sioux Cumming *(Publishing Support Programme Officer)*

Academic & Scholarly; Bibliography & Library Science; Educational & Textbooks; Electronic (Professional & Academic); Reference Books, Directories & Dictionaries

New Titles: 30 (2009)

Imprints, Series & ISBNs:
978 1 902928

Book Trade Association Membership:
Association of Learned & Professional Society Publishers

2411

IOP PUBLISHING
Dirac House, Temple Back, Bristol BS1 6BE
Telephone: 0117 929 7481
Fax: 0117 929 4318
Email: custserv@iop.org
Web Site: www.iop.org

Personnel:
Jerry Cowhig *(Managing Director)*
Michael Bray *(Financial Director)*
Karen O'Flaherty *(Group Human Resources Director)*
Nicola Gulley *(Editorial Director)*
James Walker *(Group IT Director)*

Computer Science; Electronic (Professional & Academic); Mathematics & Statistics; Physics; Scientific & Technical

New Titles: 6 (2009) , 3 (2010)
No of Employees: 250
Annual Turnover: £37.8M

Parent Company:
The Institute of Physics

Associated Companies:
USA: IOP Publishing Inc

Overseas Representation:
Japan (books): Eastern Book Service Inc, Tokyo, Japan
Japan (journals): Maruzen Co Ltd, Tokyo, Japan
Other Territories (books): Enquiries, Institute of Physics Publishing, Bristol, UK
Pakistan (books): Pak Book Corporation, Lahore, Pakistan
South East Asia, New Zealand & Australia (books): Hemisphere Publication Services, Singapore
USA & Canada (books): IOP Publishing, Williston, VT, USA
USA, Canada & Mexico (journals): American Institute of Physics, Melville, NY, USA

Book Trade Association Membership:
International Group of Scientific, Medical & Technical Publishers; Association of Learned & Professional Society Publishers

2412

IRISH ACADEMIC PRESS
2 Brookside, Dundrum Road, Dublin 14, Republic of Ireland
Telephone: 00353 1 298 9937

Fax: 00353 1 298 2783
Email: info@iap.ie
Web Site: www.iap.ie

*Academic & Scholarly; Biography &
Autobiography; Gender Studies; History &
Antiquarian; Literature & Criticism; Military
& War; Politics & World Affairs; Religion &
Theology; Sociology & Anthropology;
Theatre, Drama & Dance*

Imprints, Series & ISBNs:
978 0 7165

Book Trade Association Membership:
Publishing Ireland (Foilsiú Éireann)

2413

IRWELL PRESS LTD
59A High Street, Clophill, Beds MK45 4BE
Telephone: 01525 861888
Fax: 01525 862044
Email: George@irwellpress.co.uk
Web Site: www.irwellpress.co.uk

Personnel:
George Reeve *(Director)*
Chris Hawkins *(Director)*

Transport

New Titles: 12 (2009) , 12 (2010)
No of Employees: 1

Imprints, Series & ISBNs:
978 1 871608, 978 1 903266, 978 1
906919

Overseas Representation:
Australia: Train World Property, East
Brighton, Vic, Australia

2414

ISIS PUBLISHING LTD
Unit 7, Centremead, Osney Mead, Oxford
OX2 0ES
Telephone: 01865 250333
Fax: 01865 790358
Email: pauline.horne@isis-publishing.co.uk
Web Site: www.isis-publishing.co.uk

Distribution:
Ulverscroft Large Print Books Ltd,
The Green, Bradgate Road, Anstey,
Leicester LE7 7FU
Telephone: 0116 236 4325
Fax: 0116 234 0205
Email: sales@ulverscroft.co.uk
Web Site: www.ulverscroft.co.uk

Personnel:
Robert Thirlby *(Chief Executive Director)*
Pauline Horne *(Distribution, General, Sales
& Marketing Manager)*
Lorna Dubose *(Finance Manager)*
Becky Curtis *(Editorial – General Books
Manager)*
Catherine Thompson *(Studio/Post
Production Manager)*

*Audio Books; Biography & Autobiography;
Crime; Crime; Fiction; Humour; Military &
War; Poetry; Science Fiction*

Imprints, Series & ISBNs:
978 0 7531, 978 1 4450, 978 1 84559, 978
1 85089, 978 1 85695

Parent Company:
Ulverscroft Group Ltd

Overseas Representation:
Australia: Ulverscroft Large Print Books
(Australia) Pty Ltd, Crows Nest, NSW,
Australia
Canada: Stricker Books, Toronto, Ont,
Canada
Denmark: Bierman & Bierman A/S,
Grindsted, Denmark
Japan: PIC, Tokyo, Japan

New Zealand: Ulverscroft Large Print Books
Ltd, Fielding, New Zealand
Norway: Lydlitteratur, Nesoya, Norway
Republic of Ireland: Ulverscroft Large Print
Books Ltd, Dublin, Republic of Ireland
South Africa (Audio): Book Talk Pty Ltd,
Parkhurst, South Africa
Sweden: Bibliotekstjanst AB, Lund, Sweden
USA (Audio & Large print): Ulverscroft
Large Print Books (USA) Inc, West
Seneca, NY, USA

2415

THE ISLAMIC TEXTS SOCIETY
Miller's House, Kings Mill Lane,
Great Shelford, Cambridge CB22 5EN
Telephone: 01223 842425
Fax: 01223 842425
Email: mail@its.org.uk
Web Site: www.its.org.uk

Distribution:
Orca Book Services Ltd, Unit A3,
Fleets Corner, Poole, Dorset BH17 0HL
Telephone: 01202 665432
Fax: 01202 666219
Email: orders@orcabookservices.co.uk

Personnel:
Fatima Azzam *(Trust Secretary)*

*Academic & Scholarly; Law; Religion &
Theology*

Imprints, Series & ISBNs:
Al-Ghazali Series
Fundamental Rights & Liberties Series:
Principles & Applications: 978 0 946621,
978 1 903682

Overseas Representation:
USA: Independent Publishers Group (IPG),
Chicago, IL, USA

Book Trade Association Membership:
Publishers Association

2416

*ISTE LTD
6 Fitzroy Square, London W1T 5DX
Telephone: 020 7387 7333
Fax: 020 7380 1051
Email: info@iste.co.uk
Web Site: www.iste.co.uk

Book Trade Association Membership:
Publishers Association

2417

ITHACA PRESS
[Books on The Middle East]
8 Southern Court, South Street, Reading
RG1 4QS
Telephone: 0118 959 7847
Fax: 0118 959 7356 *(Trade Enquiries &
Orders)*
Email: dan@garnetpublishing.co.uk
Web Site: www.garnetpublishing.co.uk

Representation (UK):
Compass Academic,
The Barley Mow Centre,
10 Barley Mow Passage, Chiswick, London
W4 4PH
Telephone: 020 8994 6477

Personnel:
Khalil Abu Shawareb *(Managing Director)*
Dan Nunn *(Editorial, Rights & Permissions
Manager)*
Nick Holroyd *(Production Controller)*

*Academic & Scholarly; Economics; Fiction;
Gender Studies; History & Antiquarian;
Languages & Linguistics; Law; Literature &
Criticism; Politics & World Affairs; Religion
& Theology; Sociology & Anthropology*

Imprints, Series & ISBNs:
978 0 86372, 978 0 903729

Parent Company:
Garnet Publishing Ltd

Overseas Representation:
Australia: InBooks, Frenchs Forest, NSW,
Australia
Europe: Andrew Durnell Marketing Ltd,
Tunbridge Wells, UK
USA (academic): International Specialized
Book Services Inc, Portland, OR, USA
USA (trade): International Publishers
Marketing Inc, Sterling, VA, USA

Book Trade Association Membership:
Independent Publishers Guild

2418

IVP
IVP Book Centre, Norton Street,
Nottingham NG7 3HR
Telephone: 0115 978 1054
Fax: 0115 942 2694
Email: ivp@ivpbooks.com
Web Site: www.ivpbooks.com

Personnel:
Brian Wilson *(Chief Executive Officer)*
George Russell *(Finance & Operations)*

*Academic & Scholarly; Reference Books,
Directories & Dictionaries; Religion &
Theology*

Imprints, Series & ISBNs:
Apollos: 978 0 85110, 978 0 85111, 978 1
84474
Crossway Books: 978 0 85684
IVP: 978 0 85110, 978 0 85111, 978 1
84474

Distributor for:
Bible Society; Christian Medical Fellowship;
Dorling Kindersley Religious; Eagle
Publishing; Good Book Company;
Piquant
Australia: Matthias Media; Youthworks
USA: Crossway Books; IVP

Overseas Representation:
East Africa: Keswick Book Society, Nairobi,
Kenya
Netherlands: ASAF Import 3, Westervoort,
Netherlands
New Zealand: Soul Distributors, Auckland,
New Zealand
Philippines: Evangelical Outreach Inc,
Quezon City, Philippines; Overseas
Missionary Fellowship, Manila,
Philippines
Singapore: Bethesda Book Centre,
Singapore
South Africa: Protestant Book Centre, Cape
Town, South Africa
Sweden: Din Bok -
Formsamlingsbokhandeln, Goteborg,
Sweden
USA: InterVarsity Press, Downers Grove, IL,
USA

Book Trade Association Membership:
Christian Suppliers' Group; Evangelical
Christian Publishers Association

2419

IWA PUBLISHING
Alliance House, 12 Caxton Street, London
SW1H 0QS
Telephone: 020 7654 5500
Fax: 020 7654 5555
Email: publications@iwap.co.uk
Web Site: www.iwapublishing.com

Orders:
Portland Customer Services,
Commerce Way, Whitehall Industrial Estate,
Colchester CO2 8HP
Telephone: 01206 796351

Fax: 01206 799331
Email: sales@portland-services.com

Personnel:
Michael Dunn *(Publisher, Managing
Director & Commissioning Editor)*
Michelle Jones *(Publications Manager)*
Ian Morgan *(Marketing Manager)*
David Burns *(Digital Marketing & Sales
Executive)*

*Academic & Scholarly; Electronic
(Professional & Academic); Engineering;
Industry, Business & Management;
Reference Books, Directories &
Dictionaries; Scientific & Technical*

Imprints, Series & ISBNs:
978 1 84339, 978 1 900222

Parent Company:
International Water Association

Overseas Representation:
Australia & New Zealand: Australian Water
Association, Artarmon, NSW, Australia;
DA Information Services Pty Ltd,
Mitcham, Vic, Australia
India: Ravindra Saxena, Sara Books Pvt Ltd,
New Delhi, India
Japan: Kay Kato Associates, Kanagawa,
Japan
Malaysia: Tony Poh, STM Publisher Services
Pte Ltd, Singapore
North America: Martin P. Hill Consulting,
New York, NY, USA
Taiwan: Ta Tong Book Co Ltd, Taipei, Taiwan

Book Trade Association Membership:
Association of Learned & Professional
Society Publishers

2420

JAMES & JAMES (PUBLISHERS) LTD
[an imprint of Third Millennium Information
Group]
2–5 Benjamin Street, London EC1M 5QL
Telephone: 020 7336 0144
Fax: 020 7608 1188
Email: mj@tmiltd.com
Web Site: www.tmiltd.com

Personnel:
Hamish MacGibbon *(Chairman)*

*Academic & Scholarly; History &
Antiquarian; Industry, Business &
Management*

New Titles: 20 (2010)

Imprints, Series & ISBNs:
978 0 907383

Parent Company:
Third Millennium Information Ltd

2421

JANUS PUBLISHING CO LTD
105–107 Gloucester Place, London
W1U 6BY
Telephone: 020 7486 6633
Fax: 020 7486 6090
Email: publisher@januspublishing.co.uk
Web Site: www.januspublishing.co.uk

Distribution/Sales:
25 Winnock Road, Colchester, Essex
CO1 2BG
Telephone: 01206 578856
Fax: 01206 573221
Email: sales@januspublishing.co.uk
Web Site: www.januspublishing.co.uk

Personnel:
Jeannie Leung *(Managing, Rights &
Permissions Director)*
Tina Brand *(Sales Director)*

Academic & Scholarly; Biography &

Autobiography; Children's Books; Crime; Do-It-Yourself; Economics; Educational & Textbooks; Fiction; Fine Art & Art History; History & Antiquarian; Humour; Literature & Criticism; Magic & the Occult; Medical (incl. Self Help & Alternative Medicine); Military & War; Nautical; Philosophy; Poetry; Politics & World Affairs; Religion & Theology; Science Fiction; Sociology & Anthropology; Sports & Games; Theatre, Drama & Dance

New Titles: 20 (2009) , 20 (2010)
No of Employees: 5
Annual Turnover: £120,000

Imprints, Series & ISBNs:
Empiricus Books: 978 1 902835
Janus Books: 978 1 85756

Parent Company:
Junction Books Ltd

Overseas Representation:
Malaysia, Singapore & Brunei: Proof Line (M) Sdn Bhd, Petaling Jaya, Malaysia
South Africa: Vuga Booksellers, Durban, South Africa
USA & Canada: IPG, Concord, MA, USA

Book Trade Association Membership:
Booksellers Association; Independent Publishers Guild

2422 ▬▬▬

JARNDYCE BOOKSELLERS
46 Great Russell Street, London WC1B 3PA
Telephone: 020 7631 4220
Fax: 020 7631 1882
Email: books@jarndyce.co.uk
Web Site: www.jarndyce.co.uk

Personnel:
Brian Lake *(Partner)*
Janet Nassau *(Partner)*

Academic & Scholarly; Bibliography & Library Science; Economics; Fiction; Languages & Linguistics; Literature & Criticism; Poetry; Reference Books, Directories & Dictionaries; Sociology & Anthropology

Imprints, Series & ISBNs:
978 1 900718

Book Trade Association Membership:
Antiquarian Booksellers' Association; Provincial Booksellers' Fairs Association

2423 ▬▬▬

JOLLY LEARNING LTD
Tailours House, High Road, Chigwell, Essex IG7 6DL
Telephone: 020 8501 0405
Fax: 020 8500 1696
Email: chris@jollylearning.co.uk
Web Site: www.jollylearning.co.uk

Personnel:
Christopher Jolly *(Managing Director)*
Diane Harding *(Accounts Manager)*
Androula Stratton *(Marketing Manager)*
Angela Hockley *(Editorial Manager)*

Educational & Textbooks; Electronic (Educational)

New Titles: 15 (2009) , 15 (2010)
No of Employees: 10
Annual Turnover: £2.7M

Imprints, Series & ISBNs:
978 1 84414, 978 1 870946, 978 1 903619

Overseas Representation:
USA: Jolly Learning Ltd, c/o American International Distribution Corporation, Williston, VT, USA

Book Trade Association Membership:
Independent Publishers Guild

2424 ▬▬▬

JONES & BARTLETT INTERNATIONAL
The Exchange, Express Park, Bristol Road, Bridgwater TA6 4RR W6 7PA
Telephone: 01278 427800
Fax: 01278 421077
Email: ldowning@jblearning.com
Web Site: www.jblearning.com

Warehouse, Trade Enquiries & Orders:
Macmillan Distribution (MDL), Brunel Road, Houndmills, Basingstoke RG21 6XS
Telephone: 01256 329242
Fax: 01256 331413
Email: mdl@macmillan.co.uk
Web Site: www.macmillan-mdl.co.uk

Personnel:
Richard Warner *(Managing Director)*
Lorna Downing *(European Manager)*
Chris Gribble *(Sales Manager)*
Sarah Burne *(Operations Manager)*

Biology & Zoology; Chemistry; Computer Science; Educational & Textbooks; Geography & Geology; Law; Mathematics & Statistics; Medical (incl. Self Help & Alternative Medicine); Physics; Psychology & Psychiatry; Scientific & Technical; Sports & Games; Vocational Training & Careers

Imprints, Series & ISBNs:
978 0 7637, 978 0 86729

Parent Company:
USA: Jones & Bartlett Inc

2425 ▬▬▬

JORDAN PUBLISHING LTD
21 St Thomas Street, Bristol BS1 6JS
Telephone: 0117 918 1530
Fax: 0117 925 0486
Web Site: www.jordanpublishing.co.uk

Personnel:
Caroline Vandridge-Ames *(Managing Director)*
Ann-Marie Vowles *(Head of Marketing & Sales)*
Achim Bosse *(Editorial Manager)*

Accountancy & Taxation; Crime; Electronic (Professional & Academic); Industry, Business & Management; Law

Imprints, Series & ISBNs:
Family Law: 978 0 85308, 978 1 84661
Jordans: 978 0 85308, 978 1 84661

Parent Company:
West of England Trust

2426 ▬▬▬

RICHARD JOSEPH PUBLISHERS LTD
PO Box 15, Torrington, Devon EX38 8ZJ
Telephone: 01805 625750
Fax: 01805 625376
Email: office@sheppardsworld.co.uk
Web Site: www.sheppardsworld.co.uk

Personnel:
Richard Joseph *(Managing Director)* (to be appointed) *(Compiler)*
Claire Hudson *(Production Manager)*

Reference Books, Directories & Dictionaries

Imprints, Series & ISBNs:
Sheppard: 978 1 872699

2427 ▬▬▬

S. KARGER AG
c/o London Liaison Office, 4 Rickett Street, London SW6 1RU

Telephone: 020 7386 0500
Fax: 020 7610 3337
Email: uk@karger.ch
Web Site: www.karger.com

Personnel:
Dr Thomas Karger *(President)*
Gabriella Karger *(Chief Executive Officer)*
Ralph Weil *(Chief Executive Officer)*
Rolf Zurlinden *(Finance)*
Moritz Thommen *(Sales & Marketing)*
Hermann Vonlanthen *(Production)*
Thomas Nold *(Editorial & Rights)*

Mathematics & Statistics; Medical (incl. Self Help & Alternative Medicine); Psychology & Psychiatry

New Titles: 150 (2009) , 150 (2010)
No of Employees: 300

Imprints, Series & ISBNs:
978 3 8055

Parent Company:
Switzerland: S. Karger AG

Overseas Representation:
Australia: DA Information Services Pty Ltd, Mitcham, Vic, Australia
Baltic States: Bookshop Krisostomus, Tartu, Estonia
China, Taiwan: Karger China, Shanghai, P. R. of China
France: Librairie Médi-Sciences SARL, Paris, France
Germany: S. Karger GmbH, Freiburg, Germany
Gulf Council countries, Iran, Middle East, North Africa & Turkey: Trans Middle East International Distribution Co Ltd, Amman, Jordan
India, Bangladesh & Sri Lanka: Medscience India, New Delhi, India; Panther Publishers Pvt Ltd, Bangalore, India
Japan: Karger Japan Inc, Tokyo, Japan
Pakistan: Tahir M. Lodhi, Lahore, Pakistan
Republic of Ireland: S. Karger AG, London, UK
Singapore: APAC Publishers Services Pte Ltd, Singapore
South & Central America: Cranbury International LLC, Montpelier, VT, USA
South Africa: Academic Marketing Services (Pty) Ltd, Craighall, South Africa
South East Asia: Karger Regional Office, Kuala Lumpur, Malaysia
Switzerland (Head Office): S. Karger AG, Basel, Switzerland
Thailand: Karger Libri International Subscription Agency, Bangkok, Thailand
USA: S. Karger Publishers Inc, Unionville, USA

2428 ▬▬▬

KARNAC BOOKS LTD
118 Finchley Road, London NW3 5HT
Telephone: 020 7431 1075
Fax: 020 7435 9076
Email: shop@karnacbooks.com
Web Site: www.karnacbooks.com

Personnel:
Oliver Rathbone *(Managing Director)*
Alex Massey *(Sales Director)*

Gender Studies; Psychology & Psychiatry

New Titles: 78 (2009) , 100 (2010)
No of Employees: 10

Imprints, Series & ISBNs:
Clunie Press: 978 0 946439, 978 1 85575
Harris Meltzer Trust: 978 1 85575
Institute of Psycho-Analysis, London: 978 0 946439, 978 1 85575
International Psychoanalytical Association: 978 1 85575
Karnac Books: 978 0 946439, 978 1 85575
Library of Analytical Psychology: 978 0 946439, 978 1 85575

Maresfield Library: 978 0 946439, 978 1 85575
Systemic Thinking Theory & Practice Series: 978 0 946439, 978 1 85575
Tavistock Clinic Series: 978 1 85575
Tavistock Institute of Marital Studies (TIMS): 978 0 946439, 978 1 85575
UKCP Series: 978 1 85575
Winnicott Studies (Series): 978 0 946439, 978 1 85575

Distributor for:
Apex One; Carl Auer International; Rebus Press; Tavistock Institute of Marital Studies; Zeig Tucker & Co

Book Trade Association Membership:
Booksellers Association; Independent Publishers Guild

2429 ▬▬▬

KENYON-DEANE
10 Station Road Industrial Estate, Colwall, Malvern, Worcs WR13 6RN
Telephone: 01684 540154
Fax: 01684 540154
Email: simon@cressrelles.co.uk
Web Site: www.cressrelles.co.uk

Personnel:
Leslie Smith *(Finance, Production, Editorial & Rights Manager)*
Simon Smith *(Sales & Marketing Manager)*

Theatre, Drama & Dance

Imprints, Series & ISBNs:
978 0 7155

Parent Company:
Cressrelles Publishing Co Ltd

Distributor for:
USA: Anchorage Press

Overseas Representation:
Australia: Origin Theatrical, Sydney, NSW, Australia
New Zealand: Play Bureau of New Zealand Ltd, New Plymouth, New Zealand
Republic of Ireland: Drama League of Ireland, Dublin, Republic of Ireland
South Africa: Dalro (Pty) Ltd, Braamfontein, South Africa
USA: Bakers Plays, Quincy, MA, USA

2430 ▬▬▬

KEW PUBLISHING
[Royal Botanic Gardens, Kew]
Herbarium, 3rd Floor Wing E,
Royal Botanic Gardens, Kew, Richmond, Surrey TW9 3AE
Telephone: 020 8332 5751 & 5776 (trade enquiries)
Fax: 020 8332 5646
Email: publishing@kew.org & kewbooks@kew.org
Web Site: www.kew.org & www.kewbooks.com

Personnel:
Gina Fullerlove *(Head of Publishing)*
John Harris *(Sales, Marketing & Business Development)*
Lloyd Kirton *(Production Controller)*
Lydia White *(Publishing Assistant)*

Academic & Scholarly; Biology & Zoology; Fine Art & Art History; Gardening; Scientific & Technical

New Titles: 20 (2009) , 28 (2010)
No of Employees: 10
Annual Turnover: £500,000

Imprints, Series & ISBNs:
978 1 84246

Parent Company:
UK: Royal Botanic Gardens, Kew

Overseas Representation:
All territories (excluding USA, Canada & Mexico): Marston Book Services Ltd, Abingdon, Oxon, UK
USA, Canada & Mexico: University of Chicago Press, Chicago, IL, USA

Book Trade Association Membership:
Independent Publishers Guild

2431

HILDA KING EDUCATIONAL
Ashwells Manor Drive, Penn, Bucks HP10 8EU
Telephone: 01494 813947 & 817947
Fax: 01494 813947
Email: rkinged@aol.com
Web Site: www.hildaking.co.uk

Personnel:
Hilda King *(Director)*
R. E. King *(Executive)*

Educational & Textbooks

Imprints, Series & ISBNs:
978 1 873533

2432

LAURENCE KING PUBLISHING LTD
361–373 City Road, London EC1V 1LR
Telephone: 020 7841 6900
Fax: 020 7841 6939
Email: enquiries@laurenceking.com
Web Site: www.laurenceking.com

Personnel:
Nick Perren *(Chairman)*
Laurence King *(Managing Director)*
John Stoddart *(Financial Director)*
Felicity Awdry *(Production Director)*
Philip Cooper *(Editorial Director)*
Kara Hattersley-Smith *(Editorial – College & Fine Art Director)*
Janet Pilch *(Rights Manager)*
Lewis Gill *(Marketing Manager)*
Simon Gwynn *(Sales Manager)*

Architecture & Design; Fashion & Costume; Fine Art & Art History

Imprints, Series & ISBNs:
Portfolio (series)
Portfolio Skills (series)

Book Trade Association Membership:
Publishers Association

2433

THE KING'S ENGLAND PRESS
Cambertown House, Commercial Road, Goldthorpe, Rotherham S63 9BL
Telephone: 01484 663790
Fax: 01484 663790
Email: steve@kingsengland.com
Web Site: www.kingsengland.com & www.pottypoets.com

Personnel:
Steve Rudd *(Managing Director)*
Debbie Nunn *(Company Secretary)*

Archaeology; Children's Books; History & Antiquarian; Poetry; Travel & Topography

New Titles: 2 (2009) , 4 (2010)
No of Employees: 2

Imprints, Series & ISBNs:
978 1 872438

2434

JESSICA KINGSLEY PUBLISHERS
116 Pentonville Road, London N1 9JB
Telephone: 020 7833 2307
Fax: 020 7837 2917
Email: post@jkp.com
Web Site: www.jkp.com

Trade Enquiries & Orders:
Macmillan Distribution (MDL), Brunel Road, Houndmills, Basingstoke, Hants RG21 6XS
Telephone: 01256 302985
Fax: 01256 841426
Email: trade@macmillan.co.uk
Web Site: www.macmillandistribution.co.uk

Personnel:
Jessica Kingsley *(Managing Director)*
Dee Brigham *(Finance)*
Helen Longmate *(Marketing and Sales Director & Rights Manager)*
Jemima Kingsley *(Electronic Media)*
Despina Pechlivanidis *(Sales Manager)*
Octavia Kingsley *(Production Manager)*

Academic & Scholarly; Children's Books; Educational & Textbooks; Health & Beauty; Law; Medical (incl. Self Help & Alternative Medicine); Psychology & Psychiatry; Religion & Theology; Sociology & Anthropology; Sports & Games; Vocational Training & Careers

Imprints, Series & ISBNs:
Children in Charge: 978 1 85302
Community, Culture and Change: 978 1 84310
Forensic Focus: 978 1 85302
Jessica Kingsley Publishers: 978 1 84310, 978 1 85302
Research Highlights in Social Work: 978 1 85302
Singing Dragon: 978 1 84819

Associated Companies:
USA: Jessica Kingsley Publishers Inc

Overseas Representation:
Australia & New Zealand: Footprint Books Pty, Warriewood, NSW, Australia
Canada: UBC Press, Toronto, Ontario, Canada
Europe: Durnell Marketing Ltd, Tunbridge Wells, UK
Hong Kong, Taiwan, China, Philippines & Korea: Asia Publishers Services Ltd, Hong Kong
Japan: United Publishers Services Ltd, Aberdeen, Hong Kong
USA: Jessica Kingsley Publishers Inc, Philadelphia, USA

Book Trade Association Membership:
Publishers Association; Educational Publishers Council

2435

SEAN KINGSTON PUBLISHING
57 Orchard Way, Wantage, Oxon OX12 8ED
Telephone: 01235 770787
Email: mail@seankingston.co.uk
Web Site: www.seankingston.co.uk/publishing.html

Personnel:
Dr Sean Kingston *(Publisher)*

Academic & Scholarly; Sociology & Anthropology

New Titles: 3 (2009) , 7 (2010)
No of Employees: 2

Imprints, Series & ISBNs:
978 0 9545572, 978 0 9556400, 978 1 907774

2436

KNOW THE SCORE BOOKS
118 Alcester Road, Studley, Warwickshire B80 7NT
Telephone: 01527 454482
Fax: 01527 452183
Email: info@knowthescorebooks.com
Web Site: www.knowthescorebooks.com

Warehouse:
Frating Green, Colchester, Essex CO7 7DW
Telephone: 01206 255678
Fax: 01206 255930
Email: sales@tbs-ltd.co.uk

Personnel:
Simon Lowe *(Managing Director)*
Tony Lyons *(Marketing Manager)*

Sports & Games; Travel & Topography

Imprints, Series & ISBNs:
978 1 84818, 978 1 905449

Book Trade Association Membership:
Independent Publishers Guild

2437

KOGAN PAGE LTD
120 Pentonville Road, London N1 9JN
Telephone: 020 7278 0433
Fax: 020 7837 6348
Email: kpinfo@koganpage.com
Web Site: www.koganpage.com

Warehouse:
Littlehampton Book Services, Faraday Close, Durrington, Worthing, West Sussex BN13 3RB
Telephone: 01903 828800
Fax: 01903 828802

Personnel:
Philip Kogan *(Chairman)*
Helen Kogan *(Managing Director)*
Mark Briars *(Financial Director)*
Martin Klopstock *(Publishing Services Director)*
Ben Glover *(Sales Director)*
Cathy Frazer *(Marketing Director)*

Academic & Scholarly; Accountancy & Taxation; Educational & Textbooks; Electronic (Educational); Electronic (Professional & Academic); Industry, Business & Management; Reference Books, Directories & Dictionaries; Transport; Vocational Training & Careers

New Titles: 150 (2009) , 150 (2010)
No of Employees: 35

Imprints, Series & ISBNs:
978 0 7494

Distributor for:
Bloomberg Press (excluding Americas); GMB Publishing

Overseas Representation:
Australia & New Zealand: Woodslane Pty Ltd, Warriewood, NSW, Australia
Burma, China, Vietnam, Hong Kong, Taiwan, Middle East & Thailand: Publishers International Marketing, London, UK
Canada: Renouf Publishing Co Ltd, Ottawa, Ont, Canada
Caribbean: InterMedia Americana (IMA) Ltd, London, UK
India: Viva Books, New Delhi, India
Singapore, Malaysia & Brunei: Penguin Books Singapore, Jurong, Singapore
South Africa: Book Promotions Pty Ltd, Diep River, South Africa
USA: Ingram Publisher Services, La Vergne, TN, USA

Book Trade Association Membership:
Publishers Association; Data Publishers Association

2438

KUBE PUBLISHING LTD
Ratby Lane, Markfield, Leicester LE67 9SY
Telephone: 01530 249230
Fax: 01530 249656
Email: info@kubepublishing.com
Web Site: www.kubepublishing.com

Personnel:
Haris Ahmad *(Director)*
Anwar Cara *(Production Executive)*
Khalid Manzoor *(Distribution & Sales Executive)*
Miss Rufeedah Cara *(Administration)*
Yahya Birt *(Commissioning Editor)*

Academic & Scholarly; Audio Books; Children's Books; Economics; Educational & Textbooks; Law; Religion & Theology

Imprints, Series & ISBNs:
Islamic Foundation: 978 0 86037
Kube: 978 1 84774
Revival: 978 0 9536768

Distributor for:
Pakistan: Institute of Policy Studies; Islamic Book Publishers
USA: Foundation for Islamic Knowledge; Institute of Islamic Thought

Overseas Representation:
USA & Canada: Consortium Sales & Distribution, Minneapolis, MN, USA

2439

KYLE CATHIE LTD
23 Howland Street, London W1T 4AY
Telephone: 020 7692 7215
Fax: 020 7692 7260
Email: general.enquiries@kyle-cathie.com
Web Site: www.kylecathie.com

Distribution:
Littlehampton Book Services Ltd, Faraday Close, Durrington, West Sussex BN13 3RB
Telephone: 01903 828800
Fax: 01903 828801
Email: orders@lbsltd.co.uk
Web Site: www.lbsltd.co.uk

Personnel:
Kyle Cathie *(Managing Director)*
Paul Game *(Financial Director)*
Julia Barder *(Sales & Marketing Director)*
Catherine Heygate *(Rights Director)*
Gemma John *(Production Manager)*
Judith Hannam *(Senior Commissioning Editor)*
Sandy Deasey *(Export Sales Director)*

Cookery, Wines & Spirits; Crafts & Hobbies; Gardening; Health & Beauty; Reference Books, Directories & Dictionaries; Sports & Games

New Titles: 65 (2009) , 65 (2010)
No of Employees: 20
Annual Turnover: £6M

Imprints, Series & ISBNs:
Kyle Books
Kyle Cathie: 978 1 85626

Distributor for:
UK: Duncan Petersen Publishing Ltd

Overseas Representation:
Australia: Simon & Schuster (Australia) Pty Ltd, Pymble, NSW, Australia
India: Penguin Books India, New Delhi, India
New Zealand: New Holland Publishers (NZ) Ltd, Auckland, New Zealand
Singapore: Pansing Distribution, Singapore
South Africa: Penguin Books South Africa (Pty) Ltd, Johannesburg, South Africa
USA & Canada: National Book Network, Lanham, MD, USA

2440

PETER LANG LTD
Evenlode Court, Main Road, Long Hanborough, Witney, Oxon OX29 8SZ
Telephone: 01993 880088
Fax: 01993 882040
Email: oxford@peterlang.com
Web Site: www.peterlang.net

Personnel:
Graham Speake (*Publishing Director*)
Hannah Godfrey (*Commissioning Editor*)
Nick Reynolds (*Commissioning Editor*)
Mette Bundgaard (*Production Manager*)
Peggy Struck (*Sales & Marketing Manager*)

Academic & Scholarly

New Titles: 140 (2009) , 160 (2010)
No of Employees: 10
Annual Turnover: £600,000

Imprints, Series & ISBNs:
978 3 03911

Parent Company:
Switzerland: Peter Lang

Associated Companies:
Belgium: P. I. E. – Peter Lang SA
Germany: Peter Lang GmbH
USA: Peter Lang Publishing Inc

Overseas Representation:
Worldwide: Peter Lang, Pieterlen,
Switzerland

Book Trade Association Membership:
Independent Publishers Guild

2441

LAPWING PUBLICATIONS
1 Ballysillan Drive, Belfast BT14 8HQ
Telephone: 028 9050 0796
Email: lapwing.poetry@ntlworld.com
Web Site: www.lapwingpoetry.com.

Personnel:
Dennis Greig (*Editor & Production
Management*)
Rene Greig (*Editor*)
Adam Rudden (*Editor & Internet Services
Management*)

Poetry

New Titles: 26 (2009) , 30 (2010)
Annual Turnover: £12,000

Imprints, Series & ISBNs:
978 1 898472, 978 1 905425, 978 1
907276

2442

LAW REPORTS INTERNATIONAL
Eden House, 2 St Aldate's Courtyard,
Oxford OX1 1BN
Telephone: 01865 794638
Fax: 01865 794628
Email: lawreports@clara.co.uk
Web Site: www.lawreports.com

Personnel:
Mrs Sarah Smith (*Production Editor*)
Mrs Sarah Snell (*Senior Editor*)
Julia Savage (*Editor*)
Daniel McCarthy (*Editor*)
Premila Patel (*Editor*)

Law

New Titles: 10 (2009) , 9 (2010)
No of Employees: 5

Imprints, Series & ISBNs:
978 1 870584, 978 1 902907, 978 1
906585

Distributor for:
Zambia: The Zambia Law Journal

2443

LAW SOCIETY PUBLISHING
113 Chancery Lane, London WC2A 1PL
Telephone: 020 7841 5472
Fax: 020 7320 5853
Email: publishing@lawsociety.org.uk

Web Site: www.lawsociety.org.uk/
bookshop

Distribution:
Prolog, PO Box 99, Sudbury, Suffolk
CO10 2SN
Telephone: 0870 850 1422
Fax: 01787 313995

Personnel:
Stephen Honey (*Publishing Manager*)
Sarah Foulkes (*Production Manager*)
Millie Patel (*Marketing Manager*)
Janet Noble (*Commissioning Editor*)
Ben Mullane (*Commissioning Editor*)
Simon Blackett (*Commissioning Editor*)

Law

Imprints, Series & ISBNs:
The Law Society: 978 1 85328

Parent Company:
The Law Society

Book Trade Association Membership:
Data Publishers Association

2444

LEARNING MATTERS LTD
33 Southernhay East, Exeter EX1 1NX
Telephone: 01392 215560
Fax: 01392 215561
Email: info@learningmatters.co.uk
Web Site: www.learningmatters.co.uk

Distribution:
BEBC Distribution, Albion Close, Parkstone,
Poole BH12 3LL
Telephone: 0845 230 9000
Fax: 01202 715556
Email: learningmatters@bebc.co.uk
Web Site: www.bebc.co.uk

Personnel:
Jonathan Harris (*Managing Director*)
Zoe Engert (*Sales & Marketing Manager*)

*Academic & Scholarly; Educational &
Textbooks; Electronic (Professional &
Academic); Sociology & Anthropology*

New Titles: 50 (2009) , 55 (2010)
No of Employees: 13

Imprints, Series & ISBNs:
978 0 85725, 978 1 84445, 978 1 903300

Overseas Representation:
Australia: Palgrave Macmillan, South Yarra,
Vic, Australia
Barbados: Days Bookstore, Bridgetown,
Barbados
Ghana: EPP Books Services Ltd, Accra,
Ghana
Jamaica: The Book Merchant Ltd, Kingston,
Jamaica
Malaysia: APD Kuala Lumpur Pte Ltd,
Selangor, Malaysia
Singapore: APD Singapore Pte Ltd,
Singapore
USA: ISBS, Portland, OR, USA

Book Trade Association Membership:
Independent Publishers Guild

2445

LEARNING TOGETHER
18 Shandon Park, Belfast BT5 6NW
Telephone: 028 9040 2086
Fax: 028 9040 2086
Email: info@learningtogether.co.uk
Web Site: www.learningtogether.co.uk

Distribution:
Orca Book Services, Unit A3, Fleets Corner,
Poole, Dorset BH17 0HL
Telephone: 01202 665432
Fax: 01202 666219
Email: mail@orcabookservices.co.uk

Representation:
c/o Alan Goodworth, Roundhouse Group,
Millstone, Limers Lane, Northam,
North Devon EX39 2RG
Telephone: 01237 474474
Fax: 01237 474774
Email: roundhouse.group@ukgateway.net

Personnel:
Janet McConkey (*Managing Director*)
Stephen McConkey (*Author/Publisher*)

Educational & Textbooks

No of Employees: 2
Annual Turnover: £65,000

Imprints, Series & ISBNs:
Practice Tests In Series: 978 1 873385

Book Trade Association Membership:
Publishers Association; Educational
Publishers Council

2446

LEATHERHEAD FOOD RESEARCH
Randalls Road, Leatherhead, Surrey
KT22 7RY
Telephone: 01372 822556 & 822241
(Sales)
Fax: 01372 822272
Email: publications@leatherheadfood.com
Web Site: www.leatherheadfood.com

Personnel:
Dr Paul Berryman (*Chief Executive Officer*)
Victoria Emerton (*Knowledge Services
Manager*)

Law; Scientific & Technical

New Titles: 8 (2009) , 2 (2010)
No of Employees: 200

Imprints, Series & ISBNs:
978 0 905748, 978 1 904007, 978 1
905224

2447

LEGAL ACTION GROUP
242 Pentonville Road, London N1 9UN
Telephone: 020 7833 2931
Fax: 020 7837 6094
Email: lag@lag.org.uk
Web Site: www.lag.org.uk

Personnel:
Steve Hynes (*Director*)
Esther Pilger (*Publisher*)
Nim Moorthy (*Marketing Manager*)
Adam Wilson (*Customer Services Executive*)
Andrew Troszok (*Customer Services
Executive*)

Law

New Titles: 10 (2009) , 8 (2010)
No of Employees: 9

Imprints, Series & ISBNs:
978 0 905099, 978 1 903307

Book Trade Association Membership:
Independent Publishers Guild

2448

LEGEND PRESS
2 London Wall Buildings, London
EC2M 5UU
Telephone: 020 7448 5137
Email: info@legendpress.co.uk
Web Site: www.legendpress.co.uk

Personnel:
Tom Chalmers (*Managing Director*)

Fiction

Imprints, Series & ISBNs:
978 0 9551032, 978 1 906558

Book Trade Association Membership:
Independent Publishers Guild

2449

LETTERLAND INTERNATIONAL LTD
Stonebridge House, 28–32 Bridge Street,
Leatherhead, Surrey KT22 8BZ
Telephone: 01223 262675
Fax: 01223 264126
Email: info@letterland.com
Web Site: www.letterland.com

Distribution:
Grantham Book Services, Trent Road,
Grantham, Lincs NG31 7XQ
Telephone: 01476 541080
Fax: 01476 541061
Email: orders@letterland.com
Web Site:
www.granthambookservices.co.uk

Personnel:
Mark Wendon (*Director*)
Thomas Wendon (*Marketing Director*)
Jonathan Wendon (*Production Manager*)
Lisa Chapman (*Editor*)

*Children's Books; Educational & Textbooks;
Electronic (Educational); English as a
Foreign Language*

Imprints, Series & ISBNs:
978 0 907345, 978 1 86209

Overseas Representation:
Australia: Ed Source, Bassendean, WA,
Australia
Canada: Educan, Weston, Ont, Canada
China: Ian Taylor & Associates, Beijing, P. R.
of China
Hong Kong: ETC Educational Technology
Connection (HK) Ltd, Tai Koo Shing,
Hong Kong
Japan: J & N English Club, Shizuoka-ken,
Japan
Korea: Infobooks, Seoul, Republic of Korea
Middle East & North Africa: International
Publishers Representatives (IPR) Ltd,
Nicosia, Cyprus
New Zealand: Wakelin Educational Services,
Ashburton, New Zealand
Nigeria: Kcxploits, Lagos, Nigeria
Singapore: Tumble Tots (Asia) Pty Ltd,
Singapore, Singapore
South Africa: Educational Ideas,
Johannesburg, South Africa
Taiwan: Hello! Book Club, Taipei County,
Taiwan
USA: Letterland International, Enfield, NH,
USA

Book Trade Association Membership:
Publishers Association; Educational
Publishers Council; Independent Publishers
Guild; International Reading Association

2450

LETTS AND LONSDALE
4 Grosvenor Place, London SW1X 7DL
Telephone: 020 7096 2900
Fax: 020 7096 2945
Email: orders@lettsandlonsdale.co.uk
Web Site: www.lettsandlonsdale.com

Warehouse, Distribution:
HarperCollins, Campsie View,
Westerhill Road, Bishopbriggs, Glasgow
G64 2QT

Personnel:
Andrew Ware (*Managing Director*)
Helen Jacobs (*Publishing Director*)

*Biology & Zoology; Chemistry; Children's
Books; Educational & Textbooks;
Geography & Geology; History &*

Antiquarian; Languages & Linguistics; Mathematics & Statistics; Philosophy; Physics; Psychology & Psychiatry; Reference Books, Directories & Dictionaries; Scientific & Technical; Sociology & Anthropology; Sports & Games; Vocational Training & Careers

Imprints, Series & ISBNs:
978 1 84085, 978 1 84315, 978 1 85758, 978 1 85805

Associated Companies:
Leckie & Leckie

Overseas Representation:
Argentina: Edytex, Buenos Aires, Argentina
Botswana: Book Promotions Pty Ltd, Diep River, South Africa
Caribbean: The Book Merchant Ltd, Kingston, Jamaica
India: Overleaf, New Delhi, India
Malaysia: APD Kuala Lumpur Pte Ltd, Selangor, Malaysia
Middle East: Peter Ward Book Exports, London, UK
New Zealand: Addenda, Auckland, New Zealand
Pakistan: Publishers Marketing Associates, Karachi, Pakistan
Philippines: CRW Books, Rizal, Philippines
Singapore: APD Singapore Pte Ltd, Singapore
Tanzania, Uganda & Seychelles: A–Z Africa Book Services, Rotterdam, Netherlands

Book Trade Association Membership:
Educational Publishers Council

2451

DEWI LEWIS PUBLISHING
8 Broomfield Road, Heaton Moor, Stockport SK4 4ND
Telephone: 0161 442 9450
Fax: 0161 442 9450
Email: mail@dewilewispublishing.com
Web Site: www.dewilewispublishing.com

Trade Enquiries & Orders:
Turnaround, Unit 3 Olympia Trading Estate, Coburg Road, London N22 6TZ
Telephone: 020 8829 3000
Fax: 020 8881 5088
Email: orders@turnaround-uk.com
Web Site: www.turnaround-uk.com

Personnel:
Dewi Lewis *(Publisher)*
Caroline Warhurst *(Sales & Marketing Director)*

Architecture & Design; Fine Art & Art History; Illustrated & Fine Editions; Photography; Reference Books, Directories & Dictionaries; Sports & Games

Imprints, Series & ISBNs:
978 1 899235, 978 1 904587

Overseas Representation:
Germany: Visual Books Sales Agency, Berlin, Germany
New Zealand: Southern Publishers Group, Auckland, New Zealand
North America: Consortium Book Sales & Distribution Inc, St Paul, MN, USA

2452

LEXUS LTD
60 Brook Street, Glasgow G40 2AB
Telephone: 0141 556 0440
Fax: 0141 556 2202
Email: peterterrell@lexusforlanguages.co.uk
Web Site: www.lexusforlanguages.co.uk

Personnel:
Peter Terrell *(Publisher)*
Elfreda Crehan *(Typesetter & Designer)*

Educational & Textbooks; Languages & Linguistics; Reference Books, Directories & Dictionaries

New Titles: 2 (2009)
No of Employees: 3
Annual Turnover: £110,000

Imprints, Series & ISBNs:
Chinese Classroom: 978 1 904737
Travelmates: 978 1 904737

2453

LIBERTIES PRESS
Guinness Enterprise Centre, Taylor's Lane, Dublin 8, Republic of Ireland
Telephone: +353 (01) 415 1286
Email: sean@libertiespress.com
Web Site: www.libertiespress.com

Personnel:
Sean O'Keeffe *(Director)*
Peter O'Connell *(Director)*

Architecture & Design; Cookery, Wines & Spirits; Health & Beauty; History & Antiquarian; Literature & Criticism; Politics & World Affairs; Religion & Theology; Sports & Games

Imprints, Series & ISBNs:
978 0 9545335, 978 1 905483

Parent Company:
Republic of Ireland: Liberties Media Ltd

Book Trade Association Membership:
Publishing Ireland (Foilsiú Éireann)

2454

LIBRARIO PUBLISHERS LTD
Brough House, Kinloss, Moray IV36 2UA
Telephone: 01343 850178
Email: amlawson@librario.com
Web Site: www.librario.com

Personnel:
Mark Lawson *(Managing Director)*
Mrs Rosemary Lawson *(Sales Director)*
Mrs Janet Barcis *(Bookkeeper)*

Crime; History & Antiquarian; Medical (incl. Self Help & Alternative Medicine); Military & War; Natural History; Scientific & Technical

New Titles: 10 (2009) , 9 (2010)
No of Employees: 2
Annual Turnover: £60,000

Imprints, Series & ISBNs:
978 0 9542960, 978 1 904440, 978 1 906775

2455

LIFE OF RILEY PRODUCTIONS LTD
62 Wilson Street, London EC2A 2BU
Telephone: 01787 478337

Electronic (Educational)

Book Trade Association Membership:
Publishers Association

2456

THE LILLIPUT PRESS LTD
62–63 Sitric Road, Arbour Hill, Dublin 7, Republic of Ireland
Telephone: +353 (01) 671 1647
Fax: +353 (01) 671 1233
Email: info@lilliputpress.ie
Web Site: www.lilliputpress.ie

Distributors (Trade Orders):
Gill & Macmillan, Hume Avenue, Park West, Dublin 12, Republic of Ireland
Telephone: +353 (01) 500 9500
Fax: +353 (01) 500 9599

Personnel:
Antony Farrell *(Managing Director & Publisher)*
David Dickson *(Director)*
Vincent Hurley *(Director)*
Terence Brown *(Director)*
Vivienne Guinness *(Director)*
Kathy Gilfillan *(Director)*
Daniel Caffrey *(Director)*
Kitty Lyddon *(Assistant Editor)*

Academic & Scholarly; Architecture & Design; Biography & Autobiography; Fiction; Fine Art & Art History; History & Antiquarian; Illustrated & Fine Editions; Literature & Criticism; Music; Photography; Reference Books, Directories & Dictionaries

New Titles: 14 (2009) , 20 (2010)
No of Employees: 3
Annual Turnover: £300,000

Imprints, Series & ISBNs:
978 0 946640, 978 1 84351, 978 1 874675, 978 1 901866

Distributor for:
UK: The Houyhnhnm Press

Overseas Representation:
France: Lora Fountain Literary Agent, Paris, France
UK: Central Books Ltd, London, UK

Book Trade Association Membership:
Publishing Ireland (Foilsiú Éireann)

2457

FRANCES LINCOLN LTD
4 Torriano Mews, Torriano Avenue, London NW5 2RZ
Telephone: 020 7284 4009
Fax: 020 7485 0490
Email: reception@frances-lincoln.com
Web Site: www.franceslincoln.com

Warehouse, Trade Enquiries & Orders:
Bookpoint Ltd, 130 Milton Park, Abingdon, Oxon OX14 4SB
Telephone: 01235 400400
Fax: 01235 400500

Personnel:
John Nicoll *(Managing Director)*
Jon Rippon *(Finance Director)*
Sara Borthwick *(Business Manager)*
Jo Christian *(Editorial – Adult Books Manager)*
Andrew Dunn *(Editorial Manager – Adult Books)*
Maurice Lyon *(Editorial Manager – Children's Books)*
Laura Grandi *(Production Manager)*
Gail Lynch *(Sales & Marketing Manager)*

Architecture & Design; Children's Books; Cookery, Wines & Spirits; Fine Art & Art History; Gardening; Guide Books; Health & Beauty; Illustrated & Fine Editions; Religion & Theology; Sports & Games; Travel & Topography

Imprints, Series & ISBNs:
978 0 7112, 978 1 84507

Distributor for:
Allen & Unwin (Children's Books); Barn Owl Books Ltd; Boxer Books; Natural History Museum; Tara Publishing
USA: New York Review of Books

Overseas Representation:
All countries other than those listed: Frances Lincoln, London, UK
Australia (Adult Books) & New Zealand: Bookwise International, Adelaide, SA, Australia
Australia (Children's Books): Walker Books Australia, Newtown, NSW, Australia
South Africa: Pan Macmillan SA Pty Ltd, Hyde Park, South Africa

USA (Children's Books): Publishers Group West, Berkeley, CA, USA

Book Trade Association Membership:
Independent Publishers Guild

2458

LION HUDSON PLC
Wilkinson House, Jordan Hill Road, Oxford OX2 7DR
Telephone: 01865 302750
Fax: 01865 302757
Email: info@lionhudson.com
Web Site: www.lionhudson.com

Personnel:
Alice Lawhead *(Non-Executive Director)*
Paul Clifford *(Managing Director)*
Nicholas Jones *(Deputy Managing Director)*
John O'Nions *(Sales & Marketing Director)*
Roy McCloughry *(Chairman)*
Stephen Price *(Production Director)*
Robert Wendover *(Export Sales Manager)*
Paul Whitton *(International & Subsidiary Rights)*
Vicky Pulley *(Financial Controller)*

Biography & Autobiography; Children's Books; Educational & Textbooks; Religion & Theology

New Titles: 170 (2009) , 160 (2010)
No of Employees: 53
Annual Turnover: £9M

Imprints, Series & ISBNs:
Aslan: 978 0 7459, 978 0 85648
Candle: 978 1 85985
Lion: 978 0 7459, 978 0 85648
Lion Children's: 978 0 7459, 978 0 85648
Monarch: 978 1 85424

Overseas Representation:
Australia: Scribo Pty Ltd, Adelaide, SA, Australia
New Zealand: New Holland Publishers (NZ) Ltd, Auckland, New Zealand
South Africa: Pearson Education, Cape Town, South Africa

Book Trade Association Membership:
Publishers Association; Educational Publishers Council

2459

LISU
Loughborough University, Loughborough, Leics LE11 3TU
Telephone: 01509 635680
Fax: 01509 635699
Email: lisu@lboro.ac.uk
Web Site: www.lboro.ac.uk/departments/dis/lisu

Personnel:
Claire Creaser *(Director)*

Bibliography & Library Science; Reference Books, Directories & Dictionaries

Imprints, Series & ISBNs:
978 0 948848, 978 1 905499
LISU Reports: 978 1 901786

Parent Company:
Loughborough University

2460

LITTLE, BROWN BOOK GROUP
100 Victoria Embankment, London EC4Y 0DY
Telephone: 020 7911 8000
Fax: 020 7911 8100
Email: info@littlebrown.co.uk
Web Site: www.littlebrown.co.uk, www.orbitbooks.co.uk & www.virago.co.uk

Distribution Centre:
Littlehampton Book Services Ltd,
Faraday Close, Durrington, West Sussex
BN13 3RB
Telephone: 01903 828511
Fax: 01903 828801
Email: orders@lbsltd.co.uk

Personnel:
Ursula Mackenzie *(Chief Executive Officer &
Publisher)*
David Kent *(Chief Operating Officer)*
Diane Spivey *(Rights Director)*
Duncan Spilling *(Design Director)*
Robert Manser *(Group Sales & Marketing
Director)*
Richard Beswick *(Managing Director – Little
Brown & Abacus)*
Tim Holman *(Publisher – Orbit)*
Lennie Goodings *(Publisher – Virago)*
Antonia Hodgson *(Publisher – Sphere &
Piatkus)*
Nick Ross *(Production Director)*
Maddie Mogford *(Legal Director)*
Julian Shaw *(Finance Director)*

*Audio Books; Biography & Autobiography;
Crime; Fiction; History & Antiquarian;
Humour; Literature & Criticism; Military &
War; Music; Politics & World Affairs;
Psychology & Psychiatry; Science Fiction;
Sports & Games; Travel & Topography*

New Titles: 475 (2009)
No of Employees: 140

Imprints, Series & ISBNs:
Abacus: 978 0 349
Atom: 978 1 904233, 978 1 905654
Audio Books: 978 1 4055
Bulfinch: 978 0 8212
Little, Brown: 978 0 316, 978 1 4087
Orbit: 978 1 84149, 978 1 85723
Piatkus: 978 0 7499
Sphere Hardbacks: 978 1 84744
Sphere Paperbacks: 978 0 7515
Virago: 978 1 84408, 978 1 85381, 978 1
86049

Parent Company:
France: Hachette Livre Group of Companies

Overseas Representation:
Africa: A–Z Africa Book Services,
Rotterdam, Netherlands
Australia: Hachette Livre Australia, Sydney,
NSW, Australia
Canada: Hachette Canada, New York, NY,
USA
Caribbean, Central & South America: Jerry
Carrillo Inc, USA
China: Wei Zhao, New York, NY, USA
France & Scandinavia: Melanie Boesen,
Hachette US, Denmark
Germany, Sweden & Middle East: Simon
McArt, Little, Brown Book Group,
London, UK
India: Hachette India, Gurgaon, India
Italy: Penguin Italia srl, Milan, Italy
*Japan, Thailand, Indonesia, Hong Kong,
Korea & Taiwan:* Gilles Fauveau, Japan
New Zealand: Hachette Livre New Zealand,
Auckland, New Zealand
Singapore & Malaysia: Penguin Books
Singapore, Jurong, Singapore
South Africa: Penguin Books SA (Pty) Ltd,
Denver Ext 4, South Africa
Spain & Portugal: Penguin Books SA,
Madrid, Spain
*Switzerland, Belgium, Netherlands,
Gibraltar, Malta & Cyprus:* Rachel Hurn,
Little, Brown Book Group, London, UK

Book Trade Association Membership:
Publishers Association; Booksellers
Association; Book Marketing Ltd

2461

LITTLE TIGER PRESS
[an imprint of Magi Publications]

1 The Coda Centre, 189 Munster Road,
London SW6 6AW
Telephone: 020 7385 6333
Fax: 020 7385 7333
Email: info@littletiger.co.uk
Web Site: www.littletigerpress.com

Distribution:
Macmillan Distribution (MDL), Brunel Road,
Houndmills, Basingstoke, Hants RG21 6XS
Telephone: 01256 302692
Fax: 01256 812521
Email: mdl@macmillan.co.uk

Personnel:
Monty Bhatia *(Proprietor)*
David Bucknor *(Sales Director)*
Aude Lavielle *(Rights Director)*
Yolande Denny *(Production Director)*
Jude Evans *(Publisher)*

Children's Books

Imprints, Series & ISBNs:
Caterpillar Books
Little Tiger Press: 978 1 84506, 978 1 85430
Stripes Publishing: 978 1 84715

Parent Company:
Magi Publications

Overseas Representation:
Australia: Global Language Books,
Toongabbie, NSW, Australia
Malaysia: Pansing Distributors (M) Sdn Bhd,
Shah Alam, Malaysia
Singapore & Brunei: STP Distributors Pte
Ltd, Singapore
Southern Africa: Titles SA, Johannesburg,
South Africa

2462

**THE LITTMAN LIBRARY OF JEWISH
CIVILIZATION**
PO Box 645, Oxford OX2 0UJ
Telephone: 01865 514688
Fax: 01865 722964
Email: info@littman.co.uk
Web Site: www.littman.co.uk

Distribution:
NBN International, Estover Road, Plymouth
PL6 7PY
Telephone: 01752 202300
Fax: 01752 202333
Email: orders@nbninternational.com
Web Site: www.nbninternational.com

Personnel:
Ludo Craddock *(Chief Executive Officer)*
Connie Webber *(Managing Editor)*
Colette Littman *(Director)*
Robert Littman *(Director)*

*Academic & Scholarly; Biography &
Autobiography; Educational & Textbooks;
Fine Art & Art History; History &
Antiquarian; Literature & Criticism; Music;
Philosophy; Politics & World Affairs;
Religion & Theology; Sociology &
Anthropology; Theatre, Drama & Dance*

New Titles: 8 (2009) , 8 (2010)

Imprints, Series & ISBNs:
978 1 874774, 978 1 904113, 978 1
906764

Overseas Representation:
Australia & New Zealand: Peribo Pty Ltd,
Mount Kuring-Gai, NSW, Australia
Israel: The Hebrew University Magnes Press,
Jerusalem, Israel
USA & Canada: International Specialized
Book Services Inc, Portland, OR, USA

Book Trade Association Membership:
Independent Publishers Guild

2463

LIVERPOOL UNIVERSITY PRESS
4 Cambridge Street, Liverpool L69 7ZU
Telephone: 0151 794 2233
Fax: 0151 794 2235
Email: lup@liv.ac.uk
Web Site: http://www.liverpool-
unipress.co.uk

Sales & Distribution:
Marston Book Services, PO Box 269,
Abingdon, Oxon OX14 4YN
Telephone: 01235 465500
Fax: 01235 465555
Email: trade.order@marston.co.uk
Web Site: www.marston.co.uk

Personnel:
Anthony Cond *(Publisher)*
Simon Bell *(Sales & Marketing Manager)*
Tracey Mooney *(Finance Manager)*
Andrew Kirk *(Production Manager)*
Helen Tookey *(Journals Production Editor)*
Clare Hooper *(Journals Publishing Executive)*
Janet Smith *(Sales & Marketing Assistant)*

*Academic & Scholarly; Architecture &
Design; Educational & Textbooks; Fine Art &
Art History; History & Antiquarian;
Languages & Linguistics; Literature &
Criticism; Politics & World Affairs; Science
Fiction; Sociology & Anthropology*

Imprints, Series & ISBNs:
978 0 85323, 978 1 84631

Overseas Representation:
Africa & Middle East: International
Publishing Services (IPS) Middle East Ltd,
Dubai, UAE
Benelux & Germany: Roy de Boo, Hooge
Mierde, Netherlands
Central & Latin America: InterMedia
Americana (IMA) Ltd, London, UK
Far East (excluding Japan): STM Publisher
Services Pte Ltd, Singapore
France & Italy: Flavio Marcello Publishers'
Agents & Consultants, Padua, Italy
India: Viva Group, New Delhi, India
Malaysia: Yuha Associates, Selangor Darul
Ehsan, Malaysia
North America: International Specialized
Book Services Inc, Portland, OR, USA
Republic of Ireland: John Fitzpatrick, Dublin,
Republic of Ireland
Scandinavia: Jan Norbye, Ølstykke,
Denmark
Spain & Portugal: Iberian Book Services,
Madrid, Spain

Book Trade Association Membership:
Independent Publishers Guild

2464

**LIVING TIME® MEDIA
INTERNATIONAL**
Units 18c–19c, Wem Business Park,
New Street, Wem, Shropshire SY4 5JX
Telephone: 01939 236623
Fax: 01939 234873 & 01743 244921
Email: livingtime@email.com
Web Site: www.livingtime.co.uk

Global Rights (for Europe & USA):
5 Portland Crescent, Shrewsbury,
Shropshire SY2 5NG
Telephone: 07877 851410
Fax: 01743 244921
Email: livingtime@europe.com
Web Site: www.livingtime.co.uk

Personnel:
Alderson Smith *(Head of Publishing/Chief
Executive)*
Edouard d'Araille *(Editor-in-Chief)*
John Hargreaves *(International Sales
Executive)*
James Hartley *(Foreign & Subsidiary Rights
Executive)*

Jack Goldstein *(Film Rights Executive (USA))*
Carolyn Eden *(Children's Book Rights
Executive)*

*Academic & Scholarly; Biography &
Autobiography; Children's Books; Cinema,
Video, TV & Radio; Crime; Educational &
Textbooks; Electronic (Educational);
Electronic (Entertainment); English as a
Foreign Language; Fiction; History &
Antiquarian; Literature & Criticism;
Philosophy; Poetry; Psychology &
Psychiatry; Science Fiction*

New Titles: 20 (2009) , 25 (2010)
No of Employees: 3
Annual Turnover: £250,000

Imprints, Series & ISBNs:
Living Time® Digital: 978 1 906904
Living Time® Media International: 978 1
905820
Living Time® Press: 978 1 903331

Parent Company:
Living Time®

Associated Companies:
The Academy of the 3rd Millennium™;
Fortune Street®; Living Time Vision
(LTV); Living Time® America; Living
Time® Design; Living Time® Docufilms;
Living Time® Films Ltd; Living Time®
Legal; Living Time® Music

Overseas Representation:
Worldwide: Jack Goldstein, Living Time®
America, Hollywood, CA, USA

2465

LOGASTON PRESS
Little Logaston, Woonton, Almeley,
Herefordshire HR3 6QH
Telephone: 01544 327344
Email: logastonpress@btinternet.com
Web Site: www.logastonpress.co.uk

Personnel:
Andy Johnson *(Proprietor)*
Karen Johnson *(Proprietor)*

*Archaeology; Architecture & Design; Fine
Art & Art History; Guide Books; History &
Antiquarian; Natural History; Reference
Books, Directories & Dictionaries*

Imprints, Series & ISBNs:
Monuments in the Landscape Series: 978 0
9510242, 978 1 873827, 978 1 904396,
978 1 906663

2466

LOMOND BOOKS LTD
14 Freskyn Place,
East Mains Industrial Estate, Broxburn
EH52 5NF
Telephone: 01506 855955
Fax: 01506 855965
Email: sales@lomondbooks.co.uk
Web Site: www.lomondbooks.com

Personnel:
Trevor Maher *(Director)*
Duncan Baxter *(Sales Director)*
Jackie Brown *(Operations Director)*
Arthur Robertson *(Buyer)*

*Children's Books; Cookery, Wines & Spirits;
Crafts & Hobbies; Guide Books; History &
Antiquarian; Humour; Illustrated & Fine
Editions; Natural History; Reference Books,
Directories & Dictionaries*

New Titles: 25 (2009) , 30 (2010)

Imprints, Series & ISBNs:
978 1 84204

Book Trade Association Membership:
Booksellers Association

2467

LUATH PRESS LTD
543/2 Castlehill, The Royal Mile, Edinburgh
EH1 2ND
Telephone: 0131 225 4326
Fax: 0131 225 4324
Email: gavin.macdougall@luath.co.uk
Web Site: www.luath.co.uk

Distribution:
HarperCollins, Westerhill Road,
Bishopbriggs, Glasgow G64 2QR
Telephone: 0870 787 1722
Fax: 0870 787 1723
Email: enquiries@harpercollins.co.uk
Web Site: b2b.harpercollins.co.uk

Personnel:
Gavin MacDougall (*Director, Rights &
Overseas Distribution*)
Leila Cruickshank (*Production & Editorial*)
Sarah Imbert (*Sales & Marketing*)
Christine Wilson (*Press & Events*)

*Biography & Autobiography; Children's
Books; Cinema, Video, TV & Radio;
Cookery, Wines & Spirits; Crime;
Economics; Fiction; Gardening; Geography
& Geology; Guide Books; History &
Antiquarian; Humour; Languages &
Linguistics; Literature & Criticism; Magic &
the Occult; Medical (incl. Self Help &
Alternative Medicine); Military & War;
Music; Natural History; Photography;
Poetry; Politics & World Affairs; Sports &
Games; Theatre, Drama & Dance; Travel &
Topography; Veterinary Science*

New Titles: 40 (2009) , 40 (2010)

Imprints, Series & ISBNs:
Let's Explore: 978 0 946487, 978 1 84282
Luath: 978 0 946487, 978 1 84282, 978 1
906307, 978 1 905222, 978 1 906817
Luath Guides to Scotland: 978 0 946487
Luath Storyteller: 978 1 84282, 978 1
905222
On the Trail of: 978 0 946487, 978 1 84282
The Quest for: 978 0 946487, 978 1 84282
Scots in
Viewpoints
Walk with Luath: 978 0 946487
Wild Lives: 978 0 946487

Overseas Representation:
Australia & New Zealand: Luath Press Ltd,
Edinburgh, UK
USA & Canada: Ingram Publisher Services,
Nashville, TN, USA

Book Trade Association Membership:
Publishing Scotland; Independent
Publishers Guild

2468

LUND HUMPHRIES
Ashgate Publishing Group, Wey Court East,
Union Road, Farnham, Surrey GU9 7PT
Telephone: 01252 331551
Fax: 01252 736736
Email: info@lundhumphries.com
Web Site: www.lundhumphries.com

Trade Distribution:
Bookpoint Ltd, 39 Milton Park, Abingdon,
Oxon OX14 4TD
Telephone: 01235 400400
Fax: 01235 400413
Email: orders@bookpoint.co.uk

Personnel:
Nigel Farrow (*Chairman, Ashgate
Publishing*)
Lucy Myers (*Managing Director*)

*Academic & Scholarly; Antiques &
Collecting; Architecture & Design; Fine Art
& Art History; Photography*

New Titles: 30 (2009) , 30 (2010)

No of Employees: 5

Imprints, Series & ISBNs:
978 1 84822

Parent Company:
Ashgate Publishing

Overseas Representation:
Australia & Far East: Ashgate Publishing
Asia-Pacific, Warriewood, NSW, Australia
Central & Eastern Europe: Dr László Horváth
Publishers Representative, Budapest,
Hungary
*Finland, Sweden, Norway, Denmark &
Iceland:* Andrew Durnell Marketing Ltd,
Tunbridge Wells, UK
France & Netherlands: Casemate Books,
Newbury, UK
*Germany, Austria, Switzerland, Italy,
Greece, Luxembourg & Belgium:* Ted
Dougherty, London, UK
India: Maya Publishers Pvt Ltd, New Delhi,
India
Japan (stockholding agents): United
Publishers Services Ltd, Tokyo, Japan
Korea: Information & Culture Korea (ICK),
Seoul, Republic of Korea
Middle East: Publishers International
Marketing, Polfages, France
New Zealand: South Pacific Books (Imports)
Ltd, Auckland, New Zealand
South Africa: Peter Hyde Associates (Pty)
Ltd, Cape Town, South Africa
*South America & Africa (excluding South
Africa):* InterMedia Americana (IMA) Ltd,
London, UK
Spain & Portugal: Jenny Padovani,
Barcelona, Spain
USA & Canada: Lund Humphries,
Burlington, VT, USA

2469

THE LUTTERWORTH PRESS
PO Box 60, Cambridge CB1 2NT
Telephone: 01223 350865
Fax: 01223 366951
Email: publishing@lutterworth.com
Web Site: www.lutterworth.com

Trade Enquiries & Orders:
James Clarke & Co, PO Box 60, Cambridge
CB1 2NT
Telephone: (as above)
Fax: (as above)
Email: orders@jamesclarke.co.uk
Web Site: (as above)

Personnel:
Adrian Brink (*Managing Director*)
Rowan Binney (*Customer Service*)
Penny Bull (*Accounts Department*)
Ilaria Tassistro (*Sales & Publicity*)
Michelle Priestley (*Sales & Publicity*)
Aidan van de Weyer (*Editorial*)
Ian Bignall (*Editorial*)
Elaine Proudlove (*Editorial*)

*Academic & Scholarly; Antiques &
Collecting; Architecture & Design;
Biography & Autobiography; Children's
Books; Crafts & Hobbies; Educational &
Textbooks; Fine Art & Art History; History &
Antiquarian; Illustrated & Fine Editions;
Literature & Criticism; Military & War;
Natural History; Philosophy; Politics & World
Affairs; Reference Books, Directories &
Dictionaries; Religion & Theology; Sports &
Games*

New Titles: 25 (2009) , 27 (2010)
No of Employees: 8

Imprints, Series & ISBNs:
Acorn Editions: 978 0 906554
Patrick Hardy: 978 0 7444
The Lutterworth Press: 978 0 7188

Parent Company:
James Clarke & Co Ltd

Overseas Representation:
China & Asia: AA Media Services, Shanghai,
P. R. of China
Philippines: Edwin Makabenta, Quezon
City, Philippines
USA: The David Brown Book Co (DBBC),
Oakville, CT, USA

Book Trade Association Membership:
Educational Publishers Council;
Independent Publishers Guild

2470

McCRIMMON PUBLISHING CO LTD
10–12 High Street, Great Wakering, Essex
SS3 0EQ
Telephone: 01702 218956
Fax: 01702 216082
Email: info@mccrimmons.com
Web Site: www.mccrimmons.com

Bookshop:
All Saints Pastoral Centre, London Colney,
St Albans, Herts
Telephone: 01727 827612
Fax: 01727 827612
Email: (as above)
Web Site: (as above)

Personnel:
Joan McCrimmon (*Secretary*)
Don McCrimmon (*Sales Director*)
Nick Snode (*Graphic Designer*)
Sue Anderson (*Accounts*)
Louise Madden (*Bookshop Manager*)
Caroline Lee (*Sales Ledger*)
Robert Mossop (*Warehouse*)

*Children's Books; Educational & Textbooks;
Electronic (Educational); Music; Religion &
Theology*

New Titles: 6 (2009) , 10 (2010)
No of Employees: 8
Annual Turnover: £750,000

Imprints, Series & ISBNs:
978 0 85597

Distributor for:
USA: Harcourt Brace & Co; Harcourt
Religion Publishers (RE division); LTP
Publications; Printery House Inc

Overseas Representation:
Australia: John Garrett Publishing,
Mulgrave, Vic, Australia
Hong Kong: Catholic Truth Society, Hong
Kong
New Zealand: Pleroma Christian Supplies,
Otane, Central Hawkes Bay, New Zealand
South Africa: The Catholic Bookshop, Cape
Town, South Africa

2471

McGRAW-HILL EDUCATION
Shoppenhangers Road, Maidenhead, Berks
SL6 2QL
Telephone: 01628 502500
Fax: 01628 770224
Web Site: www.mcgraw-hill.co.uk

Personnel:
Simon Allen (*Senior Vice-President, Europe,
MEA & Asia Pacific*)
John Donovan (*UK/Northern & Central
Europe Managing Director*)
Thanos Blintzios (*MEA Managing Director*)
Alan Martin (*Operations/Finance, EMEA
Director*)
Lefteris Souris (*Sales & Marketing Director,
MEA*)
Emma Gibson (*General Manager
Professional/Medical & Open University
Press*)
Alice Duijser (*HE Sales & Marketing Director*)
Shona Mullen (*General Manager, Content &
Digital Development EMEA*)
Rob Ince (*UK Schools General Manager*)

*Academic & Scholarly; Accountancy &
Taxation; Architecture & Design; Aviation;
Biology & Zoology; Chemistry; Computer
Science; Economics; Educational &
Textbooks; Electronic (Educational);
Electronic (Professional & Academic);
Engineering; English as a Foreign
Language; Geography & Geology; Industry,
Business & Management; Law;
Mathematics & Statistics; Medical (incl. Self
Help & Alternative Medicine); Philosophy;
Physics; Politics & World Affairs; Psychology
& Psychiatry; Reference Books, Directories &
Dictionaries; Scientific & Technical;
Sociology & Anthropology; Transport;
Vocational Training & Careers*

Imprints, Series & ISBNs:
978 0 07

Parent Company:
USA: McGraw-Hill Inc

Associated Companies:
Open University Press
Australia: McGraw-Hill Education
Canada: McGraw-Hill Ryerson Ltd
Colombia: McGraw-Hill/InterAmericana
(Colombia) SA
India: McGraw-Hill Education (India) Pvt Ltd
Italy: McGraw-Hill Libri Italia srl
Japan: McGraw-Hill Book Co
Mexico: Libros McGraw-Hill de Mexico SA
de CV
Portugal: McGraw-Hill/Interamericana de
Portugal Ltda
Singapore: McGraw-Hill International Book
Co
Spain: McGraw-Hill Interamericana de
España SAU
USA: Wm. C. Brown; Brown & Benchmark;
Irwin; Irwin Professional; Osborne/
McGraw-Hill
Venezuela: McGraw-Hill/InterAmericana
(Venezuela) SA

Distributor for:
USA: Amacom; Berrett-Koehler; Harvard
Business School Press; R & D Books

Book Trade Association Membership:
Publishers Association; Booksellers
Association

2472

**MACMILLAN CHILDREN'S BOOKS
LTD**
20 New Wharf Road, London N1 9RR
Telephone: 020 7014 6000
Fax: 020 7014 6001
Web Site: www.panmacmillan.com

Trade Enquiries:
Macmillan Distribution (MDL), Houndmills,
Basingstoke, Hants RG21 6XS
Telephone: 01256 329242
Fax: 01256 840154
Email: mdl@macmillan.co.uk

Personnel:
Emma Hopkin (*Managing Director*)
Ian Mitchell (*Production Director*)
Kate Mackenzie (*Rights Director*)
Anne Glenn (*Art Director*)
Rebecca McNally (*Publishing Director,
Fiction*)
Suzanne Carnell (*Editorial, Picture & Gift
Books Director*)
Gaby Morgan (*Editorial, Poetry & Non-
Fiction Director*)
Martin Challis (*Publishing Director,
Kingfisher*)
Ed Ripley (*Sales Director*)

Audio Books; Children's Books; Poetry

Imprints, Series & ISBNs:
Campbell Books: 978 0 330, 978 0 333
Kingfisher: 978 0 7534
Macmillan Children's Books: 978 0 330, 978
0 333

Young Picador: 978 0 330, 978 0 333

Parent Company:
Macmillan Ltd

Associated Companies:
Macmillan Education Ltd; Macmillan Publishers Ltd; Palgrave Macmillan Ltd; Pan Macmillan Ltd

Book Trade Association Membership:
Publishers Association; Children's Book Circle; PA Children's Book Group

2473 ▬▬▬

MACMILLAN EDUCATION
Macmillan Oxford, Between Towns Road, Oxford OX4 3PP
Telephone: 01865 405700
Fax: 01865 405701
Web Site: www.macmillaneducation.com

Distribution:
Macmillan Distribution (MDL), Houndmills, Basingstoke, Hants RG21 6XS
Telephone: 01256 329242
Fax: 01256 840154
Email: mdl@macmillan.co.uk

Personnel:
Julian Drinkall (Chief Executive & Chairman)
Jeremy Dieguez (Managing Director, Europe)
Paul Emmett (Finance Director)
Mark Chalmers (Group Finance Director, Mac Ed)
John Peacock (Technology, Digital & Operations Director)
Flavio Centofanti (Regional Director, Middle East)
Cathy Smith (International ELT Sales & Marketing Director)
Steven Maginn (Regional Director, East Asia)
Angela Lilley (International ELT Publishing Director)
Sue Bale (Dictionary Publishing Director)
Sharon Servis (Publisher, Latin America)
Martin Powter (Company Secretary)
Nick Evans (Commercial Director, Africa)
Sue Jones (Managing Director, ELT Publishing)

Atlases & Maps; Biology & Zoology; Chemistry; Children's Books; Educational & Textbooks; English as a Foreign Language; Environment & Development Studies; Geography & Geology; History & Antiquarian; Languages & Linguistics; Mathematics & Statistics; Physics; Reference Books, Directories & Dictionaries; Vocational Training & Careers

Imprints, Series & ISBNs:
978 0 333
Macmillan Education
Macmillan Heinemann ELT

Parent Company:
Macmillan Ltd

Associated Companies:
Macmillan Children's Books; Macmillan Publishers Ltd; Palgrave Macmillan; Pan Macmillan

Overseas Representation:
See: Macmillan Publishers Ltd, Basingstoke, UK

Book Trade Association Membership:
Publishers Association

2474 ▬▬▬

MACMILLAN PUBLISHERS LTD
Brunel Road, Houndmills, Basingstoke, Hants RG21 6XS
Telephone: 01256 329242
Fax: 01256 842754
Web Site: www.macmillan.co.uk

Personnel:
Dr A. Thomas (Chief Executive Director)
D. J. G. Knight (Managing Director, Palgrave)
W. H. Farries (Group Central Finance Director, Macmillan)
S. C. Inchcombe (Managing Director, Nature Publishing Group)
J. Drinkall (Managing Director, Macmillan Education)
A. Forbes Watson (Managing Director, Pan Macmillan)
C. E. Fleming (Company Secretary)
J. M. Wheeldon (Chief Finance Officer)

Academic & Scholarly; Architecture & Design; Audio Books; Biography & Autobiography; Biology & Zoology; Chemistry; Children's Books; Cinema, Video, TV & Radio; Computer Science; Cookery, Wines & Spirits; Crafts & Hobbies; Crime; Economics; Educational & Textbooks; Electronic (Professional & Academic); Engineering; English as a Foreign Language; Environment & Development Studies; Fiction; Fine Art & Art History; Gardening; Gender Studies; Guide Books; Health & Beauty; History & Antiquarian; Humour; Languages & Linguistics; Law; Literature & Criticism; Mathematics & Statistics; Medical (incl. Self Help & Alternative Medicine); Military & War; Music; Natural History; Philosophy; Physics; Poetry; Politics & World Affairs; Psychology & Psychiatry; Reference Books, Directories & Dictionaries; Religion & Theology; Science Fiction; Scientific & Technical; Sociology & Anthropology; Sports & Games; Theatre, Drama & Dance; Travel & Topography

Imprints, Series & ISBNs:
Boxtree
Campbell Books
Kingfisher
Macmillan
Macmillan Children's Books
Macmillan Digital Audio
Macmillan New Writing
Nature
Nature Publishing Group
Palgrave Macmillan
Pan Macmillan
Papermac
Picador
Priddy Books
Sidgwick & Jackson

Parent Company:
Germany: Georg von Holtzbrinck GmbH

Associated Companies:
Argentina: Editorial Estrada SA; Editorial Puerto de Palos SA; Macmillan Publishers SA
Armenia: Macmillan Armenia CJS
Australia: Macmillan Distribution Services Pty Ltd; Macmillan Publishers Australia Pty Ltd; Macquarie Library Pty Ltd; Macquarie Online Pty Ltd; Pan Macmillan Australia Pty Ltd
Botswana: Macmillan Botswana Publishing Co (Pty) Ltd
Brazil: Macmillan do Brasil
Cameroon: Macmillan Publishers Cameroon Ltd
Egypt: Macmillan Publishers Egypt Ltd
Ghana: Unimax Macmillan Ltd
Greece: Macmillan Hellas SA
Hong Kong: Macmillan New Asia Publishers Ltd; Macmillan Production (Asia) Ltd Ltd; Macmillan Publishers (China) Ltd
India: Cosmic Graphic & Designs Pvt Ltd; Frank Brothers & Co (Publishers) Ltd; ICC India Pvt Ltd; Macmillan India Ltd; Macmillan Publishers india Ltd; MPS Technologies Ltd
Japan: Macmillan Language House Ltd; Nature Japan KK
Kenya: Macmillan Kenya (Publishers) Ltd
Malawi: Macmillan Malawi Ltd

Mexico: Ediciones Castillo SA de CV; Editorial Macmillan de Mexico SA de CV
Mozambique: Macmillan Mozambique Lda
Namibia: Gamsberg Macmillan Publishers (Pty) Ltd
New Zealand: Macmillan Publishers New Zealand Ltd
Nigeria: Macmillan Nigeria Publishers Ltd; Northern Nigerian Publishing Co Ltd
Peru: Macmillan Publishers SA
Poland: Macmillan Polska Sp.Z.0.0.
Republic of Ireland: Gill & Macmillan Ltd
Republic of Korea: Macmillan Korea Publishers Ltd
Romania: Macmillan Romania SRL
Rwanda: Macmillan Rwanda Publishers Ltd
South Africa: Clever Books (Pty) Ltd; Hodder & Stoughton Ed SA (Pty) Ltd; Macmillan South Africa Publishers (Pty) Ltd; Pan Macmillan South Africa Publishers (Pty) Ltd
Spain: Macmillan Iberia SA
Swaziland: Macmillan Boleswa Publishers Pty Ltd; Macmillan Swaziland National Publishing Co (Pty) Ltd
Tanzania: Macmillan Aidan Ltd
Uganda: Macmillan Uganda Ltd
UK: Boxtree Ltd; Campbell Books Ltd; Kingfisher Publications Ltd; Macmillan Children's Books; Macmillan Distribution Ltd; Macmillan Education; Macmillan English Campus; Macmillan New Writing; Nature Publishing Group Ltd; Palgrave Macmillan; Pan Macmillan; Picador; Rodale; Sidgwick & Jackson Ltd; Stockton Press Ltd; Think Books
USA: Bedford, Freeman & Worth Publishing Group LLC; Tom Doherty Associates LLC; Farrar, Straus & Giroux LLC; Henry Holt and Co LLC; Holtzbrinck Publishers LLC; ICC Inc; Macmillan Academic Publishing Inc; Macmillan Publishers Inc; Nature America Inc; St Martin's Press LLC; Stockton Press Inc
Zambia: Macmillan Publishers (Zambia) Ltd
Zimbabwe: College Press Publishers (Pvt) Ltd

Distributor for:
see: Macmillan Children's Books; Macmillan Education; Palgrave Macmillan; Pan Macmillan

Overseas Representation:
Armenia: Macmillan Armenia JV CJSC, Yerevan, Armenia
Australia: Macmillan Education Australia, South Yarra, Vic, Australia; Pan Macmillan (Australia) Pty Ltd, Sydney, NSW, Australia
Austria & Germany: Katin Lilienthal, Frankfurt am Main, Germany
Botswana: Macmillan Botswana Publishing Co Ltd, Gaborone, Botswana
Brazil: Macmillan do Brasil, São Paulo, Brazil
Cameroon: Macmillan Publishers Cameroon Ltd, Limbe, Cameroon
China: Macmillan Ltd, Beijing Office, Beijing, P. R. of China; Macmillan Publishers (China) Ltd, Hong Kong; Pan Macmillan Asia, Hong Kong
Columbia: Editorial Educativa, Santa Fe de Bogota, Columbia
Cyprus: Char. J. Philippides & Son Ltd, Nicosia, Cyprus
Dubai: Macmillan Education Dubai, Dubai, UAE
East & Central Africa: Macmillan Kenya (Publishers) Ltd, Nairobi, Kenya
Egypt: Macmillan Publishers Egypt Ltd, Cairo, Egypt
Ethiopia: Macmillan Publishers Ltd, Addis Ababa, Ethiopia
France: Laila Belyazid, Paris, France
France & Netherlands: Anne Georges, Brussels, Belgium
Gambia: Macmillan Publishers Ltd, Banjul, Gambia
Ghana: Unimax Macmillan Ltd, Accra, Ghana
Greece: Macmillan Hellas LLC, Athens, Greece

Hong Kong: Macmillan Education, East Asia, Hong Kong; Macmillan Production Asia, Hong Kong
Hungary: Edit Szabo, Budapest, Hungary
India: Books India Pvt Ltd, New Delhi, India; Macmillan Publishers India Ltd, Bangalore, India; Palgrave Macmillan, New Delhi, India
Iran: Sepehr Bookshop, Tehran, Iran
Italy: Macmillan Publishers Ltd, Milan, Italy
Japan: Macmillan Language House, Tokyo, Japan; Nature Japan, Tokyo, Japan
Kenya: Macmillan Kenya (Publishers) Ltd, Nairobi, Kenya
Korea: Macmillan Korea Publishers Ltd, Seoul, Republic of Korea
Malawi: Macmillan Malawi Ltd, Blantyre, Malawi
Mexico & Central America: Editorial Macmillan de Mexico SA de CV, Mexico DF, Mexico
Mozambique: Macmillan Mozambique Lda, Mozambique
Namibia: Gamsberg Macmillan Publishers (Pty) Ltd, Windhoek, Namibia
Netherlands, Belgium & Luxembourg: Daan Timmermans, Amsterdam, Netherlands
New Zealand: Macmillan Publishers New Zealand Ltd, Auckland, New Zealand
Nigeria: Macmillan Nigeria Publishers Ltd, Yaba - Lagos, Nigeria
Pakistan: Book Bird Publishers Representatives, Lahore, Pakistan
Peru: Macmillan Publishers SA, Lima, Peru
Poland: Macmillan Polska, Warsaw, Poland
Republic of Ireland: Gill & Macmillan Ltd, Dublin, Republic of Ireland
Romania: Macmillan Romania SRL, Bucharest, Romania
Rwanda: Macmillan Publishers Rwanda Ltd, Kigali, Rwanda
Saudi Arabia: Elmia Bookstores, Riyadh, Saudi Arabia
Sierra Leone: Macmillan Publishers Ltd, Freetown, Sierra Leone
Singapore: Pansing Distribution Sdn Bhd, Singapore
South Africa: Macmillan South Africa Publishers (Pty) Ltd, Braamfontein, South Africa; Pan Macmillan SA Pty Ltd, Hyde Park, South Africa
Swaziland: Macmillan Boleswa Publishers (Pty) Ltd, Manzini, Swaziland
Taiwan: Macmillan Education, Taipei, Taiwan
Tanzania: Macmillan Aidan Ltd, Dar es Salaam, Tanzania
Turkey: Macmillan Publishers Ltd, Istanbul, Turkey
Uganda: Macmillan Uganda Ltd, Kampala, Uganda
Zambia: Macmillan Zambia, Lusaka, Zambia
Zimbabwe: College Press Publishers (Pvt) Ltd, Harare, Zimbabwe

Book Trade Association Membership:
Publishers Association; Independent Publishers Guild

2475 ▬▬▬

MAGNA LARGE PRINT BOOKS
Magna House, Long Preston, Skipton, North Yorks BD23 4ND
Telephone: 01729 840225 & 840526
Fax: 01729 840683
Email: dallen@magnaprint.co.uk

Personnel:
Robert Thirlby (Chairman)
Diane Allen (General Manager)
David Mellin (Accounts)

Audio Books; Fiction

Imprints, Series & ISBNs:
Audio: 978 1 85903
Large Print: 978 0 7505, 978 1 84262

Parent Company:
Ulverscroft Large Print Books

Distributor for:
Mills & Boon Large Print

Overseas Representation:
Worldwide: Ulverscroft Large Print Books,
UK

2476 ▬▬▬▬▬▬▬

**MAINSTREAM PUBLISHING CO
(EDINBURGH) LTD**
7 Albany Street, Edinburgh EH1 3UG
Telephone: 0131 557 2959
Fax: 0131 556 8720
Email:
enquiries@mainstreampublishing.com
Web Site:
www.mainstreampublishing.com

Distribution, Trade Enquiries & Orders:
TBS Ltd, Colchester Road, Frating Green,
Colchester, Essex CO7 7DW
Telephone: 01206 255600
Fax: 01206 255930

Personnel:
Bill Campbell *(Joint Managing Director,
Editorial)*
Peter MacKenzie *(Joint Managing Director,
Sales)*
Fiona Brownlee *(Marketing & Rights,
Publicity Director)*
Ailsa Bathgate *(Editorial Director)*
Douglas Nicoll *(Company Accountant)*
Neil Graham *(Production Manager)*

*Biography & Autobiography; Cinema,
Video, TV & Radio; Cookery, Wines &
Spirits; Crime; Fine Art & Art History; Guide
Books; Health & Beauty; History &
Antiquarian; Humour; Illustrated & Fine
Editions; Literature & Criticism; Medical
(incl. Self Help & Alternative Medicine);
Military & War; Music; Photography;
Politics & World Affairs; Sports & Games*

No of Employees: 18
Annual Turnover: £3.2M

Imprints, Series & ISBNs:
978 0 906391, 978 1 84018, 978 1 84596,
978 1 85158

Associated Companies:
Random House UK

Overseas Representation:
Australia: Random House Australia Pty Ltd,
Sydney, NSW, Australia
Canada: Random House of Canada Ltd,
Mississauga, Ont, Canada
Caribbean & Latin America: Random House
Inc, New York, NY, USA
*Germany, Switzerland, Austria, Belgium,
Denmark, Finland & Luxembourg:* Jörg
Riekenbrauk, Cologne, Germany
Hong Kong, Taiwan, South Korea & China:
Stanson Yeung, Random House of
Canada Ltd, Toronto, Ont, Canada
India, Sri Lanka & Bangladesh: N. S.
Krishna, Random House Publishers India
Pte Ltd, New Delhi, India
New Zealand: Random House New Zealand
Ltd, Auckland, New Zealand
*Norway, Sweden, Spain, France, Italy,
Portugal, Cyprus, Greece, Malta, Middle
East, Pakistan & Africa (excluding South
Africa):* Random House Group Ltd,
London, UK
South Africa: Random House (SA) Pty Ltd,
Parktown, South Africa
USA: Trafalgar Square Publishing / IPG,
Chicago, IL, USA

Book Trade Association Membership:
Publishing Scotland; Booksellers
Association

2477 ▬▬▬▬▬▬▬

MANAGEMENT POCKETBOOKS LTD
Laurel House, Station Approach, Alresford,
Hants SO24 9JH
Telephone: 01962 735573
Fax: 01962 733637
Email: sales@pocketbook.co.uk
Web Site: www.pocketbook.co.uk

Personnel:
Ros Baynes *(Managing Director)*
Adrian Hunt *(Director)*

*Educational & Textbooks; Industry, Business
& Management*

New Titles: 5 (2010)

Imprints, Series & ISBNs:
Management Pocketbooks: 978 1 870471,
978 1 903776, 978 1 906610
Teachers' Pocketbooks: 978 1 870471, 978
1 903776, 978 1 906610

Overseas Representation:
Australia: Training Solutions Group,
Mudgeeraba, Qld, Australia
Caribbean: InterMedia Americana (IMA)
Ltd, London, UK
Far East: Publishers International Marketing,
Ferndown, Dorset, UK
India: Research Press, New Delhi, India
South Africa: Learning Resources Pty Ltd,
Johannesburg, South Africa

Book Trade Association Membership:
Independent Publishers Guild

2478 ▬▬▬▬▬▬▬

MANCHESTER UNIVERSITY PRESS
Oxford Road, Manchester M13 9NR
Telephone: 0161 275 2310
Fax: 0161 274 3346
Email: mup@manchester.ac.uk
Web Site: manchesteruniversitypress.co.uk

**Distribution (Trade Enquiries, Orders &
Warehouse):**
NBN International, Plymbridge House,
Estover Road, Plymouth, Devon PL6 7PY
Telephone: 01752 202301
Fax: 01752 202333
Email: enquiries@nbninternational.com
Web Site: www.nbninternational.com

Sales Representation (UK):
Yale University Press, 47 Bedford Square,
London WC1B 3DP
Telephone: 020 7079 4900
Fax: 020 7079 4901
Email: sales@yaleup.co.uk

Personnel:
David Rodgers *(Chief Executive Officer &
Production Director)*
Simon Bell *(Head of Sales & Marketing)*
Matthew Frost *(Head of Editorial)*

*Academic & Scholarly; Architecture &
Design; Cinema, Video, TV & Radio;
Economics; Educational & Textbooks; Gay &
Lesbian Studies; Gender Studies; History &
Antiquarian; Illustrated & Fine Editions;
Languages & Linguistics; Law; Literature &
Criticism; Politics & World Affairs;
Reference Books, Directories &
Dictionaries; Sociology & Anthropology;
Theatre, Drama & Dance; Transport*

Imprints, Series & ISBNs:
Manchester University Press: 978 0 7190
Mandolin: 978 1 901341

Parent Company:
UK: The University of Manchester

Distributor for:
Netherlands: Amsterdam University Press

Overseas Representation:
Asia & Middle East: Publishers International
Marketing, Sutton St Nicholas,
Herefordshire, UK
Australia & New Zealand: Footprint Books
Pty Ltd, Warriewood, NSW, Australia
Canada: University of British Columbia
Press, Vancouver, BC, Canada
Canada (Orders & Customer Service): cUPT
Distribution, Toronto, Ont, Canada
Europe: Andrew Durnell Marketing Ltd,
Tunbridge Wells, UK
India (Representation): Andrew White, The
White Partnership, Tunbridge Wells, UK
India (Sales): Viva Books, New Delhi, India
Japan: United Publishers Services Ltd,
Tokyo, Japan
Malaysia: Publishers Marketing Services,
Petaling Jaya, Malaysia
Republic of Ireland: Robert Towers,
Monkstown, Co Dublin, Republic of
Ireland
Singapore: Publishers Marketing Services
Pte Ltd, Singapore
USA: Palgrave, New York, NY, USA

Book Trade Association Membership:
Independent Publishers Guild; Association
of Learned & Professional Society Publishers

2479 ▬▬▬▬▬▬▬

MANDRAKE OF OXFORD
PO Box 250, Oxford OX1 1AP
Telephone: 01865 243671
Fax: 01865 432929
Email: mandrake@mandrake.uk.net
Web Site: www.mandrake.uk.net

Personnel:
Mogg Morgan *(Director)*
Kim Morgan *(Director)*

*Children's Books; Crime; Fiction; Fine Art &
Art History; Literature & Criticism; Magic &
the Occult; Medical (incl. Self Help &
Alternative Medicine); Philosophy; Poetry;
Religion & Theology; Sociology &
Anthropology*

Imprints, Series & ISBNs:
Golden Dawn: 978 1 869928
Mandrake of Oxford: 978 1 869928, 978 1
906958

Overseas Representation:
USA: Ingram Publisher Services, Nashville,
TN, USA; New Leaf Distributing Co, Lithia
Springs, GA, USA

Book Trade Association Membership:
Independent Publishers Guild

2480 ▬▬▬▬▬▬▬

MANEY PUBLISHING
Suite 1C, Joseph's Well, Hanover Walk,
Leeds LS3 1AB
Telephone: 0113 386 8154
Fax: 0113 386 8178
Email: maney@maney.co.uk
Web Site: www.maney.co.uk

Also at:
1 Carlton House Terrace, London
SW1Y 5AF
Telephone: 020 7451 7300
Fax: 020 7451 7307

Personnel:
Michael Gallico *(Managing Director)*
Mark Simon *(Publishing Director)*
Shelly Lynds *(Sales & Marketing Director)*
Liz Rosindale *(Managing Editor)*
Mark Hull *(Managing Editor)*
Lynne Medhurst *(Head of Corporate
Marketing Manager)*
Emily Simpson *(Head of Direct Marketing)*
Gaynor Redvers-Mutton *(Business
Development Manager)*
Kim Martin *(US Executive Publisher)*

*Academic & Scholarly; Archaeology;
Architecture & Design; Atlases & Maps;
Bibliography & Library Science; Biography &
Autobiography; Electronic (Professional &
Academic); Engineering; Environment &
Development Studies; Fashion & Costume;
Fine Art & Art History; Geography &
Geology; History & Antiquarian; Illustrated
& Fine Editions; Languages & Linguistics;
Literature & Criticism; Medical (incl. Self
Help & Alternative Medicine); Military &
War; Religion & Theology; Scientific &
Technical; Transport*

Imprints, Series & ISBNs:
Legenda
Maney Publishing: 978 0 901286, 978 1
902653
Northern Universities Press: 978 0 901286

Distributor for:
European Respiratory Society; Modern
Humanities Research Association; Pasold
Research Fund; Society for Italian
Studies; Society for Medieval
Archaeology

Overseas Representation:
USA: Publishers Communication Group,
Boston, MA, USA

Book Trade Association Membership:
International Group of Scientific, Medical &
Technical Publishers; Association of Learned
& Professional Society Publishers

2481 ▬▬▬▬▬▬▬

MANSON PUBLISHING LTD
73 Corringham Road, London NW11 7DL
Telephone: 020 8905 5150
Fax: 020 8201 9233
Email: manson@mansonpublishing.com
Web Site: www.mansonpublishing.com

Distribution:
NBN International, 10 Estover Road,
Plymouth, Devon PL6 7PY
Telephone: 01752 202300
Fax: 01752 802330
Email: cservs@nbninternational.com
Web Site: www.nbninternational.com

Personnel:
Michael Manson *(Managing Director)*

*Agriculture; Animal Care & Breeding;
Biology & Zoology; Geography & Geology;
Medical (incl. Self Help & Alternative
Medicine); Scientific & Technical; Veterinary
Science*

Imprints, Series & ISBNs:
978 1 84076, 978 1 874545

Associated Companies:
The Veterinary Press Ltd

Distributor for:
Germany: Schluetersche Publishers

Overseas Representation:
All other areas: NBN International,
Plymouth, UK
*Australia & New Zealand (Medical &
Veterinary titles):* All things Medical,
Collingwood, NSW, Australia
Australia & New Zealand (Science titles):
CSIRO Publishing, Collingwood, Vic,
Australia
Japan (Medical & Veterinary titles):
Nankodo Co Ltd, Tokyo, Japan
USA: Thieme Publishers, New York, NY, USA

Book Trade Association Membership:
Publishers Association; Independent
Publishers Guild

2482 ▬▬▬▬▬▬▬

MARITIME BOOKS
Lodge Hill, Liskeard, Cornwall PL14 4EL

Telephone: 01579 343663
Fax: 01579 346747
Email: sales@navybooks.com
Web Site: www.navybooks.com

Personnel:
M. Critchley (Managing Director)
S. Bush (Editor)
P. Garnett (Manager)

Military & War; Transport

New Titles: 2 (2009) , 5 (2010)
No of Employees: 2
Annual Turnover: £350,000

Imprints, Series & ISBNs:
978 0 907771, 978 1 904459

2483

MAVERICK HOUSE PUBLISHERS
Office 19, Dunboyne Business Park,
Dunboyne, Co Meath, Republic of Ireland
Telephone: +353 (01) 825 5717
Fax: +353 (01) 686 5036
Email: info@maverickhouse.com
Web Site: www.maverickhouse.com

Personnel:
Jean Harrington (Managing Director)

Biography & Autobiography; Crime;
Humour; Military & War; Politics & World
Affairs; Sports & Games

Imprints, Series & ISBNs:
978 0 9542945, 978 0 9548707, 978 0
9548708, 978 1 905379

Overseas Representation:
Australia: Tower Books Pty Ltd, Frenchs
Forest, NSW, Australia
Singapore & Malaysia: Paperclip, Singapore
UK: Turnaround Publisher Services Ltd,
London, UK

Book Trade Association Membership:
Publishing Ireland (Foilsiú Éireann)

2484

**MEADOWSIDE CHILDREN'S BOOKS
& GULLANE CHILDREN'S BOOKS**
185 Fleet Street, London EC4A 2HS
Telephone: 020 7400 1092
Fax: 020 7400 1037
Email: info@meadowsidebooks.com &
info@gullanebooks.com
Web Site: www.meadowsidebooks.com &
www.gullanebooks.com

Personnel:
Simon Rosenheim (Publisher)
Rupert Harbour (Sales Director)
Katherine Judge (Rights Director)

Children's Books

New Titles: 80 (2009) , 80 (2010)
No of Employees: 15
Annual Turnover: £2M

Imprints, Series & ISBNs:
Gullane: 978 1 86233
Meadowside: 978 1 84539

Parent Company:
UK: D. C. Thomson

2485

MEDIKIDZ LTD
1st Floor, 6 Burnsall Street, London
SW3 3ST
Telephone: 020 7376 6632
Email: jasatwal@medikidz.com
Web Site: www.medikiz.com

Personnel:
Dr Kim Chilman-Blair (Chief Executive
Officer)

Dr Kate Hersov (Deputy Chief Executive
Officer)
Jon Squires (Commercial Director)
Amanda Langerak (Managing Medical
Editor)
Agustin Larocca (Finance Director)

Children's Books; Educational & Textbooks;
Health & Beauty; Medical (incl. Self Help &
Alternative Medicine)

New Titles: 16 (2009) , 11 (2010)
No of Employees: 20
Annual Turnover: £500,000

Imprints, Series & ISBNs:
978 1 906935

Overseas Representation:
Australia: HarperCollins, Sydney, NSW,
Australia
New Zealand: HarperCollins, Auckland,
New Zealand
USA: American Cancer Society, New York,
USA; Future Horizons, Texas, USA; The
Guidance Group, New York, NY, USA;
Rosen, New York, NY, USA

Book Trade Association Membership:
Publishers Association; Booksellers
Association

2486

MEHRING BOOKS
PO Box 3978, Sheffield S1 2BS
Telephone: 0114 213 0191
Email: sales@mehringbooks.co.uk
Web Site: www.mehringbooks.co.uk

Personnel:
Richard Turner (Contact)

Economics; History & Antiquarian;
Literature & Criticism; Politics & World
Affairs

Imprints, Series & ISBNs:
978 0 929087, 978 1 873045

Distributor for:
Australia: Mehring Books
Germany: Arbeiterpresse Verlag
USA: Mehring Books

Overseas Representation:
Australia: Mehring Books, Marrickville,
NSW, Australia
Germany: Arbeiterpresse Verlag, Essen,
Germany
USA: Mehring Books, Oak Park, MI, USA

Book Trade Association Membership:
Independent Publishers Guild

2487

MELISENDE
G8 Allen House, The Maltings,
Station Road, Sawbridgeworth, Herts, UK
CM21 9JX
Telephone: 01279 721398
Email: melisende@btinternet.com
Web Site: www.melisende.com

Personnel:
Leonard Harrow (Editorial)
Alan Ball (Sales & Marketing)

Academic & Scholarly; Antiques &
Collecting; Archaeology; Architecture &
Design; Crafts & Hobbies; Fine Art & Art
History; History & Antiquarian; Illustrated &
Fine Editions; Politics & World Affairs;
Religion & Theology; Travel & Topography

New Titles: 6 (2009) , 6 (2010)

Imprints, Series & ISBNs:
Atelier: 978 1 901360
Melisende: 978 1 901764

Distributor for:
Cyprus: Rimal Publications
India: DC Books; East & West Publishing;
Orientblackswan/Universities Press;
Social Science Press; Visva-Bharati
UK: Altajir World of Islam Trust; Sangam
Books Ltd

Overseas Representation:
Middle East: Rimal Publications, Cyprus

2488

MENTOR BOOKS
43 Furze Road, Sandyford Industrial Estate,
Dublin 18, Republic of Ireland
Telephone: +353 (01) 295 2112/3
Fax: +353 (01) 295 2114
Email: all@mentorbooks.ie
Web Site: www.mentorbooks.ie

Personnel:
Daniel C. McCarthy (General Manager)

Academic & Scholarly; Biography &
Autobiography; Biology & Zoology;
Cinema, Video, TV & Radio; Crime;
Economics; Educational & Textbooks;
Fiction; Geography & Geology; Guide
Books; Health & Beauty; History &
Antiquarian; Humour; Industry, Business &
Management; Languages & Linguistics;
Mathematics & Statistics; Photography;
Poetry; Politics & World Affairs; Reference
Books, Directories & Dictionaries; Scientific
& Technical; Sports & Games; Travel &
Topography

New Titles: 36 (2009) , 42 (2010)
No of Employees: 15

Imprints, Series & ISBNs:
978 0 947548, 978 1 902586, 978 1 84210

Book Trade Association Membership:
Publishing Ireland (Foilsiú Éireann)

2489

MERCIER PRESS LTD
Unit +3, Oak House,
Riverview Business Park, Bessboro Road,
Blackrock, Cork, Republic of Ireland
Telephone: +353 (021) 461 4700
Fax: +353 (021) 461 4802
Email: info@mercierpress.ie
Web Site: www.mercierpress.ie

Personnel:
Clodagh Feehan (Managing Director)
Mary Feehan (Commissioning Editor)
Sharon O'Donovan (Rights & Permissions)
Wendy Logue (Managing Editor)
Niamh Hatton (Sales Executive)
Patrick Crowley (Marketing Co-ordinator)
Catherine Twibill (Design)

Academic & Scholarly; Biography &
Autobiography; Children's Books; Cookery,
Wines & Spirits; Crafts & Hobbies; Crime;
Fiction; History & Antiquarian; Humour;
Literature & Criticism; Poetry; Politics &
World Affairs; Religion & Theology;
Theatre, Drama & Dance

New Titles: 40 (2009) , 45 (2010)
No of Employees: 7

Imprints, Series & ISBNs:
Marino Books: 978 1 86023
Mercier Press: 978 0 85342, 978 1 85635

Overseas Representation:
Australia: Tower Books Pty Ltd, Frenchs
Forest, NSW, Australia
USA: James Trading Group, Nanuet, NY,
USA

Book Trade Association Membership:
Publishing Ireland (Foilsiú Éireann);
Independent Publishers Guild

2490

MERCURY BOOKS
20 Bloomsbury Street, London WC1B 3JH
Telephone: 020 7636 7171
Fax: 020 7636 1922

Personnel:
Finbarr McCabe (Managing Director)
James Birney (Sales Director)

Archaeology; Atlases & Maps; Geography &
Geology; History & Antiquarian; Literature
& Criticism; Military & War; Reference
Books, Directories & Dictionaries

Annual Turnover: £2.5M

Imprints, Series & ISBNs:
978 1 84560, 978 1 904668

Parent Company:
Caxton Publishing Group

Overseas Representation:
Australia & New Zealand: Bookwise
International, Wingfield, SA, Australia
Europe: Bill Bailey Publishers
Representatives, Newton Abbot, UK
Far East: Bookwise Asia, Singapore,
Singapore
South Africa: Peter Matthews Agencies,
Alberton, South Africa
USA & Canada: International Publishers
Marketing Inc, Herndon, VA, USA

2491

MERCURY JUNIOR
20 Bloomsbury Street, London WC1B 3JH
Telephone: 020 7636 7171
Fax: 020 7636 1922

Personnel:
Finbarr McCabe (Managing Director)
James Birney (Sales Director)

Children's Books; Fashion & Costume

No of Employees: 7
Annual Turnover: £2.5M

Imprints, Series & ISBNs:
978 1 84560, 978 1 904668

Parent Company:
Caxton Publishing Group

Overseas Representation:
Australia & New Zealand: Bookwise
International, Wingfield, SA, Australia
Europe: Bill Bailey Publishers
Representatives, Newton Abbot, UK
Far East: Bookwise Asia, Singapore,
Singapore
South Africa: Peter Matthews Agencies,
Alberton, South Africa
USA & Canada: International Publishers
Marketing Inc, Herndon, VA, USA

2492

THE MERLIN PRESS LTD
99b Wallis Road, London E9 5LN
Telephone: 020 8533 5800
Email: info@merlinpress.co.uk
Web Site: www.merlinpress.co.uk

Distribution:
Central Books Ltd, 99 Wallis Road, London
E9 5LN
Telephone: 020 8986 4854
Fax: 020 8533 5821
Email: orders@centralbooks.com

Personnel:
Anthony Zurbrugg (Managing Director)
Adrian Howe (Manager)

Academic & Scholarly; Biography &
Autobiography; Economics; Gender
Studies; History & Antiquarian; Politics &

World Affairs; Sociology & Anthropology

New Titles: 15 (2009) , 15 (2010)

Imprints, Series & ISBNs:
Green Print: 978 1 85284
The Merlin Press Ltd: 978 0 85036

Overseas Representation:
Australia: Eleanor Brasch Enterprises, Artarmon, NSW, Australia
Canada: Fernwood Books, Black Point, NS, Canada
South Africa: Blue Weaver Marketing, Tokai, South Africa
USA: Independent Publishers Group (IPG), Chicago, IL, USA

2493

MERLIN PUBLISHING/WOLFHOUND PRESS
Newmarket Hall, Cork Street, Dublin 8, Republic of Ireland
Telephone: +353 (01) 453 5866
Fax: +353 (01) 453 5930
Email: publishing@merlin.ie
Web Site: www.merlinwolfhound.com

Distribution:
Gill & Macmillan, Hume Avenue, Park West, Dublin 12, Republic of Ireland
Telephone: +353 (01) 500 9500
Fax: +353 (01) 500 9599
Email: info@gillmacmillan.ie
Web Site: www.gillmacmillan.ie

Personnel:
Chenile Keogh (*Publisher & Managing Director*)
Robert Doran (*Publishing Manager*)

Biography & Autobiography; Cinema, Video, TV & Radio; Cookery, Wines & Spirits; Crafts & Hobbies; Crime; Fashion & Costume; Fine Art & Art History; Guide Books; Health & Beauty; Humour; Music; Photography; Politics & World Affairs; Reference Books, Directories & Dictionaries; Sports & Games; Travel & Topography

New Titles: 8 (2009) , 10 (2010)
No of Employees: 2

Imprints, Series & ISBNs:
Merlin Publishing: 978 1 903582, 978 1 907162
Wolfhound Press: 978 0 86327

Parent Company:
Republic of Ireland: Merlin Media Ltd

Overseas Representation:
UK: Bounce! Sales & Marketing Ltd, London, UK
USA (Wolfhound & Merlin): Interlink Publishing Group Inc, Northampton, MA, USA

Book Trade Association Membership:
Publishing Ireland (Foilsiú Éireann)

2494

MERRELL PUBLISHERS LTD
81 Southwark Street, London SE1 0HX
Telephone: 020 7928 8880
Fax: 020 7928 1199
Web Site: www.merrellpublishers.com

Trade & Credit Orders, Returns:
Marston Book Services, PO Box 269, Abingdon, Oxon OX14 4YN
Telephone: 01235 465500
Fax: 01235 465555
Email: trade.order@marston.co.uk

Personnel:
Hugh Merrell (*Publisher*)
Claire Chandler (*Head of Editorial*)
Nicola Bailey (*Creative Director*)

Lulu Cane (*Sales & Marketing Manager*)
Alenka Oblak (*Production Manager*)
Ruth Tinham (*Foreign Rights Manager*)

Antiques & Collecting; Architecture & Design; Cookery, Wines & Spirits; Crafts & Hobbies; Fashion & Costume; Fine Art & Art History; Gardening; Guide Books; History & Antiquarian; Humour; Illustrated & Fine Editions; Natural History; Photography; Transport; Travel & Topography

New Titles: 27 (2009) , 25 (2010)
No of Employees: 15

Imprints, Series & ISBNs:
978 1 85894

Overseas Representation:
All other territories: Lulu Cane, Merrell Publishers, London, UK
Australia & New Zealand: Scribo Group, 18 Rodborough Rd, Frenchs Forest NSW 2086, Australia
Canada: Canadian Manda Group, Toronto, Ont, Canada
Central America & Caribbean: Chris Humphrys, Humphrys Roberts Associates, London, UK
Eastern Europe: Csaba & Jackie Lengyel de Bagota, CLB Marketing Services, Budapest, Hungary
Estonia, Latvia & Lithuania: Tony Moggach, InterMedia Americana (IMA) Ltd, London, UK
France: Critiques Livres Distribution, Bagnolet, France
Germany, Austria & Switzerland: Gabriele Kern Publishers Services, Frankfurt-am-Main, Germany
Hong Kong, Taiwan, China, Korea, Japan, Indonesia, Philippines & Thailand: Julian Ashton, Ashton International Marketing Services, Sevenoaks, Kent, UK
India, Bangladesh, Nepal, Bhutan & Sri Lanka: Surit Mitra, Maya Publishers Pvt Ltd, New Delhi, India
Italy, Greece, Spain & Portugal: Padovani Books Ltd, London, UK; Padovani Books Ltd, Montanare di Cortona, Italy
Malaysia, Singapore & Brunei: Pansing Distribution Pte Ltd, Singapore
Middle East, Turkey, Israel, Cyprus & Malta: Peter Ward Book Exports, London, UK
Netherlands, Belgium & Luxembourg: Nilsson & Lamm BV, Weesp, Netherlands
Republic of Ireland & Northern Ireland: Robert Towers, Monkstown, Co Dublin, Republic of Ireland
Scandinavia: Elisabeth Harder-Kreimann, Hamburg, Germany
South America: Terry Roberts, Humphrys Roberts Associates, Cotia SP, Brazil
Southern Africa: Shirley Cooksley, Quartet Books, Sunningdale, South Africa
USA: Perseus Group, Jackson, TN, USA

2495

MERTON PRIORY PRESS LTD
9 Owen Falls Avenue, Chesterfield S41 0FR
Telephone: 01246 554026
Email: mertonpriory@btinternet.com
Web Site: www.mertonpriory.co.uk

Personnel:
Philip Riden (*Controlling Director*)

Academic & Scholarly; Archaeology; Biography & Autobiography; History & Antiquarian; Transport

New Titles: 4 (2009) , 4 (2010)
Annual Turnover: £15,000

Imprints, Series & ISBNs:
978 1 898937

2496

MICHELIN MAPS & GUIDES
Hannay House, 39 Clarendon Road, Watford WD17 1JA
Telephone: 01923 205240
Fax: 01923 205241
Web Site: www.michelin.co.uk/travel

Warehouse/Returns:
Michelin Tyre Plc, Maps & Guides, Building 82 Campbell Road, Stoke on Trent, Staffs ST4 4EY
Telephone: 01923 205242
Fax: 01923 205241

Personnel:
I. Murray (*Commercial Director, Head of Travel Publications*)
J. Khawam (*Trade Marketing Manager*)

Atlases & Maps; Guide Books; Travel & Topography

Imprints, Series & ISBNs:
The Green Guide Series
Local Map Series: 978 2 06
National Map Series: 978 2 06
The Red Guide Series: 978 2 06
Regional Map Series: 978 2 06
Zoom Map Series: 978 2 06

Parent Company:
France: Manufacture Française des Pneumatiques Michelin

Overseas Representation:
Belgium & Luxembourg: Michelin Belux, Brussels, Belgium
Italy: Michelin Italiana SPA, Milan, Italy
Spain: Michelin Espana Portugal SA, Madrid, Spain
USA: Michelin Travel Publications, Greenville, SC, USA

Book Trade Association Membership:
Booksellers Association

2497

MICROFORM ACADEMIC PUBLISHERS
Main Street, East Ardsley, Wakefield, West Yorkshire WF3 2AP
Telephone: 01924 825700
Fax: 01924 871005
Email: map@microform.co.uk
Web Site: www.britishonlinearchives.co.uk

Personnel:
Nigel Le Page (*Managing Director*)
Roderic Vassie (*Head of Publishing*)

Academic & Scholarly; Biography & Autobiography; Economics; Electronic (Professional & Academic); History & Antiquarian; Literature & Criticism; Military & War; Politics & World Affairs; Religion & Theology; Sociology & Anthropology

New Titles: 36 (2009) , 30 (2010)

Imprints, Series & ISBNs:
British Records on the Atlantic World, 1700-1850: 978 1 85117
British Records Relating to America in Microform (BRRAM) (series)
Records of the Raj (series)

Associated Companies:
UK: Microform Imaging Ltd

Overseas Representation:
Japan: Far Eastern Booksellers, Tokyo, Japan
USA & Canada: PraXess, New York, NY, USA

2498

MIDDLETON PRESS
Easebourne Lane, Midhurst, Sussex GU29 9AZ
Telephone: 01730 813169

Fax: 01730 812601
Email: sales@middletonpress.co.uk
Web Site: www.middletonpress.co.uk

Personnel:
Dr J. C. V. Mitchell (*Author & Proprietor*)

Military & War; Nautical; Transport

New Titles: 20 (2009) , 20 (2010)

Imprints, Series & ISBNs:
978 0 906520, 978 1 873793, 978 1 901706, 978 1 904474, 978 1 906008

2499

MILESTONE PUBLICATIONS
62 Murray Road, Horndean, Waterlooville, Hants PO8 9JL
Telephone: 023 9259 7440
Fax: 023 9259 1975
Email: info@gosschinaclub.co.uk
Web Site: www.gosschinaclub.co.uk

Personnel:
Lynda Pine (*Managing Director*)
Debbie Webb (*Manageress*)

Antiques & Collecting

Imprints, Series & ISBNs:
978 1 85265, 978 1 903852

Parent Company:
Goss & Crested China Ltd

2500

J. GARNET MILLER
10 Station Road Industrial Estate, Colwall, Malvern, Worcs WR13 6RN
Telephone: 01684 540154
Fax: 01684 540154
Email: simon@cressrelles.co.uk
Web Site: www.cressrelles.co.uk

Personnel:
Leslie Smith (*Manager*)
Simon Smith (*Manager*)

Theatre, Drama & Dance

Parent Company:
Cressrelles Publishing Co Ltd

Overseas Representation:
Australia: Origin Theatrical, Sydney, NSW, Australia
New Zealand: Play Bureau of New Zealand Ltd, New Plymouth, New Zealand
Republic of Ireland: Drama League of Ireland, Dublin, Republic of Ireland
South Africa: Dalro (Pty) Ltd, Braamfontein, South Africa
USA: Bakers Plays, Quincy, MA, USA

2501

MILLER'S
Endeavour House, 189 Shaftesbury Avenue, London WC2H 8JY
Telephone: 020 7632 5400
Email: info-mb@mitchell-beazley.co.uk
Web Site: www.octopusbooks.co.uk

Distributor:
Littlehampton Book Services Ltd, Faraday Close, Durrington, Worthing, West Sussex BN13 3RB
Telephone: 01903 828500
Fax: 01903 828625

Personnel:
Judith Miller (*Publisher/Managing Director*)
Julie Brooke (*Publishing Manager*)

Antiques & Collecting

Parent Company:
Hachette

Associated Companies:
Mitchell Beazley; Octopus Publishing Group

Overseas Representation:
See: Octopus Publishing Group, London, UK

Book Trade Association Membership:
Booksellers Association

2502 ▬▬▬▬

THE MIT PRESS LTD
Fitzroy House, 11 Chenies Street, London
WC1E 7EY
Telephone: 020 7306 0603
Fax: 020 7306 0604
Email: info@HUP-MITpress.co.uk
Web Site: www-mitpress.mit.edu

Trade & Warehouse:
John Wiley & Sons Ltd, Distribution Centre,
Southern Cross Trading Estate,
1 Oldlands Way, Bognor Regis, West Sussex
PO22 9SA
Telephone: 01243 779777
Fax: 01243 820250
Email: cs-books@wiley.co.uk

Personnel:
Ann Sexsmith *(General Manager)*
Ann Twiselton *(Publicity Manager)*
Judith Bullent *(Texts/Exhibitions Manager)*

*Academic & Scholarly; Architecture &
Design; Bibliography & Library Science;
Biography & Autobiography; Biology &
Zoology; Computer Science; Economics;
Environment & Development Studies; Fine
Art & Art History; Gay & Lesbian Studies;
Gender Studies; Industry, Business &
Management; Languages & Linguistics;
Music; Natural History; Philosophy;
Photography; Politics & World Affairs;
Psychology & Psychiatry; Reference Books,
Directories & Dictionaries; Scientific &
Technical*

New Titles: 200 (2009) , 200 (2010)
No of Employees: 4

Imprints, Series & ISBNs:
American Association for Artificial
Intelligence Press: 978 0 262
Bradford Books: 978 0 262
MIT Press: 978 0 262
Semiotext(e): 978 0 936756, 978 1 57027,
978 1 58435
Zone Books: 978 0 942299, 978 1 890951

Parent Company:
USA: MIT Press

Distributor for:
Afterall; Semiotext(e); Zone Books (Urzone
Publishing Ltd)

Overseas Representation:
Australia & New Zealand: Footprint Books
Pty Ltd, Warriewood, NSW, Australia
*Belgium, France, Iceland, Netherlands,
Norway, Sweden, Finland & Denmark:*
Fred Hermans, Bovenkarspel,
Netherlands
Canada & Australia: David Stimpson,
Toronto, Ont, Canada
Caribbean: John Atkin, Norwalk, CT, USA
Central America: Jose Rios, Guatemala
China: Wei Zhao, Everest International
Publishing Services, Beijing, P. R. of China
Germany, Austria, Switzerland & Italy: Uwe
Lüdemann, Berlin, Germany
Hong Kong: Jane Lam, Kowloon, Hong
Kong
India: Mediamatics, Calcutta, India
Iran: Farhad Maftoon, Tehran, Iran
Israel: Rodney Franklin Agency, Tel Aviv,
Israel
Japan: Rockbook, Tokyo, Japan
Malaysia & Brunei: Simon Tay, Apex
Knowledge, Selangor, Malaysia
Mexico: Cynthia Zimpfer, Morelos, Mexico
Middle East (excluding Greece, Iran &

Israel): Avicenna Partnership, Oxford, UK
Pakistan: Saleem Malik, World Press,
Lahore, Pakistan
Philippines: Jean Lim, Megatexts Phil,
Makati City, Philippines
*Poland, Hungary, Croatia, Slovenia,
Slovakia, Czech Republic, Russia, Serbia,
Romania, Albania, Bosnia & Herzegovina,
Latvia, Lithuania & Estonia:* Ewa
Ledóchowicz, Konstancin-Jeziorna,
Poland
*Singapore, Indonesia, Vietnam, Laos,
Cambodia & Myanmar:* Susanne Patrick,
IGP Services, Singapore
South Africa: Cory Voigt Associates,
Johannesburg, South Africa
South Korea: Se-Yung Jun & Min-Hwa Yoo,
Seoul, Republic of Korea
Spain & Portugal: Chris Humphrys, Gaucin,
Spain
Taiwan: B. K. Norton, Taipei, Taiwan

Book Trade Association Membership:
Independent Publishers Guild

2503 ▬▬▬▬

MITCHELL BEAZLEY
Endeavour House,
189 Shaftesbury Avenue, London
WC2H 8JY
Telephone: 020 7632 5400
Web Site: www.octopusbooks.co.uk

Distribution:
Littlehampton Book Services,
Faraday Close, Durrington, Worthing,
West Sussex BN13 3RB
Telephone: 01903 828801
Fax: 01903 828802
Web Site:
www.pubeasy.books.lbsltd.co.uk

Personnel:
David Lamb *(Publisher Director)*
Tracey Smith *(Editorial Director)*

*Antiques & Collecting; Archaeology;
Architecture & Design; Cookery, Wines &
Spirits; Crafts & Hobbies; Fashion &
Costume; Fine Art & Art History;
Gardening; Health & Beauty; History &
Antiquarian; Illustrated & Fine Editions;
Medical (incl. Self Help & Alternative
Medicine); Music; Natural History;
Photography; Reference Books, Directories
& Dictionaries; Sports & Games; Travel &
Topography*

Parent Company:
Hachette UK Ltd

Overseas Representation:
See: Octopus Publishing Group, London, UK

Book Trade Association Membership:
Booksellers Association

2504 ▬▬▬▬

M&K PUBLISHING
[an imprint of M&K Update Ltd]
The Old Bakery, St John's Street, Keswick,
Cumbria CA12 5AS
Telephone: 01768 773030
Fax: 01768 781099
Email: enquiries@mkupdate.co.uk
Web Site: www.mkupdate.co.uk

Personnel:
Mike Roberts *(Co-Director)*
Ken Russell *(Co-Director)*

*Academic & Scholarly; Medical (incl. Self
Help & Alternative Medicine); Psychology &
Psychiatry*

Imprints, Series & ISBNs:
978 1 905539

Parent Company:
UK: M&K Update Ltd

Overseas Representation:
Worldwide: IMR Agency Ltd, Lancaster, UK

Book Trade Association Membership:
Publishers Association

2505 ▬▬▬▬

MOONLIGHT PUBLISHING LTD
The King's Manor, East Hendred, Oxon
OX12 8JY
Telephone: 01235 821821
Fax: 01235 821155
Email: johnclement@btconnect.com
Web Site:
www.moonlightpublishing.co.uk

Warehouse, Trade Enquiries & Orders:
BookSource, 50 Cambuslang Road,
Glasgow G32 8NB
Telephone: 0845 370 0067
Fax: 0845 370 0068
Email: moonlight@booksource.net
Web Site: www.booksource.net

Personnel:
John Clement *(Managing Director)*
Penny Clement *(Company Secretary)*

*Atlases & Maps; Children's Books; English
as a Foreign Language; Fine Art & Art
History; Music; Natural History*

New Titles: 14 (2009) , 12 (2010)
No of Employees: 2
Annual Turnover: £250,000

Imprints, Series & ISBNs:
Close-Ups: 978 1 85103
First Discovery: 978 1 85103
My First Discoveries: 978 1 85103
Torchlight: 978 1 85103

Overseas Representation:
Australia: Era, Brooklyn Park, SA, Australia
Canada: Rainbow Books, Vancouver, BC,
Canada
India: Rupa, New Delhi, India
Japan: First Discovery Japan, Tokyo, Japan
Korea: JY Books, Gyeonnggi-Do, Republic
of Korea
Malaysia: BR Group, Kuching, Sarawak,
Malaysia
South Africa: Wild Dog Press,
Johannesburg, South Africa
Spain: Distribuidora Vicens Vives,
Barcelona, Spain
Taiwan: Children's Publications Co Ltd,
Taipei, Taiwan

Book Trade Association Membership:
Publishers Association; Publishing Scotland

2506 ▬▬▬▬

**MOORLEY'S PRINT & PUBLISHING
LTD**
23 Park Road, Ilkeston, Derbyshire DE7 5DA
Telephone: 0115 932 0643
Fax: 0115 932 0643
Email: sales@moorleys.co.uk
Web Site: www.moorleys.co.uk

Personnel:
Peter R. Newberry *(Joint Managing,
Financial Director)*
Patrick Mancini *(Joint Managing,
Production Director)*

*History & Antiquarian; Music; Poetry;
Religion & Theology; Theatre, Drama &
Dance*

New Titles: 7 (2009) , 10 (2010)
No of Employees: 6

Imprints, Series & ISBNs:
978 0 86071, 978 0 901495

Distributor for:
Cliff College Publishing; Darby
Publications; Mainstream Baptists for Life

& Growth; Met Specials; Nimbus Press;
Social Work Christian Fellowship; Wesley
Fellowship Publications
Malaysia: Pustaka Sufes SDN BHD

Book Trade Association Membership:
Christian Booksellers Association;
Publishing Licensing Society

2507 ▬▬▬▬

MOTOR RACING PUBLICATIONS LTD
PO Box 1318, Croydon, Surrey CR9 5YP
Telephone: 020 8654 2711
Fax: 020 8407 0339
Email: john@mrpbooks.co.uk
Web Site: www.mrpbooks.co.uk

Orders:
Vine House Distribution Ltd,
The Old Mill House, Mill Lane, Uckfield,
East Sussex TN22 5AA
Telephone: 01825 767396
Fax: 01825 765649
Email: sales@vinehouseuk.co.uk
Web Site: www.vinehouseuk.co.uk

Personnel:
John Blunsden *(Managing Director)*

*Biography & Autobiography; Sports &
Games; Transport*

New Titles: 1 (2010)
No of Employees: 1
Annual Turnover: £44,000

Imprints, Series & ISBNs:
The Fitzjames Press: 978 0 948358
Motor Racing Publications: 978 0 900549,
978 0 947981, 978 1 899870
MRP Publishing: 978 0 900549, 978 0
947981, 978 1 899870

Associated Companies:
The Fitzjames Press

Overseas Representation:
*All territories (excluding Australia, New
Zealand, USA, Canada & Republic of
Ireland):* Gunnar Lie Associates, London,
UK
USA & Canada: MBI Distribution Services,
Osceola, WI, USA

2508 ▬▬▬▬

MP PUBLISHING LTD
12 Strathallan Crescent, Douglas,
Isle of Man IM2 4NR
Telephone: 01624 618672
Fax: 01624 620798
Web Site: www.mppublishing.co.uk

Electronic (Entertainment); Fiction

Book Trade Association Membership:
Publishers Association

2509 ▬▬▬▬

MURDOCH BOOKS UK LTD
6th Floor, Erico House,
93–99 Upper Richmond Road, London
SW15 2TG
Telephone: 020 8785 5995
Fax: 020 8785 5985

Distribution & Invoicing:
Macmillan Distribution Ltd, Brunel Road,
Houndmills, Basingstoke, Hants RG21 2XS
Telephone: 01256 329242
Fax: 01256 327961

Personnel:
Juliet Rogers *(Group Chief Executive)*
Cathy Slater *(Foreign Rights Director)*
Carrie Boyes *(UK Sales & Marketing
Director)*
John Sprinks *(UK Finance Director)*

Biography & Autobiography; Cookery,

Wines & Spirits; Crafts & Hobbies; Do-It-Yourself; Gardening; Health & Beauty; History & Antiquarian; Travel & Topography

Imprints, Series & ISBNs:
Murdoch Books: 978 1 74045, 978 1 74196, 978 1 74266
Pier 9: 978 1 74045, 978 1 74196, 978 1 74266

Parent Company:
Australia: Murdoch Books Pty Ltd

Overseas Representation:
Africa: A-Z Africa Book Services, Rotterdam, Netherlands
Asia: Pan Macmillan Asia, Hong Kong
Australia, New Zealand & USA: Murdoch Books Pty Ltd, Sydney, NSW, Australia
Europe: Angell Eurosales, Berwick-on-Tweed, UK; Gabriele Kern Publishers Services, Frankfurt-am-Main, Germany; Nilsson & Lamm, Sint-Niklaas, Belgium; Penny Padovani, London, UK
Middle East: Peter Ward Book Exports, London, UK

Book Trade Association Membership:
Independent Publishers Guild

2510 ▬▬▬▬▬▬

JOHN MURRAY PUBLISHERS
[a division of Hachette UK]
338 Euston Road, London NW1 3BH
Telephone: 020 7873 6000
Fax: 020 7873 6446
Web Site: www.johnmurray.co.uk

UK Orders & Invoicing, Payments & Credit Control & Warehouse:
Bookpoint, 130 Milton Park, Abingdon, Oxon OX14 4SB
Telephone: 01235 400400
Fax: 01235 821511

Personnel:
Roland Philipps *(Managing Director)*
James Spackman *(Sales & Marketing Director)*
Nikki Barrow *(Publicity Director)*
Jason Bartholomew *(Rights Director)*
Eleanor Birne *(Publishing Director)*

Biography & Autobiography; Fiction; Fine Art & Art History; History & Antiquarian; Humour; Military & War; Travel & Topography

Imprints, Series & ISBNs:
978 0 7195

Parent Company:
Hachette UK

Overseas Representation:
Australia: Alliance Distribution Services Pty Ltd, Tuggerah, NSW, Australia; Hachette Livre Australia, Sydney, NSW, Australia
Canada: McArthur & Co Publishers Ltd, Toronto, Ont, Canada
Hong Kong: Asia Publishers Services Ltd, Hong Kong
India: Hachette Book Publishing India Pvt Ltd, Gurgaon, India
Netherlands (Hardbacks and Trade Paperbacks): Nilsson & Lamm BV, Weesp, Netherlands
Netherlands (Paperbacks): Van Ditmar BV, Amsterdam, Netherlands
New Zealand: Hachette Livre New Zealand, Auckland, New Zealand
Pakistan: Oxford University Press Pakistan Branch, Karachi, Pakistan
Singapore & Malaysia: Pansing Distribution Sdn Bhd, Singapore
South Africa: Jonathan Ball Publishers (Pty) Ltd, Johannesburg, South Africa
USA: Trafalgar Square Publishing, North Pomfret, VT, USA

Book Trade Association Membership:
Independent Publishers Guild

2511 ▬▬▬▬▬▬

MW EDUCATIONAL
Westcliff Drive, Leigh-on-Sea, Essex SS9 2LB
Telephone: 01702 715282
Fax: 01702 715172
Email: mweducational@yahoo.co.uk
Web Site: www.mweducational.co.uk

Distribution:
Gardners Books Ltd, 1 Whittle Drive, Eastbourne, East Sussex BN23 6QH
Telephone: 01323 521555

Personnel:
Mark Chatterton *(Chief Executive Officer)*

Children's Books; Educational & Textbooks

Imprints, Series & ISBNs:
The A Plus Series of 11+ Practice Papers: 978 1 901146
The Advantage Series of SATs Practice Papers: 978 1 901146

2512 ▬▬▬▬▬▬

MYRIAD EDITIONS
59 Lansdowne Place, Brighton BN3 1FL
Telephone: 01273 720000
Email: info@MyriadEditions.com
Web Site: www.MyriadEditions.com

Personnel:
Candida Lacey *(Managing Director)*
Robert Benewick *(Director)*
Judith Mackay *(Director)*
Corinne Pearlman *(Design)*
Isabelle Lewis *(Production)*
Jannet King *(Editorial)*
Vicky Blunden *(Fiction)*
Emma Dowson *(Publicity)*
Adrian Weston *(Rights)*

Academic & Scholarly; Atlases & Maps; Electronic (Professional & Academic); Environment & Development Studies; Fiction; Gender Studies; Military & War; Politics & World Affairs

New Titles: 6 (2009) , 10 (2010)
No of Employees: 6

Overseas Representation:
China & Taiwan: Big Apple Tuttle-Mori Agency Inc, Taipei, Taiwan
Japan: Tuttle-Mori Agency Inc, Tokyo, Japan
Spain, Portugal & South America: Ilustrata Empresariale SL, Barcelona, Spain

Book Trade Association Membership:
Independent Publishers Guild

2513 ▬▬▬▬▬▬

MYRMIDON BOOKS LTD
Rotterdam House, 116 Quayside, Newcastle upon Tyne NE1 3DY
Telephone: 0191 206 4005
Email: ed@myrmidonbooks.com
Web Site: www.myrmidonbooks.com

Distribution:
Littlehampton Book Services, Faraday Close, Durrington, Worthing, West Sussex TN13 3RB
Telephone: 01903 828500
Email: enquiries@lbsltd.co.uk
Web Site: www.lbsltd.co.uk

Personnel:
Edward Handyside *(Publishing Director)*

Fiction

New Titles: 7 (2009) , 7 (2010)
No of Employees: 2
Annual Turnover: £102,000

Imprints, Series & ISBNs:
978 1 905802

Overseas Representation:
Australia & New Zealand: Bookwise International, Wingfield, SA, Australia
Singapore, Malaysia & neighbouring territories: Pansing Distribution Pte Ltd, Singapore
South Africa & neighbouring territories: Zytek Publishing (Pty) Ltd, Bedfordview, South Africa

Book Trade Association Membership:
Publishers Association; Independent Publishers Guild

2514 ▬▬▬▬▬▬

THE NATIONAL ACADEMIES PRESS
5 Victoria House, 138 Watling Street East, Towcester NN12 6BT
Telephone: 01327 357770
Fax: 01327 359572
Email: nap@oppuk.co.uk
Web Site: www.nap.edu

Warehouse & Distribution:
Marston Book Services, 160 Milton Park, PO Box 169, Abingdon, Oxon OX14 4YN
Telephone: 01235 465521
Email: direct.orders@marston.co.uk
Web Site: www.marston.co.uk

Personnel:
Gary Hall *(Marketing Manager)*

Academic & Scholarly; Agriculture; Animal Care & Breeding; Biology & Zoology; Chemistry; Educational & Textbooks; Engineering; Environment & Development Studies; Geography & Geology; Industry, Business & Management; Mathematics & Statistics; Medical (incl. Self Help & Alternative Medicine); Natural History; Nautical; Physics; Psychology & Psychiatry; Scientific & Technical; Veterinary Science

New Titles: 190 (2009) , 190 (2010)

Imprints, Series & ISBNs:
Joseph Henry Press: 978 0 309
National Academies Press: 978 0 309

Parent Company:
USA: National Academies Press

2515 ▬▬▬▬▬▬

NATIONAL ARCHIVES OF SCOTLAND
HM General Register House, Edinburgh EH1 3YY
Telephone: 0131 535 1314
Fax: 0131 535 1360
Email: enquiries@nas.gov.uk
Web Site: www.nas.gov.uk

Personnel:
George P. MacKenzie *(Keeper of the Records of Scotland)*
David Brown *(Head of Collection Development)*

History & Antiquarian

Imprints, Series & ISBNs:
978 1 870874

Book Trade Association Membership:
Publishing Scotland

2516 ▬▬▬▬▬▬

THE NATIONAL ASSOCIATION FOR THE TEACHING OF ENGLISH (NATE)
50 Broadfield Road, Sheffield S8 0XJ
Telephone: 01142 555419
Fax: 01142 555296
Email: info@nate.org.uk
Web Site: www.nate.org.uk

Personnel:
A. Fairhall *(Publications Manager)*
J. Elliott *(Senior Administrator)*
I. McNeilly *(Director)*

Academic & Scholarly; Educational & Textbooks; Literature & Criticism; Theatre, Drama & Dance

New Titles: 2 (2010)
No of Employees: 7

Distributor for:
Australia: Phoenix Books
UK: Routledge; Sage

Overseas Representation:
Australia: Phoenix Books, Putney, Australia

2517 ▬▬▬▬▬▬

THE NATIONAL AUTISTIC SOCIETY (NAS)
393 City Road, London EC1V 1NG
Telephone: 020 7833 2299
Fax: 020 7833 9666
Email: nas@nas.org.uk
Web Site: www.autism.org.uk

Trade Enquiries & Orders:
Central Books, 99 Wallis Road, London E9 5LN
Telephone: 0845 458 9911
Fax: 0845 458 9912
Email: nas@centralbooks.com
Web Site: www.autism.org.uk/pubs

Personnel:
Alex Tyla *(Marketing Officer)*
Kathryn Quinton *(Communications)*
David Mason *(Publications Sales Officer)*

Children's Books; Educational & Textbooks; Psychology & Psychiatry

New Titles: 6 (2009) , 5 (2010)

Imprints, Series & ISBNs:
978 1 899280, 978 1 905722

Book Trade Association Membership:
Publishers Form, NCVO

2518 ▬▬▬▬▬▬

NATIONAL CHILDREN'S BUREAU
NCB Publications, 8 Wakley Street, London EC1V 7QE
Telephone: 020 7843 6317
Fax: 020 7843 6087
Email: publications@ncb.org.uk
Web Site: www.ncb.org.uk/books

Distributor:
Central Books, 99 Wallis Road, London E9 5LN
Telephone: 0845 458 9912
Fax: 0845 458 9910
Email: ncb@centralbooks.com
Web Site: www.centralbooks.com

Personnel:
Paula McMahon *(Publishing Manager)*
Rebecca Mason-Bond *(Publishing Officer)*
Lydia Horstman *(Marketing Officer)*

Academic & Scholarly; Educational & Textbooks; Electronic (Professional & Academic); Vocational Training & Careers

New Titles: 4 (2009) , 5 (2010)
No of Employees: 3
Annual Turnover: £150,000

Imprints, Series & ISBNs:
978 0 902817, 978 1 870985, 978 1 874579, 978 1 900990, 978 1 904787, 978 1 905818

Book Trade Association Membership:
Independent Publishers Guild

2519

NATIONAL EXTENSION COLLEGE TRUST LTD
The Michael Young Centre, Purbeck Road, Cambridge CB2 8HN
Telephone: 01223 400200 or 2528
Fax: 01223 400399
Email: info@nec.ac.uk
Web Site: www.nec.ac.uk

Personnel:
Gavin Teasdale (Chief Executive Director)
Jorgen Clausen (Finance Director)
Tim Burton (Education Director)
Tony Hopwood (Business Development Director)

Economics; Educational & Textbooks; Electronic (Educational); Fine Art & Art History; Languages & Linguistics; Law; Mathematics & Statistics; Medical (incl. Self Help & Alternative Medicine); Physics; Psychology & Psychiatry; Religion & Theology; Sociology & Anthropology; Vocational Training & Careers

New Titles: 13 (2009), 2 (2010)
No of Employees: 42

Imprints, Series & ISBNs:
978 0 86082, 978 1 85356

Book Trade Association Membership:
Independent Publishers Guild

2520

NATIONAL GALLERIES OF SCOTLAND
Belford Road, Edinburgh EH4 3DS
Telephone: 0131 624 6257 & 6261
Fax: 0131 623 7135
Email: publications@nationalgalleries.org
Web Site: www.nationalgalleries.org

Personnel:
Janis Adams (Head of Publishing)
Christine Thompson (Publishing Manager)
Olivia Sheppard (Editorial Assistant)

Fine Art & Art History; Photography

Imprints, Series & ISBNs:
978 0 903148, 978 0 903598, 978 1 903278

Overseas Representation:
North America: ACC, Easthampton, MA, USA

Book Trade Association Membership:
Publishing Scotland

2521

NATIONAL GALLERY CO LTD
St Vincent House, 30 Orange Street, London WC2H 7HH
Telephone: 020 7747 5950
Fax: 020 7747 5951
Email: admin@nationalgallery.co.uk
Web Site: www.nationalgallery.co.uk

Distribution:
Yale University Press, 47 Bedford Square, London WC1B 3DP
Telephone: 020 7079 4900
Fax: 020 7079 4901
Email: sales@yaleup.co.uk
Web Site: www.yalebooks.co.uk

Personnel:
Louise Rice (Publishing & Logistics Director)
J. Green (Senior Project Editor)
Giselle Osborne (Project Editor)
Claire Young (Project Editor)
Alex Glen (Publishing Administrator)
Jane Hyne (Production Manager)
Penny Le Tissier (Production Controller)
Suzanne Bosman (Senior Picture Researcher)
Maria Ranauro (Picture Researcher)
Sara Purdy (Publishing Manager)

Academic & Scholarly; Children's Books; Cookery, Wines & Spirits; Electronic (Educational); Electronic (Professional & Academic); Fine Art & Art History; Guide Books

New Titles: 15 (2009), 15 (2010)
No of Employees: 10

Imprints, Series & ISBNs:
978 0 901791, 978 0 947645, 978 1 85709

Parent Company:
The National Gallery Trust

Overseas Representation:
Africa (excluding Southern Africa & Nigeria): Kelvin van Hasselt Publishing Services, Briningham, Norfolk, UK
Austria, Germany, Italy & Switzerland: Uwe Lüdemann, Berlin, Germany
Benelux, Denmark, Finland, France, Iceland, Norway & Sweden: Fred Hermans, Bovenkarspel, Netherlands
Hong Kong, China & Philippines: Ed Summerson, Asia Publishers Services Ltd, Hong Kong
India: S. Janakiraman, Book Marketing Services, Chennai, India
Iran: Farhad Maftoon, Tehran, Iran
Middle East: International Publishers Representatives (IPR) Ltd, Nicosia, Cyprus
Nigeria: Bounty Press Ltd, Ibadan, Nigeria
Pakistan: Anwer Iqbal, Book Bird Publishers Representatives, Lahore, Pakistan
Poland, Czech Republic, Hungary & Slovenia: Ewa Ledóchowicz, Konstancin-Jeziorna, Poland
Republic of Ireland & Northern Ireland: Robert Towers, Monkstown, Co Dublin, Republic of Ireland
Singapore, Malaysia, Brunei & Indonesia: APD Singapore Pte Ltd, Singapore
Southern Africa: Book Promotions Pty Ltd, Diep River, South Africa
Spain & Portugal: Chris Humphrys, Provincia de Malaga, Spain
USA, Canada, Mexico, Central & South America, Australia, New Zealand, Japan, Korea & Taiwan: Yale University Press, New Haven, CT, USA

2522

NATIONAL GALLERY OF IRELAND
National Gallery Bookshop, Merrion Square, Dublin 2, Republic of Ireland
Telephone: +353 (01) 663 3518
Fax: +353 (01) 661 9898
Email: bookshop@ngi.ie
Web Site: www.nationalgallery.ie

Personnel:
Kate Brown (Bookshop Account)
Lydia Furlong (Manager)
Marie McFeely (Rights & Reproduction)

Fine Art & Art History

Imprints, Series & ISBNs:
978 0 903162

Overseas Representation:
Worldwide: Art Books International Ltd, London, UK; Paul Holberton Ltd, UK

Book Trade Association Membership:
Booksellers Association; CLÉ (Irish PA)

2523

NATIONAL HOUSING FEDERATION
Lion Court, 25 Procter Street, Holborn, London WC1V 6NY
Telephone: 020 7067 1010
Fax: 020 7067 1011
Email: info@housing.org.uk
Web Site: www.housing.co.uk

Personnel:
Bev Markham (Head of Publications)
Fiona Shand (Production Editor)
Rick Lloyd (Publishing Coordinator)

Academic & Scholarly; Educational & Textbooks; Industry, Business & Management; Reference Books, Directories & Dictionaries; Vocational Training & Careers

Imprints, Series & ISBNs:
978 0 86297

2524

NATIONAL PORTRAIT GALLERY PUBLICATIONS
National Portrait Gallery, St Martin's Place, London WC2H 0HE
Telephone: 020 7306 0055 ext 266 & 020 7312 2482 (direct line)
Fax: 020 7321 6657
Email: pvadhia@npg.org.uk
Web Site: www.npg.org.uk/publications

Distribution:
Grantham Book Services, Trent Road, Grantham, Lincs NG31 7XG
Telephone: 01476 541080
Fax: 01476 541061
Email: orders@gbs.tbs_ltd.co.uk (UK only)
Web Site: www.granthambookservices.co.uk

Representation (UK):
Casemate Books, 17 Cheap Street, Newbury, Berks RG14 5DD
Telephone: 01635 231091
Fax: 01635 41619
Web Site: www.casematepublishing.co.uk

Personnel:
Robert Carr-Archer (Head of Trading)
Tom Morgan (Head of Rights & Reproduction)
Celia Joicey (Head of Publications)
Ruth Müller-Wirth (Production Manager)
Pallavi Vadhia (Sales & Marketing Manager)
Christopher Tinker (Managing Editor)
Claudia Bloch (Editor)
Victoria Jones (Sales & Marketing Assistant)
Robert Davies (Assistant Editor)

Academic & Scholarly; Biography & Autobiography; Fashion & Costume; Fine Art & Art History; Guide Books; History & Antiquarian; Illustrated & Fine Editions; Photography; Reference Books, Directories & Dictionaries

New Titles: 12 (2009), 15 (2010)
No of Employees: 8

Imprints, Series & ISBNs:
978 0 904017, 978 1 85514

Overseas Representation:
Australia: Peribo Pty Ltd, Mount Kuring-Gai, NSW, Australia
France: Casemate Books, Newbury, UK
Germany, Austria, Switzerland, Belgium & Luxembourg: Exhibitions International, Leuven, Belgium
Italy, Spain, Portugal & Greece: Penny Padovani, London, UK
Netherlands: Amsterdam University Press, Amsterdam, Netherlands
Republic of Ireland & Northern Ireland: Robert Towers, Monkstown, Co Dublin, Republic of Ireland
South America: David Williams, InterMedia Americana (IMA) Ltd, London, UK
USA: Antique Collectors Club Ltd, Easthampton, MA, USA

Book Trade Association Membership:
Booksellers Association; Independent Publishers Guild

2525

THE NATIONAL TRUST
Heelis, Kemble Drive, Swindon, Wilts SN2 2NA
Telephone: 01793 817400
Fax: 01793 817401
Email: grant.berry@nationaltrust.org.uk
Web Site: www.nationaltrust.org.uk

Also at:
Anova Books, 10 Southcombe Street, London W14 0RA
Telephone: 020 7605 1400
Web Site: www.anovabooks.com

Personnel:
John Stachiewicz (Publisher & Commercial Manager)
Grant Berry (Publishing Manager)
Oliver Garrett (Property Publisher)
Anna Groves (Editor)
Claire Forbes (Assistant Editor)

Academic & Scholarly; Agriculture; Antiques & Collecting; Archaeology; Architecture & Design; Biography & Autobiography; Children's Books; Cookery, Wines & Spirits; Fashion & Costume; Fine Art & Art History; Gardening; Guide Books; History & Antiquarian; Humour; Natural History; Reference Books, Directories & Dictionaries; Travel & Topography

New Titles: 25 (2009), 25 (2010)
No of Employees: 6

Imprints, Series & ISBNs:
978 0 7078

Associated Companies:
Anova Books; Gardners Books; The History Press

2526

NATURAL HISTORY MUSEUM PUBLISHING
The Natural History Museum, Cromwell Road, London SW7 5BD
Telephone: 020 7942 5060
Fax: 020 7942 5291
Email: publishing@nhm.ac.uk
Web Site: www.nhm.ac.uk/publishing

Warehouse & Distribution:
Bookpoint Ltd, 130 Milton Park, Abingdon, Oxon OX14 4SB
Telephone: 01235 400400
Fax: 01235 400500
Email: mailorder@bookpoint.co.uk

Personnel:
Lynn Millhouse (Production Manager)
Trudy Brannan (Editorial Manager)
Colin Ziegler (Head of Publishing)
Howard Trent (Sales & Marketing Executive)

Academic & Scholarly; Archaeology; Biography & Autobiography; Biology & Zoology; Children's Books; Educational & Textbooks; Fine Art & Art History; Geography & Geology; Natural History; Reference Books, Directories & Dictionaries; Scientific & Technical

Imprints, Series & ISBNs:
978 0 565

2527

NAXOS AUDIOBOOKS
40A High Street, Welwyn, Herts AL6 9EQ
Telephone: 01438 717808
Fax: 01438 717809
Email: info@naxosaudiobooks.com
Web Site: www.naxos.co.uk/audiobooks/

Distribution:
Select Music & Video, 3 Wells Place, Redhill, Surrey RH1 3SL

Telephone: 01737 645600
Fax: 01737 645600

Personnel:
Nicolas Soames *(Director)*

Audio Books

New Titles: 70 (2009) , 80 (2010)
No of Employees: 4

Imprints, Series & ISBNs:
978 962 634

Parent Company:
Hong Kong: HNH International

Associated Companies:
Naxos Classical Music
Hong Kong: Naxos Classical Music

Overseas Representation:
Australia: Select, Sydney, Australia
Austria: Gramola Co, Vienna, Australia
Brazil: RKR Musical, São Paulo, Brazil
Canada: Naxos of Canada Ltd,
  Scarborough, Ont, Canada
Czech Republic: Classic Music Distribution,
  Prague, Czech Republic
Denmark: Olga Musik, Ry, Denmark
Finland: FG Distribution, Helsinki, Finland
France: Naxos of France, Paris, France
Germany: MVD, Munich, Germany; Naxos
  Deutschland, Münster, Germany
Greece: Greek Record Club, Athens, Greece
Hungary: Phoenix Studio, Budapest,
  Hungary
Iceland: JAPIS, Reykjavik, Iceland
Israel: MCI Records, Tel Aviv, Israel
Japan: Naxos Japan, Nagoya & Tokyo, Japan
Korea: Hae Dong Co Ltd, Seoul, Republic of
  Korea
Malaysia: AV Masters Sdn Bhd, Kuala
  Lumpur, Malaysia
Netherlands: Vanguard Classics,
  Nieuwegein, Netherlands
New Zealand: Triton Music Ltd, Auckland,
  New Zealand
Norway: Musikkdistribusjon AS, Oslo,
  Norway
Philippines: Universal Records, Kalookan
  City, Philippines
Republic of Ireland: Cosmic Sounds Ltd,
  Dublin, Republic of Ireland
Singapore: Naxos Pte Ltd, Singapore
Slovak Republic: Slovart Music, Bratislava,
  Slovakia
South Africa: Booktalk (Pty) Ltd, Craighall,
  South Africa
Spain: FERYSA, Madrid, Spain
Sri Lanka: Titus Stores, Columbo, Sri Lanka
Sweden: Naxos Sweden, Orebro, Sweden
Switzerland: FAME, Meggen (Lucerne),
  Switzerland
Taiwan: Rock Records & Tapes, Taipei,
  Taiwan
Thailand: Media Plus & Broadcasting
  Network Ltd, Bangkok, Thailand
Turkey: Haci Emin Elendi Sokak, Istanbul,
  Turkey
USA: Naxos of America Inc, Pennsauken, NJ,
  USA

Book Trade Association Membership:
Spoken Word Publishers' Association

2528 ▬

NEED2KNOW
Remus House, Coltsfoot Drive, Woodston,
Peterborough PE2 9JX
Telephone: 01733 898103
Fax: 01733 313524
Email: sales@n2kbooks.com
Web Site: www.need2knowbooks.co.uk

Personnel:
Kate Gibbard *(Imprint Manager)*
Emma Gubb *(Editorial Assistant)*

Cookery, Wines & Spirits; Educational &

*Textbooks; Gardening; Health & Beauty;
Medical (incl. Self Help & Alternative
Medicine); Poetry; Vocational Training &
Careers*

New Titles: 17 (2009) , 70 (2010)

Imprints, Series & ISBNs:
Need2Know: 978 1 86144
Triumph House

Parent Company:
Forward Press Ltd

Book Trade Association Membership:
Booksellers Association

2529 ▬

NELSON THORNES LTD
[formerly Stanley Thornes Ltd & Thomas
Nelson & Sons Ltd]
Delta Place, 27 Bath Road, Cheltenham
GL53 7TH
Telephone: 01242 267100
Fax: 01242 221914 (General) & 253695
  (Orders)
Email: info@nelsonthornes.com
Web Site: www.nelsonthornes.com

Distribution:
Alexandra Way, Ashchurch, Tewkesbury,
Glos GL20 8PE

Personnel:
Mary O'Connor *(Managing Director)*
Clive Rushton *(Chief Financial Officer)*
Jim Green *(BU Director)*
Emma Bourne *(International Director)*
Margot van de Weijer *(Head of Customer
  Services & Distribution)*

*Accountancy & Taxation; Biology &
Zoology; Chemistry; Children's Books;
Computer Science; Economics; Educational
& Textbooks; Electronic (Educational);
Engineering; Environment & Development
Studies; Fashion & Costume; Geography &
Geology; Health & Beauty; History &
Antiquarian; Industry, Business &
Management; Languages & Linguistics;
Law; Literature & Criticism; Mathematics &
Statistics; Medical (incl. Self Help &
Alternative Medicine); Physics; Politics &
World Affairs; Psychology & Psychiatry;
Religion & Theology; Scientific & Technical;
Sociology & Anthropology; Sports &
Games; Theatre, Drama & Dance;
Vocational Training & Careers*

Imprints, Series & ISBNs:
978 0 17, 978 0 7487, 978 1 4085

Parent Company:
UK: Infinitas Learning

Distributor for:
Australia: Cengage; Macmillan Library

Overseas Representation:
Antigua & Montserrat: The Best of Books,
  St John's, Antigua
Argentina: Kel Ediciones SA (Agents),
  Buenos Aires, Argentina
Australia (Primary & Secondary): Cengage
  (Australia), NSW, Australia
Bahamas: Media Enterprises Ltd, Nassau,
  Bahamas
Barbados: Days Bookstore, Bridgetown,
  Barbados
Belize: The Book Center, Belize City, Belize
*Botswana, South Africa, Lesotho,
  Swaziland, Mozambique & Namibia:*
  Macmillan Education Ltd, Oxford, UK
*Canada (Primary & Secondary, excluding
  Modern Languages, & Further
  Education):* Bacon & Hughes Ltd,
  Ottawa, Ont, Canada
*Canada (Secondary Modern Languages
  only):* The Resource Centre, Waterloo,
  Canada
Chile: Books and Bits, Santiago, Chile

Colombia: The English Book Centre,
  Bogota, Colombia
Dominica: Jays Ltd, Roseau, Dominica
Egypt: Galaxy Trade, Giza, Egypt
Fiji & Pacific Islands: Premier Book Centre,
  Ba, Fiji
Ghana: EPP Book Services Ltd, Accra, Ghana
Greece: Compendium, Athens, Greece
Grenada: Grenada Teachers School
  Supplies, St George's, Grenada
*Gulf States, Iran, Syria, Libya, Jordan,
  Lebanon, Cyprus, Yemen, Tunis, Turkey,
  Morocco & Algeria (Further & Higher
  Education only):* International Publishing
  Services (IPS) Middle East Ltd, Dubai, UAE
Guyana: Austin's Book Services,
  Georgetown, Guyana
Hong Kong & Macao: Transglobal
  Publishers Services Ltd, Hong Kong
*India, Bangladesh, Sri Lanka, Nepal &
  Bhutan:* Overleaf, New Delhi, India
Jamaica: Kingston Bookshop, Kingston,
  Jamaica
Kenya: Savani's Book Centre, Nairobi, Kenya
Malawi & Zambia: Anglia Book Distributors
  Ltd, Blantyre, Malawi
Malaysia: APD Kuala Lumpur Pte Ltd,
  Selangor, Malaysia
Malta: Miller Distributors Ltd, Luqa, Malta
Mauritius: Editions le Printemps, Vacoas,
  Mauritius
New Zealand: Opus Textbooks, Auckland,
  New Zealand
Nigeria: Chelis Bookazine, Lagos, Nigeria
*North America & Canada (Higher Education
  titles only):* International Specialized
  Book Services Inc, Portland, OR, USA
Pakistan: Publishers Marketing Associates,
  Karachi, Pakistan
Philippines: M. V. Mojica, Manila,
  Philippines
*Republic of Ireland (Modern Languages
  only):* Modern Languages, Dublin,
  Republic of Ireland
*Republic of Ireland (Primary, Secondary &
  Further Education):* Carrol Educational
  Supplies, Dublin, Republic of Ireland
Singapore & Brunei: APD Singapore Pte Ltd,
  Singapore
St Vincent & The Grenadines: Gaymes Book
  Centre, St Vincent
*Sweden, Denmark, Norway, Finland,
  Iceland, Estonia, Latvia & Lithuania
  (Health Science & Science & Engineering
  titles only):* David Towle International,
  Stockholm, Sweden
*Tajikistan, Uzbekistan, Kazakhstan,
  Kyrgyzstan & Turkmenistan:* Silk Road
  Media, London, UK
Trinidad & Tobago: Books Etc, San
  Fernando, Trinidad
Uruguay: Opiciones en Educacion, Uruguay
Vietnam: Fahasa Companie, Ho Chi Minh
  City, Vietnam

Book Trade Association Membership:
Publishers Association

2530 ▬

**NETWORK CONTINUUM
EDUCATION LTD**
see: Continuum International Publishing
Group

2531 ▬

NEW CARAMEL LONDON LTD
[a division of Editions Caramel SA]
12–13 Ship Street, Brighton, East Sussex
BN1 1AD
Web Site: www.caramel.be

Contact:
Jean-Luc Dubois, Otto de Mentockplein 19,
1853 Strombeek-Bever, Belgium
Telephone: +32 2 263 20 51
Fax: +32 2 263 20 50
Email: jeanluc.dubois@caramel.be
Web Site: www.caramel.be

Personnel:
Jean-Michel d'Oultremont *(Joint Managing
  Director)*
Jean-Luc Dubois *(Joint Managing Director)*

Children's Books

Parent Company:
Belgium: Editions Caramel SA

Book Trade Association Membership:
Publishers Association

2532 ▬

**NEW HOLLAND PUBLISHERS (UK)
LTD**
Garfield House, 86–88 Edgware Road,
London W2 2EA
Telephone: 020 7724 7773
Fax: 020 7724 6184
Email: enquiries@nhpub.co.uk
Web Site:
  www.newhollandpublishers.com

Distribution:
Grantham Book Services, Trent Road,
Grantham, Lincs NG31 7XQ
Telephone: 01476 541080
Fax: 01476 541061
Email: orders@gbs.tbs-ltd.co.uk
Web Site:
www.granthambookservices.co.uk

Personnel:
Steve Connolly *(Managing Director)*
Sandy Caven *(Finance Director)*
Rosemary Wilkinson *(Publishing Director)*
Monica Meehan *(Rights Director)*
Terry Shaughnessy *(UK Sales & Marketing
  Director)*
Joan Woodruffe *(Production Manager)*

*Animal Care & Breeding; Cookery, Wines &
Spirits; Crafts & Hobbies; Crime; Do-It-
Yourself; Gardening; Guide Books; Health &
Beauty; Humour; Natural History; Politics &
World Affairs; Reference Books, Directories
& Dictionaries; Sports & Games; Travel &
Topography*

Imprints, Series & ISBNs:
Cadogan Guides: 978 1 86011
Globetrotters: 978 1 84537

Parent Company:
South Africa: Struik Group SA

Associated Companies:
Australia: New Holland Australia
New Zealand: New Holland Publishers (NZ)
  Ltd
South Africa: Random House Struik

Distributor for:
USA: Thomas Nelson Inc

Overseas Representation:
Australia: New Holland Publishers,
  Chatswood, NSW, Australia
Caribbean & Central America: Christopher
  Humphrys, Humphrys Roberts
  Associates, London, UK
China & Hong Kong: United Century Book
  Services Ltd, Hong Kong
Eastern Europe & Russia: Tony Moggach,
  InterMedia Americana (IMA) Ltd,
  London, UK
India: India Book Distributors (Bombay) Ltd,
  Mumbai, India
Japan: Yohan, Tokyo, Japan
Malaysia & Singapore: Pansing Distribution
  Pte Ltd, Singapore
Mexico: Arturo Gutierrez Hernandez,
  Mexico, Mexico
New Zealand: New Holland Publishers (NZ)
  Ltd, Auckland, New Zealand
Pakistan: Tahir M. Lodhi, Lahore, Pakistan
Republic of Ireland & Northern Ireland:
  Alasdair Verschoyle, Compass
  Independent Book Sales Ltd, Naas, Co
  Kildare, Republic of Ireland

Scandinavia: Katie McNeish, McNeish
Publishing International, East Sussex, UK
South America: Terry Roberts, Humphrys
Roberts Associates, Cotia SP, Brazil
Southern, Central & East Africa: Struik New
Holland Publishing (Pty) Ltd, Cape Town,
South Africa
Spain, Portugal & Gibraltar: Peter Prout,
Iberian Book Services, Madrid, Spain
*Thailand, Cambodia, Vietnam, Laos &
Myanmar:* Keith Hardy, Hardy Bigfoss
International Co Ltd, Bangkok, Thailand
USA (Globetrotters & Cadogan): Globe
Pequot Press, Guilford, CT, USA
USA (Lifestyle Books): Sterling Publishing
Co Inc, New York, NY, USA
Western Europe: Ted Dougherty, London,
UK

2533

NEW INTERNATIONALIST PUBLICATIONS LTD
55 Rectory Road, Oxford OX4 1BW
Telephone: 01865 811400
Fax: 01865 793152
Email: ni@newint.org
Web Site: www.newint.org

Representation (UK):
Turnaround Publisher Services Ltd, Unit 3,
Olympia Trading Estate, Coburg Road,
London N22 6TZ
Telephone: 020 8829 3000
Fax: 020 8881 5088

Personnel:
Frank Syratt *(Company Accountant)*
Fran Harvey *(Production Manager)*
Dan Raymond-Barker *(Publications
Marketing Manager)*
Troth Wells *(Publications Editor)*
Amanda Synnott *(Magazine Marketing)*

*Atlases & Maps; Cookery, Wines & Spirits;
Electronic (Educational); Environment &
Development Studies; Fiction;
Photography; Politics & World Affairs;
Reference Books, Directories & Dictionaries*

Annual Turnover: £3M

Imprints, Series & ISBNs:
No-Nonsense Series: 978 0 9540499, 978 1
869847, 978 1 904456, 978 1 906523
World Changing

Parent Company:
New Internationalist Trust Ltd

Overseas Representation:
Australia: Palgrave Macmillan, South Yarra,
Vic, Australia
Australia & Papua New Guinea: New
Internationalist Publications Ltd,
Adelaide, SA, Australia
Canada: New Internationalist Publications
Ltd, Toronto, Ont, Canada
New Zealand & Aotearoa: New
Internationalist Publications Ltd,
Christchurch, New Zealand
South Africa: Stephan Phillips (Pty) Ltd,
Cape Town, South Africa
USA: Consortium Book Sales & Distribution
Inc, St Paul, MN, USA

Book Trade Association Membership:
Independent Publishers Guild; Periodical
Publishers Association

2534

NEW ISLAND BOOKS LTD
2 Brookside, Dundrum Road, Dublin 14,
Republic of Ireland
Telephone: +353 (01) 298 3411
Fax: +353 (01) 298 2783
Email: sales@newisland.ie &
editor@newisland.ie
Web Site: www.newisland.ie

Distribution:
Gill & Macmillan, Hume Avenue,
Park West, Dublin 12, Republic of Ireland
Telephone: +353 (01) 500 9555
Fax: +353 (01) 500 9599
Email: sales@gillmacmillan.ie

**Representation (Republic of Ireland &
Northern Ireland):**
Compass Ireland, 38 Kerdiff Avenue, Naas,
Co Kildare, Republic of Ireland
Telephone: +353 (045) 880805
Fax: +353 (045) 880806
Email: alasdair@compassireland.ie

Personnel:
Edwin Higel *(Publisher)*
Deirdre O'Neill *(Editorial Manager)*
Inka Hagen *(Production & Design Manager)*
Aisling Glynn *(Accounts Manager)*
Karen O'Donoghue *(Marketing, Publicity &
Sales Manager)*
Maria White *(Rights Agent)*
Elaina O'Neill *(Editorial Assistant)*

*Biography & Autobiography; Children's
Books; English as a Foreign Language;
Fiction; Gender Studies; Guide Books;
History & Antiquarian; Humour; Literature
& Criticism; Poetry; Politics & World Affairs;
Theatre, Drama & Dance*

New Titles: 25 (2009) , 25 (2010)
No of Employees: 6

Imprints, Series & ISBNs:
Little Island: 978 1 84840
New Island: 978 1 84840, 978 1 874597,
978 1 902602, 978 1 904301, 978 1
905494

Overseas Representation:
UK: Compass DSA, Slough, UK
USA & Canada: Dufour Editions Inc, Chester
Springs, PA, USA; ISBS, Portland, OR,
USA

Book Trade Association Membership:
Publishing Ireland (Foilsiú Éireann)

2535

NEW PLAYWRIGHTS' NETWORK
10 Station Road Industrial Estate, Colwall,
Malvern, Worcs WR13 6RN
Telephone: 01684 540154
Fax: 01684 540154
Email: simon@cressrelles.co.uk
Web Site: www.cressrelles.co.uk

Personnel:
L. G. Smith *(Managing Director)*
S. R. Smith *(Sales Director)*

Theatre, Drama & Dance

Imprints, Series & ISBNs:
978 0 86319, 978 0 903653, 978 0 906660

Parent Company:
Cressrelles Publishing Co Ltd

Overseas Representation:
Australia: Origin Theatrical, Sydney, NSW,
Australia
New Zealand: Play Bureau of New Zealand
Ltd, New Plymouth, New Zealand
Republic of Ireland: Drama League of
Ireland, Dublin, Republic of Ireland
South Africa: Dalro (Pty) Ltd, Braamfontein,
South Africa
USA: Bakers Plays, Quincy, MA, USA

2536

NEWPRO UK LTD
Old Sawmills Road, Faringdon, Oxon
SN7 7DS
Telephone: 01367 242411
Fax: 01367 241124
Email: sales@newprouk.co.uk
Web Site: www.newprouk.co.uk

Personnel:
Christopher J. Coleman *(Managing Director
& Publisher)*
Beryl L. Coleman *(Company Secretary)*

*Antiques & Collecting; Natural History;
Photography*

Imprints, Series & ISBNs:
978 0 86343, 978 0 906447
Fountain Press
Hove Foto Books

Distributor for:
Classic Collection; Fountain Press; Hove
Foto Books; Van Hasbroeck
Italy: Editrice Reflex
USA: Centennial Photo Service; Marling
Menu Masters; McKeown's Price Guides

Overseas Representation:
Far East, Near East & Middle East:
Publishers International Marketing,
Storrington, UK
South Africa: Zytek Publishing (Pty) Ltd,
Bedfordview, South Africa

2537

NHS IMMUNISATION INFORMATION
Department of Health, Wellington House,
133–155 Waterloo Road, London SE1 8UG
Telephone: 020 7972 4973
Fax: 020 7972 3989
Email: chris.owen@dh.gsi.gov.uk
Web Site: www.immunisation.nhs.uk

*Academic & Scholarly; Educational &
Textbooks; Medical (incl. Self Help &
Alternative Medicine)*

Book Trade Association Membership:
Publishers Association

2538

NIELSEN BOOK
3rd Floor, Midas House,
62 Goldsworth Road, Woking, Surrey
GU21 6LQ
Telephone: 01483 712200
Fax: 01483 712201
Email: info.book@nielsen.com
Web Site: www.nielsenbook.co.uk

Editorial:
89–95 Queensway, Stevenage, Herts
SG1 1EA
Telephone: 0845 450 0016
Fax: 01438 745578
Email: newtitles.book@nielsen.com &
pubhelp.book@nielsen.com
Web Site: www.nielsenbook.co.uk

Personnel:
Jonathan Nowell *(President)*
Richard Knight *(Operations Director)*
Ann Betts *(Commercial Director)*
Jon Windus *(Product Development Director)*
Andrew Sugden *(Financial Director)*
Graham Baker *(Human Resources Director)*
Simon Skinner *(Sales Director)*
Julie Meynink *(Business Development
Director)*
Mo Siewcharran *(Head of Marketing)*
Peter Mathews *(Senior Manager, Publishing
Services)*
Howard Willows *(Senior Manager, Data
Development)*
Gwyneth Morgan *(Editorial Systems, Senior
Manager)*
Samantha Watson *(Quality Assurance,
Senior Manager)*
Vesna Nall *(Publisher Subscriptions
Manager)*
Paul Dibble *(Head of Data Sales)*
Stephen Long *(Head of BookNet Sales)*

Bibliography & Library Science

Parent Company:
The Nielsen Company

Associated Companies:
BDS; Bookseller Publications; ISTC Agency;
Nielsen BookData; Nielsen BookData
Asia Pacific; Nielsen BookNet; Nielsen
BookScan; UK ISBN Agency; UK SAN
Agency

Overseas Representation:
South Africa: Publications Network (Pty) Ltd
(trading as SAPNet), South Africa

Book Trade Association Membership:
Publishing Scotland; Publishing Ireland
(Foilsiú Éireann); Booksellers Association;
Independent Publishers Guild; Data
Publishers Association

2539

NIGHTINGALE PRESS
6 The Old Dairy, Melcombe Road, Bath
BA2 3LR
Telephone: 01225 478444
Fax: 01225 478440
Email: sales@manning-partnership.co.uk
Web Site: www.manning-
partnership.co.uk

Distribution:
Central Books, 99 Wallis Road, London
E9 5LN
Telephone: 0845 458 9911
Fax: 0845 458 9912
Email: info@centralbooks.com
Web Site: www.centralbooks.com

Personnel:
Garry Manning *(Managing Director)*
Roger Hibbert *(Sales Director)*
Julie Pearson *(Finance Manager)*

Humour

Imprints, Series & ISBNs:
978 1 903222

Parent Company:
UK: The Manning Partnership

Distributor for:
Australia: Brimax; Five Mile Press
UK: Brown Dog Books; Carrol & Brown;
Fanahan Books; Interpet Publishing;
Search Press
USA: GPP; Sourcebooks

Overseas Representation:
USA: Richard Gay, Shepperton, Middlesex,
UK

2540

NMS ENTERPRISES LIMITED - PUBLISHING
National Museums Scotland,
Chambers Street, Edinburgh EH1 1JF
Telephone: 0131 247 4026
Fax: 0131 247 4012
Email: publishing@nms.ac.uk
Web Site: www.nms.ac.uk/books

Representation:
CPR, SPCK Head Office, 36 Causton Street,
London SW1P 4ST
Telephone: 020 7592 3900
Email: sales@spck.org.uk

Distribution (UK):
BookSource, 50 Cambuslang Road,
Glasgow G32 8NB
Telephone: 0845 370 0067
Fax: 0845 370 0068
Email: orders@booksource.net

Personnel:
Lesley A. Taylor *(Director of Publishing)*
Kate Blackadder *(Marketing Manager)*
Maggie Wilson *(Administration & Sales)*

Academic & Scholarly; Antiques &
Collecting; Archaeology; Architecture &
Design; Biography & Autobiography;
Biology & Zoology; Children's Books;
Cookery, Wines & Spirits; Educational &
Textbooks; Fine Art & Art History;
Geography & Geology; Guide Books;
History & Antiquarian; Military & War;
Natural History; Poetry; Scientific &
Technical; Sociology & Anthropology;
Transport

New Titles: 11 (2009) , 19 (2010)
No of Employees: 4
Annual Turnover: £110,000

Imprints, Series & ISBNs:
978 0 948636, 978 1 901663, 978 1
905267

Parent Company:
National Museums Scotland

Overseas Representation:
USA: Antique Collectors Club Ltd,
Easthampton, MA, USA

Book Trade Association Membership:
Publishing Scotland

2541 ▬▬▬▬

**NORTH YORK MOORS NATIONAL
PARK AUTHORITY**
The Old Vicarage, Bondgate, Helmsley,
Yorks YO62 5BP
Telephone: 01439 770657
Fax: 01439 770691
Email: J.Renney@northyorkmoors-
npa.gov.uk
Web Site: www.northyorkmoors.org.uk

Personnel:
Julie Lawrence (Head of Information
Service)
Pat Waters-Marsh (Finance Officer)
Maureen Chapman (Sales & Marketing
Assistant)
Jill Renney (Information & Interpretation
Manager)
Mark Lewis (Interpretation Officer)
Chris Pye (Sales & Marketing Assistant)

Archaeology; Biology & Zoology; Children's
Books; Educational & Textbooks;
Environment & Development Studies;
Geography & Geology; Guide Books;
History & Antiquarian; Natural History

New Titles: 1 (2010)

Imprints, Series & ISBNs:
978 0 907480, 978 1 904622

2542 ▬▬▬▬

**NORTHCOTE HOUSE PUBLISHERS
LTD**
Horndon House, Horndon, Tavistock, Devon
PL19 9NQ
Telephone: 01822 810066
Fax: 01822 810034
Email: northcote.house@virgin.net
Web Site: www.northcotehouse.co.uk

Distributors:
Combined Book Services, Unit Y,
Paddock Wood Distribution Centre,
Paddock Wood, Tonbridge, Kent TN12 6UU
Telephone: 01892 837171
Fax: 01892 837372
Email: orders@combook.co.uk
Web Site: www.combook.co.uk

Personnel:
Brian Hulme (Managing Director &
Publisher)
Sarah Piper (Marketing Manager)

Academic & Scholarly; Educational &
Textbooks; Literature & Criticism; Theatre,
Drama & Dance

New Titles: 25 (2009) , 30 (2010)

Imprints, Series & ISBNs:
Northcote House: 978 0 7463
Resources in Education: 978 0 7463
Starting Out....: 978 0 7463
Writers and Their Work: 978 0 7463

Overseas Representation:
Africa (excluding South Africa) & Eastern
Europe: Tony Moggach, IMA, London,
UK
Australia & New Zealand: Book & Volume,
Birregurra, Vic, Australia
Caribbean: Hugh Dunphy, Kingston,
Jamaica
Germany, Austria, Switzerland, France,
Japan, Italy & Benelux: Ted Dougherty,
London, UK
India: Maya Publishers Pvt Ltd, New Delhi,
India
Japan: Koro Komori, Eureka Press, Kyoto,
Japan
Middle East: Hani Kreidieh, Beirut, Lebanon
Pakistan: Book Bird Publishers
Representatives, Lahore, Pakistan
Scandinavia: David Towle International,
Stockholm, Sweden
Spain & Portugal: Peter Prout Iberian Book
Services, Madrid, Spain
USA, Canada & Mexico: David Brown Book
Co, Oakville, CT, USA

Book Trade Association Membership:
Independent Publishers Guild

2543 ▬▬▬▬

NORTHUMBRIA UNIVERSITY PRESS
Trinity Building, Northumbria University,
Newcastle upon Tyne NE1 8ST
Telephone: 0191 227 3382
Fax: 0191 227 3387
Email: andrew.peden-
smith@northumbria.ac.uk
Web Site: www.northumbriapress.co.uk

Orders::
Littlehampton Book Services,
Faraday Close, Durrington, Worthing,
West Sussex BN13 3RB
Telephone: 01903 828500
Fax: 01903 828511
Email: orders@lbsltd.co.uk
Web Site: www.lbsltd.co.uk

Personnel:
Andrew Peden Smith (Head of Publishing)
Mark Stafford (Marketing/Publishing
Assistant)

Biography & Autobiography; Cookery,
Wines & Spirits; Fine Art & Art History;
Guide Books; History & Antiquarian;
Music; Photography; Politics & World
Affairs; Reference Books, Directories &
Dictionaries; Theatre, Drama & Dance

New Titles: 4 (2009) , 10 (2010)
No of Employees: 2
Annual Turnover: £150,000

Imprints, Series & ISBNs:
Northumbria Press: 978 0 85716
Northumbria University Press: 978 1
904794

Overseas Representation:
North America: Independent Publishers
Group, Chicago, IL, USA

Book Trade Association Membership:
Independent Publishers Guild

2544 ▬▬▬▬

W. W. NORTON & COMPANY LTD
Castle House, 75–76 Wells Street, London
W1T 3QT
Telephone: 020 7323 1579
Fax: 020 7436 4553
Email: office@wwnorton.co.uk

Web Site: www.wwnorton.co.uk

Distribution:
John Wiley & Sons Ltd, 1 Oldlands Way,
Shripney, Bognor Regis, Sussex PO22 9SA
Telephone: 01243 779777
Fax: 01243 820250
Email: cs-books@wiley.co.uk

Personnel:
R. A. Cameron (Managing Director &
Chairman)
S. King (Director)
W. D. McFeely (USA Director)
G. Luciano (USA Director)
Patrick Wright (Director)
R. Harrington (USA Director)
A. J. Llewellyn (Director)
Julia Reidhead (Director)

Architecture & Design; Biology & Zoology;
Chemistry; Cinema, Video, TV & Radio;
Computer Science; Cookery, Wines &
Spirits; Economics; Fine Art & Art History;
Gardening; Gender Studies; Geography &
Geology; History & Antiquarian; Literature
& Criticism; Mathematics & Statistics;
Military & War; Music; Natural History;
Nautical; Philosophy; Physics; Poetry;
Politics & World Affairs; Psychology &
Psychiatry; Sports & Games; Theatre,
Drama & Dance

Imprints, Series & ISBNs:
Countryman Press: 978 0 88150
Liveright: 978 0 87140
Norton: 978 0 393

Parent Company:
USA: W. W. Norton & Company

Distributor for:
USA: Dalkey Archive Press; New Directions
Publishing Corporation

Overseas Representation:
Africa & Caribbean: Kelvin van Hasselt
Publishing Services, Briningham, Norfolk,
UK
India: Viva Group, New Delhi, India
Middle East & North Africa: International
Publishers Representatives (IPR) Ltd,
Nicosia, Cyprus
Pakistan: World Press, Lahore, Pakistan
Republic of Ireland: Andrew Russell Book
Representation, Co Cork, Republic of
Ireland
South Africa: Chris Reinders, The African
Moon Press, Kelvin, South Africa

2545 ▬▬▬▬

NORWOOD PUBLISHERS LTD
3 Chapel Street, Norwood Green, Halifax,
West Yorkshire HR3 8QU
Telephone: 01274 602454
Fax: 01274 676665
Email: enquiries@norwoodpublishers.co.uk

Personnel:
M. H. Wolfenden (Partner)
Mrs A. M. Wolfenden (Partner)

Educational & Textbooks

Imprints, Series & ISBNs:
978 1 873784

2546 ▬▬▬▬

THE NOSTALGIA COLLECTION
Silver Link Publishing Ltd, The Trundle,
Ringstead Road, Great Addington,
Kettering, Northants NN14 4BW
Telephone: 01536 330543 & 330588
Fax: 01536 330588
Email: sales@nostalgiacollection.com
Web Site: www.nostalgiacollection.com

Personnel:
Peter Townsend (Managing Director,
Publisher)

Frances Townsend (Company Secretary)
Michael Sanders (Production Manager)
David Walshaw (Mail Order & Advertising
Manager)

History & Antiquarian; Military & War;
Nautical; Transport

Imprints, Series & ISBNs:
Past & Present Publishing Ltd: 978 1 85895
Silver Link Publishing Ltd: 978 0 947971,
978 1 85794

Associated Companies:
Past & Present Publishing Ltd; Silver Link
Publishing Ltd

Distributor for:
Past & Present Publishing Ltd; Silver Link
Publishing Ltd

Book Trade Association Membership:
Booksellers Association

2547 ▬▬▬▬

OAK TREE PRESS
19 Rutland Street, Cork, Republic of Ireland
Telephone: +353 (021) 431 3855
Fax: +353 (021) 431 3496
Email: info@oaktreepress.com
Web Site: www.oaktreepress.com

Personnel:
Brian O'Kane (Managing Director)
Rita O'Kane (Sales Director)

Academic & Scholarly; Accountancy &
Taxation; Educational & Textbooks;
Industry, Business & Management; Law

New Titles: 10 (2009) , 8 (2010)
No of Employees: 3

Imprints, Series & ISBNs:
Oak Tree eWare: 978 1 84621
Oak Tree Press: 978 1 86076, 978 1
872853, 978 1 904887

Parent Company:
Republic of Ireland: Cork Publishing Ltd

Book Trade Association Membership:
Publishing Ireland (Foilsiú Éireann)

2548 ▬▬▬▬

THE O'BRIEN PRESS LTD
12 Terenure Road East, Rathgar, Dublin 6,
Republic of Ireland
Telephone: +353 (01) 492 3333
Fax: +353 (01) 492 2777
Email: books@obrien.ie
Web Site: www.obrien.ie

Personnel:
Michael O'Brien (Publisher)
Ivan O'Brien (Managing Director)
Mary Webb (Editorial Director)
Kunak McGann (Rights Manager)
Erika McGann (Production Manager)
Ruth Heneghan (Marketing Manager)

Architecture & Design; Biography &
Autobiography; Children's Books; Cookery,
Wines & Spirits; Gardening; Guide Books;
Humour; Politics & World Affairs; Sports &
Games; Travel & Topography

Imprints, Series & ISBNs:
978 0 86278, 978 0 905140, 978 1 84717

Associated Companies:
Republic of Ireland: O'Brien Educational

Overseas Representation:
Britain: Francis Lincoln, UK
USA & Canada: James Trading Group,
Nanuet, NY, USA

Book Trade Association Membership:
Independent Publishers Guild

2549

OCTOPUS PUBLISHING GROUP
Endeavour House,
189 Shaftesbury Avenue, London
WC2H 8JY
Telephone: 020 7632 5400
Email: info@octopus-publishing.co.uk
Web Site: www.octopusbooks.co.uk

Distribution:
Littlehampton Book Services Ltd,
Faraday Close, Durrington, Worthing,
West Sussex BN13 3PB
Telephone: 01903 828500
Fax: 01903 828625
Email: orders@lbsltd.co.uk
Web Site: www.lbsltd.co.uk

Personnel:
Alison Goff (Chief Executive Officer)
Andrew Welham (Deputy Chief Executive
  Officer)
Angela Luxton (Commercial Director)
Steven Edney (UK Sales & Marketing
  Director)
Fiona Smith (Publicity Director)
Frances Johnson (Group Head of
  Operations)
Henri Masurel (Group Finance Director)

Animal Care & Breeding; Antiques &
Collecting; Architecture & Design; Atlases &
Maps; Cookery, Wines & Spirits; Crafts &
Hobbies; Do-It-Yourself; Fine Art & Art
History; Gardening; Health & Beauty;
History & Antiquarian; Natural History;
Sports & Games

Imprints, Series & ISBNs:
Cassell Illustrated: 978 0 600
Conran Octopus: 978 0 600
Gaia: 978 0 600
Godsfield Press: 978 0 600
Hamlyn: 978 0 600
Mitchell Beazley: 978 0 600
Philips: 978 0 600
Spruce: 978 0 600

Parent Company:
Hachette UK

Overseas Representation:
All Other Territories: Octopus Export Sales,
  Octopus Publishing Group, London, UK
Australia: Hachette Livre Australia, Sydney,
  NSW, Australia
Canada: Canadian Manda Group, Toronto,
  Ont, Canada
Caribbean: Chris Humphrys & Linda
  Hopkins, London, UK
Caribbean (for Philip's): David Williams,
  InterMedia Americana (IMA) Ltd,
  London, UK
Central America: Arturo Gutierrez
  Hernandez, Mexico, Mexico
China, Hong Kong & Taiwan: Edward
  Summerson, Asia Publishers Services Ltd,
  Hong Kong
France, Belgium, Netherlands, Scandinavia,
  Iceland, Baltics, Eastern Europe & Russia:
  Bill Bailey Publishers Representatives,
  Newton Abbot, UK
Germany, Switzerland & Austria: Gabriele
  Kern Publishers Services, Frankfurt-am-
  Main, Germany
India, Bangladesh & Sri Lanka: Hachette
  Book Publishing India Pvt Ltd, Gurgaon,
  India
Italy & Greece: Penny Padovani, London, UK
Malaysia: APD Kuala Lumpur Pte Ltd,
  Selangor, Malaysia
Middle East, North Africa, Cyprus, Malta &
  Israel: Ray Potts, Publishers International
  Marketing, Polfages, France
New Zealand: Hachette Livre New Zealand,
  Auckland, New Zealand
Philippines & Korea: Benjie Ocampo, Pasig
  City, Philippines
Singapore, Thailand, Indonesia, Vietnam,
  Brunei, Laos & Cambodia: APD
  Singapore Pte Ltd, Singapore

South Africa: Penguin Books South Africa
  (Pty) Ltd, Johannesburg, South Africa
South America: Terry Roberts, Humphrys
  Roberts Associates, Cotia SP, Brazil
Spain, Portugal & Gibraltar: Jenny
  Padovani, Barcelona, Spain
Sub-Saharan Africa: Anita Zih- De Haan,
  Rotterdam, Netherlands
USA: Octopus Books USA, c/o Hachette
  Book Group USA, Boston, MA, USA

Book Trade Association Membership:
Publishers Association

2550

OLD HOUSE BOOKS
The Old Police Station,
Moretonhampstead, Devon TQ13 8PA
Telephone: 01647 440707
Fax: 01647 440202
Email: edward@allhusen.co.uk
Web Site: www.oldhousebooks.co.uk

Personnel:
Edward Allhusen (Managing Director)

Atlases & Maps; Crafts & Hobbies;
Geography & Geology; Guide Books;
History & Antiquarian; Languages &
Linguistics; Natural History; Reference
Books, Directories & Dictionaries; Sports &
Games; Transport; Travel & Topography

New Titles: 6 (2009) , 5 (2010)
No of Employees: 1

Imprints, Series & ISBNs:
978 1 873590

Overseas Representation:
USA: Parkwest Publications Inc, Miami, FL,
  USA

2551

OLD POND PUBLISHING LTD
Dencora Business Centre,
36 White House Road, Ipswich IP1 5LT
Telephone: 01473 238200
Fax: 01473 238201
Email: sales@oldpond.com
Web Site: www.oldpond.com

Personnel:
Roger Smith (Director & Publisher)
Heather Jarrold (Marketing Manager)

Agriculture; Transport; Veterinary Science

Imprints, Series & ISBNs:
978 0 9533651, 978 1 903366, 978 1
  905523, 978 1 906853

Book Trade Association Membership:
Independent Publishers Guild

2552

THE OLD STILE PRESS
Catchmays Court, Llandogo,
Monmouthshire NP25 4TN
Telephone: 01291 689226
Email: oldstile@dircon.co.uk
Web Site: www.oldstilepress.com

Personnel:
Nicolas McDowall (Partner)
Frances McDowall (Partner)

Illustrated & Fine Editions; Literature &
Criticism; Poetry; Theatre, Drama & Dance

Imprints, Series & ISBNs:
978 0 907664

Book Trade Association Membership:
Fine Press Book Association

2553

THE OLEANDER PRESS
16 Orchard Street, Cambridge CB1 1JT
Telephone: 01638 500784
Email: editor@oleanderpress.com
Web Site: www.oleanderpress.com

Personnel:
Jon Gifford (Managing Director & Publisher)
Jane Doyle (Sales Manager)
Will Marston (Rights Manager)

Biography & Autobiography; History &
Antiquarian; Humour; Languages &
Linguistics; Literature & Criticism; Poetry;
Reference Books, Directories &
Dictionaries; Sports & Games; Travel &
Topography

New Titles: 5 (2009) , 5 (2010)
No of Employees: 3

Imprints, Series & ISBNs:
978 0 900891, 978 0 902675, 978 0
  906672

2554

OMNIBUS PRESS
14–15 Berners Street, London W1T 3LJ
Telephone: 020 7612 7400
Fax: 020 7612 7545
Email: richard.hudson@musicsales.co.uk
Web Site: www.omnibuspress.co.uk

Warehouse:
Book Sales Ltd, Newmarket Road,
Bury St Edmunds, Suffolk IP33 3YB
Telephone: 01284 702600
Fax: 01284 768301
Email: music@musicsales.co.uk
Web Site: www.musicsales.co.uk

Personnel:
Robert Wise (Managing Director)
Tony Latham (Financial Director)
Richard Hudson (Sales Director)
Mark Pickard (Production Manager)
Chris Charlesworth (Editor)
David Barraclough (Commissioning Editor)

Biography & Autobiography; Music

Imprints, Series & ISBNs:
Music Sales: 978 0 7119, 978 1 84938
Omnibus Press: 978 0 7119, 978 1 84449,
  978 1 84609, 978 1 84772, 978 1 84938
Sanctuary
Wise Publications: 978 0 7119, 978 1
  84938

Parent Company:
Music Sales Ltd

Associated Companies:
Australia: Music Sales (Pty) Ltd
USA: Music Sales Corp

Distributor for:
Dover Books; IMP; Parker Mead Ltd; Rogan
  House; Schirmer Books

Overseas Representation:
Australia: Macmillan Distribution, South
  Yarra, Vic, Australia
Australia (for Music Shops): Music Sales
  (Australia), Rosebery, NSW, Australia
Belgium: Exhibitions International, Leuven,
  Belgium
Canada: Login Canada, Winnipeg,
  Manitoba, Canada
Central America, Mexico & Caribbean:
  Humphrys Roberts Associates, London,
  UK
Eastern Europe: Tony Moggach, InterMedia
  Americana (IMA) Ltd, London, UK
France: Music Sales Ltd, UK
Germany, Austria & Switzerland: Gabriele
  Kern Publishers Services, Frankfurt-am-
  Main, Germany
Greece, Turkey, Cyprus, Malta & Middle

East: Peter Ward Book Exports, London,
  UK
Indian Sub Continent: Publishers
  International Marketing, Storrington, UK
Netherlands & Luxembourg: Nilsson &
  Lamm BV, Weesp, Netherlands
New Zealand: Macmillan Publishers New
  Zealand Ltd, Auckland, New Zealand
Scandinavia: McNeish Publishing
  International, East Sussex, UK
South Africa: Trinity Books CC, Randburg,
  South Africa
South America: Humphrys Roberts
  Associates, Cotia SP, Brazil
South East & North Asia: Chris Ashdown
  Publishers International Marketing,
  London, UK
Spain, Portugal, Gibraltar & Italy: Penny
  Padovani, London, UK
USA: Music Sales Corporation, New York,
  NY, USA

Book Trade Association Membership:
BA (Associate Member)

2555

ON STREAM PUBLICATIONS LTD
Currabaha, Cloghroe, Co Cork,
Republic of Ireland
Telephone: +353 (021) 438 5798
Email: info@onstream.ie
Web Site: www.onstream.ie

Personnel:
Roz Crowley (Managing Director & Editor)

Academic & Scholarly; Biography &
Autobiography; Cookery, Wines & Spirits;
Environment & Development Studies;
Health & Beauty; Reference Books,
Directories & Dictionaries

Imprints, Series & ISBNs:
978 1 897685

Book Trade Association Membership:
Publishing Ireland (Foilsiú Éireann)

2556

ONEWORLD CLASSICS
London House,
243–253 Lower Mortlake Road, Richmond,
Surrey TW9 2LL
Telephone: 020 8948 9550
Fax: 020 8948 5599
Email: info@oneworldclassics.com
Web Site: www.oneworldclassics.com

Personnel:
Alessandro Gallenzi (Publishing Director)
Elisabetta Minervini (Associate Publisher)

Fiction; Literature & Criticism; Poetry

New Titles: 40 (2009) , 40 (2010)
No of Employees: 4
Annual Turnover: £250,000

Imprints, Series & ISBNs:
Calder Publications: 978 0 7145
One World Classics: 978 1 84749

Associated Companies:
UK: Calder Publications Ltd

Overseas Representation:
Australia: Macmillan, Australia
South Africa: SG Distributors, South Africa
USA & Canada: Trafalgar Square Publishing
  / IPG, Chicago, IL, USA

Book Trade Association Membership:
Independent Publishers Guild

2557

ONLYWOMEN PRESS LTD
40 St Lawrence Terrace, London W10 5ST
Telephone: 020 8354 0796
Fax: 020 8960 2817

Email: onlywomenpress@btconnect.com
Web Site: www.onlywomenpress.com

Trade Distribution:
Central Books Ltd, 99 Wallis Road, London
E9 5LN
Telephone: 0845 458 9911
Fax: 0845 458 9912
Web Site: www.centralbooks.com

Personnel:
L. Mohin (Managing Director)
V. J. Lee (Director)

Academic & Scholarly; Biography &
Autobiography; Children's Books; Crime;
Fiction; Gay & Lesbian Studies; Gender
Studies; Literature & Criticism

Imprints, Series & ISBNs:
978 0 906500

Overseas Representation:
Australia: Bulldog Books, Beaconsfield,
NSW, Australia
North America: Alamo Square Distribution,
USA

Book Trade Association Membership:
Independent Publishers Guild

2558 ▬▬

THE OPEN BIBLE TRUST
Fordland Mount, Upper Basildon, Reading
RG8 8LU
Telephone: 01491 671357
Email: admin@obt.org.uk
Web Site: www.obt.org.uk

Personnel:
Michael Penny (Administrator, Editor)
Sylvia Penny (Treasurer)

Religion & Theology

Imprints, Series & ISBNs:
978 0 947778, 978 1 902859

Associated Companies:
USA: Bible Search Publications Inc

Overseas Representation:
Australia: Benean Bible Fellowship of
Australia, Glendale, NSW, Australia
Canada: Lloyd Allen, Scarborough, Ont,
Canada
New Zealand: Graeme Abbott, Hamilton,
New Zealand
USA: Bible Search Publications, Brookfield,
WI, USA

2559 ▬▬

OPEN GATE PRESS
[incorporating Centaur Press (1954)]
51 Achilles Road, London NW6 1DZ
Telephone: 020 7431 4391
Fax: 020 7431 5129
Email: books@opengatepress.co.uk
Web Site: www.opengatepress.co.uk

Trade Enquiries & Orders:
Central Books Ltd, 99 Wallis Road, London
E9 5LN
Telephone: 0845 458 9911
Fax: 0845 458 9912
Email: sales@centralbooks.com
Web Site: www.centralbooks.com

Personnel:
Jeannie Cohen (Editorial)
Elisabeth Petersdorff (Production)

Academic & Scholarly; Environment &
Development Studies; Philosophy; Politics &
World Affairs; Psychology & Psychiatry;
Religion & Theology

Imprints, Series & ISBNs:
978 0 900001, 978 1 871871

Associated Companies:
Centaur Press; Linden Press (imprint of
Centaur Press)

Book Trade Association Membership:
Publishers Association; Independent
Publishers Guild

2560 ▬▬

OPEN UNIVERSITY WORLDWIDE
Michael Young Building, Walton Hall,
Milton Keynes, Bucks MK7 6AA
Telephone: 01908 858785
Web Site: www.ouw.co.uk

Academic & Scholarly; Biology & Zoology;
Chemistry; Computer Science; Economics;
Educational & Textbooks; Electronic
(Educational); Engineering; English as a
Foreign Language; Environment &
Development Studies; Fine Art & Art
History; Geography & Geology; History &
Antiquarian; Industry, Business &
Management; Languages & Linguistics;
Literature & Criticism; Mathematics &
Statistics; Medical (incl. Self Help &
Alternative Medicine); Natural History;
Physics; Politics & World Affairs; Psychology
& Psychiatry; Religion & Theology; Scientific
& Technical; Sociology & Anthropology;
Theatre, Drama & Dance

New Titles: 127 (2009), 150 (2010)

Imprints, Series & ISBNs:
978 0 7492, 978 1 84873

2561 ▬▬

**OPTIMUS PROFESSIONAL
PUBLISHING**
33–41 Dallington Street, London EC1V 0BB
Telephone: 0845 450 6404
Fax: 0845 450 6410
Email: info@teachingexpertise.com
Web Site: www.optimus-education.com

Personnel:
Russell Lawson (Managing Director)
Frances Peel-Yates (Managing Editor)

Educational & Textbooks; Electronic
(Educational); Geography & Geology;
History & Antiquarian; Vocational Training
& Careers

New Titles: 20 (2009), 15 (2010)
No of Employees: 136
Annual Turnover: £16M

Imprints, Series & ISBNs:
978 1 899857, 978 1 904677, 978 1
905538, 978 1 906517
Chris Kington Publishing
Optimus Education
Teach to Inspire

Parent Company:
Electric Word PLC

Book Trade Association Membership:
Educational Publishers Council

2562 ▬▬

O'REILLY UK LTD
4 Castle Street, Farnham, Surrey GU9 7HS
Telephone: 01252 711776
Fax: 01252 734211
Email: information@oreilly.co.uk
Web Site: www.oreilly.com

Distributors:
John Wiley, 1 Oldlands Way, Bognor Regis
PO22 9SA
Telephone: 01243 779777
Fax: 01243 843303
Email: cs-books@wiley.co.uk

Personnel:
Graham Cameron (Managing Director)

Josette Garcia (Public Relations Manager)
Simon Chappell (Sales Director)

Computer Science

Parent Company:
USA: O'Reilly Media Inc

Distributor for:
UK: microsoft press; pragmatic bookshelf;
rocky nook

Book Trade Association Membership:
Independent Publishers Guild

2563 ▬▬

ORION BOOKS LTD
Orion House, 5 Upper St Martins Lane,
London WC2H 9EA
Telephone: 020 7240 3444
Fax: 020 7240 4822

Trade Counter & Warehouse:
Littlehampton Book Services Ltd,
Faraday Close, Durrington, Worthing,
West Sussex BN13 3RB
Telephone: 01903 828500
Fax: 01903 828625
Web Site: www.orionbooks.co.uk

Personnel:
Lisa Milton (Trade Managing Director)
Susan Lamb (Managing Director Paperback
Division)
Jon Wood (Publishing Director – Fiction)
Fiona Kennedy (Children's Publisher &
Rights Director)

Biography & Autobiography; Children's
Books; Fiction; Science Fiction

Imprints, Series & ISBNs:
Gollancz: 978 1 85798
Orion: 978 1 85797
Orion Children's: 978 1 84255, 978 1
85881
Orion Paperbacks: 978 1 85797
Phoenix: 978 1 85799
Phoenix House

Parent Company:
The Orion Publishing Group Ltd

Overseas Representation:
see: The Orion Publishing Group Ltd,
London, UK

2564 ▬▬

THE ORION PUBLISHING GROUP LTD
Orion House, 5 Upper St Martins Lane,
London WC2H 9EA
Telephone: 020 7240 3444
Fax: 020 7240 4822

Trade Counter & Warehouse:
Littlehampton Book Services Ltd,
Faraday Close, Durrington, Worthing,
West Sussex BN13 3RB
Telephone: 01903 828500
Fax: 01903 828625
Email: ...@lbsltd.co.uk
Web Site: www.lbsltd.co.uk

Personnel:
Arnaud Nourry (Chairman)
Peter Roche (Chief Executive)
Malcolm Edwards (Deputy Chief Executive &
Publisher)
Susan Lamb (Managing Director – Mass
Market)
Lisa Milton (Managing Director – Orion
Books)
Dallas Manderson (Group Sales Director)
Dominic Smith (Home Sales Director)
Mark Streatfeild (Export Sales Director)
Fiona McIntosh (Production Director)
Mark Prior (Finance Director)
Chris Emerson (Distribution Director)
Lord George Weidenfeld (Director)
Susan Howe (Group Rights Director)

Tim Hely Hutchinson (Director)
Pierre de Cacqueray (Director)
Richard Kitson (Director)

Antiques & Collecting; Archaeology; Audio
Books; Biography & Autobiography;
Children's Books; Cinema, Video, TV &
Radio; Cookery, Wines & Spirits; Crafts &
Hobbies; Crime; Fashion & Costume;
Fiction; Fine Art & Art History; Gardening;
Guide Books; Health & Beauty; History &
Antiquarian; Humour; Illustrated & Fine
Editions; Military & War; Natural History;
Nautical; Philosophy; Politics & World
Affairs; Reference Books, Directories &
Dictionaries; Science Fiction; Sports &
Games; Travel & Topography

Imprints, Series & ISBNs:
Cassell: 978 0 304
J M Dent: 978 0 460
Everyman Paperbacks: 978 0 460
First Time Authors Fiction
Gollancz: 978 0 575, 978 1 85797, 978 1
85798
Oriel
Orion: 978 1 85797
Orion Children's: 978 1 84255, 978 1
85881
Orion Fiction: 978 0 7528
Orion Media: 978 0 7528
Orion Paperbacks: 978 0 460, 978 0 7528,
978 1 85797
Phoenix House
Phoenix Mass Market: 978 0 7538
Phoenix Press: 978 1 84212
W & N Illustrated: 978 0 297
Weidenfeld & Nicolson: 978 0 297

Parent Company:
France: Hachette Livre

Associated Companies:
Cassell plc; J M Dent Ltd; Victor Gollancz;
Littlehampton Book Services Ltd; Orion
Books Ltd; George Weidenfeld &
Nicolson Ltd

Distributor for:
Peter Halban Publishers

Overseas Representation:
Australia: Hachette Livre Australia (Orion
Division), Sydney, NSW, Australia
Austria, Belgium, Cyprus, France, Germany,
Greece, Italy, Luxembourg, Netherlands,
Portugal, Spain & Switzerland: Kim Tyler,
The Orion Publishing Group Ltd, London,
UK
Canada: Hachette Book Group, Toronto,
Ont, Canada
Caribbean: Chris Humphrys, Humphrys
Roberts Associates, London, UK
Eastern Europe: Csaba & Jackie Lengyel de
Bagota, Budapest, Hungary
India: Hachette India, New Delhi, India
India, Pakistan, South America, Singapore,
Hong Kong, Thailand, Japan, Indonesia &
Malaysia: Michael Goff, The Orion
Publishing Group Ltd, London, UK
New Zealand: Hachette New Zealand (Orion
Division), Auckland, New Zealand
Philippines, Korea & Taiwan: Ralph & Sheila
Summers, Woodford Green, Essex, UK
Scandinavia, Middle East, Turkey, Malta,
Russia, North Africa & Baltic States:
Jennie McCann, The Orion Publishing
Group Ltd, London, UK
South Africa: Jonathan Ball Publishers (Pty)
Ltd, Johannesburg, South Africa

2565 ▬▬

OSPREY PUBLISHING LTD
Midland House, West Way, Botley, Oxford
OX2 0PH
Telephone: 01865 727022
Fax: 01865 727017
Email: info@ospreypublishing.com
Web Site: www.ospreypublishing.com

Distribution:
Grantham Book Services, Trent Road,
Grantham, Lincs NG31 7XQ
Telephone: 01476 541080
Fax: 01476 541061
Email: orders@gbs-tbs-ltd.co.uk

Personnel:
Rebecca Smart (Managing Director)
Chris Tinsley (Finance Director)
Joanna Sharland (Rights Director)
Kate Moore (Publisher)

Aviation; History & Antiquarian; Military &
War

Imprints, Series & ISBNs:
978 0 85045, 978 1 84176, 978 1 84603,
978 1 84908, 978 1 85532

Overseas Representation:
Australia: Capricorn Link (Australia) Pty Ltd,
Windsor, NSW, Australia
Belgium, Netherlands & Switzerland:
Robbert J. Pleysier, Heerde, Netherlands
Central & Eastern Europe: Tony Moggach,
London, UK
Far East: Ashton International Marketing
Services, Sevenoaks, Kent, UK
France: Ted Dougherty, London, UK
Germany & Austria: Gabriele Kern, PS
Publishers Services, Frankfurt, Germany
Greece & Italy: Sandro Salucci, Florence,
Italy
Middle East: Peter Ward Book Exports,
London, UK
New Zealand: David Bateman Ltd,
Auckland, New Zealand
Scandinavia: Katie McNeish, East Sussex,
UK
Spain, Portugal & Gibraltar: Peter Prout,
Iberian Book Services, Madrid, Spain
Turkey: Ayse Lale Colakoglu, Istanbul,
Turkey
USA, Caribbean & Latin America: Random
House Publishing Services, New York, NY,
USA

2566 ▬▬

*OUTSELL INC / EPS
[formerly Electronic Publishing Services]
26 Rosebery Avenue, London EC1R 4SX
Telephone: 020 7837 3345
Fax: 020 7837 8901
Email: dworlock@outsellinc.com
Web Site: www.outsellinc.com

Electronic (Professional & Academic)

Book Trade Association Membership:
Publishers Association

2567 ▬▬

PETER OWEN PUBLISHERS
73 Kenway Road, London SW5 0RE
Telephone: 020 7373 5628 & 7370 6093
Fax: 020 7373 6760
Email: admin@peterowen.com
Web Site: www.peterowen.com

Trade Counter & Warehouse:
Central Books, 99 Wallis Road, London
E9 5LN
Telephone: 020 8986 4854
Fax: 020 8533 5821
Email: orders@centralbooks.com
Web Site: www.centralbooks.com

Personnel:
Peter Owen (Managing Director)
Antonia Owen (Editorial Director)
Nick Pearson (Production Manager)
Michael O'Connell (Sales & Publicity
Manager)
Simon Smith (Rights & Editorial Manager)

Biography & Autobiography; Cinema,
Video, TV & Radio; Fashion & Costume;
Fiction; Gay & Lesbian Studies; History &

Antiquarian; Literature & Criticism; Music;
Theatre, Drama & Dance

Imprints, Series & ISBNs:
Peter Owen Modern Classics: 978 0 7206

Overseas Representation:
Australia: Peribo Pty Ltd, Mount Kuring-Gai,
NSW, Australia
Canada: Scholarly Book Services Inc,
Toronto, Canada
Europe, Scandinavia & Iceland: Books for
Europe, Massagno, Switzerland
New Zealand: Addenda Ltd, Grey Lynn,
New Zealand
South Africa: Stephan Phillips (Pty) Ltd,
Cape Town, South Africa
USA: Dufour Editions Inc, Chester Springs,
PA, USA

Book Trade Association Membership:
Independent Publishers Guild

2568 ▬▬

OXFAM PUBLISHING
Oxfam House, John Smith Drive, Cowley,
Oxford OX4 2JY
Telephone: 01865 472188
Fax: 01865 472393
Email: publish@oxfam.org.uk
Web Site: www.oxfam.org.uk/publications

Personnel:
Robert Cornford (Communications
Manager: Content Promotion)
Claire Harvey (Communications Manager:
Content Development)
Helen Moreno (Online Communications
Executive)

Academic & Scholarly; Agriculture;
Economics; Environment & Development
Studies; Gender Studies; Politics & World
Affairs

New Titles: 150 (2009) , 150 (2010)
No of Employees: 12

Imprints, Series & ISBNs:
Oxfam Online: 978 1 81814
Oxfam Publications: 978 0 85598

Associated Companies:
UK: Practical Action Publishing

Book Trade Association Membership:
Independent Publishers Guild; Association
of Learned & Professional Society Publishers

2569 ▬▬

OXFORD UNIVERSITY PRESS
Great Clarendon Street, Oxford OX2 6DP
Telephone: 01865 556767
Fax: 01865 557746
Web Site: www.oup.com

Personnel:
Nigel Portwood (Chief Executive)
David Gillard (Finance Director)
Kate Harris (Managing Director: Educational
Division)
Peter Marshall (Managing Director: ELT)
Tim Barton (Managing Director: Academic
& Journals and President OUP USA)
Neil Tomkins (Managing Director:
International Division)
Jesus Lezcano (Managing Director: OUP
Spain)

Academic & Scholarly; Biology & Zoology;
Children's Books; Economics; Educational &
Textbooks; Electronic (Professional &
Academic); English as a Foreign Language;
Industry, Business & Management;
Languages & Linguistics; Law; Mathematics
& Statistics; Medical (incl. Self Help &
Alternative Medicine); Music; Philosophy;
Physics; Politics & World Affairs; Psychology
& Psychiatry; Reference Books, Directories &
Dictionaries; Religion & Theology

New Titles: 6000 (2009)
No of Employees: 1500
Annual Turnover: £579M

Book Trade Association Membership:
Publishers Association

2570 ▬▬

PACKARD PUBLISHING LTD
Forum House, Stirling Road, Chichester,
West Sussex PO19 7DN
Telephone: 01243 537977
Fax: 01243 537977
Email: packardpublishing@googlemail.com
Web Site: www.packardpublishing.com

Personnel:
Michael Packard (Managing Director, Sales,
Rights & Permissions)

Academic & Scholarly; Agriculture;
Architecture & Design; Biology & Zoology;
Educational & Textbooks; Environment &
Development Studies; Gardening;
Geography & Geology; Languages &
Linguistics; Natural History; Reference
Books, Directories & Dictionaries; Scientific
& Technical; Sports & Games

New Titles: 2 (2009) , 4 (2010)
No of Employees: 1

Imprints, Series & ISBNs:
Packard: 978 0 906527, 978 1 85341
Packard (Arabic titles): 978 0 948690

Distributor for:
USA: Carolina Biological Supply Co Inc
(Biology Readers only); Stipes Publishing
LLC

Overseas Representation:
North America: Stipes Publishing LLC,
Champaign, IL, USA

2571 ▬▬

PAGODA TREE PRESS
4 Malvern Buildings, Fairfield Park, Bath
BA1 6JX
Telephone: 01225 463552
Fax: 01225 463552
Email: enquiries@pagodatreepress.com
Web Site: www.pagodatreepress.com

Personnel:
Hugh Rayner (Managing Director)
Jane Murphy (Creative Director)

Academic & Scholarly; Atlases & Maps;
Geography & Geology; Guide Books;
Photography; Politics & World Affairs;
Reference Books, Directories &
Dictionaries; Travel & Topography

New Titles: 9 (2009) , 6 (2010)
No of Employees: 2
Annual Turnover: £25,000

Imprints, Series & ISBNs:
978 0 9529782, 978 1 904289

Distributor for:
India: Library of Numismatic Studies
USA: Amur Maple Books
Zimbabwe: CBC Publishing

Book Trade Association Membership:
Provincial Booksellers' Fairs Association

2572 ▬▬

PALAZZO EDITIONS LTD
2 Wood Street, Bath BA1 2JQ
Telephone: 01225 326444
Fax: 01225 330209
Email: info@palazzoeditions.com
Web Site: www.palazzoeditions.com

Architecture & Design; Children's Books;
History & Antiquarian

Book Trade Association Membership:
Publishers Association

2573 ▬▬

PALGRAVE MACMILLAN
Houndmills, Basingstoke, Hants RG21 6XS
Telephone: 01256 329242
Fax: 01256 479476
Web Site: www.palgrave.com

Warehouse, Trade Enquiries & Orders:
Macmillan Distribution (MDL), Brunel Road,
Houndmills, Basingstoke, Hants RG21 6XS
Telephone: 01256 329242 & 302692
Email: mdl@macmillan.co.uk

Personnel:
Annette Thomas (Chief Executive Officer)
D. J. G. Knight (Managing Director)
S. Burridge (Publishing Director, Scholarly &
Reference)
M. Hewinson (Publishing Director, College)
D. Bull (Publishing Director, Journals)
L. Keelan (Sales Director)
V. Capstick (Marketing Director)
A. J. Jones (Digital Development Director)
R. A. Mathias (Finance Director)
J. W. Peacock (Operations Director)

Academic & Scholarly; Accountancy &
Taxation; Biology & Zoology; Chemistry;
Computer Science; Economics; Educational
& Textbooks; Electronic (Educational);
Engineering; Environment & Development
Studies; Gender Studies; Geography &
Geology; History & Antiquarian; Industry,
Business & Management; Languages &
Linguistics; Law; Literature & Criticism;
Mathematics & Statistics; Medical (incl. Self
Help & Alternative Medicine); Philosophy;
Physics; Politics & World Affairs; Psychology
& Psychiatry; Reference Books, Directories &
Dictionaries; Religion & Theology; Scientific
& Technical; Sociology & Anthropology;
Theatre, Drama & Dance; Vocational
Training & Careers

New Titles: 1233 (2009) , 1322 (2010)

Imprints, Series & ISBNs:
978 0 333, 978 1 4039

Parent Company:
Macmillan Ltd

Associated Companies:
Macmillan Children's Books; Macmillan
Education; Macmillan Publishers Ltd; Pan
Macmillan Ltd; Stockton Press Ltd
USA: Stockton Press Inc

Distributor for:
Bedford; W. H. Freeman; Sinauer
Associates; Spectrum; University Science
Books; Worth Publishers

Overseas Representation:
Africa (excluding areas listed): Africa Dept,
Palgrave Macmillan Ltd, Basingstoke,
Hants, UK
Australia: Palgrave Macmillan, South Yarra,
Vic, Australia
Austria & Germany: Katrin Lilienthal,
Frankfurt-am-Main, Germany
Central & Eastern Europe: Jacek Lewinson,
Warsaw, Poland
China: Macmillan Publishers China Ltd,
Kowloon, P. R. of China
Colombia: Grupo K-T-Dra Ltda, Santa Fe de
Bogota, Colombia
Denmark, Norway, Finland, Sweden &
Iceland: Ben Greig, Cambridge, UK
East Asia (including Hong Kong, Philippines,
Thailand, Vietnam & Indonesia): Palgrave
Macmillan, Hong Kong
Europe (excluding areas listed): Jo Waller,
Palgrave Macmillan Ltd, Basingstoke,
Hants, UK
Greece & Cyprus: Zitsa Seraphimidi, P.
Faliro, Greece
India: Ajit De, Calcutta, India; Anand

Vithalkar, Mumbai, India; Kalpana Shukla, Sunil Sharma, Jagat Bahadur, Palgrave Macmillan, New Delhi, India; V. Ravi, Palgrave Macmillan, Chennai, India
Iran: Sepehr Bookshop, Tehran, Iran
Italy & France: David Pickering, Mare Nostrum Publishing Consultants, Rome, Italy
Japan: Palgrave Macmillan Ltd, Basingstoke, Hants, UK
Kenya: Macmillan Kenya (Publishers) Ltd, Nairobi, Kenya
Korea: Macmillan Publishers, Jongro-Gu, Seoul, Republic of Korea
Latin America & Caribbean: Palgrave Macmillan Ltd, Basingstoke, Hants, UK
Malaysia: UBSD Distribution Sdn Bhd, Selangor, Malaysia
Middle East (all areas not listed): Middle Eastern Dept, Palgrave Macmillan Ltd, Basingstoke, Hants, UK
Netherlands, Belgium, Luxembourg, France & Switzerland: Daan Timmermans, Amsterdam, Netherlands
New Zealand: Macmillan Publishers New Zealand Ltd, Auckland, New Zealand
Nigeria: Macmillan Nigeria Publishers Ltd, Yaba - Lagos, Nigeria
Pakistan: Book Bird Publishers Representatives, Lahore, Pakistan
Singapore & Brunei: Pansing Distribution Sdn Bhd, Singapore
Southern Africa (including Botswana, Lesotho & Swaziland): Cory Voigt, Palgrave Macmillan, Johannesburg, South Africa
Spain: Trinidad Lopez, Madrid, Spain
Sweden: Steven Haslemere, Cambridge, UK
USA & Canada: Palgrave Macmillan, New York, NY, USA

Book Trade Association Membership:
Publishers Association; BDPA; STM

2574 ▬

PAN MACMILLAN
20 New Wharf Road, London N1 9RR
Telephone: 020 7014 6000
Fax: 020 7014 6001
Email: books@macmillan.co.uk
Web Site: www.panmacmillan.com

Warehouse, Trade Enquiries & Orders:
Macmillan Distribution (MDL), Houndmills, Basingstoke, Hants RG21 6XS
Telephone: 01256 329242
Fax: 01256 840154
Email: mdl@macmillan.co.uk

Personnel:
Anthony Forbes Watson *(Managing Director)*
Annette Thomas *(Chief Executive Officer, Macmillan Publishers Ltd)*
Emma Hopkin *(Managing Director, Macmillan Children's Books)*
Jane Carlin *(Financial Director)*
Anna Bond *(UK Sales Director)*
Aimee Roche *(International Sales Director)*
Ian Mitchell *(Production Director)*
Geoff Duffield *(Sales & Marketing Director)*
Camilla Elworthy *(Publicity Director)*
Paul Baggaley *(Publisher – Picador)*
Maria Rejt *(Publisher – Mantle)*
Jeremy Trevathan *(Publisher, Fiction – Macmillan, Pan)*
Georgina Morley *(Editorial Director, Non-Fiction)*
Harriet Sanders *(Rights Director)*
Jon Butler *(Publisher, Non-Fiction)*
Sara Lloyd *(Digital Director)*

Biography & Autobiography; Children's Books; Cinema, Video, TV & Radio; Fiction; Gardening; Guide Books; Health & Beauty; History & Antiquarian; Literature & Criticism; Poetry; Science Fiction; Sports & Games; Travel & Topography

Imprints, Series & ISBNs:
Boxtree

Campbell: 978 0 333
Macmillan: 978 0 230
Macmillan Children's Books: 978 0 230
Mantle
Pan: 978 0 330
Picador: 978 0 330
Sidgwick & Jackson: 978 0 283
Tor: 978 0 230

Parent Company:
Macmillan Ltd

Associated Companies:
Boxtree Ltd; Macmillan Children's Books; Macmillan Education; Macmillan Publishers Ltd; Palgrave Macmillan; Pan Books Ltd; Sidgwick & Jackson Ltd

Overseas Representation:
All other areas - send orders to: International Department, Pan Macmillan, Basingstoke, UK
Australia: Pan Macmillan (Australia) Pty Ltd, Sydney, NSW, Australia
Canada: H. B. Fenn & Co Ltd, Bolton, Ont, Canada
Hong Kong: Publishers' Associates Ltd, Hong Kong
India: Pan Macmillan, New Delhi, India
Japan: Shino Yasuda, Tokyo, Japan
New Zealand: Macmillan Publishers New Zealand Ltd, Auckland, New Zealand
Republic of Ireland: David Adamson, Dublin, Republic of Ireland
South Africa, Botswana, Lesotho, Swaziland, Namibia & Zimbabwe: Pan Macmillan SA Pty Ltd, Hyde Park, South Africa
South East Asia: Pansing Distribution Sdn Bhd, Singapore
West Indies & Caribbean: Macmillan Education Ltd, Oxford, UK

Book Trade Association Membership:
Publishers Association

2575 ▬

PANAF BOOKS
19 Muirfield, Biddenham, Bedford MK40 4FB
Telephone: 01234 340430
Fax: 0870 333 1196
Email: zakakembo@yahoo.co.uk
Web Site: www.panafbooks.com

Distribution:
W & G Foyles Ltd, Dept No 19, 113–119 Charing Cross Road, London WC2H 0EB
Telephone: 020 7440 3245 & (020) 7437 5660

Distribution & Stockist:
Gardners Books, 1 Whittle Drive, Eastbourne BN23 6QH
Telephone: 01323 521555
Fax: 01323 525502 & 521666
Email: customercare@gardners.com

Personnel:
S. S. Kakembo *(Publisher)*
C. W. Little *(Group Financial Adviser)*
E. R. Kakembo *(Director)*
E. Nani-Kofi *(Sales)*
J. Milne *(Consultant)*

Academic & Scholarly; Biography & Autobiography; Politics & World Affairs; Sociology & Anthropology

Imprints, Series & ISBNs:
Panaf: 978 0 901787
PGL – Autobiographies & Biographies Series: 978 0 901787

Parent Company:
Panaf Ltd

Overseas Representation:
East Africa (including Uganda, Kenya &

Tanzania): Crane Publishers Ltd, Kampala, Uganda
Ghana: Hensteve Publications Ltd, Accra, Ghana
USA: Lightning Source Inc (US), Lavergne, TN, USA

2576 ▬

PAPADAKIS PUBLISHER
[a member of New Architecture Group Ltd]
Kimber Studio, Winterbourne, Newbury, Berkshire RG20 8AN
Telephone: 01635 248833
Fax: 01635 248595
Email: info@papadakis.net
Web Site: www.papadakis.net

Personnel:
Alexandra Papadakis *(Publishing Director)*
Sarah Roberts *(Editor)*

Architecture & Design; Fine Art & Art History; Natural History; Photography; Scientific & Technical

New Titles: 9 (2009) , 12 (2010)
No of Employees: 3

Parent Company:
New Architecture Group Ltd

Book Trade Association Membership:
Publishers Association

2577 ▬

PAUPERS' PRESS
37 Quayside Close, Trent Bridge, Nottingham NG2 3BP
Telephone: 0115 986 3334
Fax: 0115 986 3334
Email: books@pauperspress.com
Web Site: www.pauperspress.com

Personnel:
Colin Stanley *(Managing Editor)*

Academic & Scholarly; Literature & Criticism; Philosophy

New Titles: 5 (2009) , 6 (2010)

Imprints, Series & ISBNs:
978 0 946650

2578 ▬

PC PUBLISHING
Keeper's House, Merton, Thetford, Norfolk IP25 6QH
Telephone: 01953 889900
Email: info@pc-publishing.com
Web Site: www.pc-publishing.com

Distribution:
Littlehampton Book Services, Faraday Close, Durrington, Worthing, West Sussex BN13 3RB
Telephone: 01903 828500
Fax: 01903 828625

Personnel:
Philip Chapman *(Director & Publisher)*

Music; Scientific & Technical

New Titles: 6 (2009) , 6 (2010)
No of Employees: 2

Imprints, Series & ISBNs:
978 1 870775, 978 1 906005

Parent Company:
UK: Music Technology Books Ltd

Overseas Representation:
Australia: Woodslane Pty Ltd, Warriewood, NSW, Australia
USA: O'Reilly Associates, Sebastopol, CA, USA

2579 ▬

PCCS BOOKS LTD
2 Cropper Row, Alton Road, Ross-on-Wye HR9 5LA
Telephone: 01989 763900
Fax: 01989 763901
Email: contact@pccs-books.co.uk
Web Site: www.pccs-books.co.uk

Editorial:
The Old Police House, Llangarron, Ross-on-Wye HR9 6PT
Telephone: 01989 770270
Fax: 01989 770700
Email: pete@pccs-books.co.uk
Web Site: www.pccs-books.co.uk

Personnel:
Maggie Taylor-Sanders *(Director)*
Peter J. Sanders *(Director)*

Academic & Scholarly; Gender Studies; Medical (incl. Self Help & Alternative Medicine); Psychology & Psychiatry; Religion & Theology

New Titles: 10 (2009) , 12 (2010)
No of Employees: 7

Imprints, Series & ISBNs:
Critical Psychology Division (Series): 978 1 898059
PCCS Books: 978 1 898059
Person-Centred Approach & Client-Centred Therapy Essential Readers (Series): 978 1 898059
Primers Series: 978 1 898059
Rogers' Therapeutic Conditions Series (Vols 1–4): 978 1 898059
Steps in Counselling Series: 978 1 898059
Straight Talking Introductions Series: 978 1 906254

Book Trade Association Membership:
Independent Publishers Guild

2580 ▬

PEARSON EDUCATION
Edinburgh Gate, Harlow, Essex CM20 2JE
Telephone: 01279 623623
Fax: 01279 431059
Web Site: www.pearson.com

Academic & Scholarly; Educational & Textbooks; Electronic (Professional & Academic); Law

Parent Company:
UK: Pearson Group

Book Trade Association Membership:
Publishers Association

2581 ▬

THE PENGUIN GROUP (UK) LTD
80 Strand, London WC2R 0RL
Telephone: 020 7010 3000
Fax: 020 7010 6060
Web Site: www.penguin.co.uk

Distribution Centre:
Penguin UK, Central Park, Rugby, Warwickshire CV23 0WB
Telephone: 01788 514300

Also at:
Pearson Shared Services/Pearson Education, Edinburgh Gate, Harlow, Essex CM20 2JE
Telephone: 01279 623102
Fax: 0870 850 5255
Email: veronica.reeve@pearsontc.co.uk

Personnel:
John Makinson *(Chairman & Chief Executive)*
Peter Field *(Penguin UK Chief Executive Officer & Dorling Kindersley Worldwide Chief Executive Officer)*

Tom Weldon (*Penguin Deputy Chief Executive Officer*)
John Duhigg (*Dorling Kindersley Deputy Chief Executive Officer*)
Stephanie Barton (*Managing Director, Penguin Children's*)
Francesca Dow (*Puffin Managing Director*)
Suzi Brennan (*Finance Director, Penguin*)
Sally Johnson (*Finance Director, Dorling Kindersley*)
Helena Peacock (*Legal & Human Resources Director*)
Chantal Noel (*Rights Director – Penguin*)
Mike Symons (*Group Sales Director*)
Deborah Wright (*Group Operations Director*)
Simon Prosser (*Publishing Director – Hamish Hamilton*)
Tony Lacey (*Publishing Director – Viking*)
Juliet Annan (*Publishing Director – Fig Tree*)
Louise Moore (*Publishing Director – Michael Joseph*)
Joanna Prior (*Managing Director, Penguin General*)

Academic & Scholarly; Antiques & Collecting; Archaeology; Atlases & Maps; Audio Books; Biography & Autobiography; Children's Books; Cinema, Video, TV & Radio; Cookery, Wines & Spirits; Crafts & Hobbies; Crime; Do-It-Yourself; Fiction; Gardening; Guide Books; Health & Beauty; History & Antiquarian; Humour; Industry, Business & Management; Literature & Criticism; Medical (incl. Self Help & Alternative Medicine); Military & War; Music; Natural History; Philosophy; Photography; Poetry; Politics & World Affairs; Psychology & Psychiatry; Reference Books, Directories & Dictionaries; Religion & Theology; Travel & Topography

No of Employees: 850

Imprints, Series & ISBNs:
Allen Lane: 978 0 14
Arkana: 978 0 14
Joint ventures with BBC Paperbacks
Hamish Hamilton: 978 0 241
Michael Joseph: 978 0 7181
Ladybird: 978 0 14
Penguin: 978 0 14
Penguin Audiobooks: 978 0 14
Penguin Classics: 978 0 14
Penguin Music Classics: 978 0 14
The Penguin Press: 978 0 14
Puffin: 978 0 14
Viking: 978 0 670
Frederick Warne: 978 0 14

Associated Companies:
Dorling Kindersley Ltd; Hamish Hamilton Ltd; Michael Joseph Ltd; Ladybird Books Ltd; Rough Guides; Ventura Publishing Ltd; Viking Ltd; Frederick Warne (& Co) Ltd
Australia: Penguin Books Australia Ltd
Canada: Penguin Books Canada Ltd
New Zealand: Penguin Books (NZ) Ltd
USA: Penguin Putnam Inc

Distributor for:
Which; Wisden

Overseas Representation:
All other areas: Penguin International Sales, London, UK
Australia: Penguin Books Australia Ltd, Camberwell, Vic, Australia
Canada: Penguin Group Canada, Toronto, Ont, Canada
France: Penguin France SA, Blagnac, France
Germany & Austria: Penguin Books Deutschland GmbH, Frankfurt am Main, Germany
India, Bangladesh, Sri Lanka & Nepal: Penguin Books India, New Delhi, India
Italy: Penguin Italia srl, Milan, Italy
Netherlands: Penguin Books BV, Amsterdam, Netherlands
New Zealand: Penguin Books (New Zealand) Ltd, Auckland, New Zealand

Poland, Baltic States, Slovenia, Slovakia & Ukraine: Grazyna Soszynska, Poznan-Baranowo, Poland
Singapore & Malaysia: Penguin Books Singapore & Malaysia, Singapore
South Africa: Penguin Group SA, Rosebank, South Africa
Spain & Portugal: Penguin Books SA, Madrid, Spain
USA: Penguin Group USA, New York, NY, USA

2582 ▬▬▬▬

PENNANT BOOKS LTD
PO Box 5675, London W1A 3FB
Telephone: 020 7387 6400
Email: info@pennantbooks.com
Web Site: www.pennantbooks.com

Distribution, Trade Enquiries & Orders:
Littlehampton Book Services,
Faraday Close, Worthing, West Sussex BN13 3RB
Telephone: 01903 828500
Fax: 01903 828801
Email: enquiries@lbsltd.co.uk
Web Site: www.lbsltd.co.uk

Personnel:
Cass Pennant (*Managing Director*)
Paul Boon (*Marketing Director*)
Caxley Pennant (*Director*)
Paul A. Woods (*Editor*)
Philomena Muinzer (*PR – Events & Publicity*)

Academic & Scholarly; Biography & Autobiography; Crime; Humour; Music; Sociology & Anthropology; Sports & Games

Imprints, Series & ISBNs:
978 1 906015

Associated Companies:
UK: Pennant Publishing Ltd

Overseas Representation:
Republic of Ireland: Compass Independent Book Sales Ltd, Naas, Co Kildare, Republic of Ireland

Book Trade Association Membership:
Independent Publishers Guild

2583 ▬▬▬▬

PENTATHOL PUBLISHING
40 Gibson Street, Wrexham,
Wrexham County LL13 7NS

Personnel:
Athol E. Cowen (*Owner/Chief Executive*)

Poetry

Book Trade Association Membership:
Publishers Association; Booksellers Association

2584 ▬▬▬▬

PHAIDON PRESS LTD
18 Regent's Wharf, All Saints Street,
London N1 9PA
Telephone: 020 7843 1000
Fax: 020 7843 1010
Web Site: www.phaidon.com

Orders:
Phaidon Customer Services
Telephone: 020 7843 1234
Fax: 020 7843 1111
Email: sales@phaidon.com
Web Site: www.phaidon.com

Warehouse:
Grove Lane, Marston Trading Estate, Frome, Somerset BA11 4AT
Telephone: 01373 474710
Fax: 01373 474711
Web Site: www.phaidon.com

Personnel:
Andrew Price (*Chairman*)
James Booth-Clibborn (*International Sales & Marketing Director*)
Amanda Renshaw (*Editorial Director*)
Emilia Terragni (*Editorial Director*)
Jonathan Feinmesser (*Financial Director*)
Simon Gwynn (*UK Sales Director*)
Paul Hammond (*Production Director*)

Academic & Scholarly; Architecture & Design; Children's Books; Cinema, Video, TV & Radio; Cookery, Wines & Spirits; Fashion & Costume; Fine Art & Art History; Illustrated & Fine Editions; Music; Photography

Imprints, Series & ISBNs:
978 0 7148

Associated Companies:
France: Phaidon Sarl
Germany: Phaidon Verlag
Japan: Phaidon KK
USA: Phaidon Press Inc

Overseas Representation:
Australia: United Book Distributors, Scoresby, Vic, Australia
France: Phaidon SARL, Paris, France
Germany: Phaidon Verlag GmbH, Berlin, Germany
Italy: Messagerie Libri, Assago, Italy
New Zealand: Pearson New Zealand, Auckland, New Zealand
Other Territories: Phaidon Press Ltd, London, UK
South Africa: Book Promotions Pty Ltd, Cape Town, South Africa
Spain: Logista Librodis, Madrid, Spain
USA: Phaidon Press Inc, New York, NY, USA

2585 ▬▬▬▬

THE PHARMACEUTICAL PRESS
1 Lambeth High Street, London SE1 7JN
Telephone: 020 7735 9141
Fax: 020 7572 2509
Email: pharmpress@rpsgb.org
Web Site: www.pharmpress.com

Orders:
The Pharmaceutical Press, c/
o Turpin Distribution,
Stratton Business Park, Pegasus Drive,
Biggleswade, Beds SG18 8TQ
Telephone: 01767 604971
Fax: 01767 601640
Email: rps@turpin-distribution.com
Web Site: www.pharmpress.com

Representation (UK):
Compass Academic Ltd,
Barley Mow Centre,
10 Barley Mow Passage, London W4 4PH
Telephone: 020 8994 6477
Fax: 020 8400 6132
Email: ca@compass-academic.co.uk

Personnel:
R. Bolick (*Managing Director, Publications*)
P. J. Weller (*Development Director*)
J. Wilson (*Production Manager*)
J. Mulholland (*Licensing Manager*)
J. Dargan (*Marketing Manager*)
C. Watling (*Sales Manager*)

Academic & Scholarly; Electronic (Professional & Academic); Medical (incl. Self Help & Alternative Medicine); Scientific & Technical; Veterinary Science

Imprints, Series & ISBNs:
978 0 85369

Parent Company:
The Royal Pharmaceutical Society of Great Britain

Overseas Representation:
Australia: Australian Pharmaceutical

Publishing Co Ltd, Hawthorn, Australia; Pharmaceutical Society of Australia, Curtin, Australia
Canada: Login Bros Canada, Winnipeg, Man, Canada
Germany, Austria & Switzerland: Deutscher Apotheker Verlag, Stuttgart, Germany
Greece: J & L Watt, Paleo Faliro, Greece
Israel: Probook, Tel Aviv, Israel
Italy: David Pickering, Rome, Italy
Japan: Maruzen Co Ltd, Tokyo, Japan
Middle East: James & Lorin Watt Ltd, Publishing Consultants, Oxford, UK
New Zealand: Pharmaceutical Society of New Zealand, Wellington, New Zealand
Republic of Ireland: Brookside Publishing Services, Dublin, Republic of Ireland
Scandinavia, Finland, Iceland & Baltic States: David Towle International, Stockholm, Sweden
South Africa: Pharmaceutical Society of South Africa, Pretoria, South Africa
Spain & Portugal: Christina de Lara Ruiz, Madrid, Spain
USA: Pharmaceutical Press, Grayslake, IL, USA

Book Trade Association Membership:
International Group of Scientific, Medical & Technical Publishers; Association of Learned & Professional Society Publishers

2586 ▬▬▬▬

PHILIP'S
Endeavour House,
189 Shaftesbury Avenue, London
WC2H 8JY
Telephone: 020 7632 5400
Web Site: www.octopusbooks.co.uk

Distribution:
Littlehampton Book Services,
Faraday Close, Durrington, West Sussex BN13 3RP
Telephone: 01903 828500
Fax: 01903 828625
Email: orders@lbsltd.co.uk
Web Site: www.lbsltd.co.uk

Personnel:
Victoria Dawbarn (*Rights & Contract Sales Director*)
David Gaylard (*Mapping Director*)

Atlases & Maps; Educational & Textbooks; Natural History; Reference Books, Directories & Dictionaries

Imprints, Series & ISBNs:
978 0 540

Parent Company:
Octopus Publishing Group

Overseas Representation:
See: Octopus Publishing Group, London, UK

Book Trade Association Membership:
International Map Traders Association

2587 ▬▬▬▬

PIATKUS BOOKS
[a division of Little, Brown Book Group]
Little, Brown Book Group,
100 Victoria Embankment, London
EC4Y 0DY
Telephone: 020 7911 8030
Fax: 020 7911 8100
Web Site: www.littlebrown.co.uk & www.piatkus.co.uk

Distribution:
Littlehampton Book Services,
Faraday Close, Durrington, Worthing,
West Sussex BN13 3RB
Telephone: 01903 828511
Fax: 01903 828801
Email: orders@lbsltd.co.uk
Web Site: www.lbsltd.co.uk

Personnel:
Ursula Mackenzie *(Chief Executive Officer & Publisher)*
Gill Bailey *(Non-Fiction Editorial Director)*
Robert Manser *(UK Sales & Marketing Director)*
Nick Ross *(Production Director)*
Emma Beswetherick *(Fiction Director)*
Julian Shaw *(Finance Director)*
Diane Spivey *(Rights Director)*

Biography & Autobiography; Cookery, Wines & Spirits; Crime; Fiction; Gender Studies; Health & Beauty; History & Antiquarian; Humour; Industry, Business & Management; Magic & the Occult; Medical (incl. Self Help & Alternative Medicine); Military & War; Music; Psychology & Psychiatry; Sociology & Anthropology

New Titles: 180 (2009) , 200 (2010)
No of Employees: 9

Imprints, Series & ISBNs:
Piatkus Books: 978 0 7499, 978 0 86188
Portrait Books: 978 0 7499

Parent Company:
France: Hachette Livre
UK: Little, Brown Book Group

Overseas Representation:
Australia: Hachette Livre Australia, Sydney, NSW, Australia
Canada: Hachette, Montreal, Canada
New Zealand: Hachette Livre New Zealand, Auckland, New Zealand
Singapore & Malaysia: Pansing Distribution Sdn Bhd, Singapore
South Africa: Penguin Books SA (Pty) Ltd, Denver Ext 4, South Africa

Book Trade Association Membership:
Publishers Association; Booksellers Association

2588 ▬▬

PICCADILLY PRESS
5 Castle Road, London NW1 8PR
Telephone: 020 7267 4492
Fax: 020 7267 4493
Email: books@piccadillypress.co.uk
Web Site: www.piccadillypress.co.uk

Warehouse & Distribution:
Grantham Book Services, Trent Road, Grantham, Lincs NG31 7XQ
Telephone: 01476 541080
Fax: 01476 541061

UK Sales & Key Accounts:
Bounce Sales & Marketing Ltd,
14 Greville Street, London EC1N 8SB
Telephone: 020 7138 3650
Fax: 020 7138 3658
Email: sales@bouncemarketing.co.uk
Web Site: www.bouncemarketing.co.uk

Personnel:
Brenda Gardner *(Publisher & Managing Director)*
Anne Clark *(Editorial/Commissioning)*
Ruth Williams *(Editorial/Commissioning)*
Melissa Hyder *(Assistant Editor)*
Margot Edwards *(Foreign Rights Consultant)*
Geoffrey Lill *(Financial Controller)*
Mary Byrne *(Publicity Consultant)*
Geoff Barlow *(Production Consultant)*
Vivien Tesseras *(Publishing Administration)*
Robert Snuggs *(Sales Manager, Bounce)*

Children's Books

New Titles: 33 (2009) , 34 (2010)
No of Employees: 6
Annual Turnover: £1.1M

Imprints, Series & ISBNs:
978 1 84812, 978 1 85340

Overseas Representation:
All other Export enquiries: Bounce Sales & Marketing Ltd, London, UK
Australia: Peribo Pty Ltd, Mount Kuring-Gai, NSW, Australia
New Zealand: South Pacific Book Distributors, Auckland, New Zealand

Book Trade Association Membership:
Independent Publishers Guild

2589 ▬▬

PICKERING & CHATTO (PUBLISHERS) LTD
21 Bloomsbury Way, London WC1A 2TH
Telephone: 020 7405 1005
Fax: 020 7405 6216
Email: info@pickeringchatto.co.uk
Web Site: www.pickeringchatto.com

Distribution & Orders:
Turpin Distribution Ltd,
Stratton Business Park, Pegasus Drive, Biggleswade, Beds SG18 8QT
Telephone: 01767 604800
Fax: 01767 601640
Web Site: www.turpin-distribution.com

Personnel:
James Powell *(Director)*
Lord Rees-Mogg *(Chairman)*
Mark Pollard *(Editorial & Rights)*
Neil O'Regan *(Production)*
Stephen Warren *(Finance)*

Academic & Scholarly; Economics; History & Antiquarian; Literature & Criticism; Religion & Theology; Scientific & Technical

New Titles: 58 (2009) , 65 (2010)
No of Employees: 11
Annual Turnover: £1.25M

Imprints, Series & ISBNs:
978 1 84893, 978 1 85196

Overseas Representation:
China: Meme Media, Beijing, P. R. of China
India: Applied Media, New Delhi, India
Japan: Japan Book Associates, Kyoto, Japan
Spain & Portugal: Iberian Book Services, Madrid, Spain
Taiwan: Unifacmanu Trading Co Ltd, Taipei, Taiwan
USA: Ashgate Publishing Co, Burlington, VT, USA

Book Trade Association Membership:
Independent Publishers Guild

2590 ▬▬

PIER PROFESSIONAL LTD
[formerly Pavilion Journals (Brighton) Ltd]
Suite N4, The Old Market,
Upper Market Street, Hove BN3 1AS
Telephone: 01273 783720
Fax: 01273 783723
Email: info@pierprofessional.com
Web Site: www.pierprofessional.com

Personnel:
Jo Sharrocks *(Publishing Manager)*
Paul Somerville *(Marketing Manager)*

Academic & Scholarly; Electronic (Professional & Academic); Psychology & Psychiatry; Sociology & Anthropology

No of Employees: 9

Book Trade Association Membership:
International Group of Scientific, Medical & Technical Publishers

2591 ▬▬

PIPERS' ASH LTD
Church Road, Christian Malford, Chippenham, Wiltshire SN15 4BW
Telephone: 01249 720563

Fax: 0870 056 8916
Email: pipersash@supamasu.com
Web Site: www.supamasu.com

Personnel:
A. Tyson *(Managing Director)*
Mrs A. M. Tyson *(Secretary)*

Academic & Scholarly; Aviation; Biography & Autobiography; Children's Books; Fiction; Literature & Criticism; Philosophy; Poetry; Psychology & Psychiatry; Science Fiction; Sports & Games; Theatre, Drama & Dance

New Titles: 12 (2009) , 12 (2010)
No of Employees: 8

Imprints, Series & ISBNs:
Biographies: 978 1 902628, 978 1 904494, 978 1 906928
Children's Libraries: 978 1 902628, 978 1 904494, 978 1 906928
Cornucopia: 978 1 902628, 978 1 904494, 978 1 906928
Kickstarters: 978 1 902628, 978 1 904494, 978 1 906928
Stagecraft: 978 1 902628, 978 1 904494, 978 1 906928
Trinity Collections: 978 1 902628, 978 1 904494, 978 1 906928

Overseas Representation:
Australia: Meagan Tyson, Sydney, Australia
Indonesia: Stephen Tyson, Jakarta, Indonesia
New Zealand: Dr Yvonne Eve Walus, Auckland, New Zealand

2592 ▬▬

PIQUANT EDITIONS
4 Thornton Road, Carlisle, Cumbria CA3 9HZ
Telephone: 01228 525075
Fax: 01228 501051
Email: info@piquant.net
Web Site: www.piquant.net

Representation (UK):
IVP, Norton Street, Nottingham NG7 3HR
Telephone: 0115 978 1054
Email: sales@ivpbooks.com
Web Site: www.piquanteditions.com

Personnel:
Pieter Kwant *(Director)*
Mrs Elria Kwant *(Publisher)*
John Bell *(Editor)*
Joshua Thompson *(Marketing Manager)*

Fiction; Fine Art & Art History; Religion & Theology

New Titles: 5 (2009) , 6 (2010)
No of Employees: 3
Annual Turnover: £100,000

Imprints, Series & ISBNs:
Piquant: 978 0 9535757
Piquant Editions: 978 1 903689

Overseas Representation:
USA & Canada: STL Inc, Waynesboro, GA, USA

Book Trade Association Membership:
Publishers Association

2593 ▬▬

THE PLAYWRIGHTS PUBLISHING CO
70 Nottingham Road, Burton Joyce, Notts NG14 5AL
Telephone: 01159 313356
Email: playwrightspublishing@yahoo.com
Web Site: www.geocities.com/playwrightspublishingco

Personnel:
Liz Breeze *(Proprietor)*
Tony Breeze *(Consultant)*

Theatre, Drama & Dance

New Titles: 6 (2009) , 6 (2010)
No of Employees: 2

Imprints, Series & ISBNs:
Playwrights Publishing Co: 978 1 873130
Ventus Books: 978 1 872758

Associated Companies:
Ventus Books

Distributor for:
The Playwrights Publishing Co; Ventus Books

2594 ▬▬

PLOWRIGHT PRESS
PO Box 66, Warwick CV34 4XE
Telephone: 01926 499433
Fax: 01926 499433
Web Site: www.plowrightpress.co.uk

Personnel:
Ruth Johns *(Director)*

Biography & Autobiography; Environment & Development Studies; Gender Studies; History & Antiquarian; Sociology & Anthropology

Imprints, Series & ISBNs:
'Ordinary' Lives Series: 978 0 9516960, 978 0 9543127
Plowright Press: 978 0 9543127, 978 0 9550940

Distributor for:
Family First Ltd; Ruth's Archive

Book Trade Association Membership:
Independent Publishers Guild; Society of Authors

2595 ▬▬

PLUTO BOOKS LTD
345 Archway Road, London N6 5AA
Telephone: 020 8374 2193
Fax: 020 8348 9133
Email: pluto@plutobooks.com
Web Site: www.plutobooks.com

Trade Enquiries & Orders:
Marston Book Services,
Unit 160 Milton Park, Abingdon, Oxon OX14 4SD
Telephone: 01235 465500
Fax: 01235 465555
Email: trade.orders@marston.co.uk
Web Site: www.marston.co.uk

Personnel:
Anne Beech *(Managing Director)*
Roger Van Zwanenberg *(Chair)*
Simon Liebesny *(Sales Director)*
Gilly Duff *(Rights & Permissions)*
Robert Webb *(Managing Editor)*
Alec Gregory *(Marketing Manager)*

Academic & Scholarly; Cinema, Video, TV & Radio; Economics; Environment & Development Studies; Gender Studies; Law; Literature & Criticism; Philosophy; Politics & World Affairs; Sociology & Anthropology

New Titles: 54 (2009) , 63 (2010)
No of Employees: 13

Imprints, Series & ISBNs:
Journeyman Press: 978 1 85172
Pluto Press: 978 0 7453, 978 0 86104

Distributor for:
Paradigm Publishers

Overseas Representation:
Australia: Palgrave Macmillan, Melbourne, Vic, Australia

Canada: Fernwood Books, Toronto, Ont, Canada
Germany (stock-holding distributor): Missing Link International Booksellers, Bremen, Germany
Germany, Austria, Switzerland, Scandinavia, Benelux, France, Italy, Greece, Malta, Central Europe & Baltic States: Andrew Durnell Marketing Ltd, Tunbridge Wells, UK
India: Maya Publishers Pvt Ltd, New Delhi, India
Japan: United Publishers Services Ltd, Tokyo, Japan
Middle East: International Publishers Representatives (IPR) Ltd, Nicosia, Cyprus
Republic of Ireland & Northern Ireland: Brookside Publishing Services, Dublin, Republic of Ireland
South Africa: Horizon Books, Plumstead, South Africa
South East Asia: Taylor & Francis Asia Pacific, Kowloon, Hong Kong; Taylor & Francis Asia Pacific, Petaling Jaya, Malaysia; Taylor & Francis Asia Pacific, Singapore; Taylor & Francis, Beijing, P. R. of China
Spain & Portugal: Iberian Book Services, Madrid, Spain
USA: Palgrave Macmillan, New York, NY, USA
USA (Orders): MPS Distribution Center, Gordonsville, VA, USA

Book Trade Association Membership:
Independent Publishers Guild

2596

THE POLICY PRESS
University of Bristol, Fourth Floor, Beacon House, Queen's Road, Bristol BS8 1QU
Telephone: 0117 331 4054
Fax: 0117 331 4093
Email: tpp-info@bris.ac.uk
Web Site: www.policypress.org.uk

Distribution:
Marston Book Services, PO Box 269, Abingdon, Oxon OX14 4YN
Telephone: 01235 465500
Fax: 01235 465556
Email: direct.orders@marston.co.uk
Web Site: www.marston.co.uk/

UK Representation:
Compass Academic Ltd,
13 Progress Business Centre, Whittle Parkway, Slough SL1 6DQ
Telephone: 01628 559500
Fax: 01628 663876
Email: ca@compass-academic.co.uk
Web Site: www.academic.compass-booksales.co.uk

Personnel:
Alison Shaw *(Director)*
Julia Mortimer *(Assistant Director)*

Academic & Scholarly; Economics; Educational & Textbooks; Gender Studies; Politics & World Affairs; Sociology & Anthropology

Imprints, Series & ISBNs:
978 1 84742, 978 1 86134

Parent Company:
University of Bristol

Overseas Representation:
Australia, New Zealand & Papua New Guinea: DA Information Services Pty Ltd, Mitcham, Vic, Australia
Europe (excluding UK): Durnell Marketing Ltd, Tunbridge Wells, UK
India, Sri Lanka, Nepal, Bangladesh & Bhutan: Surit Mitra, Maya Publishers Pvt Ltd, New Delhi, India

Japan: Kinokuniya Co Ltd, Tokyo, Japan; Maruzen Co Ltd, Tokyo, Japan
Malaysia & Brunei: UBSD Distribution Sdn Bhd, Selangor, Malaysia
Middle East & North Africa: Dar Kreidieh, Beirut, Lebanon
Pakistan: Tahir M. Lodhi, Lahore, Pakistan
South Africa: Blue Weaver Marketing, Tokai, South Africa
Taiwan: Unifacmanu Trading Co Ltd, Taipei, Taiwan
Thailand, Taiwan, Hong Kong, Korea, China, Singapore, Malaysia, Philippines & Vietnam: Tony Poh Leong Wah, Singapore, Singapore
USA & Canada: International Specialized Book Services Inc, Portland, OR, USA

Book Trade Association Membership:
Independent Publishers Guild

2597

POLITY PRESS
65 Bridge Street, Cambridge CB2 1UR
Telephone: 01223 324315
Fax: 01223 461385
Email: polity@politybooks.com
Web Site: www.polity.co.uk

Distribution Warehouse:
John Wiley & Sons Ltd, 1 Oldlands Way, Bognor Regis, West Sussex PO22 9SA
Telephone: 01243 843294
Fax: 01243 843303
Email: cs-books@wiley.co.uk

Publicity:
Polity Press, 9600 Garsington Road, Oxford OX4 2DQ
Telephone: 01865 476711
Fax: 01865 471711
Email: boconnor@wiley.com
Web Site: www.polity.co.uk

Personnel:
David Held *(Editorial Director)*
John Thompson *(Editorial Director)*

Academic & Scholarly; Cinema, Video, TV & Radio; Educational & Textbooks; Gender Studies; History & Antiquarian; Literature & Criticism; Philosophy; Politics & World Affairs; Sociology & Anthropology

New Titles: 103 (2009) , 117 (2010)
No of Employees: 21

Imprints, Series & ISBNs:
978 0 7456

Overseas Representation:
Australia: John Wiley & Sons Australia Ltd, Milton, Qld, Australia
Canada: John Wiley & Sons Canada Ltd, Etobicoke, Ont, Canada
Europe, Middle East & Africa: Karen Wootton, John Wiley & Sons Ltd, Chichester, UK
Germany: Wiley-VCH, Weinheim, Germany
Japan: Wiley Japan, Tokyo, Japan
Singapore: John Wiley & Sons (Asia) Pte Ltd, Singapore
USA: John Wiley & Sons Inc, Hoboken, NJ, USA

Book Trade Association Membership:
Independent Publishers Guild

2598

POLPERRO HERITAGE PRESS
Clifton-upon-Teme, Worcestershire WR6 6EN
Telephone: 01886 812304
Email: polperro.press@virgin.net
Web Site: www.polperropress.co.uk

Personnel:
Jerry Johns *(Managing Editor)*

Biography & Autobiography; History & Antiquarian; Natural History; Nautical; Photography; Reference Books, Directories & Dictionaries

New Titles: 1 (2009) , 4 (2010)
No of Employees: 2

Imprints, Series & ISBNs:
978 0 9530012, 978 0 9544233, 978 0 9549137, 978 0 9553648, 978 0 9559541

Book Trade Association Membership:
Independent Publishers Guild

2599

PORTHILL PUBLISHERS
PO Box 311, Edgware, Middx HA9 9EA
Telephone: 020 8958 6783
Fax: 020 8905 4516

Personnel:
Radomir Putnikovich *(Director)*
Penelope Putnikovich *(Secretary)*

Children's Books; Fine Art & Art History; Humour

Imprints, Series & ISBNs:
978 1 870732

2600

PORTLAND PRESS LTD
Commerce Way, Colchester CO2 8HP
Telephone: 01206 796351
Fax: 01206 799331
Email: editorial@portlandpress.com & sales@portland-services.com
Web Site: www.portlandpress.com & www.portland-services.com

Personnel:
Rhonda Oliver *(Managing Director)*
John Misselbrook *(Financial Director)*
Adam Marshall *(Marketing & Sales Director)*
John Day *(IT Director)*

Academic & Scholarly; Biology & Zoology; Educational & Textbooks; Electronic (Professional & Academic); Medical (incl. Self Help & Alternative Medicine); Reference Books, Directories & Dictionaries; Scientific & Technical

Imprints, Series & ISBNs:
Biochemical Society: 978 0 904498
Portland Press: 978 1 85578

Parent Company:
The Biochemical Society

Distributor for:
Antiquity Publications Ltd; Bioscientifica Ltd; Earthscan; Energy Institute; Expert Information; International Water Association Publishing; The Policy Press; Practical Action Publishing; Professional Engineering Publishing; The Royal Society; Royal Society of Chemistry; Royal Society of Medicine; SCR Publishing; The Society for Endocrinology; Vathek Publishing; WEF Publishing

Overseas Representation:
Australia: DA Information Services Pty Ltd, Mitcham, Vic, Australia
India: Affiliated East-West Press Pvt Ltd, New Delhi, India
Japan: USACO Corporation, Tokyo, Japan

Book Trade Association Membership:
International Group of Scientific, Medical & Technical Publishers; Independent Publishers Guild; Association of Learned & Professional Society Publishers; UK Serials Group

2601

PORTOBELLO BOOKS LTD
12 Addison Avenue, Holland Park, London W11 4QR
Telephone: 020 7605 1380
Fax: 020 7605 1361
Email: mail@portobellobooks.com
Web Site: www.portobellobooks.com

Personnel:
Laura Barber *(Editorial Director)*
Angela Rose *(Rights Director)*
Pru Rowlandson *(Publicity Director)*
Brigid Macleod *(Sales Director)*
Philip Gwyn Jones *(Publisher)*
Iain Chapple *(Marketing & Digital Director)*

Biography & Autobiography; Fiction; History & Antiquarian; Politics & World Affairs; Travel & Topography

New Titles: 22 (2009) , 21 (2010)
No of Employees: 12
Annual Turnover: £1M

Imprints, Series & ISBNs:
978 1 84627

Associated Companies:
UK: Granta

Overseas Representation:
Australia & New Zealand: Allen & Unwin Pty Ltd, Sydney, NSW, Australia
Canada: House of Anansi, Toronto, Ont, Canada
European Union: Faber & Faber, London, UK
Far East: Julian Ashton, Sevenoaks, Kent, UK
Netherlands: Nilsson & Lamm BV, Weesp, Netherlands
South Africa: Penguin Books South Africa (Pty) Ltd, Johannesburg, South Africa

Book Trade Association Membership:
Independent Publishers Guild; Independent Alliance

2602

POSITIVE PRESS LTD
28a Gloucester Road, Trowbridge, Wilts BA14 0AA
Telephone: 01225 719204
Fax: 01225 712187
Email: dankat@jennymosley.co.uk
Web Site: www.circle-time.co.uk

Personnel:
Jenny Mosley *(Managing Director)*
Danka Tadd *(Sales Account Manager)*

Children's Books; Educational & Textbooks

New Titles: 4 (2009) , 1 (2010)
No of Employees: 3
Annual Turnover: £245,000

Imprints, Series & ISBNs:
978 0 09

Book Trade Association Membership:
Booksellers Association

2603

PRACTICAL PRE-SCHOOL BOOKS
St Jude's Church, Dulwich Road, Herne Hill, London SE24 0PB
Telephone: 020 7738 5454
Fax: 020 7733 2325
Email: orders@practicalpreschoolbooks.com
Web Site: www.practicalpreschoolbooks.com

Distributors:
Mark Allen Distribution, Jesses Farm, Dinton, Wilts SP3 5HN

Telephone: 01722 716935
Email:
orders@practicalpreschoolbooks.com

Personnel:
Rebecca Linssen *(Group Editorial Director)*
Mark Allen *(Managing Director)*
Rebecca Haworth *(Associate Publisher)*
Tracey Mills *(Customer Services Manager)*

*Educational & Textbooks; Vocational
Training & Careers*

New Titles: 16 (2009) , 26 (2010)

Imprints, Series & ISBNs:
978 1 902438, 978 1 904575

Parent Company:
UK: Mark Allen Group

Book Trade Association Membership:
Independent Publishers Guild; British
Educational Suppliers Association (BESA)

2604 ▬▬▬▬▬▬

PRESTEL PUBLISHING LTD
4 Bloomsbury Place, London WC1A 2QA
Telephone: 020 7323 5004
Fax: 020 7636 8004
Email: sales@prestel-uk.co.uk
Web Site: www.prestel.com

Warehouse, Trade Enquiries & Orders:
Macmillan Distribution Ltd, Brunel Road,
Houndmills, Basingstoke, Hants RG21 6XS
Telephone: 01256 302692
Fax: 01256 812588
Email: orders@macmillan.co.uk
Web Site:
www.macmillandistribution.co.uk

Personnel:
Andrew Hansen *(Managing Director)*
Philippa Hurd *(Commissioning Editor
(London))*
Anna Kenning *(Sales, Marketing & Publicity
Executive)*
Oliver Barter *(UK Sales Manager)*

*Antiques & Collecting; Archaeology;
Architecture & Design; Children's Books;
Fashion & Costume; Fine Art & Art History;
Photography*

New Titles: 105 (2009) , 100 (2010)
No of Employees: 4

Imprints, Series & ISBNs:
13... Children Should Know: 978 3 7913
50... You Should Know: 978 3 7913
Adventures in Art Series: 978 3 7913

Parent Company:
Germany: Verlagsgruppe Random House
Bertelsmann

Associated Companies:
USA: Prestel Publishing

Distributor for:
Switzerland: Lars Müller Publishers
USA: Periscope Publishing Ltd

Overseas Representation:
Africa (excluding South Africa): Tony
Moggach, InterMedia Americana (IMA)
Ltd, London, UK
*Asia (including China, Hong Kong, Korea,
Philippines & Taiwan):* Ed Summerson,
Asia Publishers Services Ltd, Hong Kong
Australia: Peribo Pty Ltd, Mount Kuring-Gai,
NSW, Australia
Canada: Canadian Manda Group, Toronto,
Ont, Canada
France: Interart SARL, Paris, France
Israel: Lonnie Kahn & Co Ltd, Rishon Lezion,
Israel
Italy & Greece: Sandro Salucci, Italy
Japan: Andrew Hansen, Prestel, London, UK
Malta, Cyprus, Turkey, Middle East & North

Africa: Peter Ward Book Exports, London,
UK
Netherlands & Belgium: Nilsson & Lamm BV,
Weesp, Netherlands
Scandinavia: Elisabeth Harder-Kreimann,
Hamburg, Germany
South & Central America: David Williams,
InterMedia Americana (IMA) Ltd,
London, UK
South Africa: Zytek Publishing, Germiston,
South Africa
South East Asia: Peter Couzens, Sales East,
Bangkok, Thailand
Spain & Portugal: Christopher Humphrys,
UK
Switzerland: Buchzentrum AG, Hägendorf,
Switzerland
USA: Prestel Publishing, New York, NY, USA

2605 ▬▬▬▬▬

PRINCETON UNIVERSITY PRESS
6 Oxford Street, Woodstock, Oxon
OX20 1TW
Telephone: 01993 814500
Fax: 01993 814504
Email: admin@pupress.co.uk
Web Site: press.princeton.edu

Personnel:
Caroline Priday *(European Director of
Publicity)*
Ian Malcolm *(Executive Editor)*
Benjamin Tate *(Director of Subsidiary Rights)*

*Academic & Scholarly; Biology & Zoology;
Economics; Educational & Textbooks;
Electronic (Professional & Academic);
Environment & Development Studies;
History & Antiquarian; Industry, Business &
Management; Law; Mathematics &
Statistics; Natural History; Philosophy;
Politics & World Affairs; Reference Books,
Directories & Dictionaries; Scientific &
Technical; Sociology & Anthropology*

Imprints, Series & ISBNs:
978 0 691

Parent Company:
USA: Princeton University Press

Overseas Representation:
All other countries: Export Department,
Princeton University Press, Ewing, NJ,
USA
Continental Europe & Israel: Customer
Service Operations, Princeton University
Press, c/o John Wiley & Sons Ltd, Bognor
Regis, UK

Book Trade Association Membership:
Independent Publishers Guild

2606 ▬▬▬▬▬

PROFILE BOOKS
3A Exmouth House, Pine Street, London
EC1R 0JH
Telephone: 020 7841 6300
Fax: 020 7841 3969
Email: info@profilebooks.com
Web Site: www.profilebooks.com

Personnel:
Andrew Franklin *(Managing Director)*
Stephen Brough *(Editorial Director)*
Claire Beaumont *(Sales Director)*
Ruth Killick *(Publicity Director)*
Penny Daniel *(Rights Director)*
Pete Ayrton *(Publisher, Serpent's Tail)*
Daniel Crewe *(Associate Publisher)*
Mark Ellingham *(Publisher)*
Rebecca Gray *(Publicity Director, Serpent's
Tail)*

*Biography & Autobiography; Crime;
Economics; Fiction; History & Antiquarian;
Industry, Business & Management; Politics
& World Affairs*

No of Employees: 24

Imprints, Series & ISBNs:
The Economist Books
Profile Books
Serpent's Tail

Overseas Representation:
Australia & New Zealand: Allen & Unwin Pty
Ltd, Sydney, NSW, Australia
Europe: Faber & Faber, London, UK
Hong Kong, China, Taiwan & Philippines:
Asia Publishers Services Ltd, Hong Kong
India & Pakistan: Viva Books, New Delhi,
India
Middle East, North Africa & Turkey: Peter
Ward Book Exports, London, UK
Singapore, Malaysia, Thailand & Vietnam:
APD Singapore Pte Ltd, Singapore
South Africa: Book Promotions Pty Ltd,
Cape Town, South Africa
USA & Canada: Consortium Book Sales &
Distribution, Minneapolis, MN, USA

Book Trade Association Membership:
Publishers Association; Independent
Publishers Guild

2607 ▬▬▬▬▬

PROQUEST
International Office, The Quorum,
Barnwell Road, Cambridge CB5 8SW
Telephone: 01223 215512
Fax: 01223 215513
Email: marketing@proquest.co.uk
Web Site: www.proquest.co.uk

Personnel:
T. Robinson *(Sales)*
J. Taylor *(General Manager & Vice-President
Technology & Operations)*
S. Tilley *(Marketing)*

*Academic & Scholarly; Accountancy &
Taxation; Agriculture; Architecture &
Design; Bibliography & Library Science;
Biology & Zoology; Cinema, Video, TV &
Radio; Computer Science; Economics;
Electronic (Educational); Electronic
(Professional & Academic); Engineering;
Fashion & Costume; Fine Art & Art History;
History & Antiquarian; Industry, Business &
Management; Literature & Criticism;
Mathematics & Statistics; Medical (incl. Self
Help & Alternative Medicine); Music;
Natural History; Physics; Poetry; Politics &
World Affairs; Psychology & Psychiatry;
Reference Books, Directories &
Dictionaries; Religion & Theology; Scientific
& Technical; Sociology & Anthropology;
Theatre, Drama & Dance*

Imprints, Series & ISBNs:
978 0 85964

Parent Company:
USA: ProQuest

Overseas Representation:
Australia & New Zealand: ProQuest,
Melbourne, Vic, Australia
Canada: ProQuest, Toronto, Ont, Canada
China: ProQuest, Beijing, P. R. of China
Europe: ProQuest, Cambridge, UK
Germany: ProQuest, Berlin, Germany
Hong Kong, Macau & Taiwan: ProQuest,
Wanchai, Hong Kong
Japan: ProQuest, Yokohama, Japan
Korea: ProQuest, Seoul, Republic of Korea
Latin America: ProQuest, Rio de Janeiro,
Brazil
North America: ProQuest, Ann Arbor, MI,
USA
South East Asia & Far East: ProQuest,
Petaling Jaya, Malaysia
Spain: ProQuest España, Madrid, Spain
United Arab Emirates: ProQuest, Dubai
Media City, UAE

2608 ▬▬▬▬▬

PROSPECT BOOKS
Allaleigh House, Blackawton, Totnes, Devon
TQ9 7DL
Telephone: 01803 712269
Fax: 01803 712311
Email: tom.jaine@prospectbooks.co.uk
Web Site: www.prospectbooks.co.uk

Distribution:
Central Books, 99 Wallis Road, London
E9 5LN
Telephone: 020 8986 4854

Personnel:
Tom Jaine *(Owner)*

Cookery, Wines & Spirits

New Titles: 6 (2009) , 6 (2010)

2609 ▬▬▬▬▬

PROSPERA PUBLISHING
Longreach, 36 Ashley Road, Berkhamsted,
Herts HP4 3BL
Telephone: 020 7935 7750
Fax: 020 7935 7793
Email: suzybrownlee@prospera.co.uk
Web Site: www.prosperapublishing.co.uk

*Children's Books; Fiction; Travel &
Topography*

Book Trade Association Membership:
Publishers Association

2610 ▬▬▬▬▬

PUBLISHING HOUSE
Trinity Place, Barnstaple EX32 9HG
Telephone: 01271 328892
Fax: 01271 328768
Email: mail@vernoncoleman.com
Web Site: www.vernoncoleman.com

Personnel:
Sue Ward *(Publishing Director)*

*Fiction; Medical (incl. Self Help & Alternative
Medicine); Politics & World Affairs*

Imprints, Series & ISBNs:
Blue Books: 978 1 899726
Chilton Designs: 978 0 9503527, 978 1
898146
European Medical Journal: 978 0 9521492,
978 1 898947
Great Fiction: 978 1 904001

2611 ▬▬▬▬▬

PUNK PUBLISHING LTD
3 The Yard, Pegasus Place, London
SE11 5SD
Telephone: 020 7820 9333
Email: sophie@punkpublishing.co.uk
Web Site: www.punkpublishing.com &
www.coolcamping.co.uk

Personnel:
Jonathan Knight *(Publisher)*
Shelley Bowdler *(Marketing Manager)*

Travel & Topography

New Titles: 5 (2009) , 5 (2010)
No of Employees: 4
Annual Turnover: £500,000

Imprints, Series & ISBNs:
978 0 9552036, 978 1 906889

Book Trade Association Membership:
Independent Publishers Guild

2612 ▬▬▬▬▬

PUSHKIN PRESS
12 Chester Terrace, London NW1 4ND
Telephone: 020 7730 0750

Email: books@pushkinpress.com
Web Site: www.pushkinpress.com

Personnel:
Melissa Ulfane (Executive)

Fiction

Imprints, Series & ISBNs:
978 1 901285, 978 1 906548

2613 ━━━━━━

QUADRILLE PUBLISHING LTD
5th Floor, Alhambra House,
27–31 Charing Cross Road, London
WC2H 0LS
Telephone: 020 7839 7117
Fax: 020 7839 7118
Email: enquiries@quadrille.co.uk

Personnel:
Alison Cathie (Managing Director)
Jane O'Shea (Publishing Director)
Vincent Smith (Deputy Managing Director)
Helen Lewis (Creative Director)
Ian West (Sales Director)
Melanie Gray (International Sales Director)
Clare Lattin (Head of Publicity)

Architecture & Design; Biography & Autobiography; Cookery, Wines & Spirits; Crafts & Hobbies; Do-It-Yourself; Fashion & Costume; Gardening; Health & Beauty; Humour; Magic & the Occult; Medical (incl. Self Help & Alternative Medicine); Photography; Travel & Topography

New Titles: 30 (2009) , 30 (2010)
No of Employees: 30

Imprints, Series & ISBNs:
978 1 84400, 978 1 899988, 978 1
    902757, 978 1 903845

Book Trade Association Membership:
Booksellers Association

2615 ━━━━━━

QUARTET BOOKS
27 Goodge Street, London W1T 2LD
Telephone: 020 7636 3992
Fax: 020 7637 1866
Email: info@quartetbooks.co.uk
Web Site: www.quartetbooks.co.uk

Warehouse:
NBN International, Estover Road, Plymouth
PL6 7PZ
Telephone: 01752 202300
Fax: 01752 202330
Web Site: www.nbninternational.com

Personnel:
David Elliott (Director)

Biography & Autobiography; Fiction; History & Antiquarian; Music

Imprints, Series & ISBNs:
Robin Clark: 978 0 86072

Parent Company:
Namara Group

Associated Companies:
Robin Clark; The Women's Press

Overseas Representation:
Australia: Tower Books Pty Ltd, Frenchs
    Forest, NSW, Australia
Caribbean & South America: InterMedia
    Americana (IMA) Ltd, London, UK
*France, Belgium, Germany, Austria,
    Switzerland, Italy & Greece:* Ted
    Dougherty, London, UK
India, Denmark, Finland, Norway & Sweden:
    Quartet Books Ltd, London, UK
Japan: Japan/English Service Inc, Chiba-ken,
    Japan

Middle East: Peter Ward Book Exports,
    London, UK
Netherlands: Nilsson & Lamm BV, Weesp,
    Netherlands
New Zealand: Southern Publishers Group,
    Auckland, New Zealand
South Africa: Trinity Books CC, Randburg,
    South Africa
Spain & Portugal: Iberian Book Services,
    Madrid, Spain
*Sub-Saharan Africa (excluding South Africa)
    & Eastern Europe:* InterMedia Americana
    (IMA) Ltd, London, UK
USA: Interlink Publishing Group Inc,
    Northampton, MA, USA

2616 ━━━━━━

QUILLER PUBLISHING LTD
Wykey House, Wykey, Shrewsbury SY4 1JA
Telephone: 01939 261616
Fax: 01939 261606
Email: info@quillerbooks.com
Web Site: www.countrybooksdirect.com

**Warehouse, Distribution, Orders &
Sales Enquiries:**
Grantham Book Services, Trent Road,
Grantham, Lincolnshire NG31 7XQ
Telephone: 01476 541080
Fax: 01476 541061
Email: orders@gbs.tbs-ltd.co.uk

Personnel:
Andrew Johnston (Managing Director)
John Beaton (Editorial Director)
Julie Ward (Marketing Manager)
Jonathan Heath (Sales Manager)
Rob Dixon (Production Manager)

Animal Care & Breeding; Antiques & Collecting; Biography & Autobiography; Cookery, Wines & Spirits; Crafts & Hobbies; Fine Art & Art History; Gardening; Humour; Illustrated & Fine Editions; Military & War; Natural History; Nautical; Reference Books, Directories & Dictionaries; Sports & Games; Transport; Travel & Topography; Veterinary Science

Imprints, Series & ISBNs:
Kenilworth Press: 978 0 901366, 978 1
    872082, 978 1 872119, 978 1 905693
Quiller Press: 978 0 907621, 978 1 84689,
    978 1 904057
The Sportsman's Press: 978 0 948253
Swan Hill Press: 978 1 84037, 978 1 85310

Distributor for:
South Africa: Rowland Ward
UK: The Pony Club
USA: Half Halt Press; Stackpole Books

Overseas Representation:
Australia: Peribo Pty Ltd, Mount Kuring-Gai,
    NSW, Australia
Europe & Scandinavia: Jonathan Heath,
    Quiller Publishing Ltd, Shrewsbury, UK
South Africa: Trinity Books CC, Randburg,
    South Africa
USA & Canada: Half Halt Press, Boonsboro,
    MD, USA; Stackpole Books Inc,
    Mechanicsburg, PA, USA

Book Trade Association Membership:
Independent Publishers Guild

2617 ━━━━━━

**RACEFORM LTD / RACING POST
BOOKS**
RFM House, High Street, Compton,
Newbury, Berks RG20 6NL
Telephone: 01933 304858
Fax: 01635 578101
Email: shop@racingpost.com
Web Site: www.racingpost.com/shop

Fulfilment House:
Raceform, Sanders Road, Wellingborough,
Northamptonshire NN8 4BX
Telephone: 01933 304858

Fax: 01933 270300
Email: shop@racingpost.com
Web Site: www.racingpost.com/shop

Personnel:
Julian Brown (Publishing Director)
James de Wesselow (Managing Director)
Liz Ampairee (Sales & Marketing Director)

Sports & Games

New Titles: 50 (2009) , 52 (2010)
No of Employees: 12
Annual Turnover: £2M

Imprints, Series & ISBNs:
Highdown Books / Racing Post: 978 1
    905156
Raceform: 978 1 904317, 978 1 905153,
    978 1 906820

Parent Company:
Racing Post

Book Trade Association Membership:
Independent Publishers Guild

2618 ━━━━━━

THE RADCLIFFE PRESS
6 Salem Road, London W2 4BU
Telephone: 020 7243 1225
Fax: 020 7243 1226

Distributor:
Macmillan Distribution Ltd, Brunel Road,
Houndmills, Basingstoke, Hants RG21 6XS

Personnel:
Dr Lester Crook (Publisher)
Liz Stuckey (Finance Manager)
Stuart Weir (Production Director)
Charlotte Humphrey (Rights Manager)
Paul Davighi (Sales & Marketing Director)
Jaime Frost (Publicity Manager)

Biography & Autobiography; History & Antiquarian; Military & War; Politics & World Affairs; Travel & Topography

Imprints, Series & ISBNs:
978 1 84511, 978 1 85043, 978 1 86064

Overseas Representation:
Australia: Palgrave Macmillan, South Yarra,
    Vic, Australia
USA: Palgrave Macmillan, New York, NY,
    USA

2619 ━━━━━━

RADCLIFFE PUBLISHING LTD
18 Marcham Road, Abingdon, Oxon
OX14 1AA
Telephone: 01235 528820
Fax: 01235 528830
Email: contact.us@radcliffepublishing.com
Web Site: www.radcliffepublishing.com

Personnel:
Gregory Moxon (Managing Director)
Gillian Nineham (Editorial Director)
Margaret McKeown (Financial Director)
Jamie Etherington (Editorial Manager)
Steve Bonner (Production Manager)
Dan Allen (Marketing Executive)
Carlos Sejournant (Sales Executive)

Educational & Textbooks; Electronic (Educational); Electronic (Professional & Academic); Industry, Business & Management; Medical (incl. Self Help & Alternative Medicine); Reference Books, Directories & Dictionaries; Scientific & Technical; Vocational Training & Careers

Imprints, Series & ISBNs:
978 1 84619, 978 1 85775, 978 1 870905

Overseas Representation:
Australia: Elsevier Australia, Marrickville,
    NSW, Australia

---

*India, Bangladesh, Sri Lanka, Nepal &
    Pakistan:* Jaypee Brothers Medical
    Publishers (Pte) Ltd, New Delhi, India
Middle East: International Publishing
    Services (IPS) Middle East Ltd, Dubai, UAE
Scandinavia: David Towle International,
    Stockholm, Sweden
*Singapore, Malaysia, Thailand, Vietnam,
    Cambodia, Laos, Myanmar, Brunei,
    Indonesia, Philippines & Taiwan:* Alkem
    Co (S) Pte Ltd, Singapore
USA: Martin P. Hill Consulting, New York,
    NY, USA

Book Trade Association Membership:
Independent Publishers Guild

2620 ━━━━━━

RAND PUBLICATIONS
5 Victoria House, 138 Watling Street East,
Towcester NN12 6BT
Telephone: 01327 357770
Fax: 01327 359572
Email: rand@oppuk.co.uk
Web Site: www.rand.org

Warehouse & Distribution:
NBN International, Estover Road, Plymouth
PL6 7PY
Telephone: 01752 202301
Fax: 01752 202331
Email: orders@nbninternational.com
Web Site: www.nbninternational.com

Personnel:
Gary Hall (Manager)

Academic & Scholarly; Economics; Educational & Textbooks; Military & War; Politics & World Affairs

New Titles: 100 (2009) , 100 (2010)

Imprints, Series & ISBNs:
978 0 8330

Parent Company:
USA: Rand Publications

2621 ━━━━━━

**RANDOM HOUSE CHILDREN'S
BOOKS**
61–63 Uxbridge Road, London W5 5SA
Telephone: 020 8579 2652
Fax: 020 8231 6767
Web Site: www.kidsatrandomhouse.co.uk

Personnel:
Philippa Dickinson (Managing Director)
Helen Randles (Sales Director)
Barry O'Donovan (Marketing Director)
Jane Seery (Production Director)
Bronwen Bennie (Rights Director)
Annie Eaton (Fiction Publisher)
Fiona Macmillan (Colour & Custom
    Publishing)

Children's Books

Parent Company:
UK: Random House Group Ltd

Associated Companies:
UK: Bodley Head; Jonathan Cape; Corgi;
    Doubleday; David Fickling Books;
    Hutchinson; Red Fox; Tamarind

Book Trade Association Membership:
Publishers Association

2622 ━━━━━━

RANDOM HOUSE UK LTD
20 Vauxhall Bridge Road, London
SW1V 2SA
Telephone: 020 7840 8400
Fax: 020 7233 8791
Web Site: www.randomhouse.co.uk

Personnel:
Gail Rebuck *(Chair & Chief Executive Officer)*
Ian Hudson *(Deputy Chief Executive Officer)*
Mark Gardiner *(Group Finance Director)*
Garry Prior *(Group Sales Director)*
Stephen Esson *(Group Production Director)*
Maureen Corish *(Group Communications Director)*

Architecture & Design; Children's Books; Cookery, Wines & Spirits; Crafts & Hobbies; Crime; Do-It-Yourself; Economics; Fiction; Fine Art & Art History; Gardening; Guide Books; Health & Beauty; History & Antiquarian; Humour; Illustrated & Fine Editions; Literature & Criticism; Military & War; Music; Natural History; Philosophy; Photography; Poetry; Politics & World Affairs; Science Fiction; Sports & Games; Transport

Parent Company:
UK: Random House Group Ltd

Associated Companies:
UK: Arrow; BBC Books; Black Lace; Bodley Head; Jonathan Cape; Century; Chatto & Windus; Ebury; Everyman; Fodor; Harvill Secker; William Heinemann; Hutchinson; Mainstream; Pimlico; Preface; Random House Books; Rider; Time Out; Vermilion; Vintage; Virgin Books; Yellow Jersey

Book Trade Association Membership:
Publishers Association

2623 ━━━

RANSOM PUBLISHING LTD
Radley House, 8 St Cross Road, Winchester, Hampshire SO23 9HX
Telephone: 01962 862307
Email: ransom@ransom.co.uk
Web Site: www.ransom.co.uk

Personnel:
Jenny Ertle *(Managing Director/Marketing)*
Stephen Rickard *(Creative Director)*

Audio Books; Children's Books; Educational & Textbooks; Electronic (Educational)

New Titles: 40 (2009) , 40 (2010)
No of Employees: 5

Imprints, Series & ISBNs:
321 Go!: 978 1 84167, 978 1 900127
Boffin Boy: 978 1 84167, 978 1 900127
Cutting Edge: 978 1 84167, 978 1 900127
Dark Man: 978 1 84167, 978 1 900127
Goal!: 978 1 84167, 978 1 900127
Siti's Sisters: 978 1 84167, 978 1 900127
Starchasers: 978 1 84167, 978 1 900127
Trailblazers: 978 1 84167, 978 1 900127

Book Trade Association Membership:
Independent Publishers Guild

2624 ━━━

RAVEN'S QUILL LTD
63 High Street, Billingshurst, West Sussex RH14 9QP
Telephone: 01403 782489
Email: info@ravensquill.com
Web Site: www.ravensquill.com

Personnel:
Mrs Emily Henderson *(Director)*
Alan Gilliland *(Director)*

Children's Books; Fiction

New Titles: 1 (2010)
No of Employees: 2
Annual Turnover: £16,000

Imprints, Series & ISBNs:
Raven's Quill Ltd: 978 0 9555486

Shabby Tattler Press: 978 0 9555486

Overseas Representation:
Far East: Big Apple Tuttle-Mori, Shanghai, P. R. of China
Korea: Amo Agency, Seoul, Republic of Korea
Spain, Portugal & Latin America: Ilustrata, Barcelona, Spain

Book Trade Association Membership:
Publishers Association; Independent Publishers Guild

2625 ━━━

RAVETTE PUBLISHING LTD
PO Box 876, Horsham, West Sussex RH12 9GH
Telephone: 01403 711443
Fax: 01403 711554
Email: ravettepub@aol.com

Warehouse, Invoicing & Accounts:
Orca Book Services, 160 Milton Park, Abingdon, Oxon OX14 4SD
Telephone: 01202 665432
Fax: 01235 465555
Email: tradeorders@orcabookservices.co.uk
Web Site: www.orcabookservices.co.uk

Personnel:
Mrs M. Lamb *(Managing Director)*
Miss I. Parris *(Company Secretary)*

Children's Books; Humour; Military & War

New Titles: 15 (2009) , 19 (2010)
No of Employees: 3

Imprints, Series & ISBNs:
Born to Shop: 978 1 84161
Garfield: 978 1 84161
Hackman: 978 1 84161
Juicy Lucy: 978 1 84161
The Odd Squad: 978 1 84161, 978 1 85304
Odd Streak: 978 1 84161
Peanuts: 978 1 84161

Overseas Representation:
Australia: Peribo Pty Ltd, Mount Kuring-Gai, NSW, Australia
Denmark, Sweden, Norway & Finland: Angell Eurosales, UK
Eastern Europe: InterMediaAmericana, UK
France, Belgium, Germany, Switzerland & Austria: Anselm Robinson, UK
Hong Kong, Philippines, Korea, Taiwan, Thailand & Indonesia: Ashton International Marketing Services, Sevenoaks, Kent, UK
Japan: Yasmy International Marketing, Ageo, Japan
Middle East: Peter Ward Book Exports, London, UK
Singapore & Malaysia: Pansing Distribution Sdn Bhd, Singapore
South Africa: Bag of Books, Park Town, South Africa
Spain, Portugal, Italy & Malta: Bookport Associates, Italy

Book Trade Association Membership:
Independent Publishers Guild

2626 ━━━

REARDON PUBLISHING
[also known as Reardon & Son Publishers]
PO Box 919, Cheltenham, Glos GL50 9AN
Telephone: 01242 231800
Email: reardon@bigfoot.com
Web Site: www.reardon.co.uk & www.cotswoldbookshop.com

Personnel:
Nicholas Reardon *(Director)*

Archaeology; Atlases & Maps; Audio Books; Children's Books; Cinema, Video, TV

& Radio; Guide Books; History & Antiquarian; Humour; Magic & the Occult; Military & War; Natural History; Nautical; Travel & Topography

Imprints, Series & ISBNs:
Driveabout Series: 978 1 874192
Rideabout Series: 978 0 9508674
Walkabout Series: 978 1 873877
Walkcards (series)

Distributor for:
Cheltenham Tourism; Cicerone Press; Cordee; Corinium Publications; Estate Publications; Flukes UK; Harvey Maps; OS Maps; Philips Maps; Rambler Association; Video Ex

Book Trade Association Membership:
Outdoor Writers Guild

2627 ━━━

REDCLIFFE PRESS LTD
81g Pembroke Road, Bristol BS8 3EA
Telephone: 0117 973 7207
Fax: 0117 923 8991
Email: info@redcliffepress.co.uk
Web Site: www.redcliffepress.co.uk

Trade Orders:
Orca Book Services Ltd, Unit A3, Fleets Corner, Poole, Dorset BH17 0HL
Telephone: 01202 665432
Fax: 01202 666219
Email: orders@orcabookservices.co.uk

Personnel:
A. N. Sansom *(Sales Director)*
John Sansom *(Publishing Director)*
Clara Sansom *(Production Director)*

Architecture & Design; Fine Art & Art History; History & Antiquarian; Literature & Criticism; Poetry

Imprints, Series & ISBNs:
978 1 900178, 978 1 904537, 978 1 906593

Associated Companies:
Art Dictionaries Ltd; Sansom & Co Ltd; Westcliffe Books

Overseas Representation:
USA: Antique Collectors Club Ltd, Easthampton, MA, USA

2628 ━━━

REDEMPTORIST PUBLICATIONS
Alphonsus House, Chawton, Hants GU34 3HQ
Telephone: 01420 88222
Fax: 01420 88805
Email: rp@rpbooks.co.uk
Web Site: www.rpbooks.co.uk

Personnel:
Rev Denis McBride *(Publishing Director)*
Andrew Lane *(Head of Operations)*
Michael Roberts *(Sales & Service Manager)*
Christine Thirkell *(Financial Controller)*
Patricia Wilson *(Marketing Manager)*
Andrew Lyon *(Editorial Manager)*

Religion & Theology

New Titles: 14 (2009) , 11 (2010)
No of Employees: 30

Imprints, Series & ISBNs:
978 0 85231

Distributor for:
USA: Abbey Press; Creative Communications; Dimension Books; HarperCollins; ICS Publications; Liguori/Triumph; Loyola Press; Peter Pauper Press; RCL (Resources for Christian

Living); Regina Press (Malhame); Resurrection Press; Servant Publications; Sophia Institute; St Anthony Messenger Press/Franciscan Catholic Book Publishing Co

Book Trade Association Membership:
Booksellers Association

2629 ━━━

REFLECTIONS OF A BYGONE AGE
15 Debdale Lane, Keyworth, Notts NG12 5HT
Telephone: 0115 937 4079
Fax: 0115 937 6197
Email: reflections@postcardcollecting.co.uk

Personnel:
Brian Lund *(Contact)*
F. Mary Lund *(Contact)*

History & Antiquarian; Sports & Games; Transport

New Titles: 6 (2009) , 6 (2010)
No of Employees: 2

Imprints, Series & ISBNs:
978 0 946245, 978 1 900138, 978 1 905408

2630 ━━━

RIPLEY PUBLISHING LTD
22 The Causeway, Bishop's Stortford, Herts CM23 2EJ
Telephone: 01279 502910
Web Site: www.ripleybooks.com

Personnel:
Anne Marshall *(Publisher)*
Becky Miles *(Editorial Director)*
Amanda Dula *(Foreign Rights Manager)*

Children's Books; Fiction

New Titles: 10 (2009) , 30 (2010)
No of Employees: 5

Parent Company:
Canada: The Jim Pattison Group

2631 ━━━

RISING STARS UK LTD
22 Grafton Street, London W1S 4EX
Telephone: 020 7495 6793
Fax: 020 7495 6796
Email: info@risingstars-uk.com
Web Site: www.risingstars-uk.com

Customer Service, Trade Enquiries & Warehouse:
Grantham Book Services, Trent Road, Grantham, Lincs NG31 7XQ

Personnel:
Andrea Carr *(Managing Director)*
Tim Pearce *(Production Director)*
Camilla Erskine *(Publishing Director)*

Children's Books; Educational & Textbooks; Electronic (Educational); Fiction

New Titles: 75 (2009) , 70 (2010)
No of Employees: 12
Annual Turnover: £4M

Imprints, Series & ISBNs:
978 1 84680, 978 1 905056

Overseas Representation:
Contact: English Language International, Dunstable, UK

Book Trade Association Membership:
Publishers Association; Educational Publishers Council; Independent Publishers Guild

2632

RNIB
105 Judd Street, London WC1H 9NE
Telephone: 020 7388 1266
Fax: 020 7388 2034
Web Site: www.rnib.org.uk

Book Trade Association Membership:
Publishers Association

2633

ROADMASTER PUBLISHING
PO Box 176, Chatham, Kent ME5 9AQ
Telephone: 01634 862843
Fax: 01634 862843
Email:
roadmasterpublishing@blueyonder.co.uk

Personnel:
Malcolm Wright *(Sales Director)*

*Geography & Geology; Guide Books;
Nautical; Transport; Travel & Topography*

Imprints, Series & ISBNs:
978 1 871814

Distributor for:
Nostalgia Road Publications; Trans-Pennine
Publishing

2634

ROBINSWOOD PRESS LTD
30 South Avenue, Stourbridge,
West Midlands DY8 3XY
Telephone: 01384 397475
Fax: 01384 440443
Email: publishing@robinswoodpress.com
Web Site: www.robinswoodpress.com

Personnel:
Christopher Marshall *(Managing Director)*
Susan Marshall *(Company Secretary /
Finance Director)*
Sally Connolly *(Editorial)*
Henry Marshall *(Non-Executive Director)*

*Children's Books; Educational & Textbooks;
Electronic (Educational); English as a
Foreign Language; Fiction*

New Titles: 2 (2009) , 12 (2010)
No of Employees: 5
Annual Turnover: £100,000

Imprints, Series & ISBNs:
978 1 869981, 978 1 906053

Associated Companies:
Republic of Ireland: Robinswood Press
(Dublin) Ltd

Overseas Representation:
Australia: Lefty's, Sydney, Australia
Republic of Ireland: STA Ltd, Dublin,
Republic of Ireland
Singapore: Knowledge Tree Resources

2635

ALAN ROGERS GUIDES LTD
[part of the Mark Hammerton Group]
Spelmonden Old Oast, Goudhurst,
Cranbrook, Kent TN17 1HE
Telephone: 01580 214000
Email: russell@alanrogers.com
Web Site: www.alanrogers.com

Personnel:
Russell Wheldon *(Marketing Director)*

Travel & Topography

Parent Company:
Mark Hammerton Group

Book Trade Association Membership:
Booksellers Association

2636

ROTOVISION SA
Sheridan House, 114 Western Road, Hove,
East Sussex BN3 1DD
Telephone: 01273 727268 & 716010/11/
12 (Customer Services)
Fax: 01273 727269
Email: sales@rotovision.com
Web Site: www.rotovision.com

Personnel:
Piers Spence *(Managing Director)*
Nicole Kemble *(Rights Director)*
Mari Ahlfeld-Smith *(Financial Controller)*
April Sankey *(Publisher)*

*Architecture & Design; Cinema, Video, TV &
Radio; Fashion & Costume; Fine Art & Art
History; Music; Photography; Reference
Books, Directories & Dictionaries; Theatre,
Drama & Dance*

Imprints, Series & ISBNs:
978 2 88046

Parent Company:
Quarto Group

Overseas Representation:
Australia: Thames & Hudson (Australia) Pty
Ltd, Fishermans Bend, Vic, Australia
France: Interart SARL, Paris, France
Germany, Switzerland & Austria: Michael
Klein, Vilsbiburg, Germany
Middle East: International Publishing
Services (IPS) Middle East Ltd, Dubai, UAE
South East Asia: APD Singapore Pte Ltd,
Singapore

Book Trade Association Membership:
Booksellers Association

2637

ROUND HALL LTD
43 Fitzwilliam Place, Dublin 2,
Republic of Ireland
Telephone: +353 (01) 662 5301
Fax: +353 (01) 662 5302
Email: roundhall.info@thomson.com
Web Site: www.roundhall.thomson.com

Distribution:
Gill & Macmillan, Hume Avenue,
Park West, Dublin 12, Republic of Ireland
Telephone: +353 (01) 500 9500

Personnel:
Julie Clarke *(Director)*
Anne Waters *(Finance Manager)*
Terri McDonnell *(Production Manager)*
Martin McCann *(Editorial Manager)*
Catherine Dolan *(Commercial Manager)*
Brendan Reid *(Sales Manager)*
Pauline Ward *(Sales Manager)*
Maura Smyth *(Marketing Manager)*

*Academic & Scholarly; Accountancy &
Taxation; Educational & Textbooks;
Electronic (Professional & Academic);
Industry, Business & Management; Law;
Medical (incl. Self Help & Alternative
Medicine); Reference Books, Directories &
Dictionaries*

Imprints, Series & ISBNs:
Round Hall: 978 1 85800, 978 1 899738
Round Hall Professional: 978 1 86089

Parent Company:
USA: Thomson Reuters Corp

Associated Companies:
Australia: LBC
Canada: Carswell
New Zealand: Brookers
UK: Sweet & Maxwell
USA: West Group

2638

ROUNDHOUSE PUBLISHING LTD
Roundhouse Group, Unit B,
18 Marine Gardens, Brighton BN2 1AH
Telephone: 01273 603717
Fax: 01273 697494
Email: sales@roundhousegroup.co.uk
Web Site: www.roundhousegroup.co.uk

Warehouse & Distribution:
Orca Book Services, Unit A3, Fleets Corner,
Poole BH17 0HL
Telephone: 01202 665432
Fax: 01202 666219
Email: orders@orca-book-services.co.uk

Personnel:
Alan Goodworth *(Managing Director)*
Matt Goodworth *(Marketing Manager)*

*Academic & Scholarly; Animal Care &
Breeding; Archaeology; Architecture &
Design; Atlases & Maps; Biography &
Autobiography; Children's Books; Cinema,
Video, TV & Radio; Cookery, Wines &
Spirits; Crafts & Hobbies; Do-It-Yourself;
Fashion & Costume; Fine Art & Art History;
Gardening; Guide Books; Health & Beauty;
History & Antiquarian; Industry, Business &
Management; Literature & Criticism;
Medical (incl. Self Help & Alternative
Medicine); Military & War; Music; Natural
History; Philosophy; Photography; Politics &
World Affairs; Psychology & Psychiatry;
Reference Books, Directories &
Dictionaries; Religion & Theology; Sports &
Games; Theatre, Drama & Dance; Travel &
Topography*

New Titles: 1000 (2009) , 1200 (2010)
No of Employees: 3

Imprints, Series & ISBNs:
Roundabout: 978 1 85710
Roundhouse Publishing: 978 1 85710

Associated Companies:
Roundabout Books; Roundhouse Arts;
Roundtrip Travel; Windsor Books
International

Distributor for:
Australia: Allen & Unwin
Canada: Crabtree Publishing
Italy: Charta Art Books; Giunti Editore
Republic of Ireland: Irish Museum of
Modern Art
Spain: Poligrafa; Santana Books
UK: Age UK
USA: ABC-Clio & Greenwood International;
Allworth Press; C&T Publishing;
Capstone Press; David Godine
Publishers; Getty Museum; J Ross
Publishing; Martingale & Co; Pelican
Publishing Co; Prometheus Books;
Quality Medical Publishing; University
Press of Mississippi

Overseas Representation:
Europe (East) & Scandinavia: Bill Bailey
Publishers Representatives, Totnes, UK
Europe (South): Bookport Associates,
Milan, Italy
Europe (Spain & Portugal only): Iberian
Book Services, Madrid, Spain
Europe (West) (excluding Scandinavia): Ted
Dougherty, London, UK

2639

ROUTE PUBLISHING LTD
PO Box 167, Pontefract WF8 4WW
Telephone: 01977 797695
Email: info@route-online.com
Web Site: www.route-online.com

Distribution:
Central Books, 99 Wallis Road, London
E9 5LN
Telephone: 020 8986 4854

Fax: 020 8533 5821
Email: bill@centralbooks.com
Web Site: www.centralbooks.com

Personnel:
Ian Daley *(Editor)*
Isabel Galan *(Public Relations Director)*

*Biography & Autobiography; Cinema,
Video, TV & Radio; Fiction; Music; Poetry*

New Titles: 6 (2009) , 6 (2010)
No of Employees: 2
Annual Turnover: £100,000

Imprints, Series & ISBNs:
978 1 901927

Overseas Representation:
USA: Dufour Editions Inc, Chester Springs,
PA, USA

Book Trade Association Membership:
Independent Publishers Guild

2640

JOSEPH ROWNTREE FOUNDATION
The Homestead, 40 Water End, York
YO30 6WP
Telephone: 01904 629241
Fax: 01904 620072
Email: sharon.telfer@jrf.org.uk
Web Site: www.jrf.org.uk

Personnel:
Julia Unwin CBE *(Director)*
Julia Lewis *(Communications Director)*
Paul Dack *(Finance Director)*
Sharon Telfer *(Head of Publishing)*

*Academic & Scholarly; Architecture &
Design; Economics; Politics & World Affairs;
Sociology & Anthropology*

New Titles: 100 (2009) , 100 (2010)

2641

ROYAL COLLECTION PUBLICATIONS
Stable Yard House, St James's Palace,
London SW1A 1JR
Telephone: 020 7024 5584
Fax: 020 7839 8168
Email:
jacky.collissharvey@royalcollection.org.u
k
Web Site: www.royalcollection.org.uk

Distribution:
Thames & Hudson Ltd, 181a High Holborn,
London WC1V 7QX
Telephone: 020 7845 5000
Fax: 020 7845 5055
Web Site: www.thamesandhudson.com

Personnel:
Jacky Colliss Harvey *(Publisher)*
Kate Owen *(Commissioning Editor)*
Debbie Bogard *(Publishing Assistant)*
Nina Chang *(Publishing Assistant)*

*Academic & Scholarly; Antiques &
Collecting; Architecture & Design;
Biography & Autobiography; Fashion &
Costume; Fine Art & Art History; Guide
Books; History & Antiquarian; Illustrated &
Fine Editions; Natural History; Photography*

New Titles: 7 (2009) , 10 (2010)
No of Employees: 3
Annual Turnover: £34.4M

Imprints, Series & ISBNs:
978 1 902163, 978 1 905686

Overseas Representation:
Rest of World: Thames & Hudson Ltd,
London, UK
USA & Canada: University of Chicago Press,
Chicago, IL, USA

2642

ROYAL COLLEGE OF GENERAL PRACTITIONERS
14 Princes Gate, Hyde Park, London
SW7 1PU
Telephone: 020 7581 3232
Fax: 020 7225 3047
Email: hfarrelly@rcgp.org.uk
Web Site: www.rcgp.org.uk

Personnel:
Ms Helen Farrelly *(Publishing Manager)*

Academic & Scholarly; Medical (incl. Self Help & Alternative Medicine)

Imprints, Series & ISBNs:
978 0 85084

Book Trade Association Membership:
Association of Learned & Professional
Society Publishers

2643

ROYAL COLLEGE OF PSYCHIATRISTS
17 Belgrave Square, London SW1X 8PG
Telephone: 020 7235 2351
Fax: 020 7259 6507
Email: publications@rcpsych.ac.uk
Web Site: www.rcpsych.ac.uk

Warehouse:
Turpin Distribution, Customer Services,
Pegasus Drive, Stratton Business Park,
Biggleswade, Beds SG18 8TQ
Telephone: 01767 604951
Fax: 01767 601640
Email: custserv@turpin-distribution.com
Web Site: www.turpin-distribution.com

Personnel:
Dave Jago *(Head of Publications)*
Daniel Tomkins *(Sales & Marketing Manager)*

Academic & Scholarly; Medical (incl. Self Help & Alternative Medicine); Psychology & Psychiatry

New Titles: 10 (2009) , 10 (2010)

Imprints, Series & ISBNs:
Gaskell: 978 0 902241, 978 1 901242
RCPsych Publications: 978 0 902241, 978 1 901242

Overseas Representation:
Australia & New Zealand: All things Medical, Sydney University, Sydney, NSW, Australia
Republic of Ireland: Compass Academic, London, UK
Scandinavia (including Iceland & Estonia): David Towle International, Stockholm, Sweden
USA & Canada: Princeton Selling Group Inc, Wayne, PA, USA

Book Trade Association Membership:
Independent Publishers Guild; Association of Learned & Professional Society Publishers

2644

ROYAL GEOGRAPHICAL SOCIETY (WITH INSTITUTE OF BRITISH GEOGRAPHERS)
1 Kensington Gore, London SW7 2AR
Telephone: 020 7591 3022
Fax: 020 7591 3001
Email: journals@rgs.org
Web Site: www.rgs.org

Personnel:
David Riviere *(Head of Finance & Services)*
Madeleine Hatfield *(Managing Editor: Journal)*

Academic & Scholarly; Electronic (Educational); Electronic (Professional &
Academic); Environment & Development Studies; Geography & Geology

Imprints, Series & ISBNs:
RGS-IBG Book Series (academic/scholarly texts only)

2645

ROYAL IRISH ACADEMY
Academy House, 19 Dawson Street,
Dublin 2, Republic of Ireland
Telephone: +353 (01) 676 2570 & 676 4222
Fax: +353 (01) 676 2346
Email: publications@ria.ie
Web Site: www.ria.ie/Publications

Send trade orders to:
Gill & Macmillan Distribution,
Hume Avenue, Park West Industrial Park,
Dublin 12, Republic of Ireland
Telephone: +353 (01) 500 9500
Fax: +353 (01) 500 9599
Email: sales@gillmacmillan.ie
Web Site: www.gillmacmillan.ie

Personnel:
Patrick Buckley *(Rights & Permissions, Executive Secretary)*
Ruth Hegarty *(Production & Sales, Managing Editor)*

Academic & Scholarly; Archaeology; Atlases & Maps; Biology & Zoology; History & Antiquarian; Languages & Linguistics; Mathematics & Statistics; Politics & World Affairs; Reference Books, Directories & Dictionaries

New Titles: 6 (2009) , 7 (2010)
No of Employees: 6

Imprints, Series & ISBNs:
978 0 901714, 978 0 9543855, 978 1 874045, 978 1 904890
Prism: 978 1 904890

Overseas Representation:
North America: International Specialized Book Services Inc, Portland, OR, USA

Book Trade Association Membership:
Publishing Ireland (Foilsiú Éireann);
Association of Learned & Professional
Society Publishers

2646

THE ROYAL SOCIETY OF CHEMISTRY
Sales & Customer Care,
Thomas Graham House, Science Park,
Milton Road, Cambridge CB4 0WF
Telephone: 01223 420066
Fax: 01223 426017
Email: sales@rsc.org
Web Site: www.rsc.org

Warehouse:
Portland Customer Services, Portland Press,
Commerce Way, Colchester CO2 8HP
Telephone: 01206 226050
Fax: 01206 799331
Email: sales@portland-services.com
Web Site: www.portlandpress.com

Personnel:
Robert Parker *(Publishing Director)*
Simon Thomson *(Sales Director)*
Nichole Gibson *(Operations Manager)*

Academic & Scholarly; Chemistry; Educational & Textbooks; Electronic (Educational); Electronic (Professional & Academic); Reference Books, Directories & Dictionaries; Scientific & Technical

Imprints, Series & ISBNs:
978 0 85186, 978 0 85404

Overseas Representation:
Asia, Australia & New Zealand: Clarke Associates Ltd, Bristol, UK
Australia, New Zealand & Papua New Guinea: DA Information Services Pty Ltd, Mitcham, Vic, Australia
Hungary: Dr László Horváth Publishers Representative, Budapest, Hungary
India: S. Janakiraman, Book Marketing Services, Chennai, India
Italy: Flavio Marcello Publishers' Agents & Consultants, Padua, Italy
Japan: Aiko Hoyosa, Tokyo, Japan
Middle East, Malta, Greece, Turkey, Cyprus & Iran: Anthony Rudkin Associates, Oxford, UK; Farhad Maftoon, Tehran, Iran
Nigeria: Olu Anulopo, Bounty Books, Ibadan, Nigeria
North America & Mexico: Springer-Verlag New York Inc, Secaucus, NJ, USA
Scandinavia & Iceland: Colin Flint Ltd, Harlow, UK
South America: Terry Roberts, Humphrys Roberts Associates, Cotia SP, Brazil
Spain & Portugal: Arie Ruitenbeek, Madrid, Spain

Book Trade Association Membership:
Association of Learned Society Publishers;
STM (European Group)

2647

ROYAL SOCIETY OF MEDICINE PRESS LTD
1 Wimpole Street, London W1G 0AE
Telephone: 020 7290 3945
Fax: 020 7290 2929
Email: ian.jones@rsm.ac.uk
Web Site: www.rsmpress.co.uk

Warehousing & Distribution:
Marston Book Services, PO Box 269,
Abingdon, Oxon OX14 4YN
Telephone: 01235 465500
Fax: 01235 465555

Personnel:
Peter Richardson *(Managing Director)*
Ian Jones *(Head of Sales & Marketing)*
Mark Johnstone *(Finance)*
Mark Sanderson *(Production Manager)*
Lucy McIvor *(Journals Development Manager)*
Alison Campbell *(Managing Editor)*
Sarah Ogden *(Commissioning Editor)*

Medical (incl. Self Help & Alternative Medicine)

Imprints, Series & ISBNs:
Controversies and Dilemmas Series: 978 1 85315
Eponymists in Medicine Series: 978 1 85315
Get Through Series: 978 1 85315
In Practice Series: 978 1 85315
International Congress and Symposium Series: 978 1 85315
Key Advances Series: 978 1 85315
Key Paper Conferences Series: 978 1 85315
Recent Advances Series: 978 1 85315
Round Table Series: 978 1 85315

Parent Company:
Royal Society of Medicine

Overseas Representation:
USA: Bookmasters Inc, Ashland, OH, USA

Book Trade Association Membership:
Association of Learned & Professional
Society Publishers

2648

RUSSELL HOUSE PUBLISHING LTD
4 St George's House,
Uplyme Road Business Park, Lyme Regis
DT7 3LS
Telephone: 01297 443948
Fax: 01297 442722

Email: help@russellhouse.co.uk
Web Site: www.russellhouse.co.uk

Personnel:
Geoffrey Mann *(Managing Director)*
Martin Jones *(Director)*
Terry Nemko *(Director)*

Academic & Scholarly; Educational & Textbooks; Electronic (Educational); Electronic (Professional & Academic); Gender Studies; Industry, Business & Management; Law; Medical (incl. Self Help & Alternative Medicine); Psychology & Psychiatry; Sociology & Anthropology; Sports & Games; Theatre, Drama & Dance; Vocational Training & Careers

New Titles: 17 (2009) , 15 (2010)
No of Employees: 5

Imprints, Series & ISBNs:
978 1 898924, 978 1 903855, 978 1 905541

Overseas Representation:
Australia: Psychoz, Vic, Australia
North America: International Specialized Book Services Inc, Portland, OR, USA

2649

SAGE PUBLICATIONS LTD
1 Oliver's Yard, 55 City Road, London
EC1Y 1SP
Telephone: 020 7324 8500
Fax: 020 7324 8600
Email: info@sagepub.co.uk
Web Site: www.sagepub.co.uk

Warehouse:
Unit 11, Keirbeck Business Centre,
North Woolwich Road, Silvertown, London
E16 2BG

Personnel:
Stephen Barr *(Managing Director)*
Katherine Jackson *(Financial & Deputy Managing Director)*
Ziyad Marar *(Deputy Managing Director)*
Clive Parry *(Marketing & Sales Director)*
Phil Denvir *(IT Director)*
Richard Fidczuk *(Production Director)*
Sara Miller McCune *(Director)*
Blaise Simqu *(Director)*
Paul Chapman *(Director)*
Tony Histed *(Associate Director, Sales)*
Anne Farlow *(Non-Executive Director)*
Brenda Gowley *(Non-Executive Director)*
Alison Browne *(Customer Service (Books) Manager)*
Huw Alexander *(Rights & Permissions Manager)*

Academic & Scholarly; Bibliography & Library Science; Economics; Educational & Textbooks; Electronic (Educational); Gender Studies; Industry, Business & Management; Mathematics & Statistics; Politics & World Affairs; Psychology & Psychiatry; Reference Books, Directories & Dictionaries; Religion & Theology; Scientific & Technical; Sociology & Anthropology

Imprints, Series & ISBNs:
978 0 7619, 978 0 8039, 978 1 4129

Parent Company:
USA: SAGE Publications Inc

Associated Companies:
Paul Chapman Publishing Ltd
India: SAGE Publications Pvt Ltd
USA: Corwin Press Inc; Pine Forge Press Inc;
Sage Publications Inc

Overseas Representation:
Australia & New Zealand: Footprint Books Pty Ltd, Sydney, NSW, Australia
South Africa: Academic Marketing Services (Pty) Ltd, Craighall, South Africa

Book Trade Association Membership:
Publishers Association; Independent
Publishers Guild

2650

SAINT ALBERT'S PRESS
[British Province of Carmelites]
Carmelite Projects & Publications Office,
More House, Heslington, York YO10 5DX
Telephone: 01904 411521
Email: projects@carmelites.org.uk
Web Site: www.carmelite.org

Orders & Book Deposit:
Saint Albert's Press Book Distribution,
Carmelite Friars, 34 Tanners Street,
Faversham, Kent ME13 7JN
Telephone: 01795 537038
Fax: 01795 539511
Email: saintalbertspress@carmelites.org.uk
Web Site: www.carmelite.org

Personnel:
Johan Bergström-Allen (Director)
Kevin Bellman (Sales)
Richard Copsey (Bursar)

Academic & Scholarly; History &
Antiquarian; Poetry; Religion & Theology

New Titles: 2 (2009) , 3 (2010)
No of Employees: 2

Imprints, Series & ISBNs:
978 0 904849

Parent Company:
UK: Carmelite Charitable Trust

Associated Companies:
UK: The Carmelite Press; Whitefriars Press

Distributor for:
Italy: Edizioni Carmelitane
USA: Carmelite Institute

Book Trade Association Membership:
Independent Publishers Guild

2651

ST JEROME PUBLISHING LTD
2 Maple Road West, Brooklands,
Manchester M23 9HH
Telephone: 0161 973 9856
Fax: 0161 905 3498
Email: ken@stjeromepublishing.com
Web Site: www.stjerome.co.uk

Personnel:
Ken Baker (Managing Director)

Academic & Scholarly; Educational &
Textbooks; Electronic (Professional &
Academic); Gay & Lesbian Studies; Gender
Studies; Languages & Linguistics; Reference
Books, Directories & Dictionaries

New Titles: 15 (2009) , 15 (2010)

Imprints, Series & ISBNs:
978 1 900650, 978 1 905763

Book Trade Association Membership:
Publishers Association; Independent
Publishers Guild

2652

ST PAULS PUBLISHING
187 Battersea Bridge Road, London
SW11 3AS
Telephone: 020 7978 4300
Fax: 020 7978 4370
Email: editorial@stpaulspublishing.com
Web Site: www.stpaulspublishing.com

Personnel:
Celso Godilano (Director)
Annabel Robson (Commissioning Editor)

Paul Tennant (Sales & Marketing)
Pamela Tamburini (Permissions & Foreign
Rights)

Biography & Autobiography; Children's
Books; Philosophy; Psychology &
Psychiatry; Religion & Theology

Imprints, Series & ISBNs:
978 0 85439

Associated Companies:
Argentina: Ediciones San Pablo
Australia: St Pauls Publications
Brazil: Edições San Pablo
Canada: Medias Paul
Colombia: Ediciones San Pablo
France: Editions Mediaspaul
India: Better Yourself Books; St Pauls
Italy: Edizioni San Paolo
Japan: Chuoshuppan-Sha
Kenya: St Pauls Publications
Mexico: Ediciones San Pablo
Philippines: St Pauls
Portugal: Edições San Pablo
Republic of Ireland: St Pauls
Republic of Korea: St Pauls
Spain: Ediciones San Pablo
USA: Alba House
Venezuela: Ediciones San Pablo

Distributor for:
St Pauls

Overseas Representation:
Australia: St Pauls Publications, Homebush,
Australia
Kenya: St Paul Book Centre, Nairobi, Kenya
Nigeria: St Paul Book Centre, Oke-Padi,
Nigeria
Tanzania: St Paul Book Centre, Dar-es-
Salaam, Tanzania
Uganda: St Paul Book Centre, Kampala,
Uganda

Book Trade Association Membership:
Booksellers Association

2653

SALT PUBLISHING LTD
14A High Street, Fulbourn, Cambridge
CB21 5DH
Telephone: 01223 882220
Fax: 01223 882260
Web Site: www.saltpublishing.com

Personnel:
Chris Hamilton-Emery (Editor)
Jennifer Hamilton-Emery (General Manager)
Charlotte Prince (Publishing Assistant)

Biography & Autobiography; Fiction;
Literature & Criticism; Poetry

Imprints, Series & ISBNs:
Folio (Salt): 978 0 646
Salt Publishing: 978 1 84471, 978 1 876857

Overseas Representation:
Australia: Inbooks, c/o James Bennett Pty
Ltd, Belrose, NSW, Australia
USA: Small Press Distribution Inc, Berkeley,
CA, USA

Book Trade Association Membership:
Independent Publishers Guild

2654

SANDSTONE PRESS LTD
PO Box 5725, 1 High Street, Dingwall,
Ross-shire IV15 9WJ
Telephone: 01349 862583
Fax: 01349 862583
Email: info@sandstonepress.com
Web Site: www.sandstonepress.com

Personnel:
Robert Davidson (Managing Director)
Iain Gordon (Company Secretary)
Moira Forsyth (Director)

Academic & Scholarly; Biography &
Autobiography; Crime; English as a Foreign
Language; Environment & Development
Studies; Fiction; Humour; Illustrated & Fine
Editions; Literature & Criticism; Politics &
World Affairs; Science Fiction; Sports &
Games

Imprints, Series & ISBNs:
Sandstone Meanmnach Series: 978 1
905207
Sandstone Vista Series: 978 1 905207

Overseas Representation:
USA & Canada: Silvermibe International
Books Inc

Book Trade Association Membership:
Publishing Scotland

2655

SANSOM & CO LTD
81g Pembroke Road, Clifton, Bristol
BS8 3EA
Telephone: 0117 973 7207
Fax: 0117 923 8991
Email: johnsansom@aol.com &
info@sansomandcompany.co.uk
Web Site: www.sansomandcompany.co.uk

Trade Orders:
Orca Book Services, Unit A3, Fleets Corner,
Poole, Dorset BH17 0HL
Telephone: 01202 665432
Fax: 01202 666219
Email: orders@orcabookservices.co.uk
Web Site: www.orcabookservices.co.uk

Personnel:
A. N. Sansom (Sales Director)
John Sansom (Publishing Director)
Clara Sansom (Production Director)

Architecture & Design; Fine Art & Art
History; Literature & Criticism

Imprints, Series & ISBNs:
978 1 900178, 978 1 904537, 978 1
906593

Associated Companies:
Art Dictionaries Ltd; Redcliffe Press Ltd

Overseas Representation:
USA: Antique Collectors' Club,
Woodbridge, Suffolk, UK

2656

SAQI BOOKS
26 Westbourne Grove, London W2 5RH
Telephone: 020 7221 9347
Fax: 020 7229 7492
Web Site: www.saqibooks.com

Distribution:
Marston Book Services OX14 4SD
Telephone: 01235 465500
Fax: 01235 465555
Email: client.orders@marston.co.uk
Web Site: www.marston.co.uk

Personnel:
André Gaspard (Publisher/Director)
Lynn Gaspard (Commissioning Editor/Rights
Manager)
Ashley Biles (Sales and Marketing Manager)
Kelly Pike (Publicity Manager)
Shikha Sethi (Production Manager)

Academic & Scholarly; Architecture &
Design; Biography & Autobiography;
Cookery, Wines & Spirits; Economics;
Educational & Textbooks; Environment &
Development Studies; Fashion & Costume;
Fiction; Fine Art & Art History; Gay &
Lesbian Studies; Gender Studies; History &
Antiquarian; Humour; Illustrated & Fine
Editions; Languages & Linguistics; Law;
Literature & Criticism; Mathematics &

Statistics; Music; Philosophy; Photography;
Poetry; Politics & World Affairs; Religion &
Theology; Sociology & Anthropology

New Titles: 22 (2010)
No of Employees: 5

Imprints, Series & ISBNs:
978 0 86356
Brief Introduction (series)
Saqi Essentials

Associated Companies:
Lebanon: Dar Al Saqi Sarl

Overseas Representation:
Australia: Palgrave Macmillan, South Yarra,
Vic, Australia
USA: Consortium Publishers, St Paul, MN,
USA

Book Trade Association Membership:
Booksellers Association; Independent
Publishers Guild

2657

ALASTAIR SAWDAY PUBLISHING
The Old Farmyard, Yanley Lane,
Long Ashton, Bristol BS41 9LR
Telephone: 01275 395430
Fax: 01275 393388
Email: info@sawdays.co.uk
Web Site: www.sawdays.co.uk/bookshop

Distribution & Sales:
Penguin (UK), 80 The Strand, London
WC2R 0RL
Telephone: 020 7010 3000
Fax: 020 7010 3198
Email: sales@penguin.co.uk

Personnel:
Alastair Sawday (Publisher/Chairman)
Annie Shillito (Editorial Director)
Toby Sawday (Business Development
Director)
Julia Richardson (Production, Web/IT
Manager)
Bridget Bishop (Finance Manager)
Rob Richardson (Sales & Marketing
Manager)
Sue Bourner (Editorial, Web/IT Manager)
Joe Green (Web/IT Manager)

Environment & Development Studies;
Guide Books; Travel & Topography

Imprints, Series & ISBNs:
Alastair Sawday's Special Places to Stay: 978
1 901970, 978 1 906136
Fragile Earth: 978 1 901970, 978 1 906136

Overseas Representation:
USA & Canada: Globe Pequot Press,
Guilford, CT, USA
Worldwide (excluding USA & Canada):
Penguin Books Ltd, London, UK

Book Trade Association Membership:
Independent Publishers Guild

2658

S. B. PUBLICATIONS
14 Bishopstone Road, Seaford, East Sussex
BN25 2UB
Telephone: 01323 893498
Fax: 01323 893860
Email: sbpublications@tiscali.co.uk
Web Site: www.sbpublications.co.uk

Personnel:
Mrs L. S. Woods (Owner/Manager)
Mrs D. Quick (Finance)
Lindsay Woods (Sales Manager)
Ms E. Howe (Editorial)
C. Howden (Proofreader)
Miss C. Gillett (Sales & Administration)

Guide Books; History & Antiquarian;
Natural History; Travel & Topography

Imprints, Series & ISBNs:
978 1 85770

2659

SCALA PUBLISHERS LTD
Northburgh House, 10 Northburgh Street,
London EC1V 0AT
Telephone: 020 7490 9900
Fax: 020 7336 6870
Email: jmckinley@scalapublishers.com
Web Site: www.scalapublishers.com

All orders (excluding Australia):
ACC Distribution, Sandy Lane,
Old Marlesham, Woodbridge, Suffolk
IP12 4SD
Telephone: 01394 389950
Fax: 01394 389999
Email: sales@antique-acc.com
Web Site: www.antiquecollectorsclub.com

Personnel:
David Campbell (Chairman)
Jennifer Wright (Museum Publications
(USA) Director)
Jenny McKinley (Marketing & Publications
(excl. USA) Director)
Oliver Craske (Editorial Director)
Tim Clarke (Production Director)
Mark Bicknell (Finance Director)

Antiques & Collecting; Architecture &
Design; Children's Books; Fine Art & Art
History; Guide Books; Illustrated & Fine
Editions; Sports & Games; Travel &
Topography

New Titles: 40 (2009) , 50 (2010)

Imprints, Series & ISBNs:
978 1 85759

Overseas Representation:
Australia (Sales): In Books, NSW, Australia
Worldwide: ACC Distribution, Woodbridge,
Suffolk, UK

2660

SCHOLASTIC UK LTD
Euston House, 24 Eversholt Street, London
NW1 1DB
Telephone: 020 7756 7756
Fax: 020 7756 7795
Web Site: www.scholastic.co.uk

Scholastic Book Clubs:
(as above)

Scholastic Children's Books:
(as above)

Scholastic Book Fairs:
(as above)

Scholastic Education:
Book End, Range Road, Witney, Oxon
OX29 0YD
Fax: 01993 893222

Personnel:
Hilary Murray Hill (Scholastic Children's
Books – Managing Director)
Alan Hurcombe (Group Managing Director)
Denise Cripps (Education – Managing
Director)
Nicola Dixon (Finance Director)
Steve Thompson (Managing Director, Fairs)
Julie Randles (Managing Director, Clubs)

Children's Books; Educational & Textbooks

Parent Company:
USA: Scholastic Inc

Associated Companies:
Australia: Scholastic Australia Pty Ltd
Canada: Scholastic Canada Ltd
New Zealand: Scholastic New Zealand Ltd
UK: Chicken House Publishing

Overseas Representation:
Australia: Scholastic Australia Ltd, Gosford,
NSW, Australia
Canada: Scholastic Canada Ltd, Markham,
Ont, Canada
Far East (excluding Singapore, Malaysia &
Indonesia): Scholastic Hong Kong, Hong
Kong
New Zealand: Scholastic NZ, Auckland, New
Zealand

Book Trade Association Membership:
Publishers Association; Educational
Publishers Council; Periodical Publishers
Association

2661

SCHOOLPLAY PRODUCTIONS LTD
15 Inglis Road, Colchester, Essex CO3 3HU
Telephone: 01206 540111
Fax: 01206 766944
Email: schoolplay@inglis-
house.demon.co.uk
Web Site:
www.schoolplayproductions.co.uk

Personnel:
J. R. Lucas (Managing Director)
W. Baker (Director)
Mrs C. S. Wenden (Administrator)

Educational & Textbooks; Music; Theatre,
Drama & Dance

New Titles: 1 (2009) , 1 (2010)
No of Employees: 2

Imprints, Series & ISBNs:
978 1 872475, 978 1 902472

Book Trade Association Membership:
Publishers Association

2662

SCHOTT MUSIC LTD
48 Great Marlborough Street, London
W1F 7BB
Telephone: 020 7534 0700
Fax: 020 7534 0719
Email: info@schott-music.com
Web Site: www.schott-music.com

Trade Enquiries & Orders:
MDS Service Centre,
5–6 Raywood Office Complex,
Leacon Lane, Charing, Ashford, Kent
TN27 0EN
Telephone: 01233 712233
Fax: 01233 714948
Email: orders.uk@mds-partner.com
Web Site: www.smdextranet.schott-
extranet.de

Personnel:
Judith Webb (Joint Managing Director)
Roberto Garcia (Sales & Marketing Director)
Guy Thomas (Buying Manager)
Wendy Lampa (Head of International
Publishing)

Academic & Scholarly; Music

New Titles: 20 (2009) , 25 (2010)
No of Employees: 25

Imprints, Series & ISBNs:
Apollo-Verlag Paul Lincke GmbH: 978 3
920030
Ars-Viva-Verlag: 978 3 920045
Atlantis Musikbuch-Verlag AG: 978 3 254
Anton J. Benjamin GmbH: 978 3 923051
Boosey & Hawkes Music Publishers Ltd: 978
0 85162
Bote & Bock GmbH & Co KG: 978 3 7931,
978 3 87090
Cranz GmbH: 978 3 920201
Matth. Hohner AG: 978 3 920468, 978 3
937315
Schott London: 978 0 901938, 978 0
946535, 978 1 902455

Schott Music & Media GmbH (Intuition):
978 3 932398
Schott Music GmbH & Co KG: 978 3 7957
Schott USA: 978 0 930448
Richard Strauss GmbH & Co KG: 978 3
901974

Parent Company:
Germany: Schott Music GmbH & Co KG

Associated Companies:
Ernst Eulenburg Ltd

Distributor for:
A piacere; Ars viva; Bardic Edition; Boosey &
Hawkes Music Publishers Ltd; Delius
Trust; Edition HH; Finzi Trust; Hyperion;
Itchy Fingers Publications; Universal
Edition Ltd
Austria: Amadeus; Apollo-Verlag Paul
Lincke GmbH; Ars-Viva-Verlag; Atlantis-
Musikbuch-Verlag; Anton J. Benjamin
GmbH; Boosey & Hawkes GmbH; Bote &
Bock GmbH & Co KG; Cranz GmbH; G.
Henle Verlag; Matth. Hohner AG

Overseas Representation:
Europe: Schott Music GmbH & Co KG,
Mainz, Germany
Japan: Schott Japan Co Ltd, Tokyo, Japan
USA: Hal Leonard Corporation, Milwaukee,
WI, USA

2663

SCION PUBLISHING LTD
The Old Hayloft, Vantage Business Park,
Bloxham Road, Banbury, Oxon OX16 9UX
Telephone: 01295 258577
Fax: 01295 275624
Web Site: www.scionpublishing.com

Distribution:
NBN International, Estover Road, Plymouth
PL6 7PZ

Personnel:
Dr Jonathan Ray (Managing Director)
Simon Watkins (Sales & Marketing Director)

Academic & Scholarly; Biology & Zoology;
Chemistry; Medical (incl. Self Help &
Alternative Medicine); Scientific & Technical

New Titles: 6 (2009) , 8 (2010)
No of Employees: 3
Annual Turnover: £450,000

Imprints, Series & ISBNs:
978 1 904842

Distributor for:
Brazil: Artes Medicas
UK: Acheron Press; Medical Partners
Publishing; The Ray Society

Overseas Representation:
Americas (North & South): Cold Spring
Harbor Laboratory Press, Woodbury, NY,
USA
Australia & New Zealand: Macmillan
Education Australia, South Yarra, Vic,
Australia
Europe: Andrew Durnell Marketing Ltd,
Tunbridge Wells, UK
Far East: The White Partnership, Tunbridge
Wells, UK
South Africa: Mike Brightmore, Academic
Marketing Services, Johannesburg, South
Africa

2664

SCOTTISH CHILDREN'S PRESS
Unit 6, Newbattle Abbey Business Park,
Newbattle Road, Dalkeith EH22 3LJ
Telephone: 0131 660 6366 (editorial) &
4666 (orders)
Fax: 0870 285 4846
Email: info@scottishbooks.com &
orders@scottishbooks.com
Web Site: www.scottishbooks.com

Personnel:
Brian Pugh (Company Secretary)
Avril Gray (Director)

Archaeology; Biography & Autobiography;
Children's Books; Cookery, Wines & Spirits;
Fiction; History & Antiquarian; Languages &
Linguistics; Natural History; Poetry; Religion
& Theology; Sports & Games

Imprints, Series & ISBNs:
978 1 899827

Associated Companies:
S.C.P. Publishers Ltd (trading as Scottish
Cultural Press)

2665

SCOTTISH CULTURAL PRESS
Unit 6, Newbattle Abbey Business Park,
Newbattle Road, Dalkeith EH22 3LJ
Telephone: 0131 660 6366 (editorial) &
4666 (orders)
Fax: 0870 285 4846
Email: info@scottishbooks.com &
orders@scottishbooks.com
Web Site: www.scottishbooks.com

Personnel:
Brian Pugh (Company Secretary)
Avril Gray (Director)

Archaeology; Audio Books; Biography &
Autobiography; Cookery, Wines & Spirits;
Environment & Development Studies;
Geography & Geology; History &
Antiquarian; Languages & Linguistics;
Literature & Criticism; Military & War;
Natural History; Nautical; Poetry; Reference
Books, Directories & Dictionaries; Religion &
Theology; Sociology & Anthropology;
Theatre, Drama & Dance

Imprints, Series & ISBNs:
Scottish Children's Press: 978 1 899827
Scottish Cultural Press: 978 1 84017, 978 1
898218

Associated Companies:
S.C.P. Childrens Ltd (trading as Scottish
Children's Press)

2666

SCOTTISH TEXT SOCIETY
School of English Studies,
University of Nottingham, Nottingham
NG7 2RD
Telephone: 0115 951 5922
Fax: 0115 951 5924
Email:
editorialsecretary@scottishtextsociety.org
Web Site: www.scottishtextsociety.org

Registered Office:
Basement Flat, 25 Buccleuch Place,
Edinburgh EH8 9LN

Personnel:
Sally Mapstone (President)
Nicola Royan (Editorial Secretary)

Academic & Scholarly; History &
Antiquarian; Literature & Criticism; Poetry

Imprints, Series & ISBNs:
978 1 897976

Overseas Representation:
Worldwide: Boydell & Brewer Ltd,
Woodbridge, Suffolk, UK

Book Trade Association Membership:
Publishing Scotland

2667

SCRIPTURE UNION PUBLISHING
Scripture Union, 207–209 Queensway,
Bletchley, Milton Keynes, Bucks MK2 2EB
Telephone: 01908 856000

Fax: 01908 856111
Email: info@scriptureunion.org.uk
Web Site: www.scripture.org.uk/

Warehouse:
Marston Book Services
Telephone: 01235 465579
Fax: 01235 465518
Email: christian.orders@marston.co.uk

Mail Order:
PO Box 5148, Milton Keynes MLO
MK2 2YX
Telephone: 01908 856006
Fax: 01908 856020
Email: subs@scriptureunion.org.uk

Personnel:
Terry Clutterham *(Director of Ministry
Delivery)*
Dave Parsons *(Publishing Accounts
Manager)*
Rosemary North *(Rights Manager)*
Clive Cornelius *(Production Manager)*

*Children's Books; Educational & Textbooks;
Music; Religion & Theology*

New Titles: 30 (2009) , 42 (2010)

Imprints, Series & ISBNs:
Scripture Union: 978 0 85421, 978 0 86201

Overseas Representation:
Australasia, East Asia & Pacific: Resources
for Ministry, Gosford, NSW, Australia
Canada: Scripture Union, Pickering, Canada
New Zealand: Scripture Union Wholesale,
Wellington, New Zealand
USA: Scripture Union, Wayne, PA, USA

Book Trade Association Membership:
Booksellers Association; Educational
Publishers Council

2668 ▬▬▬

SEASQUIRT PUBLICATIONS
18d Church Gate, Loughborough, Leics
LE11 1UD
Telephone: 01509 219633
Fax: 01509 264441
Web Site: www.jimjazzmouse.com &
www.infestedwaters.co.uk

Personnel:
David Hughes *(Executive)*

Children's Books

Book Trade Association Membership:
Publishers Association; Booksellers
Association; Independent Publishers Guild

2669 ▬▬▬

SEDA PUBLICATIONS
[Staff & Educational Development
Association]
Woburn House, 20–24 Tavistock Square,
London WC1H 9HF
Telephone: 020 7380 6767
Fax: 020 7387 2655
Email: office@seda.ac.uk
Web Site: www.seda.ac.uk

Personnel:
Julie Hall *(Co-chair of SEDA)*

Academic & Scholarly

New Titles: 4 (2009) , 3 (2010)
Annual Turnover: £300,000

Book Trade Association Membership:
Association of Learned & Professional
Society Publishers

2670 ▬▬▬

SEREN
57 Nolton Street, Bridgend CF31 3AE

Telephone: 01656 663018
Web Site: www.seren-books.com

Distribution:
Central Books, 99 Wallis Road, London
E9 5LN
Telephone: 020 8986 4854
Fax: 020 8533 5821
Email: orders@centralbooks.com
Web Site: www.centralbooks.com

Personnel:
Mick Felton *(Managing Director)*
Simon Hicks *(Marketing Manager)*
Victoria Humphreys *(Marketing Officer)*
Amy Wack *(Poetry Editor)*
Penny Thomas *(Fiction Editor)*

*Biography & Autobiography; Fiction; Fine
Art & Art History; Literature & Criticism;
Photography; Poetry*

Imprints, Series & ISBNs:
978 0 907476, 978 1 85411

Parent Company:
Poetry Wales Press Ltd

Overseas Representation:
Australia: Eleanor Brasch Enterprises,
Artarmon, NSW, Australia
USA & Canada: Independent Publishers
Group (IPG), Chicago, IL, USA

2671 ▬▬▬

SESSIONS OF YORK
The Ebor Press, Huntington Road, York
YO31 9HS
Telephone: 01904 659224
Fax: 01904 637068
Email: ebor.info@sessionsofyork.co.uk
Web Site: www.sessionsofyork.co.uk

Personnel:
W. Mark Sessions *(Chairman & Managing
Director)*
Bob Jarrett *(Publishing Manager)*

*Archaeology; Biography & Autobiography;
Children's Books; History & Antiquarian;
Industry, Business & Management; Natural
History; Poetry; Politics & World Affairs;
Religion & Theology*

Imprints, Series & ISBNs:
978 1 85072

Parent Company:
William Sessions Holdings Ltd

Book Trade Association Membership:
Quakers Uniting in Publishing

2672 ▬▬▬

SGC BOOKS
PO Box 49, Spalding, Lincs PE11 1NZ
Telephone: 01775 712424
Fax: 01775 762618
Email: chalksoft@clara.co.uk
Web Site: www.chalksoft.clara.co.uk

Personnel:
David Baldwin *(Managing Director)*
Gillian Baldwin *(Home Sales, Rights
Director)*

*Children's Books; Gardening; Health &
Beauty; Natural History*

Imprints, Series & ISBNs:
978 1 85116

Parent Company:
Chalksoft Ltd

Associated Companies:
Nene Valley Publishing

Book Trade Association Membership:
Independent Publishers Guild

2673 ▬▬▬

SHARON HOUSE PUBLISHING
152 Wakefield Road, Ossett,
West Yorkshire WF5 9AQ
Telephone: 01924 279966
Fax: 01924 279966
Email: books@sharonhousepublishing.com
Web Site:
www.sharonhousepublishing.com

Personnel:
Anna McKann *(Director)*
Tim Wicks *(Director)*

Children's Books

Imprints, Series & ISBNs:
978 0 9554438

Book Trade Association Membership:
Publishers Association

2674 ▬▬▬

SHEAF PUBLISHING
Beehive Works, Milton Street, Sheffield
S3 7WL
Telephone: 0114 273 9067
Fax: 0114 270 6888
Email: sheafgraphics@btconnect.com

Personnel:
T. Cooper *(Manager)*

History & Antiquarian; Transport

No of Employees: 4

Imprints, Series & ISBNs:
978 0 9505458, 978 1 85048

2675 ▬▬▬

SHELDON PRESS
36 Causton Street, London SW1P 4ST
Telephone: 020 7592 3900
Fax: 020 7592 3939
Email: jmoriarty@spck.org.uk
Web Site: www.sheldonpress.co.uk

Personnel:
Joanna Moriarty *(Publishing Director)*
Alan Mordue *(Sales & Marketing Director)*
Fiona Marshall *(Editor)*
Sophie Dean *(Rights Manager)*

*Gender Studies; Health & Beauty; Medical
(incl. Self Help & Alternative Medicine);
Psychology & Psychiatry*

Imprints, Series & ISBNs:
Azure Books: 978 1 902694
Sheldon Press: 978 0 85969

Parent Company:
The Society for Promoting Christian
Knowledge (SPCK)

Overseas Representation:
Australia: Willow Connection Pty Ltd,
Brookvale, NSW, Australia
India: ISPCK, Delhi, India

2676 ▬▬▬

SHELDRAKE PRESS
188 Cavendish Road, London SW12 0DA
Telephone: 020 8675 1767
Fax: 020 8675 7736
Email: enquiries@sheldrakepress.co.uk
Web Site: www.sheldrakepress.co.uk

Distribution:
NBN International Ltd, Estover Road,
Plymouth PL6 7PY
Telephone: 01752 202300
Fax: 01752 202330
Email: enquiries@nbninternational.com
Web Site: www.nbninternational.com

Personnel:
Simon Rigge *(Publisher Director)*
Roger Rigge *(Company Secretary)*

*Architecture & Design; Children's Books;
Cookery, Wines & Spirits; Guide Books;
History & Antiquarian; Humour; Transport;
Travel & Topography*

Imprints, Series & ISBNs:
978 1 873329

Parent Company:
Sheldrake Holdings Ltd

Overseas Representation:
USA: Interlink Publishing Group Inc,
Northampton, MA, USA

2677 ▬▬▬

**SHEPHEARD-WALWYN
(PUBLISHERS) LTD**
107 Parkway House, Sheen Lane, London
SW14 8LS
Telephone: 020 8241 5927
Email: books@shepheard-walwyn.co.uk
Web Site: www.shepheard-walwyn.co.uk

Orders:
NBN International, Plymbridge House,
Estover Road, Plymouth PL6 7PY
Telephone: 01752 202301
Fax: 01752 202330
Email: orders@nbninternational.com
Web Site: www.nbninternational.com

Personnel:
Anthony R. A. Werner *(Managing Director)*

*Academic & Scholarly; Biography &
Autobiography; Economics; History &
Antiquarian; Illustrated & Fine Editions;
Philosophy; Politics & World Affairs;
Religion & Theology*

New Titles: 7 (2009) , 9 (2010)
No of Employees: 29
Annual Turnover: £90,000

Imprints, Series & ISBNs:
978 0 85683
The Letters of Marsilio Ficino
Marsilio Ficino's Commentaries on Plato's
Writings
Who's Who in British History series

Overseas Representation:
Australia & New Zealand: John Reed Book
Distribution, Brookvale, NSW, Australia
USA & Canada: Independent Publishers
Group (IPG), Chicago, IL, USA

2678 ▬▬▬

SHERWOOD PUBLISHING
Wildhill, Broadoak End, Hertford SG14 2JA
Telephone: 01992 550246
Fax: 01992 535283
Email: sherwood@adinternational.com
Web Site: www.sherwoodpublishing.com

Personnel:
Mrs Julie Hay *(Chief Executive)*

*Industry, Business & Management;
Psychology & Psychiatry*

New Titles: 2 (2009) , 4 (2010)
No of Employees: 1

Imprints, Series & ISBNs:
978 0 9521964, 978 0 9539852

Parent Company:
UK: Psychological Intelligence Ltd

Book Trade Association Membership:
Independent Publishers Guild

2679

THE SHETLAND TIMES LTD
Gremista, Lerwick, Shetland ZE1 0PX
Telephone: 01595 693622
Fax: 01595 694637
Email: publishing@shetland-times.co.uk
Web Site: www.shetland-books.co.uk

Scottish Agent:
BookSource, 50 Cambuslang Road,
Glasgow G32 8NB

Personnel:
Charlotte Black (Publications Manager)

Biography & Autobiography; Guide Books;
Music; Natural History

New Titles: 10 (2009) , 8 (2010)

Imprints, Series & ISBNs:
978 0 900662, 978 1 898852, 978 1
904746

Book Trade Association Membership:
Booksellers Association

2680

SHIRE PUBLICATIONS LTD
Midland House, West Way, Botley, Oxford
OX2 0PH
Telephone: 01865 727022
Fax: 01865 727017
Email: shire@shirebooks.co.uk
Web Site: www.shirebooks.co.uk

Personnel:
Rebecca Smart (Managing Director)
Sue Ross (Sales Manager)
Nicholas Wright (Publisher)

Antiques & Collecting; Archaeology;
Architecture & Design; Biography &
Autobiography; Gardening; Guide Books;
History & Antiquarian; Military & War;
Natural History; Sociology & Anthropology;
Transport; Travel & Topography

New Titles: 60 (2009) , 60 (2010)
No of Employees: 4
Annual Turnover: £500,000

Imprints, Series & ISBNs:
978 0 7478, 978 0 85263

Parent Company:
UK: Osprey Publishing Group

2681

SHORT BOOKS LTD
3A Exmouth House, Pine Street, London
EC1R 0JH
Telephone: 020 7833 9429
Fax: 020 7833 9500
Email: info@shortbooks.co.uk
Web Site: www.theshortbookco.com

Distribution:
TBS, Colchester Road, Frating Green,
Colchester CO7 7DW
Telephone: 01206 255678
Fax: 01206 255930

Personnel:
Rebecca Nicolson (Publisher)
Catherine Gibbs (Managing Director)
Aurea Carpenter (Editor)

Biography & Autobiography; Children's
Books; Fiction; History & Antiquarian;
Humour; Philosophy; Sports & Games

Imprints, Series & ISBNs:
978 0 904095, 978 0 904977, 978 0
906021, 978 0 907595

Overseas Representation:
Australasia: Allen & Unwin, Sydney, NSW,
Australia

Rest of World: Intercontinental Literature
Agency, London, UK
USA: Inkwell Management, New York, NY,
USA

Book Trade Association Membership:
Independent Publishers Guild

2682

SHU PUBLICATIONS LTD
437A Sandygate Road, Sheffield S10 5UD
Telephone: 0114 230 5104

Academic & Scholarly; Educational &
Textbooks

Book Trade Association Membership:
Publishers Association

2683

SIGEL PRESS
51A Victoria Road, Cambridge CB4 3BW
Telephone: 01223 303303
Fax: 01223 303303
Email: info@sigelpress.com
Web Site: www.sigelpress.com

Also at:
4403 Belmont Court, Medina, OH 44256,
USA
Telephone: 00 1 330 722 2541
Fax: 00 1 330 722 2541
Email: info@sigelpress.com
Web Site: www.sigelpress.com

Personnel:
Thomas Sigel (Managing & Publisher
Director)
Andrew Hogbin (Operations Director)

Academic & Scholarly; Accountancy &
Taxation; Audio Books; Children's Books;
Educational & Textbooks; Environment &
Development Studies; Fiction; Industry,
Business & Management; Military & War;
Science Fiction

New Titles: 4 (2009) , 4 (2010)
No of Employees: 2

Imprints, Series & ISBNs:
978 1 905941

Associated Companies:
USA: Sigel Press

Book Trade Association Membership:
Independent Publishers Guild

2684

SIGMA PRESS
Stobart House, Pontyclerc, Penybanc Road,
Ammanford, Carmarthenshire SA18 3HP
Telephone: 01269 593100
Fax: 01269 596116
Email: info@sigmapress.co.uk
Web Site: www.sigmapress.co.uk

Personnel:
Nigel Evans (Managing Director)
Jane Evans (Managing Editor)

Cookery, Wines & Spirits; Crafts & Hobbies;
Guide Books; Sports & Games; Travel &
Topography

Imprints, Series & ISBNs:
Sigma Leisure: 978 0 905104, 978 1 85058
Sigma Press: 978 0 905104, 978 1 85058

Parent Company:
UK: Stobart Davies Ltd

Overseas Representation:
USA: Barnes & Noble Distribution,
Jamesburg, NJ, USA

Book Trade Association Membership:
Booksellers Association; Independent
Publishers Guild

2685

SILVER MOON BOOKS
108c Goldhurst Terrace, London NW6 3HR
Telephone: 020 7625 7592

Trade Enquiries & Orders:
Turnaround Publisher Services, Unit 3,
Olympia Trading Estate, Coburg Road,
London N22 6TZ
Telephone: 020 8829 3000
Fax: 020 8881 5088

Personnel:
Jane Cholmeley (Director)

Fiction; Gay & Lesbian Studies

Imprints, Series & ISBNs:
978 1 872642

2686

SIMON & SCHUSTER (UK) LTD
1st Floor, 222 Gray's Inn Road, London
WC1X 8HB
Telephone: 020 7316 1900
Fax: 020 7316 0331
Email: @simonandschuster.co.uk
Web Site: www.simonsays.co.uk

**Customer Services & Distribution
Centre:**
HarperCollins, Customer Service Centre,
Westerhill Road, Bishopbriggs, Glasgow
G64 2QT
Telephone: 0141 306 3100
Fax: 0141 306 3767

Personnel:
Ian Stewart Chapman (Managing Director)
Suzanne Baboneau (Adult Publishing
Director)
Kerr MacRae (Executive Director)
Mike Jones (Editorial – Non-Fiction Director)
Ingrid Selberg (Children's Publishing
Director)
Maxine Hitchcock (Editorial – Fiction
Director)
Hannah Corbett (Publicity – Adult Trade
Director)
David Hyde (Production Director)
Sarah Birdsey (Rights Director)
Nick Hayward (Export Sales Director)
Stuart Mullin (Finance & Operations
Director)
Dawn Burnett (Marketing Director)

Audio Books; Biography & Autobiography;
Children's Books; Cinema, Video, TV &
Radio; Cookery, Wines & Spirits; Crime;
Fiction; Guide Books; Health & Beauty;
Humour; Industry, Business &
Management; Medical (incl. Self Help &
Alternative Medicine); Military & War;
Music; Politics & World Affairs; Religion &
Theology; Science Fiction; Sports & Games;
Travel & Topography

Imprints, Series & ISBNs:
Free Press: 978 0 671, 978 0 684, 978 0
7432, 978 1 4165
Pocket: 978 0 671, 978 0 7434, 978 1
4165, 978 1 84739, 978 1 84983
Scribner: 978 0 671, 978 0 684, 978 0
7432, 978 1 4165
Simon & Schuster: 978 0 671, 978 0 684,
978 0 7432, 978 0 85720, 978 1 4165,
978 1 84737
Simon & Schuster Audio: 978 0 7435, 978 0
85720
Simon & Schuster Children's: 978 0 689,
978 0 85707, 978 1 4169, 978 1 84738

Parent Company:
USA: Simon & Schuster Inc

Distributor for:
UK: Duncan Baird; BL Publishing
USA: Andrews McMeel; Atria; Fireside; Free
Press; Gallery; Pocket; Scribner; Simon &
Schuster Audio; Simon & Schuster Inc;
Touchstone; VIZ Media

Overseas Representation:
Australia: Simon & Schuster (Australia) Pty
Ltd, Pymble, NSW, Australia
Canada: Simon & Schuster (Canada),
Markham, Ont, Canada
New Zealand: HarperCollins (NZ) Ltd,
Glenfield, Auckland, New Zealand
Singapore: Penguin Books Singapore,
Jurong, Singapore
South Africa: Jonathan Ball Publishers (Pty)
Ltd, Johannesburg, South Africa
USA: Trafalgar Square Publishing / IPG,
Chicago, IL, USA

Book Trade Association Membership:
Publishers Association

2687

SINGING DRAGON PUBLISHERS
116 Pentonville Road, London N1 9JB
Telephone: 020 7833 2307
Fax: 020 7837 2917
Email: post@singing-dragon.com
Web Site: www.jkp.com/singingdragon/

Trade Enquiries & Orders:
Macmillan Distribution (MDL), Brunel Road,
Houndmills, Basingstoke, Hants RG21 6XS
Telephone: 01256 302985
Fax: 01256 841426
Email: trade@macmillan.co.uk
Web Site:
www.macmillandistribution.co.uk

Personnel:
Jessica Kingsley (Managing Director)
Dee Brigham (Finance)
Helen Longmate (Marketing & Sales
Director, Rights Manager)
Jemima Kingsley (Electronic Media)
Despina Pechlivanidis (Sales Manager)
Octavia Kingsley (Production Manager)

Educational & Textbooks; Health & Beauty;
Medical (incl. Self Help & Alternative
Medicine); Psychology & Psychiatry

Imprints, Series & ISBNs:
Jessica Kingsley: 978 1 84310, 978 1 85302
Singing Dragon: 978 1 84819

Associated Companies:
USA: Jessica Kingsley Publishers Inc

Overseas Representation:
Australia & New Zealand: Footprint Books
Pty, Warriewood, Australia
Canada: UBC Press, Toronto, Ont, Canada
Europe: Durnell Marketing Ltd, Tunbridge
Wells, UK
Hong Kong, Taiwan, China, Philippines &
Indonesia: Asia Publishers Services Ltd,
Hong Kong
Japan: United Publishers Services Ltd,
Aberdeen, Hong Kong
USA: Jessica Kingsley Publishers Inc,
Philadelphia, USA

Book Trade Association Membership:
Publishers Association; Educational
Publishers Council

2688

CHARLES SKILTON LTD
2 Caversham Street, London SW3 4AH
Telephone: 020 7351 4995
Fax: 020 7351 4995
Email: leonard.holdsworth@btinternet.com

Personnel:
James Hughes (Managing Director)
Margaret Fletcher (Sales Director)
Leonard Holdsworth (Editor)

Cinema, Video, TV & Radio; Cookery, Wines & Spirits; Fashion & Costume; Fiction; Fine Art & Art History; Gay & Lesbian Studies; Guide Books; Illustrated & Fine Editions; Literature & Criticism; Military & War; Poetry; Theatre, Drama & Dance; Transport; Travel & Topography

Imprints, Series & ISBNs:
Christchurch: 978 1 901846
Skilton: 978 0 284

Parent Company:
Christchurch Publishers Ltd

Associated Companies:
Caversham Communications Ltd; Christchurch Publishers Ltd; Luxor Press

Book Trade Association Membership:
Independent Publishers Guild

2689

SLIGHTLY FOXED
67 Dickinson Court, 15 Brewhouse Yard, London EC1V 4JX
Telephone: 020 7549 2121
Fax: 0870 199 1245
Email: all@foxedquarterly.com
Web Site: www.foxedquarterly.com

Personnel:
Gail Pirkis (Managing Director)
Hazel Wood (Co-Editor)
Stephanie Allen (Marketing Manager)
Jennie Paterson (Administrator)

Academic & Scholarly; Biography & Autobiography; Children's Books; Fiction; Gardening; History & Antiquarian; Illustrated & Fine Editions; Travel & Topography

Imprints, Series & ISBNs:
978 1 906562

Book Trade Association Membership:
Independent Publishers Guild

2690

SLS LEGAL PUBLICATIONS (NI)
Lansdowne House, 50 Malone Road, Belfast BT9 5BS
Telephone: 028 9066 7711
Fax: 028 9066 7733
Email: s.gamble@qub.ac.uk
Web Site: www.sls.qub.ac.uk

Personnel:
Miss M. Dudley (Director)
Mrs S. Gamble (Publications Editor)

Academic & Scholarly; Law

New Titles: 2 (2009), 2 (2010)
No of Employees: 5

Imprints, Series & ISBNs:
978 0 85389

Book Trade Association Membership:
Publishers Association; Independent Publishers Guild

2691

SMITH SETTLE PRINTING & BOOKBINDING LTD
Gateway Drive, Yeadon, West Yorkshire LS19 7XY
Telephone: 0113 250 9201
Fax: 0113 250 9223
Email: sales@smithsettle.com
Web Site: www.smithsettle.com

Personnel:
Donald Waters (Managing Director)
Tracey Thorne (Finance Director)

Academic & Scholarly; Agriculture; Archaeology; Biography & Autobiography; History & Antiquarian; Illustrated & Fine Editions; Sports & Games; Travel & Topography

Imprints, Series & ISBNs:
978 1 84103

Associated Companies:
Westbury

Distributor for:
Ken Smith Publishing Ltd; Woodstock Books Ltd

Book Trade Association Membership:
Independent Publishers Guild

2692

COLIN SMYTHE LTD
38 Mill Lane, Gerrards Cross, Bucks SL9 8BA
Telephone: 01753 886000
Fax: 01753 886469
Email: sales@colinsmythe.co.uk
Web Site: www.colinsmythe.co.uk

Warehouse & Despatch only:
Print on Demand, 9 Culley Court, Bakewell Road, Orton Southgate, Peterborough PE2 6WA
Telephone: 01733 237867
Fax: 01733 234309

Personnel:
Colin Smythe (Managing Director)
Leslie Hayward (Production)

Academic & Scholarly; Bibliography & Library Science; Biography & Autobiography; Literature & Criticism; Theatre, Drama & Dance

New Titles: 3 (2009), 2 (2010)
No of Employees: 3
Annual Turnover: £2.06M

Imprints, Series & ISBNs:
978 0 86140, 978 0 900675, 978 0 901072
Dolmen Press: 978 0 85105
Van Duren: 978 0 905715

Distributor for:
Republic of Ireland: Tir Eolas
USA: ELT Press

Overseas Representation:
Republic of Ireland: Hibernian Book Services, Dublin, Republic of Ireland
USA & Canada: Dufour Editions Inc, Chester Springs, PA, USA
USA & Canada (recent academic titles): Oxford University Press Inc USA, New York, NY, USA

Book Trade Association Membership:
Publishers Association; Booksellers Association; Independent Publishers Guild

2693

SOCCER BOOKS LTD
72 St Peter's Avenue, Cleethorpes, Lincs DN35 8HU
Telephone: 01472 696226
Fax: 01472 698546
Email: info@soccer-books.co.uk
Web Site: www.soccer-books.co.uk

Personnel:
John Robinson (Managing Director)
Michael Robinson (Director)

Sports & Games; Transport

New Titles: 9 (2009), 21 (2010)
No of Employees: 4
Annual Turnover: £350,000

Imprints, Series & ISBNs:
Complete Results & Line-ups (Series): 978 1 86223
Football In (Series): 978 1 86223
Supporters' Guide (Series): 978 1 86223

2694

SOCIAL AFFAIRS UNIT
10/11 Morley House, 314–322 Regent Street, London W1B 5SA
Telephone: 020 7637 4356
Fax: 020 7436 8530
Email: mosbacher@socialaffairsunit.org.uk
Web Site: www.socialaffairsunit.org.uk

Personnel:
Michael Mosbacher (Director)

Academic & Scholarly; Crime; Economics; Educational & Textbooks; Environment & Development Studies; Industry, Business & Management; Medical (incl. Self Help & Alternative Medicine); Politics & World Affairs; Reference Books, Directories & Dictionaries; Sociology & Anthropology

Imprints, Series & ISBNs:
978 0 907631, 978 1 904863

2695

THE SOCIETY FOR PROMOTING CHRISTIAN KNOWLEDGE (SPCK)
36 Causton Street, London SW1P 4ST
Telephone: 020 7592 3900
Fax: 020 7592 3939
Email: publishing@spck.org.uk
Web Site: www.spckpublishing.co.uk

Warehouse & Distribution:
Marston Book Services, Unit 160, Milton Park, Abingdon, Oxon OX14 4SD
Telephone: 01235 465500
Fax: 01235 465555

Personnel:
Simon Kingston (Chief Executive Officer)
Joanna Moriarty (Publishing Director)
Alan Mordue (Sales Director)
Barry Finch (Production Director)
Alison Barr (Editor)
Fiona Marshall (Editor)
Ruth McCurry (Editor)
Alexandra McDonald (Rights Manager)
Cynthia Hamilton (Senior Marketing & Publicity Manager)

Academic & Scholarly; Illustrated & Fine Editions; Medical (incl. Self Help & Alternative Medicine); Psychology & Psychiatry; Religion & Theology

New Titles: 125 (2009), 125 (2010)
No of Employees: 29

Imprints, Series & ISBNs:
Azure Books: 978 1 902694
Lynx Communication: 978 0 7459
Sheldon Press: 978 0 85969, 978 1 84709
SPCK: 978 0 281
Triangle Books: 978 0 281

Overseas Representation:
Australia & New Zealand (SPCK, Triangle, Azure): Willow Connection Pty Ltd, Brookvale, NSW, Australia
USA & Canada (SPCK, Triangle, Azure): Lightning Source UK Ltd, Milton Keynes, UK

Book Trade Association Membership:
Publishers Association

2696

SOCIETY OF ANTIQUARIES OF SCOTLAND
NMS, Chambers Street, Edinburgh EH1 1JF
Telephone: 0131 247 4145
Fax: 0131 247 4163
Email: publications@socantscot.org

Web Site: www.socantscot.org

Personnel:
Dr Simon Gilmour (Director)
Erin Osborne-Martin (Managing Editor Sales & Publicity)

Academic & Scholarly; Archaeology; History & Antiquarian

Imprints, Series & ISBNs:
978 0 903903

2697

SOCIETY OF GENEALOGISTS ENTERPRISES LTD
14 Charterhouse Buildings, London EC1M 7BA
Telephone: 020 7251 8799
Fax: 020 7250 1800
Email: sales@sog.org.uk
Web Site: www.sog.org.uk/

Personnel:
June Perrin (Chief Executive)
Anthony Mortimer (Retail Manager)

History & Antiquarian

Imprints, Series & ISBNs:
978 1 903462

Parent Company:
Society of Genealogists

Book Trade Association Membership:
Booksellers Association

2698

THE SOCIETY OF METAPHYSICIANS LTD
Archers' Court, Stonestile Lane, The Ridge, Hastings, East Sussex TN35 4PG
Telephone: 01424 751577
Fax: 01424 751577
Email: newmeta@btinternet.com
Web Site: www.metaphysicians.org.uk

Personnel:
Dr J. J. Williamson (Managing Director)
Ms C. Yuen (Secretary)
D. Cumberland (Scientific & Literary Research)
Miss D. Harris (Paranormal Research)
Mervin Gould (Tutor)
David Servera-Williamon (Web)

Academic & Scholarly; Educational & Textbooks; Electronic (Educational); Environment & Development Studies; Magic & the Occult; Medical (incl. Self Help & Alternative Medicine); Philosophy; Scientific & Technical

Imprints, Series & ISBNs:
978 0 900680, 978 1 85228, 978 1 85810

Associated Companies:
Metaphysical Research Group
Argentina: Sociedad de Metafisica Inglesa
Belgium: Society of Metaphysicians
Italy: Istituto Italiano di Ricerche Metafisiche
Nigeria: Society of Metaphysicians (Nigeria) Ltd

Distributor for:
USA: Ars Obscura; Health Research

Overseas Representation:
Australia: Magic Circle Bookshop, Perth, Australia
Belgium: Ignoramus, As, Belgium; L' Univers Particulier, Brussels, Belgium
Netherlands: Boekhandel Synthese, 's Gravenhage, Netherlands
New Zealand: Bennet's Bookshop, Palmerston North, New Zealand
Spain: Eyras Editorial, Madrid, Spain
Tenerife: Soluciones, Spain
USA: H.R., Pomeroy, WA, USA

2699

SOLIDUS
Hope Springs, Far End, Sheepscombe,
Stroud, Glos GL6 7RL
Telephone: 01452 758940
Email: info@soliduspress.com
Web Site: www.soliduspress.com

Personnel:
Helen Miles *(Proprietor)*

Children's Books; Fiction

New Titles: 10 (2009) , 8 (2010)
No of Employees: 1

Imprints, Series & ISBNs:
Back to Front: 978 1 904529
Solidus: 978 1 904529

2700

SOUTHGATE PUBLISHERS
The Square, Sandford, Crediton, Devon
EX17 4LW
Telephone: 01363 776888
Fax: 01363 776889
Email: info@southgatepublishers.co.uk
Web Site: www.southgatepublishers.co.uk

Personnel:
Drummond Johnstone *(Managing Director)*
Marlene Buckland *(Production Manager)*

*Educational & Textbooks; Environment &
Development Studies; Vocational Training &
Careers*

New Titles: 11 (2009) , 10 (2010)
No of Employees: 3

Imprints, Series & ISBNs:
978 1 85741

Associated Companies:
Mosaic Educational Publications

Distributor for:
Campaign for Learning; Learning Through
Landscapes Trust

Book Trade Association Membership:
Independent Publishers Guild

2701

SOUVENIR PRESS LTD
43 Great Russell Street, London WC1B 3PD
Telephone: 020 7580 9307/8 & 7637
5711/2/3
Fax: 020 7580 5064
Email: souvenirpress@ukonline.co.uk

Distributors & Warehouse:
Bookpoint Ltd, 130 Milton Trading Estate,
Abingdon, Oxon OX14 4SB
Telephone: 01235 400400
Fax: 01235 400413

Personnel:
Ernest Hecht *(Managing Director &
Chairman)*

*Academic & Scholarly; Animal Care &
Breeding; Antiques & Collecting;
Archaeology; Biography & Autobiography;
Crafts & Hobbies; Gardening; Gender
Studies; Health & Beauty; Humour;
Industry, Business & Management;
Literature & Criticism; Magic & the Occult;
Medical (incl. Self Help & Alternative
Medicine); Military & War; Music; Natural
History; Philosophy; Psychology &
Psychiatry; Religion & Theology; Sociology
& Anthropology; Sports & Games; Theatre,
Drama & Dance; Travel & Topography;
Veterinary Science*

Imprints, Series & ISBNs:
Condor Books: 978 0 285
Human Horizons: 978 0 285

Souvenir Press (Educational & Academic)
Ltd: 978 0 285
Souvenir Press Ltd: 978 0 285

Associated Companies:
Pictorial Presentations Ltd; Pop Universal
Ltd; Souvenir Press (Educational &
Academic) Ltd

Overseas Representation:
Australia: Tower Books Pty Ltd, Brookvale,
NSW, Australia
*Austria, Benelux, France, Germany,
Switzerland, Greece & Italy:* Ted
Dougherty, London, UK
India: Rupa, New Delhi, India
Middle East: Peter Ward Book Exports,
London, UK
New Zealand: Addenda, Auckland, New
Zealand
Scandinavia: John Edgeler, London, UK
South Africa: Trinity Books CC, Randburg,
South Africa

2702

**SPARTAN PRESS MUSIC
PUBLISHERS LTD**
Strathmashie House, Laggan,
Inverness-shire PH20 1BU
Telephone: 01528 544770
Fax: 01528 544771
Email: sales@spartanpress.co.uk
Web Site: www.spartanpress.co.uk

Personnel:
Mark Goddard *(Managing Director)*
Pat Goddard *(Director)*
Sandra Grant *(Sales Manager)*
Ian Stevenson *(IT Manager)*

Music

New Titles: 12 (2009) , 12 (2010)

Imprints, Series & ISBNs:
ISMN: 57 999

Distributor for:
Netherlands: European Music Centre
UK: Camden Music; CelloLid; Colne
Edition; G. S. Music; Hunt Edition;
Múzicas Editions; Nova Music; Pan
Educational Music; Queen's Temple
Publications; Sunshine Music Co; Useful
Music; Waveney Music Publishing Ltd;
Yorke Edition

Overseas Representation:
Netherlands: European Music Centre,
Huizen, Netherlands
USA & Canada: Theodore Presser Co, King
of Prussia, PA, USA

2703

**SPECIAL INTEREST MODEL BOOKS
LTD**
PO Box 327, Poole, Dorset BH15 2RG
Telephone: 01202 649930
Fax: 01202 649950
Email: chrlloyd@globalnet.co.uk
Web Site:
www.specialinterestmodelbooks.co.uk

Personnel:
Chris Lloyd *(Managing Director)*

*Aviation; Cookery, Wines & Spirits; Crafts &
Hobbies; Engineering; Nautical; Transport*

New Titles: 4 (2009) , 4 (2010)

Imprints, Series & ISBNs:
Amateur Winemaker Books: 978 0 900841
formerly Argus Books: 978 1 85486
formerly MAP (Model & Allied Publications):
978 1 85486
formerly Nexus Special Interest Books: 978 1
85486
Workshop Practice Series: 978 0 85242

Overseas Representation:
Australia: Capricorn Link (Australia) Pty Ltd,
Windsor, NSW, Australia
Eastern Europe, East & West Africa:
Anthony Moggach, InterMedia
Americana (IMA) Ltd, London, UK
New Zealand: South Pacific Books (Imports)
Ltd, Auckland, New Zealand
*Scandinavia (including Denmark, Sweden,
Norway, Finland & Iceland) &
Netherlands:* Angell Eurosales, Berwick-
on-Tweed, UK
South Africa: Everybody's Books, Kwa Zulu
Natal, South Africa
South & Central America & Caribbean:
David Williams, InterMedia Americana
(IMA) Ltd, London, UK
*South East Asia (including Singapore,
Malaysia, Brunei, Indonesia, Hong Kong,
Taiwan, China, Philippines, Thailand &
Japan):* Ashton International Marketing
Services, Sevenoaks, Kent, UK
*Southern Europe (including Spain, Portugal,
Italy, Malta & Greece):* Joe Portelli,
Bookport Associates, Corsico (MI), Italy
*Western Europe (including France, Belgium,
Germany, Switzerland & Austria):*
Anselm Robinson, European Marketing
Services, London, UK

2704

SPEECHMARK PUBLISHING LTD
70 Alston Drive, Bradwell Abbey,
Milton Keynes MK13 9HG
Telephone: 0845 034 4610
Fax: 0845 034 4649
Email: info@speechmark.net
Web Site: www.speechmark.net

Customer Service:
(as above)
Telephone: 0800 243755 & 0845 034
4610
Fax: 0845 034 4649
Email: sales@speechmark.net
Web Site: www.speechmark.net

Personnel:
Liz Lane *(Managing Director)*
Su Wheeler *(Marketing Manager)*
Tanya Dean *(Publishing)*

*Children's Books; Educational & Textbooks;
English as a Foreign Language; Health &
Beauty; Languages & Linguistics; Medical
(incl. Self Help & Alternative Medicine);
Psychology & Psychiatry*

Imprints, Series & ISBNs:
978 0 86388
ColorCards
Helping Children with Feelings
Speechmark Editions

Parent Company:
UK: Electric Word Plc

2705

SPOKESMAN
Russell House, Bulwell Lane, Nottingham
NG6 0BT
Telephone: 0115 978 4504 & 970 8318
Fax: 0115 942 0433
Email: elfeuro@compuserve.com
Web Site: www.spokesmanbooks.com

Personnel:
Ken Fleet *(General Manager)*
Tony Simpson *(Publisher)*
Ken Coates *(Editor)*

*Economics; Fiction; History & Antiquarian;
Military & War; Philosophy; Poetry; Politics
& World Affairs; Sociology &
Anthropology; Theatre, Drama & Dance*

New Titles: 14 (2009) , 12 (2010)
No of Employees: 4

Imprints, Series & ISBNs:
Socialist Renewal: 978 0 85124
The Spokesman: 978 0 85124

Associated Companies:
Bertrand Russell Peace Foundation Ltd

2706

SPORTSBOOKS LTD
1 Evelyn Court, Malvern Road, Cheltenham
GL50 2JR
Telephone: 01242 256755
Fax: 01242 254694
Email: randall@sportsbooks.ltd.uk
Web Site: www.sportsbooks.ltd.uk

Distribution:
Turnaround Publisher Services Ltd, Unit 3,
Olympia Industrial Estate, Coburg Road,
London N22 6TZ
Telephone: 020 8829 3000
Fax: 020 8881 5088
Email: orders@turnaround-uk.com
Web Site: www.turnaround-psl.com

Personnel:
Randall Northam *(Chairman)*
Veronica Northam *(Director)*

*Fiction; History & Antiquarian; Sports &
Games*

New Titles: 12 (2009) , 12 (2010)
No of Employees: 2

Imprints, Series & ISBNs:
BMM: 978 0 9541544, 978 1 899807
Sportsbooks: 978 0 9541544, 978 1
899807

Overseas Representation:
Australia & New Zealand: Landmark Press,
Drovin, Vic, Australia
South Africa: Zytek Publishing (Pty) Ltd,
Bedfordview, South Africa

Book Trade Association Membership:
Publishers Association; Independent
Publishers Guild

2707

SPRINGER LONDON
Ashbourne House, The Guildway,
Old Portsmouth Road, Guildford GU3 1LP
Telephone: 01483 734646
Fax: 01483 734411
Web Site: www.springer.com

Personnel:
Beverley Ford *(General Manager)*
Gabrielle Bunning *(Finance Manager)*

*Academic & Scholarly; Chemistry;
Computer Science; Engineering;
Mathematics & Statistics; Medical (incl. Self
Help & Alternative Medicine)*

Book Trade Association Membership:
Publishers Association

2708

STACEY INTERNATIONAL
128 Kensington Church Street, London
W8 4BH
Telephone: 020 7221 7166
Fax: 020 7792 9288
Email: info@stacey-international.co.uk
Web Site: www.stacey-international.co.uk

Distribution:
Central Books, 99 Wallis Road,
Hackney Wick, London E9 5LN
Telephone: 0845 458 9911
Fax: 0845 458 9912
Email: orders@centralbooks.com
Web Site: www.centralbooks.com

Personnel:
T. C. G. Stacey *(Chairman)*

Max Scott (Director)
Christopher Ind (Editor)
Charlie Powell (Editor)
David Birkett (Sales & Marketing)

Academic & Scholarly; Archaeology; Architecture & Design; Biography & Autobiography; Children's Books; Cookery, Wines & Spirits; Economics; Educational & Textbooks; Fine Art & Art History; Gardening; Geography & Geology; Guide Books; History & Antiquarian; Illustrated & Fine Editions; Languages & Linguistics; Magic & the Occult; Military & War; Natural History; Photography; Poetry; Politics & World Affairs; Reference Books, Directories & Dictionaries; Religion & Theology; Scientific & Technical; Travel & Topography

Parent Company:
Stacey Arts Ltd

Associated Companies:
Capuchin Classics; Gorilla Guides; Rubicon Press

Overseas Representation:
Asia: PIM, London, UK
Australia: Peribo Pty Ltd, Mount Kuring-Gai, NSW, Australia
Europe: Durnell Marketing Ltd, Tunbridge Wells, UK
South Africa: Stephan Philips, Cape Town, South Africa
South America & Caribbean: Intermedia Americana, London, UK
USA: The David Brown Book Co, Oakville, CT, USA; Interlink Publishing Group Inc, Northampton, MA, USA

Book Trade Association Membership:
Independent Publishers Guild

2709

STAINER & BELL LTD
PO Box 110, 23 Gruneisen Road, London N3 1DZ
Telephone: 020 8343 3303
Fax: 020 8343 3024
Email: post@stainer.co.uk
Web Site: www.stainer.co.uk

Personnel:
Keith Wakefield (Joint Managing Director, Marketing, Permissions, Accounts & Distribution)
Carol Wakefield (Joint Managing Director)
Antony Kearns (Deputy Managing Director)
Nicholas Williams (Publishing Director)
Amanda Aknai (Production Director)

Academic & Scholarly; Biography & Autobiography; History & Antiquarian; Music; Reference Books, Directories & Dictionaries; Religion & Theology; Theatre, Drama & Dance

New Titles: 36 (2009) , 30 (2010)
No of Employees: 10
Annual Turnover: £793,000

Imprints, Series & ISBNs:
Augener: 978 0 85249
Early English Church Music: 978 0 85249
Galliard: 978 0 85249
Music for London Entertainment: 978 0 85249
Musica Britannica: 978 0 85249
Purcell Society Edition: 978 0 85249
Stainer & Bell: 978 0 85249
Weekes: 978 0 85249
Joseph Williams: 978 0 85249

Distributor for:
USA: ECS Publishing Co (Rental Library only)

Overseas Representation:
USA (hymn copyrights & selected titles): Hope Publishing, Carol Stream, IL, USA
USA (Rental Library): ECS Publishing Co, Boston, MA, USA

Book Trade Association Membership:
The Music Publishers Association Ltd

2710

RUDOLF STEINER PRESS
Hillside House, The Square, Forest Row, East Sussex RH18 5ES
Telephone: 01342 824433
Fax: 01342 826437
Email: office@rudolfsteinerpress.com
Web Site: www.rudolfsteinerpress.com

Trade Enquiries & Orders:
BookSource, 50 Cambuslang Road, Glasgow G32 8NB
Telephone: 0845 370 0063
Fax: 0845 370 0064
Email: orders@booksource.net
Web Site: www.booksource.net

Personnel:
Sevak Gulbekian (Chief Editor)

Biography & Autobiography; Educational & Textbooks; Fine Art & Art History; Magic & the Occult; Medical (incl. Self Help & Alternative Medicine); Music; Philosophy; Politics & World Affairs; Religion & Theology; Sociology & Anthropology; Theatre, Drama & Dance

New Titles: 20 (2009) , 20 (2010)
No of Employees: 2
Annual Turnover: £175,000

Imprints, Series & ISBNs:
Anthroposophic Press: 978 0 88010
Mercury Arts Publications: 978 0 85440, 978 1 85584
New Knowledge Books: 978 0 85440, 978 1 85584
Sophia Books: 978 0 85440, 978 1 85584
Steiner Books: 978 0 88010, 978 0 09
Rudolf Steiner Press: 978 0 85440, 978 1 85584

Distributor for:
Mercury Arts Publications; New Knowledge Books
Australia: Completion Press
USA: Steinerbooks

Overseas Representation:
Australia: Rudolf Steiner Book Centre, Sydney, NSW, Australia
Canada: Tri-fold Books, Guelph, Ont, Canada
New Zealand: Ceres Books, Ellerslie, New Zealand
South Africa: Rudolf Steiner Publications, Bryanston, South Africa
USA: Steiner Books Inc, Herndon, VA, USA

Book Trade Association Membership:
Independent Publishers Guild

2711

STENLAKE PUBLISHING LTD
54–58 Mill Square, Catrine, Ayrshire KA5 6RD
Telephone: 01290 551122
Fax: 01290 551122
Email: enquiries@stenlake.co.uk
Web Site: www.stenlake.co.uk

Personnel:
David Pettigrew (Editorial)
Richard Stenlake (Managing Director)
Alex F. Young (Sales)

Aviation; Crafts & Hobbies; History & Antiquarian; Literature & Criticism; Nautical; Poetry; Transport

Imprints, Series & ISBNs:
Alloway Publishing: 978 0 907526
Stenlake Publishing: 978 1 84033, 978 1 872074

2712

STOBART DAVIES LTD
Stobart House, Pontyclerc, Penybanc Road, Ammanford, Carmarthenshire SA18 3HP
Telephone: 01269 593100
Fax: 01269 596116
Email: sales@stobartdavies.com
Web Site: www.stobartdavies.com

Personnel:
Jane Evans (Director)
Nigel Evans (Director)

Archaeology; Cookery, Wines & Spirits; Crafts & Hobbies; Do-It-Yourself; Guide Books; Natural History; Scientific & Technical; Travel & Topography

New Titles: 9 (2009) , 29 (2010)
No of Employees: 5
Annual Turnover: £285,000

Imprints, Series & ISBNs:
Sigma Leisure / Sigma Press: 978 1 85058
Stobart Davies Ltd: 978 0 85442

Parent Company:
Stobart Davis (2002) Ltd

Overseas Representation:
Australia & New Zealand: Footprint Books Pty Ltd, Warriewood, NSW, Australia
Europe & Far East: Saltway Publishing Ltd, Cirencester, UK
South Africa: Peter Hyde Associates (Pty) Ltd, Cape Town, South Africa
USA: David Brown Book Co, Oakville, CT, USA

Book Trade Association Membership:
Booksellers Association; Independent Publishers Guild

2713

STOTT'S CORRESPONDENCE COLLEGE
PO Box 35488, St John's Wood, London NW8 6WD
Telephone: 020 7586 4499
Email: microworld@ndirect.co.uk
Web Site: www.microworld.uk.com

Personnel:
S. C. Albert (Director)

Academic & Scholarly; Crafts & Hobbies; Fashion & Costume; Health & Beauty

Distributor for:
Australia: Stott's Correspondence College

2714

STRI (SPORTS TURF RESEARCH INSTITUTE)
St Ives Estate, Bingley, West Yorks BD16 1AU
Telephone: 01274 565131
Fax: 01274 561891
Email: info@stri.co.uk
Web Site: www.stri.co.uk

Personnel:
Dr Gordon McKillop (Chief Executive)
Mark Godfrey (Financial Director)
Richard Hayden (Director of Operations)
Carolyn Beadsmoore (Head of Sales & Marketing)

Educational & Textbooks; Environment & Development Studies; Reference Books, Directories & Dictionaries; Scientific & Technical; Sports & Games

Imprints, Series & ISBNs:
978 0 9503647, 978 1 873431

2715

STRONG OAK PRESS
PO Box 728, Crawley, West Sussex RH10 7WD
Telephone: 01293 552727
Email: strongoakpress@hotmail.com

Personnel:
Steven Apps (Managing Director)

Biography & Autobiography; Fine Art & Art History; History & Antiquarian; Military & War; Travel & Topography

Imprints, Series & ISBNs:
Spa Books: 978 0 907590
The Strong Oak Press: 978 1 871048

Distributor for:
South Africa: William Waterman Publications
UK: Spa Books Ltd; The Strong Oak Press Ltd

2716

SUBBUTEO NATURAL HISTORY BOOKS
[a division of C J Wild Bird Foods Ltd]
The Rea, Upton Magna, Shrewsbury SY4 4UR
Telephone: 01743 708017
Fax: 01743 709504
Email: joy.enston@birdfood.co.uk
Web Site: www.wildlifebooks.com

Personnel:
Tony Cordery (Senior Executive)
Paul Humber (Finance)
Claire Smith (Marketing Manager)

Natural History

New Titles: 1 (2009) , 2 (2010)
No of Employees: 80

Parent Company:
UK: C J Wild Bird Foods Ltd

Distributor for:
South Africa: Avian Demography Unit
South America: Rainforest Expeditions SAC Publications; Thomas Velqui
Spain: Arts Grafiques Delmau; Nayade Editorial
UK: Arlequin Press; Dizzy Daisy Books; Hobby Publications; Osmia Publications; Wings Plants & Paws
USA: American Birding Association

Book Trade Association Membership:
Booksellers Association

2717

SUMMER PALACE PRESS
31 Stranmillis Park, Belfast BT9 5AU
Telephone: 028 9066 7759
Email: cladnageeragh@eircom.net

Also at:
Cladnageeragh, Kilbeg, Kilcar, Co Donegal, Republic of Ireland
Telephone: +353 (0)749 738448
Email: cladnageeragh@eircom.net

Personnel:
Joan Newmann (Co-Director)
Kate Newmann (Co-Director)

Biography & Autobiography; Poetry

New Titles: 6 (2009) , 4 (2010)
No of Employees: 2

Imprints, Series & ISBNs:
978 0 9535912, 978 0 9544752, 978 0 9552122, 978 0 9560995

Book Trade Association Membership:
Publishing Ireland (Foilsiú Éireann)

2718

SUMMERSDALE PUBLISHERS LTD
46 West Street, Chichester, West Sussex
PO19 1RP
Telephone: 01243 771107
Fax: 01243 786300
Email: enquiries@summersdale.com
Web Site: www.summersdale.com

Warehouse, Trade Enquiries & Orders:
Littlehampton Book Services,
Faraday Close, Durrington, Worthing,
West Sussex BN13 3RB
Telephone: 01903 828500
Fax: 01903 828625
Email: orders@lbsltd.co.uk
Web Site: www.lbsltd.co.uk

Personnel:
Alastair Williams *(Managing Director)*
Nicky Douglas *(Sales & Marketing Director)*
Jennifer Barclay *(Editorial & Rights Director)*

*Audio Books; Biography & Autobiography;
Cookery, Wines & Spirits; Crafts & Hobbies;
Crime; Electronic (Educational); Electronic
(Entertainment); Electronic (Professional &
Academic); Guide Books; History &
Antiquarian; Humour; Sports & Games;
Travel & Topography*

New Titles: 70 (2009) , 75 (2010)
No of Employees: 12
Annual Turnover: £2M

Imprints, Series & ISBNs:
978 1 84024, 978 1 84953, 978 1 873475

Distributor for:
Protection Publications

Overseas Representation:
Australia & New Zealand: Peribo Pty Ltd,
Mount Kuring-Gai, NSW, Australia
India: Surit Mitra, New Delhi, India
Northern Europe: Michael Geoghegan,
London, UK
Scandinavia: McNeish Publishing
International, East Sussex, UK
*South East & North East Asia, Middle East &
Africa:* Chris Ashdown, Publishers
International Marketing, Ferndown,
Dorset, UK
Southern Africa: Zytek Publishing (Pty) Ltd,
Bedfordview, South Africa
Southern Europe: Bookport Associates,
Milan, Italy

Book Trade Association Membership:
Independent Publishers Guild

2719

**SUPPORTIVE LEARNING
PUBLICATIONS (SLP)**
23 West View, Chirk, Wrexham LL14 5HL
Telephone: 01691 774778
Fax: 01691 774849
Web Site: www.slpeducation.co.uk

Personnel:
Phil Roberts *(Marketing Director)*

*Educational & Textbooks; English as a
Foreign Language; Geography & Geology;
History & Antiquarian; Humour;
Mathematics & Statistics; Sports & Games;
Theatre, Drama & Dance*

No of Employees: 3
Annual Turnover: £50,000

Imprints, Series & ISBNs:
978 1 871585

Overseas Representation:
All other areas: Blackwell Publishing Ltd,
Oxford, UK
USA, Canada & Puerto Rico: Blackwell

Publishing Inc, Malden, MA, USA;
Blackwell Publishing Professional, Ames,
IA, USA

Book Trade Association Membership:
Educational Publishers Council

2720

SUSSEX ACADEMIC PRESS
PO Box 139, Eastbourne, East Sussex
BN24 9BP
Telephone: 01323 479220
Fax: 01323 478185
Email: edit@sussex-academic.co.uk
Web Site: www.sussex-academic.co.uk

Warehouse, Trade Enquiries & Orders:
Gazelle Book Services, White Cross Mills,
Hightown, Lancaster LA1 4XS
Telephone: 01524 68765
Fax: 01524 63232

Personnel:
Anthony Grahame *(Editorial Director)*
Anita Grahame *(Finance Director)*

*Academic & Scholarly; Archaeology;
Bibliography & Library Science; Biography &
Autobiography; Economics; Educational &
Textbooks; Environment & Development
Studies; Fine Art & Art History; Gender
Studies; Geography & Geology; History &
Antiquarian; Industry, Business &
Management; Law; Literature & Criticism;
Military & War; Music; Philosophy; Politics &
World Affairs; Psychology & Psychiatry;
Religion & Theology; Sociology &
Anthropology; Sports & Games; Theatre,
Drama & Dance*

New Titles: 50 (2010)
No of Employees: 4
Annual Turnover: £240,000

Imprints, Series & ISBNs:
The Alpha Press: 978 1 898595
Sussex Academic: 978 1 84519, 978 1
898723, 978 1 902210, 978 1 903900

Parent Company:
UK: The Alpha Press

Associated Companies:
Canada: Sussex Academic Press (Canada)

Overseas Representation:
Canada: University of Toronto Distribution,
Canada
*Rest of the World (excluding USA &
Canada):* Gazelle Book Services Ltd,
Lancaster, UK
USA: International Specialized Book
Services Inc, Portland, OR, USA

2721

SUSSEX PUBLICATIONS
World Microfilms, PO Box 35488,
St John's Wood, London NW8 6WD
Telephone: 020 7586 4499
Email: microworld@ndirect.co.uk
Web Site: www.microworld.uk.com

Personnel:
S. C. Albert *(Director)*

*Academic & Scholarly; Audio Books;
Cinema, Video, TV & Radio; Fine Art & Art
History; History & Antiquarian; Literature &
Criticism; Music*

Imprints, Series & ISBNs:
978 0 905272, 978 1 86013

2722

THE SWEDENBORG SOCIETY
20–21 Bloomsbury Way, London
WC1A 2TH
Telephone: 020 7405 7986
Fax: 020 7831 5848

Email: richard@swedenborg.org.uk
Web Site: www.swedenborg.org.uk

Personnel:
Richard Lines *(Company Secretary)*
Stephen McNeilly *(Publications Manager)*
Eoin Mcmahon *(Property Manager)*
James Wilson *(Assistant Editor & Librarian)*
Nora Foster *(Sales & Marketing
Representative)*

*Academic & Scholarly; Literature &
Criticism; Religion & Theology*

Imprints, Series & ISBNs:
978 0 85448

2723

**SYMPOSIUM PUBLICATIONS
LITERARY & ART**
37 Chepstow Road, London W2 5BP
Telephone: 020 7792 3762
Email: sympo@sympo.fsworld.co.uk
Web Site: www.sympo.co.uk

Personnel:
Mrs L. A. Melech *(Director)*
J. Wheeler-Melech *(Editorial Consultant)*

*Academic & Scholarly; Children's Books;
Educational & Textbooks; English as a
Foreign Language; Fine Art & Art History;
Literature & Criticism; Poetry*

New Titles: 2 (2010)

Imprints, Series & ISBNs:
Sympo Sunrise (Children's Stories): 978 0
9547757
Symposium Brush-Up Shakespeare Series:
978 0 9524749
Symposium Gem Art Series: 978 0 9524749

Overseas Representation:
Spain: Débora Vázquez Padín, Pontevedra,
Spain

2724

TA HA PUBLISHERS LTD
Unit 4, The Windsor Centre,
Windsor Grove, West Norwood, London
SE27 9NT
Telephone: 020 8670 1888
Fax: 020 8670 1998
Email: sales@taha.co.uk
Web Site: www.taha.co.uk

Personnel:
A. Siddiqui *(Director)*
Dr Abia A. Siddiqui *(Editor & Director)*
Dr J. U. N. Rafai *(Rights)*

*Children's Books; Languages & Linguistics;
Religion & Theology*

Imprints, Series & ISBNs:
978 0 907461, 978 1 84200, 978 1 897940

Associated Companies:
Diwan Press Ltd

Overseas Representation:
USA: Islamic Bookstore.com, Baltimore,
MD, USA

2725

TABB HOUSE
7 Church Street, Padstow, Cornwall
PL28 8BG
Telephone: 01841 532316
Fax: 01841 532316
Email: tabbhousebooks@talktalk.net
Web Site: tabbhousebooks.com

**Distributor (for West Country titles in
Cornwall, Devon & Somerset):**
Tor Mark Press, PO Box 4, Redruth,
Cornwall TR16 5YX
Telephone: 01209 822101

Fax: 01209 822035
Email: sales@tormarkpress.prestel.co.uk
Web Site: www.willowbooks.co.uk

**Wholesaler (for all titles for
Waterstone's):**
Gardners Books Ltd, 1 Whittle Drive,
Willingdon Drove, Eastbourne, Sussex
BN23 6QH
Telephone: 01323 521555
Fax: 01323 521666
Email: sales@gardners.com
Web Site: www.gardners.com

Personnel:
Caroline White *(Editorial Director)*
K. Bickmore *(Promotion & Marketing
Assistant)*

*Biography & Autobiography; Children's
Books; Fiction; Literature & Criticism;
Medical (incl. Self Help & Alternative
Medicine); Poetry*

New Titles: 2 (2010)

Imprints, Series & ISBNs:
978 0 907018, 978 1 873951
Tabb House Originals

Book Trade Association Membership:
Independent Publishers Guild

2726

TAIGH NA TEUD MUSIC PUBLISHERS
13 Upper Breakish, Isle of Skye IV42 8PY
Telephone: 01471 822528
Fax: 01471 822811
Email: sales@scotlandsmusic.com
Web Site: www.scotlandsmusic.com &
www.playscottishmusic.com

Personnel:
Alasdair Martin *(Sales Manager)*
Christine Martin *(Music Editor)*

Languages & Linguistics; Music

Imprints, Series & ISBNs:
978 1 871931, 978 1 906804

Overseas Representation:
Australia: Celtic Southern Cross, Bracknell,
Tasmania, Australia
North America: Music Sales Corporation,
Chester, NY, USA

2727

TANGERINE DESIGNS LTD
1 Limpley Mill, Lower Stoke, Bath BA2 7EJ
Telephone: 01225 720001
Web Site: www.tangerinedesigns.co.uk

Personnel:
Christine Swift *(Managing Director)*
Trish Pugsley *(Co-edition Sales Agent)*
Rachel Pidcock *(Co-edition Sales Agent)*
Catherine Lyn Jones *(Rights Manager)*

Children's Books

Distributor for:
UK: Alligator Books; Pinwheel

Book Trade Association Membership:
Publishers Association

2728

TANGO BOOKS LTD
PO Box 32595, London W4 5YD
Telephone: 020 8996 9970
Fax: 020 8996 9977
Email: info@tangobooks.co.uk
Web Site: www.tangobooks.co.uk

Sales & Marketing:
Bounce!, 14 Greville Street, London
EC1N 8SB
Telephone: 020 7138 3650

Fax: 020 7138 3658
Email: sales@bouncemarketing.co.uk
Web Site: www.bouncemarketing.co.uk

Personnel:
Sheri Safran *(Director/Publisher)*
David Fielder *(Director/Publisher)*

*Children's Books; Educational & Textbooks;
Environment & Development Studies;
Natural History*

New Titles: 12 (2009) , 15 (2010)
No of Employees: 5
Annual Turnover: £1M

2729

TARQUIN PUBLICATIONS
99 Hatfield Road, St Albans, Herts AL1 4JL
Telephone: 0870 143 2568
Fax: 0845 456 6385
Email: sales@tarquinbooks.com
Web Site: www.tarquinbooks.com

Personnel:
Andrew Griffin *(Editorial)*
Peter Watson *(Sales & Promotion)*

*Atlases & Maps; Children's Books; Crafts &
Hobbies; Educational & Textbooks;
Mathematics & Statistics*

Imprints, Series & ISBNs:
978 0 906212, 978 1 899618

Parent Company:
Richard Griffin (1820) Ltd

Overseas Representation:
Australia: H. E. Wootton & Sons, Toorak,
Vic, Australia; W & G Education Pty Ltd,
Berwick, Vic, Australia
New Zealand: Eton Press (Auckland) Ltd,
Auckland, New Zealand; Mahobe
Resources (NZ), Newmarket, New
Zealand
Portugal: Editôra Replicação, Lisbon,
Portugal
Singapore: Nature Craft Pte Ltd, Singapore
USA: Parkwest Publications Inc, Jersey City,
NJ, USA

Book Trade Association Membership:
Independent Publishers Guild

2730

TATE PUBLISHING
[a division of Tate Enterprises Ltd]
Millbank, London SW1P 4RG
Telephone: 020 7887 8869/70/71
Fax: 020 7887 8878
Email: tgpl@tate.org.uk

Warehouse, Trade Enquiries & Orders:
Telephone: 020 7887 8869 (5 lines)
Fax: 020 7887 8878
Email: tgpl@tate.org.uk
Web Site: www.tate.org.uk

Personnel:
Laura Wright *(Chief Executive)*
James Attlee *(Sales & Marketing Director)*
Sarah Rogers *(Head of Finance)*
Roger Thorp *(Publishing Director)*
Emma Woodiwiss *(Production Manager)*

*Children's Books; Fine Art & Art History;
Photography*

New Titles: 35 (2009) , 35 (2010)
No of Employees: 20
Annual Turnover: £3M

Imprints, Series & ISBNs:
British Artists Series
Essential Artists Series: 978 0 905005, 978 0
946590, 978 1 85437
Modern Artists Series: 978 1 85437
Movements in Modern Art Series
St Ives Artists Series

Parent Company:
Tate Enterprises Ltd

Overseas Representation:
*Asia (including Hong Kong, Taiwan, China,
Korea & Philippines):* Asia Publishers
Services Ltd, Hong Kong
Australia: Thames & Hudson (Australia) Pty
Ltd, Fishermans Bend, Vic, Australia
*Austria, Belgium, Germany, Netherlands &
Switzerland:* Exhibitions International,
Leuven, Belgium
*Denmark, Finland, Iceland, Norway &
Sweden:* Elisabeth Harder-Kreimann,
Hamburg, Germany
Eastern Europe: Phil Tyers, Athens, Greece
*Far East (including Japan, Vietnam,
Singapore, Malaysia, Indonesia &
Thailand):* Andrew Hansen, London, UK
France: Interart SARL, Paris, France
Italy, Greece, Spain & Portugal: Penny
Padovani, London, UK
Mexico, Central America & Caribbean:
Chris Humphrys, Humphrys Roberts
Associates, London, UK
Middle East: Ray Potts, Villanton, France
North & South America & Canada: Harry N.
Abrams Inc, New York, NY, USA
Republic of Ireland & Northern Ireland:
Gabrielle Redmond, Dublin, Republic of
Ireland
South Africa: David Krut Publishing,
Johannesburg, South Africa
South America: David Williams, InterMedia
Americana (IMA) Ltd, London, UK

Book Trade Association Membership:
Booksellers Association

2731

I. B. TAURIS & CO LTD
6 Salem Road, London W2 4BU
Telephone: 020 7243 1225
Fax: 020 7243 1226
Email: mail@ibtauris.com
Web Site: www.ibtauris.com

Distribution:
Macmillan Distribution Ltd, Brunel Road,
Houndmills, Basingstoke, Hants RG21 6XS

Personnel:
Iradj Bagherzade *(Chairman & Publisher)*
Jonathan McDonnell *(Managing Director)*
Stuart Weir *(Production Director)*
Liz Stuckey *(Financial Manager)*
Paul Davighi *(Sales & Marketing Director)*
Rachel Maconachy *(Publicity Manager)*

*Academic & Scholarly; Archaeology;
Architecture & Design; Biography &
Autobiography; Cinema, Video, TV &
Radio; Fine Art & Art History; Gender
Studies; Geography & Geology; Guide
Books; History & Antiquarian; Military &
War; Politics & World Affairs; Reference
Books, Directories & Dictionaries; Religion &
Theology; Sociology & Anthropology*

New Titles: 190 (2009) , 220 (2010)

Imprints, Series & ISBNs:
International Library of African Studies: 978
1 84511, 978 1 85043, 978 1 86064
International Library of Historical Studies:
978 1 84511, 978 1 85043, 978 1 86064
International Library of Human Geography:
978 1 84511, 978 1 85043, 978 1 86064
International Library of Political Studies: 978
1 84511, 978 1 85043, 978 1 86064
Isma'ili Heritage Series: 978 1 84511, 978 1
85043, 978 1 86064
Library of International Relations: 978 1
84511, 978 1 85043, 978 1 86064
Library of Middle East History: 978 1 84511,
978 1 85043, 978 1 86064
Library of Modern Middle East Studies: 978
1 84511, 978 1 85043, 978 1 86064
Library of Ottoman Studies: 978 1 84511,
978 1 85043, 978 1 86064

Tauris Parke Paperbacks: 978 1 84511, 978
1 85043, 978 1 86064

Associated Companies:
British Academic Press; Tauris Academic
Studies; Tauris Parke Books

Distributor for:
Federal Trust; Libri Publications; The
Radcliffe Press; Philip Wilson Publishers
UAE: The Emirates Center for Strategic
Studies & Research

Overseas Representation:
*Africa (excluding South Africa &
Zimbabwe):* InterMedia Americana (IMA)
Ltd, London, UK
Australia: Palgrave Macmillan, South Yarra,
Vic, Australia
India: Viva Group, New Delhi, India
Iran: Behruz Neirami, Tehran, Iran
Japan: United Publishers Services Ltd,
Tokyo, Japan
Korea, China, Hong Kong & Taiwan: Taylor
& Francis Asia Pacific, Singapore
New Zealand: Macmillan Publishers New
Zealand Ltd, Auckland, New Zealand
Northern Europe: Andrew Durnell
Marketing Ltd, Tunbridge Wells, UK
South America & Caribbean: Palgrave
Macmillan, London, UK
USA & Canada: Palgrave Macmillan, New
York, NY, USA

Book Trade Association Membership:
Independent Publishers Guild

2732

TAYLOR & FRANCIS
2 & 4 Park Square, Milton Park, Abingdon,
Oxford OX14 4RN
Telephone: 020 7017 6000
Fax: 020 7017 6336
Email: jackie.benoist@tandf.co.uk
Web Site: www.taylorandfrancis.com

Warehouse, Trade Enquiries & Orders:
Bookpoint, 130 Milton Park, Abingdon,
Oxon OX14 4SB
Telephone: 01235 400400

Personnel:
Roger Horton *(Chief Executive)*
Jeremy North *(Managing Director – Books)*
Christoph Chesher *(Sales Director)*
Stuart Dawson *(Finance Director)*
Ian Bannerman *(Managing Director –
Journals)*
Mark Majurey *(Digital Development
Director – Books)*
David Green *(Publishing Director – Journals)*
Catriona Hauer *(Global Marketing &
Customer Services Director – Journals)*
Matt Howells *(Production Director –
Journals)*
Claire L'Infant *(Director: Humanities –
Books)*
Alan Jarvis *(Director: Social Sciences –
Books)*
Nigel Eyre *(Director: Production – Books)*
Jackie Harbor *(Global Marketing Director –
Books)*
Adele Parker *(Rights Manager – Books)*
Paulette Dooler *(Rights Manager – Journals)*

*Academic & Scholarly; Archaeology;
Architecture & Design; Biology & Zoology;
Chemistry; Economics; Educational &
Textbooks; Electronic (Professional &
Academic); Engineering; Environment &
Development Studies; Gay & Lesbian
Studies; Gender Studies; Geography &
Geology; History & Antiquarian; Industry,
Business & Management; Languages &
Linguistics; Law; Literature & Criticism;
Mathematics & Statistics; Medical (incl. Self
Help & Alternative Medicine); Military &
War; Music; Philosophy; Physics; Politics &
World Affairs; Psychology & Psychiatry;
Reference Books, Directories &
Dictionaries; Religion & Theology; Scientific*

*& Technical; Sociology & Anthropology;
Sports & Games; Theatre, Drama & Dance*

New Titles: 3100 (2009) , 3300 (2010)
No of Employees: 800

Imprints, Series & ISBNs:
CRC: 978 0 8493
Dekker: 978 0 8247
Lawrence Erlbaum Associates: 978 0 8058
Garland: 978 0 8153
Psychology Press: 978 0 415
Routledge: 978 0 415
Routledge-Cavendish: 978 0 415
Taylor & Francis: 978 0 415

Parent Company:
Informa Plc

Associated Companies:
India: Routledge India Office
Norway: Taylor & Francis AS
Singapore: Taylor & Francis Asia Pacific
Sweden: Taylor & Francis AB
USA: Garland Science; Taylor & Francis
Group LLC

Distributor for:
Guildford Press; Swedish Pharmaceutical
Press

Overseas Representation:
Australia: Palgrave Macmillan, South Yarra,
Vic, Australia
Austria, Switzerland & Germany: Gabriela
Mauch, Area Sales Manager, Central
Europe, Stuttgart, Germany
*Belgium, Netherlands, France &
Luxembourg:* Liza Walraven, Sales
Representative, Amsterdam, Netherlands
Botswana: Arthur Oageng, Book
Promotions/Horizon Books, Botswana
China: Taylor & Francis, Beijing, P. R. of
China
Eastern Europe: Marek Lewinson, Warsaw,
Poland
Greece: Ryan Cooper, Taylor & Francis
Group, Abingdon, UK
India: Taylor & Francis Books India Pvt Ltd,
New Delhi, India
Israel: Franklins International, Tel Aviv, Israel
Japan: Hans Van Ess, Sales & Marketing
Executive, Tokyo, Japan
Korea: Information & Culture Korea (ICK),
Seoul, Republic of Korea
Malaysia & Brunei: David Yeong, General
Manager, Petaling Jaya, Malaysia
Mexico, Central & South America:
Cranbury International LLC, Montpelier,
VT, USA
Middle East & North Africa: International
Publishing Services (IPS) Middle East Ltd,
Dubai, UAE
New Zealand: Victoria Johnson, Macmillan
Publishers New Zealand Ltd, Auckland,
New Zealand
Nigeria: Publisher Support Services Ltd,
Ikeja, Nigeria
North America: Taylor & Francis Group LLC,
Boca Raton, FL, USA
Pakistan: M. Anwer Iqbal, Book Bird
Publishers Representatives, Lahore,
Pakistan
Republic of Ireland: Brookside Publishing
Services, Dublin, Republic of Ireland
*Singapore, Hong Kong, Vietnam,
Philippines, Indonesia, Taiwan &
Thailand:* Taylor & Francis Asia Pacific,
Singapore
*South Africa, Namibia, Lesotho &
Swaziland:* Book Promotions Pty Ltd,
Diep River, South Africa
Spain, Portugal & Italy: Philip Veysey, Area
Sales Manager, Madrid, Spain
West Indies & Caribbean: Jasmina Basic,
Taylor & Francis Group, Abingdon, UK

Book Trade Association Membership:
International Group of Scientific, Medical &
Technical Publishers

2733 ▄▄▄

TEACHIT (UK) LTD
1 Widcombe Parade, Bath BA2 4JT
Telephone: 01225 788850
Email: membership@teachit.co.uk
Web Site: www.teachit.co.uk

*Educational & Textbooks; Electronic
(Professional & Academic)*

Book Trade Association Membership:
Publishers Association

2734 ▄▄▄

TELEGRAM
26 Westbourne Grove, London W2 5RH
Telephone: 020 7229 2911
Fax: 020 7229 7492
Email: lynn@telegrambooks.com
Web Site: www.telegrambooks.com

Distribution (UK):
Marston Book Services Ltd,
160 Milton Park, Abingdon, Oxon
OX14 4SD
Telephone: 01235 465500
Fax: 01235 465555
Web Site: www.marston.co.uk

Sales (UK):
Compass, The Barley Mow Centre,
10 Barley Mow Passage, Chiswick W4 4PH
Telephone: 020 8994 6477
Fax: 020 8400 6132
Web Site: www.compass-booksales.co.uk

Personnel:
André Gaspard *(Director)*
Shikha Sethi *(Editor / Production Manager)*
Lynn Gaspard *(Rights Manager)*
Ashley Biles *(Sales Manager)*
Kelly Pike *(Publicity Manager)*

Fiction

New Titles: 12 (2009) , 8 (2010)
No of Employees: 5

Imprints, Series & ISBNs:
978 1 84659

Parent Company:
Saqi Books

Overseas Representation:
Australia & New Zealand: Palgrave
Macmillan, South Yarra, Vic, Australia
Europe: Andrew Durnell, Andrew Durnell
Marketing Ltd, Tunbridge Wells, UK
India: Pradeep Kumar, Viva Marketing, New
Delhi, India
Italy: Agnese Incisa, Letteraria Agnese
Incisa, Turin, Italy
Middle East: Dar al Saqi SARL, Beirut,
Lebanon
Pakistan: Mohammad Eusoph, Mr Books,
Islamabad, Pakistan
Singapore: Nelson Koh, Horizon Books Pte
Ltd, Singapore
South Africa: Stephan Phillips (Pty) Ltd,
Cape Town, South Africa
Spain, Portugal & Germany: Anna Soler-
Pont, Pontas Literary & Film Agency,
Barcelona, Spain
USA & Canada: Consortium Publishers, St
Paul, MN, USA

Book Trade Association Membership:
Independent Publishers Guild

2735 ▄▄▄

TELOS PUBLISHING LTD
17 Pendre Avenue, Prestatyn, Denbighshire
LL19 9SH
Telephone: 07905 311733
Email: david@telos.co.uk
Web Site: www.telos.co.uk

Business/Accounts:
5a Church Road, Shortlands, Bromley, Kent
BR2 0HP
Telephone: 020 8466 1115
Email: stephen@telos.co.uk

Personnel:
David J. Howe *(Publisher)*
Stephen James Walker *(Publisher)*

Cinema, Video, TV & Radio; Crime; Fiction

New Titles: 1 (2009) , 10 (2010)

Imprints, Series & ISBNs:
978 1 84583, 978 1 903889

Overseas Representation:
Australia & New Zealand: Bookwise
International, Wingfield, SA, Australia
USA & Canada: Fitzhenry & Whiteside Ltd,
Markham, Ont, Canada

2736 ▄▄▄

TEMPLAR PUBLISHING
The Granary, North Street, Dorking, Surrey
RH4 1DN
Telephone: 01306 876361
Fax: 01306 889097
Web Site: www.templarco.co.uk

Sales & Marketing:
Bounce Sales & Marketing,
14 Greville Street, London EC1N 8SB

Distribution:
Grantham Book Services, Trent Road,
Grantham, Lincs NG31 7XG

Personnel:
Amanda Wood *(Managing Director)*
Ruth Huddleston *(Sales & Marketing
Director)*
Karen Ellison *(Production Director)*
Odile Louis-Sidney *(Foreign Rights Director)*

Children's Books; Fiction

New Titles: 86 (2009) , 98 (2010)
No of Employees: 48
Annual Turnover: £15M

Imprints, Series & ISBNs:
978 1 84011, 978 1 898784
Amazing Baby: 978 1 904513

Parent Company:
Bonnier Publishing Ltd

Book Trade Association Membership:
Booksellers Association; Independent
Publishers Guild

2737 ▄▄▄

TEMPLE LODGE PUBLISHING
Hillside House, The Square, Forest Row,
East Sussex RH18 5ES
Telephone: 01342 824000
Fax: 01342 826437
Email: office@templelodge.com
Web Site: www.templelodge.com

Distribution:
BookSource, 50 Cambuslang Road,
Glasgow G32 8NB
Telephone: 0141 643 3955
Fax: 0845 370 0068
Email: orders@booksource.net
Web Site: www.booksource.net

Personnel:
S. E. Gulbekian *(Chief Editor)*

*Health & Beauty; Magic & the Occult;
Medical (incl. Self Help & Alternative
Medicine); Philosophy; Politics & World
Affairs; Religion & Theology*

New Titles: 10 (2009) , 10 (2010)
No of Employees: 1

Annual Turnover: £65,000

Imprints, Series & ISBNs:
978 0 904693, 978 1 902636, 978 1
906999

Overseas Representation:
Australia: Rudolf Steiner Book Centre,
Sydney, NSW, Australia
Canada: Tri-fold Books, Guelph, Ont,
Canada
New Zealand: Steinerbooks, Auckland, New
Zealand
South Africa: Rudolf Steiner Publications,
Bryanston, South Africa
USA: Steiner Books Inc, Herndon, VA, USA

Book Trade Association Membership:
Independent Publishers Guild

2738 ▄▄▄

TENEUES PUBLISHING UK LTD
21 Marlowe Court, Lymer Avenue, London
SE19 1LP
Telephone: 0208 670 7522
Fax: 0208 670 7523
Email: bclark@teneues.co.uk
Web Site: www.teneues.com

Trade Enquiries & Orders:
Combined Book Services, Unit Y,
Paddock Wood Distribution Centre,
Tonbridge, Kent TN12 6UU
Telephone: 01892 835599
Fax: 01892 837272
Email: orders@combook.co.uk

Personnel:
Hendrik Teneues *(Chairman)*
Bridget Clark *(Director of Sales &
Marketing)*
Elaine Hyde *(Administrator)*

*Architecture & Design; Photography; Travel
& Topography*

Imprints, Series & ISBNs:
Stern Portfolios: 978 3 570
Teneues: 978 1 60160, 978 3 8238, 978 3
8327

2739 ▄▄▄

TFM PUBLISHING LTD
Castle Hill Barns, Harley, Shrewsbury,
Shropshire SY5 6LX
Telephone: 01952 510061
Fax: 01952 510192
Email: nikki@tfmpublishing.com
Web Site: www.tfmpublishing.com

Representation (UK):
Gazelle, Lancaster

Personnel:
Nikki Bramhill *(Director)*
Paul Lawrence *(Director)*

*Academic & Scholarly; Medical (incl. Self
Help & Alternative Medicine)*

New Titles: 7 (2009) , 8 (2010)
No of Employees: 2
Annual Turnover: £350,000

Imprints, Series & ISBNs:
978 1 903378

Overseas Representation:
Australia & New Zealand: Elsevier Australia,
Chatswood, NSW, Australia
Europe: Gazelle, Lancaster, UK
Hong Kong: MacBarron Book Co, Kowloon,
Hong Kong
India & Sri Lanka: Thieme Medical &
Scientific Publishers Pte Ltd, Noida, India
Japan: Igaku-Shoin Ltd, Tokyo, Japan;
Nankodo Co Ltd, Tokyo, Japan
Middle East & North Africa: International
Publishing Services, Dubai, UAE

South Africa: Academic Marketing Services
(Pty) Ltd, Johannesburg, South Africa
South East Asia: Elsevier (Singapore) Pte
Ltd, Singapore
Taiwan: Unifacmanu Trading Co Ltd, Taipei,
Taiwan
USA, Canada & South America: Martin P
Hill Consulting, New York, NY, USA

Book Trade Association Membership:
Booksellers Association

2740 ▄▄▄

THAMES & HUDSON LTD
181A High Holborn, London WC1V 7QX
Telephone: 020 7845 5000
Fax: 020 7845 5050
Email: l.willis@thameshudson.co.uk
Web Site: www.thamesandhudson.com

Warehouse, Accounts & Returns:
Thames & Hudson (Distributors) Ltd,
44 Clockhouse Road, Farnborough, Hants
GU14 7QZ
Telephone: 01252 541602
Fax: 01252 377380
Email:
customerservices@thameshudson.co.uk

Personnel:
Thomas Neurath *(Chairman)*
Constance Kaine *(Deputy Chairman)*
Jamie Camplin *(Managing Director)*
Peter Meades *(Financial Director)*
Christopher Ferguson *(Operations Director)*
Neil Palfreyman *(Production Director)*
Brian Meek *(Company Secretary)*
Johanna Neurath *(Design Director)*
Christian Frederking *(Rights Director)*
Stephen Embrey *(Export Area Manager)*
Sara Ticci *(Export Area Manager)*
Scipio Stringer *(Export Area Manager)*
Laura Willis *(Marketing Manager)*
Melanie Stacey *(UK Sales Manager)*
Collette Hutchinson *(Media)*
Jonathan Earl *(Sales)*
Ian Bartley *(Export Sales)*

*Academic & Scholarly; Antiques &
Collecting; Archaeology; Architecture &
Design; Biography & Autobiography;
Children's Books; Crafts & Hobbies;
Educational & Textbooks; Environment &
Development Studies; Fashion & Costume;
Fine Art & Art History; Gardening; Gay &
Lesbian Studies; Guide Books; History &
Antiquarian; Illustrated & Fine Editions;
Literature & Criticism; Magic & the Occult;
Military & War; Music; Natural History;
Philosophy; Photography; Reference Books,
Directories & Dictionaries; Religion &
Theology; Sociology & Anthropology;
Theatre, Drama & Dance; Travel &
Topography*

Imprints, Series & ISBNs:
Aperture: 978 0 89381, 978 1 59711, 978 1
931788
Art Gallery of NSW: 978 0 7847
Ava Publishing: 978 2 88479, 978 2 940373
Mark Batty Publisher
Chris Boot: 978 0 9542813, 978 0
9546894, 978 1 905712
Booth-Clibborn: 978 1 86154
Braun Verlagshaus: 978 3 938780
British Museum Press: 978 0 7141
Dakini
Flammarion SA, France: 978 2 08
Frieze
Guggenheim Museum Publications: 978 0
89207
Ilex Press: 978 1 904705
Institute for Archaeo-Metallurgical Studies:
978 0 906183
Laurence King: 978 1 85669
Museum of Modern Art, New York: 978 0
87070
National Gallery of Australia: 978 0 642
River Books
The Royal Academy of Arts: 978 0 900946,
978 1 903973

The Royal Collection: 978 1 902163
Scriptum: 978 1 900826, 978 1 902686
Skira Editore: 978 3 87624, 978 88 8118,
978 88 8491
Steidl: 978 3 86521, 978 3 88243, 978 3
905509, 978 3 931141
Thames & Hudson: 978 0 500
Vendome: 978 0 86565
Violette Editions: 978 1 900828

Parent Company:
T & H Holdings Ltd

Associated Companies:
Thames & Hudson (Distributors) Ltd
Australia: Thames & Hudson (Australia) Pty
Ltd
France: Editions Thames & Hudson sarl
P. R. of China: Thames & Hudson China Ltd
Singapore: Thames & Hudson (S) Pte Ltd
USA: Thames & Hudson Inc

Distributor for:
British Museum Press; Laurence King
Australia: National Gallery of Australia
France: Flammarion SA
Germany: Braun Verlagshaus
Israel: Institute for Archaeo-Metallurgical
Studies
Italy: Skira Editore
USA: Mark Batty Publisher; Museum of
Modern Art, New York

Overseas Representation:
*Africa, Caribbean, Central America, Eastern
Europe, Eastern Mediterranean,
Germany (South), Italy, Japan, Mexico,
Middle East, Portugal & Spain:* Export
Sales Department, Thames & Hudson
Ltd, London, UK
*Australia, New Zealand, Papua New Guinea
& Pacific Islands:* Thames & Hudson
(Australia) Pty Ltd, Fishermans Bend, Vic,
Australia
*Austria, Switzerland & Germany (excluding
South):* Michael Klein, Vilsiburg,
Germany
Bangladesh: Zeenat Book Supply Ltd,
Dhaka, Bangladesh
Brazil & South America: Terry Roberts, Cotia
SP, Brazil
China, Hong Kong & Macau: Thames &
Hudson China Ltd, Aberdeen, Hong
Kong
France: Interart SARL, Paris, France
India, Pakistan & Sri Lanka: Raj Rupam Bora,
New Delhi, India
Iran: Book City, Tehran, Iran
Israel: Lonnie Kahn & Co Ltd, Rishon Lezion,
Israel
Korea & Taiwan: Asia Publishers Services
Ltd, Hong Kong
Lebanon: Levant Distributors, Beirut,
Lebanon
Malaysia: Thames & Hudson (S) Pte Ltd,
Petaling Jaya, Malaysia
Netherlands: Sebastian van der Zee,
Amsterdam, Netherlands
Republic of Ireland: UK Sales Department,
Thames & Hudson Ltd, London, UK
Scandinavia & Baltic States: Per Burell,
Stocksund, Sweden
Singapore & South East Asia: Thames &
Hudson (S) Pte Ltd, Singapore
*South Africa, Swaziland, Lesotho, Namibia,
Botswana & Zimbabwe:* Peter Hyde
Associates (Pty) Ltd, Cape Town, South
Africa
Thailand: Asia Book Co Ltd, Bangkok,
Thailand

Book Trade Association Membership:
Publishers Association

2741

THARPA PUBLICATIONS
Conishead Priory, Ulverston, Cumbria
LA12 9QQ
Telephone: 01229 588599
Fax: 01229 483919
Email: sales.uk@tharpa.com

Web Site: www.tharpa.com

Personnel:
Murdo McNab *(Distribution Manager)*
Manuel Rivero-Demartine *(Production
Manager)*
Steph Atkinson *(Finance Director; Sales &
Marketing Manager)*
Jim Bliether *(Editorial)*

Philosophy; Religion & Theology

New Titles: 1 (2009) , 1 (2010)
No of Employees: 4

Imprints, Series & ISBNs:
978 0 948006, 978 0 9548790

Parent Company:
New Kadampa Tradition

Overseas Representation:
Australia: Gary Allen Pty Ltd, Smithfield,
NSW, Australia
Canada: Tharpa Canada, Toronto, Ont,
Canada
Singapore & Malaysia: Tharpa Asia, Hong
Kong
South Africa: Bacchus Books, Gauteng,
South Africa
USA (Office): Tharpa Publications, New
York, NY, USA

Book Trade Association Membership:
Booksellers Association; Independent
Publishers Guild

2742

**THIRD MILLENNIUM PUBLISHING
LTD**
2–5 Benjamin Street, London EC1M 5QL
Telephone: 020 7336 0144
Fax: 020 7608 1188
Email: info@tmiltd.com
Web Site: www.tmiltd.com

Personnel:
Julian Platt *(Chairman)*
Christopher Fagg *(Publisher)*
Joel Burden *(Business Development
Director)*
David Burt *(Director)*
Michael D. Jackson *(Marketing Manager)*
Bonnie Murray *(Production Manager)*

*Antiques & Collecting; Educational &
Textbooks; Fine Art & Art History; Guide
Books; Illustrated & Fine Editions; Military &
War; Photography*

New Titles: 15 (2009) , 20 (2010)
No of Employees: 8
Annual Turnover: £1.2M

Imprints, Series & ISBNs:
978 1 906507

Distributor for:
UK: Pardoe Blacker Design

Overseas Representation:
USA & Canada: John Bramcati, Antique
Collectors Club Ltd, Easthampton, MA,
USA

2743

**THOMSON INTERNATIONAL LEGAL
& REGULATORY**
100 Avenue Road, Swiss Cottage, London
NW3 3PF
Telephone: 020 7393 7000
Fax: 020 7393 7010
Web Site: www.sweetandmaxwell.co.uk

Law

Associated Companies:
UK: Current Law Publishers; ESC
Publishing; W. Green & Son; Information
for Industry; Legal Information

Resources; Morgan Hill; Pensions
Research; Professional Publishing; Steven
& Sons; Sweet & Maxwell; Thomson Tax;
Westlaw UK

Book Trade Association Membership:
Publishers Association

2744

THOROGOOD PUBLISHING LTD
10–12 Rivington Street, London EC2A 3DU
Telephone: 020 7749 4748
Fax: 020 7720 6110
Email: info@thorogoodpublishing.co.uk
Web Site:
www.thorogoodpublishing.co.uk

Trade Orders:
Marston Book Services, 160 Milton Park,
Abingdon, Oxon OX14 4SD
Telephone: 01235 465500
Fax: 01235 465655
Email: trade.enq@marston.co.uk
Web Site: www.marston.co.uk

Personnel:
Neil Thomas *(Chairman)*
Nina Rossey *(Finance Director)*
Angela Spall *(General, Editorial, Production
Manager)*
Matthew Harris *(Marketing Manager)*
Elizabeth Hall *(Marketing Executive)*

*Accountancy & Taxation; Audio Books;
Biography & Autobiography; Electronic
(Entertainment); Electronic (Professional &
Academic); Fiction; Industry, Business &
Management; Law; Military & War; Travel &
Topography*

New Titles: 19 (2009) , 25 (2010)
No of Employees: 10

Imprints, Series & ISBNs:
978 1 85418

Associated Companies:
UK: Falconbury Ltd

Overseas Representation:
Australia & New Zealand: Woodslane Pty
Ltd, Warriewood, NSW, Australia
Europe: Andrew Durnell Marketing Ltd,
Tunbridge Wells, UK
Hong Kong, Taiwan, China & Korea: Asia
Publishers Services Ltd, Hong Kong
India: Viva Group, New Delhi, India
Latin America: InterMedia Americana (IMA)
Ltd, London, UK
Middle East, Greece & Cyprus: Ray Potts,
Publishers International Marketing,
Polfages, France
Singapore, Malaysia & South East Asia: APD
Singapore Pte Ltd, Singapore

2745

F. A. THORPE PUBLISHING
The Green, Bradgate Road, Anstey,
Leicester LE7 7FU
Telephone: 0116 236 4325
Fax: 0116 234 0205
Email: enquiries@ulverscroft.co.uk
Web Site: www.ulverscroft.com

Personnel:
Robert Thirlby *(Chief Executive)*

*Biography & Autobiography; Crime;
Fiction; Travel & Topography*

New Titles: 456 (2009) , 456 (2010)

Imprints, Series & ISBNs:
Charnwood Hardback Series: 978 0 7089,
978 1 84395, 978 1 84617, 978 1 84782
Charnwood/Ulverscroft/Linford: 978 1 4448
Linford Softcover Series: 978 0 7089, 978 1
84395, 978 1 84617, 978 1 84782
Ulverscroft Hardcover Series: 978 0 7089,
978 1 84395, 978 1 84617, 978 1 84782

Associated Companies:
Isis Publishing; Magna Large Print Books;
Ulverscroft Large Print Books Ltd

Distributor for:
Soundings Audio Books

Overseas Representation:
Australia: Sandra Lavender, Crows Nest,
Australia
Canada: Mrs Diane Van Veen, Burlington,
Ont, Canada
New Zealand: John Gregory, Feilding, New
Zealand
USA: Ulverscroft Large Print Books (USA)
Inc, West Seneca, NY, USA

2746

THOTH PUBLICATIONS
64 Leopold Street, Loughborough, Leics
LE11 5DN
Telephone: 01509 210626
Fax: 01509 238034
Email: enquiries@thoth.co.uk
Web Site: www.thoth.co.uk

Personnel:
Tom Clarke *(Senior Partner)*
Susan Attwood *(Partner)*

*Biography & Autobiography; Magic & the
Occult; Religion & Theology*

Imprints, Series & ISBNs:
978 1 870450

Distributor for:
Sun Chalice

Book Trade Association Membership:
Booksellers Association

2747

THRASS (UK) LTD
Units 1–3 Tarvin Sands, Barrow Lane,
Tarvin, Chester CH3 8JF
Telephone: 01829 741413
Fax: 01829 741419
Web Site: www.thrass.co.uk

Personnel:
Alan Davies *(Director)*
Hilary Davies *(Consultant)*
Rachel Woodward *(Office Manager)*

*Educational & Textbooks; Electronic
(Educational)*

New Titles: 4 (2009) , 4 (2010)

Imprints, Series & ISBNs:
978 1 904912, 978 1 906295

2748

TINDAL STREET PRESS
217 The Custard Factory, Gibb Street,
Birmingham B9 4AA
Telephone: 0121 773 8157
Email: alan@tindalstreet.co.uk
Web Site: www.tindalstreet.co.uk

Distribution (UK):
Turnaround, Unit 3, Olympia Trading Estate,
Coburg Road, London N22 6TZ
Telephone: 020 8829 3000
Email: orders@turnaround-uk.com
Web Site: www.turnaround-uk.com

Personnel:
Alan Mahar *(Publishing Director)*
Luke Brown *(Editor/Marketing Manager)*

Fiction

New Titles: 7 (2009) , 6 (2010)
No of Employees: 5
Annual Turnover: £300,000

Imprints, Series & ISBNs:
978 0 9556476, 978 1 906994

Overseas Representation:
Australia: Tower Books Pty Ltd, Brookvale, NSW, Australia; Tower Books Pty Ltd, Frenchs Forest, NSW, Australia
New Zealand: Addenda, Auckland, New Zealand
USA & Canada: Trafalgar Square, Independent Publishers Group, USA

Book Trade Association Membership:
Independent Publishers Guild

2749

TITAN PUBLISHING GROUP
144 Southwark Street, London SE1 0UP
Telephone: 020 7620 0200
Fax: 020 7803 1990
Email: editorial@titanemail.com
Web Site: www.titanbooks.com

Trade Enquiries & Orders:
Grantham Book Services, Trent Road, Grantham, Lincs NG31 7XG
Telephone: 01476 541080
Fax: 01476 541061
Email: orders@gbs.tbs-ltd.co.uk

Personnel:
Nick Landau *(Managing Director)*
Vivian Cheung *(Executive Director)*
Tim Whale *(Global Sales Director)*
Katy Wild *(Editorial Director)*
Chris Horn *(Head of Finance)*
Chris McLane *(Marketing Manager)*
Kevin Wooff *(Print & Paper Buyer)*
Jenny Boyce *(Rights Executive)*

Children's Books; Cinema, Video, TV & Radio

Imprints, Series & ISBNs:
978 1 84576

Overseas Representation:
All other countries: Titan Books, Sales & Marketing Department, London, UK
Central & Eastern Europe (including Poland): Csaba Lengyel de Bagota, Budapest, Hungary
Far East: Ralph & Sheila Summers, Formtone Ltd, London, UK
France, Belgium, Netherlands, Greece, Malta, Israel & South Africa: Paul Walton, Chislehurst, UK
Germany, Switzerland & Austria: Gabriele Kern Publishers Services, Frankfurt-am-Main, Germany
Middle East: Peter Ward Book Exports, London, UK
Republic of Ireland: Gill Hess Ltd, Skerries, Co Dublin, Republic of Ireland
Scandinavia & Italy: Katie McNeish, McNeish Publishing International, East Sussex, UK
Spain, Portugal & Gibraltar: Peter Prout, Iberian Book Services, Madrid, Spain

2750

TOP THAT! PUBLISHING PLC
Marine House, Tide Mill Way, Woodbridge, Suffolk IP12 1AP
Telephone: 01394 386651
Fax: 01394 386011
Email: info@topthatpublishing.com
Web Site: www.topthatpublishing.com

Personnel:
Barrie Henderson *(Managing Director)*
Dave Greggor *(Sales Director)*
Simon Couchman *(Creative Director)*
Douglas Eadie *(Finance Director)*
Daniel Graham *(Editorial Director)*
Stuart Buck *(Production Director)*
Georgina Eade *(Head of European Sales)*
David Henderson *(Digital Sales Manager)*

Children's Books; Crafts & Hobbies; Fiction; Humour; Natural History; Reference Books, Directories & Dictionaries; Sports & Games

New Titles: 30 (2009) , 120 (2010)
No of Employees: 30
Annual Turnover: £9M

Imprints, Series & ISBNs:
Kudos: 978 1 84229
Pocket Money Press: 978 1 84956
Quest: 978 1 84956
Tide Mill Press: 978 1 84956
Top That! Kids: 978 1 84956

Overseas Representation:
USA: Top That! Publishing, Valencia, CA, USA

Book Trade Association Membership:
Independent Publishers Guild

2751

TOPICAL RESOURCES
Jumps Farm, Durton Lane, Broughton, Preston, Lancs PR3 5LE
Telephone: 01772 863158
Fax: 01772 866153
Email: sales@topical-resources.co.uk
Web Site: www.topical-resources.co.uk

Personnel:
Peter Bell *(Partner)*
Heather Bell *(Partner)*
Kath Cope *(Sales Assistant)*

Audio Books; Children's Books; Educational & Textbooks

New Titles: 8 (2009) , 9 (2010)
No of Employees: 3
Annual Turnover: £200,000

Imprints, Series & ISBNs:
978 1 872977, 978 1 905509, 978 1 907269

Overseas Representation:
Australia: Ian Harding, Farr Books, Wilston, Qld, Australia
Republic of Ireland: Martin Pender, Primary Educational Resources, Enniscorthy, Co Wexford, Republic of Ireland

2752

TOTAL-E-NTWINED LTD
Think Tank, Ruston Way, Lincoln LN6 7FL
Telephone: 01522 668916
Web Site: www.total-e-bound.com

Fiction

Book Trade Association Membership:
Publishers Association

2753

TRANSWORLD PUBLISHERS LTD
[a company of the Random House Group Ltd]
61–63 Uxbridge Road, London W5 5SA
Telephone: 020 8579 2652
Fax: 020 8579 5479
Email: info@transworld-publishers.co.uk
Web Site: www.booksattransworld.co.uk

Personnel:
Larry Finlay *(Managing Director)*
Bill Scott-Kerr *(Publisher & Director)*
Sally Gaminara *(Publishing Director – Bantam Press)*
Marianne Velmans *(Publishing Director – Doubleday)*
Leon Romero Montalvo *(Head of Commercial Affairs)*
Ed Christie *(Sales & Marketing Director)*
Martin Higgins *(UK Sales Director)*
Janine Giovanni *(UK Marketing Director)*

Diana Jones *(International Sales Director)*
Alison Martin *(Production Director)*
Patsy Irwin *(Publicity Director)*
Claire Ward *(Art Director)*
Helen Edwards *(Rights Director)*

Audio Books; Biography & Autobiography; Cinema, Video, TV & Radio; Cookery, Wines & Spirits; Crime; Fiction; Gardening; Health & Beauty; History & Antiquarian; Humour; Military & War; Music; Politics & World Affairs; Science Fiction; Sports & Games; Travel & Topography

Imprints, Series & ISBNs:
Bantam: 978 0 553
Bantam Press: 978 0 593
Black Swan: 978 0 552
Channel 4 Books
Corgi: 978 0 552
Doubleday: 978 0 385
Eden Project: 978 0 593
Expert Gardening Books
Transworld Ireland

Parent Company:
USA: Random House Inc

Associated Companies:
Random House Children's Books; Random House UK Ltd
Australia: Random House Australia Pty Ltd
Canada: Random House of Canada Ltd
New Zealand: Random House New Zealand Ltd
South Africa: Random House (Pty) Ltd

Overseas Representation:
Australia: Random House Australia Pty Ltd, Sydney, NSW, Australia
Canada: Random House of Canada Ltd, Toronto, Ont, Canada
New Zealand: Random House New Zealand Ltd, Auckland, New Zealand
South Africa: Random House Struik Pty Ltd, Parktown, South Africa

Book Trade Association Membership:
BA (Associate Member)

2754

TRAVEL PUBLISHING LTD
Airport Business Centre,
10 Thornbury Road, Estover, Plymouth PL6 7PP
Telephone: 01752 697280
Fax: 01752 697299
Email: info@travelpublishing.co.uk
Web Site: www.travelpublishing.co.uk

Sales & Distribution:
Portfolio, Suite 3 & 4, Great West House, Great West Road, Brentford, Middx TW8 9DF
Telephone: 020 8326 5620
Fax: 020 8326 5621
Email: e-mail@portfoliobooks.com

Personnel:
Peter Robinson *(Director & Chairman)*
Chris Day *(Director & Company Secretary)*

Guide Books; Travel & Topography

New Titles: 10 (2009) , 10 (2010)

Imprints, Series & ISBNs:
Country Living Garden Centres & Nurseries of Britain: 978 1 904434
Country Living Rural Guides: 978 1 902007, 978 1 904434
Country Pubs & Inns: 978 1 904434
Golfers Guides: 978 1 902007, 978 1 904434
Hidden Inns: 978 1 902007, 978 1 904434
Hidden Places: 978 1 902007, 978 1 904434
Off the Motorway: 978 1 902007, 978 1 904434

Overseas Representation:
USA & Canada: Casemate Publishers & Book Distributors LLC, Havertown, PA, USA

Book Trade Association Membership:
Independent Publishers Guild

2755

TRENTHAM BOOKS
Westview House, 734 London Road, Oakhill, Stoke on Trent ST4 5NP
Telephone: 01782 745567 & 844699
Fax: 01782 745553
Email: tb@trentham-books.co.uk
Web Site: www.trentham-books.co.uk

Editorial:
28 Hillside Gardens, Highgate, London N6 5ST
Telephone: 020 8348 2174
Email: gillian@trentham-books.co.uk

Representation (UK):
Compass Academic Ltd

Personnel:
Gillian Klein *(Chairman, Rights & Permissions, Editor)*
Barbara Wiggins *(Business Manager)*

Academic & Scholarly; Educational & Textbooks; Gender Studies; Law; Politics & World Affairs; Theatre, Drama & Dance

New Titles: 20 (2009) , 25 (2010)
No of Employees: 6

Imprints, Series & ISBNs:
978 0 948080, 978 0 9507735, 978 1 85856

Associated Companies:
Trentham Print Design Ltd

Distributor for:
Arts Council; Commission for Racial Equality; Design and Technology Association; Open University
France: European Institute of Education & Social Policy; UNESCO Institute for Educational Planning

Overseas Representation:
Australia, New Zealand & South East Asia: DA Information Services Pty Ltd, Mitcham, Vic, Australia
Canada: Bacon & Hughes Ltd, Ottawa, Ont, Canada
China, Taiwan, Hong Kong & South East Asia: Tony Poh Leong Wah, Singapore, Singapore
Ireland: Ben Parker, Marketing for Publishers, Republic of Ireland
Malaysia: UBSD Distribution Sdn Bhd, Selangor, Malaysia
Philippines: Megatexts Phil Inc, Cebu City, Philippines
Spain & Portugal: Iberian Book Services, Madrid, Spain
Taiwan: Unifacmanu Trading Co Ltd, Taipei, Taiwan
USA: Stylus Publishing Inc, Sterling, VA, USA

Book Trade Association Membership:
Independent Publishers Guild

2756

TRINITARIAN BIBLE SOCIETY
Tyndale House, Dorset Road, London SW19 3NN
Telephone: 020 8543 7857
Fax: 020 8543 6370
Email: TBS@trinitarianbiblesociety.org
Web Site: www.trinitarianbiblesociety.org

Online Sales:
Web Site: www.TBS-sales.org

Personnel:
D. P. Rowland *(General Secretary)*
D. Larlham *(Assistant General Secretary)*
D. Broome *(Finance Director)*
M. Wilson *(Office Manager)*

Religion & Theology

Imprints, Series & ISBNs:
978 0 907861, 978 1 86228

Overseas Representation:
Australia: Trinitarian Bible Society (Australia), Grafton, NSW, Australia
Brazil: Sociedade Bíblica Trinitariana do Brasil, São Paulo, Brazil
Canada: Trinitarian Bible Society, Chilliwack, BC, Canada
New Zealand: Trinitarian Bible Society (New Zealand), Gisborne, New Zealand
USA: Trinitarian Bible Society (USA), Grand Rapids, MI, USA

2757

TROG ASSOCIATES LTD
PO Box 243, South Croydon, Surrey CR2 6NZ
Telephone: 020 8681 3301
Fax: 020 8681 3301
Email: ericsutherland@btinternet.com
Web Site: www.trogassociatesltd.biz

Personnel:
Eric Sutherland *(Contact)*

Accountancy & Taxation; Health & Beauty; Industry, Business & Management; Literature & Criticism

New Titles: 3 (2010)

Imprints, Series & ISBNs:
978 1 906440

Associated Companies:
UK: www.lulu.com/uk

2758

TROTMAN PUBLISHING
[an imprint of Crimson Publishing Ltd]
Crimson Publishing Ltd,
Westminster House, Kew Road, Richmond TW9 2ND
Telephone: 020 8334 1786
Fax: 020 8334 1601
Email: jessicas@crimsonpublishing.co.uk
Web Site: www.trotman.co.uk

Warehouse:
NBN International Ltd, Estover Road, Plymouth PL6 7PY
Telephone: 01752 202301
Fax: 01752 202333

Personnel:
David Lester *(Managing Director)*
Alison Yates *(Senior Commissioning Editor)*
Jessica Spencer *(Commissioning Editor)*

Educational & Textbooks; Industry, Business & Management; Reference Books, Directories & Dictionaries; Vocational Training & Careers

Imprints, Series & ISBNs:
Trotman: 978 0 85660, 978 1 84455
Trotman Education: 978 0 85660, 978 1 84455

Parent Company:
UK: Crimson Publishing Ltd

Book Trade Association Membership:
Independent Publishers Guild; Data Publishers Association

2759

TROUBADOR PUBLISHING LTD
5 Weir Road, Kibworth Beauchamp, Leics LE8 0LQ
Telephone: 0116 279 2299
Fax: 0116 279 2277
Email: books@troubador.co.uk
Web Site: www.troubador.co.uk

Personnel:
Jeremy Thompson *(Managing Director)*
Jane Rowland *(Marketing Director)*
Caroline Bromley *(Marketing Assistant)*
Terry Compton *(Assistant Publisher)*
Amy Cooke *(Production Assistant)*

Academic & Scholarly; Accountancy & Taxation; Biography & Autobiography; Children's Books; Cookery, Wines & Spirits; Crime; Economics; Fiction; Guide Books; History & Antiquarian; Humour; Industry, Business & Management; Languages & Linguistics; Literature & Criticism; Magic & the Occult; Medical (incl. Self Help & Alternative Medicine); Military & War; Natural History; Philosophy; Poetry; Politics & World Affairs; Psychology & Psychiatry; Science Fiction; Theatre, Drama & Dance; Transport; Travel & Topography

New Titles: 200 (2009) , 230 (2010)
No of Employees: 7
Annual Turnover: £900,000

Imprints, Series & ISBNs:
Italian Studies: 978 1 905237
Matador: 978 1 84876, 978 1 899293, 978 1 905886, 978 1 906221, 978 1 906510
T2: 978 1 904744

Book Trade Association Membership:
Independent Publishers Guild

2760

TRURAN
Goonance, Water Lane, St Agnes, Cornwall TR5 0RA
Telephone: 01872 553821
Email: info@truranbooks.co.uk
Web Site: www.truranbooks.co.uk

Trade Enquiries:
Tor Mark Press,
United Downs Industrial Estate, St Day, Redruth, Cornwall TR16 5HY
Telephone: 01209 822101
Fax: 01209 822035
Email: sales@tormarkpress.prestel.co.uk

Personnel:
Ivan Corbett *(Director)*
Heather Corbett *(Director)*

Aviation; Biography & Autobiography; Cookery, Wines & Spirits; Crime; Fiction; Fine Art & Art History; Gardening; Geography & Geology; Guide Books; History & Antiquarian; Languages & Linguistics; Military & War; Natural History; Nautical; Photography; Reference Books, Directories & Dictionaries

Imprints, Series & ISBNs:
978 0 9506431, 978 0 907566, 978 1 85022
Cornish Classics
Truran

2761

TSO (THE STATIONERY OFFICE LTD)
St Crispins, Duke Street, Norwich NR3 1PD
Telephone: 01603 622211
Fax: 01603 696506
Email: tsoservices@tso.co.uk
Web Site: www.tso.co.uk

Press & Offices:
Mandela Way, London SE1 5SS
Telephone: 020 7394 4200

Email: tsoservices@tso.co.uk
Web Site: www.tso.co.uk

Personnel:
Richard Dell *(Chief Executive Officer)*
Richard South *(Official Publishing Director)*
Richard Coward *(Finance Director)*
Gordon Samson *(Operations Director)*
Lisa Hallett *(Sales & Marketing Director)*
Ashley Dampier *(Head of Sales)*
David Howell *(Client Services Director)*
Terry Blake *(Technology Services Director)*

Academic & Scholarly; Accountancy & Taxation; Aviation; Computer Science; Economics; Educational & Textbooks; Electronic (Professional & Academic); Engineering; Geography & Geology; Industry, Business & Management; Law; Mathematics & Statistics; Medical (incl. Self Help & Alternative Medicine); Nautical; Politics & World Affairs; Reference Books, Directories & Dictionaries; Scientific & Technical; Transport; Veterinary Science

New Titles: 9000 (2009) , 9000 (2010)
No of Employees: 400
Annual Turnover: £68.7M

Imprints, Series & ISBNs:
Non-Parliamentary Publications: 978 0 11
Northern Ireland Publications: 978 0 337
Parliamentary Publications: 978 0 10

Parent Company:
Williams Lea

Distributor for:
Construction Industry Publications; English Heritage; International Labour Organisation
France: Council of Europe; European Pharmacopoeia Commission; Organisation for Economic Co-operation and Development; United Nations Educational, Scientific and Cultural Organisation
Germany: Deutscher Apotheker Verlag
Italy: Food and Agriculture Organisation of the United Nations
Japan: Japanese Pharmacopoeia
Luxembourg: European Communities/ Union
Spain: World Tourism Organisation
Switzerland: United Nations; World Health Organisation; World Trade Organisation
USA: Bernan Press; International Monetary Fund; United Nations; US Pharmacopoeia Convention; World Bank

Overseas Representation:
Australia: DA Information Services Pty Ltd, Mitcham, Vic, Australia
Belgium & Luxembourg: Jean de Lannoy, Brussels, Belgium
Brazil: Livraria Cultura Editora Ltda, São Paulo, Brazil; Livraria LMC LTDA, Brazil
Canada: Renouf Publishing Co Ltd, Ottawa, Ont, Canada
Croatia: VBZ d.o.o., Zagreb, Croatia
Denmark: Arnold Busck, Copenhagen, Denmark
Egypt: MERIC, Cairo, Egypt
France: Bureau D'etudes Et De, France
Germany: Deutscher Apotheker, Germany
Greece: Athenian Science, Athens, Greece
Hong Kong: Swindon Book Co Ltd, Hong Kong
Hungary: SpeedUp Ltd, Budapest, Hungary
India: Apple Books, New Delhi, India
Italy: Licosa SPA, Florence, Italy
Japan: Maruzen Co Ltd, Tokyo, Japan
Jordan: Jordan Book Centre, Amman, Jordan
Kuwait: The Kuwait Bookshop Co Ltd, Safat, Kuwait
Malaysia: Yuha Associates, Selangor Darul Ehsan, Malaysia
Mexico: Libreria Arroyave, Mexico, Mexico
Netherlands: selexyz zakelijk, Netherlands; Technische Boekhandel Waltman, Delft, Netherlands

Norway: Academic Book Centre, Oslo, Norway
Poland: Ars Plona, Poland

Book Trade Association Membership:
Booksellers Association; Educational Publishers Council; Data Publishers Association

2762

TTS GROUP
Park Lane Business Park, Kirkby-in-Ashfield, Nottinghamshire NG17 9GU
Telephone: 0800 318686
Fax: 0800 137525
Web Site: www.tts-group.co.uk

Children's Books; Educational & Textbooks; Electronic (Educational); Music

Book Trade Association Membership:
Publishers Association

2763

TWELVEHEADS PRESS
PO Box 59, Chacewater, Truro, Cornwall TR4 8ZJ
Email: enquiries@twelveheads.com
Web Site: www.twelveheads.com

Personnel:
Alan Kittridge *(Partner)*
Michael Messenger *(Partner)*
John Stengelhofen *(Partner)*

Archaeology; Guide Books; History & Antiquarian; Nautical; Transport

New Titles: 3 (2009)

Imprints, Series & ISBNs:
978 0 906294

2764

TYNE BRIDGE PUBLISHING
Newcastle Libraries, PO Box 88, Newcastle upon Tyne NE99 1DX
Telephone: 0191 277 4174
Fax: 0191 277 4137
Email: anna.flowers@newcastle.gov.uk
Web Site: www.newcastle.gov.uk/ tynebridgepublishing

Personnel:
Anna Flowers *(Publications Manager)*
Vanessa Histon *(Marketing Officer)*

Architecture & Design; Biography & Autobiography; Engineering; Fine Art & Art History; History & Antiquarian; Military & War; Nautical

New Titles: 5 (2009) , 4 (2010)
No of Employees: 2
Annual Turnover: £70,000

Imprints, Series & ISBNs:
Newcastle City Libraries: 978 0 902653
Newcastle Libraries and Information Service: 978 1 85795
Tyne Bridge Publishing: 978 1 85795

Parent Company:
City & Council of Newcastle upon Tyne

2765

UCAS
Rosehill, New Barn Lane, Cheltenham, Glos GL52 3LZ
Telephone: 01242 222444
Fax: 01242 544960
Email: publicationservices@ucas.ac.uk
Web Site: www.ucas.com

Trade Enquiries & Orders:
Publication Services, UCAS, PO Box 130, Cheltenham, Glos GL52 3ZF
Telephone: 01242 544610

Fax: 01242 544806
Email: publicationservices@ucas.ac.uk
Web Site: www.ucasbooks.com

Personnel:
Graham Bond *(Publications Production Manager)*
Steven Matthews *(Publication Sales Co-ordinator)*
Amruta Hiremath *(Senior Management Accountant)*
Joanne Voysey *(Publication Services Manager)*

Academic & Scholarly; Educational & Textbooks; Reference Books, Directories & Dictionaries; Vocational Training & Careers

New Titles: 14 (2009) , 14 (2010)

Imprints, Series & ISBNs:
978 1 84361

2766

ULVERSCROFT LARGE PRINT BOOKS LTD
The Green, Bradgate Road, Anstey, Leics
LE7 7FU
Telephone: 0116 236 4325
Fax: 0116 236 5522
Email: sales@ulverscroft.co.uk
Web Site: www.ulverscroft.co.uk

Personnel:
Robert Thirlby *(Chief Executive)*
Michele Petty *(Operations Director)*
Anna Gilbert *(General Manager)*

Audio Books; Biography & Autobiography; Crime; Fiction

New Titles: 1992 (2009) , 1809 (2010)

2767

UNICORN PRESS
47 Earlham Road, Norwich NR2 3AD
Telephone: 01603 886151
Email: unicornpress@btinternet.com
Web Site: www.unicornpress.org

Trade Distributor:
Marston Book Services, 160 Milton Park,
PO Box 269, Abingdon, Oxford OX14 4YN
Telephone: 01235 465604
Fax: 01235 465655
Email: tammy.belcher@marston.co.uk

Personnel:
Hugh Tempest-Radford *(Proprietor)*
Lucy Hulme *(Sales & Marketing)*

Antiques & Collecting; Architecture & Design; Biography & Autobiography; Crafts & Hobbies; Fashion & Costume; Fine Art & Art History; History & Antiquarian; Military & War; Nautical; Photography; Reference Books, Directories & Dictionaries

New Titles: 8 (2009) , 5 (2010)

Imprints, Series & ISBNs:
978 0 906290, 978 1 906509

Overseas Representation:
All other areas: Unicorn Press, London, UK
Germany, France, Benelux, Italy, Austria, Switzerland, Malta & Greece: Ted Dougherty, London, UK
Spain, Portugal & Gibraltar: Chris Humphrys, London, UK
USA: Antique Collectors Club Ltd, Easthampton, MA, USA

2768

UNITED WRITERS PUBLICATIONS LTD
Ailsa, Castle Gate, Penzance, Cornwall
TR20 8BG
Telephone: 01736 365954

Fax: 01736 365954
Email: sales@unitedwriters.co.uk
Web Site: www.unitedwriters.co.uk

Personnel:
M. Sheppard *(Editorial & Sales)*
T. Sully *(Production)*

Biography & Autobiography; Children's Books; Cinema, Video, TV & Radio; Educational & Textbooks; Fiction; Humour; Industry, Business & Management; Military & War; Nautical; Psychology & Psychiatry; Science Fiction; Sports & Games; Travel & Topography

New Titles: 6 (2009) , 6 (2010)

Imprints, Series & ISBNs:
978 0 901976, 978 1 85200

2769

UNIVERSITY COLLEGE OF DUBLIN PRESS
Newman House, 86 St Stephen's Green,
Dublin 2, Republic of Ireland
Telephone: +353 (01) 477 9812 & 9813
Fax: +353 (01) 477 9821
Email: ucdpress@ucd.ie
Web Site: www.ucdpress.ie

Distribution (Republic of Ireland):
Columba Mercier Distribution,
55A Spruce Avenue,
Stillorgan Industrial Park, Blackrock,
Co Dublin, Republic of Ireland
Fax: +353 (01) 294 2564

Representation (Republic of Ireland):
Hibernian Book Services,
93 Longwood Park, Rathfarnham,
Dublin 14, Republic of Ireland
Telephone: +353 (01) 493 6043
Fax: +353 (01) 493 7833

Personnel:
Barbara Mennell *(Executive Editor)*
Noelle Moran *(Assistant Editor)*

Academic & Scholarly

Imprints, Series & ISBNs:
978 1 900621, 978 1 904558, 978 1 906359

Overseas Representation:
Australia & New Zealand: Eleanor Brasch Enterprises, Artarmon, NSW, Australia
Germany, Austria & Switzerland: SHS Publishers' Consultants and Representatives, Oranienberg, Germany
North America: Dufour Editions Inc, Chester Springs, PA, USA
Spain & Portugal: Iberian Book Services, Madrid, Spain
UK & Benelux: Theo Van de Bilt Sales and Marketing, Sawbridgeworth, UK
UK, Europe & all other countries (distribution): Central Books Ltd, London, UK

Book Trade Association Membership:
Publishing Ireland (Foilsiú Éireann)

2770

UNIVERSITY OF EXETER PRESS
Reed Hall, Streatham Drive, Exeter EX4 4QR
Telephone: 01392 263066
Fax: 01392 263064
Email: uep@exeter.ac.uk
Web Site: www.exeterpress.co.uk

Distribution:
NBN International, Estover Road, Plymouth
PL6 7PY
Telephone: 01752 202301
Fax: 01752 202331
Email: cservs@nbninternational.com
Web Site: www.nbninternational.com

Personnel:
Simon Baker *(Publisher)*
Helen Gannon *(Sales)*

Academic & Scholarly; Archaeology; Cinema, Video, TV & Radio; History & Antiquarian; Literature & Criticism; Theatre, Drama & Dance

New Titles: 20 (2009) , 20 (2010)
No of Employees: 4

Imprints, Series & ISBNs:
Bristol Phoenix Press: 978 1 904675
The Exeter Press: 978 1 905816
University of Exeter Press: 978 0 85989

Parent Company:
The Exeter Press Ltd

Overseas Representation:
Australia & New Zealand: Footprint Books Pty, Mona Vale, NSW, Australia
China, Hong Kong, Taiwan & South East Asia: Tony Poh, Singapore
France & Italy: Flavio Marcello Publishers' Agents & Consultants, Padua, Italy
Germany, Austria & Switzerland: SHS Publishers' Consultants and Representatives, Oranienberg, Germany
Greece: Charles Gibbes Associates, Louslitges, France
India: Viva Books Pvt Ltd, New Delhi, India
Japan & Korea: United Publishers Services Ltd, Tokyo, Japan
Middle East: The Avicenna Partnership, Oxford, UK
Republic of Ireland: Quantum Publishing Solutions Ltd, Paisley, UK
Scandinavia: Jan Norbye, Ølstykke, Denmark
Spain & Portugal: Iberian Book Services, Madrid, Spain
USA & Canada, Central & South America: University of Chicago Press, Chicago, IL, USA

Book Trade Association Membership:
Independent Publishers Guild

2771

UNIVERSITY OF HERTFORDSHIRE PRESS
College Lane, Hatfield, Hertfordshire
AL10 9AB
Telephone: 01707 284654
Fax: 01707 284666
Email: UHPress@herts.ac.uk
Web Site: www.herts.ac.uk/UHPress

Trade Enquiries & Orders:
Central Books Ltd, 99 Wallis Road, London
E9 5LN
Telephone: 0845 458 9911
Fax: 0845 458 9912
Email: info@centralbooks.com
Web Site: www.centralbooks.com

Personnel:
Jane Housham *(Press Manager)*
Gill Cook *(Administration Assistant)*
Sarah Elvins *(Production Editor)*

Academic & Scholarly; Educational & Textbooks; Geography & Geology; History & Antiquarian; Literature & Criticism; Magic & the Occult; Mathematics & Statistics; Psychology & Psychiatry; Sociology & Anthropology; Theatre, Drama & Dance

Imprints, Series & ISBNs:
Guidelines for Research in Parapsychology: 978 0 900458, 978 1 905313
Hertfordshire Publications: 978 0 9542189, 978 1 905313, 978 1 907396
The Interface Collection: 978 0 900458, 978 1 905313, 978 1 907396
Regional and Local History: 978 0 900458, 978 1 905313, 978 1 907396
University of Hertfordshire (Faculties): 978 1 898543, 978 1 905313, 978 1 907396

University of Hertfordshire Press: 978 1 902806, 978 1 905313, 978 1 907396

Parent Company:
University of Hertfordshire

Overseas Representation:
Benelux: Netwerk Academic Book Agency, Rotterdam, Netherlands
Spain & Portugal: Iberian Book Services, Madrid, Spain
USA: Independent Publishers Group (IPG), Chicago, IL, USA

Book Trade Association Membership:
Independent Publishers Guild

2772

UNIVERSITY OF OTTAWA PRESS
5 Victoria House, 138 Watling Street,
Towcester NN12 6BT
Telephone: 01327 357770
Fax: 01327 359572
Email: uop@oppuk.co.uk
Web Site: www.press.uottawa.ca

Warehouse & Distribution:
Marston Book Services, 160 Milton Park,
PO Box 169, Abingdon, Oxon OX14 4YN
Telephone: 01235 465521
Email: direct.orders@marston.co.uk
Web Site: www.marston.co.uk

Personnel:
Gary Hall *(Marketing Manager)*

Academic & Scholarly; Cinema, Video, TV & Radio; Economics; Educational & Textbooks; Gender Studies; Industry, Business & Management; Languages & Linguistics; Literature & Criticism; Politics & World Affairs; Reference Books, Directories & Dictionaries; Sociology & Anthropology; Theatre, Drama & Dance

New Titles: 12 (2009) , 12 (2010)

Parent Company:
Canada: University of Ottawa Press

2773

UNIVERSITY OF WALES PRESS
10 Columbus Walk, Brigantine Place,
Cardiff CF10 4UP
Telephone: 029 2049 6899
Fax: 029 2049 6108
Email: press@press.wales.ac.uk
Web Site: uwp.co.uk

Distribution (UK):
NBN International Ltd, Estover Road,
Plymouth PL6 7PY
Telephone: 01752 202300
Fax: 01752 202330

Personnel:
Helgard Krause *(Head of the Press)*
Bethan James *(Sales & Marketing Manager)*
Sarah Lewis *(Commissioning Editor)*
Paul Folland *(Finance Manager)*
Sian Chapman *(Production Manager)*

Academic & Scholarly; Archaeology; Biography & Autobiography; Educational & Textbooks; Gender Studies; History & Antiquarian; Illustrated & Fine Editions; Languages & Linguistics; Literature & Criticism; Military & War; Music; Philosophy; Poetry; Politics & World Affairs; Reference Books, Directories & Dictionaries; Religion & Theology; Sociology & Anthropology; Sports & Games

Imprints, Series & ISBNs:
GPC Books: 978 0 7083, 978 0 900768
Gwasg Prifysgol Cymru: 978 0 7083, 978 0 900768
University of Wales Press: 978 0 7083, 978 0 900768

Parent Company:
University of Wales

Distributor for:
The Glamorgan County History Trust; Zena
Publications

Overseas Representation:
India: Maya Publishers Pvt Ltd, New Delhi,
India
Japan: United Publishers Services Ltd,
Tokyo, Japan
South East Asia: STM Publisher Services Pte
Ltd, Singapore
USA, Canada & Australia: Chicago
University Press, Chicago, IL, USA

Book Trade Association Membership:
Independent Publishers Guild; Literary
Publishers (Wales) Ltd

2774

MERLIN UNWIN BOOKS LTD
Palmers House, 7 Corve Street, Ludlow,
Shropshire SY8 1DB
Telephone: 01584 877456
Fax: 01584 877457
Email: books@merlinunwin.co.uk
Web Site: www.merlinunwin.co.uk

Warehouse & Returns:
Merlin Unwin Books Warehouse, c/
o Wow Distribution, The Yard,
Woofferton Grange, Brimfield, Ludlow
SY8 4NP

Personnel:
Merlin Unwin (*Design Director*)
Karen McCall (*Managing Director, Editorial*)
Joanne Potter (*Marketing & Production*)
Sue Bradley (*Finance*)

*Biography & Autobiography; Cookery,
Wines & Spirits; Crime; Humour; Medical
(incl. Self Help & Alternative Medicine);
Natural History; Reference Books,
Directories & Dictionaries; Sports & Games*

Imprints, Series & ISBNs:
978 1 873674, 978 1 906122

Book Trade Association Membership:
Independent Publishers Guild

2775

USBORNE PUBLISHING LTD
Usborne House, 83–85 Saffron Hill, London
EC1N 8RT
Telephone: 020 7430 2800
Fax: 020 7242 0974 & 7430 1562
Email: mail@usborne.co.uk
Web Site: www.usborne.com

Warehouse:
HarperCollins, Westerhill Road,
Bishopsbriggs, Glasgow G64 2QT
Telephone: 0141 306 3100
Fax: 0141 306 3767

Personnel:
T. P. Usborne (*Managing Director*)
R. Jones (*General Manager*)
J. Tyler (*Editorial Director*)
D. Harte (*Director*)
L. Hunt (*Director*)
K. M. Ball (*Company Secretary*)
E. Wright (*Rights Controller*)
C. Herisson (*UK Marketing*)
M. Larkin (*Fiction*)
G. Lewis (*Editorial*)

*Children's Books; Computer Science; Crafts
& Hobbies; Fiction; Languages &
Linguistics; Music; Natural History;
Reference Books, Directories &
Dictionaries; Scientific & Technical; Sports &
Games*

New Titles: 324 (2009) , 347 (2010)
No of Employees: 180

Annual Turnover: £35.9M

Imprints, Series & ISBNs:
978 0 7460, 978 0 86020

2776

V&A PUBLISHING
Victoria & Albert Museum,
South Kensington, London SW7 2RL
Telephone: 020 7942 2966
Fax: 020 7942 2967
Web Site: www.vandabooks.com

Distribution:
Macmillan Distribution (MDL), Houndmills,
Basingstoke RG21 6XS
Telephone: 01256 302692
Fax: 01256 812558 (UK orders) & 842084
(Export orders)
Email: mdl@macmillan.co.uk
Web Site:
www.macmillandistribution.co.uk

Personnel:
Mark Eastment (*Head of Publishing*)
Anjali Bulley (*Managing Editor*)
Nina Jacobson (*Rights Manager*)
Julie Chan (*PR & Marketing Manager*)
Clare Davis (*Production Manager*)
Clare Faulkner (*Marketing Manager*)

*Academic & Scholarly; Antiques &
Collecting; Architecture & Design;
Biography & Autobiography; Crafts &
Hobbies; Fashion & Costume; Fine Art & Art
History; Guide Books; Photography;
Theatre, Drama & Dance*

New Titles: 30 (2009) , 28 (2010)
No of Employees: 10

Imprints, Series & ISBNs:
978 0 905209, 978 0 948107, 978 1 85177

Parent Company:
Victoria & Albert Museum

Overseas Representation:
Australia & New Zealand: Allen & Unwin Pty
Ltd, Sydney, NSW, Australia
Central & Eastern Europe: Grazyna
Soszynska, Poznan-Baranowo, Poland
France: Critiques Livres Distribution,
Bagnolet, France
Germany & Austria: Penguin Books
Deutschland GmbH, Frankfurt-am-Main,
Germany
India: Maya Publishers Pvt Ltd, New Delhi,
India
Italy: Penguin Italia srl, Milan, Italy
Netherlands, Belgium & Luxembourg:
Penguin Books BV, Amsterdam,
Netherlands
Singapore, Indonesia & Thailand: APD
Singapore Pte Ltd, Singapore
South America & Central America: David
Williams, InterMedia Americana (IMA)
Ltd, London, UK
Southern Africa: Book Promotions Pty Ltd,
Cape Town, South Africa
Spain & Portugal: Penguin Books SA,
Madrid, Spain
*Turkey, Africa, Middle East, Japan, Hong
Kong, Taiwan, Korea, Scandinavia,
Switzerland, Malta, Greece, Cyprus,
Israel, China & Philippines:* International
Sales Department, Penguin Books Ltd,
London, UK
USA: Harry N. Abrams Inc, New York, NY,
USA

Book Trade Association Membership:
Independent Publishers Guild; International
Association of Museum Publishers

2777

VALLENTINE MITCHELL PUBLISHERS
29–45 High Street, Edgware, Middx
HA8 7UU
Telephone: 020 8952 9526

Fax: 020 8952 9242
Email: info@vmbooks.com
Web Site: www.vmbooks.com

Personnel:
Stewart Cass (*Managing Director*)
Jenni Tinson (*Editor & Production*)
Toby Harris (*Sales & Marketing, Publicity*)

*Academic & Scholarly; Biography &
Autobiography; History & Antiquarian;
Politics & World Affairs; Religion &
Theology*

New Titles: 25 (2010)

Imprints, Series & ISBNs:
978 0 85303

Book Trade Association Membership:
Independent Publishers Guild

2778

VELOCE PUBLISHING LTD
Veloce House,
Parkway Farm Business Estate,
Middle Farm Way, Poundbury, Dorchester
DT1 3AR
Telephone: 01305 260068
Fax: 01305 268864
Email: veloce@veloce.co.uk
Web Site: www.veloce.co.uk

Personnel:
Rod Grainger (*Publisher*)
Judith Brooks (*Company Secretary*)

*Animal Care & Breeding; Biography &
Autobiography; Illustrated & Fine Editions;
Military & War; Reference Books,
Directories & Dictionaries; Sports & Games;
Transport*

Imprints, Series & ISBNs:
978 1 84584, 978 1 874105, 978 1
901295, 978 1 903706, 978 1 904788

Overseas Representation:
Australia & New Zealand: Capricorn Link
(Australia) Pty Ltd, Windsor, NSW,
Australia
France: Editions du Palmier, Nîmes, France;
Librairie du Collectionneur, Paris, France
Germany: Heel-Verlag, Konigswinter,
Germany
Germany, Austria & Benelux: Anselm
Robinson, London, UK
Japan: Shimada & Co Inc, Tokyo, Japan;
Takahara Bookstore Co Ltd, Aichi-ken,
Japan
New Zealand: South Pacific Books (Imports)
Ltd, Auckland, New Zealand; TechBooks,
Auckland, New Zealand
Scandinavia: Angell Eurosales, Berwick-on-
Tweed, UK; MarGie Bookshop,
Stockholm, Sweden
South Africa: Motor Books, Johannesburg,
South Africa
South East Asia: Ashton International
Marketing Services, Sevenoaks, Kent, UK
Spain & Italy: Bookport Associates, Corsico
(MI), Italy; Libro Motor SI, Madrid, Spain
USA: Motorbooks International Inc,
Osceola, WI, USA

2779

VERITAS PUBLICATIONS
Veritas House, 7–8 Lower Abbey Street,
Dublin 1, Republic of Ireland
Telephone: +353 (01) 878 8177
Fax: +353 (01) 878 6507
Email: publications@veritas.ie
Web Site: www.veritas.ie

Personnel:
Caitriona Clarke (*Manager of Publications*)
Donna Doherty (*Commissioning Editor*)
Maureen Sanders (*Commercial Manager*)
Amanda Conlon-McKenna (*Publicity &
Marketing*)

Maura Hyland (*Director*)
Liam McCabe (*Sales Representative*)
Raymond Nedas (*Sales Representative*)
Eamonn Connelly (*Financial Controller*)

*Academic & Scholarly; Biography &
Autobiography; Children's Books;
Educational & Textbooks; Philosophy;
Religion & Theology*

New Titles: 30 (2009) , 30 (2010)
No of Employees: 20

Imprints, Series & ISBNs:
978 0 85390, 978 0 86217, 978 1 84730,
978 1 85390

Parent Company:
Republic of Ireland: Veritas
Communications

Distributor for:
USA: Abbey Press; ACTA Publications;
Baronius Press; Candle Books; Catholic
Word; Crossroads Publishing; Darton
Longman & Todd; Ignatius Press

Overseas Representation:
Australia: John Garrett Publishing,
Mulgrave, Vic, Australia
Malta: Libreria Taghlim Nisrani, Sliema,
Malta
New Zealand: Catholic Supplies (NZ) Ltd,
Wellington, New Zealand
South Africa: The Catholic Bookshop, Cape
Town, South Africa; St Augustine's
Catholic Bookshop, Port Elizabeth, South
Africa
USA: Acta, Chicago, IL, USA; Dufour
Editions Inc, Chester Springs, PA, USA;
Ignatius Press, San Francisco, CA, USA

Book Trade Association Membership:
Publishing Ireland (Foilsiú Éireann)

2780

VERTICAL EDITIONS
Unit 4a, Snaygill Industrial Estate, Skipton,
North Yorkshire BD23 2QR
Telephone: 01756 790362
Fax: 01756 798618
Email: custserv@verticaleditions.com
Web Site: www.verticaleditions.com

Personnel:
Karl Waddicor (*Publisher*)
Diane Evans (*Editor*)

*Biography & Autobiography; Sports &
Games*

Imprints, Series & ISBNs:
978 1 904091

Book Trade Association Membership:
Independent Publishers Guild

2781

VIRGIN BOOKS LTD
20 Vauxhall bridge Road, London
SW1V 2SA
Telephone: 020 7840 8400
Web Site: www.virginbooks.com

Personnel:
John Sadler (*Managing Director*)
Clare Pierotti (*Publicity Director*)
Vickie Boff (*Marketing Director*)
Han Ismail (*Home Sales Director*)
Phil Brown (*Production Director*)
Ed Faulkner (*Editorial Director – Non-Fiction
Editor*)
Adam Nevill (*Commissioning – Erotic
Fiction, Horror Editor*)
Louisa Joyner (*Editorial Director – non-
fiction Editor*)

*Audio Books; Biography & Autobiography;
Cinema, Video, TV & Radio; Cookery, Wines
& Spirits; Economics; Gay & Lesbian*

Studies; Health & Beauty; Humour;
Illustrated & Fine Editions; Military & War;
Music; Politics & World Affairs; Reference
Books, Directories & Dictionaries; Sports &
Games

Imprints, Series & ISBNs:
Black Lace (heteroerotic fiction by women):
978 0 352
Nexus (heteroerotic fiction): 978 0 352
Virgin (hardback): 978 1 85227
Virgin (paperback): 978 0 86369

Parent Company:
Virgin Group Ltd

Overseas Representation:
Australia: Random House Australia Pty Ltd,
Sydney, NSW, Australia
Canada: H. B. Fenn & Co Ltd, Bolton, Ont,
Canada
*Caribbean, South & Central America,
Middle East, Pakistan & Africa (excluding
South Africa):* Felicity Smith, Random
House Group Ltd, London, UK
*Eastern Europe, Baltic States, Israel, Belarus,
Russia, Turkey & Ukraine:* Mariann
Kenedi, Budapest, Hungary
*Germany, Austria, Norway, Denmark,
Finland:* Jörg Riekenbrauk, Cologne,
Germany
India: Random House Publishers India Pte
Ltd, New Delhi, India
Japan: Akiko Iwamoto, Tokyo, Japan
*Netherlands, Belgium, Luxembourg, France,
Switzerland:* Pauline Konink, Hilversum,
Netherlands
New Zealand: Random House New Zealand
Ltd, Auckland, New Zealand
*Philippines, Guam, Thailand, Indonesia,
Singapore, Malaysia, Hong Kong,
Taiwan, South Korea & China:*
Transworld Publishers Ltd, London, UK
South Africa: Random House South Africa
Pty Ltd, Houghton, South Africa
*Sweden, Iceland, Spain, Portugal, Gibraltar,
Italy, Malta, Cyprus, Greece:* Andrew
Wyman, Random House Group Ltd,
London, UK
USA: Macmillan, New York, NY, USA

Book Trade Association Membership:
Booksellers Association

2782

VOLTAIRE FOUNDATION LTD
University of Oxford, 99 Banbury Road,
Oxford OX2 6JX
Telephone: 01865 284600
Fax: 01865 284610
Email: email@voltaire.ox.ac.uk
Web Site: www.voltaire.ox.ac.uk

Distribution:
Marston Book Services, 160 Milton Park,
Abingdon, Oxon OX14 4YN
Telephone: 01235 465521 (Trade) &
465500 (Direct Sales)
Fax: 01235 465555 (Trade) & 465556
(Direct Sales)
Email: trade.orders@marston.co.uk &
direct.orders@marston.co.uk
Web Site: www.marston.co.uk

Personnel:
Prof Nicholas Cronk *(Director)*
Clare Fletcher *(Sales, Marketing, Publisher)*
Janet Godden *(Editorial Manager)*
Lyn Roberts *(Senior Publishing, SVEC
Manager)*
Liz Hancock *(Sales, Marketing, Rights &
Permissions, Admin Support)*

*Academic & Scholarly; Bibliography &
Library Science; Biography &
Autobiography; Electronic (Professional &
Academic); Fiction; History & Antiquarian;
Languages & Linguistics; Literature &
Criticism; Philosophy; Reference Books,
Directories & Dictionaries; Religion &
Theology*

Imprints, Series & ISBNs:
Correspondance complète de Françoise de
Graffigny: 978 0 7294
Correspondance complète de Jean Jacques
Rousseau: 978 0 7294
Correspondance complète de Pierre Bayle:
978 0 7294
Correspondance générale de La Beaumelle:
978 0 7294
Œuvres complètes de Montesquieu: 978 0
7294
Œuvres complètes de Voltaire: 978 0 7294
SVEC (Studies on Voltaire and the
Eighteenth Century): 978 0 7294
Vif Une nouvelle collection en livre de
poche: 978 0 7294

Parent Company:
University of Oxford

Overseas Representation:
France: Aux Amateurs de Livres, Paris,
France

2783

WALLFLOWER PRESS
6 Market Place, London W1W 8AF
Telephone: 020 7436 9494
Email: yoram@wallflowerpress.co.uk
Web Site: www.wallflowerpress.co.uk

Representation (UK):
Signature Book Representation, PO Box 12,
York YO1 7WD
Telephone: 01904 631320
Fax: 01904 675445
Email: admin@signaturebooks.co.uk

Personnel:
Yoram Allon *(Commissioning Editor)*
Amanda O'Boyle *(Sales & Marketing
Manager)*
Tom Cabot *(Production Manager)*
Jackie Downs *(Editorial Manager)*
Lucy Hurst *(Publicity & Marketing Manager)*

*Academic & Scholarly; Cinema, Video, TV &
Radio; Educational & Textbooks*

Imprints, Series & ISBNs:
978 1 903364, 978 1 904764, 978 1
905674, 978 1 906660

Overseas Representation:
Australia & New Zealand: Woodslane Pty
Ltd, Warriewood, NSW, Australia
Europe: Andrew Durnell Marketing Ltd,
Tunbridge Wells, UK
Middle East: Avicenna Partnership, Oxford,
UK
South East Asia: Taylor & Francis, Singapore
USA & Canada: Columbia University Press,
Irvington, NY, USA

2784

WARBURG INSTITUTE
University of London, Woburn Square,
London WC1H 0AB
Telephone: 020 7862 8949
Fax: 020 7862 8955
Email: warburg.books@sas.ac.uk
Web Site: warburg.sas.ac.uk

Personnel:
E. Witchell *(Administrative Assistant)*

*Academic & Scholarly; Archaeology;
Architecture & Design; Bibliography &
Library Science; Biography &
Autobiography; Fine Art & Art History;
History & Antiquarian; Magic & the Occult;
Philosophy; Religion & Theology*

Imprints, Series & ISBNs:
Special Publications (Warburg): 978 0
85481
Studies of the Warburg Institute: 978 0
85481
Warburg Institute Colloquia: 978 0 85481

Warburg Institute Surveys and Texts: 978 0
85481
Warburg Studies and Texts: 978 0 85481

Overseas Representation:
Italy: Nino Aragno Editore, Savigliano, Italy

2785

WARD LOCK EDUCATIONAL CO LTD
Bic Ling Kee House, 1 Christopher Road,
East Grinstead, West Sussex RH19 3BT
Telephone: 01342 318980
Fax: 01342 410980
Web Site: www.wardlockeducational.com

Personnel:
Au Bak Ling *(Chairman - Hong Kong)*
Eileen Parsons *(Company Secretary & Sales,
Rights & Permissions)*

*Biology & Zoology; Chemistry; Educational
& Textbooks; Geography & Geology;
Mathematics & Statistics; Music; Physics;
Religion & Theology*

No of Employees: 2

Imprints, Series & ISBNs:
978 0 7062

Parent Company:
Ling Kee (UK) Ltd

Associated Companies:
BLA Publishing Ltd

Overseas Representation:
Australia (KMP only): Concept Mathematics
Pty Ltd, Frankston, Vic, Australia
Canada: Bacon & Hughes Ltd, Ottawa, Ont,
Canada
Republic of Ireland: International
Educational Services, Leixlip, Republic of
Ireland

2786

WATERSIDE PRESS
Sherfield Gables, Reading Road,
Sherfield-on-Loddon, Hook, Hants
RG27 0JG
Telephone: 0845 2300 733
Fax: 0845 230 0744
Email: enquiries@watersidepress.co.uk
Web Site: www.watersidepress.co.uk

Personnel:
Bryan Gibson *(Proprietor)*
Jane Green *(Editor)*

*Academic & Scholarly; Biography &
Autobiography; Crime; Educational &
Textbooks; Electronic (Educational);
Electronic (Professional & Academic);
History & Antiquarian; Law; Reference
Books, Directories & Dictionaries; Sociology
& Anthropology*

New Titles: 14 (2009) , 10 (2010)

Imprints, Series & ISBNs:
978 1 872870, 978 1 904380, 978 1
906534

Overseas Representation:
USA: International Specialized Book
Services Inc, Portland, OR, USA

2787

PAUL WATKINS PUBLISHING
1 High Street, Donington, Lincs PE11 4TA
Telephone: 01775 821542
Email:
pwatkins@pwatkinspublishing.fsnet.co.u
k

Personnel:
Dr Shaun Tyas *(Proprietor)*

Academic & Scholarly; Architecture &

Design; Fine Art & Art History; History &
Antiquarian; Languages & Linguistics;
Nautical

New Titles: 7 (2009) , 7 (2010)
No of Employees: 1

Imprints, Series & ISBNs:
Shaun Tyas: 978 1 900289
Paul Watkins: 978 1 871615

Distributor for:
Caedmon of Whitby; English Place-Name
Society; Richard III and Yorkist History
Trust; Society for Name Studies in Britain
and Ireland

Book Trade Association Membership:
Small Press Centre

2788

WEIDENFELD & NICOLSON
[imprint of The Orion Publishing Group Ltd]
Orion House, 5 Upper St Martin's Lane,
London WC2H 9EA
Telephone: 020 7240 3444
Fax: 020 7240 4822

Trade Counter & Warehouse:
Littlehampton Book Services Ltd,
Faraday Close, Durrington, Worthing,
West Sussex BN13 3RB
Telephone: 01903 828500
Fax: 01903 828802

Personnel:
~Lisa Milton *(Managing Director)*
Alan Samson *(Publisher – Non-Fiction)*
Kirsty Dunseath *(Publishing Director –
Fiction)*
Michael Dover *(Editor-in-Chief)*
Rowland White *(Publisher – Non-Fiction)*

*Biography & Autobiography; Fiction;
Humour; Illustrated & Fine Editions;
Industry, Business & Management; Law;
Philosophy; Photography; Politics & World
Affairs; Sports & Games; Travel &
Topography*

Imprints, Series & ISBNs:
978 0 297

Parent Company:
The Orion Publishing Group Ltd

Overseas Representation:
see: The Orion Publishing Group Ltd,
London, UK

2789

JOSEPH WEINBERGER LTD
12–14 Mortimer Street, London W1T 3JJ
Telephone: 020 7580 2827
Fax: 020 7436 9616
Email: general.info@jwmail.co.uk
Web Site: www.josef-weinberger.com

Personnel:
Sean Gray *(Managing Director)*
Robert Heath *(Financial Director)*
Michael Callahan *(Plays Division Manager)*

Theatre, Drama & Dance

New Titles: 15 (2009) , 20 (2010)

Imprints, Series & ISBNs:
Dramatists Play Service Inc: 978 0 8222
Josef Weinberger Plays: 978 0 85676

Distributor for:
USA: Dramatists Play Service Inc

Overseas Representation:
Australia: Hal Leonard (Australia),
Melbourne, Vic, Australia
New Zealand: Play Bureau of New Zealand
Ltd, New Plymouth, New Zealand

Republic of Ireland & Northern Ireland:
Drama League of Ireland, Dublin,
Republic of Ireland
South Africa: Dalro (Pty) Ltd, Braamfontein,
South Africa
USA: Dramatists Play Service Inc, New York,
NY, USA

2790

WHICH? LTD
2 Marylebone Road, London NW1 4DF
Telephone: 020 7770 7000
Fax: 020 7770 7600
Email: which@which.co.uk
Web Site: www.which.co.uk

Personnel:
Angela Newton *(Head of Book Publishing)*

*Accountancy & Taxation; Guide Books;
Law; Reference Books, Directories &
Dictionaries; Vocational Training & Careers*

Imprints, Series & ISBNs:
978 1 84490

2791

THE WHITE ROW PRESS
135 Cumberland Road, Dundonald, Belfast
BT16 2BB
Telephone: 028 9087 4861
Email: info@whiterowpress.com
Web Site: www.whiterowpress.com

New Titles: 1 (2009) , 1 (2010)

Imprints, Series & ISBNs:
978 1 870132

2792

WHITING & BIRCH LTD
90 Dartmouth Road, London SE23 3HZ
Telephone: 020 8244 2421
Fax: 020 8244 2448
Email: enquiries@whitingbirch.net
Web Site: www.whitingbirch.net

Personnel:
David Whiting *(Director)*
Diana Birch *(Director)*

*Academic & Scholarly; Medical (incl. Self
Help & Alternative Medicine); Psychology &
Psychiatry; Sociology & Anthropology*

Imprints, Series & ISBNs:
978 1 86177, 978 1 871177

Overseas Representation:
USA: Ingram Publisher Services Inc,
Chambersburg, PA, USA; Lightning
Source Inc (US), Lavergne, TN, USA

2793

WHITTET BOOKS LTD
1, St John's Lane, Stansted, Essex
CM24 8JU
Telephone: 01279 815871
Fax: 01279 647564
Email: mail@whittetbooks.com
Web Site: www.whittetbooks.com

Warehouse:
BSP, BSP House, Station Road, Linton,
Cambs CB21 4NW
Telephone: 01223 894870
Fax: 01223 894871

Personnel:
George Papa *(Managing Director)*
Shirley Greenall *(Publisher)*

*Agriculture; Animal Care & Breeding;
Biology & Zoology; Gardening; Illustrated &
Fine Editions; Natural History; Veterinary
Science*

Imprints, Series & ISBNs:
978 0 905483, 978 1 873580

Parent Company:
Book Systems Plus Ltd

Overseas Representation:
USA & Canada: Diamond Farm Book
Publishers, Brighton, Canada

2794

WHITTLES PUBLISHING
Dunbeath Mill, Dunbeath, Caithness
KW6 6EG
Telephone: 01593 731333
Fax: 01593 731400
Email: info@whittlespublishing.com
Web Site: www.whittlespublishing.com

Warehouse/Distributor:
BookSource, 50 Cambuslang Road,
Glasgow G32 8NB
Telephone: 0845 370 0063
Fax: 0845 370 0064
Email: customerservice@booksource.net
Web Site: www.booksource.net

Personnel:
Dr Keith Whittles *(Publisher)*
Mrs Sue Steven *(Sales & Promotions
Manager)*
Mrs Linsey Hague *(Production Editor)*

*Academic & Scholarly; Biography &
Autobiography; Educational & Textbooks;
Engineering; Geography & Geology;
Military & War; Natural History; Nautical;
Reference Books, Directories &
Dictionaries; Scientific & Technical*

Imprints, Series & ISBNs:
978 1 84995, 978 1 870325, 978 1 904445

Distributor for:
Talisman Publishing

Overseas Representation:
*Australia, New Zealand & Papua New
Guinea:* James Bennett Pty Ltd, Belrose,
NSW, Australia
Germany, Austria & Switzerland: Missing
Link International Booksellers, Bremen,
Germany
Hong Kong, China, Taiwan & Korea: Asia
Publishers Services Ltd, Hong Kong
India: Sara Books Pvt Ltd, New Delhi, India
*Latin America, Caribbean & Sub-Saharan
Africa:* InterMedia Americana (IMA) Ltd,
London, UK
*Middle East (including Greece, Turkey &
Iran):* Avicenna Partnership, Dumfries, UK
*Singapore, Malaysia, Brunei, Philippines,
Indonesia, Thailand, Laos, Cambodia &
Vietnam:* APD Singapore Pte Ltd,
Singapore
South Africa: Book Promotions (Pty) Ltd,
South Africa

Book Trade Association Membership:
Publishing Scotland

2795

WILD GOOSE PUBLICATIONS
4th Floor, Savoy House,
140 Sauchiehall Street, Glasgow G2 3DH
Telephone: 0141 332 6292
Fax: 0141 332 1090
Email: admin@ionabooks.com
Web Site: www.ionabooks.com

Trade Orders:
BookSource, 50 Cambuslang Road,
Glasgow G32 8NB
Email: orders@booksource.net
Web Site: www.booksource.net

Personnel:
Sandra Kramer *(Publishing Manager)*
Alex O'Neill *(Assistant Publishing Manager
(Marketing))*

Jane Riley *(Production)*
Lorna Rae Sutton *(Publishing Officer
(Marketing))*
Neil Paynter *(Project Editor)*

Music; Religion & Theology

New Titles: 9 (2009) , 10 (2010)
No of Employees: 4

Imprints, Series & ISBNs:
978 0 947988, 978 1 901557, 978 1
905010

Parent Company:
The Iona Community

Overseas Representation:
Australia & New Zealand: Willow
Connection Pty Ltd, Brookvale, NSW,
Australia
Canada: Novalis Inc, Toronto, Ont, Canada
New Zealand: Pleroma Christian Supplies,
Otane, Central Hawkes Bay, New Zealand
USA: GIA Publications, Chicago, IL, USA

Book Trade Association Membership:
Independent Publishers Guild

2796

**WILEY BLACKWELL PUBLISHING
LTD**
9600 Garsington Road, Oxford OX4 2DP
Telephone: 01865 776865
Fax: 01865 476774
Email:
general@oxonblackwellpublishing.com
Web Site: www.blackwellpublishing.com

*Academic & Scholarly; Educational &
Textbooks*

Book Trade Association Membership:
Publishers Association

2797

JOHN WILEY & SONS LTD
The Atrium, Southern Gate, Chichester,
West Sussex PO19 8SQ
Telephone: 01243 779777
Fax: 01243 775878
Web Site: www.wiley.com

European Distribution Centre:
Southern Cross Trading Estate,
1 Oldlands Way, Bognor Regis, West Sussex
PO22 9SA
Telephone: 01243 779777
Fax: 01243 820250
Email: customer@wiley.com
Web Site: www.wiley.com

STMS Publishing (in the UK):
John Wiley & Sons, 9600 Garsington Road,
Oxford OX4 2DQ
Telephone: 01865 776868
Web Site: www.wiley.com

Personnel:
C. J. Dicks *(Managing Director, International
Finance & Operations)*
P. Kisray *(Vice-President, International
Development)*
C. Nobbs *(Vice-President, Distribution,
Europe, Middle East & Africa)*

*Academic & Scholarly; Accountancy &
Taxation; Agriculture; Animal Care &
Breeding; Antiques & Collecting;
Archaeology; Architecture & Design;
Atlases & Maps; Aviation; Biography &
Autobiography; Biology & Zoology;
Chemistry; Children's Books; Computer
Science; Cookery, Wines & Spirits; Do-It-
Yourself; Economics; Educational &
Textbooks; Electronic (Educational);
Electronic (Professional & Academic);
Engineering; Environment & Development
Studies; Gardening; Geography & Geology;
Guide Books; Health & Beauty; History &*

*Antiquarian; Humour; Industry, Business &
Management; Languages & Linguistics;
Literature & Criticism; Magic & the Occult;
Mathematics & Statistics; Medical (incl. Self
Help & Alternative Medicine); Military &
War; Music; Natural History; Philosophy;
Photography; Physics; Poetry; Politics &
World Affairs; Psychology & Psychiatry;
Reference Books, Directories &
Dictionaries; Religion & Theology; Scientific
& Technical; Sociology & Anthropology;
Sports & Games; Travel & Topography;
Veterinary Science; Vocational Training &
Careers*

Imprints, Series & ISBNs:
978 0 470, 978 0 471

Parent Company:
USA: John Wiley & Sons Inc

Associated Companies:
Capstone Publishing Ltd; Inpharm-Internet
Services Ltd; Whurr Publishers Ltd; Wiley
Distribution Services Ltd; Wiley Heyden
Ltd; Wiley Interface Ltd; Wiley Pharmafile
Ltd; Wiley-Blackwell Ltd
Germany: Wiley-VCH Verlag GmbH

Distributor for:
USA: California University Press; Columbia
University Press; Harvard University
Press; Johns Hopkins University Press;
Loeb Classical Library; The MIT Press; W.
W. Norton & Co Ltd; O'Reilly UK Ltd;
Princeton University Press; Sybex
International Corp; The University of
Chicago Press; Yale University Press

Overseas Representation:
Australia: John Wiley & Sons Australia Ltd,
Milton, Qld, Australia
Canada: John Wiley & Sons Canada Ltd,
Etobicoke, Ont, Canada
Japan: John Wiley & Sons Ltd, Tokyo, Japan
*Mexico & Latin America, Pakistan & North
Africa:* John Wiley & Sons Inc, Hoboken,
NJ, USA
Singapore & Asia: John Wiley & Sons (Asia)
Pte Ltd, Singapore

Book Trade Association Membership:
Publishers Association; Booksellers
Association; Educational Publishers
Council; International Group of Scientific,
Medical & Technical Publishers

2798

WILLOW ISLAND EDITIONS
41 Water Lane, Middlestown, Wakefield,
West Yorkshire WF4 4PX
Telephone: 01924 270723
Email: richard@willowisland.co.uk
Web Site: www.willowisland.co.uk

Personnel:
Richard Bell *(Contact)*

*Crafts & Hobbies; Gardening; Guide Books;
Natural History; Travel & Topography*

Imprints, Series & ISBNs:
978 1 902467

2799

NEIL WILSON PUBLISHING LTD
O/2 19 Netherton Avenue, Glasgow
G13 1BQ
Telephone: 0141 954 8007
Fax: 0560 150 4806
Email: info@nwp.co.uk
Web Site: www.nwp.co.uk

**Distribution, Sales Ledger & Trade
Orders:**
BookSource, 50 Cambuslang Road,
Glasgow G32 5NB
Telephone: 0845 370 0067
Fax: 0845 370 0068

Email: orders@booksource.net
Web Site: www.booksource.net

Representation (Scotland):
Don Morrison

Personnel:
Neil Wilson *(Managing Director, Sales, Rights & Permissions)*

Biography & Autobiography; Cookery, Wines & Spirits; Crime; Guide Books; History & Antiquarian; Humour; Military & War; Music; Nautical; Travel & Topography

New Titles: 7 (2009) , 3 (2010)
No of Employees: 1
Annual Turnover: £100,000

Imprints, Series & ISBNs:
978 1 897784, 978 1 903238, 978 1 906476
11:9
The Angel's Share
The In Pinn
The Vital Spark

Overseas Representation:
Republic of Ireland: Geoff Bryan, Dublin, Republic of Ireland
USA: Interlink Publishing Group Inc, Northampton, MA, USA

Book Trade Association Membership:
Publishing Scotland

2800

WINDHORSE PUBLICATIONS
169 Mill Road, Cambridge CB1 3AN
Telephone: 01223 911997
Email: info@windhorsepublications.com
Web Site:
www.windhorsepublications.com

UK Trade Orders:
BookSource, 50 Cambuslang Road, Cambuslang, Glasgow G32 8NB
Telephone: 0845 370 0063
Fax: 0845 370 0064
Email: customerservice@booksource.net
Web Site: www.booksource.net

Personnel:
Caroline Jestaz *(General Manager)*
Sarah Ryan *(Publishing Assistant)*
Peter Joseph *(Publishing Director)*

Biography & Autobiography; Medical (incl. Self Help & Alternative Medicine); Philosophy; Religion & Theology

New Titles: 6 (2009) , 10 (2010)
No of Employees: 4

Imprints, Series & ISBNs:
978 0 904766, 978 1 899579

Overseas Representation:
Asia: Horizon Books Pte Ltd, Singapore
Australia & New Zealand: Windhorse Books, Newtown, NSW, Australia
South Africa: Stephan Phillips (Pty) Ltd, Cape Town, South Africa
USA: Consortium Book Sales & Distribution Inc, St Paul, MN, USA

2801

WIT PRESS
Ashurst Lodge, Ashurst, Southampton, Hampshire SO40 7AA
Telephone: 023 8029 3223
Fax: 023 8029 2853
Email: witpress@witpress.com
Web Site: www.witpress.com

Personnel:
Prof. C. A. Brebbia *(Chairman)*
David Anderson *(Chief Executive Officer)*
B. Privett *(Production Manager)*
Ms Lorraine Carter *(Sales Co-ordinator)*

Academic & Scholarly; Archaeology; Architecture & Design; Biology & Zoology; Computer Science; Electronic (Professional & Academic); Engineering; Environment & Development Studies; Geography & Geology; Industry, Business & Management; Mathematics & Statistics; Medical (incl. Self Help & Alternative Medicine); Scientific & Technical; Transport

New Titles: 45 (2009) , 45 (2010)
No of Employees: 11

Imprints, Series & ISBNs:
978 0 905451, 978 1 84564, 978 1 85312

Parent Company:
USA: Computational Mechanics International Ltd

Book Trade Association Membership:
LAPSLD

2802

WITHERBY SEAMANSHIP INTERNATIONAL
4 Dunlop Square, Deans, Livingston, West Lothian EH54 8SB
Telephone: 01506 463227
Fax: 01506 468999
Email: info@emailws.com
Web Site: www.witherbyseamanship.com

Personnel:
Iain Macneil *(Managing Director)*
Kat Heathcote *(Director)*
Stewart Heney *(General Manager)*
Alison Hunter Gordon *(Personal Assistant to Director)*

Law; Nautical; Reference Books, Directories & Dictionaries; Transport; Travel & Topography

New Titles: 30 (2009) , 35 (2010)
No of Employees: 30
Annual Turnover: £3M

Imprints, Series & ISBNs:
978 0 900886, 978 0 948691, 978 1 85609

Distributor for:
Chartered Institute of Loss Adjustors; Chemical Distribution Institute; Institute of Chartered Shipbrokers; Institute of Risk Management; Intercargo; International Association of Classification Societies; International Institute of Marine Surveying; International Marine Pilots Association; International Maritime Organisation; International Tanker Owners' Pollution Federation; INTERTANKO; Nautical Institute; Oil Companies International Marine Forum; Skuld; Society of International Gas Tanker & Terminal Operators

Overseas Representation:
Australia: Boat Books, St Kilda, Vic, Australia
Belgium: Bogerd Martin NV
Canada: Marine Press of Canada
Denmark: Iver Weilbach & Co A/S
Greece: Vanos SA
Hong Kong: Hong Kong Ships Supplies Co, Hong Kong
India: C & C Marine Combine
Italy: C.A.I.M. ARL
Japan: Cornes & Co, Tokyo, Japan
Norway: Nautisk Forlag A/S
Singapore: DPM Singapore Pte Ltd; E W Liner Charts And Publications; Motion Smith; Nautisk Forlag AS (Singapore)
South Korea: Korea Ocean Development
Taiwan: Hong Yunn Sea Professional Co Ltd
USA: New York Nautical, New York, USA

Book Trade Association Membership:
Publishing Scotland; Independent Publishers Guild

2803

WOLTERS KLUWER HEALTH (P & E) LTD
250 Waterloo Road, London SE1 8RD
Telephone: 020 7981 0500
Fax: 020 7981 0565
Email: enquiry@lww.co.uk
Web Site: www.lww.co.uk

Orders to:
NBN International, Estover Road, Plymouth PL6 7PY
Telephone: 01752 202301
Fax: 01752 202331
Email: lww.orders@nbninternational.com
Web Site: www.nbninternational.com

Personnel:
Mrs Linda Albin *(Regional Director, Europe)*
Mr Andrew Davis *(Marketing Services Director)*
Mr Carlos Davis *(Vice-President & General Manager, International)*
Ms Sharon Zinner *(Senior International Director of Marketing & Business Development)*
Mr John Youens *(Sales Director: Middle East, Africa & Latin America)*
Ms Rachel Hendrick *(Acquisitions Editor)*
Ms Gemma Gillen *(Senior Sales Co-ordinator)*
Ms Alison Major *(Marketing Executive-Medical Education, Health Professions, Anatomical Charts & Nursing)*
Mr Daniel Raphael *(Marketing Executive-Clinical)*
Ms Jessica Buckingham *(Marketing Executive- Exhibitions)*

Academic & Scholarly; Educational & Textbooks; Electronic (Professional & Academic); Medical (incl. Self Help & Alternative Medicine); Psychology & Psychiatry; Reference Books, Directories & Dictionaries; Scientific & Technical

New Titles: 400 (2009) , 400 (2010)

Imprints, Series & ISBNs:
AmirSys: 978 1 931884
Blackwell's (transferred list): 978 1 4051
Facts & Comparisons: 978 1 5121, 978 1 57439
Lippincott Raven: 978 0 316, 978 0 397
Lippincott Williams & Wilkins: 978 0 7817, 978 1 4051, 978 1 4511, 978 1 58255, 978 1 60547, 978 1 60831, 978 1 60913
Lippincott Williams & Wilkins – Spanish Language: 978 84 96921
Springhouse: 978 0 7817, 978 1 58255
Williams & Wilkins: 978 0 316, 978 0 683

Parent Company:
Netherlands: Wolters Kluwer

Associated Companies:
USA: Lippincott Williams & Wilkins / Wolters Kluwer Health (Professional & Education); Ovid / Wolter Kluwer Health (Market Research); Wolters Kluwer Health

Distributor for:
USA: AmirSys

Overseas Representation:
Eastern Europe: Jacek Lewinson, Publisher's Agents, Warsaw, Poland
Scandinavia: Colin Flint Ltd, Cambridge, UK
Spain: Lippincott Williams & Wilkins / Wolters Kluwer Health (Professional & Education), Barcelona, Spain

Book Trade Association Membership:
Publishers Association

2804

THE WOMEN'S PRESS
27 Goodge Street, London W1T 2LD
Telephone: 020 7636 3992

Fax: 020 7637 1866
Email: david@the-womens-press.com
Web Site: www.the-womens-press.com

Warehouse:
NBN International Ltd, Estover Road, Plymouth PL6 7PY
Telephone: 01752 202300
Fax: 01752 202330
Email: control@nbninternational.com
Web Site: www.nbninternational.com

Personnel:
David Elliott *(Director)*

Biography & Autobiography; Crime; Fiction; Gay & Lesbian Studies; Gender Studies; Health & Beauty; Literature & Criticism; Politics & World Affairs; Psychology & Psychiatry; Reference Books, Directories & Dictionaries

Overseas Representation:
Africa, Eastern Europe, Caribbean & South America: InterMedia Americana (IMA) Ltd, London, UK
Australia: The Scribo Group, Frenchs Forest, NSW, Australia
Europe: Ted Dougherty, London, UK
USA: Interlink Publishing Group Inc, Northampton, MA, USA

2805

WOODHEAD PUBLISHING LTD
[incorporating Chandos Publishing]
Abington Hall, Granta Park, Great Abington, Cambridge CB21 6AH
Telephone: 01223 891358
Fax: 01223 893694
Email: custserv@woodhead-publishing.com
Web Site: www.woodheadpublishing.com

Warehouse & Distribution:
Combined Book Services, Units I/K, Paddock Wood Distribution Centre, Paddock Wood, Tonbridge, Kent TN12 6UU
Telephone: 01892 837171
Fax: 01892 837272
Email: (as above)

Personnel:
Martin Woodhead *(Managing Director)*
R. Burleigh *(Finance Director)*
Francis Dodds *(Editorial Director)*
Neil MacLeod *(Marketing Manager)*
Mary Campbell *(Production Manager)*
Sarah Whitworth *(Commissioning Editor)*
Kathryn Picking *(Commissioning Editor)*
Jess Rowley *(Commissioning Editor)*
Sheril Leich *(Commissioning Editor)*
Cliff Elwell *(Commissioning Editor)*
Laura Bunney *(Commissioning Editor)*
Ian Borthwick *(Commissioning Editor)*
Glyn Jones *(Publisher, Chandos Publishing)*

Bibliography & Library Science; Electronic (Professional & Academic); Engineering; Environment & Development Studies; Industry, Business & Management; Law; Mathematics & Statistics; Scientific & Technical

New Titles: 120 (2009) , 135 (2010)
No of Employees: 34
Annual Turnover: £3M

Imprints, Series & ISBNs:
Abington Publishing: 978 1 85573
Chandos Publishing: 978 1 84334
Gresham Books: 978 1 85573
Woodhead Publishing: 978 1 84569, 978 1 85573

Distributor for:
Germany: Beuth (The German Standards Institute); Stahleisen (The German Iron & Steel Institute); VDI (The Association of German Engineers)

Overseas Representation:
China: Ian Taylor & Associates, Beijing, P. R. of China
Eastern Europe & Russia: Dr László Horváth Publishers Representative, Budapest, Hungary
Germany, Austria & Switzerland: Bernd Feldmann, Oranienburg, Germany
Greece, Middle East, Turkey, Cyprus & Malta: Avicenna Partnership, Oxford, UK
India: Sara Books Pvt Ltd, New Delhi, India
Iran: Farhad Maftoon, Tehran, Iran
Italy, Spain, Portugal & France: Flavio Marcello Publishers' Agents & Consultants, Padua, Italy
Japan: Ben Kato, Tokyo, Japan; United Publishers Services Ltd, Tokyo, Japan
Korea: Information & Culture Korea (ICK), Seoul, Republic of Korea
Mexico, Central & South America: Cranbury International LLC, Montpelier, VT, USA
Netherlands, Belgium & Luxembourg: Netwerk Academic Book Agency, Rotterdam, Netherlands
Nigeria: Bounty Books, Ibadan, Nigeria
Pakistan: Tahir M. Lodhi, Lahore, Pakistan
Scandinavia: Jan Norbye, Ølstykke, Denmark
South Africa: Academic Marketing Services, Johannesburg, South Africa
South East Asia: APAC Publishers Services Pte Ltd, Singapore

Book Trade Association Membership:
International Group of Scientific, Medical & Technical Publishers; Independent Publishers Guild

2806

WORDSWORTH EDITIONS LTD
8b East Street, Ware, Herts SG12 9HJ
Telephone: 01920 465167
Fax: 01920 462267
Email: enquiries@wordsworth-editions.com
Web Site: www.wordsworth-editions.com

Personnel:
Helen Trayler *(Managing Director)*
Derek Wright *(Finance Director)*

Children's Books; Fiction; Literature & Criticism; Philosophy; Poetry; Reference Books, Directories & Dictionaries

New Titles: 22 (2009) , 29 (2010)
No of Employees: 3
Annual Turnover: £2M

Imprints, Series & ISBNs:
978 1 84022, 978 1 85326

Overseas Representation:
Australia & Papua New Guinea: Peribo Pty Ltd, Mount Kuring-Gai, NSW, Australia
Czech Republic: Bohemian Ventures sro, Prague, Czech Republic
Germany & Austria: Buchvertrieb Blank GmbH, Vierkirchen, Germany
India: OM Book Services, Delhi, India
Malta & Gozo: Audio Visual Centre Ltd, Sliema, Malta
Poland: Top Mark Centre, Warsaw, Poland
Romania: Depositol De Carte Distribute, Bucharest, Romania
Slovak Republic: Slovak Ventures sro, Nitra, Slovakia
Spain: Ribera Libros, SL, Arrigorriaga, Spain
USA: L. B. May & Associates, Knoxville, TN, USA

2807

WORLD MICROFILMS
PO Box 35488, St John's Wood, London NW8 6WD
Telephone: 020 7586 4499
Email: microworld@ndirect.co.uk
Web Site: www.microworld.uk.com, www.pidgeondigital.com

Personnel:
S. C. Albert *(Director)*

Academic & Scholarly; Architecture & Design; Cinema, Video, TV & Radio; History & Antiquarian

Imprints, Series & ISBNs:
978 1 85035

Distributor for:
UK: Masters of Architecture; Pidgeon Digital at www.pidgeondigital.com

2808

WORTH PRESS LTD
34 South End, Bassingbourn, Herts SG8 5NJ
Telephone: 01763 248075
Fax: 01763 248155
Email: info@worthpress.co.uk
Web Site: www.worthpress.co.uk

Warehouse:
Antony Rowe Ltd, Units 3 & 4, Pegasus Way, Bowerhill, Melksham SN12 6TR
Telephone: 01225 703691
Fax: 01225 704518

Personnel:
Ken Webb *(Contact)*
Rupert Webb *(Contact)*

Architecture & Design; Aviation; Fiction; Literature & Criticism; Military & War; Religion & Theology

New Titles: 10 (2009) , 10 (2010)
No of Employees: 5

Imprints, Series & ISBNs:
978 1 84931, 978 1 903025

Overseas Representation:
Asia: John Beaufoy, Oxford, UK
Europe: Cristina Galimberti, Bristol, UK
Scandinavia: Anglo-Nordic Books, Godalming, UK

2809

XPL PUBLISHING
99 Hatfield Road, St Albans, Herts AL1 4EG
Telephone: 0870 143 2569
Fax: 0845 456 6385
Email: sales@xplpublishing.com
Web Site: www.xplpublishing.com

Personnel:
Andrew Griffin *(Managing Director)*

Academic & Scholarly; Accountancy & Taxation; Industry, Business & Management; Law; Medical (incl. Self Help & Alternative Medicine)

Imprints, Series & ISBNs:
978 1 85811

Parent Company:
Richard Griffin (1820) Ltd

Overseas Representation:
Hong Kong: Bloomsbury Books Ltd, Hong Kong
Republic of Ireland: Brookside Publishing Services, Dublin, Republic of Ireland
USA: International Specialized Book Services Inc, Portland, OR, USA

Book Trade Association Membership:
Independent Publishers Guild

2810

Y LOLFA CYF
Hen Swyddfa'r Heddlu, Talybont, Ceredigion SY24 5HE
Telephone: 01970 832304
Fax: 01970 832782

Email: ylolfa@ylolfa.com
Web Site: www.ylolfa.com

Personnel:
Garmon Gruffudd *(Director)*
Sonia Hughes *(Administrator)*
Lefi Gruffudd *(Editor)*
Morgan Tomos *(Marketing)*
Paul Williams *(Production)*

Biography & Autobiography; Children's Books; Cookery, Wines & Spirits; Crafts & Hobbies; Fiction; Guide Books; Humour; Languages & Linguistics; Music; Poetry; Politics & World Affairs; Sports & Games

New Titles: 80 (2009) , 85 (2010)
No of Employees: 20
Annual Turnover: £1.1M

Imprints, Series & ISBNs:
Alcemi
Dinas
Y Lolfa: 978 0 86243, 978 0 904864

Book Trade Association Membership:
Union of Welsh Publishers & Booksellers

2811

YALE UNIVERSITY PRESS LONDON
47 Bedford Square, London WC1B 3DP
Telephone: 020 7079 4900
Fax: 020 7079 4901
Web Site: www.yalebooks.co.uk

Warehouse & Fulfilment:
John Wiley & Sons Ltd, Distribution Centre, Shripney Road, Bognor Regis, West Sussex PO22 9SA
Telephone: 01243 829121
Fax: 01243 820250

Personnel:
Robert Baldock *(Managing Director)*
Kate Pocock *(Sales & Marketing Director)*
Gillian Malpass *(Art & Architecture Publisher)*
Sally Salvesen *(Decorative Arts Publisher)*
Heather McCallum *(Trade Books Publisher)*
Katie Harris *(Publicity Manager)*
Charlotte Stafford *(Promotion & Direct Mail Manager)*
Anne Bihan *(Head of Rights)*
Andrew Jarmain *(Sales Manager)*
Stephen Kent *(Production & Design Manager)*
Donal Burke *(Accountant)*
Phoebe Clapham *(Politics, Economics & Current Affairs Editor)*

Academic & Scholarly; Archaeology; Architecture & Design; Biography & Autobiography; Economics; Fashion & Costume; Fine Art & Art History; Gender Studies; History & Antiquarian; Illustrated & Fine Editions; Languages & Linguistics; Military & War; Music; Natural History; Philosophy; Photography; Politics & World Affairs; Religion & Theology; Theatre, Drama & Dance

Imprints, Series & ISBNs:
978 0 300

Parent Company:
USA: Yale University Press

Associated Companies:
Yale Representation Ltd

Overseas Representation:
Africa (excluding Southern Africa & Nigeria): Kelvin van Hasselt Publishing Services, Briningham, Norfolk, UK
Austria, Germany, Italy & Switzerland: Uwe Lüdemann, Berlin, Germany
Benelux, Denmark, Finland, France, Iceland, Norway & Sweden: Fred Hermans, Bovenkarspel, Netherlands
Hong Kong, China & Philippines: Asia Publishers Services Ltd, Hong Kong

India: S. Janakiraman, Book Marketing Services, Chennai, India
Iran: Farhad Maftoon, Tehran, Iran
Middle East: International Publishers Representatives (IPR) Ltd, Nicosia, Cyprus
Nigeria: Bounty Books, Ibadan, Nigeria
Pakistan: Anwer Iqbal, Book Bird Publishers Representatives, Lahore, Pakistan
Poland, Czech Republic, Croatia, Hungary, Slovakia & Slovenia: Ewa Ledóchowicz, Konstancin-Jeziorna, Poland
Republic of Ireland & Northern Ireland: Robert Towers, Monkstown, Co Dublin, Republic of Ireland
Singapore, Malaysia, Brunei & Indonesia: APD Singapore Pte Ltd, Singapore
Southern Africa: Book Promotions Pty Ltd, Diep River, South Africa
Spain & Portugal: Chris Humphrys, Gaucin, Spain
USA, Central & South America, Mexico, Canada, Australia, New Zealand, Japan, Korea & Taiwan: Yale University Press, New Haven, CT, USA

Book Trade Association Membership:
Independent Publishers Guild

2812

YORE PUBLICATIONS
12 The Furrows, Harefield, Middx UB9 6AT
Telephone: 01895 823404
Fax: 01895 823404r2865
Email: fay.twydell@blueyonder.co.uk
Web Site: www.yore.demon.co.uk/index.html

Personnel:
Dave Twydell *(Partner)*
Fay Twydell *(Partner)*
Kara Matthews *(Typist/Secretary)*

Sports & Games

New Titles: 8 (2009) , 6 (2010)

Imprints, Series & ISBNs:
978 1 874427

2813

ZAMBEZI PUBLISHING LTD
22 Second Avenue, Camels Head, Plymouth, Devon PL2 2EQ
Telephone: 01752 367300
Fax: 01752 350453
Email: info@zampub.com
Web Site: www.zampub.com

Business:
PO Box 221, Plymouth, Devon PL2 2YJ
Telephone: 01752 367300
Fax: 01752 350453
Email: (as above)
Web Site: (as above)

Personnel:
Sasha Fenton *(Chief Executive Officer)*
Jan Budkowski *(Managing Director)*

Industry, Business & Management; Magic & the Occult; Medical (incl. Self Help & Alternative Medicine)

Imprints, Series & ISBNs:
978 0 9533478, 978 1 903065

Overseas Representation:
Europe: Gardners Books Ltd, Eastbourne, UK
USA & Rest of the World: Sterling Publishing Co Inc, New York, NY, USA

Book Trade Association Membership:
PMA (USA)

2814

ZED BOOKS LTD
7 Cynthia Street, London N1 9JF
Telephone: 020 7837 4014 & 8466

Fax: 020 7833 3960
Web Site: www.zedbooks.co.uk

Distribution:
NBN International Ltd, Estover, Plymouth
PL6 7PZ
Telephone: 01752 202301
Fax: 01752 202331

**Trade Representation - UK & Republic of
Ireland:**
Compass Academic
Telephone: 020 8994 6477
Email: ca@compass-academic.co.uk
Web Site: www.academic.compass-
booksales.co.uk/academic

Personnel:
Julian Hosie *(Marketing Director)*
Margaret Ling *(Finance & Company
    Secretary)*
Tamsine O'Riordan *(Senior Commissioning
    Editor)*
Ken Barlow *(Commissioning Editor)*
Ruvani de Silva *(Publicity Officer)*
Ruben Mootoosamy *(Sales Executive)*
Jakob Horstmann *(Production Editor)*
Anneberth Lux *(Sales Manager)*
Dan Och *(Production Manager)*
Federico Campagna *(Rights Executive)*

*Academic & Scholarly; Economics;
Environment & Development Studies;
Gender Studies; Politics & World Affairs;
Sociology & Anthropology*

New Titles: 46 (2009) , 48 (2010)
No of Employees: 10
Annual Turnover: £1.2M

Imprints, Series & ISBNs:
978 0 86232, 978 0 905762, 978 1 84277,
978 1 84813, 978 1 85649

Overseas Representation:
Australia & New Zealand: Palgrave
    Macmillan, South Yarra, Vic, Australia
Bangladesh: The University Press Ltd,
    Dhaka, Bangladesh
Canada: Fernwood Books Ltd, Halifax, NS,
    Canada
Fiji: University Book Centre, Suva, Fiji
Germany: Missing Link International
    Booksellers, Bremen, Germany
Ghana: EPP Books Services Ltd, Accra,
    Ghana
Hong Kong: Hong Kong University Press,
    Hong Kong
India: Madhyam International, New Delhi,
    India
Japan: Far Eastern Booksellers, Tokyo, Japan
Lebanon: Levant Distributors, Beirut,
    Lebanon
Malaysia: Gerakbudaya Enterprise,
    Selangor, Malaysia
Nepal: Everest Media International,
    Kathmandu, Nepal
Singapore: Publishers Marketing Services
    Pte Ltd, Singapore
Uganda: Aristoc Booklex Ltd, Kampala,
    Uganda

USA: Palgrave Macmillan, New York, NY,
    USA
West Africa: EPP Books Services Ltd, Accra,
    Ghana

Book Trade Association Membership:
Independent Publishers Guild

2815 ■■■■■■■■

ZERO TO TEN
Evans Publishing Group, Suite 1.3,
Coomb House, 7 St John's Road, Isleworth,
Middx TW7 6NH
Telephone: 020 8758 9777
Fax: 020 8758 9888
Email: tradesales@zerototen.co.uk
Web Site: www.evansbooks.co.uk

Personnel:
Andrew Macmillan *(Sales Director)*

Children's Books

Imprints, Series & ISBNs:
Cherrytree: 978 1 84234
Evans: 978 0 237
Zero to Ten: 978 1 84089

Associated Companies:
Kenya: Evans Brothers (Kenya) Ltd
Nigeria: Evans Brothers (Nigeria Publishers)
    Ltd

Sierra Leone: Evans Brothers (Sierra Leone)
    Ltd

Book Trade Association Membership:
Educational Publishers Council

2816 ■■■■■■■■

ZYMURGY PUBLISHING
Hoults Estate, Walker Road,
Newcastle upon Tyne NE6 2HL
Telephone: 0191 276 2425
Fax: 0191 276 2425
Email:
ZymurgyPublishing@googlemail.com
Web Site: Zymurgypublishing.co.uk

Personnel:
Martin Ellis *(Publisher)*

*Biography & Autobiography; Children's
Books; Gardening; Health & Beauty;
Humour; Illustrated & Fine Editions; Music;
Natural History; Photography*

New Titles: 2 (2009) , 3 (2010)

Imprints, Series & ISBNs:
978 1 903506

Book Trade Association Membership:
Independent Publishers Guild; Publishers
Publicity Circle

3   Packagers

3001 ▬▬

ALBION PRESS LTD
Spring Hill, Idbury, Oxon OX7 6RU
Telephone: 01993 831094

Personnel:
Emma Bradford *(Managing Director)*
Neil Philip *(Editorial Director)*

Children's Books

3002 ▬▬

AMBER BOOKS LTD
Bradley's Close, 74–77 White Lion Street,
London N1 9PF
Telephone: 020 7520 7600
Fax: 020 7520 7606 & 7607
Email: enquiries@amberbooks.co.uk
Web Site: www.amberbooks.co.uk

Personnel:
Stasz Gnych *(Managing Director)*
Sara Ballard *(Rights Director)*
Peter Thompson *(Head of Production)*
Charles Catton *(Publishing Manager)*

*Animal Care & Breeding; Atlases & Maps;
Aviation; Crafts & Hobbies; Crime; Fashion
& Costume; History & Antiquarian; Military
& War; Nautical; Reference Books,
Directories & Dictionaries; Sports & Games;
Transport*

New Titles: 55 (2009) , 55 (2010)
No of Employees: 16

Imprints, Series & ISBNs:
978 1 906626, 978 1 907446

Book Trade Association Membership:
Book Packagers Association

3003 ▬▬

AMOLIBROS
Loundshay Manor Cottage,
Preston Bowyer, Milverton, Taunton,
Somerset TA4 1QF
Telephone: 01823 401527
Fax: 01823 401527
Email: amolibros@aol.com
Web Site: www.amolibros.co.uk

Trade Enquiries & Orders:
Gardners Books, 1 Whittle Drive,
Eastbourne BN23 6QH
Telephone: 01323 521555
Fax: 01323 521666

Personnel:
Jane Tatam *(Managing Consultant)*

Academic & Scholarly; Biography &
*Autobiography; Biology & Zoology;
Children's Books; Fiction; Gardening;
Geography & Geology; History &
Antiquarian; Literature & Criticism; Magic &
the Occult; Medical (incl. Self Help &
Alternative Medicine); Music; Nautical;
Philosophy; Physics; Poetry; Politics & World
Affairs; Sports & Games; Theatre, Drama &
Dance; Travel & Topography*

3004 ▬▬

ANNO DOMINI PUBLISHING (ADPS)
Book House, Orchard Mews,
18 High Street, Tring, Herts HP23 5AH
Telephone: 0845 868 1333
Email: info@ad-publishing.com
Web Site: www.ad-publishing.com

Children's Books; Religion & Theology

3005 ▬▬

BENDER RICHARDSON WHITE
PO Box 266, Uxbridge UB9 5NX
Telephone: 01895 832444
Fax: 01895 835213
Email: brw@brw.co.uk
Web Site: www.brw.co.uk

Personnel:
Lionel Bender *(Editorial Director)*
Kim Richardson *(Sales & Production
Director)*
Ben White *(Art & Design Director)*

*Biology & Zoology; Children's Books;
Educational & Textbooks; Natural History;
Reference Books, Directories &
Dictionaries; Religion & Theology*

3006 ▬▬

BLA PUBLISHING LTD
1 Christopher Road, East Grinstead,
West Sussex RH19 3BT
Telephone: 01342 318980
Fax: 01342 410980
Email: eileen@wleducat.freeserve.co.uk

Personnel:
Au Bak Ling *(Chairman)*
Eileen Parsons *(Company Secretary, Sales,
Rights & Permissions)*

*Antiques & Collecting; Aviation; Biology &
Zoology; Chemistry; Children's Books;
Computer Science; Gardening; Medical
(incl. Self Help & Alternative Medicine);
Military & War; Music; Natural History;
Nautical; Physics; Reference Books,
Directories & Dictionaries; Religion &
Theology*

No of Employees: 2

Imprints, Series & ISBNs:
Thames Head

Parent Company:
Ling Kee (UK) Ltd

Associated Companies:
Ward Lock Educational Co Ltd

3007 ▬▬

BLUE BEYOND BOOKS
1 Paget Road, Ipswich IP1 3RP
Telephone: 01473 423247
Fax: 01473 214096
Email: martin.spettigue@virgin.net

Personnel:
Martin Spettigue *(Manager)*
Mark Thomas *(Sales Representative)*
Nelly Coudoa *(Sales Representative)*
Hita Hirons *(Sales Representative)*

*Magic & the Occult; Music; Philosophy;
Poetry; Religion & Theology*

Associated Companies:
USA: Aum Publications; McKeever
Publishing

Distributor for:
USA: Aum Publications; McKeever
Publishing

Overseas Representation:
Australia: Wisdom's Delight, Brisbane, Qld,
Australia
Canada: Peace Publishing, Ottawa, Ont,
Canada
France: Editions Sri Chinmey, Paris, France
Germany: The Golden Shore, Nurnberg,
Germany
USA: Heart-Light Distributors, Seattle, WA,
USA

3008 ▬▬

BOOKPOWER
[formerly ELST]
120 Pentonville Road, London N1 9JN
Telephone: 020 7843 1938
Fax: 020 7837 6348
Email: BookPower@mistral.co.uk
Web Site: www.BookPower.org

Personnel:
Valerie Teague *(Chief Executive)*
Jamie Sehmer *(Trustee, Treasurer)*
Clive Bradley *(Chairman)*

*Academic & Scholarly; Accountancy &
Taxation; Animal Care & Breeding; Biology
& Zoology; Computer Science; Economics;
Educational & Textbooks; Engineering;
Industry, Business & Management; Medical*
*(incl. Self Help & Alternative Medicine);
Scientific & Technical; Veterinary Science;
Vocational Training & Careers*

New Titles: 1 (2009) , 8 (2010)
No of Employees: 1

Imprints, Series & ISBNs:
BookPower (formerly ELST)
ELST

Associated Companies:
ELST (Educational Low-Priced Sponsored
Textbooks)

Overseas Representation:
Ghana: Gibrine Adam, EPP Book Services
Ltd, Accra, Ghana
India: Vinod Vasishtha, Viva Group, New
Delhi, India
Kenya: Jimmi Makotsi, Acacia Publishers,
Nairobi, Kenya
Nigeria: Michael Adewoye, Jasper Books,
Surulere, Lagos, Nigeria
Pakistan: British Council, Karachi, Pakistan
Sri Lanka: Pitraban Books, Colombo, Sri
Lanka
Zimbabwe: Maureen Stewart, British
Council, Bulawayo, Zimbabwe

3009 ▬▬

BROWN WELLS & JACOBS LTD
2 Vermont Road, London SE19 3SR
Telephone: 020 8653 7670
Fax: 020 8653 7774
Email: graham@bwj-ltd.com
Web Site: www.bwj.org

Personnel:
Graham Brown *(Managing Director, Design,
Sales & Production)*

Children's Books; Crafts & Hobbies

New Titles: 15 (2009) , 17 (2010)
No of Employees: 4

Imprints, Series & ISBNs:
978 1 873829

Distributor for:
Brown Wells & Jacobs Ltd (Packaging)

3010 ▬▬

**CAMBRIDGE PUBLISHING
MANAGEMENT LTD**
Burr Elm Court, Main Street, Caldecote,
Cambs CB23 7NU
Telephone: 01954 214006
Fax: 01954 214001
Email: j.dobbyne@cambridgepm.co.uk
Web Site: www.cambridgepm.co.uk

Personnel:
Jackie Dobbyne *(Managing Director)*
Tim Newton *(Production Director)*
Catherine Burch *(Editorial Manager)*

Academic & Scholarly; Archaeology; Architecture & Design; Biography & Autobiography; Cookery, Wines & Spirits; Crafts & Hobbies; Educational & Textbooks; English as a Foreign Language; Fine Art & Art History; Gardening; Industry, Business & Management; Medical (incl. Self Help & Alternative Medicine); Military & War; Natural History; Reference Books, Directories & Dictionaries; Religion & Theology; Travel & Topography; Vocational Training & Careers

No of Employees: 18

Book Trade Association Membership:
Independent Publishers Guild

3011

CORPUS PUBLISHING LTD
PO Box 8, Lydney, Glos GL15 6YD
Telephone: 01594 560600
Fax: 01594 560550
Email: info@firststonepub.co.uk

Personnel:
John Sellers *(Publisher)*

Accountancy & Taxation; Animal Care & Breeding; Children's Books; Medical (incl. Self Help & Alternative Medicine); Sports & Games

Imprints, Series & ISBNs:
Corpus Publishing: 978 1 903333
First Stone Publishing: 978 1 904439

3012

COWLEY ROBINSON PUBLISHING LTD
8 Belmont, Bath BA1 5DZ
Telephone: 01225 339999
Fax: 01225 339995
Email:
stewart.cowley@cowleyrobinson.com

Personnel:
Stewart Cowley *(Director)*
D. Hawcock *(Director)*
P. Fleming *(Director)*
Leanne Down *(Production Manager)*
Anna Sainaghi *(Senior Sales Manager)*

Children's Books

New Titles: 45 (2009) , 42 (2010)
No of Employees: 9

Parent Company:
Allcloud Ltd

3013

D & N PUBLISHING
8 Fiveways, Baydon, Wilts SN8 2LH
Telephone: 01672 540556
Email: d@dnpublishing.co.uk

Personnel:
David Price-Goodfellow *(Manager/Owner)*
Namrita Price-Goodfellow *(Designer/ Owner)*

Animal Care & Breeding; Antiques & Collecting; Aviation; Biology & Zoology; Crafts & Hobbies; Do-It-Yourself; Fine Art & Art History; Guide Books; History & Antiquarian; Medical (incl. Self Help & Alternative Medicine); Military & War; Natural History; Photography; Reference Books, Directories & Dictionaries; Sports & Games; Theatre, Drama & Dance; Transport; Travel & Topography

3014

DIAGRAM VISUAL INFORMATION LTD
34 Elaine Grove, London NW5 4QH
Telephone: 020 7485 5941
Fax: 020 7485 5941
Email: info@diagramgroup.com
Web Site: www.diagramgroup.com

Personnel:
Bruce Robertson *(Managing Director)*
Patricia Robertson *(Director)*

Children's Books; Educational & Textbooks; Geography & Geology; Health & Beauty; Reference Books, Directories & Dictionaries; Sports & Games

New Titles: 10 (2010)

Overseas Representation:
Bulgaria: Nika Literary Agency, Sofia, Bulgaria
Eastern Europe: DS Druck- und Verlags Service, London, UK
Hungary: DS Budapest Kft, Budapest, Hungary
Japan: Tuttle-Mori Agency Inc, Tokyo, Japan
Korea: KCC, Seoul, Republic of Korea
Lithuania: Musa Knyga, Vilnius, Lithuania
Netherlands & Scandinavia: Kolar Rights and Translation, Feidamsee, Austria
Poland: DS Druck Warszawa, Warsaw, Poland
Romania: Mast Publishing, Bucharest, Romania
Russia: DS, Moscow, Russia
Thailand: Big Apple Tuttle-Mori Agency (Thailand) Co Ltd, Bangkok, Thailand

3015

EDDISON SADD EDITIONS LTD
St Chad's House, 148 King's Cross Road, London WC1X 9DH
Telephone: 020 7837 1968
Fax: 020 7837 2025
Email: info@eddisonsadd.co.uk
Web Site: www.eddisonsadd.com

Accounts:
Facts & Figures
Telephone: 01280 813111
Fax: 01280 817229

Personnel:
Nick Eddison *(Managing Director)*
Ian Jackson *(Editorial Director)*
Susan Cole *(Rights Director)*
David Owen *(Financial Director)*
Sarah Rooney *(Production Director)*

Children's Books; Cookery, Wines & Spirits; Health & Beauty; Magic & the Occult; Medical (incl. Self Help & Alternative Medicine)

Imprints, Series & ISBNs:
Bookinabox

Associated Companies:
Connections Book Publishing

Overseas Representation:
Worldwide: Melia Publishing Services for Connections Book Services, UK

3016

EMMA TREEHOUSE LTD
The Studio, Church Street, Nunney, Frome, Somerset BA11 4LW
Telephone: 01373 836233
Fax: 01373 836299
Email: sales@emmatreehouse.com

Personnel:
David Bailey *(Director)*
Richard Powell *(Director)*
Hilary Allom *(Director)*

Christine Barham *(Manager)*
Margret Heilegenstadt *(Manager)*

Children's Books

Imprints, Series & ISBNs:
978 1 85576
Treehouse Children's Books

Distributor for:
Macmillan Distribution

Book Trade Association Membership:
Book Packagers Association

3017

ESSENTIAL WORKS LTD
The Green, 29 Clerkenwell Green, London EC1R 0DU
Telephone: 020 7017 0890
Email: info@essentialworks.co.uk
Web Site: www.essentialworks.co.uk

Personnel:
John Conway *(Managing Director)*
Mal Peachey *(Publishing Director)*
Jackie Strachan *(Rights & Co-Editions)*
Jane Moseley *(Rights & Co-Editions)*

Biography & Autobiography; Cinema, Video, TV & Radio; Fashion & Costume; Health & Beauty; Humour; Illustrated & Fine Editions; Military & War; Music; Photography; Sports & Games; Transport

3018

FREELANCE MARKET NEWS
Sevendale House, 7 Dale Street, Manchester M1 1JB
Telephone: 0161 228 2362
Fax: 0161 228 3533
Email: fmn@writersbureau.com
Web Site: www.freelancemarketnews.com

Personnel:
Miss Angela Cox *(Editorial & Circulation)*

Educational & Textbooks; Fiction; Literature & Criticism; Photography; Poetry

Parent Company:
The Writers Bureau Ltd

3019

GRAHAM-CAMERON PUBLISHING & ILLUSTRATION
The Studio, 23 Holt Road, Sheringham, Norfolk NR26 8NB
Telephone: 01263 821333
Fax: 01263 821334
Email: enquiry@gciforillustration.com

Marketing & Sales:
Duncan Graham-Cameron,
59 Hertford Road, Brighton BN1 7GG
Telephone: 01273 385890
Email: duncan@gciforillustration.com
Web Site: www.gciforillustration.com

Personnel:
Mike Graham-Cameron *(Managing & Editorial Partner)*
Helen Graham-Cameron *(Executive, Art & Editorial Partner)*
Duncan Graham-Cameron *(Executive, Marketing & Sales Partner)*

Architecture & Design; Children's Books; Educational & Textbooks; English as a Foreign Language; Military & War; Natural History; Religion & Theology

Imprints, Series & ISBNs:
978 0 947672

Associated Companies:
Graham-Cameron Illustration

Book Trade Association Membership:
Independent Publishers Guild; Cambridge Book Association; CAMPUS; The Paternosters

3020

HART MCLEOD LTD
14A Greenside, Waterbeach, Cambridge CB25 9HP
Telephone: 01223 861495
Fax: 01223 862902
Email: inhouse@hartmcleod.co.uk
Web Site: www.hartmcleod.co.uk

Personnel:
Graham Hart *(Editorial Director)*
Joanne Barker *(Design Director)*

Academic & Scholarly; Educational & Textbooks; Electronic (Educational); Sports & Games

3021

THE IVY PRESS LTD
210 High Street, Lewes, East Sussex BN7 2NS
Telephone: 01273 487440
Fax: 01273 487441
Web Site: www.ivy-group.co.uk

Personnel:
Stephen Paul *(Managing Director)*
Nikki Tilbury *(Rights Director)*
Peter Bridgewater *(Creative Director)*

Crafts & Hobbies; Fashion & Costume; Health & Beauty; Illustrated & Fine Editions

3022

LITTLE PEOPLE BOOKS
The Home of BookBod, Knighton, Radnorshire LD7 1UP
Telephone: 01547 520925
Email: littlepeoplebooks@thehobb.tv
Web Site: www.thehobb.tv/lpb

Personnel:
Grant Jessé *(Production Director, Managing Editor)*
Helen Wallis *(Rights, Finance Director)*

Audio Books; Children's Books; Educational & Textbooks

Imprints, Series & ISBNs:
978 1 899573

Parent Company:
Grant Jessé

Associated Companies:
Karavadra: Multimedia

Book Trade Association Membership:
Independent Publishers Guild; Book Packagers Association

3023

MARKET HOUSE BOOKS LTD
Suite B, Elsinore House,
43 Buckingham Street, Aylesbury, Bucks HP20 2NQ
Telephone: 01296 484911
Fax: 01296 338934

Personnel:
Elizabeth Martin *(Chief Editor)*
Anne Stibbs/Kerr *(Production Director)*
Jonathan Law *(Editorial Director)*

Computer Science; Industry, Business & Management; Law; Medical (incl. Self Help & Alternative Medicine); Music; Psychology & Psychiatry; Reference Books, Directories & Dictionaries; Scientific & Technical; Theatre, Drama & Dance

3024

METHODIST PUBLISHING
17 Tresham Road, Orton Southgate,
Peterborough PE2 6SG
Telephone: 01733 235962
Fax: 01733 390325
Web Site:
www.methodistpublishing.org.uk

Personnel:
Jane McClean *(Manager of Commercial Services)*

No of Employees: 5

Imprints, Series & ISBNs:
Methodist Publishing House: 978 1 85852

Parent Company:
The Methodist Church

3025

NICOLA BAXTER LTD
PO Box 215, The Brew House,
Framingham Earl Road, Yelverton, Norwich
NR14 7UR
Telephone: 01508 491111
Email: nb@nicolabaxter.co.uk
Web Site: www.nicolabaxter.co.uk

Personnel:
Nicola Baxter *(Proprietor)*

Children's Books; Educational & Textbooks

3026

ORPHEUS BOOKS LTD
6 Church Green, Witney, Oxon OX28 4AW
Telephone: 01993 774949
Fax: 01993 700330
Email: nicholas@orpheusbooks.com
Web Site: www.orpheusbooks.com

Personnel:
Nicholas Harris *(Director)*
Sarah Hartley *(Director)*

Children's Books

Imprints, Series & ISBNs:
978 1 901323, 978 1 905473

3027

PARAGON PUBLISHING
4 North Street, Rothersthorpe, Northants
NN7 3JB
Telephone: 01604 832149
Email: mark.webb@tesco.net
Web Site: www.intoprint.net

Personnel:
Mark Webb *(Proprietor)*

Academic & Scholarly; Architecture & Design; Biography & Autobiography; Children's Books; Computer Science; Cookery, Wines & Spirits; Crime; Educational & Textbooks; Electronic (Educational); Electronic (Professional & Academic); English as a Foreign Language; Environment & Development Studies; Fiction; Industry, Business & Management; Languages & Linguistics; Magic & the Occult; Medical (incl. Self Help & Alternative Medicine); Military & War; Natural History; Nautical; Poetry; Religion & Theology; Science Fiction; Scientific & Technical; Sports & Games; Theatre, Drama & Dance

New Titles: 23 (2009) , 50 (2010)
No of Employees: 2

Imprints, Series & ISBNs:
Into Print: 978 1 899820
KinderKlub
Primary Modern Language
Stadium & Arena

3028

PLAYNE BOOKS LTD
Park Court Barn, Trefin, Haverfordwest,
Pembrokeshire SA62 5AU
Telephone: 01348 837073
Fax: 01348 837063
Email: info@playnebooks.co.uk

Personnel:
Gill Davies *(Editorial Director)*
David Playne *(Design & Production)*

Children's Books; History & Antiquarian; Theatre, Drama & Dance; Travel & Topography

New Titles: 4 (2009) , 8 (2010)
No of Employees: 2
Annual Turnover: £60,000

Associated Companies:
Playne Plays; SpinfoldsWorld

Overseas Representation:
Worldwide (excluding UK & USA): April
Showers, Cheltenham, Gloucestershire,
UK

3029

TONY POTTER PUBLISHING
1 Stairbridge Court,
Bolney Grange Business Park,
Stairbridge Lane, Bolney, Haywards Heath,
West Sussex RH17 5PA
Telephone: 01444 232889
Fax: 01444 232142
Email: pat@tonypotter.com
Web Site: www.tonypotter.com

Personnel:
Dr Tony Potter *(Managing Director)*
Pat Hegarty *(Managing Editor)*
Susannah Moore *(Rights Consultant)*
Zöe Fawcett *(Head of Production)*

Children's Books; Humour

Imprints, Series & ISBNs:
Over the Moon: 978 1 905288
Potter Books: 978 1 906824
Teapot Press: 978 1 906013

Book Trade Association Membership:
Independent Publishers Guild

3030

QUANTUM PUBLISHING
6 Blundell Street, London N7 9BH
Telephone: 020 7700 6700
Fax: 020 7700 4191
Email: sarah.bloxham@quarto.com
Web Site: www.quarto.com

Personnel:
Anastasia Cavouras *(Publisher)*

Animal Care & Breeding; Antiques & Collecting; Architecture & Design; Atlases & Maps; Aviation; Children's Books; Cookery, Wines & Spirits; Crafts & Hobbies; Crime; Do-It-Yourself; Fashion & Costume; Fine Art & Art History; Gardening; Health & Beauty; History & Antiquarian; Industry, Business & Management; Magic & the Occult; Medical (incl. Self Help & Alternative Medicine); Military & War; Music; Natural History; Nautical; Photography; Sports & Games; Transport

Imprints, Series & ISBNs:
Cartographica Press
Oceana
Quantum

Parent Company:
Quarto Publishing Plc

3031

READER'S DIGEST CHILDREN'S PUBLISHING LTD
The Ice House, 124–126 Walcot Street,
Bath BA1 5BG
Telephone: 01225 473200
Fax: 01225 460942

Personnel:
Paul E. Stuart *(Commercial Director)*
Jennifer Fifield *(International Sales Director)*

Children's Books

Imprints, Series & ISBNs:
978 1 84880, 978 1 85724

Parent Company:
USA: The Reader's Digest Association Inc

Associated Companies:
USA: Reader's Digest Children's Publishing
Inc

3032

REGENCY HOUSE PUBLISHING LTD
The Red House, 84 High Street,
Buntingford, Herts SG9 9AJ
Telephone: 01763 274666
Fax: 01763 273501
Email: regency-house@btconnect.com

Personnel:
Miss N. Trodd *(Managing Director)*
B. H. Trodd *(Manager)*
Annabel Trodd *(Manager)*

Animal Care & Breeding; Architecture & Design; Aviation; Children's Books; Crafts & Hobbies; Magic & the Occult; Military & War

Imprints, Series & ISBNs:
978 1 85361

3033

Tangerine Designs Ltd

1 Limpley Mill, Lower Stoke, Bath BA2 7JF
Telephone: 01225 720001
Web Site: www.tangerinedesigns.co.uk

Personnel:
Christine Swift *(Managing Director)*
Trish Pugsley *(Co-edition Sales Agent)*
Rachel Pidcock *(Co-edition Sales Agent)*
Catherine Lyn Jones *(Rights Manager)*

Children's Books

Distributor for:
Alligator Books Ltd; Pinwheel

Book Trade Association Membership:
Publishers Association

3034

TOUCAN BOOKS LTD
Third Floor, 89 Charterhouse Street,
London EC1M 6PE
Telephone: 020 7250 3388
Fax: 020 7250 3123
Email: ellen@toucanbooks.co.uk

Personnel:
Ellen Dupont *(Managing Director)*
Robert Sackville-West *(Director)*

Animal Care & Breeding; Architecture & Design; Atlases & Maps; Children's Books; Cookery, Wines & Spirits; Crafts & Hobbies; Fine Art & Art History; Gardening; History & Antiquarian; Illustrated & Fine Editions; Military & War; Natural History; Reference Books, Directories & Dictionaries; Travel & Topography

Book Trade Association Membership:
Book Packagers Association

3035

TUCKER SLINGSBY LTD
Fifth Floor, Regal House, 70 London Road,
Twickenham TW1 3QS
Telephone: 020 8744 1007
Fax: 020 8744 0041
Email: info@tuckerslingsby.co.uk
Web Site: www.tuckerslingsby.co.uk

Personnel:
Del Tucker *(Director)*
Janet Slingsby *(Director)*

Children's Books; Crafts & Hobbies; Health & Beauty

New Titles: 30 (2009) , 30 (2010)

Imprints, Series & ISBNs:
978 1 902272, 978 1 905844, 978 1
907358

Overseas Representation:
Spain, Portugal & Latin America: I E Ilustrata
SL, Barcelona, Spain

3036

WATERSIDE PRESS
Sherfield Gables, Sherfield-on-Loddon,
Hook RG27 0JG
Telephone: 0845 2300 733
Fax: 01256 882250
Email: enquiries@watersidepress.co.uk
Web Site: www.watersidepress.co.uk

Personnel:
Bryan Gibson *(Managing Editor)*

Academic & Scholarly; Biography & Autobiography; Crime; Educational & Textbooks; Electronic (Professional & Academic); Fiction; History & Antiquarian; Law; Literature & Criticism; Reference Books, Directories & Dictionaries; Sociology & Anthropology; Theatre, Drama & Dance

New Titles: 14 (2009) , 10 (2010)

Imprints, Series & ISBNs:
978 1 872870, 978 1 904380, 978 1
906534

Associated Companies:
UK: Bryan Gibson Publications

Overseas Representation:
North America: International Specialized
Book Services Inc, Portland, OR, USA

3037

DAVID WEST CHILDREN'S BOOKS
7 Princeton Court, 55 Felsham Road,
London SW15 1AZ
Telephone: 020 8780 3836
Fax: 020 8780 9313
Email: dww@btinternet.com
Web Site:
www.davidwestchildrensbooks.com

Personnel:
David West *(Proprietor/Publisher)*
Lynn Lockett *(Publisher)*

Architecture & Design; Children's Books; Cinema, Video, TV & Radio; Crafts & Hobbies; Fashion & Costume; Geography & Geology; History & Antiquarian; Military & War; Music; Natural History; Scientific & Technical; Sports & Games; Transport

3038

PHILIP WILSON PUBLISHERS
109 Drysdale Street, The Timber Yard,
London N1 6ND
Telephone: 020 7033 9900

Fax: 020 7033 9922
Email: sales@philip-wilson.co.uk
Web Site: www.philip-wilson.co.uk

Personnel:
Philip Wilson *(Director)*
Slobodan Prohaska *(Finance Director)*

*Antiques & Collecting; Architecture &
Design; Fine Art & Art History; History &
Antiquarian*

New Titles: 10 (2009) , 10 (2010)

No of Employees: 5

Imprints, Series & ISBNs:
978 0 85667

Distributor for:
India: Niyogi Books

Overseas Representation:
USA: Palgrave Macmillan, New York, NY,
    USA
Worldwide: I. B. Tauris & Co Ltd, London,
    UK

3039 ▬▬▬▬▬▬▬

YOUNG PEOPLE IN FOCUS
23 New Road, Brighton, East Sussex
BN1 1WZ
Telephone: 01273 693311 & 647325
Fax: 01273 647322
Email:
    publications@youngpeopleinfocus.org.u
    k
Web Site:
    www.youngpeopleinfocus.org.uk

Personnel:
Kevin Lane *(Co-Director)*
Debi Roker *(Co-Director)*

Educational & Textbooks

No of Employees: 11

Imprints, Series & ISBNs:
978 1 871504

4 Authors' Agents

4001

AITKEN ALEXANDER ASSOCIATES
18–21 Cavaye Place, London SW10 9PT
Telephone: 020 7373 8672
Fax: 020 7373 6002
Email: reception@gillonaitken.co.uk
Web Site: www.aitkenalexander.co.uk

Personnel:
Gillon Aitken (Chairman)
Clare Alexander (Joint Managing Director)
Sally Riley (Joint Managing Director)
Joaquim Fernandes (Company Secretary)
Sally Riley (Foreign Rights)
Lesley Shaw (Film/TV)
Andrew Kidd (Director)

All MSS except plays, film & TV scripts, short stories & articles if not by existing clients.

Specialization: quality full-length fiction & non-fiction.

4002

THE AMPERSAND AGENCY LTD
Ryman's Cottages, Little Tew, Oxon OX7 4JJ
Telephone: 01608 683677 & 683898
Fax: 01608 683449
Email: info@theampersandagency.co.uk
Web Site:
www.theampersandagency.co.uk

Personnel:
Peter Buckman (Managing Director)
Peter Janson-Smith (Consultant)
Anne-Marie Doulton (Editor & Director)
Patrick Neale (Consultant)

All MSS except poetry, science fiction, horror, fantasy or illustrated children's books.

Specialization: literary and commercial fiction and non-fiction for all markets. A full range of services including foreign and media rights is offered. Member of the Association of Authors' Agents.

Overseas Representation:
Worldwide: The Buckman Agency, Oxford, UK

4003

DARLEY ANDERSON LITERARY, TV & FILM AGENCY
Estelle House, 11 Eustace Road, London SW6 1JB
Telephone: 020 7386 2674
Fax: 020 7386 5571
Email: enquiries@darleyanderson.com
Web Site: www.darleyanderson.com

Personnel:
Darley Anderson (Sole Proprietor)
Zoë King (Non-Fiction Associate Agent)
Steve Fisher (Film & TV)
Camilla Bolton (Crime/Thriller Associate Agent)
Madeleine Buston (Head of Rights, Women's Fiction Agent & Deputy Managing Director, Children's Books)
Sophie Gordon (Office Manager)

All MSS except short stories, academic or poetry.

Specialization: fiction: all types of thrillers & all types of fiction including contemporary, 20th century romantic sagas, chick lit, bonkbusters, women in jeopardy; also crime (cosy/hard-boiled/historical), horror, comedy & Irish novels; popular culture; accessible literary, historical, exotic sagas, psychological suspense, paranormal, supernatural and cross-over fiction, children's, young adult and picture books; non-fiction: celebrity autobiographies, biographies, 'true life' women in jeopardy, popular psychology, self-improvement, diet, health, beauty & fashion, gardening, cookery, inspirational & religious.

Overseas Representation:
Bulgaria: Anthea Literary Agency, Sofia, Bulgaria
China & Taiwan: The Grayhawk Agency, Taipei, Taiwan
Czech & Slovak Republics: Andrew Nurnberg Associates, Prague, Czech Republic
Germany: Thomas Schlück Literary Agency, Garbsen, Germany
Greece: O A Literary Agency, Markopoulo, Athens, Greece
Hungary: Kàtai & Bolza Literary Agents, Budapest, Hungary
Israel: I. Pikarski Literary Agency, Tel Aviv, Israel
Italy: Natoli, Stefan & Oliva Agenzia Letteraria, Milan, Italy
Japan: Japan Uni Agency, Tokyo, Japan; Tuttle-Mori Agency Inc, Tokyo, Japan
Korea: Danny Hony Agency, Republic of Korea
Poland: Graal Ltd, Warsaw, Poland
Romania: International Copyright Agency, Bucharest, Romania
Russia: Synopsis Literary Agency, Moscow, Russia
Serbia: PLIMA Literary Agency, Belgrade, Serbia
Turkey: Akcali Copyright Agency, Istanbul, Turkey
USA: Darley Anderson Books, London, UK
USA (for film): Steve Fisher APA Talent & Literary Agency, Los Angeles, CA

4004

AQUARIUS LIBRARY
[a division of SPM London Ltd]
PO Box 5, 136 Emmanuel Road, Hastings TN34 3ZY
Telephone: 01424 721196
Email: aquarius.lib@clara.net
Web Site: www.aquariuscollection.com

Postal Address:
PO Box 5, Hastings, East Sussex TN34 1HR
Telephone: 01424 721196
Email: aquarius.lib@clara.net
Web Site: www.aquariuscollection.com

Personnel:
Gilbert Gibson (Managing Director)
David Corkill (Picture Library Director)

Specialization: Hollywood candid photography, film stills (old & new, colour & b/w), showbusiness personalities and all other aspects of international showbusiness and mass entertainment.

Parent Company:
Sun-Pacific Music (London) Ltd

Associated Companies:
Sun-Pacific Music (London) Ltd

4005

ARTELLUS LTD
30 Dorset House, Gloucester Place, London NW1 5AD
Telephone: 020 7935 6972
Fax: 020 7487 5957
Web Site: www.artellusltd.co.uk

Personnel:
Leslie Gardner (Director)
Darryl Samaraweera (Company Secretary)
Gabriele Pantucci (Chair)

All MSS except film scripts.

Specialization: speculative fiction, thrillers, fiction – commercial and literary, self-help, history, science, art history, politics, economics.

Rights Representative in UK for:
Eastern Europe: Prava i Prevodi, Belgrade, Serbia
Far East: Big Apple Tuttle-Mori Agency Inc, Shanghai, P. R. of China
Spain & Portugal: Carmen Balcells Agencia Literaria SA, Barcelona, Spain

4006

TASSY BARHAM ASSOCIATES
23 Elgin Crescent, London W11 2JD
Telephone: 020 7229 8667
Fax: 020 7229 8667
Email: tassy@tassybarham.com

Personnel:
Tassy Barham (Agent)

Specialization: Brazil. Representing European and American agencies and publishers in Brazil, and Portuguese-language writers into the UK.

4007

LORELLA BELLI LITERARY AGENCY (LBLA)
54 Hartford House, 35 Tavistock Crescent, Notting Hill, London W11 1AY
Telephone: 020 7727 8547
Fax: 0870 787 4194
Email: info@lorellabelliagency.com
Web Site: www.lorellabelliagency.com

Personnel:
Lorella Belli (Proprietor)

All MSS except children's books, science fiction, fantasy, academic, poetry, original scripts. No reading fee. May suggest revision.

Specialization: general fiction and non-fiction (particularly interested in first-time writers, commercial women's fiction, crime, thrillers, historical, international and multicultural writing, journalists with original book ideas, books on/about Italy, current affairs, pop history, pop science, pop music, lifestyle, memoirs, biography, autobiography, MBS, cookery, fashion, personal finance, business, travel). The agency represents a number of international bestselling and award-winning authors of fiction and non-fiction. Also represents leading American agencies in the UK. Commission: 15% home; 20% overseas and dramatic rights. Works with co-agents abroad; film & TV rights handled by an associate agency.

Rights Representative in UK for:
USA: Creative Culture Agency, New York, NY, USA; Fine Print Agency, New York, NY, USA; Mildred Marmur Associates, Larchmont, NY, USA; Paula Balzer Literary Agency, New York, NY, USA; Sarah Lazin Books, New York, NY, USA; Susan Schulman Agency, New York, NY, USA

4008

BLAKE FRIEDMANN LITERARY AGENCY LTD
122 Arlington Road, London NW1 7HP
Telephone: 020 7284 0408
Fax: 020 7284 0442

Email: firstname@blakefriedmann.co.uk
Web Site: www.blakefriedmann.co.uk

Personnel:
Carole Blake (*Book Sales Director & Agent*)
Julian Friedmann (*Film & TV Director & Agent*)
Isobel Dixon (*Book Sales Director & Agent*)
Conrad Williams (*Film, TV & Radio Sales*)
Adrian Clark (*Accounts Manager*)
Oli Munson (*Book Sales Agent*)
Katie Williams (*Film & TV Agent*)

All MSS except science fiction, fantasy, children's books, plays, poetry & short stories (excluding existing clients).

Specialization: placing book rights internationally; film, television & radio rights.

Overseas Representation:
Bulgaria: Anthea Literary Agency, Sofia, Bulgaria
China, Taiwan & Hong Kong: Andrew Nurnberg Associates, Beijing, P. R. of China; Andrew Nurnberg Literary Agency, Taipei, Taiwan
France: La Nouvelle Agence, Paris, France
Germany: Liepman AG, Zurich, Switzerland
Hungary: Kátai & Bolza, Literary Agents, Budapest, Hungary
Italy: Natoli, Stefan & Oliva Agenzia Letteraria, Milan, Italy
Japan: The English Agency Japan Ltd, Tokyo, Japan
Korea: KCC International Ltd, Seoul, Republic of Korea
Poland: Graal Ltd, Warsaw, Poland
Romania: S. Kessler International Copyright Agency, Bucharest, Romania
Russia: Andrew Nurnberg Associates, Moscow, Russia
Scandinavia: Leonhardt & Hoier Literary Agency, Copenhagen, Denmark
Spain, Brazil & Portugal: The Foreign Office, Spain
Turkey: Anatolialit Agency, Turkey
USA, Canada & Greece: Blake Friedmann Literary Agency, London, UK

4009

LUIGI BONOMI ASSOCIATES LTD
91 Great Russell Street, London WC1B 3PS
Telephone: 020 7637 1234
Fax: 020 7637 2111
Email: info@bonomiassociates.co.uk
Web Site: www.bonomiassociates.co.uk

Personnel:
Luigi Bonomi (*Director*)
Amanda Preston (*Director*)
Ajda Vucicevic (*Administration Assistant*)

All MSS except poetry, children's stories or adult science fiction/fantasy.

Specialization: fiction: commercial and literary fiction, thrillers, crime, women's fiction. Non-fiction: history, science, parenting, lifestyle, diet, health, TV tie-ins. Keen to find new authors and help them develop their careers. Send preliminary letter, synopsis and first three chapters. No reading fee. Will suggest revision. Works with foreign agencies and has links with TV presenters' agencies and production companies. Authors include Will Adams, James Barrington, Chris Beardshaw, Sean Black, Gennaro Contaldo, Nick Foulkes, David Gibbins, Richard Hammond, Jane Hill, Matt Hilton, John Humphrys, Graham Joyce, Simon Kernick, Colin McDowell, Dr Gillian McKeith, Richard Madeley and Judy Finnigan, James May, Nicola Monaghan, Mike Morley, Sue Palmer, Andrew Pepper, Melanie Phillips, Jem Poster, Esther Rantzen, John Rickards, Mike Rossiter, Catherine Sampson, Prof Bryan Sykes, Alan Titchmarsh, Martin Townsend, Sir Terry Wogan, Sally Worboyes. Founded 2005.

Fiction and non-fiction (home 15%, overseas 20%).

Overseas Representation:
Worldwide: Intercontinental Literary Agency, London, UK

4010

JENNY BROWN ASSOCIATES
33 Argyle Place, Edinburgh EH9 1JT
Telephone: 0131 229 5334
Email: jenny@jennybrownassociates.com
Web Site: www.jennybrownassociates.com

Personnel:
Jenny Brown (*Agent*)
Mark Stanton (*Agent*)
Lucy Juckes (*Children's Agent*)
Allan Guthrie (*Agent*)
Kevin Pocklington (*Foreign Rights Agent*)

All MSS except academic, poetry, science fiction, horror & fantasy. Submissions: see website for submission information.

Specialization: non-fiction (including sport & music), literary fiction (including crime & thrillers) and writing for children. Many of the agency's clients are based in Scotland, but the company represents writers from all over the UK, and sells their work worldwide.

4011

FELICITY BRYAN
2a North Parade, Banbury Road, Oxford OX2 6LX
Telephone: 01865 513816
Fax: 01865 310055
Email: agency@felicitybryan.com
Web Site: www.felicitybryan.com

Personnel:
Felicity Bryan (*Director*)
Caroline Wood (*Director*)

All MSS except science fiction, fantasy, romance, gardening, memoirs, self-help, picture/illustrated books, film, TV and play scripts or poetry.

Specialization: adult fiction & general non-fiction, history & popular science, children 8–12 upwards.

Overseas Representation:
China: Andrew Nurnberg Associates, Beijing, P. R. of China; Big Apple Tuttle-Mori Agency Inc, Shanghai, P. R. of China
Europe, Russia & China: Andrew Nurnberg Associates, London, UK
Japan: Japan Uni Agency, Tokyo, Japan; Tuttle-Mori Agency Inc, Tokyo, Japan
Korea: EYA, Seoul, Republic of Korea

4012

THE BUCKMAN AGENCY
Ryman's Cottage, Little Tew, Oxford OX7 4JJ
Telephone: 01608 683677
Fax: 01608 683449
Email: r.buckman@talk21.com

Also at:
Jessica Buckman, 118 Effra Road, Wimbledon, London SW19 8PR
Telephone: 020 8544 2674
Fax: 020 8543 9653
Email: j.buckman@talk21.com

Personnel:
Rosemarie Buckman (*Partner*)
Jessica Buckman (*Partner*)

Specialization: handling of translation rights in all foreign rights markets for fiction and non-fiction, working on behalf of UK and US agencies.

4013

BRIE BURKEMAN & SERAFINA CLARKE LTD
14 Neville Court, Abbey Road, London NW8 9DD
Telephone: 0870 199 5002
Fax: 0870 199 1029
Email: info@burkemanandclarke.com
Web Site: www.burkemanandclarke.com

Personnel:
Brie Burkeman (*Proprietor*)
Elizabeth Simpson

All MSS except academic, text, poetry, short stories, musicals or short films. No reading fee but return postage essential. Unsolicited e-mail attachments will be deleted without opening. Please see website for submission guidelines.

Specialization: commercial and literary full-length fiction and non-fiction books, as well as full length scripts for film and theatre. Worldwide representation, works with sub-agents where necessary. Also independent film and TV consultant to literary agents and publishers. Commission: 15% home, 20% overseas. Member of AAA and PMA.

Overseas Representation:
Worldwide – contact: Brie Burkeman & Serafina Clarke Ltd, London, UK

4014

CAMPBELL THOMSON & MCLAUGHLIN LTD
50 Albemarle Street, London W1S 4BD
Telephone: 020 7493 4361
Fax: 020 7495 8961
Email: cbruton@ctmcl.co.uk
Web Site: www.ctmcl.co.uk

Personnel:
Charlotte Bruton (*Agent*)
John McLaughlin (*Consultant*)

All MSS except children's, poetry, SF; book length MSS only.

Rights Representative in UK for:
USA: The Fox Chase Agency Inc, Chesterbrook, PA, USA; Raines & Raines Agency, Medusa, NY, USA

Overseas Representation:
Worldwide (all translation rights): The Marsh Agency, London, UK

4015

CASAROTTO RAMSAY & ASSOCIATES LTD
Waverley House, 7–12 Noel Street, London W1F 8GQ
Telephone: 020 7287 4450
Fax: 020 7287 9128
Email: agents@casarotto.co.uk
Web Site: www.casarotto.uk.com

Personnel:
Giorgio Casarotto (*Director*)
Tom Erhardt (*Director*)
Jenne Casarotto (*Director*)
Mel Kenyon (*Director*)
Jodi Shields (*Director*)
Rachel Holroyd (*Director*)

Specialization: film scripts, TV scripts, play scripts, radio scripts only after preliminary letter. No books.

4016

CHAPMAN & VINCENT
7 Dilke Street, London SW3 4JE
Telephone: 020 7352 5582
Email: chapmanvincent@hotmail.co.uk

Personnel:
Jennifer Chapman (*Director*)
Gilly Vincent (*Director*)

All MSS except fiction of any kind, writing for children, poetry, scripts, domestic tragedies or academic work.

Specialization: non-fiction illustrated work in the areas of interiors, gardening, cookery, heritage and fashion. Write with two sample chapters and SAE. E-mail submissions without attachments can be considered. A small agency whose clients come mainly from personal recommendation. The agency is not actively seeking clients but is happy to consider really original work. Clients include George Carter, Leslie Geddes-Brown, Lucinda Lambton, Rowley Leigh and Eve Pollard. Commission: Home 15%; US & Europe 20%. Member of the Association of Authors' Agents.

Overseas Representation:
USA: Elaine Markson Literary Agency, New York, NY, USA

4017

MARY CLEMMEY LITERARY AGENCY
6 Dunollie Road, London NW5 2XP
Telephone: 020 7267 1290
Fax: 020 7813 9757
Email: mcwords@googlemail.com

Personnel:
Mary Clemmey (*Literary Agent*)

All MSS except science fiction, horror, fantasy, poetry or children's books. No unsolicited e-mail submissions.

Specialization: fiction and non-fiction, high quality work with an international market. TV, film, radio and theatre scripts from existing clients only. Please approach only by preliminary letter and synopsis (SAE essential for response).

Rights Representative in UK for:
USA: Betsy Amster Literary Enterprises, Los Angeles, CA, USA; Frederick Hill Bonnie Nadell Associates Literary Agency, San Francisco, CA, USA; Lynn C. Franklin Associates Ltd, New York, NY, USA; The Miller Agency, New York, NY, USA; Roslyn Targ Literary Agency Inc, New York, NY, USA; The Weingel Fidel Agency, New York, NY, USA

Overseas Representation:
USA: Elaine Markson Literary Agency, New York, NY, USA

4018

ELSPETH COCHRANE PERSONAL MANAGEMENT
16 Trinity Close, The Pavement, London SW4 0JD
Telephone: 020 7622 3566
Email: elspethcochrane@talktalk.net

Personnel:
Elspeth Cochrane (*Managing Director*)
Tony Barlow (*Director*)

Specialization: fiction, non-fiction, biographies, screenplays. Subjects have included Richard Burton, Marlon Brando, Sean Connery, Clint Eastwood, Lord Olivier. Also scripts for all media, with special interest in drama. No unsolicited MSS. Preliminary letter, synopsis and SAE are essential in the first instance. Clients include Royce Ryton, Robert Tanitch. Commission: 12.5%.

4019

JANE CONWAY-GORDON LTD
38 Cromwell Grove, London W6 7RG
Telephone: 020 7602 4690
Email: jane@conway-gordon.co.uk

Personnel:
Jane Conway-Gordon (Company Director)

All MSS except science fiction, poetry, children's, short pieces; return postage essential.

Overseas Representation:
Europe (excluding Germany & France): Intercontinental Literary Agency, London, UK
Germany: Liepman AG, Zurich, Switzerland
USA: Lyons Literary LLC, New York, NY, USA

4020

COOMBS MOYLETT LITERARY AGENCY
120 New Kings Road, London SW6 4LZ
Telephone: 020 8740 0454
Email: lisa.moylett@btopenworld.com

Personnel:
Lisa Moylett (Proprietor)
Juliet van Oss (Editor)
Sara Stanford (Submissions)

All MSS except science fiction, poetry or children's.

Specialization: commercial and literary fiction and non-fiction. Special interests in fiction are thrillers, crime/mystery; women's literary and contemporary and in non-fiction: biography; history and current affairs. The agency is particularly interested in finding and developing new talent. Services include the selling of subsidiary rights such as film & TV and translation. The agency has good relations with US publishers and is represented in both Japan by Tuttle Mori and in Germany by the Michael Meller Literary Agency. Guidelines for submission: first three chapters, a short synopsis and SAE (essential for the return of material). No e-mail or disc submissions.

Overseas Representation:
Germany: Michael Meller Literary Agency, Munich, Germany
Japan: Tuttle-Mori Agency Inc, Tokyo, Japan

4021

RUPERT CREW LTD
[International Literary Representation]
1a King's Mews, London WC1N 2JA
Telephone: 020 7242 8586
Fax: 020 7831 7914
Email: info@rupertcrew.co.uk
Web Site: www.rupertcrew.co.uk

Personnel:
Doreen Montgomery (Chairman & Joint Managing Director)
Caroline Montgomery (Company Secretary & Joint Managing Director)

All MSS except science fiction, fantasy, short stories, poetry, film & TV scripts (although at the present time we are unable to accept unsolicited MSS of any kind).

Specialization: international business management for authors desiring world representation. Preliminary letter with SAE required. Also acts as publishers' consultants.

Overseas Representation:
China: Big Apple Agency Inc, Shanghai, P. R. of China
Eastern Europe: Andrew Nurnberg Associates, London, UK

France: Eliane Benisti, Paris, France
Germany: Paul & Peter Fritz AG Literary Agency, Zurich, Switzerland
Hungary: Kàtai & Bolza Literary Agents, Budapest, Hungary
Israel: The Deborah Harris Agency, Israel
Italy: Agenzia Letteraria Internazionale srl, Milan, Italy
Japan: The English Agency Japan Ltd, Tokyo, Japan; Tuttle-Mori Agency Inc, Tokyo, Japan
Scandinavia & Spain: Sane Töregård Agency, Karlshamn, Sweden
Taiwan: Big Apple Tuttle-Mori Associates, Shin-Juang, Taiwan
Turkey: The Kayi Literary Agency, Turkey
USA: The Martell Agency, New York, NY, USA
Worldwide (Film/TV): MBA Literary Agents, London, UK

4022

CURTIS BROWN
Haymarket House, 28–29 Haymarket, London SW1Y 4SP
Telephone: 020 7393 4400
Fax: 020 7393 4401/2
Email: cb@curtisbrown.co.uk
Web Site: www.curtisbrown.co.uk

Personnel:
Jonathan Lloyd (Chief Executive Officer)
Jonny Geller (Managing Director – Book Department)
Nick Marston (Managing Director – Theatre, Film & TV Department)
Vivienne Schuster (Literary Agent)
Ben Hall (Chief Operating Officer)
Jacquie Drewe (Director)
Carol Jackson (Rights Agent)
Elizabeth Scheinkman (Literary Agent)
Sarah Spear (Director)
Craig Dickson (Head of Legal and Business Affairs)
Emma Bailey (Operations Manager)
Felicity Blunt (Literary Agent)
Sheila Crowley (Literary Agent)
Karolina Sutton (Literary Agent)
Stephanie Thwaites (Literary Agent)
Kate Cooper (Joint Head of Foreign Rights)
Betsy Robbins (Joint Head of Foreign Rights)
Daisy Meyrick (Rights Agent)
Katie McGowan (Rights Agent)
Helen Manders (Rights Agent)
Elizabeth Iveson (Rights Agent)

All MSS except short stories & poetry.

Specialization: negotiation in all publishing markets; and television, film & dramatic writing, directing, presenting & acting.

Rights Representative in UK for:
USA: Gelfman Schneider Literary Agents Inc, New York, NY, USA; ICM, New York, NY, USA

4023

FELIX DE WOLFE LTD
Kingsway House, 103 Kingsway, London WC2B 6QX
Telephone: 020 7242 5066
Fax: 020 7242 8119
Email: info@felixdewolfe.com

Personnel:
Caroline de Wolfe (Director)

All MSS except non-fiction, children's.

Overseas Representation:
France: Michelle Lapautre, Paris, France
Italy: Liepman AG, Zurich, Switzerland

4024

ROBERT DUDLEY AGENCY
50 Rannoch Road, London W6 9SR
Telephone: 07879 426574

Email: info@robertdudleyagency.co.uk
Web Site: www.robertdudleyagency.co.uk

Personnel:
Robert Dudley (Agent)

All MSS except film scripts.

Specialization: Robert Dudley Agency looks after a variety of authors of both fiction and non-fiction. Non-fiction subjects include sport, management, history, militaria, politics, health and well-being, travel, biography, film and archaeology.

Parent Company:
Bowerdean Publishing Co Ltd

Associated Companies:
Bowerdean Publishing Co Ltd

4025

EDWARDS FUGLEWICZ
49 Great Ormond Street, London WC1N 3HZ
Telephone: 020 7405 6725
Fax: 020 7405 6726
Email: ros@efla.co.uk

Personnel:
Ros Edwards (Partner)
Helenka Fuglewicz (Partner)

All MSS except children's books, science fiction, fantasy or horror. No unsolicited MSS.

Specialization: fiction and non-fiction: biography, history, and popular culture. Founded in 1996.

Rights Representative in UK for:
Republic of Ireland: Poolbeg Press, Dublin, Republic of Ireland
UK: The Bodleian Library, Oxford, UK

4026

FAITH EVANS ASSOCIATES
27 Park Avenue North, London N8 7RU
Telephone: 020 8340 9920
Email: faith@faith-evans.co.uk

Specialization: Small agency. No phone calls or unsolicited MSS. Submissions will not be acknowledged.

4027

FOX & HOWARD LITERARY AGENCY
4 Bramerton Street, Chelsea, London SW3 5JX
Telephone: 020 7352 8691
Fax: 020 7352 8691

Personnel:
Chelsey Fox (Agent)
Charlotte Howard (Agent)

Specialization: general non-fiction: biography, history and popular culture, reference, business, mind, body and spirit, health (home 15%, overseas 20%). No reading fee, but preliminary letter and synopsis with SAE essential. Founded 1992.

4028

FRASER ROSS ASSOCIATES
6 Wellington Place, Edinburgh EH6 7EQ
Telephone: 0131 657 4412
Email: kjross@tiscali.co.uk
Web Site: www.fraserross.co.uk

Personnel:
Lindsey Fraser (Partner)
Kathryn Ross (Partner)

All MSS except poetry, short stories & science fiction.

Specialization: representing writers and illustrators for children's books, and writers for adults (home 10–15%, overseas 20%). Send the first three chapters (or equivalent), a synopsis, CV and covering letter. Return postage is essential. Submissions from overseas will not be returned – senders should include an email contact address. Current clients include Ella Burfoot, Thomas Bloor, Joan Lingard, Tanya Landman, Vivian French, Lynne Rickards, Dugald Steer and Jamie Rix.

4029

JÜRI GABRIEL
35 Camberwell Grove, London SE5 8JA
Telephone: 020 7703 6186
Email: Juri@JuriGabriel.com

Personnel:
Jüri Gabriel (Proprietor)

All MSS except screenplays, tele or radio scripts (only handles performance rights in existing works for existing clients); science fantasy; children's books, poetry, short stories or articles.

Specialization: literary fiction, popular academic and anything that combines intellect, originality and wit. In first instance please send a two page synopsis, three sample chapters, a brief c.v. and return postage if you want the material back. No submissions by fax or e-mail. Clients include Maurice Caldera, Diana Constance, Miriam Dunne, Matt Fox, Paul Genney, Pat Gray, Mikka Haugaard, Robert Irwin, Andrew Killeen, John Lucas, David Madsen, Richard Mankiewicz, David Miller, Andy Oakes, John Outram, Phil Roberts, Roger Storey, Dr Stefan Szymanski, Jeremy Weingard, Dr Terence White. Commission: home 10%, US & translation 20%.

4030

DAVID GODWIN ASSOCIATES
55 Monmouth Street, London WC2H 9DG
Telephone: 020 7240 9992
Fax: 020 7395 6110
Web Site:
www.davidgodwinassociates.co.uk

Personnel:
David Godwin (Literary Agent)
Heather Godwin (Company Secretary)
Kirsty McLachlan (Film & TV Rights Manager)
Charlotte Knight (Assistant)
Anna Watkins (Assistant)

All MSS except science fiction & children's.

Specialization: UK, US and translation rights, TV & film.

4031

GRAHAM MAW CHRISTIE
19 Thornhill Crescent, London N1 1BJ
Telephone: 020 7609 1326
Email: enquiries@grahammawchristie.com
Web Site: www.grahammawchristie.com

Personnel:
Jane Graham Maw (Director)
Jennifer Christie (Director)

All MSS except fiction, children's or poetry.

Specialization: literary agents for general non-fiction: autobiography/memoir, humour and gift, business, web-to-book, food and drink, health, lifestyle, parenting, personal development, popular culture, popular science and popular philosophy, reference, TV tie-in. No reading fee. Will suggest revision. See website for guidance on submissions.

4032 ■■■■■■■■

LOUISE GREENBERG BOOKS LTD
The End House, Church Crescent, London
N3 1BG
Telephone: 020 8349 1179
Fax: 020 8343 4559
Email: louisegreenberg@msn.com

All MSS except sport, leisure, poetry,
children's. No telephone approaches from
authors.

Specialization: full length literary fiction and
serious non-fiction. Screen work for book
clients only.

Rights Representative in UK for:
USA: Rosalie Siegel International Literary
Agent, Penington, NJ, USA

4033 ■■■■■■■■

**GREGORY & COMPANY AUTHORS'
AGENTS**
3 Barb Mews, London W6 7PA
Telephone: 020 7610 4676
Fax: 020 7610 4686
Email: info@gregoryandcompany.co.uk
Web Site: www.gregoryandcompany.co.uk

Personnel:
Jane Gregory (Proprietor)
Stephanie Glencross (Editorial)
Claire Morris (Rights)
Terry Bland (Accounts)
Virginia Ascione (Rights Assistant)
Mary Jones (Submissions)

All MSS except children's, juvenile,
academic & technical books, poetry & plays,
TV & film scripts, science fiction, short
stories. Preliminary letter with synopsis, in
the first instance either to
maryjones@gregoryandcompany.co.uk or
to the company address above.

Specialization: fiction: commercial, crime,
literary, suspense and thrillers. Editorial
advice given to own authors. Film & TV
rights for own published authors only, no
original scripts.

Overseas Representation:
Brazil: Tassy Barham Associates, London, UK
Bulgaria: Interrights Literary & Translation
Agency, Sofia, Bulgaria
China: Big Apple Associates, Zhonghe City,
Taiwan
Croatia: Zvonimir Majdak, Zagreb, Croatia
Czech Republic & Slovakia: Andrew
Nurnberg Associates, Prague, Czech
Republic
France: La Nouvelle Agence, Paris, France
Hungary: Lex Copyright, Budapest, Hungary
Israel: Pikarski Agency, Tel Aviv, Israel
Japan: Japan Uni Agency Inc, Tokyo, Japan;
Tuttle-Mori Agency Inc, Tokyo, Japan
Korea: EYA, Seoul, Republic of Korea
Poland: Andrew Nurnberg Associates,
Warsaw, Poland
Romania: Simona Kessler International
Copyright Agency Ltd, Bucharest,
Romania
Russia: Andrew Nurnberg Associates,
Moscow, Russia
Scandinavia: Leonhardt & Hoier Literary
Agency, Copenhagen, Denmark
Spain: Carmen Balcells Agencia Literaria SA,
Barcelona, Spain
Thailand: Tuttle Mori Thailand, Bangkok,
Thailand
Turkey: Akcali Copyright Trade & Tourism
Co Ltd, Istanbul, Turkey

4034 ■■■■■■■■

THE HANBURY AGENCY
28 Moreton Street, London SW1V 2PE
Telephone: 020 7630 6768

Email: enquiries@hanburyagency.com
Web Site: www.hanburyagency.com

Personnel:
Margaret Hanbury (Managing Director)
Stuart Rushworth (Assistant Agent)
Henry de Rougemont (Media Manager)

Specialization: commercial fiction and
quality non-fiction (home 15%, overseas
20%). See website for submission details.
Authors include George Alagiah, Simon
Callow, Judith Lennox, Katie Price. Founded
in 1983.

Overseas Representation:
Brazil: Tassy Barham, London, UK
Eastern Europe, Russia & Baltic States:
Prava i Prevodi, Belgrade, Serbia
France: Michelle Lapautre, Paris, France
Germany: Mohrbooks Literary Agency,
Zurich, Switzerland
Greece: JLM Literary Agency, Athens,
Greece
Hungary: Lex Copyright, Budapest, Hungary
Israel: Ilana Pikarski Literary Agency, Tel Aviv,
Israel
Italy: Luigi Bernabó Associates Srl, Milan,
Italy
Japan: The English Agency Japan Ltd, Tokyo,
Japan
Korea: The Eric Yang Agency, Seoul,
Republic of Korea
Netherlands: Direct
Scandinavia: Licht & Burr Literary Agency,
Copenhagen, Denmark
Spain & Portugal: International Editors Co,
Barcelona, Spain
Turkey: Akcali Copyright Agency, Istanbul,
Turkey
USA: Robin Straus Inc, New York, NY, USA

4035 ■■■■■■■■

ANTONY HARWOOD LTD
103 Walton Street, Oxford OX2 6EB
Telephone: 01865 559615
Fax: 01865 310660
Email: mail@antonyharwood.com
Web Site: www.antonyharwood.com

Personnel:
Antony Harwood (Agent)
James MacDonald Lockhart (Agent)

All MSS except screenwriting, poetry.

Specialization: handles fiction and non-
fiction. Founded 2000.

4036 ■■■■■■■■

A. M. HEATH & CO LTD
6 Warwick Court, London WC1R 5DJ
Telephone: 020 7242 2811
Fax: 020 7242 2711
Web Site: www.amheath.com

Personnel:
William Hamilton (Managing Director)
Euan Thorneycroft (Director / Company
Secretary)
Victoria Hobbs (Director)
Jennifer Custer (Foreign Rights Director)
Sarah Molloy (Children's Agent)

All MSS except plays, scripts, poetry,
scientific, technical for the layman only.

Rights Representative in UK for:
USA: Anne Edelstein Literary Agency, New
York, NY, USA; Brandt & Hochman Inc,
New York, NY, USA; Gina Maccoby
Literary Agency, New York, NY, USA;
Jane Chelius Literary Agency, Brooklyn,
NY, USA; Lescher & Lescher Ltd, New
York, NY, USA; Miriam Altshuler Literary
Agency, Red Hook, NY, USA

Overseas Representation:
Brazil: Tassy Barham, London, UK

Bulgaria & Serbia: Andrew Nurnberg
Literary Agency, Sofia, Bulgaria
China & Taiwan: Andrew Nurnberg Literary
Agency, Shanghai, P. R. of China;
Andrew Nurnberg Literary Agency,
Taipei, Taiwan
Czech & Slovak Republics & Slovenia:
Andrew Nurnberg Associates, Prague,
Czech Republic
France: La Nouvelle Agence, Paris, France
Germany, Switzerland & Austria:
Mohrbooks Literary Agency, Zurich,
Switzerland
Hungary & Croatia: Andrew Nurnberg Ltd,
Budapest, Hungary
Israel: Deborah Harris Agency, Jerusalem,
Israel
Italy: Luigi Bernabó Associates Srl, Milan,
Italy
Japan (fiction): The English Agency Japan
Ltd, Tokyo, Japan
Japan (non-fiction): Tuttle-Mori Agency Inc,
Tokyo, Japan
Korea: EYA, Seoul, Republic of Korea
Poland: ANAW Literary Agency, Warsaw,
Poland
Romania: Simona Kessler International
Copyright Agency Ltd, Bucharest,
Romania
Russia: Andrew Nurnberg Associates,
Moscow, Russia
Scandinavia: Licht & Burr Literary Agency,
Copenhagen, Denmark
Turkey, Greece, Indonesia, Portugal, Latvia,
Lithuania, Estonia, Spain & Netherlands:
A. M. Heath & Co Ltd, London, UK

4037 ■■■■■■■■

DAVID HIGHAM ASSOCIATES
5–8 Lower John Street, Golden Square,
London W1F 9HA
Telephone: 020 7434 5900
Fax: 020 7437 1072
Email: dha@davidhigham.co.uk
Web Site: www.davidhigham.co.uk

Specialization: agents for the negotiation of
all rights in fiction, general non-fiction,
children's fiction and picture books, plays,
film and TV scripts. Represented in all
foreign markets. Please see website for
submissions guidelines. No reading fee.
Founded 1935.

4038 ■■■■■■■■

KATE HORDERN LITERARY AGENCY
18 Mortimer Road, Clifton, Bristol BS8 4EY
Telephone: 0117 923 9368
Email: katehordern@blueyonder.co.uk &
annewilliamskhla@googlemail.com

Personnel:
Kate Hordern (Proprietor)
Anne Williams (Associate Agent)

Specialization: quality literary and
commercial fiction, including women's
fiction, crime and thrillers, and general non-
fiction. Clients include Richard Bassett, Jeff
Dawson, Kylie Fitzpatrick, Duncan Hewitt,
Julian Lees, Will Randall, Dave Roberts, John
Sadler.

4039 ■■■■■■■■

VALERIE HOSKINS ASSOCIATES
20 Charlotte Street, London W1T 2NA
Telephone: 020 7637 4490
Fax: 020 7637 4493
Email: vha@vhassociates.co.uk

Personnel:
Valerie Hoskins (Managing Director)
Rebecca Watson (Agent)
Sara Moore (Assistant)

Specialization: film & television rights for
published work. The company is not a
publishing agency.

4040 ■■■■■■■■

IMG UK LTD
McCormack House, Burlington Lane,
London W4 2TH
Telephone: 020 8233 5300
Fax: 020 8233 5268
Email: sarah.wooldridge@imgworld.com
Web Site: www.imgworld.com

Personnel:
Sarah Wooldridge (Consultant)
Sally Matthews (Accountant)

All MSS except science fiction, fiction,
children's, short stories and poetry.

Specialization: non-fiction. No reading fee.
Please send synopsis with sample chapter
and SAE. Also handle IMG speakers. 20%
commission.

4041 ■■■■■■■■

THE INSPIRA GROUP
5 Bradley Road, Enfield, Middx EN3 6ES
Telephone: 020 8292 5163
Fax: 0870 139 3057
Email: darin@theinspiragroup.com
Web Site: www.theinspiragroup.com

Personnel:
Darin Jewell (Managing Director)
Shaun Ebelthite (Rights)
Charlene Webber (Administration)

Specialization: children's books, fantasy/sci-
fi, and general fiction. Manuscripts in all
genres are considered. Clients include
Michael Tolkien, Simon Hall, John Wilson
and Simon Brown. Authors should e-mail
their full MSS, synopsis and short literary CV
(with their postal address and landline tel.
no.) to darin@theinspiragroup.com

4042 ■■■■■■■■

**INTERCONTINENTAL LITERARY
AGENCY LTD**
Centric House, 390 Strand, London
WC2R 0LT
Telephone: 020 7379 6611
Fax: 020 7240 4724
Email: ila@ila-agency.co.uk
Web Site: www.ila-agency.co.uk

Personnel:
Nicki Kennedy (Agent)
Sam Edenborough (Agent)
Mary Esdaile (Agent)
Tessa Girvan (Agent)
Katherine West (Agent)
Jenny Robson (Agent)

Specialization: translation rights exclusively.

Rights Representative in UK for:
see website at:: Intercontinental Literary
Agency, London, UK

4043 ■■■■■■■■

JANKLOW & NESBIT (UK) LTD
33 Drayson Mews, London W8 4LY
Telephone: 020 7376 2733
Fax: 020 7376 2915
Email: queries@janklow.co.uk
Web Site: www.janklowandnesbit.co.uk

Personnel:
Claire Paterson (Literary Agent)
Will Francis (Literary Agent)
Tim Glister (Literary Agent)
Rebecca Folland (Foreign Rights Director)

All MSS except poetry, plays, film & TV
scripts.

Specialization: fiction and non-fiction;
commercial and literary. Send full outline
(non-fiction), synopsis and first three sample

chapters (fiction) plus informative covering letter and return postage.

Overseas Representation:
USA: Janklow & Nesbit Associates, New York, NY, USA

4044 ▬

JOHNSON & ALCOCK LTD
Clerkenwell House,
45–47 Clerkenwell Green, London
EC1R 0HT
Telephone: 020 7251 0125
Fax: 020 7251 2172
Email: info@johnsonandalcock.co.uk
Web Site: www.johnsonandalcock.co.uk

Personnel:
Andrew Hewson (Director)
Michael Alcock (Director)
Anna Power (Agent)
Ed Wilson (Agent)

All MSS except technical or academic material, poetry, plays. No unsolicited manuscripts; please send synopsis, full CV, sample opening chapters and SAE in the first instance. No reading fee.

Specialization: fiction and non-fiction. General non-fiction, biography, history, current affairs, health and lifestyle; literary and commercial fiction; sci-fi and graphic novels; 9+ children's and young adult.

Rights Representative in UK for:
USA: Soho Press, New York, NY, USA; Vendome Press, New York, NY, USA

Overseas Representation:
Worldwide - contact: Johnson & Alcock Ltd, London, UK

4045 ▬

JANE JUDD LITERARY AGENCY
18 Belitha Villas, London N1 1PD
Telephone: 020 7607 0273
Fax: 020 7607 0623
Web Site: www.janejudd.com

Personnel:
Jane C. Judd (Proprietor)

All MSS except plays, poetry and short stories.

Specialization: general non-fiction & fiction.

Rights Representative in UK for:
USA: Marian Young, New York, NY, USA; Mercury House, San Francisco, CA, USA; Permanent Press, Sag Harbor, NY, USA; RLR Associates, New York, NY, USA

Overseas Representation:
Eastern Europe: Prava i Prevodi Agency, Belgrade, Serbia
France: La Nouvelle Agence, Paris, France
Germany: Thomas Schlück Literary Agency, Garbsen, Germany
Italy: Stefania Fietta ALI, Milan, Italy
Netherlands & Scandinavia: Jan Michael, Amsterdam, Netherlands
Spain & Portugal: Julio F Yañez Literary Agency, Barcelona, Spain
USA: The Unter Agency, New York, NY, USA

4046 ▬

MICHELLE KASS ASSOCIATES
85 Charing Cross Road, London
WC2H 0AA
Telephone: 020 7439 1624
Fax: 020 7734 3394
Email: office@michellekass.co.uk

Personnel:
Michelle Kass (Agent)
Andrew Mills (Agent)

Specialization: an agency representing novelists, writers and directors for film, TV and theatre. No unsolicited MSS without preliminary phone call.

4047 ▬

THE FRANCES KELLY AGENCY
111 Clifton Road, Kingston-upon-Thames, Surrey KT2 6PL
Telephone: 020 8549 7830
Fax: 020 8547 0051

Personnel:
Frances Kelly (Proprietor)

Specialization: general non-fiction, all academic & professional disciplines; return postage & preliminary letter requested.

4048 ▬

KNIGHT FEATURES LTD
20 Crescent Grove, London SW4 7AH
Telephone: 020 7622 1467
Fax: 020 7622 1522
Email: info@knightfeatures.co.uk
Web Site: www.knightfeatures.co.uk

Personnel:
Peter Knight (Proprietor)
Gaby Martin (Associate)
Andrew Knight (Associate)
Samantha Ferris (Associate)

All MSS except short stories, poetry & unsolicited MSS (reading fee). No e-mail submissions.

Specialization: worldwide selling of strip cartoons, major features and serializations. Exclusive syndication agent in UK & Irish Republic for United Feature Syndicate (Peanuts, Dilbert, etc.) & Newspaper Enterprise Association (Frank & Ernest, Born Loser, King Baloo, etc.), also Paws Inc (Garfield), Creators Syndicate (The Far Side).

Rights Representative in UK for:
New Zealand: The Puzzle Co, New Zealand
USA: Paws Inc, USA; United Media Inc, New York, NY, USA

4049 ▬

LENZ-MULLIGAN RIGHTS & CO-EDITIONS
15 Sandbourne Avenue, London
SW19 3EW
Telephone: 020 8543 7846
Email: lenzmulligan@btinternet.com

Personnel:
Gundhild Lenz-Mulligan (Rights Manager)

All MSS except poetry and film scripts.

Specialization: sale of co-editions and rights in the Nordic countries and Dutch, English and German-speaking markets. Particularly interested in children's books. Also offers proofreading and translation services of German language material. Represents European, American and Australian publishers, packagers and authors.

Rights Representative in UK for:
Australia: Tracy Marsh Publications, West Beach, SA, Australia
Germany: Ars Edition, Germany
Netherlands: Image Books Factory, Eindhoven, Netherlands

4050 ▬

BARBARA LEVY LITERARY AGENCY
64 Greenhill, Hampstead High Street, London NW3 5TZ
Telephone: 020 7435 9046
Fax: 020 7431 2063

Personnel:
John F. Selby (Solicitor Associate)

Specialization: general fiction & non-fiction, and TV presenters.

Rights Representative in UK for:
USA: Arcadia, Danbury, CT, USA; Richard Parks, New York, NY, USA

Overseas Representation:
Foreign Language Markets: The Buckman Agency, London, UK
USA: Marshall Rights, London, UK

4051 ▬

LIMELIGHT CELEBRITY MANAGEMENT LTD
33 Newman Street, London W1T 1PY
Telephone: 020 7637 2529
Fax: 020 7637 2538
Email: limelight.management@virgin.net
Web Site:
www.limelightmanagement.com

Personnel:
Fiona Lindsay (Managing Director, Owner/Founder)
Mary Bekhait (Agent)
Maclean Lindsay (Operations Manager)
Alison Lindsay (Executive Assistant)

Specialization: full-length book MSS. Commercial fiction and non-fiction. Food, wine, health, crafts, gardening, biography/memoirs, popular culture, travel, women's interest (home 15%, overseas 20%), TV and radio rights (15–20%); will suggest revision where appropriate. No reading fee.

4052 ▬

CHRISTOPHER LITTLE LITERARY AGENCY
10 Eel Brook Studios,
125 Moore Park Road, London SW6 4PS
Telephone: 020 7736 4455
Fax: 020 7736 4490
Email: info@christopherlittle.net
Web Site: www.christopherlittle.net

Personnel:
Christopher Little (Agent Proprietor)
Caroline Hardman (Agent)

All MSS except poetry, plays, science fiction, fantasy, textbooks, illustrated children's or short stories. Film scripts for established clients only.

Specialization: full length commercial fiction and non-fiction. No reading fee. Send detailed letter plus synopsis and three sample chapters, and SAE in first instance.

4053 ▬

LONDON INDEPENDENT BOOKS
26 Chalcot Crescent, London NW1 8YD
Telephone: 020 7706 0486
Fax: 020 7724 3122

Personnel:
Carolyn Whitaker (Literary Agent)

All MSS except computers & young children's.

Specialization: fiction & non-fiction, particularly travel & fantasy.

4054 ▬

ANDREW LOWNIE LITERARY AGENCY LTD
36 Great Smith Street, London SW1P 3BU
Telephone: 020 7222 7574
Fax: 020 7222 7576
Email: lownie@globalnet.co.uk
Web Site: www.andrew.lownie.co.uk

Personnel:
Andrew Lownie (Proprietor)

Specialization: history, biography, packaging celebrities for book market and representing book projects for journalists. Titles agented include the Oxford Classical Dictionary, Cambridge Guide to Literature in English, Norma Major's books on Joan Sutherland and Chequers, Juliet Barker, Duncan Falconer, Laurence Gardner, Lawrence James, Christopher Lloyd, Sian Rees, David Stafford, Christian Wolmar, Sir John Mills, authorized lives of Sir Henry Cooper and Dick Emery, Desmond Seward, Daniel Tammet, Cathy Glass, Joyce Cary and Julian Maclaren - Ross Estates, numerous books about the SAS. Return postage essential. No reading fee. Commission 15% worldwide.

Overseas Representation:
Worldwide (excluding USA & Japan): The Marsh Agency, London, UK

4055 ▬

LUTYENS & RUBINSTEIN
21 Kensington Park Road, London
W11 2EU
Telephone: 020 7792 4855
Fax: 020 7792 4833
Email: info@lutyensrubinstein.co.uk

Submissions only to:
Email:
submissions@lutyensrubinstein.co.uk

Personnel:
Felicity Rubinstein (Partner)
Sarah Lutyens (Partner)

All MSS except poetry, screenplays, scripts for theatre and/or TV and radio.

Specialization: general adult non-fiction and fiction.

Overseas Representation:
France: La Nouvelle Agence, Paris, France
Germany: Eggers & Landwehr, Berlin, Germany
Italy: Grandi & Associates, Milan, Italy
USA: Inkwell Management, New York, NY, USA

4056 ▬

DUNCAN MCARA LITERARY AGENCY
28 Beresford Gardens, Edinburgh EH5 3ES
Telephone: 0131 552 1558
Email: duncanmcara@mac.com

All MSS except 'genre' fiction, educational & children's.

Specialization: literary fiction; non-fiction: art, architecture, archaeology, biography, history, military, Scottish. Home: 15%; Overseas: 20%. Preliminary email or letter with SAE essential. No reading fee. Also acts as editorial consultant on all aspects of general trade publishing. Editing, re-writing, copy-editing, proof correction for wide range of UK publishers.

4057 ▬

THE MCKERNAN LITERARY AGENCY & CONSULTANCY
5 Gayfield Square, Edinburgh EH1 3NW
Telephone: 0131 557 1771
Email: maggie@mckernanagency.co.uk
Web Site: www.mckernanagency.co.uk

Personnel:
Maggie McKernan (Agent)

All MSS except film scripts, screenplays, picture books for children.

Specialization: assisting and developing writers, as well as representing their interests in their dealings with publishers, selling rights and handling negotiations of contracts. Handle fiction and non-fiction (commercial and literary novels of all kinds, including crime, historical, contemporary). Consideration will be given to novels for children over the age of 10, but not picture books.

Overseas Representation:
USA & Worldwide (translation rights): Capel & Land Ltd, London, UK

4058

EUNICE MCMULLEN LTD
Low Ibbotsholme Cottage, off Bridge Lane, Troutbeck Bridge, Windermere, Cumbria LA23 1HU
Telephone: 01539 448551
Email: eunicemcmullen@totalise.co.uk
Web Site: www.eunicemcmullen.co.uk

Specialization: children's books (fiction only) for all ages including picture books for co-edition market and early teen fiction. No unsolicited MSS.

4059

ANDREW MANN LTD
1 Old Compton Street, London W1D 5JA
Telephone: 020 7734 4751
Fax: 020 3441 0988
Email: info@andrewmann.co.uk
Web Site: www.andrewmann.co.uk

Personnel:
Anne Dewe (Director)
Tina Betts (Director)
Louise Burns (Agent)

All MSS except poetry.

Specialization: fiction, general non-fiction & radio, television scripts. No unsolicited MSS. Preliminary letter, synopsis – first 30 pages and SAE essential. No reading fee. No e-mail submissions.

Rights Representative in UK for:
USA: Richard McDonough, Irvine, CA, USA

Overseas Representation:
China (Mainland): Big Apple Tuttle-Mori Agency Inc, Shanghai, P. R. of China
Czech Republic, Slovakia, Poland & Bulgaria': Andrew Nurnberg Associates
France: Lora Fountain Associates, Paris, France
Germany: Thomas Schlück Literary Agency, Garbsen, Germany
Hungary: Kàtai & Bolza Literary Agents, Budapest, Hungary
Israel: Deborah Harris Agency, Jerusalem, Israel
Italy: Living Literary Agency, Milan, Italy
Japan: Tuttle-Mori Agency Inc, Tokyo, Japan
Romania: Simona Kessler International Copyright Agency Ltd, Bucharest, Romania
Scandinavia, Netherlands, Spain & Portugal: Lennart Sane Agency
Taiwan: Big Apple Tuttle-Mori Associates, Shin-Juang, Taiwan
Thailand: Silk Road Agency, Bangkok, Thailand
Turkey: Asli Karasuil Agency, Istanbul, Turkey
USA: Jonathan Lyons, New York, NY, USA

4060

SARAH MANSON LITERARY AGENT
6 Totnes Walk, London N2 0AD
Telephone: 020 8442 0396
Email: info@sarahmanson.com
Web Site: www.sarahmanson.com

Personnel:
Sarah Manson (Proprietor)

All MSS except poetry and picture books.

Specialization: fiction for children and young adults. List of clients includes both well-established writers and promising new talent.

4061

MARJACQ SCRIPTS
34 Devonshire Place, London W1G 6JW
Telephone: 020 7935 9499
Fax: 020 7935 9115
Email: enquiries@marjacq.com
Web Site: www.marjacq.com

Personnel:
Philip Patterson (Literary Agent)
Luke Speed (Film Agent)
Isabella Floris (Literary Agent)

All MSS except poetry or stage plays.

Specialization: literary and commercial fiction, crime, thrillers, science fiction and women's fiction, and general non-fiction. Please submit three sample chapters and synopsis in first instance. SAE essential for return of MS.

Overseas Representation:
Austria, Germany, Switzerland & parts of Eastern Europe: Transnet Contracts Ltd, Vienna, Austria
Hungary: Kàtai & Bolza Literary Agents, Budapest, Hungary
Israel: Ilana Pikarski Literary Agency, Tel Aviv, Israel
Italy: Agenzia Piergiorgio Nicolazzini, Milan, Italy
Japan: The English Agency Japan Ltd, Tokyo, Japan
Poland: Graal Ltd, Warsaw, Poland
Scandinavia, Netherlands, Spain & Portugal: Lennart Sane Agency, Karlshamn, Sweden
Turkey: Kayi Literary & Merchandising Agency, Istanbul, Turkey

4062

THE MARSH AGENCY LTD
50 Albemarle Street, London W1S 4BD
Telephone: 020 7493 4361
Fax: 020 7495 8961
Email: enquiries@marsh-agency.co.uk
Web Site: www.marsh-agency.co.uk

Personnel:
Camilla Ferrier (Foreign Rights Director)
Jessica Woollard (Agent)
Stephanie Ebdon (Agent)

All MSS except children's, poetry, drama, TV, film & radio.

Specialization: selling of rights in the work of English-language writers throughout the world, representing a number of UK authors as well as British and American agencies and publishers.

Rights Representative in UK for:
Worldwide: see Website for full list, UK

4063

BLANCHE MARVIN
21a St Johns Wood High Street, London NW8 7NG
Telephone: 020 7722 2313
Fax: 020 7722 2313

Personnel:
Blanche Marvin (Director)

Specialization: theatre, film, TV, radio & publishing for UK & USA. MSS from published authors only.

4064

MBA LITERARY AGENTS
62 Grafton Way, London W1T 5DW
Telephone: 020 7387 2076
Fax: 020 7387 2042
Email: firstname@mbalit.co.uk
Web Site: www.mbalit.co.uk

Personnel:
Diana Tyler (Managing Director)
Meg Davis (Director)
Timothy Webb (Financial Director)
Laura Longrigg (Director)
David Riding (Director)
Susan Smith (Director)
Jean Kitson (Agent)
Sophie Gorell Barnes (Agent)
Stella Kane (Foreign Rights Manager)

All MSS except poetry, short stories.

Specialization: fiction and non-fiction. Also scripts for film, TV, radio & theatre.

Rights Representative in UK for:
USA: Beacon Artists, New York, NY, USA; Donald Maass Agency, New York, NY, USA; Frances Collin Agency, New York, NY, USA; Martha Millard Literary Agency, New York, NY, USA

Overseas Representation:
Brazil: Tassy Barham, London, UK
Eastern Europe & Greece: Prava i Prevodi, Belgrade, Serbia
France: Lora Fountain Associates, Paris, France
Germany: Mohrbooks Literary Agency, Zurich, Switzerland; Thomas Schlück Literary Agency, Garbsen, Germany
Israel: I. Pikarski Literary Agency, Tel Aviv, Israel
Italy: Vicki Satlow Literary Agency, Milan, Italy
Japan: Tuttle-Mori Agency Inc, Tokyo, Japan
Netherlands: Caroline Van Gelderen Literary Agency, Hilversum, Netherlands
Russia: Prava i Prevodi RAO, Moscow, Russia
Scandinavia: Licht & Burr Literary Agency, Copenhagen, Denmark
Spain: Carmen Balcells Agencia Literaria SA, Barcelona, Spain

4065

THE CATHY MILLER FOREIGN RIGHTS AGENCY
29A The Quadrangle, 49 Atalanta Street, London SW6 6TU
Telephone: 020 7386 5473
Fax: 020 7385 1774
Email: cathy@millerrightsagency.com

Personnel:
Mrs Cathy Miller (Principal/Managing Director)

All MSS except poetry & educational.

Specialization: foreign rights; acting as consultants to publishers on sales of foreign rights of non-fiction titles (psychoanalysis, medical, business & management, esoteric, health & general trade books); handling market research for lists or one-off projects; helping to set up rights departments; advising on all matters concerning translation rights and negotiations with foreign publishers.

Rights Representative in UK for:
Canada: Fletcher Peacock, Canada; Golden Globe Publishing, Notre Dame-de-l'Ile Perrot, PQ, Canada; Mark Fisher, Canada
UK: Ann Henning-Jocelyn, Countess of Roden, UK; Artemis Music Publishing, UK; Foulsham Publishers, UK; Free Association Books, UK; Karnac Books, UK; Phantom Genius Ltd, UK; Shepheard-Walwyn, UK; Thorogood Publishing Ltd, UK

Overseas Representation:
China: Mei Yao, New York, NY, USA
Greece: Read n Right Agency, Cahlkida, Greece
Japan: The English Agency Japan Ltd, Tokyo, Japan
Korea: EYA, Seoul, Republic of Korea
Poland: Graal Ltd, Warsaw, Poland
Russia: Alexander Korzhenevski Literary Agency, Moscow, Russia
Spain: Julio F Yañez Literary Agency, Barcelona, Spain

4066

NEW WRITING NORTH
Holy Jesus Hospital, City Road, Newcastle-upon-Tyne NE1 2AS
Telephone: 0191 233 3850
Email: claire@newwritingnorth.com
Web Site: www.newwritingnorth.com

Personnel:
Claire Malcolm (Director)
Anna Disley (Deputy Director)
Cath Robson (Finance & Administration)
Olivia Mantle (Marketing)

4067

NEW WRITING SOUTH
9 Jew Street, Brighton BN1 1UT
Telephone: 01273 735353
Email: admin@newwritingsouth.com
Web Site: www.newwritingsouth.com

Personnel:
Chris Taylor (Director)
Mark Bryant (Operations Manager)
Anna Jefferson (Creative Learning)

Specialization: nurturing and developing creative writers and their work and encouraging a thriving new writing economy in the south.

4068

THE MAGGIE NOACH LITERARY AGENCY
7 Peacock Yard, Iliffe Street, London SE17 3LH
Telephone: 020 7708 3073
Email: info@mnla.co.uk

All MSS except short stories, poetry, plays, screenplays, cookery, gardening, mind/body/spirit, illustrated children's, scientific/academic/specialist non-fiction. Absolutely no illustrated books.

Specialization: fiction, general non-fiction and children's books. No unsolicited manuscripts – submissions by arrangements only. Home 15%, USA & translation 20%.

Overseas Representation:
Worldwide: Jill Hughes, Aubourn, Lincs, UK

4069

ANDREW NURNBERG ASSOCIATES LTD
45-47 Clerkenwell Green, London EC1R 0QX
Telephone: 020 7417 8800
Fax: 020 7253 4851
Email: contact@andrewnurnberg.com
Web Site: www.andrewnurnberg.com

Personnel:
Andrew Nurnberg (Managing Director)
Sarah Nundy (Deputy Managing Director)
Vicky Mark (Director)

Specialization: representing leading British & American agents & authors throughout the world.

4070

DEBORAH OWEN LTD
78 Narrow Street, Limehouse, London
E14 8BP
Telephone: 020 7987 5119 & 5441
Fax: 020 7538 4004
Email: do@deborahowen.co.uk

Personnel:
Deborah Owen *(Literary Agent)*

*Specialization: small agency representing
Amos Oz and Delia Smith. No new authors.*

4071

PATERSON MARSH LTD
50 Albemarle Street, London W1S 4BD
Telephone: 020 7493 4361
Fax: 020 7495 8961
Web Site: www.patersonmarsh.co.uk

Personnel:
Stephanie Ebdon *(Agent)*
Mark Paterson *(Consultant)*

*All MSS except fiction, children's, poetry,
drama, TV, film & radio.*

*Specialization: professional psychology,
psychoanalysis, psychotherapy, general
non-fiction. Preliminary letter and return
postage required.*

Parent Company:
UK: The Marsh Agency Ltd

Associated Companies:
UK: The Marsh Agency Ltd

Rights Representative in UK for:
UK: Hammersmith Press, London, UK; New
Library of Psychoanalysis, London, UK;
Sigmund Freud Copyrights, London, UK
USA: The Analytic Press, New York, NY,
USA; International Universities Press,
Madison, CT, USA; Other Press LLC, New
York, NY, USA; Pitchstone Publishing, Los
Angeles, CA, USA; Routledge US, New
York, NY, USA; Zeig, Tucker & Theisen
Inc, Redding, CT, USA

4072

JOHN PAWSEY
8 Snowshill Court, Giffard Park,
Milton Keynes, Bucks MK14 5QG
Telephone: 01908 217179

Personnel:
John Pawsey *(Sole Proprietor)*

*All MSS except fiction, poetry, short stories,
journalism, children's, original film & stage
scripts.*

Specialization: sport, popular culture.

Rights Representative in UK for:
USA: Alison J. Picard, Cotuit, MA, USA;
Bobbe Siegel, New York, NY, USA

Overseas Representation:
France: Lora Fountain Associates, Paris,
France
Germany: Thomas Schlück Literary Agency,
Garbsen, Germany
Hungary: Lex Copyright, Budapest, Hungary
Italy: Living Literary Agency, Milan, Italy
Japan: The English Agency Japan Ltd, Tokyo,
Japan
Korea: Korea Copyright Center, Seoul,
Republic of Korea
Netherlands: International Literatur Bureau
BV, Hilversum, Netherlands
Russia: Prava i Prevodi RAO, Moscow, Russia
Scandinavia: Sane Töregård Agency,
Karlshamn, Sweden
Spain & South America: International
Editors Co, Barcelona, Spain

USA: Alison J. Picard, Cotuit, MA, USA
Yugoslav States: Prava i Prevodi, Belgrade,
Serbia

4073

POLLINGER LTD
9 Staple Inn, Holborn, London WC1V 7QH
Telephone: 020 7404 0342
Fax: 020 7242 5737
Email: info@pollingerltd.com
Web Site: www.pollingerltd.com

Personnel:
Lesley Pollinger *(Managing Director)*
Leigh Pollinger *(Director)*
Joanna Devereux *(Literary Agent)*
Tim Bates *(Literary Agent)*
Hayley Yeeles *(Literary Agent)*

*All MSS except poetry & articles – see
website for submission details.*

*Specialization: adult fiction and non-fiction,
children's and literary estates.*

Rights Representative in UK for:
UK: Wallflower Press, London, UK
UK (dramatic rights): Summersdale, UK
USA: New Directions Publishing
Corporation, New York, NY, USA

Overseas Representation:
China: Big Apple Tuttle-Mori Agency, Taipei,
Taiwan
Denmark, Finland, Norway & Sweden: Licht
& Burr Literary Agency, Copenhagen,
Denmark
France: Michelle Lapautre Agency, Paris,
France
Germany & Switzerland: Mohrbooks
Literary Agency, Zurich, Switzerland
Greece: Read n Right Agency, Cahlkida,
Greece
Hungary: Lex Copyright, Budapest, Hungary
Israel: The Book Publishers Association of
Israel, Tel Aviv, Israel
Japan: Tuttle-Mori Agency Inc, Tokyo, Japan
Korea: The Eric Yang Agency, Seoul,
Republic of Korea
Portugal & Brazil: Ilidio da Fonseca Matos,
Lisbon, Portugal
Spain & South America: Carmen Balcells
Agencia Literaria SA, Barcelona, Spain
Turkey: ONK Agency Ltd, Istanbul, Turkey
*Yugoslav States, Bulgaria, Poland, Czech/
Slovak Rep., Russia & Romania:* Prava i
Prevodi, Belgrade, Serbia

4074

**SHELLEY POWER LITERARY
AGENCY LTD**
13 rue du Pré Saint Gervais, 75019 Paris,
France
Telephone: +33 1 42 38 36 49
Fax: +33 1 40 40 70 08
Email: shelley.power@wanadoo.fr

Personnel:
Shelley Power *(Director, Literary Agent)*

*All MSS except children's books, poetry,
plays or film scripts. No horror, science
fiction or fantasy.*

Specialization: literary agency.

Rights Representative in UK for:
USA: The Feminist Press, New York, NY, USA

Overseas Representation:
China: Big Apple Tuttle-Mori Agency Inc,
Shanghai, P. R. of China; Big Apple
Tuttle-Mori Agency, Taipei, Taiwan
Czech Republic: Transnet Contracts, Czech
Republic
France: Lora Fountain Associates, Paris,
France
Germany: Liepman AG, Germany

Greece: JLM Literary Agency, Athens,
Greece
Hungary: Kàtai & Bolza Literary Agents,
Budapest, Hungary
Israel: Ilana Pikarski Literary Agency, Tel Aviv,
Israel
Italy: Natoli, Stefan & Oliva Agenzia
Letteraria, Milan, Italy
Japan: The English Agency Japan Ltd, Tokyo,
Japan
Korea: The Eric Yang Agency, Seoul,
Republic of Korea
Poland: Graal Ltd, Warsaw, Poland
Romania: Simona Kessler International
Copyright Agency Ltd, Bucharest,
Romania
Spain: Julio F Yañez Literary Agency,
Barcelona, Spain

4075

**REAL CREATIVES WORLDWIDE
(RCW)**
14 Dean Street, London W1D 3RS
Telephone: 020 7437 4188
Email: malcolm.rasala@realcreatives.com
Web Site: www.realcreatives.com

Personnel:
M. Rasala *(Chief Executive Officer)*
M. Maco *(COO)*
Natasha Ganea *(Sales)*

*Specialization: literary agency for books;
film agent for motion pictures (recognized
agent in Hollywood); TV agent for TV
programmes worldwide; advertiser - supply
TV programme agents; agent representing
200 professionals (directors, producers,
creatives, etc.) in the motion picture, TV and
advertising industries, 120 professors
(Harvard, Yale, MIT, Stanford, Oxford, etc.).*

Overseas Representation:
Italy: Marco Fichera, Rome, Italy

4076

REDHAMMER MANAGEMENT LTD
186 Bickenhall Mansions, London
W1U 6BX
Telephone: 020 7486 3465
Fax: 020 7000 1249
Web Site: www.redhammer.info

Personnel:
Peter Cox *(Chief Executive Officer)*

*Specialization: rights representation,
including literary and publishing, film and
TV, merchandising. The company has a
small number of successful clients who wish
to accelerate the momentum of their
success. Currently published writers can visit
our website if they would like more
information; if you have not yet been
published, your submission will be
considered if you follow the Submissions
Procedure.*

4077

ROGERS, COLERIDGE & WHITE LTD
20 Powis Mews, London W11 1JN
Telephone: 020 7221 3717
Fax: 020 7229 9084
Web Site: www.rcwlitagency.com

Personnel:
Deborah Rogers *(Chairman)*
Gill Coleridge *(Director)*
Patricia White *(Director)*
David Miller *(Director)*
Peter Straus *(Managing Director)*
Laurence Laluyaux *(Foreign Rights Director)*
Stephen Edwards *(Foreign Rights Director)*
Zoe Waldie *(Director)*
Hannah Westland *(Agent)*
Catherine Pellegrino *(Children's Agent)*
Peter Robinson *(Director)*
Sam Copeland *(Agent)*

*All MSS except screenplays, plays or
technical books. No unsolicited MSS, please
and no submissions by e-mail.*

*Specialization: handles fiction, non-fiction
and children's books. Literary agency.
Founded 1967. Rights representative in UK
and translation for several New York agents.
Commission: Home 15%; US & translation
20%.*

4078

THE SAYLE LITERARY AGENCY
1 Petersfield, Cambridge CB1 1BB
Telephone: 01223 303035
Fax: 01223 301638
Web Site: www.sayleliteraryagency.com

Personnel:
Rachel Calder *(Proprietor)*

*All MSS except children's, poetry, technical,
science fiction.*

*Specialization: fiction (literary & crime),
biography, history, current affairs, travel,
social issues.*

Rights Representative in UK for:
USA: Darhansoff Verrill Feldman Literary
Agency, New York, NY, USA; New
England Publishing Associates, CT, USA

Overseas Representation:
Europe & Rest of the World: The Marsh
Agency, London, UK
USA: Dunow, Carlson & Lerner Agency,
New York, NY, USA

4079

**CAROLINE SHELDON LITERARY
AGENCY**
71 Hillgate Place, London W8 7SS
Telephone: 020 7727 9102
Email:
carolinesheldon@carolinesheldon.co.uk &
pennyholroyde@carolinesheldon.co.uk
Web Site: www.carolinesheldon.co.uk &
www.carolinesheldonillustrators.co.uk

Personnel:
Caroline Sheldon *(Literary Agent)*
Penny Holroyde *(Literary Agent)*

All MSS except short stories.

*Specialization: fiction, women's fiction &
children's books, human interest non-
fiction.*

4080

**DORIE SIMMONDS LITERARY
AGENCY**
Riverbank House,
1 Putney Bridge Approach, London
SW6 3JD
Telephone: 020 7736 0002
Fax: 020 7736 0010
Email: dorie@doriesimmonds.com

Personnel:
Dorie Simmonds *(Proprietor)*
Frances Lubbe *(Rights Executive)*

All MSS except plays, poetry or short stories.

*Specialization: commercial fiction and non-
fiction in both the adult and children's
markets.*

4081

JEFFREY SIMMONS
15 Penn House, Mallory Street, London
NW8 8SX
Telephone: 020 7224 8917
Email: jasimmons@unicombox.co.uk

All MSS except children's books, cookery, science-fiction, romances & some specialist subjects.

Specialization: biography & memoirs; cinema, drama & the arts; general fiction; history; law & crime; literature; politics & world affairs.

Overseas Representation:
Japan: The English Agency Japan Ltd, Tokyo, Japan
Spain: Julio F Yañez Literary Agency, Barcelona, Spain

4082

SINCLAIR-STEVENSON
3 South Terrace, London SW7 2TB
Telephone: 020 7581 2550
Fax: 020 7581 2550

Translation Rights:
c/o David Higham Associates Ltd,
5–8 Lower John Street, Golden Square,
London W1F 9HA

All MSS except children's books, science fiction, science, fantasy, film or play scripts.

Specialization: non-fiction – biography and autobiography, the arts, politics and current affairs, travel, history; and fiction.

Rights Representative in UK for:
USA: T. C. Wallace Ltd, New York, NY, USA

Overseas Representation:
USA: T. C. Wallace Ltd, New York, NY, USA

4083

ROBERT SMITH LITERARY AGENCY LTD
12 Bridge Wharf, 156 Caledonian Road,
London N1 9UU
Telephone: 020 7278 2444
Fax: 020 7833 5680
Email:
robertsmith.literaryagency@virgin.net

Personnel:
Robert Smith *(Managing Director)*
Anne Smith *(Director)*

All MSS except fiction, poetry, children's books or reference. Writers may submit synopses but no unsolicited manuscripts.

Specialization: the agency sells books, series and articles to book publishers, newspapers and magazines across the world. It operates only in non-fiction. Main areas are autobiography and biography, show business, hot topics, history, health, lifestyle and true crime.

Overseas Representation:
Germany: Thomas Schlück Literary Agency, Garbsen, Germany
Italy: Natoli, Stefan & Oliva Agenzia Letteraria, Milan, Italy
Spain: RDC Agencia Literaria, Madrid, Spain

4084

SHIRLEY STEWART LITERARY AGENCY
3rd Floor, 4a Nelson Road, London SE10 9JB
Telephone: 020 8293 3000

Personnel:
Shirley Stewart *(Director)*

All MSS except children's books, poetry, plays, science fiction and fantasy.

Specialization: full-length MSS only. Fiction and non-fiction (home 10–15%, overseas 20%). No reading fee but preliminary letter and return postage essential.

Rights Representative in UK for:
USA: Curtis Brown Ltd, New York, NY, USA

4085

THE SUSIJN AGENCY LTD
3rd Floor, 64 Great Titchfield Street,
London W1W 7QH
Telephone: 020 7580 6341
Fax: 020 7580 8626
Email: info@thesusijnagency.com
Web Site: www.thesusijnagency.com

Personnel:
Laura Susijn *(Literary Agent)*
Nicola Barr *(Literary Agent)*

All MSS except children's books, sci-fi, romantic fiction, fantasy, sagas, self-help, business, military and computer books.

Specialization: selling rights world-wide in literary fiction and non-fiction. Also represents non-English language publishers and authors for UK, US and translation rights world-wide. Deals direct, using sub-agent in Eastern Europe, Israel and the Far East. Preliminary letter, synopsis and first two chapters preferred. No reading fee.

4086

THE TENNYSON AGENCY
10 Cleveland Avenue, London SW20 9EW
Telephone: 020 8543 5939
Email: submissions@tenagy.co.uk
Web Site: www.tenagy.co.uk

Personnel:
Adam Sheldon *(Partner)*

All MSS except poetry, short stories, science fiction, popular romantic and historical fiction, children's books and non-fiction unrelated to the arts.

Specialization: writing for the theatre, TV, radio and film. Related subjects and literary fiction are considered on an ad hoc basis. Commission rates: literature: 12.5%, drama: 15%, overseas: 20%. Submissions by post, on invitation, following introductory letter. Full details on the agency's website.

4087

J. M. THURLEY MANAGEMENT
Archery House, 33 Archery Square, Walmer,
Deal, Kent CT14 7AY
Telephone: 01304 371721
Email: jmthurley@aol.com
Web Site: www.thecuttingedge.biz

Personnel:
Jon Thurley *(Contact)*
Patricia Preece *(Contact)*

All MSS except short stories & poetry.

Specialization: will give editorial help by arrangement on all types of projects.

4088

LAVINIA TREVOR
29 Addison Place, London W11 4RJ
Telephone: 020 7603 5254
Fax: 0870 129 0838
Email: info@laviniatrevor.co.uk
Web Site: www.laviniatrevor.co.uk

Personnel:
Lavinia Trevor *(Agent)*

Specialization: fiction and non-fiction for the general trade market (see website). No unsolicited material.

4089

JANE TURNBULL AGENCY
58 Elgin Crescent, London W11 2JJ
Telephone: 020 7727 9409
Email: jane@janeturnbull.co.uk
Web Site: www.janeturnbull.co.uk

Mailing Address:
Barn Cottage, Veryan, Truro, Cornwall
TR2 5QA
Telephone: 01872 501317

Personnel:
Jane Turnbull *(Proprietor)*

All MSS except science or romantic fiction, children's fiction, poetry or plays.

Specialization: literary fiction, current affairs, biography, design, lifestyle, health, TV tie-ins, humour, natural history. Initial letter essential; no unsolicited MSS. Commission 15% home sales, 20% US, 20% translation, 15% radio/TV/film. Founded 1986, member of the Association of Authors' Agents.

Overseas Representation:
Worldwide: Aitken Alexander Associates, London, UK

4090

UNITED AGENTS LTD
12–26 Lexington Street, London W1F 0LE
Telephone: 020 3214 0800
Fax: 020 3214 0801
Web Site: www.unitedagents.co.uk

Personnel:
Simon Trewin *(Head, Books Department)*
Caroline Dawnay *(Agent)*
Sarah Ballard *(Agent)*
Rosemary Canter *(Agent)*
James Gill *(Agent)*
Robert Kirby *(Agent)*
Rosemary Scoular *(Agent)*
Charles Walker *(Agent)*
Anna Webber *(Agent)*
Jessica Craig *(Foreign Rights Agent)*
Jane Willis *(Foreign Rights Agent)*
Jodie Marsh *(Agent)*

Specialization: literary and talent agency, operating across books, theatre, film, TV and commercials. Offers a full service to its client base and is always interested in new clients. Please consult website at www.unitedagents.co.uk for full submission guidelines.

4091

ED VICTOR LTD
6 Bayley Street, Bedford Square, London
WC1B 3HE
Telephone: 020 7304 4100
Fax: 020 7304 4111
Email: mary@edvictor.com

Personnel:
Ed Victor *(Executive Chairman)*
Margaret Phillips *(Joint Managing Director)*
Sophie Hicks *(Foreign Rights & Joint Managing Director)*
Leon Morgan *(Director)*
Carol Ryan *(Director)*
Graham Greene *(Director)*
Hitesh Shah *(Finance Director)*

All MSS except unsolicited manuscripts.

Specialization: fiction, non-fiction, biography, children's books.

4092

WADE & DOHERTY LITERARY AGENCY LTD
33 Cormorant Lodge, Thomas More Street,
London E1W 1AU

Telephone: 020 7488 4171
Fax: 020 7488 4172
Email: rw@rwla.com
Web Site: www.rwla.com

Personnel:
Broo Doherty *(Partner)*

All MSS except scripts, poetry, plays, children's picture books or short stories.

Specialization: handles general fiction and non-fiction including children's books (but excluding picture books). Send detailed synopsis and first 10,000 words by e-mail. No reading fee. Commission: home 10%; film, TV and translation 20% (fees negotiable if a contract has already been offered). Founded 2001. Please see our website for detailed email submission guidelines.

4093

WATSON, LITTLE LTD
48–56 Bayham Place, London NW1 0EU
Telephone: 020 7388 7529
Fax: 020 7388 8501
Email: office@watsonlittle.com
Web Site: www.watsonlittle.com

Personnel:
Mandy Little *(Managing Director)*
James Wills *(Director)*
Sallyanne Sweeney *(Literary Agent)*

All MSS except short stories, plays, poetry, works for very small children & articles (except by established columnists).

Specialization: literary and commercial fiction, serious non-fiction, psychology, self-help, popular culture, celebrity, health, sport, humour, children's.

Rights Representative in UK for:
USA (children's): The Chudney Agency, New York, NY, USA

Overseas Representation:
USA (adult): Howard Morhaim Literary Agency, New York, NY, USA
USA (children's): The Chudney Agency, New York, NY, USA
Worldwide: The Marsh Agency, London, UK
Worldwide (film & TV associates): MBA Literary Agents, London, UK; The Sharland Organisation, Raunds, Northants, UK

4094

A. P. WATT LTD
20 John Street, London WC1N 2DR
Telephone: 020 7405 6774
Fax: 020 7831 2154
Email: apw@apwatt.co.uk
Web Site: www.apwatt.co.uk

Personnel:
Caradoc King *(Director)*
Linda Shaughnessy *(Director)*
Georgia Garrett *(Director)*
Derek Johns *(Director)*
Natasha Fairweather *(Director)*
Rob Kraitt *(Associate Director)*

All MSS except poetry.

Specialization: general fiction and non-fiction. No unsolicited manuscripts.

4095

JOSEF WEINBERGER PLAYS LTD
[formerly Warner/Chappell Plays Ltd]
12–14 Mortimer Street, London W1T 3JJ
Telephone: 020 7580 2827
Fax: 020 7436 9616
Email: general.info@jwmail.co.uk
Web Site: www.josef-weinberger.com

Personnel:
Michael Callahan *(Manager)*

Specialization: stage plays. Works in conjunction with overseas agents. No unsolicited manuscripts, preliminary letter essential.

Parent Company:
UK: Josef Weinberger Ltd

Associated Companies:
UK: Josef Weinberger Ltd

Rights Representative in UK for:
USA: Dramatists Play Service Inc, New York, NY, USA

Overseas Representation:
Australia: Hal Leonard (Australia) Ltd, Melbourne, Vic, Australia
Canada & USA: Dramatists Play Service Inc, New York, NY, USA
New Zealand: Play Bureau (NZ) Ltd, New Plymouth, New Zealand
South Africa: Dalro (Pty) Ltd, Johannesburg, South Africa
Zimbabwe: National Theatre Organization, Harare, Zimbabwe

4096 ▬▬▬

EVE WHITE LITERARY AGENT
54 Gloucester Street, London SW1V 4EG
Telephone: 020 7630 1155
Email: eve@evewhite.co.uk
Web Site: www.evewhite.co.uk

Personnel:
Eve White *(Director)*

All MSS except poetry, picture books, plays, screenplays.

Specialization: UK agency representing internationally published authors of commercial and literary fiction and non-fiction, children's fiction and picture books. Foreign rights handled in conjunction with Diana Mackay at Melcombe International Ltd. Film rights in conjunction with Rod Hall. Clients include: Rae Earl, Chris Pascoe, Alexander Stobbs, Ruth Saberton, Jill Marshall and Charlie Mitchell. Children's authors: Andy Stanton, Jimmy Docherty, Susannah Corbett, Gillian Rogerson, David Flavell, Kate Maryon, Carolyn Ching, Rachael Mortimer, Tracey Corderoy, Ciaran Murtagh, Miriam Halahmy & Abie

---

Longstaff. Authors wishing to submit work must consult the submission page of our website - thank you.

Overseas Representation:
Commonwealth countries & USA: Eve White, London, UK
Worldwide (excluding Commonwealth countries & USA): Melcombe International, Somerset, UK

4097 ▬▬▬

DINAH WIENER LTD
12 Cornwall Grove, London W4 2LB
Telephone: 020 8994 6011
Fax: 020 8994 6044

Personnel:
Dinah Wiener *(Director)*
D. P. Wiener *(Director)*
B. M. Wiener *(Director)*

All MSS except juvenile, plays, film scripts, poetry & short stories.

Specialization: general fiction and non-fiction.

4098 ▬▬▬

JONATHAN WILLIAMS LITERARY AGENCY
Rosney Mews, Upper Glenageary Road, Glenageary, Co Dublin, Republic of Ireland
Telephone: +353 (01) 280 3482
Fax: +353 (01) 280 3482

Personnel:
Jonathan Williams *(Director)*

All MSS except plays or film scripts. Return postage and packing is appreciated. Irish postage stamps or international postal coupons, please.

Specialization: typescripts of Irish interest.

Overseas Representation:
Italy: Agenzia Piergiorgio Nicolazzini, Milan, Italy
Japan: Tuttle-Mori Agency Inc, Tokyo, Japan
Netherlands & Germany: International Literatuur Bureau, Amsterdam, Netherlands
Spain & Spanish-speaking Latin America: Antonia Kerrigan Literary Agency, Barcelona, Spain

5 Trade & Allied Associations

5.1 INTERNATIONAL

5001

EDITEUR LTD
United House, North Road, London N7 9DP
Telephone: 020 7503 6148
Fax: 020 7503 6418
Email: info@editeur.org
Web Site: www.editeur.org

Personnel:
Mark Bide (Executive Director)
Stella Griffiths (Associate Director)
Sarah Hilderley (Accessibility Project Lead)

EDItEUR is the international group co-ordinating development of the standards infrastructure for electronic commerce in the book and serials sectors. EDItEUR provides its membership with research, standards and guidance in such diverse areas as:
– EDI and other e-commerce standards for book and serial transactions
– Bibliographic and product information
– The standards infrastructure for digital publishing
– Rights management and trading
– Radio frequency identification tags
Established in 1991, EDItEUR is a truly international organisation with 90 members from 17 countries, including Australia, Canada, Japan, South Africa, United States and most of the European countries.
A leader in global standards for the exchange of bibliographic information (particularly the ONIX for Books Product Information standard) and of e-commerce messages in the book and journal supply chains, EDItEUR is also engaged in shaping key national and international projects aimed at developing rights and permissions expressions.

5002

ENGLISH-SPEAKING UNION OF THE COMMONWEALTH
37 Charles Street, London W1J 5ED
Telephone: 020 7529 1550
Fax: 020 7495 6108
Email: esu@esu.org
Web Site: www.esu.org

Personnel:
HRH The Duke of Edinburgh KG, KT, OM (President)
The Lord Hunt of the Wirral MBE, PC (Chairman)
Mrs Valerie Mitchell OBE (Director General)

The English-Speaking Union is an international organization represented in 59 countries and with headquarters in London and New York. It is a registered charity with the aim of promoting international friendship and understanding through the English language.
The ESU runs several awards: the Duke of Edinburgh English Language Book Award, the President's Award for the best non-book language materials, the Marsh Biography Award and the Marsh Children's Literature in Translation Award.

5003

FEDERATION OF EUROPEAN PUBLISHERS
31 rue Montoyer, Box 8, 1000 Brussels, Belgium
Telephone: +32 (02) 770 11 10
Fax: +32 (02) 771 20 71
Email: info@fep-fee.eu
Web Site: www.fep-fee.eu

Personnel:
Ms Anne Bergman-Tahon (Director)

Lobbying European institutions on behalf of the European publishing community.

5004

IBBY – INTERNATIONAL BOARD ON BOOKS FOR YOUNG PEOPLE
Nonnenweg 12, Postfach, 4003 Basel, Switzerland
Telephone: +41 ((0)61) 272 29 17
Fax: +41 ((0)61) 272 27 57
Email: forest.zhang@ibby.org
Web Site: www.ibby.org

Personnel:
Elizabeth Page (Executive Director)
Patricia Aldana (President of the Executive Committee)
Forest Zhang (Deputy Director of Administration)

Promotion of children's books and reading worldwide.

5005

THE INTERNATIONAL ISBN AGENCY
United House, North Road, London N7 9DP
Telephone: 020 7503 6418
Fax: 020 7503 6418
Email: info@isbn-international.org
Web Site: www.isbn-international.org

Personnel:
Brian Green (Executive Director)
Stella Griffiths (Associate Director)

The International ISBN Agency is the registration authority for the ISBN system globally. The administration of the ISBN system is carried out on three levels:
– International agency
– Group agencies
– Publisher level
The main functions of the International ISBN Agency are:
– To promote, co-ordinate and supervise the world-wide use of the ISBN system
– To approve the definition and structure of group agencies
– To allocate group identifiers to group agencies
– To advise on the establishment and functioning of group agencies
– To advise group agencies on the allocation of international publisher identifiers
– To publish the assigned group numbers and publishers' prefixes
There are over 160 local ISBN agencies covering 200 countries. Publishers apply to their local ISBN agency to obtain ISBNs.

5006

PRIVATE LIBRARIES ASSOCIATION
Ravelston, South View Road, Pinner, Middx HA5 3YD
Email: dchambrs@aol.com
Web Site: www.plabooks.org

Personnel:
Keith Fletcher (Hon President)
Stan Brett (Hon Secretary)
David Chambers (Hon Editor & Hon Publications Secretary)
Dean A. Sewell (Hon Treasurer)

An international society of book collectors, run on a voluntary basis. Publications include a quarterly journal and The Exchange List, which circulate among member collectors throughout the world, Private Press Books, an annual bibliography, and other books concerned with book collecting.

5.2 UNITED KINGDOM & REPUBLIC OF IRELAND

5007

YR ACADEMI GYMREIG
Mount Stuart House, Mount Stuart Square, Cardiff CF10 5FQ
Telephone: 029 2047 2266
Fax: 029 2049 2930
Email: post@academi.org
Web Site: www.academi.org

Glyn Jones Centre for Writers:
Wales Millennium Centre, Bute Place, Cardiff CF10 5AL
Telephone: (as above)
Fax: 029 2047 0691
Email: (as above)
Web Site: (as above)

Personnel:
Peter Finch (Chief Executive)
Lleucu Siencyn (Deputy)

Founded in 1959, Yr Academi Gymreig / The Welsh Academy is the national society which promotes the writers and literatures of Wales. The Academi runs courses, competitions (including the Cardiff International Poetry Competition), conferences, tours by authors, international exchanges, events for schools, readings, literary performances and festivals. The Academi also offers advice to authors, a writers' critical and mentoring service and financial bursaries, and runs the annual Book of the Year Award. It works in partnership with Tŷ Newydd, the Criccieth-based residential writers' centre.
Publications include A470; Taliesin, a quarterly literary journal in the Welsh language; The Oxford Companion to the Literature of Wales; The Welsh Academy English-Welsh Dictionary; The Welsh Academy Encyclopaedia of Wales published with the support of the Lottery, and a variety of translated works.
In 2004 Academi became a resident at the Wales Millennium Centre. The Glyn Jones Centre for Writers opened in 2005.

5008

ACADEMIC AND PROFESSIONAL DIVISION OF THE PUBLISHERS ASSOCIATION
29B Montague Street, London WC1B 5BW
Telephone: 020 7691 9191
Fax: 020 7691 9199
Email: gtaylor@publishers.org.uk
Web Site: www.publishers.org.uk

Personnel:
Graham Taylor (Director)

Parent Company:
UK: The Publishers Association

The Academic and Professional Division of The Publishers Association represents the interests of publishers serving higher education, scholarly communication and the professional and commercial market. Collective activities are organized on their behalf. Membership is open to any publisher in membership of the Publishers Association who produces books, journals or similar published material for these markets.

5009

ALLIANCE OF LITERARY SOCIETIES (ALS)
59 Bryony Road, Selly Oak, Birmingham B29 4BY
Telephone: 0121 475 1805
Email: l.j.curry@bham.ac.uk
Web Site: www.allianceofliterarysocieties.org.uk

Personnel:
Linda J. Curry (Chair)
Julie Shorland (Hon Treasurer / Membership Secretary)
Anita Fernandez-Young (Secretary)

The ALS is an umbrella organization for literary societies/ groups within the UK. The AGM is hosted by different member societies each year, with accompanying talks etc covering a weekend (usually in April or May). Members of affiliated societies are welcome to attend but only the delegate of the affiliated society may have a vote. Details are on the website – including subscription rates. An annual journal (ALSo...) is also produced. This is freely available to member societies but can be purchased by non-members.

5010

ARTS COUNCIL ENGLAND
14 Great Peter Street, London SW1P 3NQ
Telephone: 0845 300 6200
Fax: 020 7973 6590
Email: enquiries@artscouncil.org.uk
Web Site: www.artscouncil.org.uk

Personnel:
Dame Liz Forgan (Chair)
Alan Davey (Chief Executive)

Arts Council England is the national development agency for the arts in England, distributing public money from government and the national lottery.
Arts Council England's main funding programme is Grants for the arts. It is open to individuals, art organizations, national touring and other people who use the arts in their work. The grants are for activities that benefit people in England or that help artists and arts organizations from England to carry out their work.
Arts Council England has one national and nine regional offices. Founded in 1946.

5011

ASSOCIATION OF AUTHORS' AGENTS
48–56 Bayham Place, London NW1 0EU
Email: jw@watsonlittle.com
Web Site: www.agentsassoc.co.uk

Personnel:
Anthony Goff (President)
Peter Straus (Vice-President)
Anna Davis (Treasurer)
James Wills (Secretary)

Founded in 1974 to institute and maintain a code of professional behaviour, to discuss matters of common professional interest and to provide a vehicle for representing the view of authors' agents in discussions on matters of common interest with other professional bodies.

5012

ASSOCIATION OF FREELANCE EDITORS, PROOFREADERS & INDEXERS (IRELAND)
11 Summerville Place, Rathmines, Dublin 16, Republic of Ireland
Telephone: +353 (0)1 295 2194 & 497 7766
Email: Brenda@ohanlonmedia.com & slq@ireland.com
Web Site: www.afepi.ie

Personnel:
Sine Quinn (Co-Chair)
Brenda O'Hanlon (Co-Chair)

The AFEPI was established to provide information to publishers on Irish freelancers working in this field, and to protect the interests of those freelancers. Membership is restricted to freelancers with experience and/or references, but skills of members are not tested or evaluated.

5013

ASSOCIATION OF ILLUSTRATORS
2nd Floor Back Building, 150 Curtain Road, London EC2A 3AT
Telephone: 020 7613 4328
Fax: 020 7613 4417
Email: info@theaoi.com
Web Site: www.theaoi.com

Personnel:
Ramon Blomfield (Managing Director)
Derek Brazell (Special Projects Manager)
Ian Veacock (Finance Officer Manager)
Becky Brown (Events & Marketing Co-ordinator Manager)
Paul Ryding (Membership Co-ordinator)

Established in 1973 to advance and protect illustrators' rights, the AOI is a non-profit making trade association dedicated to its members' professional interest and the promotion of illustration.
Corporate members (agents and clients) receive free copy of the Images Annual, discounts on events, publications and our Images competition entry, plus Varoom – the journal of illustration and made images, published three times per year.

5014

ASSOCIATION OF LEARNED & PROFESSIONAL SOCIETY PUBLISHERS
1 Abbey Cottages, The Green, Sutton Courtenay, Oxon OX14 4AF
Telephone: 01235 847776 & 0796 850 4763 (mobile)
Fax: 0870 706 0332
Email: ian.russell@alpsp.org
Web Site: www.alpsp.org

Chief Operating Officer:
Nick Evans, 9 Stanbridge Road, Putney, London SW15 1DX
Telephone: 020 8789 2394
Fax: 020 8789 2394
Email: nick.evans@alpsp.org
Web Site: www.alpsp.org

Personnel:
Ian Russell (Chief Executive)
Nick Evans (Chief Operating Officer)
Ian Hunter (Finance & Administration Manager)
Lesley Ogg (Events Co-ordinator)
Amanda Whiting (Training Co-ordinator)
Suzy Fotheringham (Marketing & Membership Co-ordinator)
Dee French (Administration Co-ordinator)
Alan Singleton (Editor-in-Chief, Learned Publishing Editor)
Isabel Czech (North American Executive Director)
Barbara Holmes (Training Administrator)

ALPSP is an international trade association for the community of not-for-profit publishers and those who work with them to disseminate academic and professional information; it was founded in 1972, and currently has over 350 members in more than 40 countries. ALPSP carries out research and other projects, monitors national and international issues and represents members' interests to the wider world. The Association provides co-operative services such as the ALPSP Learned Journals Collection. It also offers an extensive programme of courses and seminars, an informative website (www.alpsp.org), a quarterly journal, Learned Publishing, and a monthly electronic newsletter, ALPSP Alert
.

5015

ASSOCIATION OF ONLINE PUBLISHERS (AOP)
Queens House, 28 Kingsway, London WC2B 6JR
Telephone: 020 7400 7510
Fax: 020 7404 4167
Email: info@ukaop.org.uk
Web Site: www.ukaop.org.uk

Personnel:
Ruth Brownlee (Director)
Rebecca Winfied (Finance – Periodical Publishers Association Director)
Ron Nussey (Website & Database Manager)
Tilly Martin (Events & Marketing Executive)
Tim Cain (Head of Research & Insight)

Parent Company:
UK: Periodical Publishers Association

The UK Association of Online Publishers (AOP) is an industry body representing online publishing companies that create original, branded, quality content. AOP champions the interests of approximately 160 publishing companies from diverse backgrounds including newspaper and magazine publishing, TV and radio broadcasting, and pure online media.
AOP presents a unified voice to industry and Government, specifically to address issues and concerns relating to all areas of online publishing. AOP publishes original research and hosts forums, awards and conferences, covering a range of topics from paid-for-content, subscription models and data protection, through to copyright, content management, new technologies and audience measurement.
The primary mission of UK AOP is to drive standards and revenue across all areas of online publishing to raise the credibility and profile of the industry.

5016

ASSOCIATION OF SUBSCRIPTION AGENTS AND INTERMEDIARIES
Field Cottage, School Lane, Benhall, Suffolk IP17 1HE
Telephone: 01728 633196
Email: info@subscription-agents.org
Web Site: www.subscription-agents.org

Personnel:
Sarah Durrant (Secretary General)

The ASA is the international trade association serving subscription agents, sales agents and other intermediaries providing products and services within the professional and scholarly information supply chain. The ASA exists to provide information to its members from all areas of the information industry, to create a forum for exchange amongst these groups and to represent members' common interests to publishers, customers, representative and governmental organizations and associations.

5017

AUTHORS' FOUNDATION
84 Drayton Gardens, London SW10 9SB
Telephone: 020 7373 6642
Fax: 020 7373 5768
Email: info@societyofauthors.org
Web Site: www.societyofauthors.org

Personnel:
Mark Le Fanu (General Secretary)

Founded in 1984 to mark the centenary of the Society of Authors, the Foundation offers grants to published writers who need additional funding for research, travel, etc. Open to fiction, poetry and non-fiction. The Foundation incorporates the Phoenix Trust. Closing dates for applications: 30 April and 30 September.

5018

AUTHORS' LICENSING & COLLECTING SOCIETY (ALCS)
The Writers' House, 13 Haydon Street, London EC3N 1DB
Telephone: 020 7264 5700
Fax: 020 7264 5755
Email: alcs@alcs.co.uk
Web Site: www.alcs.co.uk

Personnel:
Owen Atkinson (Chief Executive)

Barbara Hayes *(Deputy Chief Executive)*
Alison Baxter *(Communications Officer)*

The Authors' Licensing & Collecting Society is the UK collective rights management society for writers of all genres. Members grant to the Society the right to administer on their behalf those rights which an author is unable to exercise as an individual or which are best handled on a collective basis. These include photocopying, rental and lending right, off-air and private recording, electronic rights, broadcast rights for BBC Prime and BBC World Service TV, cable retransmission and rights for the public reception of broadcasts. Membership costs a one-off lifetime fee of £25. Please contact the Society for further information. The ALCS administers these rights in the UK and Northern Ireland. Under reciprocal arrangements with foreign collecting societies other territories are also covered. Distributions to members are made bi-annually. For advice and further information please contact the ALCS office or click www.alcs.co.uk.

5019

BAPLA (BRITISH ASSOCIATION OF PICTURE LIBRARIES AND AGENCIES)
59 Tranquil Vale, Blackheath, London SE3 0BS
Email: enquiries@bapla.org.uk
Web Site: www.bapla.org.uk

Personnel:
Simon Cliffe *(Executive Director)*
Damalie Nakalema *(Association Administrator)*
Susanne Kittlinger *(Membership & Communications Manager)*

The British Association of Picture Libraries and Agencies, or BAPLA, is the trade association for picture libraries in the UK and one of the largest organizations of its kind in the world. With over 380 member companies, it represents the vast majority of commercial picture libraries and agencies in the UK. Please see the website for details: www.bapla.org.uk

5020

THE BIBLIOGRAPHICAL SOCIETY
c/o Institute of English Studies, Senate House, Malet Street, London WC1E 7HU
Telephone: 020 7862 8679
Fax: 020 7862 8720
Email: admin@bibsoc.org.uk
Web Site: www.bibsoc.org.uk

Personnel:
Margaret Ford *(Hon Secretary)*

The Bibliographical Society promotes the study of historical, analytical, descriptive and textual bibliography. It publishes its own journal, *The Library*, and supports a publishing programme of books and monographs on bibliographical subjects.

5021

BOOK AID INTERNATIONAL
39–41 Coldharbour Lane, Camberwell, London SE5 9NR
Telephone: 020 7733 3577
Fax: 020 7978 8006
Email: info@bookaid.org
Web Site: www.bookaid.org

Personnel:
HRH The Duke of Edinburgh KG, KT, OM *(Patron)*
James Arnold Baker *(Chair)*
Clive Nettleton *(Director)*

Books change lives. Over the past 56 years, Book Aid International has sent over 25 million carefully chosen and high quality books to some of the poorest countries of the world. In villages and cities, schools and universities, libraries, reading rooms and refugee camps, Book Aid International books have been read over and over again by people looking to learn and to build themselves brighter futures.

Increasing access to books and information is about more than sending books. Book Aid International also supports a number of projects in schools, libraries and communities that ensure that the most vulnerable of people, like refugees, orphans and women, have access to books and education.

Please get in touch with our Book Trade Development Manager if you can assist by donating new books.

5022

BOOK INDUSTRY COMMUNICATION
39–41 North Road, London N7 9DP
Telephone: 020 7607 9021
Fax: 020 7607 9021
Email: info@bic.org.uk
Web Site: www.bic.org.uk

Personnel:
Peter Kilborn *(Executive Director)*

Book Industry Communication (BIC) is an independent organization set up and sponsored by the Publishers Association, Booksellers Association, the Chartered Institute of Library and Information Professionals and the British Library to promote supply chain efficiency in all sectors of the book world through e-commerce and the application of standard processes and procedures. Its subscribers include most of the UK's major publishers, booksellers and service providers.

5023

THE BOOK TRADE CHARITY (BTBS)
The Foyle Centre, The Retreat, Kings Langley, Herts WD4 8LT
Telephone: 01923 263128
Fax: 01923 270732
Email: david@btbs.org
Web Site: www.booktradecharity.org

Personnel:
David Hicks *(Chief Executive)*
Jackie Bright *(Housing Manager, The Retreat)*
Nigel Batt *(Treasurer)*
Carole Blake *(Chairman)*

The welfare charity of the book trade, offering support to colleagues in difficult personal circumstances.

The Book Trade Charity gives direct financial support, regular and one-off, to individuals, to help with a wide range of problems.

Accommodation at The Retreat, Kings Langley, offers pre-retirement and retirement housing.

The book trade Helpline (freephone 0808 100 2304) provides sympathetic, confidential help.

Anyone who has worked in the book trade (publishing, distribution, bookselling, etc. for more than one year, employed, self-employed or freelance) is eligible to apply for assistance.

5024

BOOKSELLERS ASSOCIATION OF THE UNITED KINGDOM & IRELAND LTD
Minster House, 272 Vauxhall Bridge Road, London SW1V 1BA
Telephone: 020 7802 0802
Fax: 020 7802 0803
Email: mail@booksellers.org.uk
Web Site: www.booksellers.org.uk

Personnel:
Jane Streeter *(President)*
Tim Godfray *(Chief Executive)*

Associated Companies:
UK: Batch.co.uk Ltd; Book Industry Communication Ltd; Book Tokens Ltd; Word Book Day Ltd

Founded in 1895. Represents over 4400 outlets. Promotes and looks after the interests of booksellers, helps booksellers become more efficient, fights for better distribution in the trade, helps booksellers increase sales and reduce costs and gives advice on opening and running a bookshop. Among other services, the Association produces catalogues for distribution throughout the retail trade at Christmas and directories of members, publishers and services.

5025

BOOKTRUST
Book House, 45 East Hill, London SW18 2QZ
Telephone: 020 8516 2977
Fax: 020 8516 2978
Email: query@booktrust.org.uk
Web Site: www.booktrust.org.uk

Personnel:
HRH the Prince Philip, Duke of Edinburgh *(Patron)*
Viv Bird *(Chief Executive)*

Booktrust is an independent charity dedicated to encouraging people of all ages and cultures to engage with books. The written word underpins all our activity and enables us to fulfil our vision of inspiring a lifelong love of books for all.

5026

BRITISH CENTRE FOR LITERARY TRANSLATION (BCLT)
University of East Anglia, Norwich NR4 7TJ
Telephone: 01603 592785
Fax: 01603 592737
Email: bclt@uea.ac.uk
Web Site: www.bclt.org.uk

Personnel:
Valerie Henitiuk *(Associate Director)*
Catherine Fuller *(Co-ordinator)*

Parent Company:
UK: University of East Anglia

Raises the profile of literary translation and the professional development of literary translators. Organizes events, readings, workshops aimed at translators, professionals in arts and publishing and the general public.

5027

BRITISH FANTASY SOCIETY
56 Leyton Road, Birmingham B21 9EE
Telephone: 07845 897760
Email: secretary@britishfantasysociety.org
Web Site: www.britishfantasysociety.org

Personnel:
Ramsey Campbell *(President)*
Stephen Theaker *(Chairman & Dark Horizons Editor)*
Helen Hopley *(Secretary & Treasurer)*
David Riley *(Newsletter Editor)*
Andrew Hook *(New Horizons Editor)*
Martin Roberts *(Publicity Officer)*

Formed for devotees of fantasy, horror and related fields in literature, art and the cinema. Publications include *Prism* (quarterly), featuring news and reviews, and *Dark Horizons* and *New Horizons* (every six months alternating), featuring fiction and articles from new and established authors, plus other more occasional publications listing fiction and non-fiction of interest. There is a small press library and an annual convention, 'FantasyCon', which features the British Fantasy Awards sponsored by the Society. Please visit our website for full information.

Membership fees: UK £30 (£45 joint); Europe £40 (£60 joint); Rest of World
£55 (£80 joint).

5028

THE BRITISH GUILD OF TRAVEL WRITERS
26 Needham House, Woodberry Down, London N4 2TN
Telephone: 020 8144 8713
Web Site: www.bgtw.org

Personnel:
Melissa Shales *(Chair)*

The Guild has a membership of around 230, all professional journalists, broadcasters and photographers who derive the majority of their earnings from travel writing or broadcasting. Monthly meetings are devoted to discussion of travel topics, usually with outside speakers, and take place at a variety of venues. There is a monthly *Newsletter* for members. An annual year book giving full details of all members together with comprehensive lists of PRs and other contacts in the travel trade is available for purchase.

5029

BSI GROUP
389 Chiswick High Road, London W4 4AL
Telephone: 020 8996 9000
Fax: 020 8996 7400
Email: info@bsigroup.com
Web Site: www.bsigroup.com

Personnel:
Sir David John *(Chairman)*
Howard Kerr *(Chief Executive Officer)*

BSI Group:
   – develops private, national and international standards

– certifies management systems and products
– provides testing and certification of products and services
– provides training and information on standards and international trade and
– provides performance management and supply chain management software solutions.

5030

CHARTERED INSTITUTE OF JOURNALISTS

2 Dock Offices, Surrey Quays Road, London SE16 2XU
Telephone: 020 7252 1187
Fax: 020 7232 2302
Email: memberservices@cioj.co.uk
Web Site: www.cioj.co.uk

Personnel:
Liz Justice (President)
Norman Bartlett (Treasurer)
Dominic Cooper (General Secretary)

The senior professional society of journalists worldwide. Incorporated by Royal Charter in 1890, it had its origin in the National Association of Journalists, which was founded in 1884 and converted into the Institute in 1889. Its primary object is 'the promotion by all reasonable means of the interests of journalists and journalism'. Representing the profession as a whole, it is a completely independent body free of political partiality. It gives equal rights of membership to all members of the profession, including radio and television journalists, press photographers and public relations officers with journalistic qualifications. Trade union representation is provided by the IOJ (TU), an independent certificated trade union.

5031

CHILDREN'S BOOKS IRELAND

17 North Great George's Street, Dublin 1,
Republic of Ireland
Telephone: +353 (0)1 872 7475
Fax: +353 (0)1 872 7476
Email: info@childrensbooksireland.com
Web Site: www.childrensbooksireland.com

Personnel:
Mags Walsh (Director)
Tom Donegan (Programme Officer)
Jenny Murray (Administrator)
Patricia Kennon (Editors – Inis Magazine)
Marion Keyes (Editor – Inis Magazine)

Children's Books Ireland is the national children's book organization of Ireland. The aim of Children's Books Ireland is to promote quality children's books and reading. CBI runs an annual nationwide Children's Book Festival, the Bisto/CBI Book of the Year awards, publishes Inis, a quarterly magazine, which carries a wide range of articles about children's books in Ireland and abroad as well as an extensive review section, and hosts an annual Children's Books conference.

CBI is a resource and support organization for teachers, pupils, writers, publishers, booksellers, librarians as well as an imaginative programmer of events for young readers.

5032

CHILDREN'S WRITERS & ILLUSTRATORS GROUP

The Society of Authors, 84 Drayton Gardens, London
SW10 9SB
Telephone: 020 7373 6642
Fax: 020 7373 5768
Email: ldowdeswell@societyofauthors.org
Web Site: www.societyofauthors.org

Personnel:
Lisa Dowdeswell (Secretary)

Parent Company:
UK: The Society of Authors

The Children's Writers and Illustrators Group is an organization, founded in 1963, for writers and illustrators of children's books, who are members of the Society of Authors. Meetings are held regularly, with opportunities for members to meet each other, as well as to hear talks or discussions on various aspects of their work.

5033

CILIP (CHARTERED INSTITUTE OF LIBRARY AND INFORMATION PROFESSIONALS)

7 Ridgmount Street, London WC1E 7AE
Telephone: 020 7255 0500 & (020) 7255 0505 (textphone)
Fax: 020 7255 0501
Email: info@cilip.org.uk
Web Site: www.cilip.org.uk

Personnel:
John Woolley (Managing Director, CILIP Enterprises)
Helen Carley (Publishing Director, Facet Publishing)

Associated Companies:
Facet Publishing

CILIP: the Chartered Institute of Library and Information Professionals is a leading professional body for librarians, information specialists and knowledge managers.

CILIP forms a community of around 36,000 people engaged in library and information work, of whom approximately 21,000 are CILIP members and about 15,000 are regular customers of CILIP Enterprises.

5034

COMHAIRLE NAN LEABHRAICHEAN / THE GAELIC BOOKS COUNCIL

22 Mansfield Street, Glasgow G11 5QP
Telephone: 0141 337 6211
Fax: 0141 341 0515
Email: brath@gaelicbooks.net
Web Site: www.gaelicbooks.org

Personnel:
Prof Roibeard Ó Maolalaigh (Chair)
Ian MacDonald (Director)

The Council was set up in 1968 to administer the Gaelic Books Grant awarded by the Scottish Education Department, and its purpose is to stimulate Gaelic publishing. It normally has about ten members as its board, and a paid staff of four. In April 1983 the Scottish Arts Council became its main funding body, and its Assessor attends meetings. The Council became a charitable company in July 1996.

It provides financial assistance in the form of publication grants (paid to the publisher) for individual Gaelic books, and also commission grants for authors. Editorial advice is available, and a word-processing and proof-reading service.

In 2003 it launched the highly successful Ùr-Sgeul imprint for prose work in Gaelic, with the associated books, CDs and DVDs being issued by the publisher Clàr.

As a retailer, the Council stocks all Gaelic and Gaelic-related works in print, regular lists of these being published in its catalogue, Leabhraichean Gàidhlig, and on its website. It has its own shop at the address above, and also does mail order and mobile selling at selected events, as well as running a book club (A' Chiste Leabhraichean).

5035

COPYRIGHT TRIBUNAL

2nd Floor, 21 Bloomsbury Street, London WC1B 3HB
Telephone: 020 7034 2836
Fax: 020 7034 2826
Email: catherine.worley@ipo.gov.uk
Web Site: www.ipo.gov.uk/ctribunal.htm

Personnel:
Judge Fysh QC (Chairman)
Catherine Worley (Secretary/Head)

The main function of the Tribunal is to decide, where the parties cannot agree between themselves, the terms and conditions of licences offered by, or licensing schemes operated by, collective licensing bodies in the copyright and related rights area. It has the statutory task of conclusively establishing the facts of a case and of coming to a decision which is reasonable in the light of those facts. Its decisions are appealable to the High Court only on points of law. (Appeals on a point of law against decisions of the Tribunal in Scotland are to the Court of Session.)

Broadly, the Tribunal's jurisdiction is such that anyone who has unreasonably been refused a licence by a collecting society or considers the terms of an offered licence to be unreasonable may refer the matter to the Tribunal. The Tribunal also has the power to decide some matters even though collecting societies are not involved. For example, it can settle disputes over the royalties payable by publishers of TV programme listings to broadcasting organizations.

5036

THE CRITICS' CIRCLE

48 De Waldon House, Allitsen Road, St John's Wood,
London NW8 7BA
Telephone: 020 7483 1181
Web Site: www.criticscircle.org.uk

Personnel:
Charles Spencer (President)
William Russell (Honorary General Secretary)

Founded in 1913 by J. T. Grein, S. R. Littlewood and John Parker. Aims to promote the art of criticism and to uphold its integrity in practice; to foster and safeguard the professional interests of its members and to provide opportunities for social intercourse among them and to support the advancement of the arts. Membership is only by invitation of the Council and is confined to persons engaged professionally, regularly and substantially in the writing or broadcasting of criticism of theatre, music, film, dance and art and architecture. There is no literary section per se.

5037

DATA PUBLISHERS ASSOCIATION (DPA)

Queen's House, 28 Kingsway, London WC2B 6JR
Telephone: 020 7405 0836
Fax: 020 7404 4167
Email: sarah.gooch@dpa.org.uk
Web Site: www.dpa.org.uk

Personnel:
Jerry Gosney (Executive Director)
Sarah Gooch (Marketing Co-ordinator)

The Data Publishers Association (DPA) is the industry body representing data and directory publishers in the UK. Its role is to protect and promote the interests of the industry, both in print and online.

5038

DESIGN AND ARTISTS COPYRIGHT SOCIETY

33 Great Sutton Street, London EC1V 0DX
Telephone: 020 7336 8811
Fax: 020 7336 8822
Email: info@dacs.org.uk
Web Site: www.dacs.org.uk

Personnel:
Gilane Tawadros (Chief Executive)
John Robinson (Legal & International Director)
Tania Spriggens (Communications Director)
Jane Sandeman (Finance Director)
Jeremy Stein (Services Director)

Founded in 1984 by artists for artists. DACS is a not-for-profit organization established to administer and protect the rights of artists in the UK, including copyright and Artist's Resale Right.

Membership is open to any artist of any discipline and to the estate of an artist still in copyright.

DACS represents over 52,000 artists, including Picasso, Dali, Matisse, Wadsworth, Hamilton, Spencer and Lichtenstein.

Any publisher wishing to reproduce works of art in copyright should contact DACS in the first instance to obtain clearance prior to publication.

5039

EDUCATIONAL PUBLISHERS COUNCIL

[Schools Division of The Publishers Association]
The Publishers Association, 29B Montague Street, London
WC1B 5BW
Telephone: 020 7691 9191
Fax: 020 7691 9199
Email: gtaylor@publishers.org.uk
Web Site: www.publishers.org.uk

Personnel:
Graham Taylor (Director)

Parent Company:
UK: The Publishers Association

The Educational Publishers Council is particularly concerned with making known, both to the educational system and to the general public, the nature and importance of educational publishers' work. It is charged with assessing and putting forward the co-ordinated views of educational publishers. Membership is open to any firm which is in membership of The Publishers Association and gives proof of a bona fide interest in publishing or producing books or other permanent forms of instruction intended for classroom use.

5040

EDUCATIONAL WRITERS GROUP
The Society of Authors, 84 Drayton Gardens, London SW10 9SB
Telephone: 020 7373 6642
Fax: 020 7244 0743
Email: info@societyofauthors.org
Web Site: www.societyofauthors.org

Personnel:
Elizabeth Haylett Clark *(Secretary)*

Parent Company:
UK: The Society of Authors

The Educational Writers Group is a subsidiary group of the Society of Authors. Its purpose is to advise members on their publishing problems etc, to study the conditions peculiar to the market at home and overseas, to watch developments in teaching as they affect the educational writer, and to hold meetings at which experience can be pooled, and matters of mutual interest discussed.

5041

ENGLISH ASSOCIATION
University of Leicester, University Road, Leicester LE1 7RH
Telephone: 0116 252 3982
Fax: 0116 252 2301
Email: engassoc@le.ac.uk
Web Site: www.le.ac.uk/engassoc

Personnel:
Helen Lucas *(Chief Executive)*
Julia Hughes *(Assistant)*

Founded in 1906 to promote the knowledge, enjoyment and study of the English language and its literatures.
The Year's Work in English Studies – the annual qualitative narrative bibliographical overview of scholarly work on English language and literature written in English. Published annually in December.
The Year's Work in Critical and Cultural Theory – companion volume to YWES, providing a narrative bibliography of work in the field of critical and cultural theory.
Order from: Julia Hughes.

5042

THE FEDERATION OF CHILDREN'S BOOK GROUPS
2 Bridge Wood View, Horsforth, Leeds LS18 5PE
Telephone: 0113 258 8910
Email: info@fcbg.org.uk
Web Site: www.fcbg.org.uk

A national, voluntary organization concerned with children and their books. The Federation's aim is to promote enjoyment and interest in children's books and reading, and to encourage the availability of a range of literature for all ages, from pre-school to teenage. The Federation liaises with schools, playgroups, publishers, libraries and other official bodies.
National activities include:
– organizes, annually, The Red House Children's Book Award
– promotes National Share-a-Story Month in May
– organizes an annual conference each spring.
Members are able to receive Federation publications, including the *Federation Newsletter*, the annual *Red House Children's Book Award 'Pick of the Year' Top Fifty Booklist*, and information about National Share-a-Story Month.

5043

GAY AUTHORS WORKSHOP
BM Box 5700, London WC1N 3XX
Email: eandk2@btinternet.com

Personnel:
Kathryn Bell *(Secretary)*

Associated Companies:
UK: Gay Authors Self-Publishing Society

Gay Authors Workshop is an association of lesbians, gay men and bisexuals who are creative writers – poets, drama-

tists, fiction writers. Its aim is to raise the standard of gay literature by providing opportunities for gay writers to meet, read, discuss and criticize their work in a constructive way. Monthly meetings are held at different places in the London area (and occasionally elsewhere) for that purpose, and to share information about publishing outlets and competitions. Although London-based, it is a national organization. The quarterly newsletter (print and tape) keeps members in touch with activities. Membership is open to all gay writers, beginners as well as published authors. The subscription is £7 a year, £3 unwaged, currently under review.

5044

GIBB MEMORIAL TRUST
2 Penarth Place, Cambridge CB3 9LU
Telephone: 01223 566630
Email: PRBligh@ntlworld.com
Web Site: www.gibbtrust.org

Book Distribution:
Oxbow Books Ltd, 10 Hythe Bridge Street, Oxford OX1 2BW
Telephone: 01865 241249
Fax: 01865 794449
Email: oxbow@oxbowbooks.com
Web Site: www.oxbowbooks.com

Personnel:
P. R. Bligh *(Secretary to the Trustee)*

The Trust is a registered charity whose aim is to support the publication of works of scholarly research within the areas of the history, literature, philosophy and religion of the Persians, Turks and Arabs. Its activities are in financing and organizing the production and publication of books, and in marketing the published works. The books are distributed by Oxbow Books in Oxford, UK, and Oakville, USA.

5045

GUILD OF FOOD WRITERS
255 Kent House Road, Beckenham, Kent BR3 1JQ
Telephone: 020 8659 0422
Email: gfw@gfw.co.uk
Web Site: www.gfw.co.uk

The Guild of Food Writers is the professional association of food writers and broadcasters in the UK. Established in 1984, it now has 380 authors, columnists, freelance journalists and broadcasters amongst its members.
The objectives of the Guild as set out in its constitution are as follows:
To bring together professional food writers, to print and issue an annual list of members, to extend the range of members' knowledge and experience, and to encourage the development of new writers by every means including competitions and awards. To contribute to the growth of public interest in, and knowledge of, the subject of food and to campaign for improvements in the quality of food.
The Guild is a self-supporting body that offers its members a busy calendar that includes an annual lecture dinner and AGM, annual awards, monthly workshops and occasional professional and social events. It also publishes a monthly newsletter and comprehensive and detailed annual directory of members.
The Guild offers professional support and guidance to its members. In the public forum it campaigns with authority for improvements in the awareness and quality of food in every sector of society.

5046

INDEPENDENT PUBLISHERS GUILD (IPG)
PO Box 12, Llain, Whitland SA34 0WU
Telephone: 01437 563335
Fax: 01437 562071
Email: info@ipg.uk.com
Web Site: www.ipg.uk.com

Personnel:
Bridget Shine *(Chief Executive)*

The Independent Publishers Guild (IPG) actively represents the interests of independent publishers in the UK and is represented on many committees and forums, which form the strategy for the UK book trade. The IPG helps publishers to do better business, somewhere they can find advice, ideas and information.
With over 450 members and steadily growing with combined revenues of over £500M, the IPG provides a vibrant networking base. Members receive regular e-newsletters,

training courses and seminars covering important areas. It also organizes an annual conference.
The IPG runs a collective stand for members at leading international book fairs including Frankfurt and London.

5047

INFORMATION COMMISSIONER'S OFFICE
Wycliffe House, Water Lane, Wilmslow, Cheshire SK9 5AF
Telephone: 01625 545745
Fax: 01625 524510
Email: mail@ico.gsi.gov.uk
Web Site: www.ico.gov.uk

Personnel:
Christopher Graham *(Information Commissioner)*

The Information Commissioner's Office is the UK's independent public body set up to promote access to official information and to protect personal information.
It regulates and enforces the Data Protection Act, the Freedom of Information Act, the Privacy and Electronic Communications Regulations and the Environmental Information Regulations.
The ICO provides guidance to organizations and individuals. It rules on eligible complaints and can take action when the law is broken.
Reporting directly to Parliament, the Commissioner's powers include the ability to order compliance, using enforcement and decision notices, and prosecution.

5048

INSTITUTE OF INTERNAL COMMUNICATION
Suite GA2, Oak House, Woodlands Business Park, Breckland, Milton Keynes MK14 6EY
Telephone: 01908 313755
Fax: 01908 313661
Email: enquiries@ioic.org.uk
Web Site: www.ioic.org.uk

Personnel:
Kathie Jones *(Chief Executive)*

The Institute of Internal Communication (IoIC) (formerly CiB) is one of the UK's leading professional body for in-house, freelance and agency staff involved in internal communications. Whatever your responsibility - strategy planning and delivery, writing, design, online, print, measurement, brand management - and whether you work in-house, freelance or for an agency, IoIC exists to support you.
Major activities include the annual IoIC Awards competition, annual conference and a regular programme of educational and training events as well as our ongoing professional qualifications in internal communications.

5049

INSTITUTE OF SCIENTIFIC AND TECHNICAL COMMUNICATORS (ISTC)
Airport House, Purley Way, Croydon CR0 0XZ
Telephone: 020 8253 4506
Fax: 020 8253 4510
Email: istc@istc.org.uk
Web Site: www.istc.org.uk

Personnel:
Simon Butler *(President)*
Peter Fountain *(Treasurer)*
Marian Newell *(Communicator – ISTC Journal Editor)*
Elaine Cole *(Administration)*
Paul Ballard *(Marketing)*

Formed in 1972 as a result of the amalgamation of the Presentation of Technical Information Group (1948), the Institution of Technical Authors and Illustrators (originally the Technical Publications Association), formed in 1953, and the Institute of Technical Publicity and Publications (1963).
The Institute aims to establish and maintain professional codes of practice for those employed in all branches of scientific and technical communication. It provides a forum for the exchange of views between its members, and aims to further their expectations and interests. The membership embodies a wide range of specialist knowledge of the principles and modern practices of effective communication of scientific and technical information. Through its publications and meetings, the Institute disseminates this experience to a growing profession and to those who employ the services of its members.
The Institute represents Great Britain on the International Council for Technical Communication (INTECOM).

Publications: *The Communicator* (UK subscription: £37 per year).

5050

INSTITUTE OF TRANSLATION & INTERPRETING
Fortuna House, South Fifth Street, Milton Keynes MK9 2PQ
Telephone: 01908 325250
Fax: 01908 325259
Email: info@iti.org.uk
Web Site: www.iti.org.uk

Personnel:
Mrs Pamela Mayorcas *(Chair)*

The Institute of Translation and Interpreting (ITI) is the UK's main professional association for translators and interpreters and aims to promote the highest standards in translating and interpreting. It has a strong corporate membership and runs professional development courses and conferences, sometimes in conjunction with its language, regional and subject networks. Membership is open to those with a genuine and proven involvement in translation and interpreting. As a full and active member of the International Federation of Translators, it maintains good contacts with translators and interpreters worldwide. ITI's bi-monthly bulletin is available on subscription through the ITI office in Milton Keynes.

ITI's directory of translators and interpreters may be accessed from the website at www.iti.org.uk.

5051

IP3 (INSTITUTE OF PAPER, PRINTING & PUBLISHING)
Claremont House, 70–72 Alma Road, Windsor, Berks SL4 3EZ
Telephone: 0870 330 8625
Fax: 0870 330 8615
Email: info@ip3.org.uk
Web Site: www.ip3.org.uk

Personnel:
David Pryke *(Director)*
Lynda King *(Administration Manager)*

Fostering excellence in publishing through:
 – the promotion, support and endorsement of a programme of educational training, research and development
 – the introduction of a code of practice
 – the development of standards of occupational competence
 – the publication of bulletins, handbooks, reports and research designed to assist in the improvement of individual performance
 – the development of professional publishing qualifications
 – meetings, seminars and conferences.
 The Institute will offer individuals:
 – membership of an active community of people working in publishing
 – the opportunity to participate in and influence the direction of a body that has their best interests at heart
 – a community that can raise professional standards and, as a consequence, individual and collective status
 – opportunities to network, seek advice, guidance and career counselling
 – access to career, education and training information
 – a range of cost-saving services and activities.
 The Institute of Publishing will be a forum providing opportunities for individuals in publishing to develop themselves and progress in their careers and to meet the challenges of an increasingly competitive business.

5052

ISBN AGENCY – UK AND IRISH REPUBLIC
3rd Floor, Midas House, 62 Goldsworth Road, Woking, Surrey GU21 6LQ
Telephone: 0870 777 8712
Fax: 0870 777 8714
Email: isbn.agency@nielsen.com
Web Site: www.isbn.nielsenbook.co.uk

Personnel:
Julian Sowa *(Senior Manager)*
Diana Williams *(Manager)*

Parent Company:
Nielsen Book

Associated Companies:
UK: ISTC Agency; SAN Agency

The UK International Standard Book Numbering Agency is responsible for assigning ISBN prefixes to publishers based in the UK or the Irish Republic.
 The UK ISBN Agency cannot assign ISBNs to publishers based in other countries.
 The Agency:
 – allocates ISBN publisher prefixes to eligible publishers based on the information provided by the publisher;
 – advises publishers on the correct and proper implementation of the ISBN system;
 – maintains a database of publishers and their prefixes for inclusion in the *Publishers' International ISBN Directory*;
 – encourages and promotes the use of the Bookland EAN bar code format;
 – encourages and promotes the importance of the ISBN for a proper listing of titles with bibliographical agencies;
 – provides technical advice and assistance to publishers and the booktrade on all aspects of ISBN usage.
 Any new publishers wishing to apply for an allocation of ISBNs should contact the ISBN Agency for an application pack. A registration fee is payable.

5053

ISSN UK CENTRE
The British Library, Boston Spa, Wetherby, West Yorkshire LS23 7BQ
Telephone: 01937 546959
Fax: 01937 546562
Email: issn-uk@bl.uk
Web Site: www.bl.uk/issn

Assigns ISSN (International Standard Serial Numbers) to serial titles published in the UK.

5054

ISTC AGENCY
3rd Floor, Midas House, 62 Goldsworth Road, Woking, Surrey GU21 6LQ
Telephone: 0870 777 8712
Fax: 0870 777 8714
Email: istc.agency@nielsen.com
Web Site: www.istc.nielsenbook.co.uk

Personnel:
Julian Sowa *(Senior Manager)*
Diana Williams *(Manager)*

Parent Company:
UK: Nielsen Book

Associated Companies:
UK: ISBN Agency; SAN Agency

The International Standard Text Code (ISTC) is a global identification system for textual works, i.e. the content in text-based publications. Nielsen Book operates one of the first ISTC registration agencies, enabling authors, publishers and other authorized representatives to register textual works with an ISTC. It also provides advice and guidance on how to make the most of this important new system. Nielsen Book also runs the ISBN and SAN agencies.

5055

MEDICAL WRITERS GROUP
The Society of Authors, 84 Drayton Gardens, London SW10 9SB
Telephone: 020 7373 6642
Fax: 020 7373 5768
Email: info@societyofauthors.org &
sbaxter@societyofauthors.org
Web Site: www.societyofauthors.org

Personnel:
Sarah Baxter *(Secretary)*

The Medical Writers Group, established in 1979, is a group within the Society of Authors. Its principal objects are to represent its members in all matters affecting their interests as medical writers; to hold meetings from time to time for the discussion of matters of common interest; and to provide, through the Society, advice to members on the special problems of medical authorship. Authors who have had a book accepted for publication, but not yet published, can join the Society and obtain advice. Also administers the Medical Book Awards.

5056

MUSIC PUBLISHERS ASSOCIATION
6th Floor, British Music House, 26 Berners Street, London W1T 3LR
Telephone: 020 7580 0126
Fax: 020 7637 3929
Email: info@mpaonline.org.uk
Web Site: www.mpaonline.org.uk

Personnel:
Stephen Navin *(Chief Executive)*

Associated Companies:
UK: MCPS Ltd

The Music Publishers Association (MPA) was established in 1881 and is governed by an elected Board. The MPA exists to safeguard the interests of music publishers and the writers signed to them. It provides them with a forum and a collective voice, and aims to inform and to educate the wider public in the importance and value of copyright.
 The MPA offers a range of services and publications to those interested in music publishing (including training) and participates in education and information initiatives across the music industry.

5057

NATIONAL ACQUISITIONS GROUP
12–14 King Street, Wakefield WF1 2SQ
Telephone: 01924 383010
Fax: 01924 383010
Web Site: www.nag.org.uk

Personnel:
Paul Dalton *(Chair)*
Sarah Armitage *(Hon. Secretary)*
Mark Merrill *(Publications Officer & Hon. Treasurer)*
Jane Butler *(Administrator)*

Established in 1986, NAG is a broadly based organization which stimulates, co-ordinates and publicizes developments in library acquisitions and the book trade. The membership includes individuals and organizations within publishing, bookselling and systems supply, as well as librarians responsible for choosing and buying books for academic, public, national, government and special institutions.
 NAG has two main aims:
 – to bring together all those in any way concerned with library acquisitions, to assist them in exchanging information and comment and to promote understanding and good practice between them;
 – to seek to influence other organizations and individuals to adopt its opinions and standards.
 NAG's objectives are to:
 – provide a forum for discussion and the exchange of information;
 – extend knowledge and understanding of technological developments;
 – promote the dissemination of information about library acquisitions;
 – develop the awareness of producers, suppliers and librarians;
 – act as a channel of communication with Government and other bodies.

5058

NATIONAL ASSOCIATION FOR THE TEACHING OF ENGLISH
50 Broadfield Road, Sheffield S8 0XJ
Telephone: 0114 555 419
Fax: 0114 555 296
Email: info@nate.org.uk
Web Site: www.nate.org.uk

Personnel:
Ian McNeilly *(Director)*
Anne Fairhall *(Publications Manager)*
Julia Elliott *(Senior Office Administrator)*

NATE is the UK subject association for all aspects of English teaching from pre-school to university. NATE publishes its own and distributes other titles covering:
 – *classroom resources:* primary, secondary, post 16
 – *teaching English:* theoretical titles including: language, literacy, literature, speaking and listening, media, drama, information and communications technologies, assessment, theory, equal opportunities

– management & staff development: curriculum, planning, managing the English department, whole school issues relating to English teaching.

The Association publishes four periodicals: *English in Education, NATE News, English Drama Media* and *Classroom.*

5059

NATIONAL LITERACY TRUST
68 South Lambeth Road, London SW8 1RL
Telephone: 020 7587 1842
Fax: 020 7587 1411
Email: contact@literacytrust.org.uk
Web Site: www.literacytrust.org.uk

The National Literacy Trust is an independent charity that believes that literacy transforms lives, and that with better literacy, everyone can succeed in life.

The National Literacy Trust campaigns to improve public understanding of the vital importance and impact of literacy. It uses careful, targeted communication to encourage individuals in most need of support to understand the importance of literacy in their lives and to inspire them to overcome their own anxieties or prejudices about literacy.

It also supports those trying to improve their literacy through projects, networks and communities across the UK and it delivers projects and programmes. It investigates and innovates, conducting research to improve and measure the effectiveness of services and support for people who need help with literacy. It also works in partnership, bringing together key organizations to lead literacy promotion in the UK, and it shares its knowledge as widely as possible.

For more information see www.literacytrust.org.uk

5060

NEW WRITING NORTH
Holy Jesus Hospital, City Road, Newcastle upon Tyne NE1 2AS
Telephone: 0191 233 3850
Fax: 0191 447 7686
Email: olivia@newwritingnorth.com
Web Site: www.newwritingnorth.com

Personnel:
Cath Robson *(Finance Director)*
Anna Disley *(Deputy, Theatre & Education Director)*
Olivia Mantle *(Projects & Marketing Officer)*

New Writing North is the literature development agency for the north-east of England.

5061

NIELSEN BOOKDATA
3rd Floor, Midas House, 62 Goldsworth Road, Woking, Surrey GU21 6LQ
Telephone: 01483 712200
Fax: 01483 712201
Email: info.bookdata@nielsen.com
Web Site: www.nielsenbookdata.co.uk

Personnel:
Ann Betts *(Commercial Director)*
Simon Skinner *(Sales Director)*
Mo Siewcharran *(Head of Marketing)*
Paul Dibble *(Head of Data Sales)*
Vesna Nall *(Publisher & Subscriptions Manager)*
Lucy Huddlestone *(UK Sales Manager)*
Melanie Brassington *(Export Sales Manager)*

Parent Company:
UK: Nielsen Book

Associated Companies:
UK: Nielsen BookNet; Nielsen BookScan

Nielsen BookData is an information provider worldwide. The company has a range of products and services which provide content-rich, accurate and timely book information for English-language titles published internationally. These services are sold to booksellers, libraries and publishers in over 100 countries, including the UK, Ireland, Europe, Australia, New Zealand, South Africa and the USA.

5062

PERIODICAL PUBLISHERS ASSOCIATION
Queens House, 28 Kingsway, London WC2B 6JR
Telephone: 020 7404 4166
Fax: 020 7404 4167
Web Site: www.ppa.co.uk

Personnel:
Barry McIlheney *(Chief Executive)*

Associated Companies:
Republic of Ireland: Periodical Publishers Association Ireland
UK: Association of Publishing Agencies; Periodical Publishers Association Scotland; Periodicals Training Council

Trade association representing publishers of consumer, business-to-business and customer magazines.

5063

THE POETRY SOCIETY
22 Betterton Street, London WC2H 9BX
Telephone: 020 7420 9880
Fax: 020 7240 4818
Email: info@poetrysociety.org.uk
Web Site: www.poetrysociety.org.uk

Personnel:
Judith Palmer *(Director)*
Fiona Sampson *(Editor, Poetry Review)*
Lisa Roberts *(Press & Marketing Manager)*
Paul McGrane *(Membership Manager)*
Bea Colley *(Education Manager)*
Paul Ranford *(Finance Manager)*

The Society's principal activities include: the quarterly publication of the UK's world-class poetry magazine, *Poetry Review* and the Society's newsletter, *Poetry News*; the National Poetry Competition which awards over £8000 in prizes each year and has brought many poets to national attention; the annual Foyle Young Poets of the Year Award (11–17 year olds); the Poet Laureate funded Ted Hughes Award for New Work in Poetry. The Poetry Society also produces a range of publications including *The Poetry Book for Primary Schools* and *Jumpstart: Poetry in the Secondary School* as well as books exploring the links between poetry and pop, poetry and gardens, and poetry and personal development. Other resources include *poetryclass*, an invaluable teacher-training resource for both primary and secondary school teachers.

5064

PUBLIC LENDING RIGHT
Richard House, Sorbonne Close, Stockton-on-Tees TS17 6DA
Telephone: 01642 604699
Fax: 01642 615641
Email: authorservices@plr.uk.com
Web Site: www.plr.uk.com

Personnel:
Jim Parker *(Registrar)*

Public Lending Right (PLR) exists to make payments to authors for the borrowing of their books from public libraries. PLR is funded by the Department for Culture, Media and Sport, and is headed by a Registrar. To qualify, authors must register their books with the PLR office. Payment calculations are based on book loans from a representative sample of public libraries. Payments are made annually. No author may receive more than £6600.

5065

THE PUBLISHERS ASSOCIATION
29B Montague Street, London WC1B 5BW
Telephone: 020 7691 9191
Fax: 020 7691 9199
Email: mail@publishers.org.uk
Web Site: www.publishers.org.uk

Personnel:
Simon Juden *(Chief Executive)*
Graham Taylor *(Educational, Academic & Professional Publishing Director)*
Emma House *(Trade & International Director)*

The Publishers Association is a trade organization serving book, journal and electronic publishers in the UK. It brings publishers together to discuss the main issues facing the industry and to define the practical policies that will take the industry forward. The aim of The Publishers Association is to serve and promote by all lawful means the interest of book, journal and electronic publishers and to protect their interests.

5066

PUBLISHERS LICENSING SOCIETY LTD
37–41 Gower Street WC1E 6HH
Telephone: 020 7299 7730
Fax: 020 7299 7780
Email: pls@pls.org.uk
Web Site: www.pls.org.uk

Personnel:
Graham Taylor *(Chairman)*
Tom West *(Operations Manager)*
Lydia Murray *(Finance Manager)*
David Bishop *(Licensing & Communications Manager)*
Mark Bide *(Consultant)*
Alicia Wise *(Chief Executive)*

The Publishers Licensing Society (PLS) obtains mandates from publishers which grant PLS the authority to license photocopying and digitization of pages from published works. PLS also consults with publishers on the development of licences.

PLS aims to maximize revenue from licences for mandating publishers and to expand the range and repertoire of mandated publishers available to licence holders. It supports the Copyright Licensing Agency (CLA) in its efforts to increase the number of legitimate users through the issuing of licences and pursues any infringements of copyright works belonging to rights holders.

5067

PUBLISHERS PUBLICITY CIRCLE
65 Airedale Avenue, London W4 2NN
Telephone: 020 8994 1881
Email: ppc-@lineone.net
Web Site: www.publisherspublicitycircle.co.uk

Personnel:
Heather White *(Secretary/Treasurer)*

For over 50 years, the Publishers Publicity Circle has enabled book publicists – both from publishing houses and freelance PR agencies – to meet each and share information regularly. Representatives of the media are invited to speak about the ways in which they can feature authors and their books, and how book publicists can provide most effectively the information and material needed.

Annual prizes are awarded for the best publicity campaigns of the year.

A directory of the PPC membership is published each year and distributed to over 2500 media contacts, providing the names of publicity staff, their fax and telephone numbers, and email addresses.

5068

PUBLISHING IRELAND (FOILSIÚ ÉIREANN)
Guinness Enterprise Centre, Taylor's Lane, Dublin 8, Republic of Ireland
Telephone: +353 (01) 415 1210
Email: info@publishingireland.com
Web Site: www.publishingireland.com

Personnel:
Jean Harrington *(President Publishing Ireland)*
Jolly Ronan *(Project Manager)*
Karen Kenny *(Administrator)*
Clara Schuessler *(Admin Assistant)*

Publishing Ireland promotes the publication, distribution, sale and publicity of books at home and abroad. There are over 100 members of the association. Publishing Ireland is a member of the Federation of European Publishers and of the International Publishers Association.

5069

PUBLISHING SCOTLAND
Scottish Book Centre, 137 Dundee Street, Edinburgh EH11 1BG
Telephone: 0131 228 6866
Fax: 0131 228 3220
Email: enquiries@publishingscotland.org
Web Site: www.publishingscotland.org

Personnel:
Marion Sinclair *(Chief Executive)*
Joan Lyle *(Training and Information Manager)*
Liam Davison *(BooksfromScotland.com Editor)*

Associated Companies:
BooksfromScotland.com
UK: BookSource Ltd

Publishing Scotland has grown from the work of the Scottish Publishers Association (SPA), a trade association in existence for over 30 years, representing over 65 book publishers. It also offers network membership to those individuals, organizations and companies who work with or within the publishing industry but who are not actually publishers themselves.

Publishing Scotland is an organization with responsibility for support and development of the publishing sector in Scotland. The remit is to work with companies, organizations and individuals in the industry, and to co-ordinate joint initiatives and partnerships. Publishing Scotland provides a forum for discussions, events and for linking services and skills to needs and opportunities. Publishing Scotland provides all the services for publishers that were previously the work of the SPA.

Publishing Scotland represents its members' interests in a number of capacities, in co-operative promotion and marketing of their books, attendance at international book fairs, joint catalogue mailings, export services and training.

5070

ROMANTIC NOVELISTS' ASSOCIATION
(contact by email only)
Email: RNAHonSec@o2.co.uk
Web Site: www.rna-uk.org

Personnel:
E. M. Ryle *(Secretary)*

The Romantic Novelists' Association aims to raise the prestige of romantic authorship and generally to encourage and foster the writing of romantic works. The RNA makes annual awards for the Romantic Novel of the Year, and for the Love Story of the Year (for Category Romance). The RNA runs a critique scheme for unpublished writers who may join the Association as New Writers' Scheme (non-voting) members. The Joan Hessayon Award is made annually for the best published novel to have gone through the NWS critique scheme. The RNA's annual residential conference takes place over a weekend in early July. Regional chapters, around the country, organize their own meetings and events. In addition, there are members' meetings in London, with guest speakers, and summer and winter parties where published and unpublished writers network with agents, editors and publishers. The RNA's magazine, *Romance Matters*, is published four times a year and distributed free to members.

5071

ROYAL SOCIETY OF LITERATURE
Somerset House, Strand, London WC2R 1LA
Telephone: 020 7845 4676
Fax: 020 7845 4679
Email: info@rslit.org
Web Site: www.rslit.org

Personnel:
Colin Thubron FRSL *(President)*
Anne Chisholm FRSL *(Chair)*
Maggie Fergusson FRSL *(Secretary)*

The Society's purpose is to sustain all that is best, whether traditional or experimental, in English Letters, and to encourage a catholic appreciation of literature. Lectures and poetry readings take place monthly at Somerset House. The Society administers a number of trusts for the advancement of Letters. The Royal Society of Literature Award under the Heinemann bequest is presented annually to one or more writers on the strength of a published work of high literary merit. The V. S. Pritchett Memorial Prize is a new prize for a previously unpublished short story. The Royal Society of Literature Ondaatje Prize was launched in 2003. The £10,000 prize will be awarded annually to the book of the highest literary merit, fiction or non-fiction, which evokes the spirit of a place.

5072

RSA (THE ROYAL SOCIETY FOR THE ENCOURAGEMENT OF ARTS, MANUFACTURES AND COMMERCE)
8 John Adam Street, London WC2N 6EZ
Telephone: 020 7451 6902
Fax: 020 7839 5805
Email: editor@rsa.org.uk
Web Site: www.theRSA.org

Publisher:
Wardour Publishing & Design, Elsley Court, 20–22 Great Titchfield Street, London W1W 8BE
Telephone: 020 7016 2555
Web Site: www.wardour.co.uk

Personnel:
Luke Johnson *(Chairman)*
Matthew Taylor *(Chief Executive)*
Stephen King *(Chief Operating Officer)*
Nina Bolognesi *(External Affairs Director)*
Belinda Lester *(Fellowship Director)*
Julian Thompson *(Projects Director)*
Carrie Walsh *(Commercial Director)*
Frances Hedges *(Editor)*

Publishes quarterly *RSA Journal* and reports, conference papers and occasional books.

5073

SAN AGENCY
3rd Floor, Midas House, 62 Goldsworth Road, Woking, Surrey GU21 6LQ
Telephone: 0870 777 8712
Fax: 0870 777 8714
Email: san.agency@nielsen.com
Web Site: www.san.nielsenbook.co.uk

Personnel:
Julian Sowa *(Senior Manager)*
Diana Williams *(Manager)*

Parent Company:
UK: Nielsen Book

Associated Companies:
UK: ISBN Agency; ISTC Agency

SANs, Standard Address Numbers, are unique for geographical locations and can be assigned to the addresses of organizations involved in the bookselling or publishing industries. The SAN Agency is responsible for managing the scheme on behalf of Book Industry Communication in any country except the USA, Canada, Australia and New Zealand. Nielsen Book also runs the ISBN and ISTC agencies.

5074

SCBWI (SOCIETY OF CHILDREN'S BOOK WRITERS & ILLUSTRATORS (BRITISH ISLES REGION))
36 Mackenzie Road, Beckenham, Kent BR3 4RU
Telephone: 020 8249 9716
Email: ra@britishscbwi.org
Web Site: www.britishscbwi.org

Personnel:
Natascha Biebow *(Regional Advisor (Chair))*
Stephanie Williams *(Newsletter Editor)*
Anne-Marie Perks *(Illustrator Co-ordinator)*
John Shelley *(Illustrato Co-ordinator)*
Sue Hyams *(Membership Co-ordinator)*
Candy Gourlay *(Website Co-ordinator)*

Parent Company:
USA: SCBWI

The SCBWI is an international professional organization for writers and illustrators of children's books. It is a network for the exchange of knowledge between writers, illustrators, editors, publishers, agents, librarians, educators, booksellers and others involved with literature for young people. There are currently more than 18,000 members worldwide, in over 70 regions.

The SCBWI International sponsors three annual conferences on writing and illustrating books and multimedia, one in New York in February, one in Bologna, Italy, and one in Los Angeles in August, as well as dozens of regional conferences and events throughout the world. It also publishers a bi-monthly newsletter, *The Bulletin*, awards grants for works in progress, and provides many informational publications on the art and business of writing and selling written, illustrated and electronic material. The SCBWI also presents numerous grants and awards, including the Golden Kite Award for the best fiction and non-fiction books.

The SCBWI British Isles (SCBWI-BI) region meets bi-monthly, usually in London, for a speaker or workshop event. It also sponsors local critique groups, master classes and regional networks events, and publishes a quarterly newsletter, *Words and Pictures*, which includes up-to-date events and marketing information, and articles on the craft of children's writing and illustrating. It also runs a yearly

Writers' and Illustrators' Conference with hands-on workshops on improving your craft and the opportunity to meet publishing professionals and find out what they are looking for. SCBWI-BI runs a listserve and social networking site where writers and illustrators can set up their own promotional website.

SCBWI is open to both published and unpublished writers and illustrators.

Full membership is open to those whose work for children's books, illustrations or photographs, films, electronic media, articles, poems or stories has been published or produced.

Associate membership is open to all those with an interest in children's literature or media, whether or not they have published.

To join, see our web site www.britishscbwi.org

5075

SCHOOL LIBRARY ASSOCIATION
Unit 2, Lotmead Business Village, Lotmead Farm, Wanborough, Swindon SN4 0UY
Telephone: 01793 791787
Fax: 01793 791786
Email: info@SLA.org.uk
Web Site: www.SLA.org.uk

Personnel:
Steve Hird *(Editor)*
Chris Brown *(Review Editor)*
Richard Leveridge *(Production Editor)*

The School Library Association is an independent organization working to promote the development of school libraries, primary and secondary. Services to members include advice and information, publications at reduced prices, *The School Librarian*, a quarterly journal of articles and reviews, training courses and a network of area branches. Membership includes schools, colleges, local education authorities, public libraries, publishers and individuals in the United Kingdom and overseas. Membership costs £79.50 p.a.

5076

SCOTTISH BOOK TRUST
Sandeman House, Trunks Close, 55 High Street, Edinburgh EH1 1SR
Telephone: 0131 524 0160
Fax: 0131 524 0161
Email: info@scottishbooktrust.com
Web Site: www.scottishbooktrust.com

Personnel:
Marc Lambert *(Chief Executive Officer)*
Jeanette Harris *(General Manager)*
Sophie Moxon *(Head of Programme)*
Marion Bourbouze *(Head of Marketing & Audience Development)*

Scottish Book Trust is a leading agency for the promotion of literature in Scotland, developing innovative projects to encourage adults and children to read, write and be inspired by books.

It promotes children's literature and the joys of reading and writing by organizing book awards, author tours and talks, and writing competitions, and by developing interactive online projects. It supports writers with a range of projects including skills development and bursaries, the funding of literature events, book awards and the promotion of Scottish writing to over 10 million people worldwide. It fosters readers and writers by offering a variety of events, advice and online information on books and authors. It works with learning professionals all over Scotland to create innovative and effective resources and events which inspire people through literature.

5077

SOCIETY FOR EDITORS & PROOFREADERS
Erico House, 93–99 Upper Richmond Road, London SW15 2TG
Telephone: 020 8785 5617
Fax: 020 8785 5618
Email: admin@sfep.org.uk
Web Site: www.sfep.org.uk

Personnel:
Sarah Price *(Chair)*
Justina Amenu *(Executive Secretary)*

Founded in 1988 with the twin aims of promoting high editorial standards and achieving recognition of its members' professional status, the Society works to disseminate information and training, foster good relations between members and their clients, and combat the isolation often experienced by freelances. It supports recognized standards of training and accreditation for editors and proofreaders, and is establishing recognized standards for its own members. Membership in 2008 was approximately 1400.

Benefits of membership include: annual directory of members seeking work; free regular newsletter; local groups throughout the country; online discussion group; annual conference; meetings and training sessions in several centres, covering aspects of current professional practice and business matters; legal helpline; discounts on selected products and services.

5078

SOCIETY OF ARCHIVISTS
Prioryfield House, 20 Canon Street, Taunton, Somerset TA1 1SW
Telephone: 01823 327030 & 327077
Fax: 01823 271719
Email: societyofarchivists@archives.org.uk
Web Site: www.archives.org.uk

Personnel:
John Chambers (*Executive Director*)
Lorraine Logan (*Membership Administrator*)

Publication of texts/periodicals on archives and records management. Conferences and training courses.

5079

SOCIETY OF AUTHORS
84 Drayton Gardens, London SW10 9SB
Telephone: 020 7373 6642
Fax: 020 7373 5768
Email: info@societyofauthors.org
Web Site: www.societyofauthors.org

Personnel:
Tom Holland (*Chairman*)
Mark Le Fanu (*General Secretary*)

An independent trade union for authors. Its purpose is to further the interests of its 8500 members through individual advice and general campaigning. It is controlled by an elected Committee of Management and administered by a staff with long experience in the business and legal aspects of authorship. Members have access to a comprehensive advisory service and may seek advice on all forms of contracts. The Society also serves the interests of specialist writers through a number of subsidiary groups – viz the Broadcasting Group, the Translators Association, Children's Writers and Illustrators, Educational Writers, Academic Writers and Medical Writers Groups. It makes representations to government departments and promotes campaigns on behalf of the profession as a whole (eg public lending right, tax concessions for authors, etc). It also administers literary estates, publishes a quarterly journal, *The Author*, issues numerous *Quick Guides* to its members and manages a variety of awards and trust funds for authors.

5080

SOCIETY OF AUTHORS PENSION FUND
84 Drayton Gardens, London SW10 9SB
Telephone: 020 7373 6642
Fax: 020 7373 5768
Email: info@societyofauthors.org
Web Site: www.societyofauthors.org

Personnel:
Mark Le Fanu (*Secretary*)

A small number of pensions is granted by the Pension Fund Committee to authors over the age of 60 who have been members of the Society for 10 years. Pensions are normally £1700 per annum.

5081

SOCIETY OF EDITORS
University Centre, Granta Place, Cambridge CB2 1RU
Telephone: 01223 304080
Fax: 01223 304090
Email: info@societyofeditors.org
Web Site: www.societyofeditors.org

Personnel:
Bob Satchwell (*Executive Director*)

The Society of Editors has more than 400 members in national, regional and local newspapers, magazines, broadcasting and new media, journalism, education and media law.

It campaigns for media freedom, self-regulation, the public's right to know and the maintenance of standards in journalism.

5082

SOCIETY OF INDEXERS
Woodbourn Business Centre, 10 Jessell Street, Sheffield S9 3HY
Telephone: 0114 244 9561
Email: admin@indexers.org.uk
Web Site: www.indexers.org.uk

Personnel:
John Silvester (*Company Secretary*)

Founded in 1957 as an autonomous professional body to promote greater awareness of indexing and raise standards in all forms of indexing. The Society's well-established distance learning course (with CILIP seal of recognition) now runs on a web-based platform and gives a thorough grounding in the principles (and pitfalls) of indexing. Workshops and an annual conference provide additional training opportunities. An online directory, *Indexers Available*, contains full details of qualified and experienced indexers with specialist subjects ranging from accountancy to zoology, together with advice on commissioning an indexer and guidelines on fees. The Society also publishes a quarterly international journal, *The Indexer*, plus occasional papers on specialized aspects of indexing and a newsletter for members. The Wheatley Medal is awarded annually for an outstanding index, conferring prestige on indexer, author and publisher. The Society wishes to impress on both publishers and authors the need for adequate and competent indexes in non-fiction works, whether in print or electronic format.

5083

SOCIETY OF MEDICAL WRITERS
Ashlett House, 24 Rochester Way, Sudbury, Suffolk CO10 1LP
Telephone: 01787 374879
Email: raymond.hume@btinternet.com
Web Site: www.somw.org.uk

Personnel:
Dr Raymond Hume (*Chairman*)
Dr Richard Cutler (*Finance Officer*)
Dr Michael Lasserson (*Editor*)

Membership of the Society of Medical Writers is open to anyone who publishes or aspires to publish their work of whatever nature – medical or non-medical, fact or fiction, prose or poetry. It is intended that the association should be enjoyable, stimulating and educational so that writing from medical practice, including general practice, is improved and encouraged.

The aims of the Society are therefore to:
– improve standards of writing by medical practitioners;
– encourage literacy whether in scientific papers, review articles, historical or anecdotal essays;
– provide meetings for practitioners interested in writing, for the exchange of views, skills and ideas;
– provide education on the preparation, presentation and submission of written material for publication;
– act as a means of introduction between practitioners and suitable publishers and editors;
– maintain a register of members of the SOMW, available to commissioning editors and others;
– advise on sources of assistance with regard to technical, legal and financial aspects of writing;
– consider questions of ethics relating to writing and publication;
– further developments in the art of writing and to facilitate access to educational opportunities for those motivated to become better writers.

5084

SOCIETY OF YOUNG PUBLISHERS
The Publishers Association, 29B Montague Street, London WC1B 5BW
Email: sypchair@thesyp.org.uk
Web Site: www.thesyp.org.uk

Personnel:
Angela Solomon (*Chair*)

Laura Palosuo (*Treasurer*)
Simon Hagan (*Marketing Officer*)

Established in 1949, the Society of Young Publishers is open to anyone in publishing or a related trade (in any capacity) – or who is hoping to be soon. Its aim is to assist, inform and enthuse anyone trying to break into the publishing industry or progress within it.

It organizes monthly speaker meetings which discuss different topics of relevance to the publishing industry. Guest speakers are drawn from a variety of backgrounds.

Members receive approximately five issues per year of its magazine, *InPrint*, to keep them up-to-date with the society and events and issues within the industry. The SYP receives regular notice of situations vacant which members receive through its Jobs Bulletin.

5085

TRANSLATORS ASSOCIATION
84 Drayton Gardens, London SW10 9SB
Telephone: 020 7373 6642
Fax: 020 7373 5768
Email: info@societyofauthors.org
Web Site: www.societyofauthors.org

Personnel:
Sarah Burton (*Acting Secretary*)

The Translators Association is a subsidiary of the Society of Authors and advises literary translators on such matters as contracts and fees. Publishers seeking book translators can search the online database.

5086

TRAVELLING SCHOLARSHIP FUND
Society of Authors, 84 Drayton Gardens, London SW10 9SB
Telephone: 020 7373 6642
Fax: 020 7373 5768
Email: info@societyofauthors.org
Web Site: www.societyofauthors.org

Personnel:
Mark Le Fanu (*Secretary*)

Founded in 1944 by an anonymous donor, to enable British creative writers to travel and to keep in touch with their colleagues abroad. A special committee annually reviews the field of contemporary literature before making its awards, which are not for open candidature, and are normally made to established writers of over 30 years of age. The Fund is administered by the Society of Authors.

5087

WATCH (WRITERS ARTISTS & THEIR COPYRIGHT HOLDERS)
The Library, University of Reading, PO Box 223, Whiteknights, Reading RG6 6AE
Telephone: 0118 378 8783
Fax: 0118 378 6636
Email: d.c.sutton@reading.ac.uk
Web Site: www.watch-file.com

Personnel:
Dr D. Sutton (*Director*)

WATCH provides a free online database of information about the copyright holders of literary authors, artists and prominent persons. The database is in the form of an open-access public website, jointly maintained by the Universities of Texas and Reading.

5088

WELSH BOOKS COUNCIL / CYNGOR LLYFRAU CYMRU
Castell Brychan, Aberystwyth, Ceredigion SY23 2JB
Telephone: 01970 624151
Fax: 01970 625385
Email: castellbrychan@cllc.org.uk
Web Site: www.cllc.org.uk & www.gwales.com

Personnel:
Elwyn Jones (*Director*)
Sion Ilar (*Design*)
Marian Beech Hughes (*Editorial*)
D. Philip Davies (*Information Services*)
Menna Lloyd Williams (*Children's Books*)
Dafydd Charles Jones (*Distribution*)
Arwyn Roderick (*Finance*)

Moelwen Gwyndaf *(Administration)*
Tom Ferris *(Sales & Marketing)*

The Welsh Books Council is a national organization with charitable status funded by the Welsh Assembly Government. Established in 1961, it is responsible for promoting all sectors of the publishing industry in Wales, in both languages, in conjunction with publishers, booksellers, libraries and schools. The Council is also responsible for distributing publishing grants for Welsh-language publishing and Welsh writing in English. Its Wholesale Distribution Centre stocks the vast majority of Welsh-interest titles currently available. www.gwales.com, the Council's on-line information and ordering service, is a one-stop shop for titles of relevance to Wales.

5089 ▄

WORSHIPFUL COMPANY OF STATIONERS AND NEWSPAPER MAKERS

Stationers' Hall, Ave Maria Lane, London EC4M 7DD
Telephone: 020 7248 2934
Fax: 020 7489 1975
Email: admin@stationers.org
Web Site: www.stationers.org

Personnel:
C. H. McKane *(Master)*
W. J. Alden MBE DL *(Clerk)*

The Worshipful Company of Stationers had its beginnings in a Guild dating back at least to 1403; the original Charter was granted in 1557. The Company was expanded in modern times (1933) to include the Newspaper Makers. For nearly four centuries it was essential for the protection of copyright to register books at Stationers' Hall; since 1924 an extensively used system of voluntary registration has been in force. This was discontinued in February 2000.

The Company's object has always been to promote the interests of the printing and allied trades, among them publishing and bookbinding. Its activities at the present day include the binding of apprentices and the award of scholarships to young men and women in these trades and the provision of pensions and financial help for tradesmen and their widows. The Company also plays a full part in the life of the City of London.

The Stationers' Hall may be hired for functions.

6 Trade & Allied Services

6.1 EDITORIAL SERVICES

6001

ACUPUNCTUATION LTD
4 Harbidges Lane, Long Buckby, Northampton NN6 7QL
Telephone: 01327 844119
Email: acuedit@fireflyuk.net
Web Site: www.acuedit.co.uk

Personnel:
David Price (Contact)

Writing, rewriting, editing, proofreading.
Special interests:
– Fine Art (particularly Modern Art);
– Music (particularly operettas and musicals, pop and rock music);
– Travel Guides;
– Modern European History and Politics (particularly Eastern Europe and the former Soviet Union);
– Social and Cultural History.

6002

AESOP (ALL EDITORIAL SERVICES ONLINE FOR PUBLISHERS & AUTHORS)
28 Abberbury Road, Iffley, Oxford OX4 4ES
Telephone: 01865 429563
Fax: 08700 635449
Email: mart@copyedit.co.uk
Web Site: www.copyedit.co.uk

Personnel:
Martin Noble (Owner/Editor)

AESOP provides the following editorial services to publishers, authors, academics and businesses: copy-editing; proof-reading; structural editing; rewriting; co-writing; ghost-writing; thesis and dissertation editing and printing; improving use of English of non-native English writers of academic reports and books; indexing; editorial reports and reviews; advice to publishers, authors and literary agents; novelization; research; fact-checking; bibliographical research; CRC (camera ready copy) in Word format; text capture; scanning/OCR; e-book production on CD-ROM or online; keying in MSS; audio transcription; tagging. Specializes in fiction, literature, poetry, media, music, performing arts, humour, biography, memoirs, travel, education, economics, psychology, history, alternative health, new age, esoteric and spiritual subjects, special needs.

6003

ASGARD PUBLISHING SERVICES
75 Woodside View, Leeds LS4 2QS
Telephone: 0113 274 1037
Fax: 0113 274 1037
Email: andrew.shackleton@asgardpublishing.co.uk
Web Site: www.asgardpublishing.co.uk

Also at:
Allan Scott
Telephone: 01449 741747

Fax: 01449 740118
Email: allanscott@compuserve.com

Personnel:
Philip Gardner (Personnel)
Michael Scott Rohan (Personnel)
Allan Scott (Personnel)
Andrew Shackleton (Personnel)

Established in 1984. Full editorial service, including writing and re-writing, translating, copy-editing, proof-reading, indexing, design and layout. Projects can be taken from manuscript to film, or to Quark XPress files. Extensive experience with DTP, computer-based multimedia projects (including video production) and electronic publishing. Reference material is a speciality.

6004

BBR SOLUTIONS LTD
12 Cutthorpe Road, Chesterfield S42 7AE
Telephone: 01246 271662
Email: bbr@bbr-online.com
Web Site: www.bbr-online.com

Personnel:
Chris Reed (Director)
Amanda Thompson (Director)

Associated Companies:
UK: BBR Distribution

BBR is an editorial and design consultancy with over 20 years' experience in publishing. It provides both a contract and bespoke service, proofing and editing manuscripts for publication, and creating clean typography-led designs for books and journals.
Please visit the company's website for more information and to view its portfolio.

6005

BLACK ACE BOOK PRODUCTION
PO Box 7547, Perth PH2 1AU
Telephone: 01821 642822
Fax: 01821 642101
Web Site: www.blackacebooks.com

Personnel:
Hunter Steele (Director)
Boo Wood (Director)

Book production and text processing, including text capture (or scanning), editing, proofing to camera-ready/film, printing and binding, jacket artwork and design. Delivery of finished books; can sometimes help with distribution.

6006

BOOK CREATION LTD
20 Lochaline Street, London W6 9SH
Telephone: 020 8563 9982
Fax: 020 3355 0201
Email: info@librios.com
Web Site: www.bookcreation.com

Personnel:
Hal Robinson (Managing Director)

Associated Companies:
UK: Librios Ltd

Book Creation provides editorial, translation, design and packaging/repackaging services, using Mac and PC technology, to text and layouts or final film, primarily in illustrated non-fiction, partworks, dictionaries and general reference, often involving re-use of existing illustrative or text resources.
Its sister company, Librios, provides comprehensive, XML-based electronic publishing and content management services.
With the growing importance of digital delivery, Book Creation Ltd is working ever more closely with its sister company, Librios Ltd, to provide the full range of print, e-book, website and mobile media options that publishers require.

6007

COPYTRAIN
Pitts, Great Milton, Oxford OX44 7NF
Telephone: 01844 279345
Fax: 01844 279345
Email: rbalkwill@aol.com

Personnel:
Richard Balkwill (Proprietor)

Copytrain provides a consultancy and advisory service to publishers in the training and copyright fields.
Training: Publishing Training Centre lecturer in editorial management, financial planning and copyright. Seminars in contracts, copyright and rights. Courses in all aspects of publishing and management.
Copyright: Advice to publishers on rights and copyright matters. Review of authors' and suppliers' contracts and agreements. Associate of Rightscom.
Clients include UNESCO, WIPO and the CfBT Education Trust.
Copytrain provides 'work-for-hire' writing commissions, especially in the children's reference area (non-fiction, history, railways).

6008

FIRST EDITION TRANSLATIONS LTD
6 Wellington Court, Wellington Street, Cambridge CB1 1HZ
Telephone: 01223 356733
Fax: 01223 316232
Email: info@firstedit.co.uk
Web Site: www.firstedit.co.uk

Personnel:
Sheila Waller (Director)

First Edition offers complete and specialized editorial and translation services, including all necessary liaison: translation, research, editing, Americanization, proofreading, indexing, desktop publishing, print ready PDF or CD output. Assessment of foreign language books for the market.

6009

GEO GROUP & ASSOCIATES
4 Christian Fields, London SW16 3JZ
Telephone: 020 8764 6292
Fax: 0115 981 9418
Email: Nyala.publishing@geo-group.co.uk
Web Site: www.geo-group.co.uk

Also at:
Nyala Publishing, 97 Rivermead, West Bridgford,
Nottingham NG2 7RF
Telephone: 0115 981 9418
Email: (as above)
Web Site: (as above)

Personnel:
John Douglas (Director)

Associated Companies:
UK: Nyala Publishing

Publishing services: pre-press, editing, design, proofreading, reading.

6010

ALEXANDRA NYE, LITERARY CONSULTANT
6 Kinnoull Avenue, Dunblane, Perthshire FK15 9JG
Telephone: 01786 825114

Personnel:
Alexandra Nye (Editorial Director / Literary Consultant)

Provides a consultancy service for all types of fiction, with special interest in literary fiction, Scottish history, upmarket thrillers. Children's fiction age range 9–12, teens and young adult. Will supply detailed 5-page report on MSS. Does not accept poetry, plays, TV scripts or biographies.

6011

CHRISTOPHER PICK
41 Chestnut Road, London SE27 9EZ
Telephone: 020 8761 2585
Fax: 020 8761 6388
Email: christopher@the-picks.co.uk

Personnel:
Christopher Pick (Publications Consultant)

I research, write, edit and produce information materials for public- and voluntary-sector agencies and for the corporate sector. I specialize in producing documents (e.g. policy and research reports, annual reports, handbooks) that are accessible and clearly written and that meet the needs of the target audience/readership. I also write and produce family memoirs and 'popular' histories of organizations, companies, etc.

6012

THE PUZZLE HOUSE
Ivy Cottage, Battlesea Green, Stradbroke, Suffolk IP21 5NE
Telephone: 01379 384656
Fax: 01379 384656
Email: puzzlehouse@btinternet.com
Web Site: www.thepuzzlehouse.co.uk

Personnel:
Roy Preston (Partner)
Sue Preston (Partner)

The Puzzle House supplies crossword, quiz and puzzle material for books and magazines. Full editorial service is offered on projects ranging from a one-off puzzle to full CRC book. All subject areas and age ranges catered for. Specialist interest and experience in the children's activity market. Established 1988. Puzzles available for syndication.

6013

RONNE RANDALL
26 Oak Tree Avenue, Radcliffe-on-Trent, Nottingham NG12 1AD
Telephone: 0115 933 5804
Email: ronnerandall@aol.com
Web Site: www.freelancersintheuk.co.uk/ronne-randall-i430.html

Personnel:
Ronne Randall (Proprietor)

Accurate Americanization by a native of the USA, as well as editorial services including editing, copy editing, writing, rewriting/adaptation, and proofreading. Special interest and experience in children's books (including licensed characters). Clients include Ladybird, Macmillan, Hodder Children's Books, Templar and Parragon.

6014

READING AND RIGHTING
[Robert Lambolle Services]
618b Finchley Road, London NW11 7RR
Telephone: 020 8455 4564
Email: lambhorn@gmail.com
Web Site: readingandrighting.netfirms.com

Personnel:
Robert Lambolle (Literary/Script Consultant & Managing Director)

Established in 1987, Reading & Righting is an independent script consultancy providing evaluation and editing services, based on wide-ranging agency and publishing experience. Detailed assessment, analysis of prospects and next-step guidelines for fiction, non-fiction, screenplays, plays and poetry, plus full editing service, one-to-one tutorials, mentoring, lectures, creative writing courses, and research. Prospective clients should consult website or request leaflet outlining procedure and terms.

Specialist interests include cinema, the performing arts, popular culture, psychotherapy and current affairs.

6015

SANDHURST EDITORIAL
36 Albion Road, Sandhurst, Berks GU47 9BP
Telephone: 01252 877645
Email: lionel.browne@sfep.net
Web Site: www.sandhurst-editorial.co.uk

Personnel:
Lionel Browne (Proprietor)

Sandhurst Editorial provides a complete editorial service for clients inside and outside the UK, both private sector and public sector: academic and educational publishers, research associations, commercial clients, and government departments. The skills on offer include editorial development and consultancy, project management, writing, rewriting, copy-editing and proofreading.

The company specializes in science and technology, but has handled projects as diverse as bibles, biography, travel guides and corporate reports.

6016

SUNRISE SETTING LTD
12a Fore Street, St Marychurch, Torquay, Devon TQ1 4NE
Telephone: 01803 322635
Fax: 01803 323565
Email: enquiries@sunrise-setting.co.uk
Web Site: www.sunrise-setting.co.uk

Personnel:
Jessica Stock (Finance & Marketing Director)
Alistair Smith (Technical Director)

Sunrise Setting Ltd has over 30 years' experience of providing a high-quality typesetting, editorial and project management service to STM and General publishers, including copyediting, a full XML workflow, graphics manipulation, project management of conference proceedings, books and journals, and the writing of LaTex class files and author support.

6017

HANS ZELL PUBLISHING CONSULTANTS
Glais Bheinn, Lochcarron, Ross-shire IV54 8YB
Telephone: 01520 722951
Fax: 01520 722953
Email: hanszell@hanszell.co.uk
Web Site: www.hanszell.co.uk/

Personnel:
Hans M. Zell (Proprietor)

Associated Companies:
UK: Hans Zell Publishing

Consultancy service to publishers and academic institutions, in particular providing advisory services and individual project management for publishers, research institutes, and the book community in Africa and in other developing countries.

Specialization:
– scholarly publishing, especially university press publishing, and publishing by research institutions and NGOs, including editorial and financial management, administration, marketing and promotion, pricing and distribution, general publishing management, and dealing with author and publisher
contracts
– journals publishing management, including subscription management and fulfilment, financial control, journals promotion, and market assessments- reference book publishing, particularly for reference resources focusing on Africa and the developing world, including research, project evaluations, editorial services, and market assessments
– training – in-house or through workshops and seminars – in editorial and production management, financial planning, and all areas of marketing
– marketing and distribution of books on African and development studies, and African literature and culture
– providing a range of specialist mailing list services in this area, full details available on request
– Internet training for the book professions in developing countries.

Under the Hans Zell Publishing imprint we publish a number of reference resources (print and online) on Africa, African studies and African publishing.

6.2 DESIGN & PRODUCTION SERVICES

6018

BOOK PRODUCTION CONSULTANTS LTD
25–27 High Street, Chesterton, Cambridge CB4 1ND
Telephone: 01223 352790
Fax: 01223 460718
Email: bpc@bpccam.co.uk
Web Site: www.bpccam.co.uk

Personnel:
Colin Walsh (Managing Director)
Jo Littlechild (Marketing Manager)
Susan Buck (Accounts Manager)
Jo'e Coleby (Editorial Project Manager)

Associated Companies:
UK: Book Connections; Granta Editions

A totally comprehensive publishing service including editing, sub-editing, designing, technical mark-up, illustrating, technical drawing, estimating, paper buying, typesetting and origination. BPC arranges the printing and binding of black-and-white or colour publications in the UK or overseas and supervises quality control and delivery schedules; also computer software packs including design of packaging and manufacture of boxes, tapes and discs. Other specialities include the design and production of illustrated books, music and foreign language setting projects, academic journals and institutional publications, producing company sponsored books and company histories. Electronic publishing and CD-ROM origination, particularly as joint ventures, form part of current expansion. Specialist divisions include business histories (providing authors, archivists and picture researchers), contract magazine production and company literature.

6019

BOOKCRAFT LTD
18 Kendrick Street, Stroud, Glos GL5 1AA
Telephone: 0870 1601900
Fax: 0870 1601901
Email: information@bookcraft.co.uk
Web Site: www.bookcraft.co.uk

Personnel:
John Button (Publishing Director)

Bookcraft provides publishers with a wide range of editorial, design, technical and training services.
Main areas of activity are:
– publishing consultancy
– publishing software training
– design services

– editorial and proofreading services
– project management.

6020

CHASE PUBLISHING SERVICES LTD
33 Livonia Road, Sidmouth, Devon EX10 9JB
Telephone: 01395 514709
Fax: 01395 514709
Email: r.addicott@chase-publishing.co.uk

Personnel:
Ray Addicott *(Director)*

Chase offers a complete editorial and production service to authors and publishers – from copy-editing of the author's typescript to finished books at the delivery point. It specializes in academic books. Founded in 1989.

6021

DISCRIPT LTD
24 Bedfordbury, Covent Garden, London WC2N 4BN
Telephone: 020 7240 3196
Fax: 020 7379 8559
Email: info@discript.com
Web Site: www.discript.com

Personnel:
Richard Bates *(Managing Director)*
F. R. Bates *(Finance Director)*

Discript can provide editorial, proofreading, production, book design and typography, including text keyboarding, OCR capture and indexing. Whether a large technical document, illustrated book or colour leaflet is required, Discript can provide a fast efficient service. It also helps authors to self-publish.

6022

FOTOLIBRA
22 Mount View Road, London N4 4HX
Telephone: 020 8348 1234
Email: professionals@fotoLibra.com
Web Site: www.fotoLibra.com

Personnel:
Gwyn Headley *(Director)*
Yvonne Seeley *(Director)*

Associated Companies:
USA: Idea Logical Company Inc

fotoLibra is a picture library set up by publishers for publishers. The company has 18,000+ photographers in over 150 countries ready and willing to take the required image if it is not already in the library – and there's no obligation to buy. Over 350,000 images on line.

6023

GRAHAM-CAMERON ILLUSTRATION
The Studio, 23 Holt Road, Sheringham, Norfolk NR26 8NB
Telephone: 01263 821333
Fax: 01263 821334
Email: enquiry@gciforillustration.com
Web Site: www.gciforillustration.com

Sales & Marketing:
Duncan Graham-Cameron, 59 Hertford Road, Brighton BN1 7GG
Telephone: 01273 385890
Email: duncan@gciforillustration.com
Web Site: (as above)

Personnel:
Mike Graham-Cameron *(Finance)*
Helen Graham-Cameron *(Art)*
Duncan Graham-Cameron *(Sales & Marketing)*

Parent Company:
UK: Graham-Cameron Publishing

Associated Companies:
UK: Helen Herbert, Fine Art

This agency has some 37 qualified professional illustrators who have a wide range of techniques, media and artistic skills. GCI specializes in pictures for educational and children's books, ELT and for general information publications.

6024

HOLBROOK DESIGN OXFORD LTD
Holbrook House, 105 Rose Hill, Oxford OX4 4HT
Telephone: 01865 459000
Email: info@holbrook-design.co.uk
Web Site: www.holbrook-design.co.uk

Personnel:
Peter Tucker *(Design Director)*

Holbrook Design Oxford Ltd was founded as PGT Design in 1974. It offers the following services: typography, editorial design and art direction, photography; from concept through dummies, mark-up and typesetting, page layouts to artwork, in consultation with photographers, illustrators and printers. Clients include many national and international publishers. Holbrook Design has particular experience in educational and general publishing; subject areas covered range from science to religion, cookery to history and first readers to A-level.

6025

HOLBROOK HOSTING
Holbrook House, 105 Rose Hill, Oxford OX4 4HT
Telephone: 01865 459000
Email: info@holbrookhosting.com
Web Site: www.holbrookhosting.com

Personnel:
Peter Tucker *(Consultant)*

Design Systems is a consultancy providing both technical and design expertise in the implementation and use of both Macs and PCs in graphics and publishing industries. Agents include Adobe, Quark, Ventura Software, Monotype, Linotype and other associated companies. Affiliated to Holbrook Design Oxford Ltd, for many years designers in publishing and print.

6026

HYBERT DESIGN LTD
Suite 3, Maple Court, Grove Park, White Waltham, Berks SL6 3LW
Telephone: 01628 822700
Fax: 01628 822288
Email: info@hybertdesign.com
Web Site: www.hybertdesign.com

Also at:
Buterud P1 8722, 464 91 Dals Rostock, Sweden
Telephone: +46 (0)530 30084

Personnel:
Tom Hybert *(Director)*
Kate Hybert *(Company Secretary)*
Linda Elliott *(Senior Designer)*

Established in 1975, Hybert Design specializes in marketing, promotion and cover design for publishers in all areas, including education, science and technology, journal and business publishing.

6027

IMAGO PUBLISHING LTD
Albury Court, Albury, Thame, Oxon OX9 2LP
Telephone: 01844 337000
Fax: 01844 339935
Email: reception@imago.co.uk
Web Site: www.imago.co.uk

Personnel:
Colin Risk *(Managing Director)*
Jim Allpass *(Finance Director)*
Angela Young *(Director)*
Debbie Knight *(Director)*
Cherry Jaquet *(Production Director)*
Martina Scheible *(Director)*
Paolo Scaramuzza *(Director)*

Offers production consultancy, print broking and training to the publishing industry. With offices in the UK, Paris, Hong Kong, China, Singapore, Malaysia, India, Sydney, New York and California, the group is able to locate and control sources of manufacture on a world-wide basis. The group works with a wide range of customers, and can offer its extensive expertise in many ways, from running all the production needs for small publishers/packagers, to sourcing

and arranging for the manufacture of individual projects on a competitive brokerage basis. All types of work are handled, including colour separation, children's books, novelty products, short- and long-run general books and magazines. Training courses in colour, toy safety, paper, assessing digital images, CTP, InDesign, Quark and Photoshop run regularly.

6028

MY WORD!
PO Box 4575, Rugby, Warwickshire CV21 9EH
Telephone: 01788 571294
Email: janet@myword.co.uk
Web Site: www.myword.co.uk

Personnel:
Roderick Grant *(Partner)*
Janet Grant *(Partner)*

My Word! is a family business which specializes in typesetting of materials for both printing and the Internet.
Its range includes magazines, books, newsletters, newspapers, brochures, conference and sales materials, leaflets, posters and stationery.
Clients come from both the charity and commercial sectors.

6029

ROYAL NATIONAL INSTITUTE OF BLIND PEOPLE (RNIB)
Bakewell Road, Orton Southgate, Peterborough PE2 6XU
Telephone: 0303 123 9999
Fax: 01733 375001
Email: helpline@rnib.org.uk
Web Site: rnib.org.uk

Royal National Institute of Blind People (RNIB) is one of the UK's leading charities offering information, support and advice to over two million people with sight loss.
It produces accessible format editions of publications so that blind and partially sighted people can read them in a format such as braille, large print or audio formats – from textbooks supporting children in education to a Mills and Boon romance, and everything in between. It offers transcription services for businesses and publishers.
It publishes a range of material about living with sight loss, such as eye condition leaflets and information on benefits.

6030

SMALL PRINT
The Old School House, 74 High Street, Swavesey, Cambridge CB24 4QU
Telephone: 01954 231713 (mobile: 07760 430206)
Fax: 01954 205061
Email: info@smallprint.co.uk
Web Site: www.smallprint.co.uk

Personnel:
Naomi Laredo *(Proprietor)*

A flexible publishing and translation resource for publishers and businesses producing educational, training and information material.
Project management service includes research, copywriting, editing and proofreading, design and layout for web or print, audio and video production.
Translation and language-checking covers most European and Asian languages.
Clients include ACCA, BBC, Berlitz, Cambridge University Press, Channel 4 Learning, Dorling Kindersley, Henley Management College, Nelson Thornes, Pearson Education.

6.3 ELECTRONIC PUBLISHING SERVICES

6031

ATTWOOLL ASSOCIATES LTD
90 Divinity Road, Oxford OX4 1LN
Telephone: 01865 422230
Fax: 01865 791192
Email: david@attwoollassociates.com
Web Site: www.attwoollassociates.com

Personnel:
David Attwooll (Director)
Clare Painter (Associate)

Attwooll Associates Ltd is a publishing consultancy and licensing agency specializing in electronic and print media, in North American and UK markets. It was founded in April 2002.
   Activities include:
   – publishing and media strategy
   – intellectual property exploitation and licensing
   – project management and innovation
   – market-driven content creation and acquisition
   – information mapping and knowledge management
   – mergers and acquisitions advice
   – training seminars and lectures.
   Please see www.attwoollassociates.com

6032 ▰

GLOBAL MAPPING
Glebe Farm, Turweston, Brackley, Northants NN13 5JE
Telephone: 01280 840770
Fax: 01280 840816
Email: sales@globalmapping.uk.com
Web Site: www.globalmapping.uk.com

Personnel:
Alan Smith (Managing Director)

Publishes its own range of maps. Also creates bespoke map products for other publishers including interactive map-based websites. Online retailer of map-based products such as wall maps, postcode maps, ordnance survey data, atlases, globes and guides. Global Mapping aims to be a one-stop shop for all map-based requirements.

6033 ▰

KOALA PUBLISHING LTD
Downend House, 112 North Street, Downend, Bristol BS16 5SE
Telephone: 0117 910 9111
Fax: 0117 910 9222
Email: gordon.dennis@koalapub.co.uk
Web Site: www.koalapub.co.uk

Personnel:
Gordon Dennis (Commercial Director)
Vivienne Willoughby-Ellis (Managing Director)
Robin Shobbrook (Marketing Manager)

Koala helps suppliers of complex products and services who need to:
   – create straightforward, easy to use documentation and get it to their customers in the most effective way possible – from PDAs to printer manuals;
   – efficiently organize, write and deliver their technical manuals, policies and procedures;
   – reduce the cost and time constraints on professional staff of providing information to their customers, and reduce the long-term risks of litigation caused by faulty documentation.
   Koala provides software products for publishing technical documentation including manuals, training materials, catalogues, directories and listings. Services include project management and control; analysis and design; bespoke programming; data format conversion; and full training and support.

6034 ▰

LIGHTNING SOURCE UK LTD
Chapter House, Pitfield, Kiln Farm, Milton Keynes MK11 3LW
Telephone: 0845 121 4567
Fax: 0845 121 4594
Email: enquiries@lightningsource.co.uk
Web Site: www.lightningsource.com

Personnel:
David Taylor (Group Managing Director)
Dave Piper (Managing Director)
Terry Gridley (Operations Director)
Frank Devine (Finance Director)
Lawrence Felice (Marketing Manager)

Parent Company:
USA: Ingram Content Group, Inc.

Associated Companies:
USA: Lightning Source, Inc.

Lightning Source offers quality e-book and one-off book manufacturing and access to comprehensive distribution solutions in the publishing industry.

6035 ▰

MMT
[trading as MMT Digital]
1A Uppingham Gate, Ayston Road, Uppingham, Rutland LE15 9NY
Telephone: 01572 822278
Fax: 01572 820213
Email: info@mmtdigital.co.uk
Web Site: www.mmtdigital.co.uk

London Office:
Suite 54–55, 88–90 Hatton Gardens, London EC1N 8PN
Telephone: 020 7242 5698
Fax: (as above)
Email: (as above)
Web Site: (as above)

Personnel:
Peter Cannings (Human Resources & Finance Director)
Ben Rudman (Joint Managing & Marketing Director)
James Cannings (Joint Managing & Production Director)

Currently working with Hodder on their e-titles.

6036 ▰

NIELSEN BOOKNET
3rd Floor, Midas House, 62 Goldsworth Road, Woking, Surrey GU21 6LQ
Telephone: 01483 712200
Fax: 01483 712201
Email: sales.booknet@nielsen.com
Web Site: www.nielsenbooknet.co.uk

Personnel:
Ann Betts (Commercial Director)
Stephen Long (Head of BookNet)
Mo Siewcharran (Head of Marketing)
Joanna De Courville (Business Development Manager)
Paul Dibble (Head of Data Sales)

Parent Company:
UK: Nielsen Book

Associated Companies:
UK: Nielsen BookData; Nielsen BookScan

Nielsen BookNet provides a range of e-commerce services that allow electronic trading between booksellers, distributors, publishers, libraries and other suppliers, regardless of their size and location. Services include BookNet Transaction Services for booksellers and publishers/distributors, TeleOrdering and EDI. Nielsen BookNet is uniquely placed in the book trade to be the trading hub for orders, invoices, delivery notes and other EDI messaging.

6037 ▰

TRILOGY GROUP
Aries House, 43 Selkirk Street, Cheltenham, Glos GL52 2HJ
Telephone: 01242 222132
Fax: 01242 235103
Email: alex-dare@trilogygroup.com
Web Site: www.trilogygroup.com

Personnel:
Alex Dare (Managing Director)
Simon Gough (IT Director)
Mike Ribbins (Group Chairman)

The Trilogy Group specializes in software for the specialist publisher, especially those requiring a totally integrated business solution to handle publishing management, administration, direct and distribution sales together with active marketing. Our software, which uses Microsoft SQL Server technology, offers:
   – title management
   – customer management with profiles and buying history
   – active marketing facilities
   – direct mail management with optional integration to MailSort
   – subscriptions management
   – royalties
   – integration to accounting systems
   – vast range of 'real time' management reports
   – real-time stock management
   – warehouse and despatch management

   – integrated on-line shopping facilities with web hosting
   – multi-site management
   – EPOS
   – production control, scheduling and job costing.

6.4 TRANSLATION SERVICES

6038 ▰

FIRST EDITION TRANSLATIONS LTD
6 Wellington Court, Wellington Street, Cambridge CB1 1HZ
Telephone: 01223 356733
Fax: 01223 316232
Email: info@firstedit.co.uk
Web Site: www.firstedit.co.uk

Personnel:
Sheila Waller (Director)

Translations – commercial, technical, academic and of any length – undertaken in any language according to publisher's requirements. Editing, proofreading, Americanization, indexing, typesetting/desktop publishing.
   Output to print ready PDF or CD. Quotations given without obligation.

6039 ▰

SATRAP PUBLISHING & TRANSLATION
Suite 21, London House, 271 King Street, Hammersmith, London W6 9LZ
Telephone: 020 8748 9397
Fax: 020 8748 9394
Email: satrap@btconnect.com
Web Site: www.satrap.co.uk

Personnel:
Alex Vahdat (Managing Director)
Mrs Homa Lohrasb (Technical Manager)

Satrap Publishing is a UK-based international company, specializing in the fields of translation, typesetting and print services in Oriental and East European languages.
   The company produces promotional literature, exhibition catalogues, information pamphlets, books, reports, manuals, business stationery, product labels, diaries etc for Western European companies, trade centres and various organizations which have foreign language requirements for their overseas trade links.
   The human resources and advanced technical facilities available are ideal for those clients who wish to target ethnic minorities for their social, cultural and educational programmes. Satrap Publishing offers a complete package of expert translation, typesetting, professional graphic design as well as printing. Production of exclusive greeting cards and wedding stationery in non-European languages are among other services from Satrap Publishing.

6040 ▰

SWEDISH-ENGLISH LITERARY TRANSLATORS ASSOCIATION (SELTA)
3 Roseacre Close, London W13 8DG
Telephone: 020 8997 1218
Web Site: www.selta.org.uk &
www.swedishbookreview.com

Personnel:
Peter Linton (Hon Secretary)
Sarah Death (Editor, Swedish Book Review)

SELTA aims to promote the publication of Swedish literature in English and to represent the interests of those involved in its translation. Publishes Swedish Book Review (ISSN: 0265 8119): biannual, £15 p.a.

6041 ▰

TAMR TRANSLATIONS LTD
[sister company to American Pie (American Eyes Ltd)]
197 Kings Cross Road, London WC1X 9DB
Telephone: 020 7278 9490
Fax: 020 7278 2447
Email: bacon@langservice.com
Web Site: www.tamrtranslations.com

Also at:
215 West Red Oak #I, Sunnyvale, CA 94086–6632, USA

Email: DHenderson@aol.com
Web Site: www.americanization.com

Personnel:
Josephine Bacon (*Director*)
Dan Henderson (*Director*)
Azmi Jbeily (*Director*)

Parent Company:
UK: American Pie (American Eyes Ltd)

Associated Companies:
UK: Tamr Translations Ltd

Tamr Translations Ltd specializes in work for publication, into and from English, including highly illustrated books. Specialist languages are French, Arabic and Hebrew, specialist subjects cookery, art and architecture. American Pie, with offices in London and Sunnyvale, California, translates between British and American English.

The two companies have translated more than 100 books between them, and have also published three translations. Their work has won the Gourmand Prize for Cookery Translation.

6042

UPS TRANSLATIONS
111 Baker Street, London W1U 6RR
Telephone: 020 7224 1220
Fax: 020 7486 3272
Email: info@upstranslations.com
Web Site: www.upstranslations.com

Personnel:
Bernard Silver (*Chairman & Managing Director*)
Denise McKenzie (*Company Secretary*)
Justin Silver (*Sales Director*)

Parent Company:
UK: United Publicity Services Plc

Translation of books from manuscript to final film, into and from all the languages of the world, and Americanization.

6043

SALLY WALKER LANGUAGE SERVICES
43 St Nicholas Street, Bristol BS1 1TP
Telephone: 0117 929 1594
Fax: 0117 929 0633
Email: translations@sallywalker.co.uk
Web Site: www.sallywalker.co.uk

Also at:
Perch Buildings, 9 Mount Stuart Square, Cardiff CF10 5EE
Telephone: 029 2048 0747
Fax: 029 2048 8736
Email: languages@sallywalker.co.uk
Web Site: www.sallywalker.co.uk

Personnel:
Sally Walker (*Director*)
Richard Smith (*General Manager*)

Established in 1969 Sally Walker Language Services provides a 70 language capability. Languages include all European and major Middle Eastern and Far Eastern. Additionally most Indian and African languages are offered.

6044

WESSEX TRANSLATIONS LTD
Barn 500, The Grange, Romsey Road, Michelmersh, Romsey, Hants SO51 0AE
Telephone: 0870 1669 300
Fax: 0870 1669 299
Email: sales@wt-lm.com
Web Site: www.wt-lm.com

Personnel:
Jonathan Nater (*Director*)
Robin Weber (*Director*)
Paul Stewart (*Director*)

Associated Companies:
France: Wessex Traductions

In addition to translation our services include interpreting, typesetting, DTP and artwork, editing and proofreading, copywriting, software localization, language training, audio

and video transcription, voice-overs and website translations.

Translators always work into their mother tongue, and all translations are double-checked, and then re-worked, DTPed if required and checked again before despatch. The final text is sent by email with hard copy if required to meet clients' individual software requirements, ready to print wherever possible.

A special urgent Tender Translation Service is also offered.

6.5 SALES & MARKETING SERVICES

6045

AMALGAMATED BOOK SERVICES LTD
The Old Mill House, Mill Lane, Uckfield, East Sussex TN22 5AA
Telephone: 01825 746050
Fax: 01825 764925
Email: richard@vinehouseuk.co.uk
Web Site: www.amalg.co.uk

Personnel:
Richard Squibb (*Managing Director*)
Paul Cook (*Senior Sales Executive*)
Glenn Wilson (*Senior Sales Executive*)

Associated Companies:
UK: Vine House Distribution Ltd

Sales representation for publishers covering the UK, Ireland and elsewhere.

6046

BERTOLI MITCHELL LLP
53 Chandos Place, Covent Garden, London WC2N 4HS
Telephone: 020 7812 6416
Fax: 020 7812 6677
Email: nb@bertolimitchell.co.uk
Web Site: www.bertolimitchell.co.uk

Personnel:
William Mitchell (*Managing Partner*)
Natalina Bertoli (*Partner*)
Paul Mitton (*Senior Associate*)

Bertoli Mitchell LLP is a specialist mergers and acquisitions advisory firm in the publishing and information industries.

The partnership offers corporate finance services for mergers, acquisitions and divestitures including:
– sell-side advisory representation to sellers of privately held businesses and corporate clients seeking to divest business units or assets
– buy-side advisory services and representation
– commercial and contracts due diligence
– valuations
Since Bertoli Mitchell was founded in 1994 it has advised successfully on over 80 transactions.

Bertoli Mitchell also undertakes strategic research and consultancy. Activities include:
– profiling, analysis, forecasting and recommendations for clients considering entry into specific markets or sectors
– benchmarking, cost audits and development of financial targets
– development of business plans
Clients range from large fully listed international companies to shareholders of small and medium-sized private businesses.

6047

BEST MAILING SERVICES LTD
Merlin Way, North Weald, Epping, Essex CM16 6HR
Telephone: 01992 524343
Fax: 01992 524552
Email: sales@bestmailing.co.uk
Web Site: www.bestmailing.co.uk

Personnel:
Mrs Lyn Reed (*Managing Director*)
Peter Cook (*Client Services Director*)

BMS offers a complete direct mail production facility.

Comprehensive services include database management, data capture, laser printing, mail order fulfilment, subscription management, machine and hand enclosing, bulk despatch, overseas and UK postal discounts.

BMS also provides high volume digital printing and on demand publishing, backed up with a professional finishing service which includes booklet making and collating.

6048

BOOKLINK
43 Maycock Grove, Northwood, Middx HA6 3PU
Telephone: 01923 828612
Fax: 01923 828455
Email: info@booklink.co.uk
Web Site: www.booklink.co.uk

Personnel:
Evelyne Duval (*Managing Director*)

Associated Companies:
UK: Musketeer Books Ltd

An international connection for foreign rights sales and consultancy. Representing French, English and American publishers/packagers.

6049

BOOKS ON MUSIC
3 Kendal Green, Kendal, Cumbria LA9 5PN
Telephone: 01539 740049
Fax: 01539 737744
Web Site: www.booksonmusic.co.uk

Personnel:
Rosemary Dooley (*Manager*)

Distributor for:
UK: The British Journal for Ethnomusicology; Royal Musical Association Research Chronicle (*journal*)

Books on Music runs collaborative publishers' exhibitions at academic music conferences. Specialization in music.

6050

BROOKSIDE PUBLISHING SERVICES LTD
2 Brookside, Dundrum Road, Dublin 14, Republic of Ireland
Telephone: +353 (01) 298 9937
Fax: +353 (01) 298 2783
Email: sales@brookside.ie

Personnel:
Edwin Higel (*Managing Director*)
Conor Graham (*Sales & Marketing Manager*)
Michael Darcy (*Senior Academic Sales Rep*)

Agents for various imprints in Ireland including:
Bloomsbury Professional Publishing; Cambridge University Press; Chartered Accountants Ireland; Clarus Press; Continuum; A & A Farmar; First Law; Nick Hern; Irish Academic Press; Irish Theatre Handbook; Jones & Bartlett; Jessica Kingsley; Learning Matters; Pharmaceutical Press; Pluto; Radcliffe Medical; Routledge / Taylor & Francis; Special Stories Publishing; Taxation Advice Bureau Guide

Represents both trade and academic publishers.

6052

BROOMFIELD BOOKS LTD
36 De La Warr Road, East Grinstead, West Sussex RH19 3BP
Telephone: 01342 313237
Fax: 01342 322525
Email: nic@broomfieldbooks.co.uk
Web Site: www.broomfieldbooks.co.uk

Personnel:
Nic Webb (*Director*)
Mrs Andrea Grant-Webb (*Director*)

Broomfield Books is a publishing consultancy and sales agency for small and medium publishers of non-fiction and fiction. The sales agency covers London and the south-east of England, together with UK key accounts and the export market.

6053

THE CENTRE FOR INTERFIRM COMPARISON
32 St Thomas Street, Winchester, Hants SO23 9HJ
Telephone: 01962 844144
Fax: 01962 843180

Email: mikebayliss@cifc.co.uk
Web Site: www.cifc.co.uk

Personnel:
Mr M. J. Bayliss (Director)

An independent organization established in 1959 by the British Institute of Management and the British Productivity Council specifically to meet the demand for a neutral specialist body to conduct interfirm comparisons (IFCs) and benchmarking projects on a confidential basis as a service to management.

The Centre has run a series of confidential IFCs specifically designed for book publishers in conjunction with the Publishers Association. These provided participants with measures for assessing how their overall performance compared, where and why it differed, and lines of action for improvement. More recently the Centre carried out projects for learned journal and magazine publishers. It has become a specialist in conducting in-depth and carefully defined benchmarking projects for firms and organizations of all kinds, based on information supplied confidentially by participants.

6054

COLMAN GETTY CONSULTANCY
28 Windmill Street, London W1T 2JJ
Telephone: 020 7631 2666
Fax: 020 7631 2699
Email: info@colmangetty.co.uk
Web Site: www.colmangetty.co.uk

Personnel:
Dotti Irving (Chief Executive)
Liz Sich (Managing Director)
Mark Hutchinson (Director)
Truda Spruyt (Associate Director)
Jane Acton (Associate Director)
Ruth Cairns (Associate Director)

Colman Getty is a London-based PR and communications consultancy, founded in 1987 and headed by Dotti Irving formerly publicity director of Penguin Books. The agency specializes in book publishing, cultural and campaigning PR and event management and has established a reputation for handling complex, high-profile campaigns, individual promotions, literary prizes and anniversaries and longer term consultancies. As well as offering a wide-based expertise in PR and publicity, Colman Getty offers bespoke marketing services – from copywriting and print production to sales promotion, advertising and digital and social media campaigns. Its client list includes The Man Booker Prize for Fiction, the BBC Samuel Johnson Prize for Non Fiction, National Poetry Day, *The Times* Cheltenham Literature Festival, World Book Day, award-winning bookseller Foyles and a number of individual writers such as J.K. Rowling, Nigella Lawson, Charlie Higson, Val McDermid and Patricia Cornwell. Other clients include the Association of Graduate Recruiters and *Management Today*.

6055

THE COLUMBA BOOKSERVICE
55A Spruce Avenue, Stillorgan Industrial Park, Blackrock, Co Dublin, Republic of Ireland
Telephone: +353 (01) 294 2556
Fax: +353 (01) 294 2564
Email: info@columba.ie
Web Site: www.columba.ie

Personnel:
Séan O Boyle (Managing Director)
Cecilia West (Sales Director)

UK distributor/representative for:
Canada: Novalis
Republic of Ireland: The Columba Press
USA: Michael Glazier Books; The Liturgical Press; Loyola Press; Paraclete Press; Paulist Press; Pueblo Books; Resource Publications; Twenty-third Publications

The Columba Bookservice provides trade representation, sales and marketing services for a number of religious publishers.

6056

COMPASS DSA LTD
13 Progress Business Park, Whittle Parkway, Slough SL1 6DQ
Telephone: 01628 559500

Fax: 01628 663876
Email: alan@compass-dsa.co.uk
Web Site: www.compass-dsa.co.uk

Personnel:
Alan Jessop (Joint Managing Director)
Derek Searle (Joint Managing Director)
June Searle (Director)

Associated Companies:
Republic of Ireland: Compass Ireland Ltd
UK: Compass Academic Ltd

Client publishers:
Republic of Ireland: The Collins Press; New Island Books Ltd
UK: Absolute Press; Accent Press; ALMA Books; Assouline; Benefactum; Birlinn Ltd; Black & White Publishing; Carcanet Press; Comma Press; Compendium Publishing; Enitharmon Press; Gibson Square; Good Hotel Guide; Hay House Publishers; Nick Hern Books; Hesperus Press; How to Books / Springhill; Interact; Little Books; Malavan Media; Myrmidon Books; Oldie Publications; Peter Owen; Oxygen Books; Plexus; Polygon Ltd; Pomona Books; Pushkin Press; Radio Times; Ryland, Peter & Small / Cico; Saqi / Telegram; Sport Media; Summersdale; Thorogood; TMI; Visit Britain; Which?

Compass DSA is one of the leading independent sales companies, providing sales and marketing services for publishers to both the traditional and non-traditional markets across the UK and Ireland.

6057

DAVENPORT PUBLISHING SERVICES
11 Silbury Rise, Keynsham, Bristol BS31 1JP
Telephone: 0117 986 2914
Fax: 0117 986 2074
Email: anne@annedavenport.demon.co.uk

Personnel:
Anne Davenport (Proprietor & Consultant)

Davenport Publishing Services offers consultancy in marketing, promotion, sales and distribution for academic, STM and society publishers.

Projects successfully completed include marketing planning and market research, promotion planning, copywriting for print and electronic media, sales advice, sourcing of overseas agents, representatives and distributors, and lapsed subscriber chasing. Davenport Publishing Services offers a full service from consultancy to implementation of marketing campaigns. Long-term or short-term projects are welcome.

Clients include society publishers, university presses and independent institutions with publishing interests.

6058

DURNELL MARKETING LTD
2 Linden Close, Tunbridge Wells, Kent TN4 8HH
Telephone: 01892 544272
Fax: 01892 511152
Email: admin@durnell.co.uk & orders@durnell.co.uk
Web Site: www.durnell.co.uk

Personnel:
Andrew Durnell (Managing Proprietor/Director)
Julia Lippiatt (Finance Proprietor/Director)

Durnell Marketing provides a solution for publishers wishing to maximize their sales – via a single sales force – to all of Central, Eastern and Western Europe's diverse markets, including Ireland (but excluding the UK). A team of multilingual sales representatives ensures maximum, effective and personal coverage of publishers' potential customers, be they library suppliers, general wholesalers, bookshop chains, specialist independents, campus bookshops, non-trade, museum or institutional accounts. Travelling representatives are supported by office-based multilingual sales specialists who provide extra sales backup by promoting trade books, potential textbooks and major reference works to the trade, individual academics and institutions. In addition, Durnell Marketing organizes specific promotions, exhibitions, mailings, author signings and more.

6059

EDUCATION DIRECT
Riverside House, Sir Thomas Longley Road, Rochester, Kent ME2 4FN
Telephone: 01634 291122

Fax: 01634 720269
Email: info@education.co.uk
Web Site: www.education.co.uk

Personnel:
Jason Gould (Managing Director)
David Edwards (Operations Director)
Tim Roger (Finance Director)
Martin Thorpe (Company Secretary)

Education Direct provides a complete range of services for companies promoting their products and services to schools, colleges and universities, including:
  – a list of educational establishments and contact names;
  – award-winning marketing software;
  – direct mail services to the education sector;
  – project management;
  – dedicated telesales and customer services department.

6060

GAZELLE ACADEMIC
White Cross Mills, Hightown, Lancaster LA1 4XS
Telephone: 01524 68765
Fax: 01524 63232
Email: sales@gazellebooks.co.uk
Web Site: www.gazellebookservices.co.uk

Personnel:
Trevor Witcher (Managing Director)
Brian Haywood (Finance Director)
Mark Trotter (Sales & Distribution Director)

Parent Company:
UK: Gazelle Book Services Ltd

Clients:
Australia: FHA Publishing & Communication
Belgium: EuroComment
Canada: Calgary University Press; Canadian Humanist Publications; Wilfrid Laurier University Press; Museum of New Mexico Press; New Society Publishers
Denmark: Aarhus University Press; Museum Tusculanum Press
Finland: Finnish Literature Society; PG-Team Oy; Sophi Academic Press
Germany: Ontos-verlag.de
Israel: Yad Ben Zvi
Netherlands: Aspekt Uitgeverij BV; Nova Vista Publishing; VU University Press
Norway: Tapir Academic Press
Sweden: International Idea; Nordic Academic Press; Student Litteratur
Switzerland: INU Press
UK: Arabian Publishing; Boulevard Books; Clinical Press – Europe; Elector Electronics; William Harvey Press Ltd; Institute of Economic Affairs; Merit Publishing (Medical); Sponsorship Unit; Sussex Academic Press; TFM Publishing Ltd (Medical); World Council of Churches
USA: Ariadne Press; Colorado University Press; Current Clinical Strategies Publishing; Darwin Press; Duquesne University Press; Encounter Books; Feminist Press; Hackett Publishing Co; Harlan Davidson Inc; Ibex Publishers; J & S Publishing Co Inc; Liberty Fund; Mage Publishers; MediPress; Nova Science Publishers Inc; Scientific Publishing Co; Truman State University Press; University of Alberta Press; University of New Mexico Press; Woodbine House Inc

Gazelle Academic is now a division of Gazelle Book Services.

6061

GLOBAL BOOK MARKETING LTD
99B Wallis Road, London E9 5LN
Telephone: 020 8533 5800
Fax: 020 8533 5800
Email: info@globalbookmarketing.co.uk

Personnel:
A. Zurbrugg (Managing Director)
A. Howe (Sales Manager)
A. Hanson (IT Manager)

European agents for:
Canada: Between the Lines; Fernwood Publishing
France: Cacimbo Editions
Germany: Bayreuth African Studies; Barbara Budrich; LIT Verlag
Jamaica: Ian Randle Publishers; Universities of the Caribbean Press
Kenya: Camerapix

Netherlands: International Books (Utrecht); Techne
Nigeria: Kachifo
South Africa: Blue Weaver Marketing; Briza; Briza
    Publications; Fernwood Press; Human & Rousseau;
    Jacana Education; Kwela Books; Pharos; David Philip /
    Spearhead / New Africa Books Consortium; Tafelberg
Switzerland: Basler Afrika Bibliografien
Tanzania: Blue Mango Publishing
UK: Battlebridge; Eastern Arts / Saffron; Horniman Museum
    Publications
USA: International Publishers (New York)
Zimbabwe: African Publishing Group

Agents and representatives. Many publishers are distributed
by Central Books Ltd.

6062

HAWKINS PUBLISHING SERVICES
12 Parkview Cottages, Crowhurst Lane End, Oxted, Surrey
RH8 9NT
Telephone: 01342 893029
Fax: 01342 893316
Email: gill.hawkins@virgin.net

Personnel:
Gillian Hawkins *(Director)*

Distributor for:
Australia: Sibling Press
UK: Dynasty Press; Full Circle Editions; Gullane; Inside
    Pocket; Meadowside; Shepheard Walwyn

Sales, marketing, publicity, rights and distribution.

6063

HUMPHRYS ROBERTS ASSOCIATES
5 Voluntary Place, Wanstead, London E11 2RP
Telephone: 020 8530 5028
Fax: 020 8530 7870
Email: humph4hra@aol.com

Also at:
Terry Roberts, Humphrys Roberts Associates,
Caixa Postal 801, Agencia Jardim da Gloria,
06700–990 Cotia SP, Brazil
Telephone: +55 (11) 4702 4496 & 4702 6997
Fax: +55 (11) 4702 6896
Email: hrabrasil@intercall.com.br

Personnel:
Christopher Humphrys *(Joint Managing Director)*
Terry Roberts *(Joint Managing Director)*

Publishers' agents and representatives, representing UK and
US publishers in South America, Central America, Mexico,
the Caribbean, Spain, Portugal and Gibraltar.

6064

BRIAN INNS BOOKSALES & SERVICES
9 Ashley Crescent, Warwick CV34 6QH
Telephone: 01926 498428
Fax: 01926 498428
Email: brian.inns@btinternet.com

Personnel:
Brian Inns *(Managing Director)*

Specialization: general non-fiction and technical books.
    Services: consultancy and solutions for publishers. Devel-
opment of business with multiple bookselling groups and
key accounts handled personally by Brian Inns. Specialist at
improving market penetration.
    Representation in UK. Distribution arranged.

6065

CHRIS LLOYD SALES & MARKETING SERVICES
50a Willis Way, Poole, Dorset BH15 3SY
Telephone: 01202 649930
Fax: 01202 649950
Email: chrlloyd@globalnet.co.uk
Web Site: www.chrislloydsales.co.uk

Distribution:
Orca Book Services
Telephone: 01202 665432

Personnel:
Christopher Lloyd *(Proprietor)*

Publishers & Imprints represented include:
Belgium: Tectum; Versant Sud
Canada: Annick Press; Boston Mills Press; Firefly Books;
    Master Point Press; Robert Rose
France: Heimdal Editions; Herrisey Editions; Histoire &
    Collections
Netherlands: Miller Books
New Zealand: Ventura Publications
Spain: Andrea Press; Udyat Books
UK: Amateur Winemaker Books; Argus Books; Book Guild
    Publishing; Bromley Books; D & B Publishing; Finesse
    Bridge Books; Galago Books; Herridge & Sons; Jaguar
    Daimler Heritage Trust; Key Books; LDA (Learning
    Development Aids); Mindsports; Mushroom Model
    Publications; Plane Essentials; Ravette; Reynolds & Hearn;
    Special Interest Model Books *(formerly Nexus Special
    Interests);* Veloce Publishing
USA: Black Dog & Leventhal; Cycle Publishing / van der Plas
    Publications; Meadowbrook Press; Mikaya; Potomac
    Books *(formerly Brasseys Inc);* Marianne Richmond
    Studios

An independent sales and marketing agency for small and
medium sized publishers.

6066

THE MANNING PARTNERSHIP LTD
6 The Old Dairy, Melcombe Road, Oldfield Park, Bath
BA2 3LR
Telephone: 01225 478444
Fax: 01225 478440
Email: karen@manning-partnership.co.uk
Web Site: www.manning-partnership.co.uk

Personnel:
Garry Manning *(Joint Managing Director)*
Roger Hibbert *(Joint Managing Director)*
James Wheeler *(Sales Manager)*
Karen Twissell *(Office Manager)*

Associated Companies:
UK: Brown Dog Books; Nightingale Press

UK Distributor for:
UK: Brimax; Carroll & Brown; Five Mile Press; G2; Globe
    Pequot Press; Interpet Publishing; Ivy Press; Oval Books;
    Tony Potter; Mathew Price; Search Press; Selectabook;
    Source Books

The Manning Partnership Ltd offers a total sales, marketing
and distribution solution for publishers both in the UK and in
English-language export markets. Formed in March 1997.
Traditional and non-traditional markets are serviced.

6067

MARKETABILITY (UK) LTD
12 Sandy Lane, Teddington, Middx TW11 0DR
Telephone: 020 8977 2741
Fax: 020 8977 2741
Email: rachel@marketability.info
Web Site: www.marketability.info

Personnel:
Rachel Maund *(Director)*

Current and recent clients include:
Australia: Australian Publishers Association
Canada: B. C. Decker
China: Elsevier; Higher Education Press
Mexico: CANIEM (Mexican Publishers Association)
Republic of Ireland: CLÉ (Irish Publishers Association); New
    Island
Russia: Guild of Book Dealers
Singapore: National Book Development Council; Singapore
    Book Publishers' Association; Taylor & Francis; Wiley Asia;
    World Scientific
UK: ALPSP; Ashgate Publishing; BBC Active; A. & C. Black;
    Bradt Travel Guides; Brilliant Publications; Cambridge
    University Press; Centre for Alternative Technology;
    Continuum; Dundee University Press; Elsevier; European
    Database of Libraries; HarperCollins Publishers; Hodder
    Education; Hymns Ancient and Modern; Institute of
    Physics; Learning Matters; Little, Brown Book Group;
    Lonely Planet; Macmillan; McGraw Hill; Natural History
    Museum Publications; NBN International; NCVO
    (National Council for Voluntary Organisations); Oxford
    University Press; Palgrave Macmillan; Paperless Proofs;
    Pearson Education; Pen and Sword Books; Pluto Press;
    ProQuest; Publishing Scotland; Publishing Training

Centre; Random House Group; Roots for Churches;
    Royal Society; Sage Publications; Specialist Schools &
    Academies Trust; Taylor & Francis Group; University
    College London; University of Wales Press; John Wiley &
    Sons; World Scientific

Marketability is a group of experienced publishing consultants, all ex-publishers, providing complete support to publishers' marketing departments, from campaigns to
consultancy. It supplies resources when needed: to manage
catalogue or direct marketing campaigns, devise and conduct market research, or provide consultancy and advice on
strategic and practical issues. Its experience is across all publishing sectors, and with both small and large organizations.
    Also provides in-company and external training courses –
see our separate entry under Training.

6068

MIDAS PUBLIC RELATIONS LTD
10–14 Old Court Place, Kensington, London W8 4PL
Telephone: 020 7361 7860
Fax: 020 7938 1268
Email: info@midaspr.co.uk
Web Site: www.midaspr.co.uk

Personnel:
Tony Mulliken *(Chairman)*
Steven Williams *(Chief Executive Officer)*
Jacks Thomas *(Chief Executive Officer)*
Fiona Marsh *(New Business Manager)*

Midas Public Relations, a PR Week Top 50 consumer agency
and a fully accredited member of the PRCA, has established
a reputation as one of the leading PR agencies for the book,
magazine and publishing industry, through its work with
major publishing houses, high profile authors, corporate
communications, trade and consumer events and awards,
and the Direct Marketing Industry. Originally formed in 1990
to service the publishing industry, its areas of expertise now
span related sectors including the arts, awards, events,
media, entertainment, online, music and children's. Specialists in creative, original and award-winning PR campaigns –
traditional and online – and named in The Bookseller Magazine's Top 100 'most influential in publishing' Midas Public
Relations has a strong reputation for understanding the
commercial reality of the arts and publishing world with
numerous contacts in the industry.

6069

MOMENTA PUBLISHING LTD
2 Moorlands Close, Hindhead, Surrey GU26 6SY
Telephone: 01428 606339
Fax: 01428 606339
Email: roblmomenta@compuserve.com

Personnel:
Robert Leech *(Director)*
Mahara Collier *(Company Secretary)*

Founded 1972. Momenta represents various publishing
houses, mainly specializing in academic, scholastic, technical, architectural, scientific and medical books, located in
continental Europe and the USA as well as the UK.
    Momenta offers the following services:
    – full sales representation in the UK and Western Europe;
    – visits to bookshops, sci-tech, academic and medical cen-
tres, universities, libraries;
    – medical and sci-tech lecturers and personnel;
    – participation in book fairs, congresses and exhibitions;
    – detailed visit reports containing comments, impressions
and recommendations;
    – market research;
    – contact with overdue debtors;
    – book distribution if required.
    Momenta is a dynamic company with a wide experience
in book sale and promotion.

6070

NIELSEN BOOKSCAN
3rd Floor, Midas House, 62 Goldsworth Road, Woking,
Surrey GU21 6LQ
Telephone: 01483 712222
Fax: 01483 712220
Email: info.bookscan@nielsen.com
Web Site: www.nielsenbookscan.co.uk

Personnel:
Mo Siewcharran *(Head of Marketing)*
Ann Betts *(Commercial Director)*

Julie Meynink *(UK Business Director)*
Reeta Windsor *(Business Development Manager)*
Carol Brownlee *(Retail Account Manager)*
Paul Dibble *(Head of Data Services)*

Parent Company:
UK: Nielsen Book

Associated Companies:
UK: Nielsen BookData; Nielsen BookNet

Nielsen BookScan is a continuous book sales tracking service operating in the UK, Ireland, Australia, the USA, South Africa, Italy, New Zealand, Denmark and Spain. BookScan collects total transaction data at the point of sale directly from tills and dispatch systems of all major book retailers. This ensures that detailed and highly accurate sales information on what books are selling, and at what price, is available to the book trade. LibScan measures book borrowings in public libraries.

6071

OXFORD CREATIVE MARKETING
12 Hids Copse Road, Oxford OX2 9JJ
Telephone: 01865 861669
Email: sue.miller@oxfordcreative.com
Web Site: www.oxfordcreative.com

Personnel:
Sue Miller *(Managing Director)*

Oxford Creative Marketing provides wide-ranging marketing, publicity and consultancy services for academic, educational, professional and trade publishers.
Services include:
– marketing planning and new strategy advice;
– copywriting for corporate material, catalogues, fliers, newsletters, etc;
– direct mail campaigns;
– publicity campaigns for trade and academic books, and any work that is usually handled by an in-house marketing department.
As well as handling one-off projects, OCM can provide on-going marketing support for publishers looking for more regular help.

6072

THE OXFORD PUBLICITY PARTNERSHIP LTD
5 Victoria House, 138 Watling Street East, Towcester NN12 6BT
Telephone: 01327 357770
Fax: 01327 359572
Email: info@oppuk.co.uk
Web Site: www.oppuk.co.uk

Personnel:
Gary Hall *(Director)*

Launched in 1989, the Oxford Publicity Partnership provides a comprehensive range of sales and marketing services for general non-fiction, academic and professional publishers on an on-going or freelance basis.
OPP acts as the UK and European sales and marketing office for a number of British and North American publishers and its focus is on the development of their presence in these markets to achieve wider recognition and enhanced sales.
OPP's team of experienced marketing staff work with clients to achieve the best combination of publicity and PR, direct mail, electronic marketing, advertising, and exhibition participation. It also has close links with reps, distributors, and the book trade.

6073

PARKER ASSOCIATES
Cedar House, 35 Chichele Road, Oxted, Surrey RH8 0AE
Telephone: 01883 730207
Email: 101341.1235@compuserve.com

Personnel:
Adrian Parker *(Managing Director)*

Representing:
UK: Sheldrake Press

Sales and marketing group for publishers. Selling to the UK and Ireland book trade and also to the European book trade.

Four representatives sell to the UK book trade and two to the Irish book trade. Four representatives sell to the European book trade.

6074

JOHN RULE, PUBLISHERS SALES AGENT
40 Voltaire Road, London SW4 6DH
Telephone: 020 7498 0115
Email: johnrule@johnrule.co.uk

Personnel:
John Rule *(Manager)*

Sales and distribution services for small publishers into UK and export markets.

6075

SALT WAY PUBLISHING (TORPEDO GLOBAL SALES NETWORK) LTD
33 Hatherop Nr Cirencester Gloucestershire GL7 3NA
Telephone: 01285 750212
Email: chris.mclaren@saltwaypublishing.co.uk
Web Site: http://torpedo-global.com

Personnel:
Mr Chris McLaren *(Managing Director)*
Mr Peter Couzens *(Manager South East Asia)*
Mr Peter Matthews *(Manager South Africa)*
Mr Tom McGorry *(Manager North America)*

Parent Company:
Salt Way Publishing Ltd

Associated Companies:
Gunpowder Press; Torpedo Global Sales Network; Watling Street Publishers

Salt Way Publishing Ltd provides highly professional sales representation, for Adult and Children's Trade lists, in the UK and Ireland.
The company has seven highly experienced sales personnel covering all areas of retailer and wholesale and works very closely with its publishing clients. Salt Way Publishing also publishes its own lists under the Watling Street imprint and (in joint venture with Bookcraft Ltd) the Gunpowder Press imprint.
Salt Way also acts as managing partner for Torpedo Global Sales Network, which is a federation of long-established and experienced independent publishers' sales agencies, operating in all the major English Language markets across the world.
In addition Torpedo has strong working relationships with other agents in key foreign language territories.
Torpedo Global Sales Network can also offer assistance in regard to shipping, printing, book production and distribution.
The aim of Salt Way and Torpedo is to provide bespoke international sales solutions to client publishers whose lists are appropriate to our experience, customer base and overall offer.

6076

SEOL LTD
West Newington House, 10 Newington Road, Edinburgh EH9 1QS
Telephone: 0131 668 1456
Fax: 0131 668 4466
Email: info@seol.co.uk

Personnel:
Hugh Andrew *(Joint Managing Director)*
Carol Crawford *(Joint Managing Director)*
Harry Ward *(Joint Managing Director)*
Carole Hamilton *(Joint Managing Director)*
Rona Stewart *(Financial Manager)*

Clients include:
UK: Appletree Press Ltd; Argyll Publishing; Atelier; Colin Baxter; Birlinn Ltd; Clan Books; John Donald; Fort Publishing; Goblinshead; Hallewell Publications; House of Lochar; Glen Murray Publishing; Polygon; RCAHMS (Royal Commission on the Ancient & Historical Monuments of Scotland); Rucksack Readers; Saltire Society; Usborne

A sales representation agency to the trade and non-traditional outlets in Scotland.

6077

STAR BOOK SALES
PO Box 20, Whimple, Exeter EX5 2WY
Telephone: 0845 156 7082
Fax: 01404 823820
Email: enquiries@starbooksales.com
Web Site: www.starbooksales.com

Personnel:
Dennis Buckingham *(Sales Director)*

UK distributor for:
UK: Angela Patchell Books; Ashgrove Press; Bang On Top Productions; Choc Lit; Coastal Publishing; Dimensional Entertainment; Edit Vallard; Evans Mitchell Books; Giorgio Nada; JB Publishing; Manchester Press; Nova Vista Books; Parker House Publishing; Pinter & Martin; Redcliffe Press; Tonto Books; Troubador Publishing

Providing sales, marketing and distribution services for UK and international publishers. Territories covered in primary market: UK and Europe.

Through associated organizations it can provide global coverage for English language titles.

6078

UNIVERSITY PRESSES MARKETING
The Tobacco Factory, Raleigh Road, Southville, Bristol BS3 1TF
Telephone: 0117 902 0275
Fax: 0117 902 0294
Email: sales@universitypressesmarketing.co.uk
Web Site: www.universitypressesmarketing.co.uk

Personnel:
Andrew Gilman *(Chief Executive Officer)*
Paul Skinner *(Office Manager)*
Helena Svojsikova *(Area Manager)*

Sales agent for (mainly) American university presses in the UK and Europe.

6079

THE UNIVERSITY PRESSES OF CALIFORNIA, COLUMBIA & PRINCETON LTD
John Wiley & Sons Ltd, Distribution Centre, 1 Oldlands Way, Bognor Regis, West Sussex PO22 9SA
Telephone: 01243 842165
Fax: 01243 842167
Email: lois@upccp.demon.co.uk

Personnel:
Andrew Brewer *(Managing Director)*
Lois Edwards *(Business Manager)*

6080

PETER WARD BOOK EXPORTS
Unit 3, Taylors Yard, 67 Alderbrook Road, London SW12 8AD
Telephone: 020 8772 3300
Fax: 020 8772 3309
Email: richard@pwbookex.com

Personnel:
Richard Ward *(Senior Partner)*

Publishers' sales representatives in Middle East, North Africa, Cyprus, Turkey, Malta, Greece and Israel.

6.6 DISTRIBUTORS

6081

AFRICAN BOOKS COLLECTIVE
PO Box 721, Oxford OX1 9EN
Telephone: 01869 349110
Fax: 01869 349110
Email: orders@africanbookscollective.com
Web Site: www.africanbookscollective.com

Personnel:
Mary Jay *(Chief Executive Officer)*
Justin Cox *(Marketing & Production)*

Participating publishers include:
Benin: Centre Panafricain de Prospective Sociale / Pan-African Social Prospects Centre
Botswana: Lightbooks Publishers; Pyramid Publishing
Cameroon: University of Buea
Eritrea: Hdri Publishers
Ethiopia: Development Policy Management Forum (DPMF); Forum for Social Studies; Organisation for Social Science Research in Eastern and Southern Africa (OSSREA)
Ghana: Afram Publications (Ghana) Ltd; Africa Christian Press; Association of African Universities Press; Blackmask; Freedom Publishers; Ghana Universities Press; Sedco Publishing; SEM Financial Training Centre Ltd; Sub-Saharan Publishers; Third World Network Africa; Woeli Publishing Services; Women's Health Action Research Centre
Kenya: Academy Science Publishers; East African Educational Publishers; Focus Books; Kwani Trust; LawAfrica; Nairobi University Press; Twaweza Communications
Lesotho: Institute of Southern African Studies, National University of Lesotho; Law Society of Lesotho
Liberia: Cotton Tree Press
Malawi: Central Africana; Chancellor College Publishers; Kachere Series
Mauritius: Editions Vivazi
Namibia: Reader in Namibian Sociology; University of Namibia Press
Nigeria: African Heritage Press; College Press Publishers; CSS Ltd; Enicrownfit Publishers; Fourth Dimension Publishing Co Ltd; Handel Books; Heinemann Educational Books (Nigeria); Ibadan Cultural Studies Group; Ibadan University Press; Kraft Books; Maiyati Chambers; Malthouse Press Ltd; New Horn Press Ltd; Obafemi Awolowo University Press; Onyoma Research Publications; Opon ifa Readers; Saros International Publishers; Spectrum Books Ltd; University of Lagos Press; University Press Ltd; Yintab Books
Senegal: African Renaissance; Council for the Development of Social Science Research in Africa (CODESRIA)
Sierra Leone: PenPoint Publishers
South Africa: Africa Institute of South Africa; Brenthurst Collection / Frank Horley Books; Ikhwezi Afrika Publishers; Mail and Guardian Books; Modjaji Books; Umsinsi Books; UNISA Press
Swaziland: JAN Publishing Centre
Tanzania: Centre for Energy, Environment, Science & Technology (CEEST); Dar es Salaam University Press; E & D Ltd; Mkuki na Nyota Publishers; Tanzania Publishing House
Uganda: Femrite (Uganda Women Writers' Association); Fountain Publishers
Zambia: Bookworld Publishers; Multimedia Zambia; University of Zambia; Zambia Women Writers' Association
Zimbabwe: Africa Community Publishing & Development Trust; Baobab Books; Kimaathi Publishing House; Mambo Press; Southern African Printing and Publishing House / SAPES Trust; University of Zimbabwe Publications; Weaver Press Ltd; Women and Law in South Africa Research Trust; Zimbabwe International Book Fair Trust; Zimbabwe Publishing House Ltd

African Books Collective is a major initiative to promote African-published books in Europe, North America, and in Commonwealth countries outside Africa. It is owned by the founding publishers, and is non-profit making on its own behalf. Centralized billing and shipping is provided from Oxford; and for North America by Michigan State University Press. The greater part of the list is available print-on-demand. Joint catalogues are available, and on the website for download. New title information is sent monthly to the e-subscriber list. English-language material is stocked, with an emphasis on scholarly, literature and children's titles. A small number of titles in French and children's titles in Swahili are also stocked. Standing order / blanket order plans are available and can be geared to meet libraries' specific requirements or acquisitions profiles. Trading started in May 1990.

6082

ANGLO-AMERICAN BOOKS
Crown Buildings, Bancyfelin, Carmarthen SA33 5ND
Telephone: 01267 211880
Fax: 01267 211882
Email: books@anglo-american.co.uk
Web Site: www.anglo-american.co.uk

Personnel:
Mr D. Bowman *(Managing Director)*
Mrs C. Lenton *(Marketing Director)*

UK Distributor/Representative for:
USA: Center Press; Milton H. Erickson Foundation Press; Free Spirit Publishing; Genesis II; International Society of Neuro-Semantics; Kagan & Kagan; Kendall/Hunt; Leading Edge Communications; Meta Publications; Network 3000 Publishing; NLP Comprehensive; Science and Behavior Books; Success Strategies; Teacher Created Materials; Transforming Press; Westwood Publishing

Anglo-American Books is a stockholding distributor of British and American books with particular expertise in the NLP, personal growth, hypnotherapy, accelerated learning and psychotherapy fields. Stock book orders received by 2.30 pm are dispatched the same day.
Order Department opening times: 9–5 Monday to Friday.

6083

ATLANTIC BOOKS
The Bookhouse, 18 Great Footway, Tunbridge Wells, Kent TN3 0DT
Telephone: 01892 864951
Fax: 01892 864950
Email: esther@atlanticbooks.co.uk
Web Site: www.atlanticbooks.co.uk

Personnel:
Esther Matthews *(Proprietor)*
Andy Ackerley *(Sales & Marketing Manager)*
Jayne Robinson *(Customer Service Manager)*
Joe Ackerley *(Warehouse Manager)*

Supplier of all US published material; any American title.

6084

AVANTIBOOKS LTD
Unit 9, The io Centre, Whittle Way, Arlington Business Park, Stevenage SG1 2BD
Telephone: 01438 747000
Fax: 01438 741131
Email: orders@avantibooks.com
Web Site: www.avantibooks.com

Personnel:
Hilary Rosenberg *(Director)*
Sue Ravitz *(Director)*

UK distributor/representative for:
Australia: ARIS
South Africa: University of Kwa-Zulu-Natal; Viva Books
UK: Brown & Brown Publishing; Gatehouse Media; LLU+; Newleaf Books; Suffolk Community Learning & Skills Dept; Suffolk Family Learning
USA: New Readers Press; Peppercorn Books & Press

Mail order bookshop, specializing in educational titles for basic skills teaching and ESOL/ELT.

6085

BBR DISTRIBUTION
12 Cutthorpe Road, Chesterfield S42 7AE
Telephone: 01246 271662
Email: distribution@bbr-online.com
Web Site: www.bbr-online.com/catalogue

Personnel:
Chris Reed *(Director)*

Parent Company:
UK: BBR Solutions Ltd

UK distributor for:
Australia: Aurealis; Chimaera Publications
Canada: Tesseract Books
Republic of Ireland: Aeon Press; Albedo One
UK: Bowland Press; British Association for Korean Studies (BAKS); EAHMH Publications; Endcliffe Press; European Association for the History of Medicine and Health Publications; Hilltop Press
USA: Automatism Press; Cambrian Publications; Cyber-Psycho's A.O.D.; Dreams and Nightmares; Fairwood Press; Jazz Police Books; New York Review of S.F.; Not One of Us; Nova Express; Ocean View Books; Permeable Press; Space & Time; Talebones; Wordcraft of Oregon

BBR is a mail order distributor of independent literary, speculative fiction and fringe interest publications, serving customers throughout the world.

6086

BEBC DISTRIBUTION
Albion Close, Parkstone, Poole, Dorset BH12 3LL
Telephone: 01202 715555
Fax: 01202 715556
Web Site: www.bebcdistribution.co.uk

Personnel:
John Walsh *(Managing Director)*
Charles Kipping *(Marketing Manager)*
Rosy Jones *(Operations Manager)*
Karen Bickers *(Client Manager)*

Parent Company:
UK: The Bournemouth English Book Centre Ltd

UK Distributor/Representative for:
Australia: Actual Enterprises; Adams & Austen Press; Boyer Education; Insearch Publications
Germany: Ernst Klett *(ELT Titles only)*
Netherlands: John Benjamins bv
New Zealand: Catt Publishing
UK: Academic Book Collection; Barrington Stoke *(School Orders)*; Brilliant Publications; Brookemead ELT; Coat Meur Press; College of Law Publishing; Commonwealth Secretariat; FunSongs Ltd; Gem Publishing; The Language Factory; Learning Matters; Listen & Speak Publications; Redhead Music; Reflect Press; TP Publications; York Associates

Distributors for educational publishers specializing in Business, Law, English Language Teaching, ICT books, Human Rights and Conservation. For further information or to order, please telephone 01202 715555.

6087

BETTER BOOKS
3 Paganel Drive, Dudley DY1 4AZ
Telephone: 01384 253276
Fax: 0871 715 0236
Email: sales@betterbooks.com
Web Site: www.betterbooks.com

Personnel:
P. J. Wilkes *(Proprietor)*

UK distributor/representative for:
USA: Educators Publishing Service

Mail order distributor of books relating to dyslexia and other special educational needs.

6088

THE BOOK SERVICE LTD
Colchester Road, Frating Green, Colchester, Essex CO7 7DW
Telephone: 01206 256000 (orders: 255678)
Fax: 01206 255929 (orders: 255930)
Email: sales@tbs-ltd.co.uk
Web Site: www.TheBookService.co.uk

Personnel:
Mark Williams *(Managing Director)*
Colin James *(Deputy Managing Director)*
Justin Smith *(Finance & Commercial Director)*

Parent Company:
UK: The Random House Group

Associated Companies:
UK: Grantham Book Services

Distributors for::
Andersen Press; Atlantic Books; BBC Audio Books; Nicholas Brealey; Canongate Books; Constable & Robinson; Faber & Faber; Granta Books; Icon Books; Mainstream Publishing; Methuen Publishing; Parragon; Profile Books; Quercus; Random House Group; Sort of Books; Transworld; Virgin Books

The Book Service (TBS) is the UK's leading distributor. Distributing over 100 million books per year, TBS has high-tech fully automated handling systems and offers full electronic ordering and e-Commerce capabilities. TBS operates a full sales ledger, offers cash collection, debt and stock insurance policies, telesales, royalties and sub-rights services. Ancillary work such as mailing, shrink-wrapping, re-pricing, dump-bin and counter pack make up is also offered.

6089

BOOK SYSTEMS PLUS LTD
BSP House, Station Road, Linton, Cambs CB21 4NW
Telephone: 01223 894870
Fax: 01223 894871
Email: bsp2b@aol.com
Web Site: www.booksystemsplus.com

Personnel:
George J. Papa (Managing Director)
Shirley Greenall (Marketing & New Business)

Parent Company:
UK: Whittet Books Ltd

Publishers represented:
Australia: A & B Publishers Pty Ltd; Bookbiz International
Canada: The Althouse Press; The Charlton Press; Detselig
  Enterprises Ltd; Greatest Escapes.com
Germany: Chateaux & Manoirs
Netherlands: Mo' Media
South Africa: Dreams 4 Africa
UK: Aardvark Publishing; Alice & Fred Books; Caister
  Academic Press; Chakula Press Ltd; Classic Locations;
  Cobwebs Brentwood; Cracking It; Delfryn Publications;
  EFL Ltd; Euro Impala; Fitzwarren Publishing; Focus
  Publications Ltd; Gudrun Publishing / Edda UK; Hiller
  Airguns; Hoopoe Books; Idlewild Publishers; Institute for
  Psychophysical Research; Oxford Forum; Pathfinder
  Audio; Porpoise Books; Raleo Publishing Ltd; Revenge Ink
  Ltd; Tricorn; UK International Ceramics; Vista Consulting
  Team Ltd; Whittet Books Ltd; Wild Boar Trading
USA: John F. Blair, Publisher

Book Systems Plus provides full distribution, invoicing and
customer services to publishers from the UK and overseas. It
also offers bookshop representation and marketing support.
It has particular marketing expertise with travel guides and
books on antiques and collectables. It acts as the UK sole
agent for publishers in North America, Australia, South
Africa and Europe.

6090

BOOKPOINT LTD
130 Milton Park, Abingdon, Oxon OX14 4SB
Telephone: 01235 400400
Fax: 01235 832068
Web Site: www.bookpoint.co.uk

Personnel:
Chris Emerson (Chief Operating Officer)
Martyn Burchall (Operations Director)
Ray Webb (Head of Customer Services)
Graham Money (General Manager & Director)
Lesley Morgan (Group IT Director)
Jon Swan (Head of Credit Control)

Parent Company:
UK: Hachette UK

Distributor for:
UK: Ashgate/Gower Publishing; Debretts; Facet Publishing
  (formerly Library Association); Hachette Children's;
  Headline Book Publishing; Hodder & Stoughton; Hodder
  Education; Hodder Gibson; Hodder Religious; In Easy
  Steps; Frances Lincoln; John Murray; Pedigree Books;
  Plexus Publishing; Souvenir Press; Taylor & Francis

Bookpoint services encompass a number of industry leading
initiatives, plus a full suite of EDI applications, order processing, accounting, royalty maintenance, management reporting, warehousing, despatch and ancillary functions.
Bookpoint also operate a Premier Next Day Service, and
offer PUBEASY to booksellers.

6091

BOOKSOURCE
50 Cambuslang Road, Cambuslang, Glasgow G32 8NB
Telephone: 0845 370 0063
Fax: 0845 370 0064
Email: info@booksource.net
Web Site: www.booksource.net

Personnel:
Davinder Bedi (Managing Director)
Lorraine Fannin (Director)
Mike Miller (Director)
Christian Mclean (Director)
Dr Keith Whittles (Director)

Marion Sinclair (Director)
Louise Wilson (Client Services Manager)
David Warnock (Systems & Facilities Manager)
Lavinia Drew (Credit Controller)

Distribution on behalf of:
UK: Acair Ltd; Appletree Press; Argyll Publishing;
  Association for Scottish Literary Studies; Atelier Books; B
  & W Publishing; Balnakeil Press; Benchmark Books; BILD
  Publications; Birlinn Ltd; Black & White Publishing; Books
  Noir; Carnegie Publishing; Cicerone Press; Clairview
  Books; Clan Publishers; John Donald; R. R. Donnelley (for
  the Scottish Executive); Richard Drew Ltd; Dundee
  University Press; Floris Books; Fort Publishing; Geddes &
  Grosset Ltd; Gullane Children's Books; Hallewell
  Publications; Hawthorn Press; IPC Media; Islands Book
  Trust; Librario Publishing; Little Star Creations;
  Meadowside Children's Books; Mercat Press; Moonlight
  Publishing; Glen Murray Publishing; NMS Enterprises Ltd
  Publishing; Polygon; Publishing Scotland; Real Reads;
  Rider French Publications; Roving Press; Royal
  Commission on the Ancient and Historical Monuments of
  Scotland; Rucksack Readers; Saltire Society; Sandstone
  Press; Steve Savage Publishing; Scottish Society for
  Northern Studies; Scottish Text Society; Sparkling Books;
  Rudolf Steiner Press; Strident Publishing; Sunday Herald
  Books; Temple Lodge Publishing; Tuckwell Press; Two
  Ravens Press; Waverley Press; Whittles Publishing; Wild
  Goose Publications; Neil Wilson Publishing; Windhorse
  Publications

Established in 1995, BookSource offers warehousing and
worldwide distribution services to book trade publishers,
charities and funded institutions, and other commercial
enterprises.

6092

BUSHWOOD BOOKS LTD
6 Marksbury Avenue, Kew Gardens, Surrey TW9 4JF
Telephone: 020 8392 8585
Fax: 020 8392 9876
Email: info@bushwoodbooks.co.uk
Web Site: www.bushwoodbooks.co.uk

Personnel:
Richard Hansen (Director)
Victoria Hansen (PA)
Ian McLellan (Sales)

Exclusive distributor for:
USA: Schiffer (Mind, Body, Spirit titles); Schiffer Collectibles
  Arts & Crafts; Schiffer Publishing Ltd (Military Aviation)

The company also carries in stock hundreds of titles on
antiques and collectibles, predominantly horology, jewellery,
ceramics and glass. It specializes in providing a service for UK
customers to purchase from North American publishers.
  Bushwood Books is one of the leading UK distributors of
German World War II titles in English, and also carries the
Schiffer Mind, Body, Spirit list.

6093

CENGAGE LEARNING EMEA
[a division of Cengage Learning]
Cheriton House, North Way, Andover, Hants SP10 5BE
Telephone: 01264 332424
Fax: 01264 342732
Web Site: www.cengage.co.uk

Personnel:
Jill Jones (Chief Executive Officer)
Chad Bonney (Chief Financial Officer)
Carrie Willicome (Operations Director)

Parent Company:
USA: Cengage Learning Inc

Distributors for:
UK: Cengage Learning (selected imprints); Evans Publishing
  Group; Janes

6094

CENTRAL BOOKS
99 Wallis Road, London E9 5LN
Telephone: 0845 458 9911 & 020 8986 4854
Fax: 0845 458 9912
Email: orders@centralbooks.com
Web Site: www.centralbooks.com

Personnel:
Bill Norris (Managing Director)
Mark Chilver (Magazine Director)
Bob Moheebob (Accountant)
Eric McCorkle (Warehouse Manager)
Indy Kaur Naura (Trade Returns & Customer Services
  Manager)
Graham Charnock (Trade Customer Services Manager)
Mike Drabble (Mail Order Manager)
Sasha Simic (Magazine Sales Rep Manager)
Regina Henrich (Publisher Liaison Manager)

Distribution for:
Australia: Fremantle Arts Centre Press
Canada: Black Rose Books; Fernwood Press
France: Zulma
Germany: European Photography
Italy: Giancarlo Politi Editore
Jamaica: Ian Randle
Kenya: Camerapix
Netherlands: Get Lost Publishing; International Books
Republic of Ireland: Dedalus Press; A & A Farmer; Galway
  University Press; The Lilliput Press Ltd; Oisin Publishing;
  Salmon Publishing Ltd; University College Dublin Press
South Africa: Fernwood Press; Kwela; Ravan Press
UK: 21; Absolute Press; Agraphia Press; Ambit Books;
  Amnesty International UK; Archetype; Aurora Metro
  Press; Auteur; Battlebridge; Blue Island Publishing;
  Bowerdean Publishing Co Ltd; Broadcast Books;
  Calouste Gulbenkian Foundation; Catalyst Press; Centre
  for Policy on Ageing; CILT; Comerford & Miller; Corvo
  Books; CPAG (Child Poverty Action Group); Dedalus;
  Demos; Directory of Social Change; Disability Alliance;
  English Heritage; Enitharmon Press; Five Leaves
  Publications; Flambard; Flowers East; Foreign Policy
  Centre; Format Publishing; Friction Press; Gambit;
  Golgonooza; Green Books; Greenprint; Greenwich
  Exchange; Harbord Publishing; Heretic Books Ltd
  (formerly GMP Publishers Ltd); Holo Books; Hood Hood
  Books; Human Givens; Human Rights Watch; Imprint
  Academic; Latin America Bureau; Lawrence & Wishart;
  Libris Ltd; Loki Books; London Art & Artists; Lucas
  Publications Ltd; Mares Nest; Menard Press; Merlin Press;
  Middlesex University Press; Minority Rights Group;
  Muslim Academic Trust; National Autistic Society (NAS);
  New Clarion Press; New European Publications Ltd;
  Northway; Open Gate Press; Peepal Tree Books; Pomona
  Books; Prospect Books; Quilliam; Redstone Press;
  Refugee Council; Right Angle Publishing; Route;
  Runnymede Trust; Seafarer; Seren; Serif; Smith /
  Doorstep; Smith Institute; Social Market Foundation;
  Stacey International; Totterdown Books; University of
  Hertfordshire Press; Vegan Society; Wallflower Press;
  Weston Publishing; Westworld International; Wooden
  Books; WorldView
USA: International Publishers NY; McPherson & Co;
  Monthly Review; Pamphleteer's Press

The main activity and purpose of Central Books is to assist
independent publishers to reach the widest possible audience for their books. Central Books offer warehousing, distribution, representation and some help with marketing and
promotion. It supplies booksellers and library suppliers
throughout the world. The company is one of Europe's leading distributors of magazines and journals to the book trade.

6095

COMBINED ACADEMIC PUBLISHERS LTD
15a Lewins Yard, East Street, Chesham, Bucks HP5 1HQ
Telephone: 01494 581601
Fax: 01494 581602
Email: nickesson@combinedacademic.co.uk
Web Site: www.combinedacademic.co.uk

Personnel:
Nicholas Esson (Managing Director)
Ms Julia Monk (Marketing Manager)
Ms Denise Martin (Accounts Manager)
Keith Woods (Representative)

UK & European distributor for:
Canada: McGill-Queen's University Press
USA: Duke University Press; Indiana University Press; New
  York University Press; Temple University Press; University
  of Illinois Press; University of Nebraska Press; University of
  Texas Press; University of Washington Press

Combined Academic Publishers, in association with Marston
Book Services, is a professional representation and distribution agency for academic and university presses.

UK and Republic of Ireland field sales are handled by our own representative and a team of experienced commisson agents, while agents are active in five continental European territories – Scandinavia; the Netherlands and Belgium; Southern Europe; Germany, Austria and Switzerland; Central and Eastern Europe – as well as the Middle East and Africa.

CAP has a pro-active marketing department offering direct mail campaigns, space advertising and review copy distribution.

6096

COMBINED BOOK SERVICES LTD
Unit Y, Paddock Wood Distribution Centre, Paddock Wood, Tonbridge, Kent TN12 6UU
Telephone: 01892 837171
Fax: 01892 837272
Email: info@combook.co.uk
Web Site: www.combook.co.uk

Personnel:
Keith Neale *(Joint Managing Director)*
Allan Smith *(Joint Managing Director)*

Distributors for:
Germany: earBOOKS (edel)
Italy: LEM Art Group
UK: A Jot Publishing; J. A. Allen *(Equestrian)*; Anshan Publishers; Barrington Hall Publishing; John Calder; Claerhout Publishing; Developmedica; Discovery Books; Eddington Hook; Encyclopaedia Britannica; Freehand Publishing; Robert Hale; Hammersmith Press; Hoberman Collection; Korero Books; Lotus Publishing; Management Books 2000; Momenta Publishing; NAG Publishers; New Age Science; Northcote House Publishers; Oneworld Classics; Phoenix Publishers; Pocket Issue; Pucci Books *(formerly Oblique)*; Pushkin Press; Thomas Telford Ltd *(Institute of Civil Engineers)*; teneues Publishing UK; Woodhead Publishing

Combined Book Services provides full distribution services for publishers of trade, academic and professional books. The service includes invoicing and cash collection together with a comprehensive range of management reports. CBS also distributes calendars and stationery products.

6097

CONTOUR MANAGEMENT SERVICES (CMS)
PO Box 3042, New Milton, Hants BH25 7XG
Telephone: 01425 620532
Fax: 01425 620532
Email: mikecms@btinternet.com
Web Site: www.contourmanagementservices.com

Personnel:
Mike Cranidge *(Managing Partner)*
Sue Cranidge *(Partner)*

Agent and distributor for:
Australia: Meridian Maps
Portugal: Turinta
USA: Hedberg Maps Inc; Map Link

Importers and distributors of maps with a difference.

6098

CORNERHOUSE PUBLICATIONS
70 Oxford Street, Manchester M1 5NH
Telephone: 0161 200 1503
Fax: 0161 200 1504
Email: Publications@Cornerhouse.org
Web Site: www.Cornerhouse.org/books

Personnel:
Paul Daniels *(Publications Director)*
Debbie Fielding *(Administrator)*
Suzanne Davies *(Publications Officer)*
James Brady *(Publications Officer)*

Clients include:
Germany: DuMont Buchverlag; Kerber Verlag; Richter Verlag; Verlag für moderne Kunst Nurnberg; Walther König
Switzerland: JRPRingier
UK: British Council Visual Arts & Design; Haunch of Venison; Hayward Gallery; Henry Moore Institute; ICA; Ikon; Modern Art Oxford; Photoworks; Ridinghouse

Distributor of contemporary visual arts and photography books for publishers, museums amd galleries world-wide. A full list of publishers we distribute is available in our catalogue or at our website: www.Cornerhouse.org/books.

6099

DEEP BOOKS LTD
Unit 3, Goose Green Trading Estate, 47 East Dulwich Road, London SE22 9BN
Telephone: 020 8693 0234
Fax: 020 8693 1400
Email: sales@deep-books.co.uk
Web Site: www.deep-books.co.uk

Personnel:
Chris Custance *(Managing Director)*
Alan Ritchie *(Marketing Manager)*
Paul Woodfield *(Sales Manager)*

Client Publishers include:
Australia: Michelle Anderson Publishing *(formerly Hill of Content Publishing)*; Finch Publishing; Barry Long Books (Australia); Milne Books
Austria: Ennsthaler Publishing House
Israel: Astrolog Publishing House
Italy: Lo Scarabeo
Monaco: Alpen Editions
Netherlands: Altamira-Becht; Binkey Kok Publications; Gottmer Publishing Group
Singapore: Lotus Bloom Publishing
UK: Camino Guides; Earthdancer; Findhorn Press; Gothic Image Publications; Khaniqahi Nimatullahi Publications (KNP); KNP London; Barry Long Books (Britain); Polair Publishing
USA: Acropolis Books; Alpha Books / Penguin USA; Amber Lotus; ARE Press; Ariel Press; Associates Publishing; Avery/Penguin USA; Ayerware Publishing; Basic Health Publications; Bear & Co; Bear Cub Books; Berkley Publishing Group; Best Life Media; Bindu Books; Blue Dolphin Publishing Inc; Bluestar Communications; Boys Town Press; Bristlecone Publishing; Career Press; CCNM Press; Celebra; Chamberlain Bros / Penguin USA; Chiron Publications; Chopra Centre Press; Alan Cohen Publishing; Crystal Clarity Publishers; Crystal Quartz Depot; Dawn Publications; Dawnhorse Publications; De Vorss & Co; Destiny Audio Books; Destiny Books; Destiny Recordings; Dragonhawk Publishing; Dutton / Penguin USA; Earth Magic Productions Inc; Enthea Press; Freedom Press; Glorian Publishing; Golden Sufi Center; Gotham Books / Penguin USA; Hampton Roads Publishing; Nicolas Hays; Healing Arts Press; Himalayan Institute Press; Hologram Books; Hudson Street / Penguin USA; Hunter House Inc; Ibis Press; Inner Expansion Publishing; Inner Health Books; Inner Traditions International; Inner Travel Books; Integral Yoga Publications; Jewish Light Publishing; JZK Publishing; Kali Press; Veronica Lane Books; Lantern Books; Music Design; New American Library; New Century Publishing; New Page Books; Oral Traditions; Original Publications; Park St Press; Penguin Group USA; Perigee/Penguin; Plume; Portfolio / Penguin USA; Power Press; Prentice Hall Press; Putnam / Penguin USA; Quintessential Healing; Rainbow Ridge; Richmond House Publishing; Riverhead Books / Penguin USA; Self Realization Fellowship; Sherman Asher Publishing; Silvergirl Publications; Skylight Paths; Squareone Publishers; Synergetic Press; Tallfellow Press; Jeremy P. Tarcher / Penguin USA; Three Wings Press; Threshold Books; Timeless Books; Transpersonal Publishing; Vital Health Publishing; Winged Horse Publishing; Witches' Almanac; Words of Wizdom; World Wisdom Books

Specialist mind body spirit distributors. Deep Books handles publishers lists from the UK, the USA and Australia. It provides sales and distribution for these publishers throughout the UK, Republic of Ireland, mainland Europe and Scandinavia and acts as their exclusive agents in that territory.

6100

EUROPEAN SCHOOLBOOKS LTD
Ashville Trading Estate, The Runnings, Cheltenham GL51 9PQ
Telephone: 01242 245252
Fax: 01242 224137
Email: direct@esb.co.uk
Web Site: www.eurobooks.co.uk

Personnel:
Frank Preiss *(Managing Director)*
Ruth Trippett *(Marketing)*

Distributor for:
Brazil: Pontes Editores
Denmark: Grafisk Forlag
France: 10/18; Assimil; Bordas; Casterman; CLE International; Armand Colin; Didier; Ecole des loisirs; Editions du Fallois; Editions du Seuil; Flammarion; Folio; Foucher; Gallimard; Garnier Flammarion; Gault Millau; Hachette; Hatier; J'ai lu; Larousse; Livres de poche; Minuit; Nathan; Presses de la cité; Presses Pocket; Presses Universitaires de France; Presses Universitaires de Grenoble; Le Robert
Germany: Arena; Bibliographisches Institut Mannheim; Brockhaus; Carlsen; Cornelsen; Deutscher Taschenbuch Verlag; Diogenes; Duden; Fischer; Gilde Buchhandlung; Goldmann; Heyne; Max Hueber Verlag; Insel; Kiepenheuer & Witsch; Knaur; Langenscheidt; Luchterhand; Reclam; Rowohlt; Suhrkamp; Ullstein; Verlag Dürr & Kessler; Verlag für Deutsch; Verlag Moritz Diesterweg
Italy: Alma Edizioni; Bonacci Editore; Edilingua; Einaudi; European Language Institute; Fabbri-Bompiani; Feltrinelli; Garzanti; Giunti; Guerra; Mondadori; Le Monnier; Oscar; Piemme; Rizzoli; Rux; La Spiga; Zanichelli
Netherlands: Intertaal
Portugal: Dinapress; Lidel Edições Técnicas; Porto Editora Lda; Public. Europa-America
Spain: Alfaguara; Alianza; Anaya; Anaya ELE; Austral; Catedra; Colegio de España; Destino; Difusión; EDELSA; Ediciones Edhasa; Ediciones Edinumen; Ediciones Molino; Ediciones SM; Espasa-Calpe; Everest; Grijalbo; Juventud; Mondadori España; Planeta; Plaza & Janes; Santillana; Seix Barral; SGEL; Sopena; Javier Vergara
UK: European Schoolbooks Publishing Ltd; Understanding Global Issues

Distributors of some 80,000 titles in the main European languages on behalf of over 100 publishers. Large-scale promotion in all sectors of the foreign languages educational market. Suppliers of foreign-published stock to academic and general bookshops. General wholesale service for non-stock titles.

6101

THE EUROSPAN GROUP
3 Henrietta Street, Covent Garden, London WC2E 8LU
Telephone: 020 7240 0856
Fax: 020 7379 0609
Email: info@eurospangroup.com
Web Site: www.eurospanbookstore.com

Send orders to::
Eurospan Group, c/o Turpin Distribution, Pegasus Drive, Stratton Business Park, Biggleswade SG18 8TQ
Telephone: 01767 604972
Fax: 01767 601640
Email: eurospan@turpin-distribution.com
Web Site: www.eurospanbookstore.com

Personnel:
Michael Geelan *(Managing Director & Chairman)*
Kate Fraser *(Director of Operations)*
Stephen Lustig *(Marketing Director)*

Marketing, Sales & Distribution for overseas publishers, including:
USA: American Academy of Ophthalmology; American Academy of Orthopaedic Surgeons; American Academy of Pediatrics; American Mathematical Society; American Psychological Association; American Society of Civil Engineers (ASCE); Autism Asperger Publishing Co; Broadview Press; Brookes Publishing; Facts on File; Future Horizons; Hazelden Publishing; IGI Global; Left Coast Press; Lynne Rienner Publishers; M.E. Sharpe & Co; McFarland & Co; Northwestern University Press; PennWell Books; Rutgers University Press; Slack Incorporated; Springer Publishing Company; Stanford University Press; Teachers College Press; The University of Michigan; Transaction Publishers; University of Hawai'i Press; University of North Carolina Press; University Press of New England; World Bank Publications

Eurospan Group is one of Europe's fastest-growing independent marketing, sales and distribution agencies for US book publishers seeking to expand sales and imagery in Europe, the Middle East, Africa and Asia. It provides a similar one-stop solution, in Europe and the Middle East only, for book publishers from South Africa, Asia and Australasia.

A complete list of publishers and subsidiary imprints distributed by Eurospan is available on request.

6102

FREELANCE MARKET NEWS
Sevendale House, 7 Dale Street, Manchester M1 1JB
Telephone: 0161 228 2362
Fax: 0161 228 3533
Email: fmn@writersbureau.com
Web Site: www.freelancemarketnews.com

Personnel:
Miss Angela Cox (Managing Editor)

Parent Company:
UK: The Writers Bureau Ltd

Distributor for:
USA: Writer's Digest Books (books on writing)

6103

GAZELLE BOOK SERVICES LTD
White Cross Mills, Hightown, Lancaster LA1 4XS
Telephone: 01524 68765
Fax: 01524 63232
Email: sales@gazellebooks.co.uk
Web Site: www.gazellebooks.co.uk

Personnel:
Trevor Witcher (Managing Director)
Brian Haywood (Company Secretary & Finance Director)
Mark Trotter (Distribution & Sales Director)
Kevin Dixon (Warehouse Manager)
Lee Hodgkiss (Marketing & Exhibitions Manager)
Gareth Hindson (Customer Service Manager)
Melanie Warren (Sales & Marketing Manager)
Analyn Dixon (Book-keeper)

Gazelle Book Services handles both trade and academic lists
and covers the whole of the UK and Europe. It provides:
– fast order turn-round;
– comprehensive stock and regular stock replenishment;
– efficient reporting and information service to customers;
– regular sales calling and regular liaison with booksellers
in connection with promotion, exhibitions, special events,
etc;
– following through;
– friendly, helpful service;
– regular and adaptable reporting to publishers;
– flexibility and co-operation.
Complete list of client publishers is available on request.

6104

GMC PUBLICATIONS LTD
GMC Publications Ltd, 166 High Street, Lewes, East Sussex
BN7 1XU
Telephone: 01273 402808
Fax: 01273 402866
Email: distribution@thegmcgroup.com
Web Site: www.gmcbooktrade.com

Personnel:
Mr Jonathan Phillips (Joint Managing Director)
Mr Michael Robb (Sales Director)
Mr Jonathan Bailey (Associate Publisher)
Ms Melanie Arora (Books Marketing Manager)

Associated Companies:
Ammonite Press; Guild of Master Craftsman Publications;
The Photographer's Institute Press

Book publisher and distributor (via Orca):
UK: Rowan
USA: Fox Chapel Publishing; Potter Craft (The Crown
Publishing Group); Sterling Publishing co. Inc (This
includes their imprints); The Taunton Press Inc; Watson-
Guptill (The Crown Publishing Group)

GMC is one of the UK's leading publishers and distributors
of craft & leisure books and magazines. GMC Publications
produces approximately 50 illustrated books a year and has
8 magazines. Established in 2006, GMC Distribution carries
3000 books for other publishers, including Ammonite Press,
Sterling Publishing, The Taunton Press, Watson-Guptill, Pot-
terCraft and Fox Chapel.

6105

GRANTHAM BOOK SERVICES
Trent Road, Grantham, Lincs NG31 7XQ
Telephone: 01476 541000 (orders: 541080)
Fax: 01476 541060 (orders: 541061)

Email: orders@gbs.tbs-ltd.co.uk
Web Site: www.granthambookservices.co.uk

Personnel:
Mark Williams (Managing Director)
Colin James (Deputy Managing Director)
Justin Smith (Finance & Commercial Director)
Andy Willis (Client Services Director)

Parent Company:
UK: Random House Group

Associated Companies:
UK: The Book Service

Clients include::
France: La Martiniere
UK: AA Special Sales; Alma Books; Bounce Sales &
Marketing; Chronicle; Compass Maps; Crown House;
The Crowood Press; David & Charles; Footprint
Handbooks; Geocentre International UK Ltd; Gerald
Duckworth & Co.; Hay House; Nick Hern Books;
Hesperus Press; Horizon Press; Horizon To Books; Lerner;
Lonely Planet; Manchester United; Manning Partnership;
Melia Publishing Services; National Archives; National
Portrait Gallery; New Holland; Oneworld Publications;
Osprey; Osprey Publishing; Oval; Perseus Books; PGUK;
Piccadilly Press; Quarto Group; Quayside Publishing;
Quiller Publishing; Reaktion Books; Rotovision; Running
Press; Severn House Publishers; Templar Publishing;
Thomas Cook; Timber Press; Titan Books
USA: Everyman; MBI; Rockport; Workman Publishing

Grantham Book Services (GBS) is the UK's Independent's
Specialist.
Distributing over 26 million books per year, GBS offers a
bespoke book distribution service with full electronic ordering and e-Commerce capabilities. GBS operates a full sales
ledger, cash collection service, debt and stock insurance policies, telesales, royalties and sub-rights services.
Ancillary work such as mailing, shrink-wrapping, re-pricing, dump-bin and counter pack make up is also offered.

6106

KUPERARD PUBLISHERS
59 Hutton Grove, London N12 8DS
Telephone: 020 8446 2440
Fax: 020 8446 2441
Email: enquiries@kuperard.co.uk
Web Site: www.kuperard.co.uk

Personnel:
Joshua Kuperard (Chief Executive)
Martin Kaye (Sales & Marketing Manager)
Linda Tenenbaum (Special Sales Manager)

Publisher/Distributor of:
Chic Guides; Culture Smart! Guides; Customs & Etiquette;
FHG Guides; Kuperard Books; NFT Guides; Simple Guides
Israel: Koren Publishers; Toby Press
USA: HarperCollins; Lerner Books; Living Language
(Random House); The Modern Library (Random House);
Penguin; Schocken Books / Random House

Kuperard, a division and imprint of Bravo Ltd, acts as publishers, co-publishers and distributors, handling marketing
and representation. Kuperard handle over 30 UK and overseas publishers. Stocklists, catalogues and brochures are
available upon request.
Travel subjects include leisure guides covering a wide variety of destinations and markets. Kuperard publishes cross-
cultural guides for business people and travellers. Religion
subjects covered include art, cookery, the Holy Land, history,
language, mysticism, holocaust, faith and spirituality.

6107

LITTLEHAMPTON BOOK SERVICES LTD
Faraday Close, Durrington, Worthing, West Sussex
BN13 3RB
Telephone: 01903 828500
Fax: 01903 828625
Email: enquiries@lbsltd.co.uk
Web Site: www.lbsltd.co.uk

Personnel:
Chris Emerson (Chief Executive Officer)
Simon Davidson (Managing Director)
Matt Wright (Finance Director)
Lesley Morgan (Group IT Director)
Bridget Radnedge (Publishing Services Director)

Alan Rakes (Inventory Director)
Issy Harrash (General Manager – Operations)

Parent Company:
UK: Hachette UK Publishing Group

Clients include:
3C Publishing (Columbia Marketing Ltd); Ian Allan; Anvil
Poetry Press; Aurum Press, Apple & JR Books;
Automobile Association; Barefoot Books; John Blake
Publishing; Bloodaxe; Carcanet; Crombie Jardine
Publishing; DAAB; Express Newspapers; Eye Books Ltd;
Gallic Books; Gibson Square Publishing; Gloucester
Publishers (formerly Everyman); The Good Hotel Guide
Ltd; Grub Street; Haus Publishing; Heritage House;
Infinite Ideas Co; Interact Publishing Ltd; Kogan Page;
Kyle Cathie; Make Believe Ideas Ltd; Max Press;
Myrmidon Books; Northumbria University Publishing;
Michael O'Mara Books; Octopus Publishing Group; Old
St Publishing; Oldie Publications; Orion Group; PC
Publishing; Pitch Publishing Ltd; Private Eye; Raceform /
Highdown Publishing; Radio Times; Snowbooks Ltd;
Sport Media; Summersdale; Tantor Media Inc; Taschen;
Thames & Hudson; Transit Publishing; Vertigo
Communications LLB; Vision; Which? The Consumer
Association

Littlehampton Book Services provides publishers with full
warehouse management and distribution services that
include credit control and trust accounting, sophisticated
management reporting, telesales, customer service and royalty accounting.

6108

B. McCALL BARBOUR
28 George IV Bridge, Edinburgh EH1 1ES
Telephone: 0131 225 4816
Fax: 0131 225 4816
Web Site: www.mccallbarbour.co.uk

Personnel:
Rev Dr T. C. Danson-Smith (Managing Partner)
Miss G. A. Danson-Smith (Despatch Manager)

USA companies represented:
USA: AMG Publishers; Chick Publications; Dake Bible Sales;
Discovery House; Harvest-House; Kirkbride Bible Co;
Kregel Publishers; Living Stories Inc; Thomas Nelson &
Sons; Oxford University Press (Bibles); John Peterson
Music; Rainbow Study Bibles; Schoettle Publishing
House; Singspiration Inc; Sword of the Lord Publishers;
Zondervan Corporation

Distributor of Bibles, Christian books and greeting cards,
also videos, DVDs, gifts.

6109

MACMILLAN DISTRIBUTION (MDL)
Brunel Road, Houndmills, Basingstoke, Hants RG21 6XS
Telephone: 01256 302840
Fax: 01256 841426
Email: www-mdl@macmillan.co.uk
Web Site: www.macmillandistribution.co.uk

Personnel:
Lawrence Jennings (Chairman)
David Smith (Managing Director)
Andrew May-Miller (Information Services Director)
Guy Browning (Distribution Director)

Parent Company:
UK: Macmillan Ltd

Distributor for:
Accent Press Ltd; Arcturus Publishing Ltd; Arden
Shakespeare; Barrington Stoke; Berg Publishers; A. & C.
Black; Bloomsbury Publishing Plc; Boxtree; Camra; Cico
Books; Class Publishing (London) Ltd; CRW Publishing
Ltd; Earthscan / James & James; Elliott & Thompson Ltd;
Fairchild; Featherstone; First Second Editions; W.
Foulsham & Co Ltd; W. H. Freeman & Worth Publishers;
Guinness World Records Ltd; Jones & Bartlett; Jessica
Kingsley Publishers; Little Tiger Press (Magi); Macmillan
Children's Books; Macmillan Digital Audio; Macmillan
Education; Methuen Drama; Murdoch Books (UK) Ltd;
Nature Publishing Group; Office for National Statistics
(ONS); Palgrave; Pan Macmillan; Panini Books;
Persephone Book Ltd; Pharmaceutical Press; Picador;
Prestel Publishing Ltd; Priddy Books; Quadrille Publishing
Ltd; Ryland Peters & Small; Sinauer Associates; I. B.

Tauris; V & A Publications; Walker Books Ltd; John Wisden & Co Ltd

Macmillan Distribution (MDL) offers a full book distribution service to the Macmillan publishers as well as a wide range of third-party clients. It provides order fulfilment in a variety of electronic formats as well as more traditional forms, cash collection and information provision through its sophisticated sales analysis system. MDL was one of the first publisher's distribution companies to obtain ISO9000 certification, the internationally recognized standard for quality systems, and is fully e4 books commended. It consciously looks for ways to expand and improve the services it offers, which include printing, catalogue despatch A.I. provision and links with reps using PDAs for order transfer and title and price availability. It recently invested in 120,000 sq feet of new state-of-the-art warehousing, and refinements of its warehousing and stock systems are ongoing.

6110

MARSTON BOOK SERVICES LTD
160 Milton Park, Abingdon, Oxon OX14 4SD
Telephone: 01235 465604
Fax: 01235 465655
Email: monica.harding@marston.co.uk
Web Site: www.marston.co.uk

Personnel:
John Holloran (Chairman)
Ross Clayton (Managing Director)
Graham Cooper (Financial Director)
Melanie Khosla (Customer Service Manager)
Donna Green (Trade Manager)
Monica Harding (Client Development & Service Manager)

Associated Companies:
UK: Orca Book Services

Clients represented:
Belgium: Brepols Publishing; Harvey Miller Publishers
Denmark: Copenhagen Business School Press
Germany: ACTAR-D; Berghahn; Boerm Bruckmeier Verlag GmbH; Fraunhofer Verlag; Hogrefe Publishing
Italy: Damiani Editore
Netherlands: Asian Studies Book Services
Republic of Ireland: Cork University Press / Attic Press
Singapore: World Scientific Publishing
UK: Actar D; Acumen Publishing; Adamson Publishing; Alban Books; Alpha Science International Ltd; Anthem Press; Arts Council of England; Assouline Publishing Inc; Atrium Group; The Barbirolli Society; Bennett & Bloom; Berghahn Books; Bibles for Children; Biteback Publishing Ltd; Black Dog Publishing Ltd; Bloomsbury Professional; Bonnier Books; Burke Publishing; CIPAC; Clinical Publishing; Combined Academic Publishers Ltd; Compass – DSA; James Currey Publishers; Edinburgh University Press; Edward Elgar Publishing Ltd; Equinox; Flame Tree Publishing; Gestalten UK; Harriman House Ltd; The History Press; Hurst & Co (Publishers) Ltd; ICSA; Imaginative Minds; Institute of Physics (education only); Island Press; Peter Lang Ltd; Library Reference; Lion Hudson Plc; Liverpool University Press; Manchester University Press; Manticore Books Ltd; Mapin; Marshall Cavendish; Merrell Publishers Ltd; Multilingual Matters Ltd / Channel View Publications; NIAS; Now Publishing; Oberon; Orthodox Christian Books Ltd; Permillion; Pluto Press; The Policy Press; Public Catalogue Foundation; The Royal Society of Medicine Press Ltd; John Rule Sales & Marketing; Saint Andrew Press; Saqi Books; Scottish Council for Law Reporting; Scripture Union for England & Wales; Society for Promoting Christian Knowledge; Terra Publishing; Third Millennium Publishing Ltd; Thorogood Publishing; Turning Point; Unicorn Press; University of Buckingham; Verso; The Voltaire Foundation
USA: ABC-CLIO; CQ Press; Enisen Publishing; National Academies Press; Omnigraphics; Rizzoli International Publications; University of Pennsylvania Press

Provides fulfilment services to the publishing world.
Services available include: order processing; customer service; credit control; management reporting; production of royalty statements; pick, pack and despatch (automated warehouse management system); digital print facility; journal fulfilment; ancillary work; exhibition services; EDI; IT support and development.

6111

MDS BOOK SALES
128 Pikes Lane, Glossop, Derbys SK13 8EH
Telephone: 01457 861508

Fax: 01457 868332
Email: enquiries@mdsbooks.co.uk
Web Site: www.mdsbooks.co.uk

Personnel:
Mark Senior (Proprietor)

Associated Companies:
UK: Venture Publications Ltd

Distributor for:
UK: Birmingham Transport Historical Group; DTS Sales; Earlswood Press; John Hambley Books; Robin Hood Publishing; Senior Publications; Venture Publications Ltd; Peter Watts Publishing; Woodpecker Publications

Book wholesalers and distributors specializing in transport related lists.

6112

MELIA PUBLISHING SERVICES LTD
The White House, 2A Meadrow, Godalming, Surrey GU7 3HN
Telephone: 01483 869839
Fax: 01483 869845
Email: melia@melia.co.uk
Web Site: www.melia.co.uk

Personnel:
Terry Melia (Managing Director)
Billy Adair (Sales Director)
Cleve Vine (Finance Director)
Joanna Melia (Sales Manager)
Linda West (Accounts Manager)

Distributor for:
UK: Connections; Ivy Press; Psychology News; Snake River Press; Worth Press Ltd
USA: Algonquin; Artisan; Tom Doherty Association; Farrar, Straus & Giroux; Filipacchi; Forgie; Griffin; Harcourt Trade Books; Henry Holt; Houghton Mifflin Harcourt; Kensington Publishing Corporation; Minotaur; Newmarket Press; Owl; Papercutz; Picador; Rodale; Seven Seas; St Martins Press; Storey Books; Time Inc Home Entertainment; Toby Press LLC; Tor; Workman Publishing

Sales and distribution for English language publishers.

6113

METANOIA BOOK SERVICE
[Book service of the London Mennonite Centre]
14 Shepherds Hill, London N6 5AQ
Telephone: 020 8340 8775
Fax: 020 8341 6807
Email: metanoia@menno.org.uk
Web Site: www.metanoiabooks.org.uk

Personnel:
Will Newcomb (Manager)

Parent Company:
UK: London Mennonite Centre

Associated Companies:
UK: Bridge Builders

Distributor for:
Canada: Pandora Press
USA: Cascadia; Good Books; Herald Press (Sole UK distributor); The Alban Institute (Sole UK distributor); Wipf & Stock

To raise awareness of Mennonite and Anabaptist distinctives through the selling of Mennonite/Anabaptist and radical discipleship literature/publications.
To distribute Christian titles to help congregations transform their conflict and culture.

6114

MK BOOK SERVICE
7 East Street, Hartford Road, Huntingdon PE29 1WZ
Telephone: 01480 353710
Fax: 01480 431703
Email: mkbooks@tiscali.co.uk

Personnel:
M. R. King (Owner)

UK distributor/representative for clients including:
Argentina: Del Nuevo Extremo; Lola
Australia: Academic English Press; Gary Allen Pty Ltd NSW; Art Media; Ausmed; Australian Medical Publications; Blue Cat Books; E. J. Bowles; Coffee School Melbourne; Corkwood Press; Crossing Press; Ken Duncan Panographs; Eagles Nest Golf Guides; East Street Publications; Golden Point Press; Haese & Harris; Hobby Investment; IBID Press; Indo Lingo Surf; JB Books; Linford; Melting Pot Press; Mitchell Wordsmith; Parrot Books; Perfect Potion; Piscean Books; Slouch Hat Publications; Wizard Study Guides; Woodmore
Bangladesh: University Press Dhaka
Canada: Creative Newfoundland; Empty Mirror Press; Fitzhenry & Whiteside; St James Publishing BC
Estonia: Periodika
France: Editions Pelisser
Germany: ADAC
Iceland: Forglaid; Iceland Review; Mimir
India: Aditya Prakashan; Allied Publications; Anmol; Asa; Ashish/APH; Asia Bookclub; Atlantic Publishing; Authors Press; Best Books Kolkata; Biotech; Book Enclave; Concord Press; Daya; Deep & Deep; Diamond Pocket Books; DK Printworld Pty Ltd; Galaxy; Gene-Tech Books; India Research Press; Indus; Intellectual Book Corner; ISPCK; Kaushal; Low Price Publications; Mahaveer & Sons; Minerva Associates; Modern Publishers; National Book Trust; Papyrus; Prestige; Rajesh; Regency; South Asian Publications
Israel: Ben Zvi Press; Bible Lands Museum; Carta; Francisian Printing Press; Gefen; Israel Academy of Sciences; Israel Exploration Society; Magnes Press; Rubin Mass Publishing Jerusalem; Yad Vaschem
Italy: Biblico Pontificio
Latvia: Avots
New Zealand: Hyndmans
USA: Eisenbrauns; Kendall Hunt

Distributor for overseas publishers; importer from overseas, for whom we are not agents; distributor for selected UK publishers; library supply; booksearch for out of print UK books.

6115

MOTILAL (UK) – BOOKS OF INDIA
367 High Street, London Colney, St Albans, Herts AL2 1EA
Telephone: 01727 761677
Fax: 01727 761357
Email: info@mlbduk.com

Personnel:
R. J. McLennan (Managing Director)
Ms Ann Moister (Finance)
Richard Neil (Customer Service)
Barbara Doffman (Customer Service)

Parent Company:
UK: Moneysavers (Ldn) Ltd

Associated Companies:
UK: Ahimsa Books

Indian publishers represented include:
India: Abhinav Publications; Amexfel Publishers; Anmol Publications; Aravali Books International; Aryan Books International; Asian Educational Services; Asiatic Publishing House; Banjara Academy; Bihar School of Yoga; Bookwell Publications; Brijbasi Art Press; Centre for Studies in Civilizations; Commonwealth Youth Programme; Cosmo Publications; Crest Publishing House; Deep & Deep Publications; DK Printworld; Excel Books; Foundation Books; Full Circle Publishing Ltd; Gemini Books; Gulshan Publishers; Gyan Publishing House; HarperCollins India; Hind Pocket Books; Indian Book Centre; Indiana Publishing House; Indica Books; Indus Publishing; Institute for Human Development; Jaico Publishing House; Jaya Books; Jaypee Brothers Medical Publishers; Kalpaz Publications; Katha; Kitab Bhavan; Laxmi Publications; Low Price Publications; Malhotra Publishing; Manas Publications; Manohar Publishers; Motilal Banarsidass; New Age Books; Orient Paperbacks; Paljor Publications; Pentagon Press; Pragati Publications; Sandeep Prakashan; Prentice-Hall of India Pvt Ltd; Pustak Mahal; Rawat; Readworthy Publications Pvt Ltd; Sahasrara Publications; Sanskrit Religious Institute; Sanskriti; Shubhi Publications; Spectrum Publications; Sura Books; Torchlight Publishing; Unisun Publications; Universal Law Publishing; Vanity Books International; Wordspeak; Worldview Publications; Zubaan

Distributor of books and other materials dealing with the philosophies, religions and cultures of India.

In November 1998 the company took over Motilal Books, who are the European distributors for Motilal Banarsidass Ltd (MLBD) of New Delhi. MLBD are the foremost publishers for the academic market on the topics of Hinduism, Buddhism, Jainism and all subjects unique to India. We supply all markets with titles in all fields, books from India in general, representing all major Indian publishers.

The company now represents over 300 Indian publishers as their UK distributor, with over 35,000 English titles listed on Nielsen BookData.

6116

NMD TRADING CO
[trading as Mayfield Books & Gifts]
9 Orgreave Close, Sheffield S13 9NP
Telephone: 0114 288 9522
Fax: 0114 269 1499
Email: sales@mayfield-books.co.uk

Personnel:
David N. Smith (Managing Director)
Andrew Smith (Sales Director)

Supply bookshops and other trade outlets through the Midlands and Northern England with maps and guides and local book product. Specialize in walking and outdoor activity books. Four representatives call regularly throughout the year. Main suppliers are Ordnance Survey, George Philips, Collins and Geographers A-Z Map Co. Provide a service for small publishers into the multiple chains, e.g. W. H. Smith, Waterstone's. Distributor for Myriad Books and a growing range of nostalgia products from the Frith Collection.

Sole supplier of LAM-fold maps. Also supply laminated flat maps and other special product, such as library supply.

6117

OHL GLOBAL FREIGHT MANAGEMENT & LOGISTICS
Action Court, Ashford Road, Ashford, Middx TW15 1XS
Telephone: 01784 890005
Fax: 01784 890013
Email: pbarrett@ohl.com
Web Site: www.activair.ohl.com

Oceanfreight Division:
OHL Global Freight Management & Logistics,
Watkins Close, Burnt Mills Industrial Estate, Basildon, Essex
SS13 1TL
Telephone: 01268 724400
Fax: 01268 728226
Email: mcaines@ohl.com
Web Site: www.activair.ohl.com

Personnel:
Geoff Corpe (President)
Steve Lai (Finance Director)
Paul Barrett (International Sales Director)
Martin Caines (Oceanfreight Director)
Chris Packwood (Airfreight Director)

Parent Company:
USA: OHL Inc

Freight forwarder to the publishing industry, providing efficient cost-effective services specifically designed for the worldwide movement of trade and academic books. Services offered are by air, sea and road between publisher's warehouse and bookshop door. Sponsor of the British Book Awards.

6118

ORCA BOOK SERVICES LTD
Unit A3, Fleets Corner, Poole, Dorset BH17 0HL
Telephone: 01202 665432
Fax: 01202 666219
Email: orders@orcabookservices.co.uk
Web Site: www.orcabookservices.co.uk

Orders to:
Orca Book Services, 160 Milton Park, Abingdon, Oxon
OX14 4SD

Personnel:
Martyn Chapman (Commercial Director)
Denise Shonfeld (Publisher Services Manager)
Ian Whyte (Logistics Director)
Trish Clapp (Publisher Services Development Manager)

Parent Company:
UK: Marston Book Services Ltd

UK distributor for:
Age Concern; Amberley Publishing; Ammo Books; Arris Publishing; Black Dog & Leventhal; Blue Ibex; Book Foundation; Book Guild; Compendium; Continuum International Publishing Group; CSA Word; Dimensional Entertainment; Dynasty Press; Evans Mitchell Books; Family Doctor Publications; Firefly Books; Global Oriental; Guild of Master Craftsman Publications; Histoires et Collections; John Hunt Publishing; Industrial Press; Islamic Texts; JB Publishing; Kuperard Publishers; Lark Books; Learning Development Aids; Lifetime Careers Publishing; Management Briefs; Maverick Arts; O Books; Palazzo Editions; Parkstone Press; Pepin Press; A. K. Peters; Potomac Books; Ravette Publishing; Redcliffe Press; Reynolds & Hearn; Romain Pages; Roundhouse Publishing; Special Interest Model Books; Sterling Publishing; Taunton Press; Ticktock Books; Tonto; Trolley Books; Troubador; Veloce Publishing; Vine House; White Star Publishers

Orca Book Services provides a full distribution service to general, academic and specialist publishers. A comprehensive package of management reports comes as standard. Royalty accounting is also available as well as representation through the various sales agencies with which we have arrangements.

6119

ORTHODOX CHRISTIAN BOOKS LTD
c/o St Matthias Church, Burton Road, Lincoln LN1 3TX
Telephone: 01782 444561
Fax: 01782 624106
Email: orthbook@aol.com
Web Site: www.orthodoxbooks.co.uk

Personnel:
Nicholas Chapman (Managing Director)

UK distributor for:
Greece: Denise Harvey
USA: Antiochian Archdiocese Publications Department; Conciliar Press; Holy Cross Press; Holy Trinity Monastery; St Herman of Alaska Press; St Nectarios Press; St Nikodemos Orthodox Publication Society; St Tikhon's Seminary Press; St Vladimir's Seminary Press

Specialist distributor, wholesaler and retailer of books and other items pertaining to the faith, life and worship of the Orthodox Christian Churches. For some publishers it has exclusive distribution rights for the UK, European Union and British Commonwealth.

6120

POMEGRANATE EUROPE LTD
Unit 1, Hurlbutt Road, Heathcote Business Centre, Warwick
CV34 6TD
Telephone: 01926 430111
Fax: 01926 430888
Email: sales@pomeurope.co.uk
Web Site: www.pomegranate.com

Personnel:
Thomas Burke (Managing Director)
Ley S. Bricknell (Sales Director)
Katie Burke (Publisher Director)

Associated Companies:
USA: Pomegranate Communications Inc

UK Distributor for:
USA: Pomegranate

Pomegranate (Europe) Ltd represent, distribute and publish a high-quality range of fine art and photographic calendars, posters, cards, diaries, books of days, postcards, books and much more.

6121

REARDON PUBLISHING
PO Box 919, Cheltenham, Glos GL50 9AN
Telephone: 01242 231800
Email: reardon@bigfoot.com
Web Site: www.reardon.co.uk &
www.cotswoldbookshop.com

Personnel:
Nicholas Reardon (Director)

UK distributor for:
UK: Cassell (selected publications); Cicerone (selected publications); Cordee (selected publications); Corinium Publications; Estate Publications; Flukes UK (illustrated maps); The Gloucestershire Ramblers Association; Harvey Maps (all maps); Ordnance Survey (all maps); Orion (selected publications); Philips Maps; Video Ex (selected titles)

Reardon Publishing offers a wide range of Costwold books, maps, videos, CDs and postcards and prints mostly in the specialized areas of walking, cycling, driving, folklore, leisure and tourism in both the Cotswold and associated counties, plus a new range of books on Antarctica and Antarctic heroes.

6122

SCANDINAVIA CONNECTION
26 Woodsford Square, London W14 8DP
Telephone: 020 7602 0657
Email: books@scandinavia-connection.co.uk
Web Site: www.scandinavia-connection.co.uk

Personnel:
Max Morgan-Witts (Chairman)

Parent Company:
UK: Max Morgan-Witts Productions Ltd

UK distributor for:
Denmark: Aschehoug; Borgen; Nyt Nordisk
Finland: Otava
Iceland: EDDA; Forlagid; JPV
Norway: Cappelen; Index; KOM; Normann's; Wennergren-Cappelen
Sweden: Atlantis; ICA; J-P Lahall
USA: Pelican (for Norway B&B Book)

Sole UK supplier for various Scandinavian publishers of non-fiction

English edition Scandinavian books, maps, videos and CD-ROMs; UK book

distributor for non-fiction English editions by Norwegian, Finnish,

Icelandic, Danish and Swedish publishers.

6123

TRADE COUNTER DISTRIBUTION
Mendlesham Industrial Estate, Norwich Road, Mendlesham,
Norfolk IP14 5NA
Telephone: 01449 766629
Fax: 01449 767122
Email: patrick.curran@tradecounter.co.uk
Web Site: www.tradecounter.co.uk

Personnel:
Patrick Curran (Managing Director)
Martin Leigh (General Manager)
Brian Barron (Chairman)

Distributor:
UK: Capital Transport; Miles Kelly

Storage, packing and distribution of books for publishers. Order processing and credit control. Operates both full service and fulfilment.

6124

TRANSATLANTIC PUBLISHERS GROUP LTD
Unit 242, 235 Earls Court Road, London SW5 9FE
Telephone: 020 7373 2515
Fax: 020 7244 1018
Email: Richard@TPGLtd.co.uk
Web Site: www.TransatlanticPublishers.com

Personnel:
Richard Williamson (Managing Director)
Mark Chaloner (Sales & Marketing Director)

UK distributor for:
INDIA: I.K. INTERNATIONAL
USA: American Institute of Aeronautics & Astronautics; American Institute of Mathematical Sciences; American

Pharmacists Associations; American Society of Health Systems Pharmacists (ASHP); Business Expert Press Inc; Demos Medical Publishers; Destech Publishers; Franklin Beedle & Associates; Industrial Press; Joint Commission Resources; Lexicomp Inc; Momentum Press; A. K. Peters; Potomac Books; Zero to Three Press

Distributors and agents for scientific, technical and medical, and academic publishers in the UK, Europe and the Middle East.

6125

TURNAROUND PUBLISHER SERVICES LTD
Unit 3, Olympia Trading Estate, Coburg Road, London N22 6TZ
Telephone: 020 8829 3000
Fax: 020 8881 5088
Email: sales@turnaround-uk.com
Web Site: www.turnaround-uk.com

Personnel:
Bill Godber *(Managing & Sales Director)*
Claire Thompson *(Marketing Director & Company Secretary)*
Sue Gregg *(Finance Director)*
Andy Webb *(UK Sales Director)*

Clients include:
Australia: 4 Ingredients; Etram Publishing; Outre Gallery & Publishing
Canada: Tradewind Books
Czech Republic: Magic Realist Press
France: BIGfib; Editions Intervalles; Heolis; JNF Productions
Germany: Editions Braus; From Here to Fame; Kehrer Verlag; Konkursbuch Verlag; Mannerschwarm; Mix of Pix
Italy: Europa Editions
Jamaica: LMH Publishing Ltd
Japan: Kumon Publishing Group
Republic of Ireland: Maverick House
Sweden: Dokument; Nicotext; Premium Publishing
Thailand: Creation; Creation / Oneiros Books; Creation / Solar Books; Creation / Wet Angel
UK: Adelita Ltd; AK Press; The Aquarium; Arcadia Books; Arcadia E-Books; Artists' & Photographers' Press Ltd; Ayebia Clarke Publishing Ltd; B A for Adoption & Fostering; Black Spring; Blackamber Books; Bliss; Bloody Books; Bookmarks; Borderline Publications; Burning House; Cinebook; Creative Essentials; Creme de la Crime Ltd; Crocus Books; Dalen Books; Dexter Haven Publishing; Education Now Books; Emerald Publishing; Erotic Review Books; Eurocrime; Facts, Figures & Fun; Fanfare; Guerilla Books; Hansib Publications; Helter Skelter; High Stakes Publishing; Honno Welsh Women's Press; Inglis Publications; Kamera; Dewi Lewis Publishing; Lifeguides; Little Roots; London Books; LVSC; Monday Books; Myriad Editions; New Internationalist; Noir Publishing; Rankin Photography Ltd; Susan Russell Publishing; SAF Publishing Ltd; Satchel; Selfmadehero; Sorted; Southbank Publishing; Sportsbooks; Straightforward Publishing; Strange Attractor; Suitcase Press; True Crime Library; Vice UK; Zidane Press; Ziji Publishing
USA: Africa World Press Inc; Angel City Press; Arcata Arts; Atlas & Co; Barricade Books; Berkley Boulvard *(select stock holdings only)*; Blood Moon Productions; Bywater Books; Catbird Press; Checker Publishing; Consafos Books; Counterpoint; Demo; DGN Productions Inc; Disinformation Co Ltd; Disney Editions *(select stock holdings only)*; Dominion Press; Doubleday *(select stock holdings only)*; Exact Change; Fantagraphics; Fulcrum; Green Candy Press; Green Integer; Hachette Book Group USA *(select stock holdings only)*; HarperCollins US *(select stock holdings only)*; Haymarket Books; Holloway House Publishing; Hyperion *(select stock holdings only)*; IG Publishing; Intrigue Press; Last Gasp; Lee & Low; Majority Press; Manic D Press; Melville House; The Nazca Plains; NBM; The New Press; Penguin Book Group USA *(select stock holdings only)*; Process; Random House Group USA *(select stock holdings only)*; The Red Sea Press; Santa Monica Press; Sierra Club Books; Simon & Schuster Group USA *(select stock holdings only)*; Speck Press; St Martins Press Group *(select stock holdings only)*; Starbooks; Steerforth Press; Testify Books; Turtle Point Press; Van Patten

Turnaround provides a sales, marketing and distribution service for a range of UK, US and Irish publishers in the UK and Europe.

6126

TURPIN DISTRIBUTION SERVICES LTD
Pegasus Drive, Stratton Business Park, Biggleswade, Beds SG18 8TQ
Telephone: 01767 604868
Fax: 01767 604949
Email: neil.castle@turpin-distribution.com
Web Site: www.turpin-distribution.com

Also at:
Turpin North America, The Bleachery, 143 West Street, New Milford, CT 06778, USA
Telephone: +1 (860) 350 0041
Fax: +1 (860) 350 0039
Email: turpinna@turpin-distribution.com
Web Site: www.turpin-distirbution.com

Personnel:
Lorna Summers *(Managing Director)*
Richard Stroud *(Company Accountant)*
Neil Castle *(Head of Customer Relations & Distribution)*
Alan Medd *(Head of IT)*
Elizabeth Just *(Head of Operations, Turpin USA)*

Parent Company:
UK: Eurospan Group

Clients include:
France: Organisation for Economic Co-operation and Development (OECD)
Germany: Dechema
Greece: Adcotec
Japan: Japanese Society for Analytical Chemistry
Netherlands: Brill Academic Publishers; Hes en de Graaf; Kluwer Law International; New in Chess
UK: Adcotec; Philip Allan Updates; Association of Learned and Professional Society Publishers (ALPSP); The Association of Project Managers; Beech Tree Publishing; Berg Publishing; Biohealthcare; The Bodleian Library; The British Library; British Psychological Society; Dunedin Academic Press; Euromoney PLC; Eurospan Group; Fiscal Publications; John Harper Publishing; The HotHive; The Institute of Cast Metal Engineers; Intellect Journals; Internet Archaeology; IP Publishing; Journal of Transport & Economic Policy; Pickering & Chatto; Pion Publishers; Royal College of Obstetricians and Gynaecologists; The Royal College of Psychiatrists; Sapiens; Spiramus; Way; White Horse Press
USA: ABC-Clio; American Association Cancer Research; American School of Classical Studies; Aspen Publishers Inc; Berghahn Journals; The Freer Gallery of Art; United Nations

Turpin Distribution is an international fulfilment and distribution company providing services to the academic, scholarly and professional publishing industry. We provide solutions for book, journal and online publishers that include:
– Global fulfilment and distribution
– UK and US offices with multilingual customer care advisors
– Order and renewals processing
– Billing and account collection
– Comprehensive warehouse services with global distribution for books and journals
– Full subscription management for print and online journals with e-commerce ordering
– Online sales reporting with data manipulation for analysis and customer management
Turpin can accommodate any business model and pricing policy, enabling publishers to retain control of their products; develop collections; set multiple pricing options; use a variety of routes to market; and manage its customers successfully.

6127

VINE HOUSE DISTRIBUTION LTD
Waldenbury, North Chailey, East Sussex BN8 4DR
Telephone: 01825 723398
Fax: 01825 724188
Email: richard@vinehouseuk.co.uk
Web Site: www.vinehouseuk.co.uk

Customer Services:
The Old Mill House, Mill Lane, Uckfield, East Sussex TN22 5AA
Telephone: 01825 767396
Fax: 01825 765649
Email: sales@vinehouseuk.co.uk
Web Site: www.vinehouseuk.co.uk

Personnel:
Richard Squibb *(Director)*
Sarah Squibb *(Director)*
Tara Horwood *(Director)*
Pauline Gosden *(Customer Services Manager)*

Associated Companies:
UK: Vine House Book Promotion

Clients include:
Australia: Clockwork Media; Epic Guides; Inn Australia
Finland: Fine Publishing
Italy: Mediane
Monaco: Christian Philippsen
New Zealand: Travelwise
South Africa: Outstanding 100
Spain: Editorial Moll
Sweden: MagDig Media
Switzerland: Chronosports; Editions J. R. Piccard
UK: Ashgrove Publishing; Association of Illustrators; At Heart Publishing; Bearmondsey Publishing; Berkut International; Boleyn Books; The Book Guild; British Institute of Radiology; Dance Books; Delancey Press *(imprint of The Book Guild)*; Dove Publishing; Fitzjames Press; Football World; Good Life Press; Haldane Mason; Hochland Communications; Martin Holmes Rallying; Honeyglen Publishing; Horse's Mouth Publications; Immel Publishing; Jaspal Jandu Photography; Sheila Markham Rare Books; Andrew Martin International; Masquerade Publications; Motor Racing Publications; Oxbridge Applications; Park Lane Books; Picnic Publishing; PMM Books; Puck Books; Julian Richer Publishing; Royal Academy of Dancing; Safety House; Saxon Books; R. D. & A. S. Shepherd Partnership; Silent But Deadly Publications; Superbrands; Sylph Editions; Tartarus Press; Temple House Books; Tiger Books; Tonto Books; Touchstone Books; Troubador Publishing; John van Weenen; Wooden Dragon Press
USA: Dance Horizons; Princeton Book Co; Wine Appreciation Guild

Vine House Distribution provides a comprehensive range of services for small and medium sized book publishers, including representation, distribution, marketing, publicity and promotion, and mail order fulfilment.

6128

VIRTUE BOOKS LTD
Edward House, Tenter Street, Rotherham S60 1LB
Telephone: 01709 365005
Fax: 01709 829982
Email: info@virtue.co.uk
Web Site: www.virtue.co.uk

Personnel:
Richard Russum *(Commercial Director)*
Peter Russum *(Managing Director)*

Parent Company:
UK: E. Russum & Sons Ltd

Specialist distributor, concentrating almost exclusively on books on cookery, food and drink. Virtue holds stocks of over 300 titles and supplies mainly to professional and domestic kitchen shops, cook shops, food shops, delicatessens, etc. Some of the titles on its list are exclusive to Virtue, but the majority are sourced from British, American and some continental publishers.

6129

WINDSOR BOOKS LTD
31 Furze Platt Road, Maidenhead, Berkshire SL6 7NE
Telephone: 01628 770542
Fax: 01628 770546
Email: geoffcowen@windsorbooks.co.uk
Web Site: www.windsorbooks.co.uk

Personnel:
Geoff Cowen *(Managing Director)*
Angela Prysor-Jones *(Publicity Manager)*

Associated Companies:
UK: Meyer & Meyer Sport (UK); Star Book Sales

UK Distributor/Representative for:
Germany: Meyer & Meyer Verlag

Windsor Books Ltd, through its subsidiary, Star Book Sales, provides distribution combined with sales representation and marketing in the UK and European markets for publishers based in the UK and Europe, linked to physical distribution through Orca Distribution Services Ltd. The Star sales team consists of nine representatives in the UK and Republic of Ireland and eight covering West and Eastern Europe.

6.7 REMAINDER MERCHANTS

6130

BOOKMARK REMAINDERS LTD
Rivendell, Illand, Launceston, Cornwall PL15 7LS
Telephone: 01566 782728
Fax: 01566 782059
Email: andrew.rattray@book-bargains.co.uk
Web Site: www.book-bargains.co.uk

Personnel:
Andrew Rattray (Director)
Carol Rattray (Director)

A wide range of genuine remainders and bargain books. Prompt payment to publishers, authors for surplus stocks.

6131

FANSHAW BOOKS LTD
Unit 7, Lysander Mews, Lysander Grove, London N19 3QP
Telephone: 020 7281 9387
Fax: 020 7561 3502
Email: info@roybloom.com
Web Site: www.roybloom.com

Personnel:
Adam Bloom (Managing Director)
Roy Bloom (Chairman)

Remainder company specializing in real UK publishers' books, mainly non-fiction, art, military, history, etc. It also has a number of retail stores, so customers can buy from one to 50,000 copies of a book.

6132

OCTAGON BOOKS (WHOLESALE) LTD
The Old Exchange, New Pond Road, Holmer Green, High Wycombe, Bucks HP15 6SU
Telephone: 01494 711717 (mobile: 07718 364857)
Fax: 01494 711176
Email: ronive@lineone.net

Personnel:
Ron Ive (Director)
Bernard McDonnell (Commercial Director)

All types of remainders and promotional reprints.

6133

JIM OLDROYD BOOKS
The Old Town Jail, 14–18 London Road, Sevenoaks, Kent TN13 1AJ
Telephone: 01732 463356
Fax: 01732 464486
Email: Stephen@oldroyd.co.uk
Web Site: www.oldroyd.co.uk

Personnel:
Jim Oldroyd (Director)
Stephen Bryan (Manager)
Niki Oldroyd (Buyer Manager)
Sally Millest (Assistant)
Tim Finch (Sales)
Colin Gower (Sales)
Margaret Walker (Sales)
Hugh Llewellyn-Jones (Director)

Remainders, bargain books and overstocks of adult and children's books. All ages and all interests.

6134

PR BOOKS LTD
Unit 2, Mealbank Trading Estate, Mealbank, Kendal, Cumbria LA8 9DL
Telephone: 01539 733332
Fax: 01539 733375
Email: info@prbooks.co.uk
Web Site: www.prbooks.co.uk

Personnel:
Paul Farrar (Joint Managing Director)
Ruth Farrar (Joint Managing Director)
Thomas Seddon (Regional Sale)
Mark Farrar (Sales Director)

Associated Companies:
UK: Caxton Publishing Ltd; Greenwich Book Time; Henry Roberts Bookshops

PR Books Ltd is an international book wholesaler. It is located in the north-west of England and has been in business for 20 years. It currently has close to 6000 remainder titles, covering the following subjects: children's, educational, natural history, military history, fiction, non-fiction, cookery, travel, arts & crafts, social, reference, dictionaries, language packs, fitness, wellbeing, gardening and interior design.

6135

SANDPIPER BOOKS LTD
24 Langroyd Road, London SW17 7PL
Telephone: 020 8767 7421
Fax: 020 8682 0280
Email: enquiries@sandpiper.co.uk
Web Site: www.sandpiper.co.uk & www.psbooks.co.uk

Distribution::
Alton Logistics Ltd, Unit 4 Heathfield Industrial Estate, Battle Road, Heathfield, Newton Abbot TQ12 6RY
Telephone: 01626 832225
Fax: 01626 832398
Email: enquiries@altonlogistics.co.uk

Personnel:
Robert Collie (Managing Director)
Simon Lang (Mail Order (Postscript))

Hardback reprints exclusive to Sandpiper of Oxford University Press monographs in classical and mediaeval studies, philosophy and history, retailing at paperback prices and retaining the Clarendon / OUP imprint. The company also buys remainders exclusively from university presses and the scholarly divisions of major publishers as well as from smaller companies, and supplies an extensive network of trade and non-trade outlets both in the UK and overseas.

6.8 MAIN WHOLESALERS

6136

ARGOSY LIBRARIES LTD
Unit 12, North Park, North Road, Finglas, Dublin 11, Republic of Ireland
Telephone: +353 (01) 823 9500
Fax: +353 (01) 823 9599
Email: info@argosybooks.ie
Web Site: www.argosybooks.ie

Personnel:
Fergal Stanley (Managing Director)
Eddie Walsh (General Manager)
Ronan Richmond (Sales Manager)
Mary Healy (Buyer)

Trade book wholesaler specializing in books of Irish interest and maps and guides to Ireland. Export service available.

6137

BAKER & TAYLOR UK LTD
Unit B, Charbridge Way, Bicester, Oxon OX26 4ST
Telephone: 01869 363500
Fax: 01869 363555

Personnel:
Diane White (Buying Director)
Annette Burgess (Commercial Director)
Gareth Powell (Managing Director)

Parent Company:
USA: Baker & Taylor

Baker & Taylor offers book distribution and merchandising service. A full-time sales force covers the entire UK and Northern Ireland, supported by five senior managers.
Operating from its computerized distribution centre at Bicester, Baker & Taylor offers over 10,000 titles from stock totally geared to the specialist markets it services, delivered fast. Baker & Taylor's range extends to gardening, DIY and

the home, cookery, natural history, travel and leisure, illustrated stationery, gift books and children's books. It supplies books mainly to garden centres, home and DIY outlets, department stores, the natural history / heritage markets and the gift sector, and offers a specialist service to non-traditional children's book outlets and club warehouses.

6138

BERTRAMS
1 Broadland Business Park, Norwich NR7 0WF
Telephone: 0871 803 6666
Fax: 0871 803 6709 (customer services)
Email: sales@bertrams.com
Web Site: www.bertrams.com

Personnel:
Michael Neil (Managing Director)
Ian Hendrie (Finance & Commercial Director)
Chris Rushby (Buying & Marketing Director)

Parent Company:
UK: Smiths News Plc

Bertrams is wholly owned by Smiths News Plc, one of the UK's leading wholesalers of newspapers and magazines. It celebrated 40 years of trading in 2008. Bertrams has a stockholding of over 920,000 titles from over 6000 publishers and can source over 5 million English language titles from both the UK and USA. Customers, from independent booksellers to online retailers, multinationals to non-book trade outlets in both the UK and international markets, can access availability of stock, product information, ordering and shipping details in real time through Bertrams.com, Bertmail, Bertrams' ordering system, as well as Bertrams' Customer Services department. A proactive marketing program enables publishers to market their titles effectively and efficiently through all sales channels, both business to business and to the end consumer. The warehouse works at 24/7 at peak capacity and provides an accurate and robust service in a secure site.
Bertram Library Services business in Leeds provides stock and selection advice for public libraries throughout the country. Bertram Publisher Services, the distribution arm of the group, provides distribution facilities for a range of publishers and retailers.
Bertrams is a key industry player with membership of the BA and BIC, working towards improving the supply chain throughout the book industry.

6139

BOOKSPEED
16 Salamander Yards, Edinburgh EH6 7DD
Telephone: 0131 467 8100
Fax: 0131 467 8008
Email: sales@bookspeed.com
Web Site: www.bookspeed.com

Personnel:
Kingsley Dawson (Director)
Fiona Stout (Director of Sales)
Matthew Perren (Director of Buying & Logistics)
Shona Rowan (Marketing & Bibliographic Manager)

Parent Company:
UK: Rhodawn Ltd

Consultants and suppliers of books to specialist retailers in the gift, leisure and heritage markets.

6140

BOOKWORLD WHOLESALE LTD
Unit 10, Hodfar Road, Sandy Lane Industrial Estate, Stourport-on-Severn, Worcs DY13 9QB
Telephone: 01299 823330
Fax: 01299 829970
Email: info@bookworldws.co.uk
Web Site: www.bookworldws.co.uk

Personnel:
Justin Gainham (Sales Director)
Andrea Gainham (Director)

Transport, military, aviation and modelling book wholesaler and distributor. Mail order department worldwide.
Minimum order one book, full trade terms given but postage added to orders under £50 in value. Teleordering mnemonic BK WORLD.
Range of distribution whole of UK. Number of publishers for whom we distribute is in excess of 70.

6141

GARDNERS BOOKS LTD
1 Whittle Drive, Eastbourne, East Sussex BN23 6QH
Telephone: 01323 521555
Fax: 01323 521666
Email: sales@gardners.com
Web Site: www.gardners.com

Personnel:
Alan Little *(Chairman)*
Jonathan Little *(Managing Director)*
Nicky Little *(Finance Director)*
Andrew Little *(Technical Director)*
Bob Jackson *(Commercial Director)*
Simon Morley *(Buying Director)*
David O'Reilly *(Warehouse Director)*
Gary Sheppard *(Marketing Manager)*
Phil Edwards *(Senior Buying Manager)*
Gail Harbour *(Buying Manager)*

Gardners Books is a leading independent book and entertainment product wholesaler offering one of the largest
stock ranges available from any UK wholesaler, with in
excess of 2 million titles available from over 5000 publishers,
80,000+ eBook files and 45,000 DVDs and Blu-ray discs.
Gardners offers a comprehensive range of e-commerce
solutions including bespoke data feeds and drop-ship fulfilment to meet retailers' business requirements. Orders can be
placed 24 hours a day via its account holders' website,
Gardlink electronic ordering system, Gardcall automated telephone enquiry service, fax and EDI. Its experienced customer care team is available from Monday to Saturday
between 9am and 6pm to take orders and assist customers.
Gardners Books trade website, www.gardners.com, is
free to account holders and features data on over 1.2 million
British books in print, as well as real-time stock figures,
invoices, backorders and promotional offers. Information on
additional services Gardners offers, such as B2B and B2C
home delivery fulfilment to marketing materials, distribution
services and print on demand can also be found on the site.

6142

SHOGUN INTERNATIONAL LTD
87 Gayford Road, London W12 9BY
Telephone: 020 8749 2022
Fax: 020 8740 1086
Email: info@shoguninternational.com

Personnel:
G. Blanc *(Manager)*

Shogun International deals exclusively with wholesaling of
martial arts goods and related sports books.

6.9 MAIN LIBRARY SUPPLIERS

6143

THE HOLT JACKSON BOOK CO LTD
Park Mill, Great George Street, Preston PR1 1TJ
Telephone: 01772 798000
Email: info@holtjackson.co.uk
Web Site: www.holtjackson.co.uk

Personnel:
Yvette Stafford *(Chairman)*
Kathryn Pattinson *(Managing Director)*
J. Little *(Director)*
A. Little *(Director)*
Mrs J. Holborn *(Director)*

Parent Company:
UK: The Little Group Ltd

Booksellers.

6144

STEVEN SIMPSON BOOKS
5 Hardingham Road, Hingham, Norwich NR9 4LX
Telephone: 01953 850471
Fax: 01953 850471
Web Site: www.aquariumatlas.co.uk

Trade Webshop:
AquariumAtlas.EU, 5 Hardingham Road, Norwich NR9 4LX

Telephone: 01953 850471
Fax: 01953 850471
Email: info@aquariumatlas.eu
Web Site: www.aquariumatlas.eu

Personnel:
S. J. Simpson *(Proprietor)*

UK distributor for:
Germany: Hans A. Baenasch / Mergus Verlag GmbH
(exclusive); Birgit Schmettkamp Verlag *(exclusive);* Verlag
ACS Aqualog GmbH *(exclusive);* Verlag Eugen Ulmer KG
(exclusive)
Italy: Aquapress Publishers *(exclusive);* FAO (Food &
Agriculture Organization of the United Nations)
Nepal: T. K. Shrestha *(exclusive)*

Distributor to the trade for overseas publishers in the field of
natural history.

6145

STARKMANN LTD
6 Broadley Street, London NW8 8AE
Telephone: 020 7724 5335
Fax: 020 7724 9863
Email: orders@starkmann.co.uk
Web Site: www.starkmann.com

Delivery Address:
6 Plympton Place, London NW8 8AD

Personnel:
Dr Bernard Starkmann *(Managing Director)*
Sheikh Obarey *(Accounts Manager)*
Martin Illmann *(Sales Manager)*
Steven Wright *(Operations Manager)*
Rodney Latham *(IT Manager)*
Kerstin Peter *(Customer Service Manager)*

Suppliers of academic and scientific books and ebooks to
university, college, industrial and research libraries in Europe.
Customers and potential customers receive frequent and
accurate new book information. Distribution of the main
line publishers from UK, USA, Netherlands, Germany and
Switzerland. Supplies made at publisher's list price. Fast airfreight service of US books. Comprehensive website featuring bibliographic database, online ordering, order tracking,
new title alert service and special offers.

6146

ROY YATES BOOKS
Smallfields Cottage, Cox Green, Rudgwick, Horsham,
West Sussex RH12 3DE
Telephone: 01403 822299
Fax: 01403 823012
Email: royyatesbooks@btconnect.com

Personnel:
Roy Yates *(Managing Director)*

Specialist supplier of children's books to schools and libraries; distributes multilingual books; distributes foreign-lan-
guage books.

6.10 BOOK CLUBS

6147

ARTISTS' CHOICE LTD
The Old Post Office, Bythorn, Huntingdon, Cambs
PE28 0QN
Telephone: 01832 710201
Fax: 01832 710488
Email: henry@artists-choice.co.uk
Web Site: www.artists-choice.co.uk

Personnel:
Henry Malt *(Managing Director)*

Book club aimed at the amateur artist.

6148

BIBLIOPHILE BOOKS
Unit 5 Datapoint Business Centre, 6 South Crescent,
London E16 4TL
Telephone: 020 7474 2474
Fax: 020 7474 8589

Email: orders@bibliophilebooks.com
Web Site: www.bibliophilebooks.com

Personnel:
Jackie McDaid *(General Manager)*
Steven Lee *(Distribution)*
Anne Quigley *(Director)*

Produces 10 catalogues a year, offering books at bargain
prices to private buyers. Range: general, eg biography, history, travel, handicrafts, humour, literature.

6149

LETTERBOX LIBRARY
71–73 Allen Road, Stoke Newington, London N16 8RY
Telephone: 020 7503 4801
Fax: 020 7503 4800
Email: info@letterboxlibrary.com
Web Site: www.letterboxlibrary.com

Personnel:
Kerry Mason *(Contact)*
Fen Coles *(Contact)*

Letterbox Library is a children's bookseller specializing in children's books which celebrate equality and diversity. Quarterly catalogues are produced with up to 70 new titles,
offered at discounts to members. Books are multicultural
and non-sexist, and also show groups of people traditionally
under-represented in children's books, e.g. different faith
groups, disabled children, refugees. All books are approved
by an independent team of reviewers. Subscription is £5 a
year and entitles members to discounts. Non-members can
buy books at the retail price. Letterbox Library also provides
book displays for schools and libraries and attends exhibitions. Letterbox Library is a not-for-profit social enterprise.

6150

POETRY BOOK SOCIETY
Dutch House, 307–308 High Holborn, London WC1V 7LL
Telephone: 020 7831 7468
Fax: 020 7833 5990
Email: info@poetrybooks.co.uk
Web Site: www.poetrybooks.co.uk &
www.poetrybookshoponline.com

Personnel:
Chris Holifield *(Director)*

Publicly funded charity, membership organization, mail
order book club promoting contemporary poetry titles to an
international readership. Quarterly publication of *Bulletin*
magazine featuring selected new poetry titles. Also has Children's Poetry Bookshelf, relaunched 2005 with new website
(www.childrenspoetrybookshelf.co.uk) and parent and
library memberships. The Society also acts as sole distributor
for The Poetry Archive CDs, and awards the annual T. S. Eliot
Prize for Poetry.
Membership from £12 p.a.
Also runs www.poetrybookshoponline.com, selling a
wide range of poetry and SoundBlast performance poets'
CDs.

6.11 LITERARY & TRADE EVENTS

6151

**BOOKSELLERS ASSOCIATION ANNUAL
CONFERENCE**
Minster House, 272 Vauxhall Bridge Road, London
SW1V 1BA
Telephone: 020 7802 0802
Fax: 020 7802 0803
Email: naomi.gane@booksellers.org.uk
Web Site: www.booksellers.org.uk

Personnel:
Tim Godfray *(Chief Executive)*
Naomi Gane *(Conference Organizer)*
Alan Staton *(Head of Marketing & Events)*

Major UK book trade event. The Conference provides
opportunity for those supplying or serving the retail book
trade to meet trade customers and for both to learn from
business programme. **Details from:** above address.

6152

THE TIMES CHELTENHAM LITERATURE FESTIVAL
Cheltenham Festivals Ltd, 109 Bath Road, Cheltenham,
Glos GL53 7LS
Telephone: 01242 774967
Fax: 01242 256457
Email: judith.ludenbach@cheltenhamfestivals.com
Web Site: www.cheltenhamfestivals.com

Personnel:
Donna Renney (Chief Executive)
Sarah Smyth (Artistic Director)
Clair Greenaway (Executive Director)

Annual in October. Promoted by Cheltenham Festivals Ltd.
Performances, poetry readings, talks and discussions by liter-
ary personalities. Includes Book It! Festival for Children,
Voices Off Fringe Festival and Write Away creative writing
workshops.
Details from: Artistic Director: Sarah Smyth or Executive
Director: Clair Greenaway.

6153

CHILDREN'S BOOK WEEK
Booktrust, Book House, 45 East Hill, Wandsworth, London
SW18 2QZ
Telephone: 020 8516 2976
Fax: 020 8516 2992
Email: education@booktrust.org.uk
Web Site: www.booktrust.org.uk

Personnel:
HRH The Prince Philip, Duke of Edinburgh (Patron)
Viv Bird (Chief Executive)
Sue Horner (Chair)

Children's Book Week is an annual event which takes place
every October. It is a national event promoting the idea that
reading and books are fun!
Promotional resource materials are sent to schools and
libraries in England.

6154

CIANA LTD
24 Langroyd Road, London SW17 7PL
Telephone: 020 8682 1969
Fax: 020 8682 1997
Email: enquiries@ciana.co.uk
Web Site: www.ciana.co.uk

Personnel:
Robert Collie (Director)
Sarah Weedon (Director)

Organizers of two annual trade fairs for the remainder, over-
stock and promotional book market. Over 100,000 discounted books, stationery items, CDs and DVDs. The
September Fair is held in London Islington. The January Fair
is in the Barbican in the City of London.

6155

EDINBURGH INTERNATIONAL BOOK FESTIVAL
5A Charlotte Square, Edinburgh EH2 4DR
Telephone: 0131 718 5666
Email: admin@edbookfest.co.uk
Web Site: www.edbookfest.co.uk

Personnel:
Nick Barley (Director)
Sara Grady (Children & Education Programme Director)
Andrew Coulton (Administrative Director)
Amanda Barry (Marketing & PR Manager)
Lois Wolffe (Sponsorship & Development Manager)
James Shaw (Book Sales Manager)

The Edinburgh International Book Festival is a public celebra-
tion of the written word and takes place every August. Over
800 events feature writers from across the globe, bringing
authors together with their readers to talk about books, discuss ideas and share the latest thinking on a range of subjects from the environment to poetry.
The festival runs its own independent book sales operation on the site – a tented village in Edinburgh's Charlotte
Square Gardens – offering three large retail outlets including
a bookshop dedicated to children's books.

6156

FRANKFURT BOOK FAIR
Reineckstrasse 3, 60313 Frankfurt am Main, Germany
Telephone: +49 69 2102 0
Fax: +49 69 2102 227 & 277
Email: info@book-fair.com
Web Site: www.book-fair.com

Personnel:
Juergen Boos (Chief Executive Officer)
Katja Böhne (Director, Marketing & Communication)

Parent Company:
Germany: Börsenverein des Deutschen Buchhandels

The Frankfurt Book Fair is one of the largest book fairs in the
world with more than 7000 exhibitors from over 100 countries. Open exclusively to the trade for the first three days
and to the public for the last two days it attracts publishers,
booksellers, authors, agents, distributors and the whole
range of multimedia companies.
The Frankfurt Book Fair also organizes the participation of
German publishers at more than 25 international book fairs
and is associated with the Cape Town Book Fair in South
Africa and the Abu Dhabi International Book Fair. The Frankfurt Book Fair is a subsidiary of the German Publishers &
Booksellers Association.

6157

**GENERAL DIRECTORATE OF INTERNATIONAL
BOOK EXHIBITIONS & FAIRS**
Malaya Dmitrovka Street 16, Moscow 127006, Russia
Telephone: +7 (495) 699 4034, 699 9790 & 699 3466
Fax: +7 (495) 699 2539 & 299 1110
Email: mibf@mibf.ru & vBelov@mibf.ru
Web Site: www.mibf.ru

Personnel:
Nikolay Ph. Ovsyannikov (General Director)
Nina Sudjina (Head of Foreign Relations Department)
Valery Belov (Project Manager)

Organization of annual Moscow International and Russian
National Book Fairs, as well as collective and national book
stands of Russian publishers at the international book fairs.

6158

GÖTEBORG BOOK FAIR
412 94 Göteborg, Sweden
Telephone: +46 (031) 708 8400
Fax: +46 (031) 209103
Email: info@goteborg-bookfair.com
Web Site: www.goteborg-bookfair.com

Personnel:
Birgitta Jacobsson Ekblom (Public Relations Manager)
Anna Falck (Managing Director)

Göteborg Book Fair is one of the biggest bookfairs in northern Europe; 100,000 visits in four days, 900 exhibitors, 450
seminars and more than 1000 journalists covering the fair.
Göteborg Book Fair is arranged annually in September,
and takes place at the Swedish Exhibition Centre located in
the centre of the city of Göteborg.

6159

LEIPZIG BOOK FAIR
Leipziger Messe GmbH, Messe-Allee 1, 04356 Leipzig,
Germany
Telephone: +49 (0)341 678 8240
Fax: +49 (0)341 678 8242
Email: info@leipziger-buchmesse.de
Web Site: www.leipziger-buchmesse.de

Personnel:
Oliver Zille (Exhibition Director)

The Leipzig Book Fair is an independent, general book fair
concentrating on the German-speaking countries of Europe
(Germany, Austria and Switzerland, also the Central and
Eastern European countries). It also features international
book art and is additionally characterized by general themes
(e.g. audio books, travelling, music) which change from year
to year and which are highlighted by special events relating
to these themes. The commercial aspect of the Leipzig Book
Fair is accompanied by a wide range of fringe events, including a section for antique books and prints.

Visitors to the Leipzig Book Fair are mainly made up of
representatives from publishers, the book trade, libraries,
the newer media, the printing industry, and all other areas
connected with the production of books, including book
illustrators and graphic designers.
2011 dates: 17–20 March.

6160

THE LONDON BOOK FAIR
Gateway House, 28 The Quadrant, Richmond, Surrey
TW9 1DN
Telephone: 020 8271 2124
Fax: 020 8910 7930
Email: lbf.helpline@reedexpo.co.uk
Web Site: www.londonbookfair.co.uk

Personnel:
Alistair Burtenshaw (Group Exhibition Director)
Amy Webster (International Key Accounts Manager)
Emma Lowe (Sales Manager)
Matt Colgan (Sales Manager)
Barbara Davis (International Sales Manager)
Orna O'Brien (Conference Manager)
Rebecca Hearn (Marketing Executive)
Christine Dolan (Exhibition Co-ordinator)
Lucy Holland-Smith (Marketing Manager)

The London Book Fair is a global marketplace for rights
negotiation and the sale and distribution of content across
print, audio, TV, film and digital channels, bringing three
days of focused access to customers content and emerging
markets.
2011 Fair: 11–13 April at Earls Court, London. For further
information, please visit our website www.londonbook-
fair.co.uk

6161

THE LONDON LITERARY MAFIA
618b Finchley Road, London NW11 7RR
Telephone: 020 8455 4564
Email: lambhorn@gmail.com
Web Site: www.phantomcaptain.netfirms.com

Personnel:
Neil Hornick (Artistic Director)

Parent Company:
UK: The Phantom Captain

'Are You Reading Me?' – Established in 1997, The London
Literary Mafia (a.k.a. The Phantom Captain Literary Lions) is
a performance company specializing in entertainments,
talks and readings devised to brighten up literature festivals,
conferences, book launches, award ceremonies, promotions, luncheons and dinners, book fairs, writing courses
and related writer/reader-themed events. Activities draw on
the extensive experience of Neil Hornick, artistic director of
the company, as writer-director-actor and (under a pen-
name) as a professional literary consultant. Events can be
commissioned and designed for specific occasions.

6162

SALON DU LIVRE DE MONTREAL
300 rue St-Sacrement, Bureau 430, Montreal, PQ,
H2Y 1X4, Canada
Telephone: +1 (514) 845 2365
Fax: +1 (514) 845 7119
Email: slm.info@videotron.ca
Web Site: www.salondulivredemontreal.com

Personnel:
Francine Bois (General Manager)

The Salon du Livre de Montréal is a public book fair which
aims to promote reading.
2010 Fair: 17–22 November.

6163

TOKYO INTERNATIONAL BOOK FAIR
Reed Exhibitions Japan Ltd, 18F Shinjuku Nomura Building,
1-26-2 Nishi-Shinjuku, Shinjuku-ku, Tokyo 163-0570, Japan
Telephone: +81 3 3349 8507
Fax: +81 3 3345 7929
Email: tibf-eng@reedexpo.co.jp
Web Site: www.bookfair.jp/english

Personnel:
Kaoru Iwata (International Sales Director)

Janet Or *(International Sales Manager)*
Keisuke Amano *(Show Director)*

Parent Company:
UK: Reed Exhibition Companies

Tokyo International Book Fair (TIBF) represents the world's second largest single publishing market - Japan. TIBF has built its success upon the full support of its joint organization committee comprising the seven most influential Japanese publishing trade associations.

TIBF offers exhibitors opportunities to meet major book publishers, literary agents, distributors and booksellers from all over Japan and neighbouring countries such as Korea, Taiwan, Hong Kong and China, and develop extensive business opportunities including:
– international rights negotiation
– joint publishing projects
– direct book exports.
2011 Fair: 7–10 July at Tokyo Big Sight.
For more information, please contact Reed Exhibitions in Tokyo.

6164 ▬▬▬▬▬▬▬▬▬▬▬▬▬▬▬▬

WOMEN IN PUBLISHING
London
Email: info@wipub.org.uk
Web Site: www.womeninpublishing.org.uk

Women in Publishing works to promote the status of women working in publishing and related areas by helping them to develop their careers.

6165 ▬▬▬▬▬▬▬▬▬▬▬▬▬▬▬▬

WORLD BOOK DAY
c/o Booksellers' Association, 272 Vauxhall Bridge Road, London SW1V 1BA
Telephone: 020 7802 0802
Email: cathy.schofield@blueyonder.co.uk
Web Site: www.worldbookday.com

Personnel:
Cathy Schofield *(Word Book Day Co-ordinator)*

One of the UK's biggest celebrations of books and reading, held on the first Thursday in March. It is a partnership of publishers, booksellers and interested parties who work together to promote books and reading for the personal enrichment and enjoyment of all. One of the main aims of World Book Day is to encourage children to explore the pleasures of reading by providing them with the opportunity to have a book of their own. Thanks to the generosity of National Book Tokens and participating booksellers, schoolchildren are entitled to receive a World Book Day £1 book token, which can be exchanged for one of the specially published £1 books or is redeemable against a book or audiobook of their choice.

6.12 PUBLISHING REFERENCE BOOKS & PERIODICALS

6166 ▬▬▬▬▬▬▬▬▬▬▬▬▬▬▬▬

THE AUTHOR
84 Drayton Gardens, London SW10 9SB
Telephone: 020 7373 6642
Fax: 020 7373 5768
Email: TheAuthor@societyofauthors.org
Web Site: www.societyofauthors.org

Personnel:
Andrew Rosenheim *(Editor)*
Kate Pool *(Manager)*

Parent Company:
UK: The Society of Authors

Free to members. £12, post free, per copy for others. Annual subscription: £30, post free.

The quarterly journal of the Society of Authors. Articles on the legal, commercial and technical side of authorship.

6167 ▬▬▬▬▬▬▬▬▬▬▬▬▬▬▬▬

BOOKS FOR KEEPS
1 Effingham Road, London SE12 8NZ
Telephone: 020 8852 4953
Fax: 020 8318 7580
Email: enquiries@booksforkeeps.co.uk
Web Site: www.booksforkeeps.co.uk

Personnel:
Richard Hill *(Managing Director)*
Rosemary Stones *(Editor)*

ISSN: 0143-909X

Available to all via website.

Reviews all children's books and carries articles/features about authors, publishing, education, etc. Main readership - teachers, librarians and parents.

6168 ▬▬▬▬▬▬▬▬▬▬▬▬▬▬▬▬

BOOKS IN PRINT 2.0
Bowker (UK) Ltd, St Andrew's House, 18–20 St Andrew Street, London EC4A 3AG
Telephone: 020 7832 1770
Fax: 020 7832 1710
Email: sales@bowker.co.uk
Web Site: www.bowker.com

Personnel:
Doug McMillan *(Managing Director)*
Pam Roud *(Sales Director)*
Jo Grange *(Marketing Manager)*

Associated Companies:
USA: R. R. Bowker LLC; Cambridge Information Group

Annual subscription: from £2290.

Books in Print 2.0 has a new search and discovery interface that gives a faster and more efficient way to build collections and help users find the books they need. It incorporates global data; users may choose to subscribe to the international or USA side.

6169 ▬▬▬▬▬▬▬▬▬▬▬▬▬▬▬▬

BOOKS IN PRINT 2010–2011
Grey House Publishing, 4919 Route 22, PO Box 56, Amenia, NY 12501, USA
Telephone: +1 (518) 789 8700
Fax: +1 (518) 789 0556
Email: books@greyhouse.com
Web Site: www.greyhouse.com

Personnel:
Richard Gottlieb *(President)*
Leslie Mackenzie *(Publisher)*
Jessica Moody *(Vice-President, Marketing)*

Associated Companies:
USA: R. R. Bowker LLC; Cambridge Information Group

ISBN: 978 1 59237 636 0

Published August 2010, 7 volumes, hbk, $1045.

Full bibliographic and ordering information for over two million titles published or distributed in the USA.

6170 ▬▬▬▬▬▬▬▬▬▬▬▬▬▬▬▬

THE BOOKSELLER
5th Floor, Endeavour House, 189 Shaftesbury Avenue, London WC2H 8TJ
Telephone: 020 7420 6006
Fax: 020 7420 6103
Email: firstname.surname@bookseller.co.uk
Web Site: www.theBookseller.com

Personnel:
Nigel Roby *(Managing Director)*
Nicola Chin *(Advertising Manager)*
Samantha Missingham *(Head of Audience Marketing)*
Neill Denny *(Editor-in-Chief)*
Marzia Ghiselli *(Business Development Director)*

Parent Company:
UK: Bookseller Media Group Ltd

ISSN: 0006-7539

Weekly £4.40. Annual subscription: £177 (UK: public libraries), £186 (UK: all other businesses), £192 (Europe – airmail), £264 (rest of world – airmail).

The weekly newspaper of the book trade, offering in the course of a year over 7000 pages of news, analysis, features, letters, advertising and lists of books published in the UK. Major national and international events reported, regular authoritative articles on matters of trade, special features, book features and rights, stock market, legal and financial pages. Twice a year a six-month special issue of over 700 pages provides the best reference source for British publishers' publishing plans. Regular supplements in specialist areas.

6171 ▬▬▬▬▬▬▬▬▬▬▬▬▬▬▬▬

BOOKSELLER + PUBLISHER
Thorpe-Bowker, PO Box 6509, St Kilda Road Central, Vic 8008, Australia
Telephone: +61 (03) 8517 8333
Fax: +61 (03) 8517 8399
Email: bookseller.publisher@thorpe.com.au
Web Site: www.booksellerandpublisher.com.au

Personnel:
Gary Pengelly *(General Manager)*
Tim Coronel *(Publisher)*
Xeverie Swee *(Advertising Manager)*
Silvana Paolini *(Production & Design)*
Matthia Dempsey *(Editor in Chief)*

Parent Company:
Australia: Thorpe-Bowker
USA: R. R. Bowker LLC

Published continuously since 1921, *Bookseller + Publisher* magazine (and its offshoots the *Weekly Book Newsletter*, *WBN Media Extra* and *Australian Library News*) is the trade publication of the book industry for Australia and the region.

6172 ▬▬▬▬▬▬▬▬▬▬▬▬▬▬▬▬

BRITISH COPYRIGHT COUNCIL
Copyright House, 29–33 Berners Street, London W1T 3AB
Telephone: 01986 788122
Email: info@britishcopyright.org
Web Site: www.britishcopyright.org

The BCC was founded in 1965 and incorporated in 2007. It is a national consultative and advisory body representing those who create, hold interests in or manage rights in literary, dramatic, musical and artistic works, films, sound recordings, broadcasts and other material in which there are rights of copyright or related rights; and those who perform such works.

6173 ▬▬▬▬▬▬▬▬▬▬▬▬▬▬▬▬

CHILDREN'S BOOKS IN PRINT 2010
Grey House Publishing, 4919 Route 22, PO Box 56, Amenia, NY 12501, USA
Telephone: +1 (518) 789 8700
Fax: +1 (518) 789 0556
Email: books@greyhouse.com
Web Site: www.greyhouse.com

Personnel:
Richard Gottlieb *(President)*
Leslie Mackenzie *(Publisher)*
Jessica Moody *(Vice-President, Marketing)*

Associated Companies:
USA: R. R. Bowker LLC; Cambridge Information Group

ISBN: 978 0 8352 5025 2

Published December 2009, 2 volumes, $455.

Most complete list of currently available children's books published in the USA.

6174 ▬▬▬▬▬▬▬▬▬▬▬▬▬▬▬▬

CHILDREN'S WRITERS' & ARTISTS' YEARBOOK
A. & C. Black Publishers Ltd, 36 Soho Square, London W1D 3QY
Telephone: 020 7758 0201
Fax: 020 7758 0222

Email: wayb@acblack.com
Web Site: www.acblack.com &
www.writersandartists.co.uk

Personnel:
Jill Coleman *(Managing Director)*
Jonathan Glasspool *(Deputy Managing Director)*

Parent Company:
UK: Bloomsbury Publishing Plc

ISBN: 978 1 4081 28596

Annual. 2011 edition, published August 2010, £14.99.

A comprehensive guide to markets in all areas of children's media. Contains articles and information on a wide range of topics written by well-known authors and illustrators, best-selling publishers and editors, leading figures in TV and radio and other children's media experts. Also contains market contacts including book publishers and packagers, literary and art agents, magazines, TV and radio, festivals, courses and bookshops.

6175

THE COMPLETE DIRECTORY OF LARGE PRINT BOOKS AND SERIALS 2010

Grey House Publishing, 4919 Route 22, PO Box 56, Amenia, NY 12501, USA
Telephone: +1 (518) 789 8700
Fax: +1 (518) 789 0556
Email: books@greyhouse.com
Web Site: www.greyhouse.com

Personnel:
Richard Gottlieb *(President)*
Leslie Mackenzie *(Publisher)*
Jessica Moody *(Vice-President, Marketing)*

Associated Companies:
USA: R. R. Bowker LLC; Cambridge Information Group

ISBN: 978 1 59237 612 4

Published January 2010, 1 volume, $415.

Bigger than ever, this invaluable guide covers the large print field like no other resource. Inside you'll discover current, accurate bookfinding and ordering information on some 32,000 titles.

6176

DIRECTORY OF UK & IRISH BOOK PUBLISHERS

The Booksellers Association of UK & Ireland,
272 Vauxhall Bridge Road, London SW1V 1BA
Telephone: 020 7802 0802
Fax: 020 7802 0803
Email: mail@booksellers.org.uk
Web Site: www.booksellers.org.uk

Personnel:
Tim Godfray *(Chief Executive)*

BA online Directory of UK & Irish Book Publishers
(www.ukpublishers.net)

£25 (BA members), £50 (non-members).

Contains addresses and comprehensive information (including personnel, e-mail and www sites) about UK and Irish publishers, sales agents, remainder dealers, distributors and book wholesalers, including distribution arrangements in the UK for overseas publications. Also includes trade terms and returns information, details of product specialization such as audio books, electronic publishing and maps, plus a subject specialization index and ISBN prefixes.

6177

DIY: BOOKFINDING AND BOOKSELLING

Magna Graecia's Publishers, PO Box 342, Oxford OX2 7YF
Telephone: 01865 553653
Fax: 01865 553653
Email: info@magnagraeciaspublishers.co.uk
Web Site: www.magnagraeciaspublishers.co.uk

Personnel:
Luigi Gigliotti *(Research Editor Director)*

Single parts: £29.95 each, except Volume 5: £19.95. Complete set: £229.60 plus p&p.
   List of titles reported wanted by our members, clients in the UK and worldwide. The Register is updated daily. It is available on-line or in print format.
   Set of eight parts: Volume One (3 parts) by authors; Volume Two (2 parts) by titles; Volume Three (1 part) by categories; Volume Four (1 part) by subjects; Volume Five (1 part) by subjects.

6178

THE NEW WALFORD: GUIDE TO REFERENCE RESOURCES

Facet Publishing, 7 Ridgmount Street, London WC1E 7AE
Telephone: 020 7255 0597
Fax: 020 7255 0591
Email: info@facetpublishing.co.uk
Web Site: www.facetpublishing.co.uk

Personnel:
John Woolley *(Managing Director)*
Lena Stuart *(Marketing Manager)*
Rohini Ramachandran *(Sales Manager)*
Helen Carley *(Publisher)*
Kathryn Beecroft *(Production)*
Louise Le Bas *(Commissioning Editor)*
Lin Franklin *(Desk Editor)*

In three volumes. Vol. 1: Science, Technology and Medicine (**ISBN:** 978 1 85604 495 0, June 2005, 848 pp, hbk, £149.95). Vol. 2: The Social Sciences (**ISBN:** 978 1 85604 498 1, 2007, 720 pp, hbk, £159.95). Vol. 3: Arts, Humanities and General Reference (**ISBN:** 978 1 85604 499 8, 2010, 800 pp, hbk, £159.95).

6179

NEW WELSH REVIEW

PO Box 170, Aberystwyth, Ceredigion SY23 1WZ
Telephone: 01970 628410
Email: admin@newwelshreview.com
Web Site: www.newwelshreview.com

Personnel:
Kathryn Gray *(Editor)*
Sue Fisher *(Development Manager)*

New Welsh Review is a quarterly magazine which brings its readers a selection of new writing from Wales and the UK. Each issue includes a range of critical articles, book reviews, fiction and poetry. While the magazine's focus is on Welsh writing in English, its outlook is deliberately eclectic, encompassing broader European and international literary contexts.

6180

PUBLISHING, BOOKS & READING IN SUB-SAHARAN AFRICA: A CRITICAL BIBLIOGRAPHY

Hans Zell Publishing, Glais Bheinn, Lochcarron, Ross-shire IV54 8YB
Telephone: 01520 722951
Fax: 01520 722953
Email: hanszell@hanszell.co.uk
Web Site: www.hanszell.co.uk/pbrssa/index.shtml

Personnel:
Hans Zell *(Editor & Publisher)*

ISBN: 978 0 9541029 5 1

Published October 2008, 762 pp, cased, £130/€195/$260. Print and online (online access bundled with print). Online only £65/€97.50/$130.

This is a new, completely revised and fully updated edition of a much acclaimed bibliography published over ten years ago. Covering both print and online resources, it charts the growth of publishing and book development in the countries of Africa south of the Sahara, as well as including a very large number of entries on many other topics as they relate to books and reading in Africa. With over 2500 critically annotated citations, it is a detailed documentation resource on the current state of the book on the African continent. The annotations aim to provide informed commentary and critical analysis, and draw attention to particularly important contributions of the literature on publishing and the book in Africa. The bibliography is arranged under five major parts: (1) Serials and reference; (2) General, comparative and regional studies; (3) Country studies; (4) Studies by topic,

listing material by 30 topic headings; (5) Book industry training/Self-publishing

6181

SHEPPARD'S WORLD

Richard Joseph Publishers Ltd, PO Box 15, Torrington, Devon EX38 8ZJ
Telephone: 01805 625750
Email: office@sheppardsworld.co.uk
Web Site: www.sheppardsworld.co.uk

Personnel:
Richard Joseph *(Managing Director)*

Sheppard's World is a central reference source for businesses in the secondhand and antiquarian book trades, and includes dealers in antique maps, prints and ephemera. Subscribers can search on line (and in printed directories as and when published) covering all the details previously found in our printed directories – full contact details, opening hours, size of stock, major subjects stocked, credit cards accepted, and membership of trade associations. Details are posted to www.sheppardsworld.co.uk
   Dealers, collectors and members of the trade can receive our free trade newsletter Sheppard's Confidential which carries the latest trade news, news about forthcoming trade fairs and auctions – and reviews of fairs and auctions. The website www.sheppardsconfidential.com includes dealers' catalogues, calendar of fairs and auctions, and books wanted.

6182

THE TIMES LITERARY SUPPLEMENT

Times House, 1 Pennington Street, London E98 1BS
Telephone: 020 7782 5000
Fax: 020 7782 4966
Email: letters@the-tls.co.uk
Web Site: www.the-tls.co.uk

Personnel:
Sir Peter Stothard *(Editor)*
Alan Jenkins *(Deputy Editor)*
Robert Potts *(Managing Editor)*

The *TLS* is a weekly literary review, which carries reviews by leading authorities on up to 3000 books a year on literature and language, history, politics, philosophy, the arts and music, social studies, economics, natural history and many other subjects. It also reviews exhibitions and performing arts, carries articles of general interest, publishes poetry and has a letters page which is the principal forum for literary debate. It is essential reading for librarians, booksellers and academics, and also for its broad, worldwide general readership.

6183

WRITERS' & ARTISTS' YEARBOOK

A. & C. Black Publishers Ltd, 36 Soho Square, London W1D 3QY
Telephone: 020 7758 0201
Fax: 020 7758 0222
Email: wayb@acblack.com
Web Site: www.acblack.com &
www.writersandartists.co.uk

Personnel:
Jill Coleman *(Managing Director)*
Jonathan Glasspool *(Deputy Managing Director)*

Parent Company:
UK: Bloomsbury Publishing Plc

Annual. 2011 edition, published June 2010, £14.99.

A guide for freelance writers and artists. Details of English-language periodicals; of British, American and Commonwealth publishers; of British, American and Continental literary agents; and of press, art and photographic agencies. Practical information on such topics as copyright, libel and income tax; and on the Internet. Articles on writing for newspapers and the periodical press, on films, television, radio, artists, and markets for verse and drama.

6184

WRITERS' FORUM

[owned by Select Publisher Services Ltd]
PO Box 6337, Bournemouth BH1 9EH
Telephone: 01202 586848

Email: www.selectps.com
Web Site: www.writers-forum.com

Advertisement & PR Manager:
Wendy O'Brien, 3 Sandypark Farm, Old Rydon Lane, Exeter
EX2 7JW
Telephone: 01392 873270
Email: wendy.obrien99@googlemail.com

Personnel:
Tim Harris *(Publisher)*
Carl Styants *(Editor)*
Wendy O'Brien *(Advertising & PR Manager)*
Chris Wigg *(Subscriptions Manager)*

Parent Company:
UK: Select Publisher Services

Associated Companies:
UK: The Flower Press

12 issues a year. Subscription: UK £36; Europe £46; Rest of
World £52.

Writers' Forum is a major resource for all writers; covering
the who, why, where, what and how on the craft and business of writing; it runs monthly story and poetry competitions featuring large cash prizes where the winners are
printed in the magazine.
   Welcomes articles on any aspect of the craft and business
of writing. Length: 800–2000 words. Payment: by arrangement. Founded 1993.

6.13 TRAINING

6185

**CENTRE FOR PUBLISHING, UNIVERSITY COLLEGE
LONDON**
Department of Information Studies, UCL, Gower Street,
London WC1E 6BT
Telephone: 020 7679 2473
Fax: 020 7383 0557
Email: ma-publishing@ucl.ac.uk
Web Site: www.publishing.ucl.ac.uk

Personnel:
Prof Iain Stevenson *(Teaching Director)*
Prof David Nicholas *(Director)*
Dr Ian Rowlands *(Research Director)*
Prof Anthony Watkinson *(Industry Liaison)*
Ms Kerstin Michaels *(Administrator)*
Ms Lucy Lyons *(Administration Secretary)*
Dr Claire Warwick *(Electronic Publishing)*

Research and education in publishing. Offers a taught MA in
Publishing with pathways in Publishing, Electronic Publish-
ing and Magazine Publishing (from 2010). Also Mphil and
PhD research in publishing.

6186

CITY UNIVERSITY LONDON
Department of Journalism and Publishing,
Northampton Square, London EC1V 0HB
Telephone: 020 7040 0100
Fax: 020 7040 8594
Email: maryann.kernan.1@city.ac.uk
Web Site: www.city.ac.uk/journalism

Personnel:
Mary Ann Kernan *(Programme Director)*
Max Adam *(Visiting Lecturer)*
Richard Balkwill *(Visiting Lecturer)*
Brenda Stones *(Visiting Lecturer)*
Dominic Vaughan *(Visiting Lecturer)*
Stephen Mesquita *(Visiting Lecturer)*

Offers a full-time one year Master's Degree (MA) in Publishing Studies to prepare entrants and re-entrants to the industry. Comprises nine taught units, a 5–6 week industrial
placement and a dissertation. The department has close
industry links and the course is supervised by leading industry professionals.
   Also conducts research into publishing and supervises
research students.
   The MSc in Electronic Publishing offers a practical introduction to digital media, information management and
multi-media production. Please contact Dr Vesna Brujic-

Okretic in the Department of Informatics: 020 7040 8551 or
v.brujic-okretic@city.ac.uk.

6187

**EDINBURGH NAPIER UNIVERSITY, SCHOOL OF
ARTS & CREATIVE INDUSTRIES**
Craighouse Campus, Craighouse Road, Edinburgh
EH10 5LG
Telephone: 0131 455 6133
Fax: 0131 455 6193
Email: de.allan@napier.ac.uk
Web Site: www.napier.ac.uk\sci

Personnel:
Avril Gray *(MSc Publishing full and part-time Programme
Leader)*

BA and MSc Publishing. Higher education full and part-time
qualifications.

6188

GERMAN TUITION – BARBARA CLASSEN
2 Blackall Street, London EC2A 4AD
Telephone: 020 7613 3177
Email: barbara@germantuition.com
Web Site: www.germantuition.com

Personnel:
Barbara Classen *(Director/Tutor)*
Nicole Nagel *(Co-Tutor)*
Itamar Groisman *(Co-Tutor)*
Eva Friedrich *(Co-Tutor)*
Marina de Quay *(Co-Tutor)*
Janka Troeber *(Co-Tutor)*

The company offers lively German tuition at all levels and
specializes in German for the book trade. Students can
choose between one-to-one tuition or small groups of 4–6.
German Tuition also offers short-term tailor-made intensive
courses.
   Tutors are professional, experienced native speakers and
offer free consultations with trial lesson. Students may work
towards one of many recognized exams.
   Clients include publishers, booksellers, journalists and
other professionals.
   Classes are held in the central London German Tuition
office or in client's office/home 7 days a week.
   German Tuition London has a small branch in Freiburg,
Germany, offering tailor-made German language holidays
and Business German courses for the book trade, usually
over one week.

6189

LONDON COLLEGE OF COMMUNICATION
Elephant & Castle, London SE1 6SB
Telephone: 020 7514 6569
Fax: 020 7514 2035
Email: info@lcc.arts.ac.uk
Web Site: www.lcc.arts.ac.uk

Personnel:
Sandra Kemp *(Head of College)*

Parent Company:
UK: University of the Arts, London

MA, BA Hons Publishing.

6190

MARKETABILITY (UK) LTD
12 Sandy Lane, Teddington, Middx TW11 0DR
Telephone: 020 8977 2741
Fax: 020 8977 2741
Email: rachel@marketability.info
Web Site: www.marketability.info

Personnel:
Rachel Maund *(Director)*

Marketability provides practical training to publishers, both
through its small-group open workshop programme and
through tailored in-house training. These flexible courses
can be devised to cover a wide range of publishing issues. All
tutors are actively working for publishers in the areas in
which they are training. Our clients represent all areas of
publishing, from large academic, STM and university
presses, to small institutes, to large and small trade publishers. We devise and deliver training programmes for publish-

ers' associations internationally as well as in the UK. (See our
client list in our other entry under section 6.5 of this directory for more details.)
   The open course programme includes: academic marketing, e-marketing, copywriting, copywriting for the web,
schools marketing, direct mail, marketing to the book trade,
marketing planning, introduction to marketing in publishing, publicity, essential editorial skills, profitable commissioning. There are numerous in-house course options including
market research, working with authors, grammar and proofreading.
   Also provides marketing support and consultancy. See
separate entry under 6.5 Sales and Marketing Services.

6191

**OXFORD INTERNATIONAL CENTRE FOR
PUBLISHING STUDIES**
Oxford Brookes University, Buckley Building, Gipsy Lane,
Headington, Oxford OX3 0BP
Telephone: 01865 484967
Fax: 01865 484082
Email: angus.phillips@brookes.ac.uk
Web Site: www.brookes.ac.uk/publishing

Personnel:
Angus Phillips *(Director)*

The Oxford International Centre for Publishing Studies is
renowned for its degree programmes at both undergradu-
ate and postgraduate level. It is also active in the areas of
consultancy and professional development. It has excellent
contacts throughout the industry and already works closely
with industry organizations such as the Publishers Association, Independent Publishers Guild, and the London Book
Fair. Through organizations such as the Arts Council, British
Council and UK Trade & Investment, it is well known for its
work around the world. Staff have published widely on the
history and future of publishing. Its website has podcasts,
the latest news about the Centre, and listings of job vacan-
cies and work experience opportunities:
www.brookes.ac.uk/publishing

6192

**THE PUBLISHING TRAINING CENTRE AT BOOK
HOUSE**
45 East Hill, Wandsworth, London SW18 2QZ
Telephone: 020 8874 2718
Fax: 020 8870 8985
Email: publishing.training@bookhouse.co.uk
Web Site: www.train4publishing.co.uk

Personnel:
John Whitley *(Chief Executive)*
Orna O'Brien *(Course Administration Manager)*
Edelweiss Arnold *(Marketing Manager)*

The Publishing Training Centre was set up in 1979 as an educational charity for book and journal publishers.
   It offers over 60 different courses, most of which are run
several times a year. Courses are between one and five days
long and cover a wide range of publishing and management
skills.
   Most courses are held at The Publishing Training Centre's
London premises, though some are residential, and are
based mainly in the Oxford area.
   In addition, The Publishing Training Centre offers:
   – in-company courses in the UK and overseas;
   – distance learning courses in proofreading, editing, picture research, editorial project management and copywriting;
   – consultancy service;
   – training needs analysis;
   – books.
   The Publishing Training Centre is responsible for the development and updating of the industry-agreed standards for
each job function specific to publishing.

6193

SOCIETY FOR EDITORS AND PROOFREADERS
Erico House, 93–99 Upper Richmond Road, London
SW15 2TG
Telephone: 020 8785 5617
Fax: 020 8785 5618
Email: admin@sfep.org.uk
Web Site: www.sfep.org.uk

Personnel:
Sarah Price *(Chair)*
Justina Utuka *(Company Secretary)*

One of the major aims of the Society for Editors and Proofreaders is to help editorial freelances and staff to improve and update their skills. It is gradually building up a wide range of one-day courses, from 'Introduction to Proofreading' to 'Project Management' and 'On-Screen Editing', as well as more specialized courses. Most of its courses are run in London. About twice a year, two or three courses are run in Edinburgh, York and Bristol. Discounts are offered to members of the SFEP and to SI and NUJ members. Current details can be found on our website.

6194

STIRLING CENTRE FOR INTERNATIONAL PUBLISHING & COMMUNICATION
Department of English Studies, University of Stirling, Stirling FK9 4LA
Telephone: 01786 467510
Fax: 01786 466210
Email: alison.scott@stir.ac.uk
Web Site: www.publishing.stir.ac.uk

Personnel:
Prof Claire Squires (Director)
Dr Padmini Ray Murray (Lecturer)
Frances Sessford (Lecturer)

The Stirling Centre for International Publishing and Communication at the University of Stirling was established in 1982, and has since developed a global reputation for its postgraduate degrees in publishing, its research activities, and its industry links. Focusing on book, magazine, journal and digital publishing, the Centre trains the publishers of the future, provides opportunities for those currently working in the industry to reflect on their professional practice and, through its research, critically analyses the past, present and future of publishing.

The Centre offers an Mlitt in Publishing Studies and an MSc in International Publishing Management (one year full time or two years part time), as well as an Mres in Publishing Studies and possibilities for research at PhD level.

7 Appendices

7.1 PUBLISHERS CLASSIFIED BY FIELDS OF ACTIVITY

The categories shown below are those in which the publishers listed have declared their interest. The list is intended to be neither exclusive nor comprehensive.

Packagers are shown in *italic* print.

ACADEMIC & SCHOLARLY

Acumen Publishing Ltd
Adam Matthew Digital Ltd
Adam Matthew Publications Ltd
Age UK books
Al-Furqan Islamic Heritage Foundation
Alban Books Ltd
Alpha Science International Ltd
American Psychiatric Publishing Inc
Amnesty International International Secretariat
Amolibros
Peter Andrew Publishing Co Ltd
Anglo-Saxon Books
Ann Arbor Publishers Ltd
Anshan Ltd
Anthem Press
Apex Publishing Ltd
Archetype Publications Ltd
Arena Books (Publishers)
Ashgate Publishing Ltd
Ashmolean Museum Publications
Association for Learning Technology
Association for Scottish Literary Studies
Audio-Forum – The Language Source
Aurora Metro Publications Ltd
Austin & Macauley Publishers Ltd
Authentic Media
B & D Publishing
Ruth Bean Publishers
Bedford Freeman Worth (BFW)
Berg Publishers
Berghahn Books
Joseph Biddulph Publisher
Biohealthcare Publishing (Oxford) Ltd
Black Ace Books
Blackhall Publishing
Blackstaff Press
Blue Ocean Publishing
BML
Bodleian Library Publishing
BookPower
Borthwick Publications
Bowker (UK) Ltd
Boydell & Brewer Ltd
Brandbooks
British Association for Adoption & Fostering
British Library
British Museum Press

Business Education Publishers
CABI
Calypso Publications
Cambridge Archive Editions Ltd
Cambridge Publishing Management Ltd
Cambridge University Press
Capstone Global Library Ltd
Carnegie Publishing Ltd
Jon Carpenter Publishing
John Catt Educational Ltd
Cengage Learning EMEA Ltd
Centre for Economic Policy Research
Centre for Policy on Ageing
Chalksoft Ltd
Channel View Publications Ltd
Chartered Institute of Personnel & Development
Christian Education
Church of Ireland Publishing
CILT, the National Centre for Languages
James Clarke & Co
Clear Answer Medical Publishing Ltd
Coachwise Ltd
Coastal Publishing
Cois Life
Commonwealth Secretariat
The Continuum International Publishing Group Ltd
Cork University Press
Countyvise Ltd
Crossbow Education Ltd
Crown House Publishing Ltd
Dance Books Ltd
Darton, Longman & Todd Ltd
The Davenant Press
Richard Dennis Publications
Denor Press Ltd
J M Dent
Ditto International Ltd
Ashley Drake Publishing Ltd
Gerald Duckworth & Co Ltd
Dunedin Academic Press
Earthscan
Edinburgh University Press
Electric Word PLC
Edward Elgar Publishing Ltd
Elsevier Ltd
Emerald Group Publishing Ltd
Energy Institute
English Heritage
Equinox Publishing Ltd
The Erskine Press
Ethics International Press Ltd
Everyman's Library
Fabian Society
Facet Publishing
A. & A. Farmar
Feather Books
Five Leaves Publications
Floris Books
Four Courts Press
Friends of the Earth

Garnet Publishing Ltd
GeoCenter International Ltd
Geography Publications
Geological Society Publishing House
Gill & Macmillan Ltd
GLMP Ltd
The Goldsmith Press Ltd
Gracewing Publishing
Granta Editions
Greenleaf Publishing
Guildhall Press
Gwasg Gwenffrwd
John Harper Publishing
HarperCollins Publishers Ltd
Hart McLeod Ltd
Hart Publishing
Harvard University Press
Hawthorn Press
Roger Heavens
Helion & Co Ltd
Historical Publications Ltd
Hobnob Press
Hodder Education
Hodder Gibson
Holo Books
Human Kinetics Europe Ltd
C. Hurst & Co (Publishers) Ltd
Hymns Ancient & Modern Ltd
Hypatia Publications
Icon Books Ltd
Immunisation Information
Imperial College Press
Imprint Academic
Institute of Acoustics
Institute of Development Studies
Institute of Education (Publications), University of London
Institute of Employment Rights
Institution of Engineering and Technology (IET)
Intellect Ltd
International Medical Press
International Network for the Availability of Scientific Publications (INASP)
Irish Academic Press
The Islamic Texts Society
Ithaca Press
IVP
IWA Publishing
James & James (Publishers) Ltd
Janus Publishing Co Ltd
Jarndyce Booksellers
Kew Publishing
Jessica Kingsley Publishers
Sean Kingston Publishing
Kogan Page Ltd
Kube Publishing Ltd
Peter Lang Ltd
Learning Matters Ltd
The Lilliput Press Ltd
The Littman Library of Jewish Civilization
Liverpool University Press

Living Time® Media International
Lund Humphries
The Lutterworth Press
McGraw-Hill Education
Macmillan Publishers Ltd
Manchester University Press
Maney Publishing
Melisende
Mentor Books
Mercier Press Ltd
The Merlin Press Ltd
Merton Priory Press Ltd
Microform Academic Publishers
The MIT Press Ltd
M&K Publishing
Myriad Editions
The National Academies Press
The National Association for the Teaching of English (NATE)
National Children's Bureau
National Gallery Co Ltd
National Housing Federation
National Portrait Gallery Publications
The National Trust
Natural History Museum Publishing
NHS Immunisation Information
NMS Enterprises Limited - Publishing
Northcote House Publishers Ltd
Oak Tree Press
On Stream Publications Ltd
Onlywomen Press Ltd
Open Gate Press
Open University Worldwide
Oxfam Publishing
Oxford University Press
Packard Publishing Ltd
Pagoda Tree Press
Palgrave Macmillan
Panaf Books
Paragon Publishing
Paupers' Press
PCCS Books Ltd
Pearson Education
The Penguin Group (UK) Ltd
Pennant Books Ltd
Phaidon Press Ltd
The Pharmaceutical Press
Pickering & Chatto (Publishers) Ltd
Pier Professional Ltd
Pipers' Ash Ltd
Pluto Books Ltd
The Policy Press
Polity Press
Portland Press Ltd
Princeton University Press
ProQuest
Rand Publications
Round Hall Ltd
Roundhouse Publishing Ltd
Joseph Rowntree Foundation
Royal Collection Publications
Royal College of General Practitioners

Royal College of Psychiatrists
Royal Geographical Society (with Institute of British Geographers)
Royal Irish Academy
The Royal Society of Chemistry
Russell House Publishing Ltd
Sage Publications Ltd
Saint Albert's Press
St Jerome Publishing Ltd
Sandstone Press Ltd
Saqi Books
Schott Music Ltd
Scion Publishing Ltd
Scottish Text Society
SEDA Publications
Shepheard-Walwyn (Publishers) Ltd
SHU Publications Ltd
Sigel Press
Slightly Foxed
SLS Legal Publications (NI)
Smith Settle Printing & Bookbinding Ltd
Colin Smythe Ltd
Social Affairs Unit
The Society for Promoting Christian Knowledge (SPCK)
Society of Antiquaries of Scotland
The Society of Metaphysicians Ltd
Souvenir Press Ltd
Springer London
Stacey International
Stainer & Bell Ltd
Stott's Correspondence College
Sussex Academic Press
Sussex Publications
The Swedenborg Society
Symposium Publications Literary & Art
I. B. Tauris & Co Ltd
Taylor & Francis
tfm publishing Ltd
Thames & Hudson Ltd
Trentham Books
Troubador Publishing Ltd
TSO (The Stationery Office Ltd)
UCAS
University College of Dublin Press
University of Exeter Press
University of Hertfordshire Press
University of Ottawa Press
University of Wales Press
V&A Publishing
Vallentine Mitchell Publishers
Veritas Publications
Voltaire Foundation Ltd
Wallflower Press
Warburg Institute
Waterside Press
Waterside Press
Paul Watkins Publishing
Whiting & Birch Ltd
Whittles Publishing
Wiley Blackwell Publishing Ltd
John Wiley & Sons Ltd

WIT Press
Wolters Kluwer Health (P & E) Ltd
World Microfilms
XPL Publishing
Yale University Press London
Zed Books Ltd

ACCOUNTANCY & TAXATION

Age UK books
Peter Andrew Publishing Co Ltd
Austin & Macauley Publishers Ltd
Blackhall Publishing
BookPower
Cambridge University Press
Cengage Learning EMEA Ltd
The Chartered Institute of Public
  Finance & Accountancy
Corpus Publishing Ltd
Emerald Group Publishing Ltd
W. Foulsham & Co Ltd
Gower Publishing Co Ltd
Granta Editions
Harriman House
Hodder Education
In Easy Steps Ltd
Jordan Publishing Ltd
Kogan Page Ltd
McGraw-Hill Education
Nelson Thornes Ltd
Oak Tree Press
Palgrave Macmillan
ProQuest
Round Hall Ltd
Sigel Press
Thorogood Publishing Ltd
Trog Associates Ltd
Troubador Publishing Ltd
TSO (The Stationery Office Ltd)
Which? Ltd
John Wiley & Sons Ltd
XPL Publishing

AGRICULTURE

Austin & Macauley Publishers Ltd
Blackstaff Press
CABI
Cambridge University Press
Carnegie Publishing Ltd
Clairview Books Ltd
Commonwealth Secretariat
The Crowood Press Ltd
Earthscan
Eco-logic Books
Edward Elgar Publishing Ltd
Food Trade Press Ltd
Granta Editions
Institute of Development Studies
Manson Publishing Ltd
The National Academies Press
The National Trust
Old Pond Publishing Ltd
Oxfam Publishing
Packard Publishing Ltd
ProQuest
Smith Settle Printing &
  Bookbinding Ltd
Whittet Books Ltd
John Wiley & Sons Ltd

ANIMAL CARE & BREEDING

J. A. Allen
Amber Books Ltd
Anova Books
Austin & Macauley Publishers Ltd
BookPower
CABI
Calypso Publications
Capall Bann Publishing
Carroll & Brown Ltd
Chalksoft Ltd
Collins & Brown
Corpus Publishing Ltd
The Crowood Press Ltd
D & N Publishing
The Davenant Press
Findhorn Press Ltd
Robert Hale Ltd
HarperCollins Publishers Ltd
Haynes Publishing

Hodder Education
Manson Publishing Ltd
The National Academies Press
New Holland Publishers (UK) Ltd
Octopus Publishing Group
Quantum Publishing
Quiller Publishing Ltd
Regency House Publishing Ltd
Roundhouse Publishing Ltd
Souvenir Press Ltd
Toucan Books Ltd
Veloce Publishing Ltd
Whittet Books Ltd
John Wiley & Sons Ltd

ANTIQUES & COLLECTING

Antique Collectors' Club Ltd
Austin & Macauley Publishers Ltd
Ruth Bean Publishers
BLA Publishing Ltd
Bodleian Library Publishing
British Museum Press
Cameron Books
Carlton Publishing Group
Caxton Publishing Group Ltd
The Crowood Press Ltd
D & N Publishing
Richard Dennis Publications
W. Foulsham & Co Ltd
Granta Editions
Robert Hale Ltd
HarperCollins Publishers Ltd
Hodder Education
The Horizon Press
How To Books Ltd
Lund Humphries
The Lutterworth Press
Melisende
Merrell Publishers Ltd
Milestone Publications
Miller's
Mitchell Beazley
The National Trust
Newpro UK Ltd
NMS Enterprises Limited -
  Publishing
Octopus Publishing Group
The Orion Publishing Group Ltd
The Penguin Group (UK) Ltd
Prestel Publishing Ltd
Quantum Publishing
Quiller Publishing Ltd
Royal Collection Publications
Scala Publishers Ltd
Shire Publications Ltd
Souvenir Press Ltd
Thames & Hudson Ltd
Third Millennium Publishing Ltd
Unicorn Press
V&A Publishing
John Wiley & Sons Ltd
Philip Wilson Publishers

ARCHAEOLOGY

Archaeopress Ltd
Archetype Publications Ltd
Ashmolean Museum Publications
Batsford
Blackstaff Press
Borthwick Publications
Boydell & Brewer Ltd
British Museum Press
Brown & Whittaker Publishing
*Cambridge Publishing
  Management Ltd*
Cambridge University Press
Capall Bann Publishing
Carnegie Publishing Ltd
Colour Heroes Ltd
Cork University Press
Cornwall Editions Ltd
Council for British Archaeology
The Davenant Press
The Dovecote Press
Gerald Duckworth & Co Ltd
Edinburgh University Press
Emerald Group Publishing Ltd
English Heritage
Equinox Publishing Ltd
Ex Libris Press

Four Courts Press
Geography Publications
Glasgow Museums Publishing
Granta Editions
Halsgrove
Heart of Albion Press
Hobnob Press
Hodder Education
Holo Books
The King's England Press
Logaston Press
Maney Publishing
Melisende
Mercury Books
Merton Priory Press Ltd
Mitchell Beazley
The National Trust
Natural History Museum
  Publishing
NMS Enterprises Limited -
  Publishing
North York Moors National Park
  Authority
The Orion Publishing Group Ltd
The Penguin Group (UK) Ltd
Prestel Publishing Ltd
Reardon Publishing
Roundhouse Publishing Ltd
Royal Irish Academy
Scottish Children's Press
Scottish Cultural Press
Sessions of York
Shire Publications Ltd
Smith Settle Printing &
  Bookbinding Ltd
Society of Antiquaries of Scotland
Souvenir Press Ltd
Stacey International
Stobart Davies Ltd
Sussex Academic Press
I. B. Tauris & Co Ltd
Taylor & Francis
Thames & Hudson Ltd
Twelveheads Press
University of Exeter Press
University of Wales Press
Warburg Institute
John Wiley & Sons Ltd
WIT Press
Yale University Press London

ARCHITECTURE & DESIGN

Anova Books
Antique Collectors' Club Ltd
Architectural Association
  Publications
Ashgate Publishing Ltd
Aurum Press
AVA Publishing (UK) Ltd
Duncan Baird Publishers
Batsford
Berg Publishers
Joseph Biddulph Publisher
Black Dog Publishing Ltd
A. & C. Black (Publishers) Ltd
Bodleian Library Publishing
Boydell & Brewer Ltd
*Cambridge Publishing
  Management Ltd*
Cambridge University Press
Cameron Books
Carlton Publishing Group
Caxton Publishing Group Ltd
Centre for Alternative Technology
  Publications
Compendium Publishing Ltd
Conran Octopus
Cork University Press
Countryside Books
Richard Dennis Publications
Eric Dobby Publishing Ltd
Donhead Publishing Ltd
Gerald Duckworth & Co Ltd
Earthscan
Eco-logic Books
English Heritage
Fiell Publishing Ltd
Garnet Publishing Ltd
GeoCenter International Ltd
Gower Publishing Co Ltd
Gracewing Publishing

Graffeg
*Graham-Cameron Publishing &
  Illustration*
Granta Editions
Green Books
HarperCollins Publishers Ltd
Haynes Publishing
Hayward Publishing
The Herbert Press
Historical Publications Ltd
IHS BRE Press
Intellect Ltd
Laurence King Publishing Ltd
Dewi Lewis Publishing
Liberties Press
The Lilliput Press Ltd
Frances Lincoln Ltd
Liverpool University Press
Logaston Press
Lund Humphries
The Lutterworth Press
McGraw-Hill Education
Macmillan Publishers Ltd
Manchester University Press
Maney Publishing
Melisende
Merrell Publishers Ltd
The MIT Press Ltd
Mitchell Beazley
The National Trust
NMS Enterprises Limited -
  Publishing
W. W. Norton & Company Ltd
The O'Brien Press Ltd
Octopus Publishing Group
Packard Publishing Ltd
Palazzo Editions Ltd
Papadakis Publisher
Paragon Publishing
Phaidon Press Ltd
Prestel Publishing Ltd
ProQuest
Quadrille Publishing Ltd
Quantum Publishing
Random House UK Ltd
Redcliffe Press Ltd
Regency House Publishing Ltd
RotoVision SA
Roundhouse Publishing Ltd
Joseph Rowntree Foundation
Royal Collection Publications
Sansom & Co Ltd
Saqi Books
Scala Publishers Ltd
Sheldrake Press
Shire Publications Ltd
Stacey International
I. B. Tauris & Co Ltd
Taylor & Francis
teNeues Publishing UK Ltd
Thames & Hudson Ltd
Toucan Books Ltd
Tyne Bridge Publishing
Unicorn Press
V&A Publishing
Warburg Institute
Paul Watkins Publishing
David West Children's Books
John Wiley & Sons Ltd
Philip Wilson Publishers
WIT Press
World Microfilms
Worth Press Ltd
Yale University Press London

ATLASES & MAPS

AA Publishing
Ian Allan Publishing Ltd
Amber Books Ltd
Anthem Press
The Belmont Press
British Geological Survey
Carel Press
Caxton Publishing Group Ltd
Collins Geo
Cork University Press
G. L. Crowther
Discovery Walking Guides Ltd
Earthscan
Encyclopaedia Britannica (UK) Ltd
Express Newspapers

Folens Ltd
Geddes & Grosset
GeoCenter International Ltd
The Geographical Association
Geography Publications
Alan Godfrey Maps
Granta Editions
HarperCollins Publishers Ltd
Harvey Map Services Ltd
Haynes Publishing
Hodder Education
Instant-Books UK Ltd
Macmillan Education
Maney Publishing
Mercury Books
Michelin Maps & Guides
Moonlight Publishing Ltd
Myriad Editions
New Internationalist Publications
  Ltd
Octopus Publishing Group
Old House Books
Pagoda Tree Press
The Penguin Group (UK) Ltd
Philip's
Quantum Publishing
Reardon Publishing
Roundhouse Publishing Ltd
Royal Irish Academy
Tarquin Publications
Toucan Books Ltd
John Wiley & Sons Ltd

AUDIO BOOKS

Ashgrove Publishing
Austin & Macauley Publishers Ltd
Barefoot Books
BBC Audiobooks Ltd
Beautiful Books Ltd
John Blake Publishing Ltd
Bloomsbury Publishing Plc
Canongate Books
Cló Iar-Chonnachta
Cois Life
CSA Word
Day One Publications
Dref Wen Cyf/Ltd
Feather Books
Filament Publishing Ltd
Gatehouse Media Ltd
GLMP Ltd
Hachette Children's Books
HarperCollins Publishers Ltd
Hodder Education
Hodder & Stoughton General
ISIS Publishing Ltd
Kube Publishing Ltd
Little, Brown Book Group
Little People Books
Macmillan Children's Books Ltd
Macmillan Publishers Ltd
Magna Large Print Books
Naxos Audiobooks
The Orion Publishing Group Ltd
The Penguin Group (UK) Ltd
Ransom Publishing Ltd
Reardon Publishing
Scottish Cultural Press
Sigel Press
Simon & Schuster (UK) Ltd
Summersdale Publishers Ltd
Sussex Publications
Thorogood Publishing Ltd
Topical Resources
Transworld Publishers Ltd
Ulverscroft Large Print Books Ltd
Virgin Books Ltd

AVIATION

A.M.S. Educational Ltd
Air-Britain (Historians) Ltd
Ian Allan Publishing Ltd
Amber Books Ltd
Ashgate Publishing Ltd
Bene Factum Publishing Ltd
BLA Publishing Ltd
Bridge Books
Brooklands Books Ltd
Caxton Publishing Group Ltd
Conway

Countryside Books
Crécy Publishing Ltd
The Crowood Press Ltd
D & N Publishing
Energy Institute
Granta Institute
Greenhill Books / Lionel Leventhal Ltd
Grub Street
Halsgrove
Haynes Publishing
Hodder Education
The Horizon Press
Icon Books Ltd
IHS Jane's
McGraw-Hill Education
Osprey Publishing Ltd
Pipers' Ash Ltd
Quantum Publishing
Regency House Publishing Ltd
Special Interest Model Books Ltd
Stenlake Publishing Ltd
Truran
TSO (The Stationery Office Ltd)
John Wiley & Sons Ltd
Worth Press Ltd

BIBLIOGRAPHY & LIBRARY SCIENCE

Ashgate Publishing Ltd
Austin & Macauley Publishers Ltd
Bowker (UK) Ltd
British Library
Cambridge University Press
James Clarke & Co
The Continuum International Publishing Group Ltd
Facet Publishing
Galactic Central Publications
Gwasg Gwenffrwd
Hypatia Publications
Institute of Development Studies
International Network for the Availability of Scientific Publications (INASP)
Jarndyce Booksellers
LISU
Maney Publishing
The MIT Press Ltd
Nielsen Book
ProQuest
Sage Publications Ltd
Colin Smythe Ltd
Sussex Academic Press
Voltaire Foundation Ltd
Warburg Institute
Woodhead Publishing Ltd

BIOGRAPHY & AUTOBIOGRAPHY

A.M.S. Educational Ltd
Accent Press Ltd
Acumen Publishing Ltd
Ian Allan Publishing Ltd
Allison & Busby
Alma Books Ltd
Amolibros
Anshan Ltd
Apex Publishing Ltd
Arcadia Books Ltd
Ashgrove Publishing
Atlantic Books
Attic Press
Aureus Publishing Ltd
Aurum Press
Austin & Macauley Publishers Ltd
Authentic Media
Authorhouse UK Ltd
Back-In-Print Books Ltd
Barny Books
Beautiful Books Ltd
Bene Factum Publishing Ltd
Berghahn Books
Black Ace Books
Black Spring Press Ltd
Blackstaff Press
John Blake Publishing Ltd
Bloomsbury Publishing Plc
Bodleian Library Publishing
Book Castle Publishing Ltd

Marion Boyars Publishers Ltd
Brandon/Mount Eagle Publications
Nicholas Brealey Publishing
Brewin Books Ltd
British Library
Brown & Whittaker Publishing
Business Education Publishers
Cambridge Publishing Management Ltd
Cambridge University Press
Camra Books
Canongate Books
Carlton Publishing Group
Catcher Ltd
The Catholic Truth Society
Christian Focus Publications
James Clarke & Co
Cló Iar-Chonnachta
Colourpoint Books
Constable & Robinson Ltd
The Continuum International Publishing Group Ltd
David C Cook (UK)
Countyvise Ltd
Crimson Publishing
Cualann Press
Currach Press
Darton, Longman & Todd Ltd
The Davenant Press
Day One Publications
Dedalus Ltd
Richard Dennis Publications
Denor Press Ltd
J M Dent
The Derby Books Publishing Co Ltd
The Dovecote Press
Ashley Drake Publishing Ltd
Gerald Duckworth & Co Ltd
Equinox Publishing Ltd
The Erskine Press
Essential Works Ltd
Ex Libris Press
Express Newspapers
Faber & Faber Ltd
Family Publications
Fastprint
Feather Books
Filament Publishing Ltd
Flambard Press
Geography Publications
Gibson Square
Gill & Macmillan Ltd
The Goldsmith Press Ltd
Gomer
Gothic Image Publications
Gracewing Publishing
Granta Books
Granta Editions
Green Books
Guildhall Press
Gwasg Gwenffrwd
Gwasg Gwynedd
Hachette Scotland
Halban Publishers
Robert Hale Ltd
Halsgrove
Hammersmith Press Ltd
HarperCollins Publishers Ltd
Harvard University Press
Haynes Publishing
Highland Books
Hodder Faith
Hodder & Stoughton General
Alison Hodge Publishers
Holo Books
Honno (Welsh Women's Press)
Hymns Ancient & Modern Ltd
Hypatia Publications
Icon Books Ltd
Independent Music Press
Indepenpress Publishing Ltd
Irish Academic Press
ISIS Publishing Ltd
Janus Publishing Co Ltd
The Lilliput Press Ltd
Lion Hudson Plc
Little, Brown Book Group
The Littman Library of Jewish Civilization
Living Time® Media International

Luath Press Ltd
The Lutterworth Press
Macmillan Publishers Ltd
Mainstream Publishing Co (Edinburgh) Ltd
Maney Publishing
Maverick House Publishers
Mentor Books
Mercier Press Ltd
The Merlin Press Ltd
Merlin Publishing/Wolfhound Press
Merton Priory Press Ltd
Microform Academic Publishers
The MIT Press Ltd
Motor Racing Publications Ltd
Murdoch Books UK Ltd
John Murray Publishers
National Portrait Gallery Publications
The National Trust
Natural History Museum Publishing
New Island Books Ltd
NMS Enterprises Limited - Publishing
Northumbria University Press
The O'Brien Press Ltd
The Oleander Press
Omnibus Press
On Stream Publications Ltd
Onlywomen Press Ltd
Orion Books Ltd
The Orion Publishing Group Ltd
Peter Owen Publishers
Pan Macmillan
Panaf Books
Paragon Publishing
The Penguin Group (UK) Ltd
Pennant Books Ltd
Piatkus Books
Pipers' Ash Ltd
Plowright Press
Polperro Heritage Press
Portobello Books Ltd
Profile Books
Quadrille Publishing Ltd
Quartet Books
Quiller Publishing Ltd
The Radcliffe Press
Roundhouse Publishing Ltd
Route Publishing Ltd
Royal Collection Publications
St Pauls Publishing
Salt Publishing Ltd
Sandstone Press Ltd
Saqi Books
Scottish Children's Press
Scottish Cultural Press
Seren
Sessions of York
Shepheard-Walwyn (Publishers) Ltd
The Shetland Times Ltd
Shire Publications Ltd
Short Books Ltd
Simon & Schuster (UK) Ltd
Slightly Foxed
Smith Settle Printing & Bookbinding Ltd
Colin Smythe Ltd
Souvenir Press Ltd
Stacey International
Stainer & Bell Ltd
Rudolf Steiner Press
Strong Oak Press
Summer Palace Press
Summersdale Publishers Ltd
Sussex Academic Press
Tabb House
I. B. Tauris & Co Ltd
Thames & Hudson Ltd
Thorogood Publishing Ltd
F. A. Thorpe Publishing
Thoth Publications
Transworld Publishers Ltd
Troubador Publishing Ltd
Truran
Tyne Bridge Publishing
Ulverscroft Large Print Books Ltd
Unicorn Press
United Writers Publications Ltd

University of Wales Press
Merlin Unwin Books Ltd
V&A Publishing
Vallentine Mitchell Publishers
Veloce Publishing Ltd
Veritas Publications
Vertical Editions
Virgin Books Ltd
Voltaire Foundation Ltd
Warburg Institute
Waterside Press
Waterside Press
Weidenfeld & Nicolson
Whittles Publishing
John Wiley & Sons Ltd
Neil Wilson Publishing Ltd
Windhorse Publications
The Women's Press
Y Lolfa Cyf
Yale University Press London
Zymurgy Publishing

BIOLOGY & ZOOLOGY

Alpha Science International Ltd
Amolibros
Austin & Macauley Publishers Ltd
Bedford Freeman Worth (BFW)
Bender Richardson White
BLA Publishing Ltd
BookPower
Brown & Whittaker Publishing
CABI
Calypso Publications
Cambridge University Press
Clear Answer Medical Publishing Ltd
D & N Publishing
Earthscan
GLMP Ltd
HarperCollins Publishers Ltd
Harvard University Press
Hodder Education
Imperial College Press
Jones & Bartlett International
Kew Publishing
Letts and Lonsdale
McGraw-Hill Education
Macmillan Education
Macmillan Publishers Ltd
Manson Publishing Ltd
Mentor Books
The MIT Press Ltd
The National Academies Press
Natural History Museum Publishing
Nelson Thornes Ltd
NMS Enterprises Limited - Publishing
North York Moors National Park Authority
W. W. Norton & Company Ltd
Open University Worldwide
Oxford University Press
Packard Publishing Ltd
Palgrave Macmillan
Portland Press Ltd
Princeton University Press
ProQuest
Royal Irish Academy
Scion Publishing Ltd
Taylor & Francis
Ward Lock Educational Co Ltd
Whittet Books Ltd
John Wiley & Sons Ltd
WIT Press

CHEMISTRY

Alpha Science International Ltd
Anshan Ltd
Anthem Press
Atlantic Europe Publishing Co Ltd
Bedford Freeman Worth (BFW)
BLA Publishing Ltd
Cambridge University Press
Elsevier Ltd
Energy Institute
Food Trade Press Ltd
GLMP Ltd
HarperCollins Publishers Ltd
Hodder Education

Icon Books Ltd
Imperial College Press
Jones & Bartlett International
Letts and Lonsdale
McGraw-Hill Education
Macmillan Education
Macmillan Publishers Ltd
The National Academies Press
Nelson Thornes Ltd
W. W. Norton & Company Ltd
Open University Worldwide
Palgrave Macmillan
The Royal Society of Chemistry
Scion Publishing Ltd
Springer London
Taylor & Francis
Ward Lock Educational Co Ltd
John Wiley & Sons Ltd

CHILDREN'S BOOKS

A.M.S. Educational Ltd
Acair Ltd
Accent Press Ltd
Alban Books Ltd
Albion Press Ltd
Amolibros
Andersen Press Ltd
Anno Domini Publishing (ADPS)
Anova Books
Antique Collectors' Club Ltd
Apex Publishing Ltd
Atlantic Europe Publishing Co Ltd
Aurora Metro Publications Ltd
Austin & Macauley Publishers Ltd
Authentic Media
Authorhouse UK Ltd
Award Publications Ltd
b small publishing ltd
Badger Publishing Ltd
Barefoot Books
Barny Books
The Belmont Press
Bender Richardson White
Bene Factum Publishing Ltd
Bible Reading Fellowship
BLA Publishing Ltd
A. & C. Black (Publishers) Ltd
Bloomsbury Publishing Plc
Blue Ocean Publishing
Bodleian Library Publishing
Marion Boyars Publishers Ltd
British Association for Adoption & Fostering
British Museum Press
Brown Dog Books
Brown Wells & Jacobs Ltd
Cambridge University Press
Carlton Publishing Group
Catcher Ltd
The Catholic Truth Society
Caxton Publishing Group Ltd
Chalksoft Ltd
Chicken House Publishing Ltd
Child's Play (International) Ltd
Christian Education
Christian Focus Publications
Classical Comics Ltd
Cló Iar-Chonnachta
Coachwise Ltd
Cois Life
Cornwall Editions Ltd
Corpus Publishing Ltd
Countyvise Ltd
Cowley Robinson Publishing Ltd
CRW Publishing Ltd
Cyhoeddiadau'r Gair
Day One Publications
Delancey Press Ltd
J M Dent
Diagram Visual Information Ltd
Ashley Drake Publishing Ltd
Dramatic Lines
Dref Wen Cyf/Ltd
Eddison Sadd Editions Ltd
Egmont UK Ltd
Emma Treehouse Ltd
Encyclopaedia Britannica (UK) Ltd
English Heritage
Evans Publishing Group
Everyman's Library
Faber & Faber Ltd

Feather Books
Five Leaves Publications
Floris Books
The Fostering Network
W. Foulsham & Co Ltd
Galore Park Publishing Ltd
Geddes & Grosset
Glowworm Books & Gifts Ltd
Gomer
Graham-Cameron Publishing & Illustration
W. F. Graham (Northampton) Ltd
Guildhall Press
Gwasg Gwenffrwd
Gwasg Gwynedd
Hachette Children's Books
Peter Haddock Publishing
Haldane Mason Ltd
HarperCollins Publishers Ltd
Hawthorn Press
Haynes Publishing
Highland Books
Hodder Faith
Holland Publishing Plc
John Hunt Publishing Ltd
Icon Books Ltd
Indepenpress Publishing Ltd
Janus Publishing Co Ltd
The King's England Press
Jessica Kingsley Publishers
Kube Publishing Ltd
Letterland International Ltd
Letts and Lonsdale
Frances Lincoln Ltd
Lion Hudson Plc
Little People Books
Little Tiger Press
Living Time® Media International
Lomond Books Ltd
Luath Press Ltd
The Lutterworth Press
McCrimmon Publishing Co Ltd
Macmillan Children's Books Ltd
Macmillan Education
Macmillan Publishers Ltd
Mandrake of Oxford
Meadowside Children's Books & Gullane Children's Books
Medikidz Ltd
Mercier Press Ltd
Mercury Junior
Moonlight Publishing Ltd
MW Educational
The National Autistic Society (NAS)
National Gallery Co Ltd
The National Trust
Natural History Museum Publishing
Nelson Thornes Ltd
New Caramel London Ltd
New Island Books Ltd
Nicola Baxter Ltd
NMS Enterprises Limited - Publishing
North York Moors National Park Authority
The O'Brien Press Ltd
Onlywomen Press Ltd
Orion Books Ltd
The Orion Publishing Group Ltd
Orpheus Books Ltd
Oxford University Press
Palazzo Editions Ltd
Pan Macmillan
Paragon Publishing
The Penguin Group (UK) Ltd
Phaidon Press Ltd
Piccadilly Press
Pipers' Ash Ltd
Playne Books Ltd
Porthill Publishers
Positive Press Ltd
Tony Potter Publishing
Prestel Publishing Ltd
Prospera Publishing
Quantum Publishing
Random House Children's Books
Random House UK Ltd
Ransom Publishing Ltd
Raven's Quill Ltd
Ravette Publishing Ltd

Reader's Digest Children's Publishing Ltd
Reardon Publishing
Regency House Publishing Ltd
Ripley Publishing Ltd
Rising Stars UK Ltd
Robinswood Press Ltd
Roundhouse Publishing Ltd
St Pauls Publishing
Scala Publishers Ltd
Scholastic UK Ltd
Scottish Children's Press
Scripture Union Publishing
Seasquirt Publications
Sessions of York
SGC Books
Sharon House Publishing
Sheldrake Press
Short Books Ltd
Sigel Press
Simon & Schuster (UK) Ltd
Slightly Foxed
Solidus
Speechmark Publishing Ltd
Stacey International
Symposium Publications Literary & Art
Ta Ha Publishers Ltd
Tabb House
Tangerine Designs Ltd
Tangerine Designs Ltd
Tango Books Ltd
Tarquin Publications
Tate Publishing
Templar Publishing
Thames & Hudson Ltd
Titan Publishing Group
Top That! Publishing Plc
Topical Resources
Toucan Books Ltd
Troubador Publishing Ltd
TTS Group
Tucker Slingsby Ltd
United Writers Publications Ltd
Usborne Publishing Ltd
Veritas Publications
David West Children's Books
John Wiley & Sons Ltd
Wordsworth Editions Ltd
Y Lolfa Cyf
Zero to Ten
Zymurgy Publishing

CINEMA, VIDEO, TV & RADIO

Anova Books
Aurora Metro Publications Ltd
Aurum Press
Austin & Macauley Publishers Ltd
AVA Publishing (UK) Ltd
Berg Publishers
Berghahn Books
Black Dog Publishing Ltd
Black Spring Press Ltd
Blackstaff Press
Bloomsbury Publishing Plc
Marion Boyars Publishers Ltd
Carlton Publishing Group
The Continuum International Publishing Group Ltd
Currach Press
Edinburgh University Press
Essential Works Ltd
Faber & Faber Ltd
Gibson Square
Robert Hale Ltd
HarperCollins Publishers Ltd
Harvard University Press
Nick Hern Books
Hodder Education
Hodder & Stoughton General
Intellect Ltd
Living Time® Media International
Luath Press Ltd
Macmillan Publishers Ltd
Mainstream Publishing Co (Edinburgh) Ltd
Manchester University Press
Mentor Books
Merlin Publishing/Wolfhound Press
W. W. Norton & Company Ltd

The Orion Publishing Group Ltd
Peter Owen Publishers
Pan Macmillan
The Penguin Group (UK) Ltd
Phaidon Press Ltd
Pluto Books Ltd
Polity Press
ProQuest
Reardon Publishing
RotoVision SA
Roundhouse Publishing Ltd
Route Publishing Ltd
Simon & Schuster (UK) Ltd
Charles Skilton Ltd
Sussex Publications
I. B. Tauris & Co Ltd
Telos Publishing Ltd
Titan Publishing Group
Transworld Publishers Ltd
United Writers Publications Ltd
University of Exeter Press
University of Ottawa Press
Virgin Books Ltd
Wallflower Press
David West Children's Books
World Microfilms

COMPUTER SCIENCE

Age UK books
Alpha Science International Ltd
Anshan Ltd
Austin & Macauley Publishers Ltd
Bernard Babani (Publishing) Ltd
BLA Publishing Ltd
BookPower
Business Education Publishers
Cambridge University Press
Emerald Group Publishing Ltd
Haynes Publishing
Hodder Education
Imperial College Press
In Easy Steps Ltd
Institution of Engineering and Technology (IET)
Intellect Ltd
IOP Publishing
Jones & Bartlett International
McGraw-Hill Education
Macmillan Publishers Ltd
Market House Books Ltd
The MIT Press Ltd
Nelson Thornes Ltd
W. W. Norton & Company Ltd
Open University Worldwide
O'Reilly UK Ltd
Palgrave Macmillan
Paragon Publishing
ProQuest
Springer London
TSO (The Stationery Office Ltd)
Usborne Publishing Ltd
John Wiley & Sons Ltd
WIT Press

COOKERY, WINES & SPIRITS

Accent Press Ltd
Anova Books
Antique Collectors' Club Ltd
Appletree Press Ltd
Ashgrove Publishing
Attic Press
Aurora Metro Publications Ltd
Aurum Press
Austin & Macauley Publishers Ltd
Authorhouse UK Ltd
Duncan Baird Publishers
Bene Factum Publishing Ltd
Blackstaff Press
John Blake Publishing Ltd
Bloomsbury Publishing Plc
Blue Ocean Publishing
Bossiney Books Ltd
Brown Dog Books
Brown & Whittaker Publishing
Cambridge Publishing Management Ltd
Camra Books
Capall Bann Publishing
Carlton Publishing Group
Carnegie Publishing Ltd

Jon Carpenter Publishing
Carroll & Brown Ltd
Caxton Publishing Group Ltd
Clairview Books Ltd
Collins & Brown
Conran Octopus
Copper Beech Publishing Ltd
Currach Press
Dedalus Ltd
Ashley Drake Publishing Ltd
Eddison Sadd Editions Ltd
Elliott & Thompson
Equinox Publishing Ltd
Ex Libris Press
Faber & Faber Ltd
Findhorn Press Ltd
W. Foulsham & Co Ltd
Garnet Publishing Ltd
Geddes & Grosset
GeoCenter International Ltd
Gill & Macmillan Ltd
The Goldsmith Press Ltd
Graffeg
Granta Editions
Green Books
Grub Street
Hachette Scotland
Haldane Mason Ltd
HarperCollins Publishers Ltd
Ian Henry Publications Ltd
Hodder Education
Hodder & Stoughton General
Alison Hodge Publishers
How To Books Ltd
Indepenpress Publishing Ltd
Kyle Cathie Ltd
Liberties Press
Frances Lincoln Ltd
Lomond Books Ltd
Luath Press Ltd
Macmillan Publishers Ltd
Mainstream Publishing Co (Edinburgh) Ltd
Mercier Press Ltd
Merlin Publishing/Wolfhound Press
Merrell Publishers Ltd
Mitchell Beazley
Murdoch Books UK Ltd
National Gallery Co Ltd
The National Trust
Need2Know
New Holland Publishers (UK) Ltd
New Internationalist Publications Ltd
NMS Enterprises Limited - Publishing
Northumbria University Press
W. W. Norton & Company Ltd
The O'Brien Press Ltd
Octopus Publishing Group
On Stream Publications Ltd
The Orion Publishing Group Ltd
Paragon Publishing
The Penguin Group (UK) Ltd
Phaidon Press Ltd
Piatkus Books
Prospect Books
Quadrille Publishing Ltd
Quantum Publishing
Quiller Publishing Ltd
Random House UK Ltd
Roundhouse Publishing Ltd
Saqi Books
Scottish Children's Press
Scottish Cultural Press
Sheldrake Press
Sigma Press
Simon & Schuster (UK) Ltd
Charles Skilton Ltd
Special Interest Model Books Ltd
Stacey International
Stobart Davies Ltd
Summersdale Publishers Ltd
Toucan Books Ltd
Transworld Publishers Ltd
Troubador Publishing Ltd
Truran
Merlin Unwin Books Ltd
Virgin Books Ltd
John Wiley & Sons Ltd
Neil Wilson Publishing Ltd

Y Lolfa Cyf

CRAFTS & HOBBIES

Accent Press Ltd
Amber Books Ltd
Anova Books
Apex Publishing Ltd
Aurum Press
Bernard Babani (Publishing) Ltd
Batsford
Ruth Bean Publishers
Black Dog Publishing Ltd
A. & C. Black (Publishers) Ltd
Blue Ocean Publishing
Brown Wells & Jacobs Ltd
Calypso Publications
Cambridge Publishing Management Ltd
Capall Bann Publishing
Carlton Publishing Group
Caxton Publishing Group Ltd
Collins & Brown
Conran Octopus
Crimson Publishing
The Crowood Press Ltd
D & N Publishing
Eco-logic Books
Eco-logic Books
F+W Media International (formerly David & Charles)
Floris Books
W. Foulsham & Co Ltd
Stanley Gibbons
Haldane Mason Ltd
Robert Hale Ltd
HarperCollins Publishers Ltd
Hawthorn Press
Haynes Publishing
Hodder Education
The Ilex Press Ltd
In Easy Steps Ltd
Indepenpress Publishing Ltd
Instant-Books UK Ltd
The Ivy Press Ltd
Kyle Cathie Ltd
Lomond Books Ltd
The Lutterworth Press
Macmillan Publishers Ltd
Melisende
Mercier Press Ltd
Merlin Publishing/Wolfhound Press
Merrell Publishers Ltd
Mitchell Beazley
Murdoch Books UK Ltd
New Holland Publishers (UK) Ltd
Octopus Publishing Group
Old House Books
The Orion Publishing Group Ltd
The Penguin Group (UK) Ltd
Quadrille Publishing Ltd
Quantum Publishing
Quiller Publishing Ltd
Random House UK Ltd
Regency House Publishing Ltd
Roundhouse Publishing Ltd
Sigma Press
Souvenir Press Ltd
Special Interest Model Books Ltd
Stenlake Publishing Ltd
Stobart Davies Ltd
Stott's Correspondence College
Summersdale Publishers Ltd
Tarquin Publications
Thames & Hudson Ltd
Top That! Publishing Plc
Toucan Books Ltd
Tucker Slingsby Ltd
Unicorn Press
Usborne Publishing Ltd
V&A Publishing
David West Children's Books
Willow Island Editions
Y Lolfa Cyf

CRIME

Accent Press Ltd
Allison & Busby
Alma Books Ltd
Amber Books Ltd

Apex Publishing Ltd
Arcadia Books Ltd
Atlantic Books
Austin & Macauley Publishers Ltd
Austin & Macauley Publishers Ltd
Authorhouse UK Ltd
Back-In-Print Books Ltd
Bitter Lemon Press
Blackstaff Press
John Blake Publishing Ltd
Canongate Books
Carlton Publishing Group
Caxton Publishing Group Ltd
CBD Research Ltd
Countyvise Ltd
Eric Dobby Publishing Ltd
Gerald Duckworth & Co Ltd
Express Newspapers
Feather Books
Five Leaves Publications
Flambard Press
W. Foulsham & Co Ltd
Gibson Square
Guildhall Press
Hachette Scotland
Robert Hale Ltd
HarperCollins Publishers Ltd
Haynes Publishing
Hodder & Stoughton General
Honno (Welsh Women's Press)
Icon Books Ltd
Indepenpress Publishing Ltd
ISIS Publishing Ltd
ISIS Publishing Ltd
Janus Publishing Co Ltd
Jordan Publishing Ltd
Librario Publishers Ltd
Little, Brown Book Group
Living Time® Media International
Luath Press Ltd
Macmillan Publishers Ltd
Mainstream Publishing Co
   (Edinburgh) Ltd
Mandrake of Oxford
Maverick House Publishers
Mentor Books
Mercier Press Ltd
Merlin Publishing/Wolfhound
   Press
New Holland Publishers (UK) Ltd
Onlywomen Press Ltd
The Orion Publishing Group Ltd
Paragon Publishing
The Penguin Group (UK) Ltd
Pennant Books Ltd
Piatkus Books
Profile Books
Quantum Publishing
Random House UK Ltd
Sandstone Press Ltd
Simon & Schuster (UK) Ltd
Social Affairs Unit
Summersdale Publishers Ltd
Telos Publishing Ltd
F. A. Thorpe Publishing
Transworld Publishers Ltd
Troubador Publishing Ltd
Truran
Ulverscroft Large Print Books Ltd
Merlin Unwin Books Ltd
Waterside Press
Waterside Press
Neil Wilson Publishing Ltd
The Women's Press

DO-IT-YOURSELF

Anova Books
Austin & Macauley Publishers Ltd
Caxton Publishing Group Ltd
Centre for Alternative Technology
   Publications
Collins & Brown
The Crowood Press Ltd
D & N Publishing
Express Newspapers
F+W Media International
   (formerly David & Charles)
Granta Editions
Green Books
HarperCollins Publishers Ltd
Haynes Publishing

Hodder Education
Indepenpress Publishing Ltd
Janus Publishing Co Ltd
Murdoch Books UK Ltd
New Holland Publishers (UK) Ltd
Octopus Publishing Group
The Penguin Group (UK) Ltd
Quadrille Publishing Ltd
Quantum Publishing
Random House UK Ltd
Roundhouse Publishing Ltd
Stobart Davies Ltd
John Wiley & Sons Ltd

ECONOMICS

Adam Matthew Publications Ltd
Peter Andrew Publishing Co Ltd
Anthem Press
Arena Books (Publishers)
Ashgate Publishing Ltd
Atlantic Books
Austin & Macauley Publishers Ltd
Berghahn Books
Blackhall Publishing
BookPower
Nicholas Brealey Publishing
Cambridge University Press
Jon Carpenter Publishing
Centre for Economic Policy
   Research
The Chartered Institute of Public
   Finance & Accountancy
Commonwealth Secretariat
The Continuum International
   Publishing Group Ltd
Delta Alpha Publishing Ltd
J M Dent
Earthscan
Edward Elgar Publishing Ltd
Emerald Group Publishing Ltd
Euromonitor International
Fabian Society
Garnet Publishing Ltd
Gibson Square
Gill & Macmillan Ltd
Granta Editions
Green Books
HarperCollins Publishers Ltd
Harriman House
Harvard University Press
Hodder Education
Icon Books Ltd
Imperial College Press
Institute of Development Studies
Institute of Employment Rights
Ithaca Press
Janus Publishing Co Ltd
Jarndyce Booksellers
Kube Publishing Ltd
Luath Press Ltd
McGraw-Hill Education
Macmillan Publishers Ltd
Manchester University Press
Mehring Books
Mentor Books
The Merlin Press Ltd
Microform Academic Publishers
The MIT Press Ltd
National Extension College Trust
   Ltd
Nelson Thornes Ltd
W. W. Norton & Company Ltd
Open University Worldwide
Oxfam Publishing
Oxford University Press
Palgrave Macmillan
Pickering & Chatto (Publishers) Ltd
Pluto Books
The Policy Press
Princeton University Press
Profile Books
ProQuest
Rand Publications
Random House UK Ltd
Joseph Rowntree Foundation
Sage Publications Ltd
Saqi Books
Shepheard-Walwyn (Publishers)
   Ltd
Social Affairs Unit
Spokesman

Stacey International
Sussex Academic Press
Taylor & Francis
Troubador Publishing Ltd
TSO (The Stationery Office Ltd)
University of Ottawa Press
Virgin Books Ltd
John Wiley & Sons Ltd
Yale University Press London
Zed Books Ltd

EDUCATIONAL & TEXTBOOKS

A.M.S. Educational Ltd
Acair Ltd
Accent Press Ltd
Acumen Publishing Ltd
Adamson Publishing Ltd
Advance Materials
Age UK books
Alban Books Ltd
Philip Allan Publishers Ltd
Alpha Science International Ltd
American Psychiatric Publishing
   Inc
Anglo-Saxon Books
Ann Arbor Publishers Ltd
Anshan Ltd
Anthem Press
Ashgate Publishing Ltd
Association for Scottish Literary
   Studies
Atlantic Europe Publishing Co Ltd
Aurora Metro Publications Ltd
Austin & Macauley Publishers Ltd
AVA Publishing (UK) Ltd
B & D Publishing
Bernard Babani (Publishing) Ltd
Back-In-Print Books Ltd
Badger Publishing Ltd
Barefoot Books
BEAM Education
Bender Richardson White
Berg Publishers
Bible Reading Fellowship
A. & C. Black (Publishers) Ltd
Blue Ocean Publishing
BookPower
Borthwick Publications
Brandbooks Ltd
Brilliant Publications
Business Education Publishers
Butterfingers Books
Calypso Publications
Cambridge Publishing
   Management Ltd
Cambridge University Press
Capall Bann Publishing
Capstone Global Library Ltd
Careers Europe
Carel Press
Catcher Ltd
The Catholic Truth Society
John Catt Educational Ltd
Cengage Learning EMEA Ltd
Centre for Alternative Technology
   Publications
Chalksoft Ltd
Channel View Publications Ltd
Chartered Institute of Personnel &
   Development
Chemcord Ltd
Christian Education
Christian Focus Publications
CILT, the National Centre for
   Languages
Claire Publications
Classical Comics Ltd
Clear Answer Medical Publishing
   Ltd
Cló Iar-Chonnachta
Coachwise Ltd
Cois Life
Collins Geo
Colour Heroes Ltd
Colourpoint Books
The Continuum International
   Publishing Group Ltd
Coordination Group Publications
   Ltd (CGP Ltd)
Crimson Publishing
Crossbow Education Ltd

Darton, Longman & Todd Ltd
The Davenant Press
Delta ELT Publishing Ltd
Denor Press Ltd
Diagram Visual Information Ltd
Ditto International Ltd
Ashley Drake Publishing Ltd
Dramatic Lines
Dref Wen Cyf/Ltd
Earthscan
ECO Publishing International Ltd
Edinburgh University Press
Educational Planning Books Ltd
Egon Publishers Ltd
Edward Elgar Publishing Ltd
Elm Publications
Elsevier Ltd
Emerald Group Publishing Ltd
English Heritage
Equinox Publishing Ltd
Ethics International Press Ltd
Evans Publishing Group
Facet Publishing
Filament Publishing Ltd
First & Best in Education
Folens Ltd
The Fostering Network
W. Foulsham & Co Ltd
Freelance Market News
Friends of the Earth
Galore Park Publishing Ltd
Gatehouse Media Ltd
The Geographical Association
Geography Publications
Gill & Macmillan Ltd
GLMP Ltd
Gower Publishing Co Ltd
Graham-Cameron Publishing &
   Illustration
Granada Learning
Granta Editions
Greenleaf Publishing
Guildhall Press
Gwasg Gwenffrwd
Hachette Children's Books
Haldane Mason Ltd
John Harper Publishing
HarperCollins Publishers Ltd
Hart McLeod Ltd
Hawthorn Press
Ian Henry Publications Ltd
Hinton House Publishers Ltd
Hodder Education
Hodder Gibson
Holland Publishing Plc
Hopscotch Educational Publishing
How To Books Ltd
Human Kinetics Europe Ltd
Hymns Ancient & Modern Ltd
Hypatia Publications
Icon Books Ltd
Immunisation Information
In Easy Steps Ltd
Indepenpress Publishing Ltd
Institute of Development Studies
Institute of Education
   (Publications), University of
   London
Institution of Engineering and
   Technology (IET)
Intellect Ltd
International Network for the
   Availability of Scientific
   Publications (INASP)
Janus Publishing Co Ltd
Jolly Learning Ltd
Jones & Bartlett International
Hilda King Educational
Jessica Kingsley Publishers
Kogan Page Ltd
Kube Publishing Ltd
Learning Matters Ltd
Learning Together
Letterland International Ltd
Letts and Lonsdale
Lexus Ltd
Lion Hudson Plc
Little People Books
The Littman Library of Jewish
   Civilization
Liverpool University Press
Living Time® Media International

The Lutterworth Press
McCrimmon Publishing Co Ltd
McGraw-Hill Education
Macmillan Education
Macmillan Publishers Ltd
Management Pocketbooks Ltd
Manchester University Press
Medikidz Ltd
Mentor Books
MW Educational
The National Academies Press
The National Association for the
   Teaching of English (NATE)
The National Autistic Society
   (NAS)
National Children's Bureau
National Extension College Trust
   Ltd
National Housing Federation
Natural History Museum
   Publishing
Need2Know
Nelson Thornes Ltd
NHS Immunisation Information
Nicola Baxter Ltd
NMS Enterprises Limited -
   Publishing
North York Moors National Park
   Authority
Northcote House Publishers Ltd
Norwood Publishers Ltd
Oak Tree Press
Open University Worldwide
Optimus Professional Publishing
Oxford University Press
Packard Publishing Ltd
Palgrave Macmillan
Paragon Publishing
Pearson Education
Philip's
The Policy Press
Polity Press
Portland Press Ltd
Positive Press Ltd
Practical Pre-School Books
Princeton University Press
Radcliffe Publishing Ltd
Rand Publications
Ransom Publishing Ltd
Rising Stars UK Ltd
Robinswood Press Ltd
Round Hall Ltd
The Royal Society of Chemistry
Russell House Publishing Ltd
Sage Publications Ltd
St Jerome Publishing Ltd
Saqi Books
Scholastic UK Ltd
SchoolPlay Productions Ltd
Scripture Union Publishing
SHU Publications Ltd
Sigel Press
Singing Dragon Publishers
Social Affairs Unit
The Society of Metaphysicians Ltd
Southgate Publishers
Speechmark Publishing Ltd
Stacey International
Rudolf Steiner Press
STRI (Sports Turf Research
   Institute)
Supportive Learning Publications
   (SLP)
Sussex Academic Press
Symposium Publications Literary &
   Art
Tango Books Ltd
Tarquin Publications
Taylor & Francis
Teachit (UK) Ltd
Thames & Hudson Ltd
Third Millennium Publishing Ltd
THRASS (UK) Ltd
Topical Resources
Trentham Books
Trotman Publishing
TSO (The Stationery Office Ltd)
TTS Group
UCAS
United Writers Publications Ltd
University of Hertfordshire Press
University of Ottawa Press

University of Wales Press
Veritas Publications
Wallflower Press
Ward Lock Educational Co Ltd
Waterside Press
Waterside Press
Whittles Publishing
Wiley Blackwell Publishing Ltd
John Wiley & Sons Ltd
Wolters Kluwer Health (P & E) Ltd
Young People in Focus

ELECTRONIC (EDUCATIONAL)

Adam Matthew Digital Ltd
Adamson Publishing Ltd
Alpha Science International Ltd
Anthem Press
Atlantic Europe Publishing Co Ltd
AVA Publishing (UK) Ltd
Bernard Babani (Publishing) Ltd
Bowker (UK) Ltd
Cambridge University Press
Carel Press
Catcher Ltd
Chalksoft Ltd
Claire Publications
Coachwise Ltd
Collins Geo
Commonwealth Secretariat
The Continuum International
  Publishing Group Ltd
Crimson Publishing
Elm Publications
Emerald Group Publishing Ltd
Encyclopaedia Britannica (UK) Ltd
Ethics International Press Ltd
Evans Publishing Group
First & Best in Education
Folens Ltd
The Geographical Association
GLMP Ltd
HarperCollins Publishers Ltd
Hart McLeod Ltd
Heart of Albion Press
Hodder Education
Holland Publishing Plc
Human Kinetics Europe Ltd
Imperial College Press
Intellect Ltd
Jolly Learning Ltd
Kogan Page Ltd
Letterland International Ltd
Life of Riley Productions Ltd
Living Time® Media International
McCrimmon Publishing Co Ltd
McGraw-Hill Education
National Extension College Trust
  Ltd
National Gallery Co Ltd
Nelson Thornes Ltd
New Internationalist Publications
  Ltd
Open University Worldwide
Optimus Professional Publishing
Palgrave Macmillan
Paragon Publishing
ProQuest
Radcliffe Publishing Ltd
Ransom Publishing Ltd
Rising Stars UK Ltd
Robinswood Press Ltd
Royal Geographical Society (with
  Institute of British
  Geographers)
The Royal Society of Chemistry
Russell House Publishing Ltd
Sage Publications Ltd
The Society of Metaphysicians Ltd
Summersdale Publishers Ltd
THRASS (UK) Ltd
TTS Group
Waterside Press
John Wiley & Sons Ltd

ELECTRONIC (ENTERTAINMENT)

Bernard Babani (Publishing) Ltd
Carlton Publishing Group
HarperCollins Publishers Ltd
Holland Publishing Plc

The Ilex Press Ltd
Living Time® Media International
MP Publishing Ltd
Summersdale Publishers Ltd
Thorogood Publishing Ltd

ELECTRONIC (PROFESSIONAL & ACADEMIC)

Adam Matthew Digital Ltd
Alpha Science International Ltd
Anthem Press
Ashgate Publishing Ltd
Bernard Babani (Publishing) Ltd
Berg Publishers
Berghahn Books
Blackhall Publishing
BML
Bowker (UK) Ltd
Cambridge University Press
Centre for Policy on Ageing
The Continuum International
  Publishing Group Ltd
Earthscan
Edinburgh University Press
Edward Elgar Publishing Ltd
Emerald Group Publishing Ltd
Energy Institute
Equinox Publishing Ltd
Ethics International Press Ltd
Facet Publishing
Filament Publishing Ltd
Garnet Publishing Ltd
Gwasg Gwenffrwd
HarperCollins Publishers Ltd
Haynes Publishing
Hodder Education
Human Kinetics Europe Ltd
IHS Jane's
Imperial College Press
In Easy Steps Ltd
Institution of Engineering and
  Technology (IET)
Intellect Ltd
International Medical Press
International Network for the
  Availability of Scientific
  Publications (INASP)
IOP Publishing
IWA Publishing
Jordan Publishing Ltd
Kogan Page Ltd
Learning Matters Ltd
McGraw-Hill Education
Macmillan Publishers Ltd
Maney Publishing
Microform Academic Publishers
Myriad Editions
National Children's Bureau
National Gallery Co Ltd
Outsell Inc / EPS
Oxford University Press
Paragon Publishing
Pearson Education
The Pharmaceutical Press
Pier Professional Ltd
Portland Press Ltd
Princeton University Press
ProQuest
Radcliffe Publishing Ltd
Round Hall Ltd
Royal Geographical Society (with
  Institute of British
  Geographers)
The Royal Society of Chemistry
Russell House Publishing Ltd
St Jerome Publishing
Summersdale Publishers Ltd
Taylor & Francis
Teachit (UK) Ltd
Thorogood Publishing Ltd
TSO (The Stationery Office Ltd)
Voltaire Foundation Ltd
Waterside Press
Waterside Press
John Wiley & Sons Ltd
WIT Press
Wolters Kluwer Health (P & E) Ltd
Woodhead Publishing Ltd

ENGINEERING

Alpha Science International Ltd
Peter Andrew Publishing Co Ltd
Anshan Ltd
Anthem Press
Bernard Babani (Publishing) Ltd
BookPower
Cambridge University Press
Conway
Earthscan
Emerald Group Publishing Ltd
Energy Institute
Geological Society Publishing
  House
Gower Publishing Co Ltd
Granta Editions
IChemE
Imperial College Press
Institute of Physics & Engineering
  in Medicine
Institution of Engineering and
  Technology (IET)
IWA Publishing
McGraw-Hill Education
Macmillan Publishers Ltd
Maney Publishing
The National Academies Press
Nelson Thornes Ltd
Open University Worldwide
Palgrave Macmillan
ProQuest
Special Interest Model Books Ltd
Springer London
Taylor & Francis
TSO (The Stationery Office Ltd)
Tyne Bridge Publishing
Whittles Publishing
John Wiley & Sons Ltd
WIT Press
Woodhead Publishing Ltd

ENGLISH AS A FOREIGN LANGUAGE

Austin & Macauley Publishers Ltd
A. & C. Black (Publishers) Ltd
*Cambridge Publishing
  Management Ltd*
Cambridge University Press
Cengage Learning EMEA Ltd
Classical Comics Ltd
Delta ELT Publishing Ltd
Folens Ltd
Gatehouse Media Ltd
GLMP Ltd
The Goldsmith Press Ltd
*Graham-Cameron Publishing &
  Illustration*
Gwasg Gwenffrwd
HarperCollins Publishers Ltd
Hodder Education
Letterland International Ltd
Living Time® Media International
McGraw-Hill Education
Macmillan Education
Macmillan Publishers Ltd
Moonlight Publishing Ltd
New Island Publishing
Open University Worldwide
Oxford University Press
Paragon Publishing
Robinswood Press Ltd
Sandstone Press Ltd
Speechmark Publishing Ltd
Supportive Learning Publications
  (SLP)
Symposium Publications Literary &
  Art

ENVIRONMENT & DEVELOPMENT STUDIES

Alpha Science International Ltd
Anshan Ltd
Anthem Press
Ashgate Publishing Ltd
Atlantic Europe Publishing Co Ltd
Austin & Macauley Publishers Ltd
Berghahn Books
Black Dog Publishing Ltd
CABI

Cambridge University Press
Capall Bann Publishing
Jon Carpenter Publishing
Centre for Alternative Technology
  Publications
Channel View Publications Ltd
Clairview Books Ltd
Collins Geo
Commonwealth Secretariat
Cork University Press
Earthscan
Eco-logic Books
ECO Publishing International Ltd
Edward Elgar Publishing Ltd
Emerald Group Publishing Ltd
Energy Institute
Ethics International Press Ltd
Fabian Society
Friends of the Earth
Geological Society Publishing
  House
Green Books
Greenleaf Publishing
HarperCollins Publishers Ltd
Hodder Education
IHS BRE Press
Imperial College Press
Instant-Books UK Ltd
Institute of Development Studies
Intellect Ltd
Macmillan Education
Macmillan Publishers Ltd
Maney Publishing
The MIT Press Ltd
Myriad Editions
The National Academies Press
Nelson Thornes Ltd
New Internationalist Publications
  Ltd
North York Moors National Park
  Authority
On Stream Publications Ltd
Open Gate Press
Open University Worldwide
Oxfam Publishing
Packard Publishing Ltd
Palgrave Macmillan
Paragon Publishing
Plowright Press
Pluto Books Ltd
Princeton University Press
Royal Geographical Society (with
  Institute of British
  Geographers)
Sandstone Press Ltd
Saqi Books
Alastair Sawday Publishing
Scottish Cultural Press
Sigel Press
Social Affairs Unit
The Society of Metaphysicians Ltd
Southgate Publishers
STRI (Sports Turf Research
  Institute)
Sussex Academic Press
Tango Books Ltd
Taylor & Francis
Thames & Hudson Ltd
John Wiley & Sons Ltd
WIT Press
Woodhead Publishing Ltd
Zed Books Ltd

FASHION & COSTUME

Amber Books Ltd
Anova Books
Antique Collectors' Club Ltd
Aurum Press
Austin & Macauley Publishers Ltd
AVA Publishing (UK) Ltd
Batsford
Ruth Bean Publishers
Berg Publishers
Black Dog Publishing Ltd
A. & C. Black (Publishers) Ltd
Carlton Publishing Group
Collins & Brown
Copper Beech Publishing Ltd
Eric Dobby Publishing Ltd
Gerald Duckworth & Co Ltd

Essential Works Ltd
Fiell Publishing Ltd
Glasgow Museums Publishing
Granta Editions
The Herbert Press
Independent Music Press
The Ivy Press Ltd
Laurence King Publishing Ltd
Maney Publishing
Mercury Junior
Merlin Publishing/Wolfhound
  Press
Merrell Publishers Ltd
Mitchell Beazley
National Portrait Gallery
  Publications
The National Trust
Nelson Thornes Ltd
The Orion Publishing Group Ltd
Peter Owen Publishers
Phaidon Press Ltd
Prestel Publishing Ltd
ProQuest
Quadrille Publishing Ltd
Quantum Publishing
RotoVision SA
Roundhouse Publishing Ltd
Royal Collection Publications
Saqi Books
Charles Skilton Ltd
Stott's Correspondence College
Thames & Hudson Ltd
Unicorn Press
V&A Publishing
David West Children's Books
Yale University Press London

FICTION

Acair Ltd
Accent Press Ltd
Alban Books Ltd
Albyn Press
Allison & Busby
Alma Books Ltd
Amolibros
Apex Publishing Ltd
Arcadia Books Ltd
Arena Books (Publishers)
Ashgrove Publishing
Atlantic Books
Aurora Metro Publications Ltd
Austin & Macauley Publishers Ltd
Authorhouse UK Ltd
Back-In-Print Books Ltd
The Banton Press
Barny Books
Beautiful Books Ltd
Birlinn Ltd
Bitter Lemon Press
Black Ace Books
Black Spring Press Ltd
Blackstaff Press
Bloomsbury Publishing Plc
Blue Sky Press
Marion Boyars Publishers Ltd
Brandon/Mount Eagle
  Publications
Brewin Books Ltd
Canongate Books
Capuchin Classics
Catcher Ltd
Caxton Publishing Group Ltd
Classical Comics Ltd
Cló Iar-Chonnachta
Cois Life
Collins & Brown
Colour Heroes Ltd
Colourpoint Books
Constable & Robinson Ltd
Cornwall Editions Ltd
Countyvise Ltd
CRW Publishing Ltd
Dedalus Ltd
Delancey Press Ltd
Denor Press Ltd
J M Dent
Dref Wen Cyf/Ltd
Gerald Duckworth & Co Ltd
Enitharmon Press
Everyman's Library
Faber & Faber Ltd

Fastprint
Feather Books
Five Leaves Publications
Flambard Press
Freelance Market News
The Gallery Press
Garnet Publishing Ltd
Victor Gollancz Ltd
Granta Books
Guildhall Press
Hachette Children's Books
Hachette Scotland
Halban Publishers
Robert Hale Ltd
Harlequin Mills & Boon Ltd
HarperCollins Publishers Ltd
Ian Henry Publications Ltd
Highland Books
Hodder Faith
Hodder & Stoughton General
Honno (Welsh Women's Press)
John Hunt Publishing Ltd
Icon Books Ltd
Indepenpress Publishing Ltd
ISIS Publishing Ltd
Ithaca Press
Janus Publishing Co Ltd
Jarndyce Booksellers
Legend Press
The Lilliput Press Ltd
Little, Brown Book Group
Living Time® Media International
Luath Press Ltd
Macmillan Publishers Ltd
Magna Large Print Books
Mandrake of Oxford
Mentor Books
Mercier Press Ltd
MP Publishing Ltd
John Murray Publishers
Myriad Editions
Myrmidon Books Ltd
New Internationalist Publications Ltd
New Island Books Ltd
Oneworld Classics
Onlywomen Press Ltd
Orion Books Ltd
The Orion Publishing Group Ltd
Peter Owen Publishers
Pan Macmillan
Paragon Publishing
The Penguin Group (UK) Ltd
Piatkus Books
Pipers' Ash Ltd
Piquant Editions
Portobello Books Ltd
Profile Books
Prospera Publishing
Publishing House
Pushkin Press
Quartet Books
Random House UK Ltd
Raven's Quill Ltd
Ripley Publishing Ltd
Rising Stars UK Ltd
Robinswood Press Ltd
Route Publishing Ltd
Salt Publishing Ltd
Sandstone Press Ltd
Saqi Books
Scottish Children's Press
Seren
Short Books Ltd
Sigel Press
Silver Moon Books
Simon & Schuster (UK) Ltd
Charles Skilton Ltd
Slightly Foxed
Solidus
Spokesman
Sportsbooks Ltd
Tabb House
Telegram
Telos Publishing Ltd
Templar Publishing
Thorogood Publishing Ltd
F. A. Thorpe Publishing
Tindal Street Press
Top That! Publishing Plc
Total-E-Ntwined Ltd
Transworld Publishers Ltd

Troubador Publishing Ltd
Truran
Ulverscroft Large Print Books Ltd
United Writers Publications Ltd
Usborne Publishing Ltd
Voltaire Foundation Ltd
Waterside Press
Weidenfeld & Nicolson
The Women's Press
Wordsworth Editions Ltd
Worth Press Ltd
Y Lolfa Cyf

FINE ART & ART HISTORY

Albyn Press
Anova Books
Antique Collectors' Club Ltd
Apex Publishing Ltd
Archetype Publications Ltd
Ashgate Publishing Ltd
Ashmolean Museum Publications
Aureus Publishing Ltd
Austin & Macauley Publishers Ltd
Duncan Baird Publishers
Bene Factum Publishing Ltd
Berg Publishers
Black Dog Publishing Ltd
A. & C. Black (Publishers) Ltd
Blackthorn Press
Bodleian Library Publishing
British Library
British Museum Press
Cambridge Publishing Management Ltd
Cambridge University Press
Cameron Books
Canongate Books
Carlton Publishing Group
Caxton Publishing Group Ltd
Cork University Press
D & N Publishing
Richard Dennis Publications
Gerald Duckworth & Co Ltd
F+W Media International (formerly David & Charles)
Flambard Press
Four Courts Press
GeoCenter International Ltd
Gibson Square
Glasgow Museums Publishing
The Goldsmith Press Ltd
Gothic Image Publications
Granta Editions
Green Books
Hachette Children's Books
Halsgrove
HarperCollins Publishers Ltd
Harvard University Press
Hayward Publishing
The Herbert Press
Alison Hodge Publishers
Hypatia Publications
The Ilex Press Ltd
Janus Publishing Co Ltd
Kew Publishing
Laurence King Publishing Ltd
Dewi Lewis Publishing
The Lilliput Press Ltd
Frances Lincoln Ltd
The Littman Library of Jewish Civilization
Liverpool University Press
Logaston Press
Lund Humphries
The Lutterworth Press
Macmillan Publishers Ltd
Mainstream Publishing Co (Edinburgh) Ltd
Mandrake of Oxford
Maney Publishing
Melisende
Merlin Publishing/Wolfhound Press
Merrell Publishers Ltd
The MIT Press Ltd
Mitchell Beazley
Moonlight Publishing Ltd
John Murray Publishers
National Extension College Trust Ltd
National Galleries of Scotland

National Gallery Co Ltd
National Gallery of Ireland
National Portrait Gallery Publications
The National Trust
Natural History Museum Publishing
NMS Enterprises Limited - Publishing
Northumbria University Press
W. W. Norton & Company Ltd
Octopus Publishing Group
Open University Worldwide
The Orion Publishing Group Ltd
Papadakis Publisher
Phaidon Press Ltd
Piquant Editions
Porthill Publishers
Prestel Publishing Ltd
ProQuest
Quantum Publishing
Quiller Publishing Ltd
Random House UK Ltd
Redcliffe Press Ltd
RotoVision SA
Roundhouse Publishing Ltd
Royal Collection Publications
Sansom & Co Ltd
Saqi Books
Scala Publishers Ltd
Seren
Charles Skilton Ltd
Stacey International
Rudolf Steiner Press
Strong Oak Press
Sussex Academic Press
Sussex Publications
Symposium Publications Literary & Art
Tate Publishing
I. B. Tauris & Co Ltd
Thames & Hudson Ltd
Third Millennium Publishing Ltd
Toucan Books Ltd
Truran
Tyne Bridge Publishing
Unicorn Press
V&A Publishing
Warburg Institute
Paul Watkins Publishing
Philip Wilson Publishers
Yale University Press London

GARDENING

Amolibros
Anova Books
Antique Collectors' Club Ltd
Aurum Press
Austin & Macauley Publishers Ltd
Batsford
Bene Factum Publishing Ltd
BLA Publishing Ltd
Black Dog Publishing Ltd
Cambridge Publishing Management Ltd
Capall Bann Publishing
Caxton Publishing Group Ltd
Centre for Alternative Technology Publications
Chalksoft Ltd
Conran Octopus
Constable & Robinson Ltd
Copper Beech Publishing Ltd
The Crowood Press Ltd
Dedalus Ltd
J M Dent
Eco-logic Books
Ex Libris Press
Express Newspapers
Findhorn Press Ltd
Floramedia UK Ltd
Floris Books
W. Foulsham & Co Ltd
Friends of the Earth
GeoCenter International Ltd
Graffeg
Green Books
HarperCollins Publishers Ltd
Hawthorn Press
Haynes Publishing
Hodder Education

Alison Hodge Publishers
How To Books Ltd
Kew Publishing
Kyle Cathie Ltd
Frances Lincoln Ltd
Luath Press Ltd
Macmillan Publishers Ltd
Merrell Publishers Ltd
Mitchell Beazley
Murdoch Books UK Ltd
The National Trust
Need2Know
New Holland Publishers (UK) Ltd
W. W. Norton & Company Ltd
The O'Brien Press Ltd
Octopus Publishing Group
The Orion Publishing Group Ltd
Packard Publishing Ltd
Pan Macmillan
The Penguin Group (UK) Ltd
Quadrille Publishing Ltd
Quantum Publishing
Quiller Publishing Ltd
Random House UK Ltd
Roundhouse Publishing Ltd
SGC Books
Shire Publications Ltd
Slightly Foxed
Souvenir Press Ltd
Stacey International
Thames & Hudson Ltd
Toucan Books Ltd
Transworld Publishers Ltd
Truran
Whittet Books Ltd
John Wiley & Sons Ltd
Willow Island Editions
Zymurgy Publishing

GAY & LESBIAN STUDIES

Arcadia Books Ltd
Aurora Metro Publications Ltd
Austin & Macauley Publishers Ltd
Cló Iar-Chonnachta
Cork University Press
Findhorn Press Ltd
Gibson Square
Guildhall Press
Hymns Ancient & Modern Ltd
Indepenpress Publishing Ltd
Manchester University Press
The MIT Press Ltd
Onlywomen Press Ltd
Peter Owen Publishers
St Jerome Publishing Ltd
Saqi Books
Silver Moon Books
Charles Skilton Ltd
Taylor & Francis
Thames & Hudson Ltd
Virgin Books Ltd
The Women's Press

GENDER STUDIES

Adam Matthew Digital Ltd
Adam Matthew Publications Ltd
Anthem Press
Arcadia Books Ltd
Ashgate Publishing Ltd
Attic Press
Aurora Metro Publications Ltd
Berghahn Books
Cambridge University Press
Capall Bann Publishing
Commonwealth Secretariat
Cork University Press
Edinburgh University Press
Equinox Publishing Ltd
Garnet Publishing Ltd
HarperCollins Publishers Ltd
Harvard University Press
Hawthorn Press
Hodder Education
Holo Books
C. Hurst & Co (Publishers) Ltd
Hymns Ancient & Modern Ltd
Icon Books Ltd
Institute of Development Studies
Intellect Ltd
Irish Academic Press

Ithaca Press
Karnac Books Ltd
Macmillan Publishers Ltd
Manchester University Press
The Merlin Press Ltd
The MIT Press Ltd
Myriad Editions
New Island Books Ltd
W. W. Norton & Company Ltd
Onlywomen Press Ltd
Oxfam Publishing
Palgrave Macmillan
PCCS Books Ltd
Piatkus Books
Plowright Press
Pluto Books Ltd
The Policy Press
Polity Press
Russell House Publishing Ltd
Sage Publications Ltd
St Jerome Publishing Ltd
Saqi Books
Sheldon Press
Souvenir Press Ltd
Sussex Academic Press
I. B. Tauris & Co Ltd
Taylor & Francis
Trentham Books
University of Ottawa Press
University of Wales Press
The Women's Press
Yale University Press London
Zed Books Ltd

GEOGRAPHY & GEOLOGY

Albyn Press
Amolibros
Anthem Press
Ashgate Publishing Ltd
Atlantic Europe Publishing Co Ltd
Bedford Freeman Worth (BFW)
Blackstaff Press
British Geological Survey
Cambridge University Press
Chalksoft Ltd
Collins Geo
G. L. Crowther
Diagram Visual Information Ltd
The Dovecote Press
Dunedin Academic Press
Earthscan
Ex Libris Press
The Geographical Association
Geography Publications
Geological Society Publishing House
Graffeg
HarperCollins Publishers Ltd
Hodder Education
Alison Hodge Publishers
Icon Books Ltd
Imray Laurie Norie & Wilson Ltd
Jones & Bartlett International
Letts and Lonsdale
Luath Press Ltd
McGraw-Hill Education
Macmillan Education
Maney Publishing
Manson Publishing Ltd
Mentor Books
Mercury Books
The National Academies Press
Natural History Museum Publishing
Nelson Thornes Ltd
NMS Enterprises Limited - Publishing
North York Moors National Park Authority
W. W. Norton & Company Ltd
Old House Books
Open University Worldwide
Optimus Professional Publishing
Packard Publishing Ltd
Pagoda Tree Press
Palgrave Macmillan
Roadmaster Publishing
Royal Geographical Society (with Institute of British Geographers)
Scottish Cultural Press

Stacey International
Supportive Learning Publications
(SLP)
Sussex Academic Press
I. B. Tauris & Co Ltd
Taylor & Francis
Truran
TSO (The Stationery Office Ltd)
University of Hertfordshire Press
Ward Lock Educational Co Ltd
David West Children's Books
Whittles Publishing
John Wiley & Sons Ltd
WIT Press

GUIDE BOOKS

AA Publishing
Accent Press Ltd
Age UK books
Albyn Press
Apex Publishing Ltd
Appletree Press Ltd
Arris Publishing Ltd
Back-In-Print Books Ltd
Birlinn Ltd
Blackstaff Press
Bossiney Books Ltd
Bradt Travel Guides Ltd
British Geological Survey
Brown & Whittaker Publishing
Camra Books
Canongate Books
Capall Bann Publishing
The Catholic Truth Society
Cicerone Press Ltd
Collins Geo
Colour Heroes Ltd
Countryside Books
Crimson Publishing
Currach Press
D & N Publishing
Day One Publications
Discovery Walking Guides Ltd
The Dovecote Press
English Heritage
Everyman's Library
Ex Libris Press
Express Newspapers
FHG Guides Ltd
Findhorn Press Ltd
Footprint Travel Guides
W. Foulsham & Co Ltd
Garnet Publishing Ltd
GeoCenter International Ltd
The Geographical Association
Gill & Macmillan Ltd
Gothic Image Publications
Gracewing Publishing
Graffeg
Granta Editions
Green Books
Guildhall Press
Halsgrove
Harden's Ltd
HarperCollins Publishers Ltd
Haynes Publishing
Heart of Albion Press
Hobnob Press
Holo Books
The Horizon Press
How To Books Ltd
Instant-Books UK Ltd
Frances Lincoln Ltd
Logaston Press
Lomond Books Ltd
Luath Press Ltd
Macmillan Publishers Ltd
Mainstream Publishing Co
(Edinburgh) Ltd
Mentor Books
Merlin Publishing/Wolfhound
Press
Merrell Publishers Ltd
Michelin Maps & Guides
National Gallery Co Ltd
National Portrait Gallery
Publications
The National Trust
New Holland Publishers (UK) Ltd
New Island Books Ltd

NMS Enterprises Limited -
Publishing
North York Moors National Park
Authority
Northumbria University Press
The O'Brien Press Ltd
Old House Books
The Orion Publishing Group Ltd
Pagoda Tree Press
Pan Macmillan
The Penguin Group (UK) Ltd
Random House UK Ltd
Reardon Publishing
Roadmaster Publishing
Roundhouse Publishing Ltd
Royal Collection Publications
S. B. Publications
Alastair Sawday Publishing
Scala Publishers Ltd
Sheldrake Press
The Shetland Times Ltd
Shire Publications Ltd
Sigma Press
Simon & Schuster (UK) Ltd
Charles Skilton Ltd
Stacey International
Stobart Davies Ltd
Summersdale Publishers Ltd
I. B. Tauris & Co Ltd
Thames & Hudson Ltd
Third Millennium Publishing Ltd
Travel Publishing Ltd
Troubador Publishing Ltd
Truran
Twelveheads Press
V&A Publishing
Which? Ltd
John Wiley & Sons Ltd
Willow Island Editions
Neil Wilson Publishing Ltd
Y Lolfa Cyf

HEALTH & BEAUTY

Age UK books
Amberwood Publishing Ltd
Peter Andrew Publishing Co Ltd
Apex Publishing Ltd
Ashgrove Publishing
Aurum Press
Austin & Macauley Publishers Ltd
Duncan Baird Publishers
A. & C. Black (Publishers) Ltd
Blackstaff Press
Bloomsbury Publishing Plc
Capall Bann Publishing
Carlton Publishing Group
Carroll & Brown Ltd
Clairview Books Ltd
Class Publishing
Collins & Brown
Crimson Publishing
Diagram Visual Information Ltd
Eddison Sadd Editions Ltd
Essential Works Ltd
Express Newspapers
Findhorn Press Ltd
Floris Books
W. Foulsham & Co Ltd
Gibson Square
Granta Editions
Green Books
Haldane Mason Ltd
Hammersmith Press Ltd
HarperCollins Publishers Ltd
Harvard University Press
Hawker Publications
Haynes Publishing
Hodder Education
Human Kinetics Europe Ltd
Icon Books Ltd
Indepenpress Publishing Ltd
The Ivy Press Ltd
Jessica Kingsley Publishers
Kyle Cathie Ltd
Liberties Press
Frances Lincoln Ltd
Macmillan Publishers Ltd
Mainstream Publishing Co
(Edinburgh) Ltd
Medikidz Ltd
Mentor Books

Merlin Publishing/Wolfhound
Press
Mitchell Beazley
Murdoch Books UK Ltd
Need2Know
Nelson Thornes Ltd
New Holland Publishers (UK) Ltd
Octopus Publishing Group
On Stream Publications Ltd
The Orion Publishing Group Ltd
Pan Macmillan
The Penguin Group (UK) Ltd
Piatkus Books
Quadrille Publishing Ltd
Quantum Publishing
Random House UK Ltd
Roundhouse Publishing Ltd
SGC Books
Sheldon Press
Simon & Schuster (UK) Ltd
Singing Dragon Publishers
Souvenir Press Ltd
Speechmark Publishing Ltd
Stott's Correspondence College
Temple Lodge Publishing
Transworld Publishers Ltd
Trog Associates Ltd
Tucker Slingsby Ltd
Virgin Books Ltd
John Wiley & Sons Ltd
The Women's Press
Zymurgy Publishing

HISTORY & ANTIQUARIAN

A.M.S. Educational Ltd
Acair Ltd
Acumen Publishing Ltd
Adam Matthew Digital Ltd
Adam Matthew Publications Ltd
Al-Furqan Islamic Heritage
Foundation
Albyn Press
Ian Allan Publishing Ltd
Amber Books Ltd
Amolibros
Anglo-Saxon Books
Anova Books
Appletree Press Ltd
Arena Books (Publishers)
Arris Publishing Ltd
Ashgate Publishing Ltd
Ashmolean Museum Publications
Atlantic Books
Atlantic Europe Publishing Co Ltd
The Banton Press
Barny Books
Batsford
BBH Publishing Ltd
The Belmont Press
Bene Factum Publishing Ltd
Berghahn Books
Birlinn Ltd
Black Ace Books
Blackstaff Press
Blackthorn Press
Bloomsbury Publishing Plc
Bodleian Library Publishing
Book Castle Publishing Ltd
Borthwick Publications
Bossiney Books Ltd
Boydell & Brewer Ltd
Brewin Books Ltd
Bridge Books
British Library
Brown & Whittaker Publishing
Business Education Publishers
Cambridge Archive Editions Ltd
Cambridge University Press
Canongate Books
Capall Bann Publishing
Carlton Publishing Group
Carnegie Publishing Ltd
Jon Carpenter Publishing
The Catholic Truth Society
Christian Focus Publications
Church of Ireland Publishing
James Clarke & Co
Cló Iar-Chonnachta
Colour Heroes Ltd
Colourpoint Books
Columba

Compendium Publishing Ltd
The Continuum International
Publishing Group Ltd
Conway
Copper Beech Publishing Ltd
Cork University Press
Cornwall Editions Ltd
Countryside Books
Countyvise Ltd
Crécy Publishing Ltd
Cualann Press
Currach Press
D & N Publishing
The Davenant Press
Richard Dennis Publications
J M Dent
The Dovecote Press
Ashley Drake Publishing Ltd
Dramatic Lines
Gerald Duckworth & Co Ltd
Edinburgh University Press
Elliott & Thompson
English Heritage
Equinox Publishing Ltd
The Erskine Press
Ex Libris Press
F+W Media International
(formerly David & Charles)
Family Publications
A. & A. Farmar
Five Leaves Publications
Four Courts Press
Garnet Publishing Ltd
Geddes & Grosset
Geography Publications
Gibson Square
Gill & Macmillan Ltd
Glasgow Museums Publishing
GLMP Ltd
Alan Godfrey Maps
Gomer
Gracewing Publishing
Granta Editions
Greenhill Books / Lionel Leventhal
Ltd
Gresham Books Ltd
Guildhall Press
Gwasg Gwenffrwd
Hachette Scotland
Halban Publishers
Halsgrove
HarperCollins Publishers Ltd
Harvard University Press
Haynes Publishing
Heart of Albion Press
Helion & Co Ltd
Ian Henry Publications Ltd
Historical Publications Ltd
Hobnob Press
Hodder Education
Hodder Faith
Hodder & Stoughton General
Holo Books
The Horizon Press
Hypatia Publications
Icon Books Ltd
Intellect Ltd
Irish Academic Press
Ithaca Press
James & James (Publishers) Ltd
Janus Publishing Co Ltd
The King's England Press
Letts and Lonsdale
Liberties Press
Librario Publishers Ltd
The Lilliput Press Ltd
Little, Brown Book Group
The Littman Library of Jewish
Civilization
Liverpool University Press
Living Time® Media International
Logaston Press
Lomond Books Ltd
Luath Press Ltd
The Lutterworth Press
Macmillan Education
Macmillan Publishers Ltd
Mainstream Publishing Co
(Edinburgh) Ltd
Manchester University Press
Maney Publishing
Mehring Books

Melisende
Mentor Books
Mercier Press Ltd
Mercury Books
The Merlin Press Ltd
Merrell Publishers Ltd
Merton Priory Press Ltd
Microform Academic Publishers
Mitchell Beazley
Moorley's Print & Publishing Ltd
Murdoch Books UK Ltd
John Murray Publishers
National Archives of Scotland
National Portrait Gallery
Publications
The National Trust
Nelson Thornes Ltd
New Island Books Ltd
NMS Enterprises Limited -
Publishing
North York Moors National Park
Authority
Northumbria University Press
W. W. Norton & Company Ltd
The Nostalgia Collection
Octopus Publishing Group
Old House Books
The Oleander Press
Open University Worldwide
Optimus Professional Publishing
The Orion Publishing Group Ltd
Osprey Publishing
Peter Owen Publishers
Palazzo Editions Ltd
Palgrave Macmillan
Pan Macmillan
The Penguin Group (UK) Ltd
Piatkus Books
Pickering & Chatto (Publishers) Ltd
Playne Books Ltd
Plowright Press
Polity Press
Polperro Heritage Press
Portobello Books Ltd
Princeton University Press
Profile Books
ProQuest
Quantum Publishing
Quartet Books
The Radcliffe Press
Random House UK Ltd
Reardon Publishing
Redcliffe Press Ltd
Reflections of a Bygone Age
Roundhouse Publishing Ltd
Royal Collection Publications
Royal Irish Academy
S. B. Publications
Saint Albert's Press
Saqi Books
Scottish Children's Press
Scottish Cultural Press
Scottish Text Society
Sessions of York
Sheaf Publishing
Sheldrake Press
Shepheard-Walwyn (Publishers)
Ltd
Shire Publications Ltd
Short Books Ltd
Slightly Foxed
Smith Settle Printing &
Bookbinding Ltd
Society of Antiquaries of Scotland
Society of Genealogists
Enterprises Ltd
Spokesman
Sportsbooks Ltd
Stacey International
Stainer & Bell Ltd
Stenlake Publishing Ltd
Strong Oak Press
Summersdale Publishers Ltd
Supportive Learning Publications
(SLP)
Sussex Academic Press
Sussex Publications
I. B. Tauris & Co Ltd
Taylor & Francis
Thames & Hudson Ltd
Toucan Books Ltd
Transworld Publishers Ltd

Troubador Publishing Ltd
Truran
Twelveheads Press
Tyne Bridge Publishing
Unicorn Press
University of Exeter Press
University of Hertfordshire Press
University of Wales Press
Vallentine Mitchell Publishers
Voltaire Foundation Ltd
Warburg Institute
Waterside Press
Waterside Press
Paul Watkins Publishing
David West Children's Books
John Wiley & Sons Ltd
Philip Wilson Publishers
Neil Wilson Publishing Ltd
World Microfilms
Yale University Press London

HUMOUR

Accent Press Ltd
Allison & Busby
Alma Books Ltd
Anova Books
Antique Collectors' Club Ltd
Apex Publishing Ltd
Appletree Press Ltd
Atlantic Books
Aurora Metro Publications Ltd
Aurum Press
Austin & Macauley Publishers Ltd
Authorhouse UK Ltd
Barny Books
Beautiful Books Ltd
Bene Factum Publishing Ltd
Birlinn Ltd
A. & C. Black (Publishers) Ltd
Blackstaff Press
John Blake Publishing Ltd
Bloomsbury Publishing Plc
Bodleian Library Publishing
Brown Dog Books
Canongate Books
Carlton Publishing Group
Constable & Robinson Ltd
Countryside Books
Countyvise Ltd
CRW Publishing Ltd
Currach Press
Delancey Press Ltd
Gerald Duckworth & Co Ltd
Essential Works Ltd
Exley Publications Ltd
Express Newspapers
F+W Media International
   (formerly David & Charles)
Feather Books
W. Foulsham & Co Ltd
Gibson Square
Gill & Macmillan Ltd
Guildhall Press
Hachette Scotland
Robert Hale Ltd
HarperCollins Publishers Ltd
Ian Henry Publications Ltd
Hodder Faith
Hodder & Stoughton General
Holo Books
Icon Books Ltd
Indepenpress Publishing Ltd
ISIS Publishing Ltd
Janus Publishing Co Ltd
Little, Brown Book Group
Lomond Books Ltd
Luath Press Ltd
Macmillan Publishers Ltd
Mainstream Publishing Co
   (Edinburgh) Ltd
Maverick House Publishers
Mentor Books
Mercier Press Ltd
Merlin Publishing/Wolfhound
   Press
Merrell Publishers Ltd
John Murray Publishers
The National Trust
New Holland Publishers (UK) Ltd
New Island Books Ltd
Nightingale Press

The O'Brien Press Ltd
The Oleander Press
The Orion Publishing Group Ltd
The Penguin Group (UK) Ltd
Pennant Books Ltd
Piatkus Books
Porthill Publishers
Tony Potter Publishing
Quadrille Publishing Ltd
Quiller Publishing Ltd
Random House UK Ltd
Ravette Publishing Ltd
Reardon Publishing
Sandstone Press Ltd
Saqi Books
Sheldrake Press
Short Books Ltd
Simon & Schuster (UK) Ltd
Souvenir Press Ltd
Summersdale Publishers Ltd
Supportive Learning Publications
   (SLP)
Top That! Publishing Plc
Transworld Publishers Ltd
Troubador Publishing Ltd
United Writers Publications Ltd
Merlin Unwin Books Ltd
Virgin Books Ltd
Weidenfeld & Nicolson
John Wiley & Sons Ltd
Neil Wilson Publishing Ltd
Y Lolfa Cyf
Zymurgy Publishing

ILLUSTRATED & FINE EDITIONS

Albyn Press
Ashgate Publishing Ltd
Bene Factum Publishing Ltd
Birlinn Ltd
Black Dog Publishing Ltd
Blackstaff Press
British Library
Canongate Books
Carlton Publishing Group
Constable & Robinson Ltd
Richard Dennis Publications
Enitharmon Press
The Erskine Press
Essential Works Ltd
Everyman's Library
Express Newspapers
Granta Editions
Halsgrove
HarperCollins Publishers Ltd
The Herbert Press
The Ivy Press Ltd
Dewi Lewis Publishing
The Lilliput Press Ltd
Frances Lincoln Ltd
Lomond Books Ltd
The Lutterworth Press
Mainstream Publishing Co
   (Edinburgh) Ltd
Manchester University Press
Maney Publishing
Melisende
Merrell Publishers Ltd
Mitchell Beazley
National Portrait Gallery
   Publications
The Old Stile Press
The Orion Publishing Group Ltd
Phaidon Press Ltd
Quiller Publishing Ltd
Random House UK Ltd
Royal Collection Publications
Sandstone Press Ltd
Saqi Books
Scala Publishers Ltd
Shepheard-Walwyn (Publishers)
   Ltd
Charles Skilton Ltd
Slightly Foxed
Smith Settle Printing &
   Bookbinding Ltd
The Society for Promoting
   Christian Knowledge (SPCK)
Stacey International
Thames & Hudson Ltd
Third Millennium Publishing Ltd
Toucan Books Ltd

University of Wales Press
Veloce Publishing Ltd
Virgin Books Ltd
Weidenfeld & Nicolson
Whittet Books Ltd
Yale University Press London
Zymurgy Publishing

INDUSTRY, BUSINESS & MANAGEMENT

Accent Press Ltd
Peter Andrew Publishing Co Ltd
Anthem Press
Arena Books (Publishers)
Ashgate Publishing Ltd
Atlantic Books
Aurelian Information Ltd
Austin & Macauley Publishers Ltd
AVA Publishing (UK) Ltd
Barny Books
Bene Factum Publishing Ltd
Biohealthcare Publishing (Oxford)
   Ltd
Blackhall Publishing
Blue Ocean Publishing
BookPower
Nicholas Brealey Publishing
Business Education Publishers
*Cambridge Publishing
   Management Ltd*
Cambridge University Press
Carnegie Publishing Ltd
Cengage Learning EMEA Ltd
Centre for Economic Policy
   Research
Chartered Institute of Personnel &
   Development
Commonwealth Secretariat
Crimson Publishing
Ashley Drake Publishing Ltd
Earthscan
Edward Elgar Publishing Ltd
Elliott & Thompson
Elm Publications
Emerald Group Publishing Ltd
Energy Institute
Ethics International Press Ltd
Euromonitor International
Executive Grapevine International
   Ltd
Filament Publishing Ltd
W. Foulsham & Co Ltd
GLMP Ltd
Gower Publishing Co Ltd
Granta Editions
Greenleaf Publishing
HarperCollins Publishers Ltd
Harriman House
Hawthorn Press
Hodder Education
How To Books Ltd
ICSA Information & Training Ltd
IHS Jane's
The Ilex Press Ltd
Imperial College Press
In Easy Steps Ltd
Indepenpress Publishing Ltd
Institute for Employment Studies
Institute of Development Studies
Institution of Engineering and
   Technology (IET)
IWA Publishing
James & James (Publishers) Ltd
Jordan Publishing Ltd
Kogan Page Ltd
McGraw-Hill Education
Management Pocketbooks Ltd
Market House Books Ltd
Mentor Books
The MIT Press Ltd
The National Academies Press
National Housing Federation
Nelson Thornes Ltd
Oak Tree Press
Open University Worldwide
Oxford University Press
Palgrave Macmillan
Paragon Publishing
The Penguin Group (UK) Ltd
Piatkus Books
Princeton University Press

Profile Books
ProQuest
Quantum Publishing
Radcliffe Publishing Ltd
Round Hall Ltd
Roundhouse Publishing Ltd
Russell House Publishing Ltd
Sage Publications Ltd
Sessions of York
Sherwood Publishing
Sigel Press
Simon & Schuster (UK) Ltd
Social Affairs Unit
Souvenir Press Ltd
Sussex Academic Press
Taylor & Francis
Thorogood Publishing Ltd
Trog Associates Ltd
Trotman Publishing
Troubador Publishing Ltd
TSO (The Stationery Office Ltd)
United Writers Publications Ltd
University of Ottawa Press
Weidenfeld & Nicolson
John Wiley & Sons Ltd
WIT Press
Woodhead Publishing Ltd
XPL Publishing
Zambezi Publishing Ltd

LANGUAGES & LINGUISTICS

Advance Materials
Anglo-Saxon Books
Association for Scottish Literary
   Studies
Audio-Forum – The Language
   Source
b small publishing ltd
Berghahn Books
Joseph Biddulph Publisher
Brilliant Publications
Cambridge University Press
Carel Press
Channel View Publications Ltd
CILT, the National Centre for
   Languages
Claire Publications
Cló Iar-Chonnachta
Cois Life
The Continuum International
   Publishing Group Ltd
Delta ELT Publishing Ltd
Ashley Drake Publishing Ltd
Dunedin Academic Press
Edinburgh University Press
Emerald Group Publishing Ltd
Equinox Publishing Ltd
GeoCenter International Ltd
Geography Publications
GLMP Ltd
Gomer
Gwasg Gwenffrwd
HarperCollins Publishers Ltd
Hinton House Publishers Ltd
Hodder Education
Icon Books Ltd
Intellect Ltd
Ithaca Press
Jarndyce Booksellers
Letts and Lonsdale
Lexus Ltd
Liverpool University Press
Luath Press Ltd
Macmillan Education
Macmillan Publishers Ltd
Manchester University Press
Maney Publishing
Mentor Books
The MIT Press Ltd
National Extension College Trust
   Ltd
Nelson Thornes Ltd
Old House Books
The Oleander Press
Open University Worldwide
Oxford University Press
Packard Publishing Ltd
Palgrave Macmillan
Paragon Publishing
Royal Irish Academy
St Jerome Publishing Ltd

Saqi Books
Scottish Children's Press
Scottish Cultural Press
Speechmark Publishing Ltd
Stacey International
Ta Ha Publishers Ltd
Taigh na Teud Music Publishers
Taylor & Francis
Troubador Publishing Ltd
Truran
University of Ottawa Press
University of Wales Press
Usborne Publishing Ltd
Voltaire Foundation Ltd
Paul Watkins Publishing
John Wiley & Sons Ltd
Y Lolfa Cyf
Yale University Press London

LAW

Amnesty International
   International Secretariat
Peter Andrew Publishing Co Ltd
Anthem Press
Ashgate Publishing Ltd
Atlantic Books
Bene Factum Publishing Ltd
Blackhall Publishing
Borthwick Publications
Business Education Publishers
Cambridge University Press
Class Publishing
Commonwealth Secretariat
Delta Alpha Publishing Ltd
J M Dent
Earthscan
Edinburgh University Press
Edward Elgar Publishing Ltd
Ethics International Press Ltd
Four Courts Press
GLMP Ltd
Granta Editions
W. Green The Scottish Law
   Publisher
Hart Publishing
Harvard University Press
Hodder Education
Holo Books
Incorporated Council of Law
   Reporting for England and
   Wales
Institute of Employment Rights
The Islamic Texts Society
Ithaca Press
Jones & Bartlett International
Jordan Publishing Ltd
Jessica Kingsley Publishers
Kube Publishing Ltd
Law Reports International
Law Society Publishing
Leatherhead Food Research
Legal Action Group
McGraw-Hill Education
Macmillan Publishers Ltd
Manchester University Press
Market House Books Ltd
National Extension College Trust
   Ltd
Nelson Thornes Ltd
Oak Tree Press
Oxford University Press
Palgrave Macmillan
Pearson Education
Pluto Books Ltd
Princeton University Press
Round Hall Ltd
Russell House Publishing Ltd
Saqi Books
SLS Legal Publications (NI)
Sussex Academic Press
Taylor & Francis
Thomson International Legal &
   Regulatory
Thorogood Publishing Ltd
Trentham Books
TSO (The Stationery Office Ltd)
Waterside Press
Waterside Press
Weidenfeld & Nicolson
Which? Ltd

Witherby Seamanship
  International
Woodhead Publishing Ltd
XPL Publishing

LITERATURE & CRITICISM

Adam Matthew Digital Ltd
Adam Matthew Publications Ltd
Albyn Press
Allison & Busby
Amolibros
Anthem Press
Arena Books (Publishers)
Ashgate Publishing Ltd
Association for Scottish Literary
  Studies
Atlantic Books
Austin & Macauley Publishers Ltd
Back-In-Print Books Ltd
Beautiful Books Ltd
Berghahn Books
Blackstaff Press
Blackthorn Press
Bloodaxe Books Ltd
Bloomsbury Publishing Plc
Bodleian Library Publishing
Marion Boyars Publishers Ltd
Boydell & Brewer Ltd
Brandon/Mount Eagle
  Publications
Cambridge University Press
Canongate Books
Carel Press
James Clarke & Co
Classical Comics Ltd
Cló Iar-Chonnachta
Cois Life
The Continuum International
  Publishing Group Ltd
Cork University Press
The Davenant Press
Dedalus Ltd
J M Dent
Dionysia Press Ltd
Ashley Drake Publishing Ltd
Gerald Duckworth & Co Ltd
Edinburgh University Press
Enitharmon Press
Everyman's Library
Faber & Faber Ltd
Feather Books
Four Courts Press
Freelance Market News
Garnet Publishing Ltd
GLMP Ltd
The Goldsmith Press Ltd
Gomer
Green Books
Guildhall Press
Gwasg Gwenffrwd
Halban Publishers
HarperCollins Publishers Ltd
Harvard University Press
Hippopotamus Press
Hobnob Press
Hodder Education
How To Books Ltd
Icon Books Ltd
Indepenpress Publishing Ltd
Intellect Ltd
Irish Academic Press
Ithaca Press
Janus Publishing Co Ltd
Jarndyce Booksellers
Liberties Press
The Lilliput Press Ltd
Little, Brown Book Group
The Littman Library of Jewish
  Civilization
Liverpool University Press
Living Time® Media International
Luath Press Ltd
The Lutterworth Press
Macmillan Publishers Ltd
Mainstream Publishing Co
  (Edinburgh) Ltd
Manchester University Press
Mandrake of Oxford
Maney Publishing
Mehring Books
Mercier Press Ltd

Mercury Books
Microform Academic Publishers
The National Association for the
  Teaching of English (NATE)
Nelson Thornes Ltd
New Island Books Ltd
Northcote House Publishers Ltd
W. W. Norton & Company Ltd
The Old Stile Press
The Oleander Press
Oneworld Classics
Onlywomen Press Ltd
Open University Worldwide
Peter Owen Publishers
Palgrave Macmillan
Pan Macmillan
Paupers' Press
The Penguin Group (UK) Ltd
Pickering & Chatto (Publishers) Ltd
Pipers' Ash Ltd
Pluto Books Ltd
Polity Press
ProQuest
Random House UK Ltd
Redcliffe Press Ltd
Roundhouse Publishing Ltd
Salt Publishing Ltd
Sandstone Press Ltd
Sansom & Co Ltd
Saqi Books
Scottish Cultural Press
Scottish Text Society
Seren
Charles Skilton Ltd
Colin Smythe Ltd
Souvenir Press Ltd
Stenlake Publishing Ltd
Sussex Academic Press
Sussex Publications
The Swedenborg Society
Symposium Publications Literary &
  Art
Tabb House
Taylor & Francis
Thames & Hudson Ltd
Trog Associates Ltd
Troubador Publishing Ltd
University of Exeter Press
University of Hertfordshire Press
University of Ottawa Press
University of Wales Press
Voltaire Foundation Ltd
Waterside Press
John Wiley & Sons Ltd
The Women's Press
Wordsworth Editions Ltd
Worth Press Ltd

MAGIC & THE OCCULT

Aeon Books
Amolibros
Austin & Macauley Publishers Ltd
Duncan Baird Publishers
The Banton Press
Blue Beyond Books
Bossiney Books Ltd
Capall Bann Publishing
Caxton Publishing Group Ltd
Collins & Brown
Eddison Sadd Editions Ltd
W. Foulsham & Co Ltd
Geddes & Grosset
Godsfield Press Ltd
Gothic Image Publications
Robert Hale Ltd
HarperCollins Publishers Ltd
Heart of Albion Press
John Hunt Publishing Ltd
Indepenpress Publishing Ltd
Janus Publishing Co Ltd
Luath Press Ltd
Mandrake of Oxford
Paragon Publishing
Piatkus Books
Quadrille Publishing Ltd
Quantum Publishing
Reardon Publishing
Regency House Publishing Ltd
The Society of Metaphysicians Ltd
Souvenir Press Ltd
Stacey International

Rudolf Steiner Press
Temple Lodge Publishing
Thames & Hudson Ltd
Thoth Publications
Troubador Publishing Ltd
University of Hertfordshire Press
Warburg Institute
John Wiley & Sons Ltd
Zambezi Publishing Ltd

MATHEMATICS & STATISTICS

Al-Furqan Islamic Heritage
  Foundation
Alpha Science International Ltd
Anshan Ltd
Anthem Press
Atlantic Books
Atlantic Europe Publishing Co Ltd
Austin & Macauley Publishers Ltd
Bernard Babani (Publishing) Ltd
BEAM Education
Bedford Freeman Worth (BFW)
Blackstaff Press
Cambridge University Press
Carel Press
Chalksoft Ltd
Claire Publications
GLMP Ltd
Hodder Education
Icon Books Ltd
Imperial College Press
The Institute of Mathematics and
  its Applications
IOP Publishing
Jones & Bartlett International
S. Karger AG
Letts and Lonsdale
McGraw-Hill Education
Macmillan Education
Macmillan Publishers Ltd
Mentor Books
The National Academies Press
National Extension College Trust
  Ltd
Nelson Thornes Ltd
W. W. Norton & Company Ltd
Open University Worldwide
Oxford University Press
Palgrave Macmillan
Princeton University Press
ProQuest
Royal Irish Academy
Sage Publications Ltd
Saqi Books
Springer London
Supportive Learning Publications
  (SLP)
Tarquin Publications
Taylor & Francis
TSO (The Stationery Office Ltd)
University of Hertfordshire Press
Ward Lock Educational Co Ltd
John Wiley & Sons Ltd
WIT Press
Woodhead Publishing Ltd

MEDICAL (INCL. SELF HELP & ALTERNATIVE MEDICINE)

Accent Press Ltd
Age UK books
Alpha Science International Ltd
Amberwood Publishing Ltd
American Psychiatric Publishing
  Inc
Amolibros
Anshan Ltd
Anthem Press
Apex Publishing Ltd
Ashgrove Publishing
Austin & Macauley Publishers Ltd
Duncan Baird Publishers
Barny Books
Bene Factum Publishing Ltd
BLA Publishing Ltd
Blackhall Publishing
Blackstaff Press
BookPower
CABI
*Cambridge Publishing
  Management Ltd*

Cambridge University Press
Capall Bann Publishing
Jon Carpenter Publishing
Carroll & Brown Ltd
Caxton Publishing Group Ltd
Clairview Books Ltd
Class Publishing
Clear Answer Medical Publishing
  Ltd
Collins & Brown
Constable & Robinson Ltd
Corpus Publishing Ltd
Crown House Publishing Ltd
D & N Publishing
Denor Press Ltd
Eddison Sadd Editions Ltd
Elsevier Ltd
The Erskine Press
Filament Publishing Ltd
Findhorn Press Ltd
Floris Books
W. Foulsham & Co Ltd
Geddes & Grosset
Gibson Square
GLMP Ltd
Godsfield Press Ltd
Granta Editions
Haldane Mason Ltd
Hammersmith Press Ltd
HarperCollins Publishers Ltd
Hawker Publications
Hawthorn Press
Haynes Publishing
Ian Henry Publications Ltd
Hinton House Publishers Ltd
Hodder Education
How To Books Ltd
Human Kinetics Europe Ltd
Immunisation Information
Imperial College Press
Indepenpress Publishing Ltd
Institute of Physics & Engineering
  in Medicine
International Medical Press
Janus Publishing Co Ltd
Jones & Bartlett International
S. Karger AG
Jessica Kingsley Publishers
Librario Publishers Ltd
Luath Press Ltd
McGraw-Hill Education
Macmillan Publishers Ltd
Mainstream Publishing Co
  (Edinburgh) Ltd
Mandrake of Oxford
Maney Publishing
Manson Publishing Ltd
Market House Books Ltd
Medikidz Ltd
Mitchell Beazley
M&K Publishing
The National Academies Press
National Extension College Trust
  Ltd
Need2Know
Nelson Thornes Ltd
NHS Immunisation Information
Open University Worldwide
Oxford University Press
Palgrave Macmillan
Paragon Publishing
PCCS Books Ltd
The Penguin Group (UK) Ltd
The Pharmaceutical Press
Piatkus Books
Portland Press Ltd
ProQuest
Publishing House
Quadrille Publishing Ltd
Quantum Publishing
Radcliffe Publishing Ltd
Round Hall Ltd
Roundhouse Publishing Ltd
Royal College of General
  Practitioners
Royal College of Psychiatrists
Royal Society of Medicine Press
  Ltd
Russell House Publishing Ltd
Scion Publishing Ltd
Sheldon Press
Simon & Schuster (UK) Ltd

Singing Dragon Publishers
Social Affairs Unit
The Society for Promoting
  Christian Knowledge (SPCK)
The Society of Metaphysicians Ltd
Souvenir Press Ltd
Speechmark Publishing Ltd
Springer London
Rudolf Steiner Press
Tabb House
Taylor & Francis
Temple Lodge Publishing
tfm publishing Ltd
Troubador Publishing Ltd
TSO (The Stationery Office Ltd)
Merlin Unwin Books Ltd
Whiting & Birch Ltd
John Wiley & Sons Ltd
Windhorse Publications
WIT Press
Wolters Kluwer Health (P & E) Ltd
XPL Publishing
Zambezi Publishing Ltd

MILITARY & WAR

A.M.S. Educational Ltd
Adam Matthew Digital Ltd
Air-Britain (Historians) Ltd
Ian Allan Publishing Ltd
Amber Books Ltd
Anglo-Saxon Books
Anova Books
Apex Publishing Ltd
Arena Books (Publishers)
Ashgate Publishing Ltd
Ashgrove Publishing
Atlantic Books
Aurum Press
Austin & Macauley Publishers Ltd
Back-In-Print Books Ltd
Barny Books
Bene Factum Publishing Ltd
Berghahn Books
Birlinn Ltd
BLA Publishing Ltd
Blackstaff Press
Bloomsbury Publishing Plc
Bodleian Library Publishing
Boydell & Brewer Ltd
Brewin Books Ltd
Bridge Books
Brooklands Books Ltd
Business Education Publishers
*Cambridge Publishing
  Management Ltd*
Carlton Publishing Group
Carnegie Publishing Ltd
Caxton Publishing Group Ltd
Chatham Publishing
Clairview Books Ltd
Colour Heroes Ltd
Compendium Publishing Ltd
Constable & Robinson Ltd
Conway
Countryside Books
Crécy Publishing Ltd
The Crowood Press Ltd
Cualann Press
D & N Publishing
Eric Dobby Publishing Ltd
The Dovecote Press
Ashley Drake Publishing Ltd
Gerald Duckworth & Co Ltd
Elliott & Thompson
English Heritage
The Erskine Press
Essential Works Ltd
F+W Media International
  (formerly David & Charles)
W. Foulsham & Co Ltd
Four Courts Press
GLMP Ltd
*Graham-Cameron Publishing &
  Illustration*
Greenhill Books / Lionel Leventhal
  Ltd
Grub Street
Hachette Scotland
Robert Hale Ltd
Halsgrove
HarperCollins Publishers Ltd

Harvard University Press
Haynes Publishing
Helion & Co Ltd
Hodder & Stoughton General
C. Hurst & Co (Publishers) Ltd
Icon Books Ltd
IHS Jane's
Indepenpress Publishing Ltd
Irish Academic Press
ISIS Publishing Ltd
Janus Publishing Co Ltd
Librario Publishers Ltd
Little, Brown Book Group
Luath Press Ltd
The Lutterworth Press
Macmillan Publishers Ltd
Mainstream Publishing Co
  (Edinburgh) Ltd
Maney Publishing
Maritime Books
Maverick House Publishers
Mercury Books
Microform Academic Publishers
Middleton Press
John Murray Publishers
Myriad Editions
NMS Enterprises Limited -
  Publishing
W. W. Norton & Company Ltd
The Nostalgia Collection
The Orion Publishing Group Ltd
Osprey Publishing Ltd
Paragon Publishing
The Penguin Group (UK) Ltd
Piatkus Books
Quantum Publishing
Quiller Publishing Ltd
The Radcliffe Press
Rand Publications
Random House UK Ltd
Ravette Publishing Ltd
Reardon Publishing
Regency House Publishing Ltd
Roundhouse Publishing Ltd
Scottish Cultural Press
Shire Publications Ltd
Sigel Press
Simon & Schuster (UK) Ltd
Charles Skilton Ltd
Souvenir Press Ltd
Spokesman
Stacey International
Strong Oak Press
Sussex Academic Press
I. B. Tauris & Co Ltd
Taylor & Francis
Thames & Hudson Ltd
Third Millennium Publishing Ltd
Thorogood Publishing Ltd
Toucan Books Ltd
Transworld Publishers Ltd
Troubador Publishing Ltd
Truran
Tyne Bridge Publishing
Unicorn Press
United Writers Publications Ltd
University of Wales Press
Veloce Publishing Ltd
Virgin Books Ltd
David West Children's Books
Whittles Publishing
John Wiley & Sons Ltd
Neil Wilson Publishing Ltd
Worth Press Ltd
Yale University Press London

MUSIC

Amolibros
Anova Books
Arc Publications Ltd
Ashgate Publishing Ltd
Atlantic Books
Attic Press
Aureus Publishing Ltd
Aurum Press
Beautiful Books Ltd
BLA Publishing Ltd
Black Dog Publishing Ltd
A. & C. Black (Publishers) Ltd
Black Spring Press Ltd
Blackstaff Press

John Blake Publishing Ltd
Bloomsbury Publishing Plc
Blue Beyond Books
Blue Sky Press
Marion Boyars Publishers Ltd
Boydell & Brewer Ltd
Cambridge University Press
Canongate Books
Capall Bann Publishing
Carlton Publishing Group
Chalksoft Ltd
Cló Iar-Chonnachta
Collins & Brown
Compendium Publishing Ltd
The Continuum International
  Publishing Group Ltd
Cork University Press
Currach Press
Dance Books Ltd
Denor Press Ltd
J M Dent
Elliott & Thompson
Equinox Publishing Ltd
Essential Works Ltd
Faber & Faber Ltd
Feather Books
Four Courts Press
Granta Editions
Gresham Books Ltd
Guildhall Press
Hachette Scotland
Robert Hale Ltd
HarperCollins Publishers Ltd
Harvard University Press
Hawthorn Press
Haynes Publishing
Helter Skelter Publishing Ltd
Hymns Ancient & Modern Ltd
Independent Music Press
Indepenpress Publishing Ltd
The Lilliput Press Ltd
Little, Brown Book Group
The Littman Library of Jewish
  Civilization
Luath Press Ltd
McCrimmon Publishing Co Ltd
Macmillan Publishers Ltd
Mainstream Publishing Co
  (Edinburgh) Ltd
Market House Books Ltd
Merlin Publishing/Wolfhound
  Press
The MIT Press Ltd
Mitchell Beazley
Moonlight Publishing Ltd
Moorley's Print & Publishing Ltd
Northumbria University Press
W. W. Norton & Company Ltd
Omnibus Press
Peter Owen Publishers
Oxford University Press
PC Publishing
The Penguin Group (UK) Ltd
Pennant Books Ltd
Phaidon Press Ltd
Piatkus Books
ProQuest
Quantum Publishing
Quartet Books
Random House UK Ltd
RotoVision SA
Roundhouse Publishing Ltd
Route Publishing Ltd
Saqi Books
SchoolPlay Productions Ltd
Schott Music Ltd
Scripture Union Publishing
The Shetland Times Ltd
Simon & Schuster (UK) Ltd
Souvenir Press Ltd
Spartan Press Music Publishers Ltd
Stainer & Bell Ltd
Rudolf Steiner Press
Sussex Academic Press
Sussex Publications
Taigh na Teud Music Publishers
Taylor & Francis
Thames & Hudson Ltd
Transworld Publishers Ltd
TTS Group
University of Wales Press
Usborne Publishing Ltd

Virgin Books Ltd
Ward Lock Educational Co Ltd
David West Children's Books
Wild Goose Publications
John Wiley & Sons Ltd
Neil Wilson Publishing Ltd
Y Lolfa Cyf
Yale University Press London
Zymurgy Publishing

NATURAL HISTORY

AA Publishing
Antique Collectors' Club Ltd
Arris Publishing Ltd
Atlantic Books
Aurum Press
Austin & Macauley Publishers Ltd
Duncan Baird Publishers
Bender Richardson White
BLA Publishing Ltd
A. & C. Black (Publishers) Ltd
Blackstaff Press
Bodleian Library Publishing
British Museum Press
Brown & Whittaker Publishing
Calypso Publications
*Cambridge Publishing
  Management Ltd*
Cambridge University Press
Cameron Books
Capall Bann Publishing
Carlton Publishing Group
Carnegie Publishing Ltd
Caxton Publishing Group Ltd
Chalksoft Ltd
Colour Heroes Ltd
Cornwall Editions Ltd
Countyvise Ltd
The Crowood Press Ltd
D & N Publishing
The Dovecote Press
Earthscan
Elliott & Thompson
The Erskine Press
Ex Libris Press
F+W Media International
  (formerly David & Charles)
Graffeg
*Graham-Cameron Publishing &
  Illustration*
Granta Editions
Green Books
Haldane Mason Ltd
Robert Hale Ltd
Halsgrove
HarperCollins Publishers Ltd
Harvard University Press
Hodder Education
Alison Hodge Publishers
Icon Books Ltd
Librario Publishers Ltd
Logaston Press
Lomond Books Ltd
Luath Press Ltd
The Lutterworth Press
Macmillan Publishers Ltd
Merrell Publishers Ltd
The MIT Press Ltd
Mitchell Beazley
Moonlight Publishing Ltd
The National Academies Press
The National Trust
Natural History Museum
  Publishing
New Holland Publishers (UK) Ltd
Newpro UK Ltd
NMS Enterprises Limited -
  Publishing
North York Moors National Park
  Authority
W. W. Norton & Company Ltd
Octopus Publishing Group
Old House Books
Open University Worldwide
The Orion Publishing Group Ltd
Packard Publishing Ltd
Papadakis Publisher
Paragon Publishing
The Penguin Group (UK) Ltd
Philip's
Polperro Heritage Press

Princeton University Press
ProQuest
Quantum Publishing
Quiller Publishing Ltd
Random House UK Ltd
Reardon Publishing
Roundhouse Publishing Ltd
Royal Collection Publications
S. B. Publications
Scottish Children's Press
Scottish Cultural Press
Sessions of York
SGC Books
The Shetland Times Ltd
Shire Publications Ltd
Souvenir Press Ltd
Stacey International
Stobart Davies Ltd
Subbuteo Natural History Books
Tango Books Ltd
Thames & Hudson Ltd
Top That! Publishing Plc
Toucan Books Ltd
Troubador Publishing Ltd
Truran
Merlin Unwin Books Ltd
Usborne Publishing Ltd
David West Children's Books
Whittet Books Ltd
Whittles Publishing
John Wiley & Sons Ltd
Willow Island Editions
Yale University Press London
Zymurgy Publishing

NAUTICAL

Adlard Coles Nautical
Ian Allan Publishing Ltd
Amber Books Ltd
Amolibros
Austin & Macauley Publishers Ltd
The Belmont Press
BLA Publishing Ltd
A. & C. Black (Publishers) Ltd
Brown, Son & Ferguson, Ltd
Chatham Publishing
Conway
Countyvise Ltd
Crécy Publishing Ltd
The Crowood Press Ltd
Ex Libris Press
Granta Editions
Haynes Publishing
The Horizon Press
IHS Jane's
Imray Laurie Norie & Wilson Ltd
Janus Publishing Co Ltd
Middleton Press
The National Academies Press
W. W. Norton & Company Ltd
The Nostalgia Collection
The Orion Publishing Group Ltd
Paragon Publishing
Polperro Heritage Press
Quantum Publishing
Quiller Publishing Ltd
Reardon Publishing
Roadmaster Publishing
Scottish Cultural Press
Special Interest Model Books Ltd
Stenlake Publishing Ltd
Truran
TSO (The Stationery Office Ltd)
Twelveheads Press
Tyne Bridge Publishing
Unicorn Press
United Writers Publications Ltd
Paul Watkins Publishing
Whittles Publishing
Neil Wilson Publishing Ltd
Witherby Seamanship
  International

PHILOSOPHY

Acumen Publishing Ltd
Alban Books Ltd
Amolibros
Apex Publishing Ltd
Arena Books (Publishers)
Ashgate Publishing Ltd

Atlantic Books
Austin & Macauley Publishers Ltd
Duncan Baird Publishers
The Banton Press
Black Ace Books
Blue Beyond Books
Marion Boyars Publishers Ltd
Boydell & Brewer Ltd
Cambridge University Press
Canongate Books
Capall Bann Publishing
Jon Carpenter Publishing
James Clarke & Co
Compendium Publishing Ltd
The Continuum International
  Publishing Group Ltd
Cork University Press
Darton, Longman & Todd Ltd
Gerald Duckworth & Co Ltd
Edinburgh University Press
Emerald Group Publishing Ltd
Equinox Publishing Ltd
Everyman's Library
Fabian Society
Filament Publishing Ltd
Floris Books
Four Courts Press
Gibson Square
Gothic Image Publications
Gracewing Publishing
Green Books
Halban Publishers
Harvard University Press
Heart of Albion Press
Hodder Education
John Hunt Publishing Ltd
Hymns Ancient & Modern Ltd
Icon Books Ltd
Imprint Academic
Indepenpress Publishing Ltd
Intellect Ltd
Janus Publishing Co Ltd
Letts and Lonsdale
The Littman Library of Jewish
  Civilization
Living Time® Media International
The Lutterworth Press
McGraw-Hill Education
Macmillan Publishers Ltd
Mandrake of Oxford
The MIT Press Ltd
W. W. Norton & Company Ltd
Open Gate Press
The Orion Publishing Group Ltd
Oxford University Press
Palgrave Macmillan
Paupers' Press
The Penguin Group (UK) Ltd
Pipers' Ash Ltd
Pluto Books Ltd
Polity Press
Princeton University Press
Random House UK Ltd
Roundhouse Publishing Ltd
St Pauls Publishing
Saqi Books
Shepheard-Walwyn (Publishers)
  Ltd
Short Books Ltd
The Society of Metaphysicians Ltd
Souvenir Press Ltd
Spokesman
Rudolf Steiner Press
Sussex Academic Press
Taylor & Francis
Temple Lodge Publishing
Thames & Hudson Ltd
Tharpa Publications
Troubador Publishing Ltd
University of Wales Press
Veritas Publications
Voltaire Foundation Ltd
Warburg Institute
Weidenfeld & Nicolson
John Wiley & Sons Ltd
Windhorse Publications
Wordsworth Editions Ltd
Yale University Press London

PHOTOGRAPHY

AA Publishing

Age UK books
Anova Books
Antique Collectors' Club Ltd
Arcadia Books Ltd
Aurum Press
AVA Publishing (UK) Ltd
BBH Publishing Ltd
Berg Publishers
Black Dog Publishing Ltd
Blackstaff Press
Carlton Publishing Group
Cló Iar-Chonnachta
Collins & Brown
Compendium Publishing Ltd
Cork University Press
Currach Press
D & N Publishing
Delta Alpha Publishing Ltd
Essential Works Ltd
F+W Media International
   (formerly David & Charles)
Fiell Publishing Ltd
Flambard Press
Freelance Market News
Garnet Publishing Ltd
GeoCenter International Ltd
Gomer
Graffeg
Granta Editions
Guildhall Press
Robert Hale Ltd
HarperCollins Publishers Ltd
Haynes Publishing
Hayward Publishing
Alison Hodge Publishers
The Ilex Press Ltd
In Easy Steps Ltd
Dewi Lewis Publishing
The Lilliput Press Ltd
Luath Press Ltd
Lund Humphries
Mainstream Publishing Co
   (Edinburgh) Ltd
Mentor Books
Merlin Publishing/Wolfhound
   Press
Merrell Publishers Ltd
The MIT Press Ltd
Mitchell Beazley
National Galleries of Scotland
National Portrait Gallery
   Publications
New Internationalist Publications
   Ltd
Newpro UK Ltd
Northumbria University Press
Pagoda Tree Press
Papadakis Publisher
The Penguin Group (UK) Ltd
Phaidon Press Ltd
Polperro Heritage Press
Prestel Publishing Ltd
Quadrille Publishing Ltd
Quantum Publishing
Random House UK Ltd
RotoVision SA
Roundhouse Publishing Ltd
Royal Collection Publications
Saqi Books
Seren
Stacey International
Tate Publishing
teNeues Publishing UK Ltd
Thames & Hudson Ltd
Third Millennium Publishing Ltd
Truran
Unicorn Press
V&A Publishing
Weidenfeld & Nicolson
John Wiley & Sons Ltd
Yale University Press London
Zymurgy Publishing

PHYSICS

Alpha Science International Ltd
Amolibros
Anshan Ltd
Anthem Press
Atlantic Europe Publishing Co Ltd
Bedford Freeman Worth (BFW)
BLA Publishing Ltd

Cambridge University Press
GLMP Ltd
Granta Editions
HarperCollins Publishers Ltd
Hodder Education
Icon Books Ltd
Imperial College Press
Institute of Physics & Engineering
   in Medicine
IOP Publishing
Jones & Bartlett International
Letts and Lonsdale
McGraw-Hill Education
Macmillan Education
Macmillan Publishers Ltd
The National Academies Press
National Extension College Trust
   Ltd
Nelson Thornes Ltd
W. W. Norton & Company Ltd
Open University Worldwide
Oxford University Press
Palgrave Macmillan
ProQuest
Taylor & Francis
Ward Lock Educational Co Ltd
John Wiley & Sons Ltd

POETRY

A.M.S. Educational Ltd
Acair Ltd
Accent Press Ltd
Albyn Press
Alma Books Ltd
Amolibros
Anglo-Saxon Books
Anthem Press
Anvil Press Poetry Ltd
Apex Publishing Ltd
Arc Publications Ltd
Association for Scottish Literary
   Studies
Atlantic Books
Austin & Macauley Publishers Ltd
Authorhouse UK Ltd
Barddas
Bene Factum Publishing Ltd
Blackstaff Press
Bloodaxe Books Ltd
Blue Beyond Books
Blue Ocean Publishing
Blue Sky Press
Brown & Whittaker Publishing
Canongate Books
Catcher Ltd
Cló Iar-Chonnachta
Cois Life
Countyvise Ltd
Enitharmon Press
Everyman's Library
Ex Libris Press
Express Newspapers
Faber & Faber Ltd
Fastprint
Feather Books
Five Leaves Publications
Flambard Press
Forward Press
W. Foulsham & Co Ltd
Freelance Market News
The Gallery Press
GLMP Ltd
The Goldsmith Press Ltd
Gomer
Green Books
Guildhall Press
Gwasg Gwenffrwd
Hachette Children's Books
HarperCollins Publishers Ltd
Hippopotamus Press
Icon Books Ltd
Indepenpress Publishing Ltd
ISIS Publishing Ltd
Janus Publishing Co Ltd
Jarndyce Booksellers
The King's England Press
Lapwing Publications
Living Time® Media International
Luath Press Ltd
Macmillan Children's Books Ltd
Macmillan Publishers Ltd

Mandrake of Oxford
Mentor Books
Mercier Press Ltd
Moorley's Print & Publishing Ltd
Need2Know
New Island Books Ltd
NMS Enterprises Limited -
   Publishing
W. W. Norton & Company Ltd
The Old Stile Press
The Oleander Press
Oneworld Classics
Pan Macmillan
Paragon Publishing
The Penguin Group (UK) Ltd
Pentathol Publishing
Pipers' Ash Ltd
ProQuest
Random House UK Ltd
Redcliffe Press Ltd
Route Publishing Ltd
Saint Albert's Press
Salt Publishing Ltd
Saqi Books
Scottish Children's Press
Scottish Cultural Press
Scottish Text Society
Seren
Sessions of York
Charles Skilton Ltd
Spokesman
Stacey International
Stenlake Publishing Ltd
Summer Palace Press
Symposium Publications Literary &
   Art
Tabb House
Troubador Publishing Ltd
University of Wales Press
John Wiley & Sons Ltd
Wordsworth Editions Ltd
Y Lolfa Cyf

POLITICS & WORLD AFFAIRS

Acumen Publishing Ltd
Amnesty International
   International Secretariat
Amolibros
Anthem Press
Apex Publishing Ltd
Arcadia Books Ltd
Arena Books (Publishers)
Arris Publishing Ltd
Ashgate Publishing Ltd
Atlantic Books
Attic Press
Austin & Macauley Publishers Ltd
Berghahn Books
Blackstaff Press
Bloomsbury Publishing Plc
Bodleian Library Publishing
Brandon/Mount Eagle
   Publications
Cambridge Archive Editions Ltd
Cambridge University Press
Canongate Books
Jon Carpenter Publishing
Centre for Economic Policy
   Research
Clairview Books Ltd
Commonwealth Secretariat
The Continuum International
   Publishing Group Ltd
Conway
The Davenant Press
Ashley Drake Publishing Ltd
Gerald Duckworth & Co Ltd
Earthscan
Edinburgh University Press
Ethics International Press Ltd
Faber & Faber Ltd
Fabian Society
Garnet Publishing Ltd
Gibson Square
Gill & Macmillan Ltd
GLMP Ltd
Gothic Image Publications
Granta Books
Green Books
Guildhall Press
Gwasg Gwenffrwd

Halban Publishers
Robert Hale Ltd
John Harper Publishing
HarperCollins Publishers Ltd
Harvard University Press
Hawthorn Press
Hodder Education
Hodder & Stoughton General
C. Hurst & Co (Publishers) Ltd
Icon Books Ltd
IHS Jane's
Imprint Academic
Indepenpress Publishing Ltd
Institute of Development Studies
Institute of Employment Rights
Irish Academic Press
Ithaca Press
Janus Publishing Co Ltd
Liberties Press
Little, Brown Book Group
The Littman Library of Jewish
   Civilization
Liverpool University Press
Luath Press Ltd
The Lutterworth Press
McGraw-Hill Education
Macmillan Publishers Ltd
Mainstream Publishing Co
   (Edinburgh) Ltd
Manchester University Press
Maverick House Publishers
Mehring Books
Melisende
Mentor Books
Mercier Press Ltd
The Merlin Press Ltd
Merlin Publishing/Wolfhound
   Press
Microform Academic Publishers
The MIT Press Ltd
Myriad Editions
Nelson Thornes Ltd
New Holland Publishers (UK) Ltd
New Internationalist Publications
   Ltd
New Island Books Ltd
Northumbria University Press
W. W. Norton & Company Ltd
The O'Brien Press Ltd
Open Gate Press
Open University Worldwide
The Orion Publishing Group Ltd
Oxfam Publishing
Oxford University Press
Pagoda Tree Press
Palgrave Macmillan
Panaf Books
The Penguin Group (UK) Ltd
Pluto Books Ltd
The Policy Press
Polity Press
Portobello Books Ltd
Princeton University Press
Profile Books
ProQuest
Publishing House
The Radcliffe Press
Rand Publications
Random House UK Ltd
Roundhouse Publishing Ltd
Joseph Rowntree Foundation
Royal Irish Academy
Sage Publications Ltd
Sandstone Press Ltd
Saqi Books
Sessions of York
Shepheard-Walwyn (Publishers)
   Ltd
Simon & Schuster (UK) Ltd
Social Affairs Unit
Spokesman
Stacey International
Rudolf Steiner Press
Sussex Academic Press
I. B. Tauris & Co Ltd
Taylor & Francis
Temple Lodge Publishing
Transworld Publishers Ltd
Trentham Books
Troubador Publishing Ltd
TSO (The Stationery Office Ltd)
University of Ottawa Press

University of Wales Press
Vallentine Mitchell Publishers
Virgin Books Ltd
Weidenfeld & Nicolson
John Wiley & Sons Ltd
The Women's Press
Y Lolfa Cyf
Yale University Press London
Zed Books Ltd

PSYCHOLOGY & PSYCHIATRY

American Psychiatric Publishing
   Inc
Ann Arbor Publishers Ltd
Anshan Ltd
Ashgrove Publishing
Atlantic Books
Austin & Macauley Publishers Ltd
Beautiful Books Ltd
Bedford Freeman Worth (BFW)
Blackhall Publishing
Nicholas Brealey Publishing
British Association for Adoption &
   Fostering
Cambridge University Press
Capall Bann Publishing
Channel View Publications Ltd
Constable & Robinson Ltd
Crown House Publishing Ltd
Currach Press
Darton, Longman & Todd Ltd
Delancey Press Ltd
Ashley Drake Publishing Ltd
Emerald Group Publishing Ltd
The Fostering Network
Gibson Square
Gill & Macmillan Ltd
Gothic Image Publications
Granta Editions
HarperCollins Publishers Ltd
Harvard University Press
Hawthorn Press
Heart of Albion Press
Hinton House Publishers Ltd
Hodder Education
Human Kinetics Europe Ltd
John Hunt Publishing Ltd
Icon Books Ltd
Imprint Academic
Jones & Bartlett International
S. Karger AG
Karnac Books Ltd
Jessica Kingsley Publishers
Letts and Lonsdale
Little, Brown Book Group
Living Time® Media International
McGraw-Hill Education
Macmillan Publishers Ltd
Market House Books Ltd
The MIT Press Ltd
M&K Publishing
The National Academies Press
The National Autistic Society
   (NAS)
National Extension College Trust
   Ltd
Nelson Thornes Ltd
W. W. Norton & Company Ltd
Open Gate Press
Open University Worldwide
Oxford University Press
Palgrave Macmillan
PCCS Books Ltd
The Penguin Group (UK) Ltd
Piatkus Books
Pier Professional Ltd
Pipers' Ash Ltd
ProQuest
Roundhouse Publishing Ltd
Royal College of Psychiatrists
Russell House Publishing Ltd
Sage Publications Ltd
St Pauls Publishing
Sheldon Press
Sherwood Publishing
Singing Dragon Publishers
The Society for Promoting
   Christian Knowledge (SPCK)
Souvenir Press Ltd
Speechmark Publishing Ltd
Sussex Academic Press

Taylor & Francis
Troubador Publishing Ltd
United Writers Publications Ltd
University of Hertfordshire Press
Whiting & Birch Ltd
John Wiley & Sons Ltd
Wolters Kluwer Health (P & E) Ltd
The Women's Press

REFERENCE BOOKS, DIRECTORIES & DICTIONARIES

Acumen Publishing Ltd
Adam Matthew Publications Ltd
Adamson Publishing Ltd
Age UK books
Alban Books Ltd
Albyn Press
Ian Allan Publishing Ltd
Alpha Science International Ltd
Amber Books Ltd
American Psychiatric Publishing Inc
Anglo-Saxon Books
Anshan Ltd
Anthem Press
Antique Collectors' Club Ltd
Apex Publishing Ltd
Appletree Press Ltd
Ashgate Publishing Ltd
Atlantic Books
Atlantic Europe Publishing Co Ltd
Aurelian Information Ltd
Aurora Metro Publications Ltd
Austin & Macauley Publishers Ltd
AVA Publishing (UK) Ltd
Duncan Baird Publishers
Bender Richardson White
Bene Factum Publishing Ltd
BLA Publishing Ltd
A. & C. Black (Publishers) Ltd
Blackstaff Press
Bloomsbury Publishing Plc
BML
Bodleian Library Publishing
Bowker (UK) Ltd
Boydell & Brewer Ltd
British Association for Adoption & Fostering
British Museum Press
Calypso Publications
Cambridge Publishing Management Ltd
Cambridge University Press
Camra Books
Carel Press
Caxton Publishing Group Ltd
CBD Research Ltd
Chambers Harrap Publishers Ltd
Church House Publishing
James Clarke & Co
Collins & Brown
Commonwealth Secretariat
The Continuum International Publishing Group Ltd
Countryside Books
Crimson Publishing
D & N Publishing
Delta Alpha Publishing Ltd
J M Dent
Diagram Visual Information Ltd
Eric Dobby Publishing Ltd
Gerald Duckworth & Co Ltd
Earthscan
Edinburgh University Press
Edward Elgar Publishing Ltd
Encyclopaedia Britannica (UK) Ltd
Energy Institute
Equinox Publishing Ltd
Euromonitor International
Executive Grapevine International Ltd
Express Newspapers
Facet Publishing
Folens Ltd
Food Trade Press Ltd
W. Foulsham & Co Ltd
Friends of the Earth
Geddes & Grosset
GeoCenter International Ltd
Geography Publications
Stanley Gibbons

Gill & Macmillan Ltd
Gomer
Granta Editions
Green Books
Gwasg Gwenffrwd
Hachette Children's Books
Peter Haddock Publishing
Robert Hale Ltd
Harden's Ltd
HarperCollins Publishers Ltd
Harvard University Press
Haynes Publishing
Hemming Information Services
Hodder Education
How To Books Ltd
Hymns Ancient & Modern Ltd
Hypatia Publications
Icon Books Ltd
IHS Jane's
In Easy Steps Ltd
Indepenpress Publishing Ltd
International Network for the Availability of Scientific Publications (INASP)
IVP
IWA Publishing
Jarndyce Booksellers
Richard Joseph Publishers Ltd
Kogan Page Ltd
Kyle Cathie Ltd
Letts and Lonsdale
Dewi Lewis Publishing
Lexus
The Lilliput Press Ltd
LISU
Logaston Press
Lomond Books Ltd
The Lutterworth Press
McGraw-Hill Education
Macmillan Education
Macmillan Publishers Ltd
Manchester University Press
Market House Books Ltd
Mentor Books
Mercury Books
Merlin Publishing/Wolfhound Press
The MIT Press Ltd
Mitchell Beazley
National Housing Federation
National Portrait Gallery Publications
The National Trust
Natural History Museum Publishing
New Holland Publishers (UK) Ltd
New Internationalist Publications Ltd
Northumbria University Press
Old House Books
The Oleander Press
On Stream Publications Ltd
The Orion Publishing Group Ltd
Oxford University Press
Packard Publishing Ltd
Palgrave Macmillan
The Penguin Group (UK) Ltd
Philip's
Polperro Heritage Press
Portland Press Ltd
Princeton University Press
ProQuest
Quiller Publishing Ltd
Radcliffe Publishing Ltd
RotoVision SA
Round Hall Ltd
Roundhouse Publishing Ltd
Royal Irish Academy
The Royal Society of Chemistry
Sage Publications Ltd
St Jerome Publishing
Scottish Cultural Press
Social Affairs Unit
Stacey International
Stainer & Bell Ltd
STRI (Sports Turf Research Institute)
I. B. Tauris & Co Ltd
Taylor & Francis
Thames & Hudson Ltd
Top That! Publishing Plc

Toucan Books Ltd
Trotman Publishing
Truran
TSO (The Stationery Office Ltd)
UCAS
Unicorn Press
University of Ottawa Press
University of Wales Press
Merlin Unwin Books Ltd
Usborne Publishing Ltd
Veloce Publishing Ltd
Virgin Books Ltd
Voltaire Foundation Ltd
Waterside Press
Waterside Press
Which? Ltd
Whittles Publishing
John Wiley & Sons Ltd
Witherby Seamanship International
Wolters Kluwer Health (P & E) Ltd
The Women's Press
Wordsworth Editions Ltd

RELIGION & THEOLOGY

Acumen Publishing Ltd
Al-Furqan Islamic Heritage Foundation
Alban Books Ltd
Anno Domini Publishing (ADPS)
Apex Publishing Ltd
Arena Books (Publishers)
Ashgate Publishing Ltd
Ashgrove Publishing
Atlantic Books
Atlantic Europe Publishing Co Ltd
Austin & Macauley Publishers Ltd
Authentic Media
Authorhouse UK Ltd
The Banner of Truth Trust
The Banton Press
Bender Richardson White
Berghahn Books
Bible Reading Fellowship
BLA Publishing Ltd
Blackstaff Press
Blue Beyond Books
Blue Ocean Publishing
Borthwick Publications
Bryntirion Press
Cambridge Publishing Management Ltd
Cambridge University Press
Capall Bann Publishing
The Catholic Truth Society
Christian Education
Christian Focus Publications
Church House Publishing
Church of Ireland Publishing
Clairview Books Ltd
James Clarke & Co
Columba
The Continuum International Publishing Group Ltd
David C Cook (UK)
Countyvise Ltd
Cyhoeddiadau'r Gair
Darton, Longman & Todd Ltd
The Davenant Press
Day One Publications
Gerald Duckworth & Co Ltd
Eagle Publishing Ltd
Edinburgh University Press
Equinox Publishing Ltd
Family Publications
Fastprint
Feather Books
Filament Publishing Ltd
Findhorn Press Ltd
Floris Books
W. Foulsham & Co Ltd
Four Courts Press
Garnet Publishing Ltd
GLMP Ltd
Godsfield Press Ltd
Gothic Image Publications
Gracewing Publishing
Graham-Cameron Publishing & Illustration
Gresham Books Ltd

Gwasg Gwenffrwd
Halban Publishers
HarperCollins Publishers Ltd
Harvard University Press
Hawthorn Press
Heart of Albion Press
Highland Books
Hodder Education
Hodder Faith
John Hunt Publishing Ltd
C. Hurst & Co (Publishers) Ltd
Hymns Ancient & Modern Ltd
Icon Books Ltd
Imprint Academic
Indepenpress Publishing Ltd
Irish Academic Press
The Islamic Texts Society
Ithaca Press
IVP
Janus Publishing Co Ltd
Jessica Kingsley Publishers
Kube Publishing Ltd
Liberties Press
Frances Lincoln Ltd
Lion Hudson Plc
The Littman Library of Jewish Civilization
The Lutterworth Press
McCrimmon Publishing Co Ltd
Macmillan Publishers Ltd
Mandrake of Oxford
Maney Publishing
Melisende
Mercier Press Ltd
Microform Academic Publishers
Moorley's Print & Publishing Ltd
National Extension College Trust Ltd
Nelson Thornes Ltd
The Open Bible Trust
Open Gate Press
Open University Worldwide
Oxford University Press
Palgrave Macmillan
Paragon Publishing
PCCS Books Ltd
The Penguin Group (UK) Ltd
Pickering & Chatto (Publishers) Ltd
Piquant Editions
ProQuest
Redemptorist Publications
Roundhouse Publishing Ltd
Sage Publications Ltd
Saint Albert's Press
St Pauls Publishing
Saqi Books
Scottish Children's Press
Scottish Cultural Press
Scripture Union Publishing
Sessions of York
Shepheard-Walwyn (Publishers) Ltd
Simon & Schuster (UK) Ltd
The Society for Promoting Christian Knowledge (SPCK)
Souvenir Press Ltd
Stacey International
Stainer & Bell Ltd
Rudolf Steiner Press
Sussex Academic Press
The Swedenborg Society
Ta Ha Publishers Ltd
I. B. Tauris & Co Ltd
Taylor & Francis
Temple Lodge Publishing
Thames & Hudson Ltd
Tharpa Publications
Thoth Publications
Trinitarian Bible Society
University of Wales Press
Vallentine Mitchell Publishers
Veritas Publications
Voltaire Foundation Ltd
Warburg Institute
Ward Lock Educational Co Ltd
Wild Goose Publications
John Wiley & Sons Ltd
Windhorse Publications
Worth Press Ltd
Yale University Press London

SCIENCE FICTION

Allison & Busby
Apex Publishing Ltd
Arena Books (Publishers)
Atlantic Books
Austin & Macauley Publishers Ltd
Authorhouse UK Ltd
Catcher Ltd
Constable & Robinson Ltd
Gerald Duckworth & Co Ltd
Everyman's Library
Victor Gollancz Ltd
HarperCollins Publishers Ltd
Hodder & Stoughton General
Icon Books Ltd
Indepenpress Publishing Ltd
ISIS Publishing Ltd
Janus Publishing Co Ltd
Little, Brown Book Group
Liverpool University Press
Living Time® Media International
Macmillan Publishers Ltd
Orion Books Ltd
The Orion Publishing Group Ltd
Pan Macmillan
Paragon Publishing
Pipers' Ash Ltd
Random House UK Ltd
Sandstone Press Ltd
Sigel Press
Simon & Schuster (UK) Ltd
Transworld Publishers Ltd
Troubador Publishing Ltd
United Writers Publications Ltd

SCIENTIFIC & TECHNICAL

Alpha Science International Ltd
Anshan Ltd
Anthem Press
Archetype Publications Ltd
Atlantic Europe Publishing Co Ltd
Austin & Macauley Publishers Ltd
Bernard Babani (Publishing) Ltd
Biohealthcare Publishing (Oxford) Ltd
BookPower
British Geological Survey
CABI
Calypso Publications
Cambridge University Press
Chalksoft Ltd
Commonwealth Secretariat
J M Dent
Donhead Publishing Ltd
Earthscan
Elsevier Ltd
Energy Institute
English Heritage
Forensic Science Society
Geological Society Publishing House
GLMP Ltd
Granta Editions
Greenleaf Publishing
HarperCollins Publishers Ltd
Haynes Publishing
Hodder Education
Human Kinetics Europe Ltd
IChemE
Icon Books Ltd
IHS BRE Press
Imperial College Press
Imprint Academic
In Easy Steps Ltd
Institute of Acoustics
Institute of Food Science & Technology
Institute of Physics & Engineering in Medicine
Institution of Engineering and Technology (IET)
Intellect Ltd
IOP Publishing
IWA Publishing
Jones & Bartlett International
Kew Publishing
Leatherhead Food Research
Letts and Lonsdale
Librario Publishers Ltd
McGraw-Hill Education

Macmillan Publishers Ltd
Maney Publishing
Manson Publishing Ltd
Market House Books Ltd
Mentor Books
The MIT Press Ltd
The National Academies Press
Natural History Museum Publishing
Nelson Thornes Ltd
NMS Enterprises Limited - Publishing
Open University Worldwide
Packard Publishing Ltd
Palgrave Macmillan
Papadakis Publisher
Paragon Publishing
PC Publishing
The Pharmaceutical Press
Pickering & Chatto (Publishers) Ltd
Portland Press Ltd
Princeton University Press
ProQuest
Radcliffe Publishing Ltd
The Royal Society of Chemistry
Sage Publications Ltd
Scion Publishing Ltd
The Society of Metaphysicians Ltd
Stacey International
Stobart Davies Ltd
STRI (Sports Turf Research Institute)
Taylor & Francis
TSO (The Stationery Office Ltd)
Usborne Publishing Ltd
David West Children's Books
Whittles Publishing
John Wiley & Sons Ltd
WIT Press
Wolters Kluwer Health (P & E) Ltd
Woodhead Publishing Ltd

SOCIOLOGY & ANTHROPOLOGY

Acumen Publishing Ltd
Arena Books (Publishers)
Ashgate Publishing Ltd
Austin & Macauley Publishers Ltd
Berg Publishers
Berghahn Books
Blackhall Publishing
British Association for Adoption & Fostering
British Museum Press
Cambridge University Press
Jon Carpenter Publishing
Centre for Policy on Ageing
Channel View Publications Ltd
Countryside Books
Dunedin Academic Press
Earthscan
Edinburgh University Press
Emerald Group Publishing Ltd
Equinox Publishing Ltd
The Fostering Network
Garnet Publishing Ltd
Gibson Square
GLMP Ltd
Granta Editions
Gwasg Gwenffrwd
Harvard University Press
Hawthorn Press
Heart of Albion Press
Hodder Education
C. Hurst & Co (Publishers) Ltd
Icon Books Ltd
Imprint Academic
Institute of Development Studies
Institute of Education (Publications), University of London
Intellect Ltd
Irish Academic Press
Ithaca Press
Janus Publishing Co Ltd
Jarndyce Booksellers
Jessica Kingsley Publishers
Sean Kingston Publishing
Learning Matters Ltd
Letts and Lonsdale

The Littman Library of Jewish Civilization
Liverpool University Press
McGraw-Hill Education
Macmillan Publishers Ltd
Manchester University Press
Mandrake of Oxford
The Merlin Press Ltd
Microform Academic Publishers
National Extension College Trust Ltd
Nelson Thornes Ltd
NMS Enterprises Limited - Publishing
Open University Worldwide
Palgrave Macmillan
Panaf Books
Pennant Books Ltd
Piatkus Books
Pier Professional Ltd
Plowright Press
Pluto Books Ltd
The Policy Press
Polity Press
Princeton University Press
ProQuest
Joseph Rowntree Foundation
Russell House Publishing Ltd
Sage Publications Ltd
Saqi Books
Scottish Cultural Press
Shire Publications Ltd
Social Affairs Unit
Souvenir Press Ltd
Spokesman
Rudolf Steiner Press
Sussex Academic Press
I. B. Tauris & Co Ltd
Taylor & Francis
Thames & Hudson Ltd
University of Hertfordshire Press
University of Ottawa Press
University of Wales Press
Waterside Press
Waterside Press
Whiting & Birch Ltd
John Wiley & Sons Ltd
Zed Books Ltd

SPORTS & GAMES

Ian Allan Publishing Ltd
J. A. Allen
Amber Books Ltd
Amolibros
Peter Andrew Publishing Co Ltd
Anova Books
Apex Publishing Ltd
Appletree Press Ltd
Atlantic Books
Aureus Publishing Ltd
Aurum Press
Austin & Macauley Publishers Ltd
A. & C. Black (Publishers) Ltd
Blackstaff Press
John Blake Publishing Ltd
Bodleian Library Publishing
Brown Dog Books
Butterfingers Books
Carel Press
Carlton Publishing Group
Christian Focus Publications
Cicerone Press Ltd
Coachwise Ltd
Collins & Brown
Copper Beech Publishing Ltd
Corpus Publishing Ltd
Countyvise Ltd
The Crowood Press Ltd
Cualann Press
Currach Press
D & N Publishing
The Derby Books Publishing Co Ltd
Diagram Visual Information Ltd
Ashley Drake Publishing Ltd
Elliott & Thompson
Essential Works Ltd
Express Newspapers
FHG Guides Ltd
Filament Publishing Ltd
Footprint Travel Guides

Gomer
Granta Editions
Hachette Scotland
Haldane Mason Ltd
HarperCollins Publishers Ltd
Hart McLeod Ltd
Harvey Map Services Ltd
Haynes Publishing
Roger Heavens
Hodder Education
Hodder & Stoughton General
Alison Hodge Publishers
Human Kinetics Europe Ltd
Icon Books Ltd
Imray Laurie Norie & Wilson Ltd
Indepenpress Publishing Ltd
Janus Publishing Co Ltd
Jones & Bartlett International
Jessica Kingsley Publishers
Know the Score Books
Kyle Cathie Ltd
Letts and Lonsdale
Dewi Lewis Publishing
Liberties Press
Frances Lincoln Ltd
Little, Brown Book Group
Luath Press Ltd
The Lutterworth Press
Macmillan Publishers Ltd
Mainstream Publishing Co (Edinburgh) Ltd
Maverick House Publishers
Mentor Books
Merlin Publishing/Wolfhound Press
Mitchell Beazley
Motor Racing Publications Ltd
Nelson Thornes Ltd
New Holland Publishers (UK) Ltd
W. W. Norton & Company Ltd
The O'Brien Press Ltd
Octopus Publishing Group
Old House Books
The Oleander Press
The Orion Publishing Group Ltd
Packard Publishing Ltd
Pan Macmillan
Paragon Publishing
Pennant Books Ltd
Pipers' Ash Ltd
Quantum Publishing
Quiller Publishing Ltd
Raceform Ltd / Racing Post Books
Random House UK Ltd
Reflections of a Bygone Age
Roundhouse Publishing Ltd
Russell House Publishing Ltd
Sandstone Press Ltd
Scala Publishers Ltd
Scottish Children's Press
Short Books Ltd
Sigma Press
Simon & Schuster (UK) Ltd
Smith Settle Printing & Bookbinding Ltd
Soccer Books Ltd
Souvenir Press Ltd
Sportsbooks Ltd
STRI (Sports Turf Research Institute)
Summersdale Publishers Ltd
Supportive Learning Publications (SLP)
Sussex Academic Press
Taylor & Francis
Top That! Publishing Plc
Transworld Publishers Ltd
United Writers Publications Ltd
University of Wales Press
Merlin Unwin Books Ltd
Usborne Publishing Ltd
Veloce Publishing Ltd
Vertical Editions
Virgin Books Ltd
Weidenfeld & Nicolson
David West Children's Books
John Wiley & Sons Ltd
Y Lolfa Cyf
Yore Publications

THEATRE, DRAMA & DANCE

Amolibros
Peter Andrew Publishing Co Ltd
Ashgate Publishing Ltd
Association for Scottish Literary Studies
Aurora Metro Publications Ltd
Austin & Macauley Publishers Ltd
Ruth Bean Publishers
Berghahn Books
A. & C. Black (Publishers) Ltd
Blackstaff Press
Bloomsbury Publishing Plc
Blue Ocean Publishing
Marion Boyars Publishers Ltd
Brown, Son & Ferguson, Ltd
Cambridge University Press
Capall Bann Publishing
Carel Press
Classical Comics Ltd
Cló Iar-Chonnachta
Cois Life
Collins & Brown
The Continuum International Publishing Group Ltd
Cressrelles Publishing Co Ltd
The Crowood Press Ltd
D & N Publishing
Dance Books Ltd
Ashley Drake Publishing Ltd
Dramatic Lines
Gerald Duckworth & Co Ltd
Faber & Faber Ltd
Feather Books
Filament Publishing Ltd
Five Leaves Publications
Samuel French Ltd
The Gallery Press
Gibson Square
GLMP Ltd
Granta Editions
Guildhall Press
Hanbury Plays
Ian Henry Publications Ltd
Nick Hern Books
Human Kinetics Europe Ltd
Indepenpress Publishing Ltd
Intellect Ltd
Irish Academic Press
Janus Publishing Co Ltd
Kenyon-Deane
The Littman Library of Jewish Civilization
Luath Press Ltd
Macmillan Publishers Ltd
Manchester University Press
Market House Books Ltd
Mercier Press Ltd
J. Garnet Miller
Moorley's Print & Publishing Ltd
The National Association for the Teaching of English (NATE)
Nelson Thornes Ltd
New Island Books Ltd
New Playwrights' Network
Northcote House Publishers Ltd
Northumbria University Press
W. W. Norton & Company Ltd
The Old Stile Press
Open University Worldwide
Peter Owen Publishers
Palgrave Macmillan
Paragon Publishing
Pipers' Ash Ltd
Playne Books Ltd
The Playwrights Publishing Co
ProQuest
RotoVision SA
Roundhouse Publishing Ltd
Russell House Publishing Ltd
SchoolPlay Productions Ltd
Scottish Cultural Press
Charles Skilton Ltd
Colin Smythe Ltd
Souvenir Press Ltd
Spokesman
Stainer & Bell Ltd
Rudolf Steiner Press
Supportive Learning Publications (SLP)
Sussex Academic Press

Taylor & Francis
Thames & Hudson Ltd
Trentham Books
Troubador Publishing Ltd
University of Exeter Press
University of Hertfordshire Press
University of Ottawa Press
V&A Publishing
Waterside Press
Joseph Weinberger Ltd
Yale University Press London

TRANSPORT

AA Publishing
Albyn Press
Ian Allan Publishing Ltd
Amber Books Ltd
Ashgate Publishing Ltd
Atlantic Books
Aurum Press
Barny Books
The Belmont Press
Brewin Books Ltd
Brooklands Books Ltd
Capital Transport Publishing
Carlton Publishing Group
Caxton Publishing Group Ltd
Chatham Publishing
Colourpoint Books
Conway
Copper Beech Publishing Ltd
Countryside Books
Countyvise Ltd
Crécy Publishing Ltd
The Crowood Press Ltd
G. L. Crowther
Currach Press
D & N Publishing
The Derby Books Publishing Co Ltd
The Dovecote Press
Earthscan
Edward Elgar Publishing Ltd
Elm Publications
Emerald Group Publishing Ltd
Essential Works Ltd
Ex Libris Press
Express Newspapers
Friends of the Earth
GeoCenter International Ltd
Glasgow Museums Publishing
Gomer
Granta Editions
Haynes Publishing
Ian Henry Publications Ltd
The Horizon Press
IHS Jane's
Imray Laurie Norie & Wilson Ltd
Irwell Press Ltd
Kogan Page Ltd
McGraw-Hill Education
Manchester University Press
Maney Publishing
Maritime Books
Merrell Publishers Ltd
Merton Priory Press Ltd
Middleton Press
Motor Racing Publications Ltd
NMS Enterprises Limited - Publishing
The Nostalgia Collection
Old House Books
Old Pond Publishing Ltd
Quantum Publishing
Quiller Publishing Ltd
Random House UK Ltd
Reflections of a Bygone Age
Roadmaster Publishing
Sheaf Publishing
Sheldrake Press
Shire Publications Ltd
Charles Skilton Ltd
Soccer Books Ltd
Special Interest Model Books Ltd
Stenlake Publishing Ltd
Troubador Publishing Ltd
TSO (The Stationery Office Ltd)
Twelveheads Press
Veloce Publishing Ltd
David West Children's Books
WIT Press

Witherby Seamanship
  International

TRAVEL & TOPOGRAPHY

AA Publishing
Amolibros
Chris Andrews Publications Ltd
Appletree Press Ltd
Arcadia Books Ltd
Arena Books (Publishers)
Arris Publishing Ltd
Aurora Metro Publications Ltd
Aurum Press
Austin & Macauley Publishers Ltd
BBH Publishing Ltd
Beautiful Books Ltd
The Belmont Press
Bene Factum Publishing Ltd
Berghahn Books
Black Dog Publishing Ltd
Blackstaff Press
Book Castle Publishing Ltd
Boydell & Brewer Ltd
Bradt Travel Guides Ltd
Brandon/Mount Eagle
  Publications
Nicholas Brealey Publishing
Bridge Books
Calypso Publications
*Cambridge Publishing
  Management Ltd*
Camra Books
Centre for Alternative Technology
  Publications
Channel View Publications Ltd
Cicerone Press Ltd
Cló Iar-Chonnachta
Collins Geo
Compendium Publishing Ltd
Countryside Books
Crimson Publishing
Cualann Press
Currach Press

D & N Publishing
Day One Publications
Dedalus Ltd
Discovery Walking Guides Ltd
The Dovecote Press
Gerald Duckworth & Co Ltd
Eland Publishing Ltd
Elm Publications
English Heritage
The Erskine Press
Everyman's Library
Ex Libris Press
Express Newspapers
FHG Guides Ltd
Fiell Publishing Ltd
Footprint Travel Guides
W. Foulsham & Co Ltd
Garnet Publishing Ltd
GeoCenter International Ltd
The Geographical Association
Gibson Square
Gothic Image Publications
Graffeg
Granta Books
Granta Editions
Green Books
Gwasg Gwenffrwd
Robert Hale Ltd
Halsgrove
HarperCollins Publishers Ltd
Haynes Publishing
Historical Publications Ltd
Hobnob Press
Alison Hodge Publishers
Holo Books
The Horizon Press
How To Books Ltd
Hymns Ancient & Modern Ltd
Imray Laurie Norie & Wilson Ltd
Indepenpress Publishing Ltd
Instant-Books UK Ltd
The King's England Press
Know the Score Books
Frances Lincoln Ltd

Little, Brown Book Group
Luath Press Ltd
Macmillan Publishers Ltd
Melisende
Mentor Books
Merlin Publishing/Wolfhound
  Press
Merrell Publishers Ltd
Michelin Maps & Guides
Mitchell Beazley
Murdoch Books UK Ltd
John Murray Publishers
The National Trust
New Holland Publishers (UK) Ltd
The O'Brien Press Ltd
Old House Books
The Oleander Press
The Orion Publishing Group Ltd
Pagoda Tree Press
Pan Macmillan
The Penguin Group (UK) Ltd
Playne Books Ltd
Portobello Books Ltd
Prospera Publishing
Punk Publishing Ltd
Quadrille Publishing Ltd
Quiller Publishing Ltd
The Radcliffe Press
Reardon Publishing
Roadmaster Publishing
Alan Rogers Guides Ltd
Roundhouse Publishing Ltd
S. B. Publications
Alastair Sawday Publishing
Scala Publishers Ltd
Sheldrake Press
Shire Publications Ltd
Sigma Press
Simon & Schuster (UK) Ltd
Charles Skilton Ltd
Slightly Foxed
Smith Settle Printing &
  Bookbinding Ltd
Souvenir Press Ltd

Stacey International
Stobart Davies Ltd
Strong Oak Press
Summersdale Publishers Ltd
teNeues Publishing UK Ltd
Thames & Hudson Ltd
Thorogood Publishing Ltd
F. A. Thorpe Publishing
Toucan Books Ltd
Transworld Publishers Ltd
Travel Publishing Ltd
Troubador Publishing Ltd
United Writers Publications Ltd
Weidenfeld & Nicolson
John Wiley & Sons Ltd
Willow Island Editions
Neil Wilson Publishing Ltd
Witherby Seamanship
  International

VETERINARY SCIENCE

J. A. Allen
BookPower
CABI
Calypso Publications
Granta Editions
Luath Press Ltd
Manson Publishing Ltd
The National Academies Press
Old Pond Publishing Ltd
The Pharmaceutical Press
Quiller Publishing Ltd
Souvenir Press Ltd
TSO (The Stationery Office Ltd)
Whittet Books Ltd
John Wiley & Sons Ltd

VOCATIONAL TRAINING &
CAREERS

Austin & Macauley Publishers Ltd
Bene Factum Publishing Ltd

BookPower
Nicholas Brealey Publishing
*Cambridge Publishing
  Management Ltd*
Cengage Learning EMEA Ltd
CILT, the National Centre for
  Languages
Crimson Publishing
Emerald Group Publishing Ltd
Ethics International Press Ltd
Filament Publishing Ltd
The Fostering Network
Gower Publishing Co Ltd
Hawker Publications
Hodder Education
How To Books Ltd
In Easy Steps Ltd
Institute of Education
  (Publications), University of
  London
Jones & Bartlett International
Jessica Kingsley Publishers
Kogan Page Ltd
Letts and Lonsdale
McGraw-Hill Education
Macmillan Education
National Children's Bureau
National Extension College Trust
  Ltd
National Housing Federation
Need2Know
Nelson Thornes Ltd
Optimus Professional Publishing
Palgrave Macmillan
Practical Pre-School Books
Radcliffe Publishing Ltd
Russell House Publishing Ltd
Southgate Publishers
Trotman Publishing
UCAS
Which? Ltd
John Wiley & Sons Ltd

7.3   INDEX OF PERSONAL NAMES

7.5   UK PUBLISHERS BY POSTCODE

LONDON & SOUTH-EAST ENGLAND

Brighton
BN1 1AD **2531**
BN1 1UJ **2399**
BN1 1WZ **3039**
BN1 9RE **2401**
BN2 1AH **2638**
BN2 1GJ **2397**
BN3 1AS **2590**
BN3 1DD **2636**
BN3 1FL **2512**
BN7 2NS **2389, 3021**
BN11 1BE **2061**
BN23 6NT **2193**
BN24 9BP **2720**
BN25 2UB **2658**
Bromley
BR3 5JS **2151**
Croydon
CR0 4PA **2275**
CR2 6NZ **2757**
CR5 2YH **2388**
CR9 5YP **2507**
Guildford
GU3 1LP **2707**
GU5 9SW **2220**
GU7 2EP **2363**
GU9 7HS **2562**
GU9 7PT **2045, 2315, 2468**
GU21 6LQ **2538**
GU29 9AZ **2498**
GU32 2EW **2347**
GU34 1HG **2213**
GU34 3HQ **2628**
Harrow
HA3 5ZH **2138**
HA3 8RU **2081**
HA8 7UU **2777**
HA9 9EA **2599**
Hemel Hempstead
HP4 3BL **2609**
HP10 8EU **2431**
HP17 8NT **2282**
HP20 2NQ **3023**
HP22 4YY **2112**
HP23 5AH **3004**
Ilford
IG7 6DL **2423**
IG8 8HD **2373**
Kingston-upon-Thames
KT11 1LG **2122**
KT12 4RG **2016**
KT22 7RY **2446**
KT22 8BZ **2449**
London
E9 5LN **2492**
E14 5LB **2058**
EC1A 9PN **2382**
EC1M 5QL **2420, 2742**
EC1M 5UX **2258**
EC1M 6BF **2234**
EC1M 6PE **3034**
EC1M 7BA **2697**

EC1N 8RT **2775**
EC1N 8SB **2341**
EC1N 8TS **2118**
EC1N 8XA **2237**
EC1R 0DU **3017**
EC1R 0HT **2018, 2338**
EC1R 0JH **2606, 2681**
EC1R 4QB **2114**
EC1R 4QL **2244**
EC1R 4SX **2566**
EC1V 0AT **2260, 2659**
EC1V 0BB **2245, 2561**
EC1V 0DG **2154**
EC1V 1LR **2432**
EC1V 1NG **2517**
EC1V 3QP **2155**
EC1V 4JX **2689**
EC1V 7QE **2518**
EC1Y 1SP **2649**
EC2A 2BU **2455**
EC2A 3AR **2092**
EC2A 3DU **2744**
EC2M 5UU **2448**
EC3R 6AE **2264**
EC3R 8DU **2409**
EC4A 2HS **2484**
EC4A 3AG **2103, 2108**
EC4Y 0DY **2460, 2587**
N1 2LZ **2219**
N1 6ND **3038**
N1 7JQ **2291**
N1 9JB **2434, 2687**
N1 9JF **2814**
N1 9JN **2437, 3008**
N1 9PA **2584**
N1 9PF **3002**
N1 9RR **2472, 2574**
N1 9UN **2447**
N3 1DZ **2709**
N6 5AA **2595**
N7 8PL **2366**
N7 9BH **3030**
N7 9DP **2385**
N12 8ZR **2222**
N13 9AJ **2239**
N19 4PT **2131**
N22 7BW **2345**
NW1 0ND **2057**
NW1 1DB **2660**
NW1 2DB **2120**
NW1 3BH **2333, 2368, 2369, 2371, 2510**
NW1 4DF **2790**
NW1 4ND **2612**
NW1 8PR **2588**
NW3 3PF **2743**
NW3 5HT **2428**
NW5 2DU **2254**
NW5 2RZ **2457**
NW5 4QH **3014**
NW6 1DZ **2559**
NW6 1LU **2054**
NW6 3HR **2685**
NW6 6RD **2146**
NW8 6WD **2053, 2713, 2721, 2807**

NW10 3YB **2337**
NW11 7DL **2481**
NW11 8ED **2324**
SE1 0HX **2494**
SE1 0UP **2749**
SE1 2BH **2251**
SE1 6LH **2390**
SE1 7HR **2170**
SE1 7JN **2585**
SE1 7NX **2191**
SE1 8HA **2033, 2287**
SE1 8RD **2803**
SE1 8UG **2537**
SE1 8XX **2354**
SE10 8RF **2035**
SE11 5AY **2148**
SE11 5SD **2611**
SE19 1LP **2738**
SE19 3SR **3009**
SE23 3HZ **2792**
SE24 0PB **2376, 2603**
SE27 9NT **2724**
SW1A 1JR **2641**
SW1H 0QS **2419**
SW1H 9BN **2267**
SW1P 3AZ **2167**
SW1P 4RG **2730**
SW1P 4ST **2675, 2695**
SW1V 2SA **2026, 2622, 2781**
SW1V 2SS **2359**
SW1X 7DL **2450**
SW1X 8PG **2643**
SW1Y 5HX **2187**
SW3 3ST **2485**
SW3 4AH **2015, 2688**
SW3 5SR **2255**
SW5 0RE **2567**
SW6 1RU **2427**
SW6 6AW **2461**
SW7 1PU **2642**
SW7 2AR **2644**
SW7 2RL **2776**
SW7 5BD **2526**
SW8 5WZ **2082**
SW11 3AS **2652**
SW11 5DH **2351**
SW11 6SS **2327**
SW12 0DA **2676**
SW14 8LS **2677**
SW15 1AZ **3037**
SW15 1NL **2109**
SW15 2PE **2209**
SW15 2TG **2509**
SW16 4ER **2011**
SW18 1YW **2066**
SW18 4JJ **2214**
SW19 1JQ **2159**
SW19 3NN **2756**
W1A 3FB **2582**
W1B 1AH **2386**
W1B 5DL **2079**
W1B 5SA **2694**
W1D 3QY **2008, 2093, 2099, 2361**
W1D 4SA **2188**

W1F 7BB **2662**
W1F 9JW **2336**
W1G 0AE **2647**
W1G 0DD **2292**
W1G 7AR **2252**
W1J 6HE **2218**
W1S 4EX **2631**
W1T 2LD **2614, 2615, 2804**
W1T 3JJ **2789**
W1T 3JW **2143**
W1T 3LJ **2554**
W1T 3QH **2068**
W1T 3QT **2544**
W1T 4AY **2439**
W1T 4EJ **2019**
W1T 5DX **2416**
W1T 5HJ **2041**
W1T 5JR **2290**
W1U 6BY **2421**
W1U 6NR **2259**
W1W 7AB **2039**
W1W 8AF **2783**
W2 2EA **2532**
W2 4BU **2618, 2731**
W2 4QS **2177**
W2 5BP **2723**
W2 5RH **2656, 2734**
W4 5TF **2319**
W4 5YD **2728**
W5 4YX **2010**
W5 5SA **2621, 2753**
W6 7NF **2065**
W6 7NJ **2404**
W6 7PA **2424**
W6 7QH **2274**
W6 8JB **2346**
W6 9ER **2190**
W8 4BH **2140, 2708**
W8 4PL **2013**
W8 6SA **2242**
W8 9FA **2358**
W10 5ST **2557**
W11 2LW **2089**
W11 4QR **2320, 2601**
W12 8QP **2362**
W14 0RA **2031, 2074, 2182, 2192**
W14 9PB **2097**
WC1A 2QA **2604**
WC1A 2TH **2589, 2722**
WC1B 3DA **2266**
WC1B 3DP **2811**
WC1B 3ES **2042**
WC1B 3JH **2150, 2490, 2491**
WC1B 3PA **2422**
WC1B 3PD **2701**
WC1B 3PL **2381**
WC1B 3QQ **2121**
WC1E 7AE **2268**
WC1E 7EY **2349, 2502**
WC1H 0AB **2784**
WC1H 0AL **2402**
WC1H 9HF **2669**
WC1H 9NE **2632**

WC1N 2BX **2046, 2247**
WC1N 3JZ **2050**
WC1V 6NY **2523**
WC1V 7QX **2740**
WC1X 0DW **2024**
WC1X 8HB **2686**
WC1X 9DH **3015**
WC1X 9NG **2091**
WC2A 1PL **2443**
WC2A 1PP **2395**
WC2H 0HE **2524**
WC2H 0LS **2613**
WC2H 7HH **2521**
WC2H 8JY **2189, 2310, 2501, 2503, 2549, 2586**
WC2H 9EA **2223, 2312, 2563, 2564, 2788**
WC2H 9HE **2391**
WC2N 6DF **2343**
WC2N 6RL **2160**
WC2R 0LX **2303**
WC2R 0RL **2581**
Luton
LU6 2ES **2117**
Medway
ME4 4HN **2022**
ME5 9AQ **2633**
Portsmouth
PO8 9JL **2499**
PO14 1BU **2101**
PO19 1RP **2718**
PO19 7DN **2570**
PO19 8SQ **2797**
Reading
RG1 4QS **2296, 2417**
RG8 8LU **2558**
RG9 4PG **2051**
RG14 5DS **2199**
RG20 6NL **2617**
RG20 8AN **2576**
RG21 4EA **2001**
RG21 6XS **2080, 2474, 2573**
RG21 6YR **2299**
RG27 0JG **2786, 3036**
Redhill
RH4 1DN **2736**
RH10 7WD **2715**
RH12 9GH **2625**
RH14 9QP **2624**
RH17 5PA **3029**
RH18 5ES **2172, 2710, 2737**
RH19 3BT **2785, 3006**
RH19 4FS **2195**
Romford
RM1 4LH **2360**
Slough
SL1 4AA **2288**
SL2 3PQ **2132**
SL6 2QL **2471**
SL9 8BA **2692**
SL9 9QE **2111**
Southall
UB9 5NX **3005**

UB9 6AT **2812**
Southampton
SO24 0BE **2380**
SO24 9JH **2477**
SO40 7AA **2801**
Southend
SS1 1EF **2405**
SS3 0EQ **2470**
SS9 2LB **2511**
St Albans
AL1 3BN **2400**
AL1 4EG **2809**
AL1 4JL **2729**
AL1 4LW **2135**
AL6 9EQ **2527**
AL8 6HG **2262**
AL10 9AB **2771**
Tonbridge
TN4 9AT **2032**
TN11 8HL **2012**
TN16 1BZ **2283**
TN17 1HE **2635**
TN18 5AD **2228**
TN30 6BW **2295, 2326**
TN35 4PG **2698**
Twickenham
TW1 3QS **3035**
TW1 4HX **2056**
TW2 5RQ **2232**
TW7 6NH **2815**
TW9 1SR **2344**
TW9 2LL **2020, 2556**
TW9 2ND **2203, 2758**
TW9 3AE **2430**
TW9 3HA **2064**
Watford
WD6 3PW **2161**
WD17 1JA **2496**
WD19 4BG **2263**
WD25 9XX **2387**

SOUTH-WEST ENGLAND

Bath
BA1 2JQ **2572**
BA1 3JN **2302**
BA1 5BG **2072, 3031**
BA1 5DZ **3012**
BA1 6JX **2571**
BA2 3AF **2238**
BA2 3BH **2075**
BA2 3DZ **2284**
BA2 3LR **2123, 2539**
BA2 4JT **2733**
BA2 7EJ **2727**
BA2 7JF **3033**
BA6 8AE **2129**
BA6 8XR **2314**
BA11 1DS **2163**
BA11 4EL **2365**
BA11 4LW **3016**
BA13 4JE **2236**
BA14 0AA **2602**
BA22 7JJ **2353**
Bournemouth
BH15 2RG **2703**

BH20 6AE **2180**
BH21 4JD **2230**
Bristol
BS1 2AW **2158**
BS1 6BE **2411**
BS1 6JS **2425**
BS8 1QU **2596**
BS8 3EA **2627, 2655**
BS16 3JG **2408**
BS41 9LR **2657**
Dorchester
DT1 3AR **2778**
DT7 3LS **2648**
Exeter
EX1 1NX **2444**
EX4 4QR **2770**
EX5 5HY **2392**
EX17 4LW **2700**
EX32 9HG **2610**
EX38 8ZJ **2426**
Jersey
JE2 3LD **2261**
Plymouth
PL2 2EQ **2813**
PL6 7PP **2754**
PL14 4EL **2482**
PL15 8LD **2107**
PL19 9NQ **2542**
PL23 1EQ **2197**
PL28 8BG **2725**
Salisbury
SP3 5QP **2076**
SP3 6FA **2367**
SP7 9LY **2229**
SP10 5BE **2152**
Swindon
SN2 2GZ **2253**
SN2 2NA **2525**
SN5 7YD **2164**
SN7 7DS **2536**
SN8 2AA **2005, 2006**
SN8 2HR **2206**
SN8 2LH **3013**
SN15 4BW **2591**
Taunton
TA4 1NE **2137**
TA4 1QF **3003**
TA6 4RR **2175**
TA19 0LE **2221**
TA21 9PZ **2339**
Torquay
TQ9 6EB **2322**
TQ9 7DL **2608**
TQ12 4PU **2265**
TQ13 8PA **2550**
Truro
TR4 8ZJ **2763**
TR5 0RA **2760**
TR18 4AW **2383**
TR20 8BG **2768**
TR20 8XA **2372**

MIDLANDS

Birmingham
B9 4AA **2748**
B29 6LB **2165**
B61 0RU **2102**
B80 7LG **2115**
B80 7NT **2436**
B91 1UE **2357**
Coventry
CV21 3HQ **2384**
CV34 4XE **2594**
CV37 1EP **2063**
CV47 0FB **2394**
Derby
DE6 1HD **2377**
DE7 5DA **2506**

DE21 4SZ **2224**
Dudley
DY8 3XY **2634**
Gloucester
GL5 1BJ **2352**
GL6 7RL **2699**
GL7 3QB **2208**
GL15 6YD **3011**
GL50 2JA **2246**
GL50 2JR **2706**
GL50 9AN **2626**
GL52 3LZ **2765**
GL53 7TH **2077, 2529**
GL56 0YN **2044**
Hereford
HR3 6QH **2465**
HR3 8QU **2545**
HR6 0QF **2316**
HR6 8NZ **2216**
HR9 5LA **2579**
Leicester
LE7 7FU **2745, 2766**
LE8 0LQ **2759**
LE11 1UD **2668**
LE11 3TU **2459**
LE11 5DN **2746**
LE12 6UJ **2355**
LE67 9SY **2438**
Milton Keynes
MK2 2EB **2667**
MK7 6AA **2560**
MK9 2BE **2059, 2060**
MK11 1EB **2227**
MK13 9HG **2704**
MK18 1NT **2364**
MK40 4FB **2575**
MK43 7LP **2078**
MK45 4BE **2413**
Northampton
NN3 6RT **2318**
NN5 7HJ **2226, 2398**
NN7 3JB **3027**
NN12 6BT **2023, 2514,
    2620, 2772**
NN12 9AR **2176**
NN14 4BW **2546**
NN17 4HH **2277**
Nottingham
NG1 9AW **2278**
NG2 3BP **2577**
NG6 0BT **2705**
NG7 2RD **2666**
NG7 3HR **2418**
NG12 5GG **2119**
NG12 5HT **2629**
NG14 5AL **2593**
NG17 9GU **2762**
NG32 2BB **2073**
Oxford
OX1 1AP **2479**
OX1 1BN **2442**
OX1 1ST **2410**
OX1 2JW **2348**
OX1 2PH **2047**
OX1 3HJ **2374**
OX1 5RP **2269**
OX2 0ES **2414**
OX2 0EW **2104**
OX2 0LX **2028**
OX2 0PH **2565, 2680**
OX2 0UJ **2462**
OX2 6DP **2569**
OX2 6JX **2782**
OX2 7DR **2458**
OX2 7ED **2040**
OX2 8EJ **2139**
OX3 0BP **2048**
OX4 1AW **2083**
OX4 1BW **2533**

OX4 1RE **2084**
OX4 2DP **2796**
OX4 2JY **2568**
OX4 2JZ **2021**
OX4 3PP **2473**
OX5 1GB **2249**
OX5 1RX **2378**
OX7 3PH **2145**
OX7 6RU **3001**
OX10 8DE **2130**
OX12 8ED **2435**
OX12 8JY **2505**
OX14 1AA **2619**
OX14 3FE **2085**
OX14 4RN **2732**
OX15 0SE **2017**
OX16 9UX **2663**
OX18 4XN **2215**
OX20 1TW **2605**
OX28 4AW **3026**
OX28 4BN **2087**
OX29 8SZ **2440**
Shrewsbury
SY3 0WN **2272**
SY4 1JA **2616**
SY4 4UR **2716**
SY4 5JX **2464**
SY5 6LX **2739**
SY6 6WZ **2396**
SY8 1DB **2774**
Stoke-on-Trent
ST4 5NP **2755**
ST17 0TE **2204**
Worcester
WR6 6EN **2598**
WR9 7EE **2342**
WR9 7RP **2027**
WR13 6RN **2202, 2429,
    2500, 2535**

EAST ANGLIA

Cambridge
CB1 1JT **2553**
CB1 2NT **2174, 2469**
CB1 3AN **2800**
CB2 1UR **2597**
CB2 8HN **2519**
CB2 8RU **2133**
CB4 0WF **2646**
CB4 0WS **2100**
CB4 1ND **2321**
CB4 3BW **2683**
CB5 8SW **2607**
CB6 2UA **2029**
CB21 5DH **2653**
CB21 6AH **2805**
CB22 5EN **2415**
CB23 7NU **3010**
CB25 9HP **3020**
Chelmsford
CM6 2PP **2147**
CM20 2JE **2580**
CM21 9JX **2487**
CM23 2EJ **2630**
CM24 8JU **2793**
Colchester
CO1 2TW **2280**
CO2 8HP **2600**
CO3 3HU **2661**
CO6 1JE **2171**
CO15 5WN **2036**
Ipswich
IP1 3RP **3007**
IP1 5LT **2551**
IP12 1AP **2750**
IP12 1BL **2149**
IP12 3DF **2110**
IP12 4SD **2034**

IP25 6QH **2578**
IP33 2BL **2043**
IP33 3PH **2257**
Lincoln
LN6 7FL **2752**
LN11 0BL **2356**
Norwich
NR2 3AD **2767**
NR3 1PD **2761**
NR3 3AX **2007**
NR14 7UR **3025**
NR16 2PB **2256**
NR26 8NB **3019**
Peterborough
PE2 6SG **3024**
PE2 6XD **2271**
PE2 9JX **2286, 2528**
PE11 1NZ **2156, 2672**
PE11 4TA **2787**
PE27 5BT **2393**
PE28 2NJ **2248**
PE28 5XE **2217**
Stevenage
SG1 2AY **2407**
SG1 2DX **2067**
SG8 5NJ **2808**
SG9 9AJ **3032**
SG12 9HJ **2806**
SG14 2JA **2678**
SG19 3JA **2009**

NORTH-EAST ENGLAND

Bradford
BD1 3PT **2141**
BD16 1AU **2714**
BD16 1WA **2250**
BD23 2QR **2780**
BD23 4ND **2475**
Doncaster
DN35 8HU **2693**
Durham
DH1 3NP **2004**
DH4 5QY **2128**
DH8 7PW **2309**
Harrogate
HG1 1BX **2285**
HG4 5DF **2105**
Leeds
LS3 1AB **2480**
LS6 4NB **2025**
LS8 2SP **2293**
LS12 4HP **2179**
LS19 7XY **2691**
LS28 6AT **2379**
Newcastle-upon-Tyne
NE1 2AJ **2279**
NE1 3DY **2513**
NE1 8ST **2543**
NE6 2HL **2816**
NE48 1RP **2098**
NE70 7JX **2030**
NE99 1DX **2764**
Sheffield
S1 2BS **2486**
S1 4BF **2300**
S3 7WL **2674**
S3 8GG **2325**
S8 0XJ **2516**
S10 5UD **2682**
S023 9HX **2623**
S32 1DJ **2241**
S41 0FR **2495**
S63 9BL **2433**
S80 3LR **2062**
Wakefield
WF1 2LT **2243**
WF3 2AP **2497**
WF4 4PX **2798**

WF5 9AQ **2673**
WF8 4WW **2639**
York
YO10 5DD **2106**
YO10 5DX **2650**
YO16 6BT **2335**
YO18 8AL **2096**
YO24 1ES **2406**
YO30 6WP **2640**
YO30 7BZ **2198**
YO31 9HS **2671**
YO61 3UZ **2184**
YO62 5BP **2541**

NORTH-WEST ENGLAND

Carlisle
CA2 5AU **2142**
CA3 9HZ **2592**
CA12 5AS **2504**
Chester
CH3 8JF **2747**
CH41 9HH **2200**
Isle of Man
IM2 4NR **2508**
Lancaster
LA1 4SL **2144**
LA7 7PY **2169**
LA12 9QQ **2741**
LA17 7WZ **2194**
Liverpool
L3 5SD **2403**
L69 7ZU **2463**
Manchester
M1 1JB **3018**
M13 9NR **2478**
M22 5LH **2201**
M23 9HH **2651**
Oldham
OL14 6DA **2038**
Preston
PR1 8JP **2207**
PR3 5LE **2751**
Stockport
SK4 4ND **2451**
Warrington
WA4 9DE **2297**

WALES

Cardiff
CF5 1GZ **2317**
CF10 4UP **2773**
CF14 2EA **2233**
CF14 7ZY **2231**
CF31 3AE **2670**
CF31 4DX **2126**
CF32 0TN **2055**
CF37 5PB **2086**
CF46 6RY **2003**
Mid-Wales
LD7 1UP **3022**
SY20 9AZ **2153**
SY23 3GL **2375**
SY24 5HE **2810**
North Wales
LL12 7AW **2116**
LL13 7NS **2583**
LL14 5HL **2719**
LL18 9AY **2307**
LL19 9SH **2735**
LL21 9WZ **2331**
LL26 0EH **2330**
LL53 5YE **2332**
LL53 6SH **2212**
Newport (Gwent)
NP25 4TN **2552**
Swansea
SA6 6AE **2071**

SA18 3HP **2684, 2712**
SA33 5ND **2205**
SA44 4JL **2313**
SA62 5AU **3028**

SCOTLAND

Dumfries
DG10 9SU **2134**
Edinburgh
EH1 1JF **2540, 2696**
EH1 1TE **2136**
EH1 2ND **2467**
EH1 3QB **2235**
EH1 3UG **2476**
EH1 3YY **2515**
EH2 4PS **2323**
EH4 3BL **2014**
EH4 3DS **2520**
EH7 4AY **2157**
EH8 9LF **2240**
EH9 1QS **2088**
EH11 1SH **2281**
EH12 6EL **2069**
EH15 1JG **2225**
EH22 3LJ **2664, 2665**
EH52 5LH **2308**
EH52 5NF **2466**
EH54 8SB **2802**
Falkirk
FK16 6BJ **2350**
Glasgow
G2 3DH **2795**
G4 0HZ **2298**
G12 8QH **2049**
G13 1BQ **2799**
G40 2AB **2452**
G41 2SD **2124**
G53 7NN **2306**
G64 2QT **2183**
G74 2JZ **2162**
Inverness
IV15 9WJ **2654**
IV20 1TW **2166**
IV36 2TF **2276**
IV36 2UA **2454**
IV42 8PY **2726**
Kilmarnock
KA5 6RD **2711**
KA27 8NQ **2070**
Kirkcaldy
KY12 7XG **2210**
Orkney
KW6 6EG **2794**
Paisley & Isles
HS1 2QN **2002**
PA1 1NB **2334, 2370**
PA1 1TJ **2273**
PA75 6PR **2125**
Perth
PH2 1AU **2090**
PH20 1BU **2702**
Shetland
ZE1 0PX **2679**

NORTHERN IRELAND

Belfast
BT3 9LE **2095**
BT5 6NW **2445**
BT7 1AP **2037**
BT9 5AU **2717**
BT9 5BS **2690**
BT14 8HQ **2441**
BT16 2BB **2791**
BT23 4YH **2185**
BT48 0LZ **2328**